MW00788166

AL ALABAMA

Houghton Mifflin Harcourt

United States History

Civil War to the Present

William Deverell
Deborah Gray White

HISTORY

Authors

William Deverell

William Deverell is Professor of History at the University of Southern California. He is the author of *Railroad Crossing: Californians and the Railroad, 1850-1910* and *Whitewashed Adobe: The Rise of Los Angeles and the Remaking of the Mexican Past.* He is the editor of the *Blackwell Companion to the American West.* With Greg Hise, he co-authored *Eden by Design: The 1930 Olmsted-Bartholomew Plan for the Los Angeles Region* and co-edited *Land of Sunshine: The Environmental History of Metropolitan Los Angeles.* He is the former chairman of the California Council for the Humanities.

Deborah Gray White

Deborah Gray White, a former New York City school teacher, is Board of Governors Professor of History at Rutgers University in New Brunswick, New Jersey. A specialist in American history and the history of African Americans, she is the author of several books, including: *Ar'n't I A Woman? Female Slaves in the Plantation South; Too Heavy a Load: Black Women in Defense of Themselves, 1894-1994*; and *Let My People Go, African Americans 1804-1860,* Volume 4 in the *Young Oxford History of African Americans.* In 2009 she received a Guggenheim Fellowship for her upcoming book *"Can't We All Just Get Along": The Cultural Awakenings of the 1990s.*

2015 Edition
Copyright © by Houghton Mifflin Harcourt Publishing Company

All rights reserved. No part of this work may be reproduced or transmitted in any form or by any means, electronic or mechanical, including photocopying or recording, or by any information storage and retrieval system, without the prior written permission of the copyright owner unless such copying is expressly permitted by federal copyright law. Requests for permission to make copies of any part of the work should be addressed to Houghton Mifflin Harcourt Publishing Company, Attn: Contracts, Copyrights, and Licensing, 9400 Southpark Center Loop, Orlando, Florida 32819-8647.

Portions © 2010 A&E Television Networks, LLC. All rights reserved.

The History Channel, History, "H" logo and History Education are trademarks of A&E Television Networks, LLC. All rights reserved.

Printed in the U.S.A.

ISBN 978-0-544-12773-9

4 5 6 7 8 9 10 0868 22 21 20 19 18 17 16 15 14

4500471296 B C D E F G

If you have received these materials as examination copies free of charge, Houghton Mifflin Harcourt Publishing Company retains title to the materials and they may not be resold. Resale of examination copies is strictly prohibited.

Possession of this publication in print format does not entitle users to convert this publication, or any portion of it, into electronic format.

© Houghton Mifflin Harcourt Publishing Company • Image Credits: (tl), Seth Joel/HRW Photo; (br), Michael Denora/HRW Photo

Program Consultants

Contributing Author

Kylene Beers, Ed.D.
Senior Reading Advisor to Secondary Schools
Teachers College Reading and Writing Project
Columbia University
New York City, New York

A former middle school teacher, Dr. Beers has turned her commitment to helping struggling readers into the major focus of her research, writing, speaking, and teaching. She is the former editor of the National Council of Teachers of English (NCTE) literacy journal *Voices from the Middle.* She has also served as the president of NCTE. Her published works include *When Kids Can't Read: What Teachers Can Do* (Heinemann, 2002).

General Editor

Frances Marie Gipson
Secondary Literacy
Los Angeles Unified School District
Los Angeles, California

In her current position, Frances Gipson guides reform work for secondary instruction and supports its implementation. She has designed curriculum at the district, state, and national levels. Her leadership of a coaching collaborative with Subject Matter Projects of the University of California at Los Angeles evolved from her commitment to rigorous instruction and to meeting the needs of diverse learners.

Senior Literature and Writing Specialist

Carol Jago
English Department Chairperson
Santa Monica High School
Santa Monica, California

An English teacher at the middle and high school levels for 26 years, Carol Jago also directs the Reading and Literature Project at UCLA. She has been published in numerous professional journals and has authored several books, including *Cohesive Writing: Why Concept Is Not Enough* (Boynton/Cook, 2002). She became president of the National Council of Teachers of English (NCTE) in 2010.

Consultants

Martha H. Ball, M.A.
Religion Consultant
Utah 3Rs Project Director
Utah State Office of Education
Salt Lake City, Utah

John Ferguson, M.T.S., J.D.
Senior Religion Consultant
Assistant Professor
Political Science/Criminal Justice
Howard Payne University
Brownwood, Texas

J. Frank Malaret
Senior Consultant
Dean, Downtown and West Sacramento Outreach Centers
Sacramento City College
Sacramento, California

Kimberly A. Plummer, M.A.
Senior Consultant
History-Social Science Educator/Advisor
Holt McDougal

Galit Reichlin
Associate Director
Middle Eastern Affairs and International Analysis
Anti-Defamation League
(Reviewed Middle East content in the chapter Searching for Order.)

Andrés Reséndez, Ph.D.
Senior Consultant,
Assistant Professor
Department of History
University of California at Davis
Davis, California

© Houghton Mifflin Harcourt Publishing Company

Academic Reviewers

Anne C. Bailey, Ph.D.
Spelman College
Atlanta, Georgia

Albert Camarillo, Ph.D.
Department of History
Stanford University

Larry Conyers, Ph.D.
Department of Anthropology
University of Denver

Willard Gatewood, Ph.D.
Emeritus Alumni Distinguished Professor, Department of History
University of Arkansas

Christopher Hendricks, Ph.D.
Department of History
Armstrong Atlantic State University
Savannah, Georgia

Skip Hyser, Ph.D.
Department of History
James Madison University
Harrisonburg, Virginia

Yasuhide Kawashima
Department of History
University of Texas at El Paso

Brenda E. Stevenson, Ph.D.
Department of History UCLA
Los Angeles, California

David Switzer, Ph.D.
Department of Social Studies
Plymouth State University

Jessica Wang, Ph.D.
Department of History UCLA
Los Angeles, California

Nan Woodruff, Ph.D
Department of History
Pennsylvania State University

Craig Yirush, Ph.D.
Department of History UCLA
Los Angeles, California

Educational Reviewers

Nelson Acevedo
New York City Alternative Schools and Programs
New York, New York

Henry Assetto
Twin Valley High School
Elverson, Pennsylvania

John Bilsky
Linton Middle School
Penn Hills, Pennsylvania

Julie Chan, Ed.D.
Director, Literacy Instruction
Newport-Mesa Unified School District
Costa Mesa, California

Kermit Cummings
Cockeysville Middle School
Baltimore County Public Schools
Baltimore, Maryland

Katherine A. DeForge
Social Studies Chair
Marcellus Central School
Marcellus, New York

Sandra Eades
Ridgely Middle School
Lutherville, Maryland

Ed Felten
Coopersville Public School District
Coopersville, Michigan

Tim Gearhart
Daniel Lewis Middle School
Paso Robles, California

Stacy Goldman
Lincoln Middle School
Berwyn, Illinois

Joseph P. Macary
Supervisor of Social Studies
Waterbury Public Schools
Waterbury, Connecticut

Carol Eiler Moore
Dundalk Middle School
Dundalk, Maryland

Tina Nelson
Baltimore County Public School District
Baltimore, Maryland

Ann-Jean Paci
Sheepshead Bay High School
Brooklyn, New York

Anthony Powell
Edmund W. Miles Middle School
Amityville, New York

Linda Prior
Floyd T. Binns Middle School
Culpeper County, Virginia

Wendy Schanberger
Hereford Middle School
Monkton, Maryland

Sua A. Shin
Culpeper Middle School
Culpeper, Virginia

Kathleen Torquata
Lincoln Middle School
Berwyn, Illinois

© Houghton Mifflin Harcourt Publishing Company

For more information go to hmhsocialstudies.com

Contents

© Houghton Mifflin Harcourt Publishing Company

For more information go to hmhsocialstudies.com

UNIT 2 A Growing America, 1850–1914

© Houghton Mifflin Harcourt Publishing Company

For more information go to hmhsocialstudies.com

© Houghton Mifflin Harcourt Publishing Company

r more information
to hmhsocialstudies.com

CHAPTER 7 America as a World Power, 1867–1920

CHAPTER 8 World War I, 1914–1920

© Houghton Mifflin Harcourt Publishing Company

For more information go to hmhsocialstudies.com

UNIT 4 Boom Times and Challenges, 1919–1945

© Houghton Mifflin Harcourt Publishing Company

For more information go to hmhsocialstudies.com

© Houghton Mifflin Harcourt Publishing Company

For more information go to hmhsocialstudies.com

© Houghton Mifflin Harcourt Publishing Company

For more information go to hmhsocialstudies.com

UNIT 6 Modern America,

References

© Houghton Mifflin Harcourt Publishing Company

Houghton Mifflin Harcourt

HISTORY® is the leading destination for revealing, award-winning, original non-fiction series and event-driven specials that connect history with viewers in an informative, immersive and entertaining manner across multiple platforms. HISTORY is part of A&E Television Networks (AETN), a joint venture of Hearst Corporation, Disney/ABC Television Group and NBC Universal, an award-winning, international media company that also includes, among others, A&E Network™, BIO™, and History International™.

HISTORY programming greatly appeals to educators and young people who are drawn into the visual stories our documentaries tell. Our Education Department has a long-standing record in providing teachers and students with curriculum resources that bring the past to life in the classroom. Our content covers a diverse variety of subjects, including American and world history, government, economics, the natural and applied sciences, arts, literature and the humanities, health and guidance, and even pop culture.

The HISTORY website, located at **www.history.com**, is the definitive historical online source that delivers entertaining and informative content featuring broadband video, interactive timelines, maps, games, podcasts and more.

"We strive to engage, inspire and encourage the love of learning..."

Since its founding in 1995, HISTORY has demonstrated a commitment to providing the highest quality resources for educators. We develop multimedia resources for K–12 schools, two- and four-year colleges, government agencies, and other organizations by drawing on the award-winning documentary programming of A&E Television Networks. We strive to engage, inspire and encourage the love of learning by connecting with students in an informative and compelling manner. To help achieve this goal, we have formed a partnership with Houghton Mifflin Harcourt.

©2010 A&E Television Networks, LLC. All Rights Reserved. 01762 © Houghton Mifflin Harcourt Publishing Company

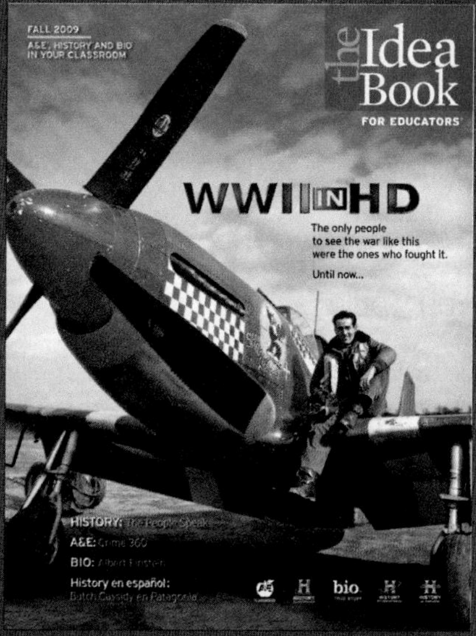

The Idea Book for Educators

Classroom resources that bring the past to life

Live webcasts

HISTORY Take a Veteran to School Day

© Houghton Mifflin Harcourt Publishing Company

In addition to premium video-based resources, **HISTORY** has extensive offerings for teachers, parents, and students to use in the classroom and in their in-home educational activities, including:

- ***The Idea Book for Educators*** is a biannual teacher's magazine, featuring guides and info on the latest happenings in history education to help keep teachers on the cutting edge.
- **HISTORY Classroom (www.history.com/classroom)** is an interactive website that serves as a portal for history educators nationwide. Streaming videos on topics ranging from the Roman aqueducts to the civil rights movement connect with classroom curricula.
- **HISTORY email newsletters** feature updates and supplements to our award-winning programming relevant to the classroom with links to teaching guides and video clips on a variety of topics, special offers, and more.
- **Live webcasts** are featured each year as schools tune in via streaming video.
- **HISTORY Take a Veteran to School Day** connects veterans with young people in our schools and communities nationwide.

In addition to **HOUGHTON MIFFLIN HARCOURT**, our partners include the *Library of Congress*, the *Smithsonian Institution, National History Day, The Gilder Lehrman Institute of American History*, the *Organization of American Historians*, and many more. HISTORY video is also featured in museums throughout America and in over 70 other historic sites worldwide.

Become an Active Reader

Did you ever think you would begin reading your social studies book by reading about reading? Actually, it makes better sense than you might think. You would probably make sure you learned some soccer skills and strategies before playing in a game. Similarly, you need to learn some reading skills and strategies before reading your social studies book. In other words, you need to make sure you know whatever you need to know in order to read this book successfully.

Tip #1

Use the Reading Social Studies Pages

Take advantage of the two pages on reading at the beginning of every chapter. Those pages introduce the chapter themes; explain a reading skill or strategy; and identify key terms, people, and academic vocabulary.

Themes

Why are themes important? They help our minds organize facts and information. For example, when we talk about baseball, we may talk about types of pitches. When we talk about movies, we may discuss animation.

Historians are no different. When they discuss history or social studies, they tend to think about some common themes: Economics, Geography, Religion, Politics, Society and Culture, and Science and Technology.

Reading Skill or Strategy

Good readers use a number of skills and strategies to make sure they understand what they are reading. These lessons will give you the tools you need to read and understand social studies.

Key Terms, People, and Academic Vocabulary

Before you read the chapter, review these words and think about them. Have you heard the word before? What do you already know about the people? Then watch for these words and their meanings as you read the chapter.

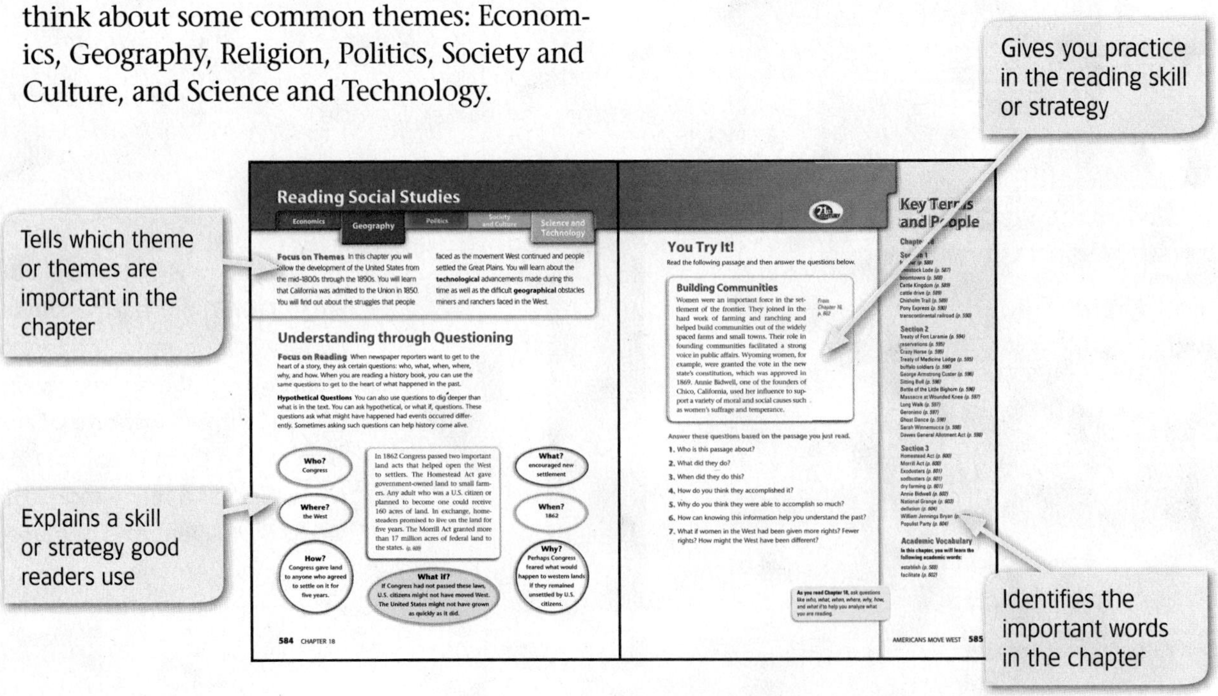
Gives you practice in the reading skill or strategy
Tells which theme or themes are important in the chapter
Explains a skill or strategy good readers use
Identifies the important words in the chapter
Reading Social Studies
Understanding through Questioning
You Try It!
Building Communities

© Houghton Mifflin Harcourt Publishing Company

Tip #2

Read like a Skilled Reader

You will never get better at reading your social studies book—or any book for that matter—unless you spend some time thinking about how to be a better reader.

Skilled readers do the following:

- They preview what they are supposed to read before they actually begin reading. They look for vocabulary words, titles of sections, information in the margin, or maps or charts they should study.
- They divide their notebook paper into two columns. They title one column "Notes from the Chapter" and the other column "Questions or Comments I Have."
- They take notes in both columns as they read.
- They read like **active readers**. The Active Reading list below shows you what that means.
- They use clues in the text to help them figure out where the text is going. The best clues are called signal words.

  Chronological Order Signal Words: *first, second, third, before, after, later, next, following that, earlier, finally*

  Cause and Effect Signal Words: *because of, due to, as a result of, the reason for, therefore, consequently*

  Comparison/Contrast Signal Words: *likewise, also, as well as, similarly, on the other hand*

READING SOCIAL STUDIES

Active Reading

Successful readers are **active readers.** These readers know that it is up to them to figure out what the text means. Here are some steps you can take to become an active, and successful, reader.

Predict what will happen next based on what has already happened. When your predictions don't match what happens in the text, reread the confusing parts.

Question what is happening as you read. Constantly ask yourself why things have happened, what things mean, and what caused certain events.

Summarize what you are reading frequently. Do not try to summarize the entire chapter! Read a bit and then summarize it. Then read on.

Connect what is happening in the part you're reading to what you have already read.

Clarify your understanding. Stop occasionally to ask yourself whether you are confused by anything. You may need to reread to clarify, or you may need to read further and collect more information before you can understand.

Visualize what is happening in the text. Try to see the events or places in your mind by drawing maps, making charts, or jotting down notes about what you are reading.

© Houghton Mifflin Harcourt Publishing Company

Tip #3

Pay Attention to Vocabulary

It is no fun to read something when you don't know what the words mean, but you can't learn new words if you only use or read the words you already know. In this book, we know we have probably used some words you don't know. But, we have followed a pattern as we have used more difficult words.

Key Terms and People

At the beginning of each section you will find a list of key terms or people that you will need to know. Be on the lookout for those words as you read through the section.

Freedmen's Bureau

In 1865 Congress established the **Freedmen's Bureau**, an agency providing relief for freedpeople and certain poor people in the South. The Bureau had a difficult job. At its high point, about 900 agents served the entire South. Bureau commissioner Oliver O. Howard eventually decided to use the Bureau's limited budget to distribute food to the poor and to provide education and legal help for freedpeople. The Bureau also helped African American war veterans.

The Freedmen's Bureau played an important role in establishing more schools in the South. Laws against educating slaves meant that most freedpeople had never learned to read or write. Before the war ended, however, northern groups, such as the American Missionary Association, began providing books and teachers to African Americans. The teachers were mostly women who were committed to helping freedpeople. One teacher said of her students, "I never before saw children so eager to learn . . . It is wonderful how [they] . . . can have so great a desire for knowledge, and such a capacity for attaining [reaching] it."

After the war, some freedpeople organized their own education efforts. For example, Freedmen's Bureau agents found that some African Americans had opened schools in abandoned buildings. Many white southerners continued to believe that African Americans should not be educated. Despite opposition, by 1869 more than 150,000 African American students were attending more than 3,000 schools. The Freedmen's Bureau also helped establish a number of universities for African Americans, including Howard and Fisk universities.

Students quickly filled the new classrooms. Working adults attended classes in the evening. African Americans hoped that education would help them to understand and protect their rights and to enable them to find better jobs. Both black and white southerners benefited from the effort to provide greater access to education in the South.

READING CHECK **Analyzing** How did the Freedmen's Bureau help reform education in the South?

Helping the Freedpeople

Congress created the Freedmen's Bureau to help freedpeople and poor southerners recover from the Civil War. The Bureau assisted people by:

- providing supplies and medical services
- establishing schools
- supervising contracts between freedpeople and employers
- taking care of lands abandoned or captured during the war

What role did the Freedmen's Bureau play during Reconstruction?

556

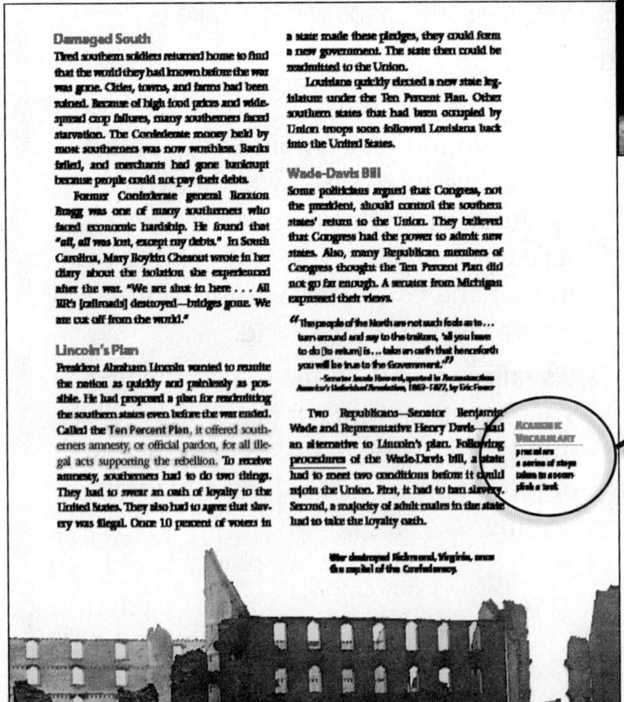

Damaged South

Tired southern soldiers returned home to find that the world they had known before the war was gone. Cities, towns, and farms had been ruined. Because of high food prices and widespread crop failures, many southerners faced starvation. The Confederate money held by most southerners was now worthless. Banks failed, and merchants had gone bankrupt because people could not pay their debts.

Former Confederate general Braxton Bragg was one of many southerners who faced economic hardship. He found that "all, all was lost, except my debts." In South Carolina, Mary Boykin Chesnut wrote in her diary about the isolation she experienced after the war. "We are shut in here . . . All RR's [railroads] destroyed—bridges gone. We are cut off from the world."

Lincoln's Plan

President Abraham Lincoln wanted to reunite the nation as quickly and painlessly as possible. He had proposed a plan for readmitting the southern states even before the war ended. Called the **Ten Percent Plan**, it offered southerners amnesty, or official pardon, for all illegal acts supporting the rebellion. To receive amnesty, southerners had to do two things. They had to swear an oath of loyalty to the United States. They also had to agree that slavery was illegal. Once 10 percent of voters in a state made these pledges, they could form a new government. The state then could be readmitted to the Union.

Louisiana quickly elected a new state legislature under the Ten Percent Plan. Other southern states that had been occupied by Union troops soon followed Louisiana back into the United States.

Wade-Davis Bill

Some politicians argued that Congress, not the president, should control the southern states' return to the Union. They believed that Congress had the power to admit new states. Also, many Republican members of Congress thought the Ten Percent Plan did not go far enough. A senator from Michigan expressed their views.

"The people of the North are not such fools as to . . . turn around and say to the traitors, 'all you have to do [to return] is . . . take an oath that henceforth you will be true to the Government.'"

—Senator Jacob Howard, quoted in *Reconstruction: America's Unfinished Revolution, 1863–1877*, by Eric Foner

Two Republicans—Senator Benjamin Wade and Representative Henry Davis—had an alternative to Lincoln's plan. Following procedures of the Wade-Davis bill, a state had to meet two conditions before it could rejoin the Union. First, it had to ban slavery. Second, a majority of adult males in the state had to take the loyalty oath.

ACADEMIC VOCABULARY
procedure a series of steps taken to accomplish a task

War destroyed Richmond, Virginia, once the capital of the Confederacy.

553

Academic Vocabulary

When we use a word that is important in all classes, not just social studies, we define it in the margin under the heading *Academic Vocabulary*. You will run into these academic words in other textbooks, so you should learn what they mean while reading this book.

READING SOCIAL STUDIES

© Houghton Mifflin Harcourt Publishing Company

Words to Know

As you read this social studies textbook, you will be more successful if you know or learn the meanings of the words on this page. There are two types of words listed here. The first list contains academic words, the words we discussed at the bottom of the previous page. These words are important in all classes, not just social studies. The second list contains words that are special to this particular topic of social studies, U.S. history.

Academic Words

abstract	expressing a quality or idea without reference to an actual thing
acquire	to get
advocate	to plead in favor of
affect	to change or influence
agreement	a decision reached by two or more people or groups
aspects	parts
authority	power, right to rule
cause	the reason something happens
circumstances	surrounding situation
classical	referring to the cultures of ancient Greece or Rome
complex	difficult, not simple
concrete	specific, real
consequences	the effects of a particular event or events
contemporary	existing at the same time
contract	a binding legal agreement
criteria	rules for defining
develop/ development	to grow or improve/ 1. The process of growing or improving; 2. Creation
distinct	separate
distribute	to divide among a group of people
effect	the results of an action or decision
efficient/ efficiency	productive not wasteful the quality of being efficient
element	part
establish	to set up or create
execute	to perform, carry out
explicit	fully revealed without vagueness
facilitate	to bring about
factor	cause
features	characteristics
function	use or purpose
ideal	ideas or goals that people try to live up to
impact	effect, result
implement	to put in place
implications	effects of a decision
implicit	understood though not clearly put into words
incentive	something that leads people to follow a certain course of action
influence	to change or have an effect on
innovation	a new idea or way of doing something
logic/logical	well-thought-out ideas/reasoned, well thought out
method	a way of doing something
motive	a reason for doing something
neutral	unbiased, not favoring either side in a conflict
policy	rule, course of action
primary	main, most important
principle	basic belief, rule, or law
procedure	a series of steps taken to accomplish a task
process	a series of steps by which a task is accomplished
purpose	the reason something is done
reaction	a response
rebel	to fight against authority
role	1. a part or function 2. Assigned behavior
strategy	a plan for fighting a battle or war
structure	the way something is set up or organized
traditional	customary, time-honored
values	ideas that people hold dear and try to live by
vary/various	1. To be different 2. of many types

Social Studies Words

AD	refers to dates after Jesus's birth
BC	refers to dates before the birth of Jesus of Nazareth
BCE	refers to "Before Common Era," dates before the birth of Jesus of Nazareth
CE	refers to "Common Era," dates after Jesus's birth
century	a period of 100 years
civilization	the culture of a particular time or place
climate	the weather conditions in a certain area over a long period of time
culture	the knowledge, beliefs, customs, and values of a group of people
custom	a repeated practice; tradition
democracy	governmental rule by the people, usually on a majority rule principle
economy	the system in which people make and exchange goods and services
geography	the study of the earth's physical and cultural features
independence	freedom from forceful rule
monarchy	governmental rule by one person, a king or queen
North	the region of the United States sometimes defined by the states that did not secede from the Union during the Civil War
rebellion	an organized resistance to the established government
society	a group of people who share common traditions
South	the region of the United States sometimes defined by the states that seceded from the Union to form the Confederate States of America

© Houghton Mifflin Harcourt Publishing Company

How to Make This Book Work for You

Studying U.S. history will be easy for you using this textbook. Take a few minutes to become familiar with the easy-to-use structure and special features of this history book. See how this U.S. history textbook will make history come alive for you!

Unit

Each chapter of this textbook is part of a unit of study focusing on a particular time period. Each unit opener provides an illustration, painting, or photograph that gives you an overview of the exciting topics that you will study in the unit.

Chapter

Each chapter begins with a chapter-opener introduction that has an Essential Question to examine while studying the chapter, and ends with Chapter Review pages and a Standardized Test Practice page.

Reading Social Studies These chapter-level reading lessons teach you skills and provide opportunities for practice to help you read the textbook more successfully. Within each chapter there is a point-of-reference *Focus on Reading* note in the margin to demonstrate the reading skill for the chapter. There are also questions in the Chapter Review activity to make sure that you understand the reading skill.

Social Studies Skills The Social Studies Skills lessons, which appear at the end of each chapter, give you an opportunity to learn and use a skill that you will most likely use again while in school. You will also be given a chance to make sure that you understand each skill by answering related questions in the Chapter Review activity.

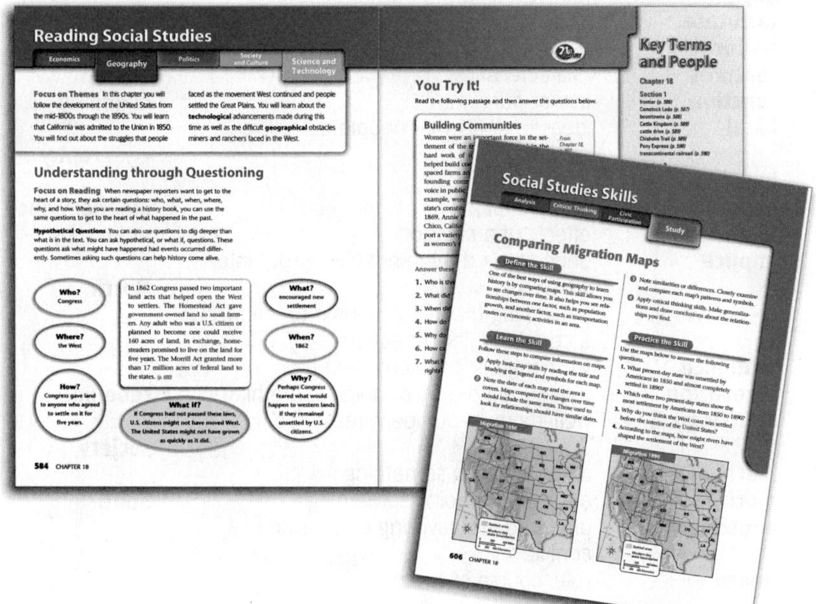

© Houghton Mifflin Harcourt Publishing Company

Section

The Section opener pages include: Main Idea statements, an overarching Big Idea statement, and Key Terms and People. In addition, each section includes the following special features.

If You Were There . . . introductions begin each section with a situation for you to respond to, placing you in the time period and in a situation related to the content that you will be studying in the section.

Building Background sections connect what will be covered in this section with what you studied in the previous section.

Short sections of content organize the information in each section into small chunks of text that you should not find too overwhelming.

The **Taking Notes** feature allows you to write down the most important information from the section in a usable format.

SECTION 1

Miners, Ranchers, and Railroads

What You Will Learn...

Main Ideas

1. A mining boom brought growth to the West.
2. The demand for cattle created a short-lived Cattle Kingdom on the Great Plains.
3. East and West were connected by the transcontinental railroad.

The Big Idea

As more settlers moved West, mining, ranching, and railroads soon transformed the western landscape.

Key Terms

frontier, *p. 586*
Comstock Lode, *p. 587*
boomtowns, *p. 588*
Cattle Kingdom, *p. 589*
cattle drive, *p. 589*
Chisholm Trail, *p. 589*
Pony Express, *p. 590*
transcontinental railroad, *p. 590*

hmhsocialstudies.com
TAKING NOTES

Use the graphic organizer online to take notes on the kinds of economic opportunities that people found in the West.

If YOU were there...

You are a cowboy in Texas in 1875. You love life on the open range, the quiet nights, and the freedom. You even like the hard work of the long cattle drives to Kansas. But you know that times are changing. Homesteaders are moving in and fencing off their lands. Some of the older cowboys say it's time to settle down and buy a small ranch. You hope that they're not right.

What would make you give up a cowboy's life?

BUILDING BACKGROUND In the years following the Civil War, the U.S. population grew rapidly. Settlements in the West increased. More discoveries of gold and silver attracted adventurers, while the open range drew others. Thousands of former Civil War soldiers also joined the move West.

Mining Boom Brings Growth

During the years surrounding the War, most Americans had thought of the Great Plains and other western lands as the Great American Desert. In the years following the Civil War, Americans witnessed the rapid growth of the U.S. population and the spread of settlements throughout the West. With the admission of the state of California to the Union in 1850, the western boundary of the American **frontier**—an undeveloped area—had reached the Pacific Ocean.

The frontier changed dramatically as more and more people moved westward. Settlers built homes, fenced off land, and laid out ranches and farms. Miners, ranchers, and farmers remade the landscape of the West as they adapted to their new surroundings. The geography of the West was further changed by the development and expansion of a large and successful railroad industry that moved the West's natural resources to eastern markets. Gold and silver were the most valuable natural resources, and mining companies used the growing railroad network to bring these precious metals to the East.

586 CHAPTER 18

Effects of the Transcontinental Railroad

QUICK FACTS

- Increased settlement of the West
- Increased business activity and East-West trade
- Helped make the railroad industry one of the most powerful in the country

Results of the Railroad

The transcontinental railroad increased both economic growth and the population in the West. Railroad companies provided better transportation for people and goods. They also sold land to settlers, which encouraged people to move West.

New railroads helped businesses. Western timber companies, miners, ranchers, and farmers shipped wood, metals, meat, and grain east by railroad. In exchange, eastern businesses shipped manufactured goods to the West. As trade between regions increased, the idea that the U.S. economy was interdependent becam... perceptions of ti... railroad schedules began to unite areas that had before existed under different times. Four continental time zones were established in 1883.

Railroad companies encouraged people to put their money into the railroad business, which they did—sometimes unwisely. Railroad speculation and the collapse of railroad owner Jay Cooke's banking firm helped start the Panic of 1873. By the 1880s, many small western railroads were deeply in debt. Despite such setbacks, Americans remained interested in railroad investments. By 1890 there were about 164,000 more miles of track in operation than in 1865. Railroads had become one of the biggest industries in the United States.

THE IMPACT TODAY

Today's businesses ship goods across the country using railroads, the interstate highway system, and airplanes.

READING CHECK **Finding Main Ideas** How did the railroad affect the development of the West?

SUMMARY In this section you learned about the increased settlement of the West.

Section 1 Assessment

hmhsocialstudies.com
ONLINE QUIZ

Reviewing Ideas, Terms, and People

1. a. **Recall** Why did Americans move West in the years following the Civil War?
   b. **Draw Conclusions** What effect did the discovery of the **Comstock Lode** have on the West?
   c. **Evaluate** Do you think women were important to the success of mining towns? Why or why not?
2. a. **Recall** What led to the cattle boom in the West?
   b. **Analyze** Why was there competition between ranchers and farmers to settle in the Great Plains?
   c. **Evaluate** What played the biggest role in ending the **Cattle Kingdom**? Why?
3. a. **Recall** When and where did the Union Pacific and Central Pacific lines meet?
   b. **Make Generalizations** How do you think the **transcontinental railroad** improved people's lives?

Critical Thinking

4. **Comparing** Review your notes about opportunities in the West. Then use a graphic organizer like the one below to list the effects of these opportunities.

Opportunity	Effect

FOCUS ON WRITING

5. **Taking Notes on Mining, Ranching, and the Railroads** As you read this section, take notes on how mining, ranching, and railroads changed the West. How might a railroad worker feel about these changes?

592 CHAPTER 18

© Houghton Mifflin Harcourt Publishing Company • Image Credits: (t), The Granger Collection, New York

Reading Check questions end each section of content so that you can test whether or not you understand what you have just studied.

Summary statements provide you with a brief review of the section's main points.

Section Assessment boxes provide an opportunity for you to make sure that you understand the main ideas of the section. We also provide assessment practice online!

© Houghton Mifflin Harcourt Publishing Company

Alabama: Physical

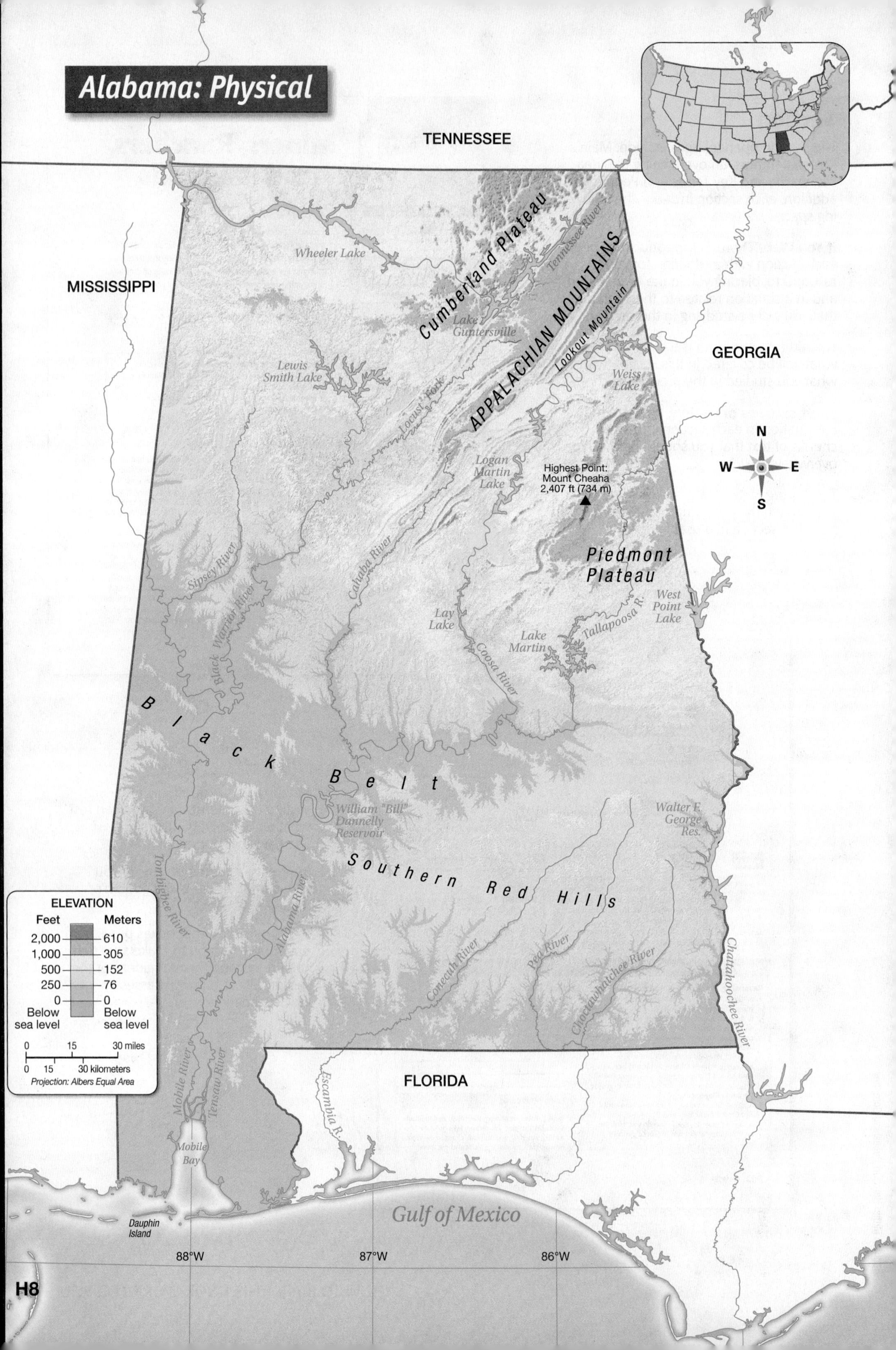
TENNESSEE
MISSISSIPPI
GEORGIA
FLORIDA
Gulf of Mexico
Wheeler Lake
Cumberland Plateau
Tennessee River
APPALACHIAN MOUNTAINS
Lookout Mountain
Lake Guntersville
Lewis Smith Lake
Weiss Lake
Locust Fork
Logan Martin Lake
Highest Point: Mount Cheaha 2,407 ft (734 m)
Piedmont Plateau
Sipsey River
Black Warrior River
Cahaba River
Lay Lake
Coosa River
Lake Martin
Tallapoosa R.
West Point Lake
Black Belt
William "Bill" Dannelly Reservoir
Walter F. George Res.
Southern Red Hills
Tombigbee River
Alabama River
Conecuh River
Pea River
Choctawhatchee River
Chattahoochee River
Escambia R.
Mobile River
Tensaw River
Mobile Bay
Dauphin Island
88°W
87°W
86°W
N
S
E
W
ELEVATION
Feet
Meters
2,000
1,000
500
250
0
Below sea level
610
305
152
76
0
Below sea level
0 15 30 miles
0 15 30 kilometers
Projection: Albers Equal Area

Alabama: Political

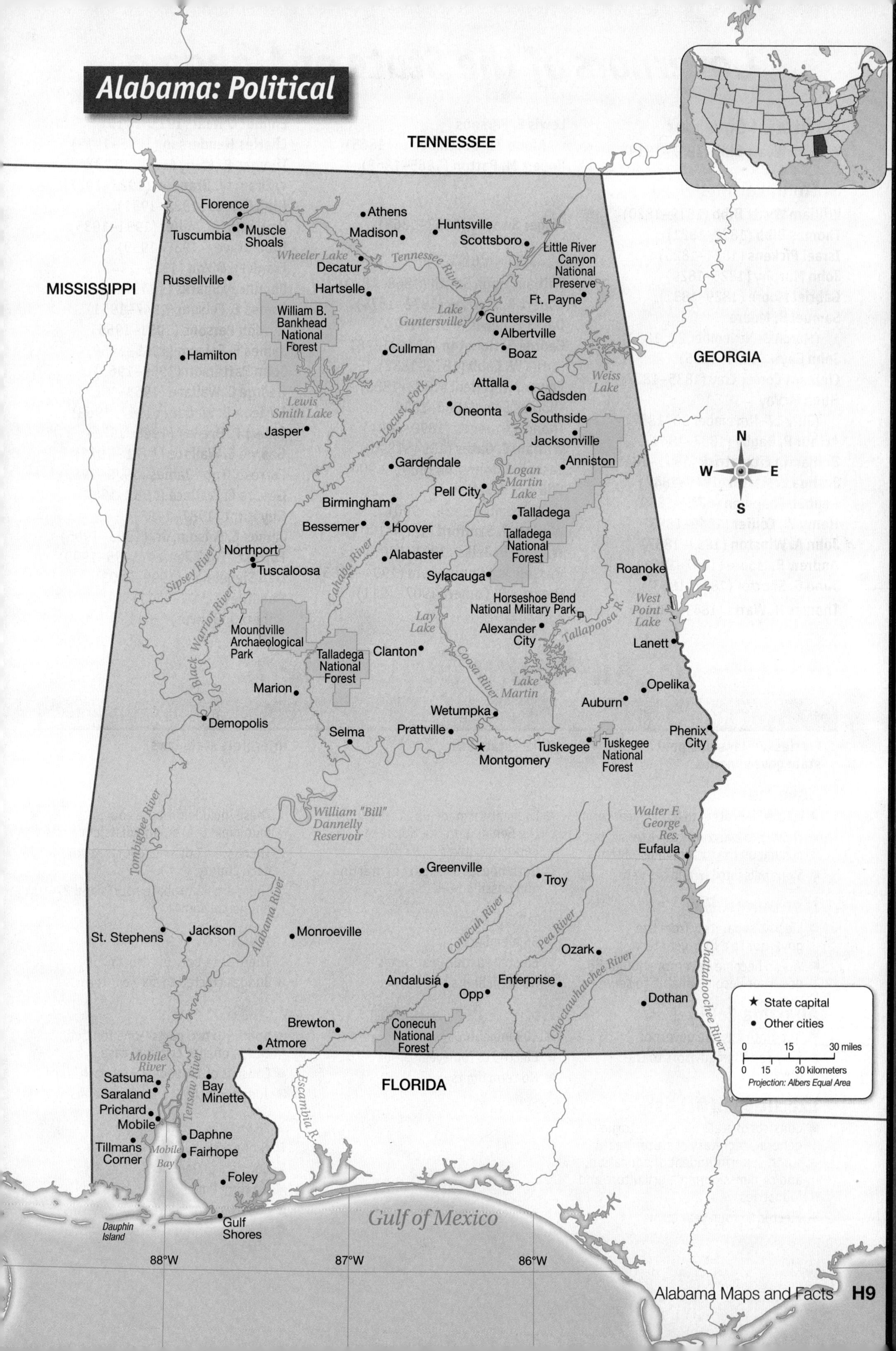

TENNESSEE
MISSISSIPPI
GEORGIA
FLORIDA
Gulf of Mexico
Florence
Athens
Tuscumbia
Muscle Shoals
Madison
Huntsville
Scottsboro
Little River Canyon National Preserve
Wheeler Lake
Decatur
Tennessee River
Russellville
Hartselle
Ft. Payne
William B. Bankhead National Forest
Lake Guntersville
Guntersville
Albertville
Cullman
Boaz
Hamilton
Attalla
Weiss Lake
Gadsden
Lewis Smith Lake
Oneonta
Southside
Locust Fork
Jasper
Jacksonville
Gardendale
Anniston
Logan Martin Lake
Pell City
Birmingham
Talladega
Bessemer
Hoover
Talladega National Forest
Northport
Alabaster
Tuscaloosa
Sipsey River
Cahaba River
Sylacauga
Roanoke
Black Warrior River
Horseshoe Bend National Military Park
West Point Lake
Moundville Archaeological Park
Lay Lake
Alexander City
Tallapoosa R.
Talladega National Forest
Clanton
Lanett
Coosa River
Lake Martin
Marion
Opelika
Auburn
Wetumpka
Demopolis
Selma
Prattville
Phenix City
Tuskegee
Tuskegee National Forest
Montgomery
Tombigbee River
William "Bill" Dannelly Reservoir
Walter F. George Res.
Eufaula
Greenville
Troy
Alabama River
Conecuh River
Pea River
St. Stephens
Jackson
Monroeville
Ozark
Chattahoochee River
Andalusia
Enterprise
Choctawhatchee River
Opp
Dothan
Brewton
Conecuh National Forest
Atmore
Mobile River
Tensaw River
Escambia R.
Satsuma
Bay Minette
Saraland
Prichard
Mobile
Daphne
Tillmans Corner
Mobile Bay
Fairhope
Foley
Dauphin Island
Gulf Shores
88°W
87°W
86°W
N
S
E
W
★ State capital
• Other cities
0 15 30 miles
0 15 30 kilometers
Projection: Albers Equal Area

Alabama Maps and Facts

Governors of the State of Alabama

Territorial Governor

William Wyatt Bibb (1817–1819)

State Governors

William Wyatt Bibb (1819–1820)
Thomas Bibb (1820–1821)
Israel Pickens (1821–1825)
John Murphy (1825–1829)
Gabriel Moore (1829–1831)
Samuel B. Moore (March 3–November 22, 1831)
John Gayle (1831–1835)
Clement Comer Clay (1835–1837)
Hugh McVay (July 17–November 30, 1837)
Arthur P. Bagby (1837–1841)
Benjamin Fitzpatrick (1841–1845)
Joshua L. Martin (1845–1847)
Reuben Chapman (1847–1849)
Henry W. Collier (1849–1853)
John A. Winston (1853–1857)
Andrew B. Moore (1857–1861)
John G. Shorter (1861–1863)
Thomas H. Watts (1863–1865)
Lewis E. Parsons (June 21–December 13, 1865)
Robert M. Patton (1865–1868)

Military Governor

Wager Swayne (1867–1868)

State Governors

William Hugh Smith (1868–1870)
Robert B. Lindsay (1872–1874)
David P. Lewis (1872–1874)
George S. Houston (1874–1878)
Rufus W. Cobb (1878–1882)
Edward A. O'Neal (1882–1886)
Thomas Seay (1886–1890)
Thomas G. Jones (1890–1894)
William C. Oates (1894–1896)
Joseph F. Johnston (1896–1900)
William D. Jelks (December 1–26, 1900)
William J. Samford (1900–1901)
William D. Jelks (1901–1907)
Russell M. Cunningham (1904–1905)
Braxton B. Comer (1907–1911)
Emmet O'Neal (1911–1915)
Charles Henderson (1915–1919)
Thomas E. Kilby (1919–1923)
William W. Brandon (1923–1927)
Bibb Graves (1927–1931)
Benjamin M. Miller (1931–1935)
Bibb Graves (1935–1939)
Frank M. Dixon (1939–1943)
Chauncey Sparks (1943–1947)
James E. Folsom (1947–1951)
Gordon Persons (1951–1955)
James E. Folsom (1955–1959)
John Patterson (1959–1963)
George C. Wallace (1963–1967)
Lurleen B. Wallace (1967–1968)
Albert P. Brewer (1968–1971)
George C. Wallace (1971 –1979)
Forrest "Fob" James (1979–1983)
George C. Wallace (1983–1987)
Guy Hunt (1987–1993)
James E. Folsom, Jr. (1993–1995)
Forrest "Fob" James (1995–1999)
Don Siegelman (1999–2003)
Bob Riley (2003–2011)
Robert J. Bentley (2011–)

Alabama Government

Executive Branch

Carries out laws and policies of state government

Governor

- Elected by voters to a four-year term
- Limited to two consecutive terms, but no limit on the total number of terms
- Signs bills into law and has veto power

Lieutenant Governor

- Elected separately from the governor to a four-year term
- Would become governor should the governor become unable to serve

Alabama Cabinet

- Appointed by the governor
- Serve as chief advisors to the governor

Executive Officials

- Consists of state auditor, attorney general, secretary of state, treasurer, superintendent of education, and commissioner of agriculture and industries
- Elected to four-year terms

Legislative Branch

Makes state laws

Bicameral System

- Legislature made up of two houses, the Senate and the House of Representatives
- Both houses take part in drafting and passing laws

State Senate

- 35 members
- Elected to four-year terms
- No term limits

House of Representatives

- 105 members
- Elected to four-year terms
- No term limits

Judicial Branch

Interprets state laws

County Courts

- These include probate courts, municipal courts, and district courts
- There are 67 district courts, 1 for each county
- There are 68 probate courts and 274 municipal courts

Circuit Courts

- There are 41 circuit courts
- Judges elected to six-year terms

Appeals Courts

- Split into two parts—one for civil cases, one for criminal cases
- Consists of 10 judges, 5 for each court
- Judges elected to six-year terms

Supreme Court

- Highest state court
- Consists of 9 justices
- No term limits
- Justices elected to six-year terms
- Justices cannot seek re-election after age 70

© Houghton Mifflin Harcourt Publishing Company

Alabama State Facts

State amphibian	Red hills salamander
State bird	Yellowhammer
State flower	Camellia
State freshwater fish	Largemouth bass
State fruit	Blackberry
State game bird	Wild turkey
State gemstone	Star blue quartz
State insect	Monarch butterfly
State mammal	Black bear
State mascot and butterfly	Eastern tiger swallowtail
State mineral	Hematite
State nut	Pecan
State reptile	Alabama red-bellied turtle
State saltwater fish	Tarpon
State tree	Southern long-leaf pine
State wildflower	Oak-leaf hydrangea
Capital	Montgomery
Motto	"We Dare Maintain Our Rights"
Song	"Alabama"
Folk dance	Square dance
Year of statehood	1819
Highest natural point	2,407 feet (Mount Cheaha)
Total area	51,701 square miles
National rank in total area	29
Population (2011 estimate)	4,802,740
National rank in population	23
Most populous city	Birmingham
Most populous metropolitan area	Greater Birmingham area
Number of counties	67
Bordering states	Florida, Georgia, Mississippi, Tennessee

State flag

Monarch butterfly

Black bear

© Houghton Mifflin Harcourt Publishing Company • Image Credits: (bkgd) ©Dave Allen Photography/Shutterstock.com; (t) ©Stockbyte/Getty Images/Houghton Mifflin Harcourt; (c) ©James Urbach/Purestock/SuperStock/Houghton Mifflin Harcourt

AL Alabama

Alabama State Capitol, Montgomery

Offshore drilling platform

Sunset at Mobile Bay

As you read the following pages and work through the unpacking of the United States Studies: Industrial Revolution to the Present Standards, you will discover the big ideas and key concepts that your teacher expects you to learn and understand.

You will see two things:

1 **>** what the standard actually says

2 **What does it mean?** an explanation to help you understand the big ideas within the standard

United States Studies: Industrial Revolution to the Present

>1. Explain the impact of industrialization, urbanization, communication, and cultural changes on life in the United States from the late nineteenth century to World War I.

What does it mean?

Identify and discuss changes that occurred in the United States from the late 1800s until the end of World War I in 1918. These changes include an growth in industrial production, the increasing population of cities, technological inventions that helped people communicate across long distances, and new forms of entertainment and social relationships. See chapters 4, The Industrial Age, and 5, Immigrants and Urban Life, for more information.

>2. Describe reform movements and changing social conditions during the Progressive Era in the United States.

- **Relating countries of origin and experiences of new immigrants to life in the United States** Examples: Ellis Island and Angel Island experiences
- **Identifying workplace reforms, including the eight-hour workday, child labor laws, and workers' compensation laws**
- **Identifying political reforms of Progressive movement leaders, including Theodore Roosevelt and the establishment of the national park system**
- **Identifying social reforms of the Progressive movement, including efforts by Jane Addams, Clara Barton, and Julia Tutwiler**

© Houghton Mifflin Harcourt Publishing Company • ©imac/Alamy Images/©Amar and Isabelle Guillen - Guillen Photography/Alamy Images/©Digital Vision/Getty Images

Camellia

Yellowhammer

- **Recognizing goals of the early civil rights movement and the purpose of the National Association for the Advancement of Colored People (NAACP)**
- **Explaining Progressive movement provisions of the Sixteenth, Seventeenth, Eighteenth, Nineteenth, and Twenty-first Amendments to the Constitution of the United States**

What does it mean?

Identify the causes that Progressive reformers worked to change during the late 1800s and early 1900s, and discuss the efforts of their reforms. These include the changes that immigration created, changes in workers' rights laws, the creation of national parks, and the early struggle for equal rights. Also describe the leaders of the Progressive movement and the Constitutional Amendments adopted during the era. See chapters 5, Immigrants and Urban Life, and 6, The Progressive Spirit of Reform, for more information.

>3. Identify causes and consequences of World War I and reasons for United States' entry into the war.
Examples: sinking of the *Lusitania*, Zimmerman Note, alliances, militarism, imperialism, nationalism

- **Describing military and civilian roles in the United States during World War I**
- **Explaining roles of important persons associated with World War I, including Woodrow Wilson and Archduke Franz Ferdinand**
- **Analyzing technological advances of the World War I era for their impact on modern warfare**
  Examples: machine gun, tank, submarine, airplane, poisonous gas, gas mask
- **Locating on a map major countries involved in World War I and boundary changes after the war**
- **Explaining the intensification of isolationism in the United States after World War I**
  Examples: reaction of the Congress of the United States to the Treaty of Versailles, League of Nations, and Red Scare
- **Recognizing the strategic placement of military bases in Alabama**

What does it mean?

Discuss the events that led to World War I, the battles of the war, changes on the home front, and how the end of the war affected the world and the United States. Identify world leaders during the war, new technology that was invented to fight the war, the countries involved in the war, and the contribution of Alabamians to the war effort. See Chapter 8, World War I, for more information.

Fall leaves

© Houghton Mifflin Harcourt Publishing Company • Image Credits: ©photolibrary. All rights reserved.

>4. Identify cultural and economic developments in the United States from 1900 through the 1930s.

- **Describing the impact of various writers, musicians, and artists on American culture during the Harlem Renaissance and the Jazz Age**
  Examples: Langston Hughes, Louis Armstrong, Ernest Hemingway, F. Scott Fitzgerald, Andrew Wyeth, Frederic Remington, W. C. Handy, Erskine Hawkins, George Gershwin, Zora Neale Hurston
- **Identifying contributions of turn-of-the-century inventors**
  Examples: George Washington Carver, Henry Ford, Alexander Graham Bell, Thomas Alva Edison, Wilbur and Orville Wright
- **Describing the emergence of the modern woman during the early 1900s**
  Examples: Amelia Earhart, Zelda Fitzgerald, Helen Keller, suffragettes, suffragists, Susan B. Anthony, flappers, Margaret Washington
- **Identifying notable persons of the early 1900s**
  Examples: Babe Ruth, Charles A. Lindbergh, W. E. B. Du Bois, John T. Scopes
- **Comparing results of the economic policies of the Warren G. Harding, Calvin Coolidge, and Herbert Hoover Administrations**
  Examples: higher wages, increase in consumer goods, collapse of farm economy, extension of personal credit, stock market crash, Immigration Act of 1924

What does it mean?

Describe the art, music, and literature that were created during the early 1900s and their effect on the United States, especially those of the 1920s. Discuss the new roles for women that arose during the period. Identify important inventors and celebrities of the time. Explain how presidents Harding, Coolidge, and Hoover affected the economy. See chapters 7, 8, 9, and 10 for more information.

Alabama cotton

>5. Explain causes and effects of the Great Depression on the people of the United States.
Examples: economic failure, loss of farms, rising unemployment, building of Hoovervilles

- **Identifying patterns of migration during the Great Depression**
- **Locating on a map the area of the United States known as the Dust Bowl**
- **Describing the importance of the election of Franklin D. Roosevelt as President of the United States, including the New Deal alphabet agencies**
- **Locating on a map river systems utilized by the Tennessee Valley Authority (TVA)**

What does it mean?

Discuss the changes in the economy that led to the Great Depression and how those changes affected people's lives, including why and where they moved during the period. Identify the region known as the Dust Bowl and the area where the Tennessee Valley Authority built dams. Describe the changes that Franklin Roosevelt made to the United States as president. See Chapter 10, The Great Depression, for more information.

>6. Identify causes and consequences of World War II and reasons for entry of the United States into the war.

- **Locating on a map Allied countries and Axis Powers**
- **Locating on a map key engagements of World War II, including Pearl Harbor; the battles of Normandy, Stalingrad, and Midway; and the Battle of the Bulge**
- **Identifying key figures of World War II, including Franklin D. Roosevelt, Sir Winston Churchill, Harry S. Truman, Joseph Stalin, Adolf Hitler, Benito Mussolini, Michinomiya Hirohito, and Hideki Tojo**
- **Describing the development of and the decision to use the atomic bomb**
- **Describing human costs associated with World War II**
  Examples: the Holocaust, civilian and military casualties
- **Explaining the importance of the surrender of the Axis Powers ending World War II**

What does it mean?

Discuss the events that led to World War II, the battles during the war, and how the end of the war affected the world and the United States. Identify the countries involved in the war, important battles, and world leaders during the war. Describe the effects of the war, including the dropping of the atomic bomb and the Holocaust. See chapters 11, World War II, and 12, Early Years of the Cold War, for more information.

© Houghton Mifflin Harcourt Publishing Company • Image Credits: ©Waldo4/Fotolia

>7. Identify changes on the American home front during World War II.
Example: rationing

- **Recognizing the retooling of factories from consumer to military production**
- **Identifying new roles of women and African Americans in the workforce**
- **Describing increased demand on Birmingham steel industry and Port of Mobile facilities**
- **Describing the experience of African Americans and Japanese Americans in the United States during World War II, including the Tuskegee Airmen and occupants of internment camps**

What does it mean?

Discuss the changes in U.S. society during World War II, including changes in what factories produced; the effects of the war on women, African Americans, and Japanese Americans; and the contributions of Alabamians to the war effort. See Chapter 11, World War II, for more information.

>8. Describe how the United States' role in the Cold War influenced domestic and international events.

- **Describing the origin and meaning of the Iron Curtain and communism**
- **Recognizing how the Cold War conflict manifested itself through sports**
  Examples: Olympic Games, international chess tournaments, Ping-Pong diplomacy
- **Identifying strategic diplomatic initiatives that intensified the Cold War, including the policies of Harry S. Truman, Dwight D. Eisenhower, and John F. Kennedy**
  Examples: trade embargoes, Marshall Plan, arms race, Berlin blockade and airlift, Berlin Wall, mutually assured destruction, North Atlantic Treaty Organization (NATO), Warsaw Pact, Cuban missile crisis, Bay of Pigs invasion
- **Identifying how Cold War tensions resulted in armed conflict**
  Examples: Korean Conflict, Vietnam War, proxy wars
- **Describing the impact of the Cold War on technological innovations**
  Examples: *Sputnik*; space race; weapons of mass destruction; accessibility of microwave ovens, calculators, and computers
- **Recognizing Alabama's role in the Cold War**
  Examples: rocket production at Redstone Arsenal, helicopter training at Fort Rucker
- **Assessing effects of the end of the Cold War Era**
  Examples: policies of Mikhail Gorbachev; collapse of the Soviet Union; Ronald W. Reagan's foreign policies, including the Strategic Defense Initiative (SDI or Star Wars)

What does it mean?

Discuss the beginning of the Cold War, and the events and effect of it. Describe how Cold War tensions affected relationships and interactions between countries, including wars. Identify the effects of inventions of the Cold War, Alabama's role in the Cold War, and the effects of the end of the Cold War. See chapters 12, 14, and 15 for more information.

American White Ibis

>9. Critique major social and cultural changes in the United States since World War II.

- **Identifying key persons and events of the modern Civil Rights Movement**
  Examples: persons—Martin Luther King Jr., Rosa Parks, Fred Shuttlesworth, John Lewis
  events—*Brown versus Board of Education*, Montgomery Bus Boycott, student protests, Freedom Rides, Selma-to-Montgomery Voting Rights March, political assassinations
- **Describing the changing role of women in United States' society and how it affected the family unit**
  Examples: women in the workplace, latchkey children
- **Recognizing the impact of music genres and artists on United States' culture since World War II**
  Examples: genres—protest songs; Motown, rock and roll, rap, folk, and country music
  artists—Elvis Presley, the Beatles, Bob Dylan, Aretha Franklin, Hank Williams
- **Identifying the impact of media, including newspapers, AM and FM radio, television, twenty-four hour sports and news programming, talk radio, and Internet social networking, on United States' culture since World War II**

What does it mean?

Describe changes in U.S. society and people's lives since the 1940s, including changing women's roles, music styles, and media available to Americans. Discuss how these changes have affected the way Americans live. See chapters 12, 13, 14, 15, and 16 for more information.

>10. Analyze changing economic priorities and cycles of economic expansion and contraction for their impact on society since World War II.
Examples: shift from manufacturing to service economy, higher standard of living, globalization, outsourcing, insourcing, "boom and bust," economic bubbles

- **Identifying policies and programs that had an economic impact on society since World War II**
  Examples: G. I. Bill of Rights of 1944, Medicare and Medicaid, Head Start programs, space exploration, Children's Health Insurance Program (CHIP), environmental protection issues
- **Analyzing consequences of immigration for their impact on national and Alabama economies since World War II**

What does it mean?

Describe changes in the U.S. economy since the end of World War II and their effect on society, including immigration. See chapters 12, 13, 15, and 16 for more information.

>11. Identify technological advancements on society in the United States since World War II.
Examples: 1950s—fashion doll, audio cassette
1960s—action figure, artificial heart, Internet, calculator
1970s—word processor, video game, cellular telephone
1980s—personal computer, Doppler radar, digital cellular telephone
1990s—World Wide Web, digital video diskette (DVD)
2000s—digital music player, social networking technology, personal Global Positioning System (GPS) device

What does it mean?

Describe technologies created since the 1940s and how they have affected life in the United States. See chapters 12, 15, and 16 for more information.

>12. Evaluate significant political issues and policies of presidential administrations since World War II.

- **Identifying domestic policies that shaped the United States since World War II**
  Examples: desegregation of the military, Interstate Highway System, federal funding for education, Great Society, affirmative action, Americans with Disabilities Act, welfare reform, Patriot Act, No Child Left Behind Act
- **Recognizing domestic issues that shaped the United States since World War II**
  Examples: McCarthyism, Watergate scandal, political assassinations, health care, impeachment, Hurricane Katrina
- **Identifying issues of foreign affairs that shaped the United States since World War II**
  Examples: Vietnam Conflict, Richard Nixon's China initiative, Jimmy Carter's human rights initiative, emergence of China and India as economic powers
- **Explaining how conflict in the Middle East impacted life in the United States since World War II**
  Examples: oil embargoes; Iranian hostage situation; Camp David Accords; Persian Gulf Wars; 1993 World Trade Center bombing; terrorist attacks on September 11, 2001; War on Terrorism; homeland security
- **Recognizing the election of Barack Obama as the culmination of a movement in the United States to realize equal opportunity for all Americans**
- **Identifying the 2008 presidential election as a watershed in the use of new technology and mass participation in the electoral process**

What does it mean?

Discuss the effects of political decisions by the United States since the 1940s, including those related to U.S. government and society as well as those relating to international relations, including the conflict in the Middle East. Describe the importance of the election of 2008. See chapters 12, 13, 14, 15, and 16 for more information.

Montgomery skyline

Bellingrath Gardens, Theodore

© Houghton Mifflin Harcourt Publishing Company • Image Credits: ©Steve McConnell/Alamy

PROLOGUE

Beginnings of a Nation:

A Review of United States History to 1860

BUILDING BACKGROUND The first settlers in the Americas came in small groups from Asia over the course of thousands of years. Much later, European colonists arrived. Europeans combined their traditions with the opportunities and environment of the Americas to create brand-new societies and, eventually, new nations.

© Houghton Mifflin Harcourt Publishing Company • Image Credits: (bkgd) © Bettmann/CORBIS

Our Colonial Heritage

Reading Focus *As you read, think about the kinds of people who arrived in the Americas to make a new home.* Most historians agree that the first people came to North America from Asia by crossing the Bering Land Bridge between 38,000 and 10,000 BC. As they spread through the Americas, these early Native Americans created many societies—groups that share a set of common values and traditions.

Land and climate had a dramatic impact on these early societies. Some places were good for farming or had a rich supply of wild animals and plants. In these areas large groups of people lived in villages. This was true in the Pacific Coast and parts of the East and Southwest. Other parts of North America had less game and were too dry and cold for farming. In these regions Native Americans lived in smaller groups and had to move often to find food. Farther south, in modern-day Mexico and Peru, Native Americans called the Aztec and the Inca each built powerful empires.

Contact and Colonies

The Atlantic and Pacific Oceans kept the Americas isolated from the rest of the world for many years. By the AD 1400s, however, Europeans were exploring the seas. They wanted to find overseas routes to the valuable Asian silk and spice trade. Portuguese sailors traveled east around the southern tip of Africa to reach Asia. Christopher Columbus convinced the king and queen of Spain to support his search for a western sea route. In 1492 Columbus's small fleet crossed the Atlantic Ocean. The ships landed not in Asia, as Columbus believed, but on an island in the Bahamas.

Ships such as these were used by European explorers.

Early Beginnings, 38,000 BC–1492

38,000 BC

c. 38,000 to 10,000 BC The first humans settle in North America.

c. AD 1200 The Aztec occupy central Mexico.

1492 Christopher Columbus sails across the Atlantic Ocean and reaches the Americas.

1492

© Houghton Mifflin Harcourt Publishing Company • Image Credits: (br), ©Jose Fuste Raga/age fotostock/SuperStock; p1 (cr), Mary Evans Picture Library; p1 (bl), © Kenneth Garrett/Getty Images

KEY FACTS

- **1620** The Pilgrims sign the Mayflower Compact, one of the first attempts at self-government in the colonies.

Other Europeans soon came to the Americas. Spanish soldiers called conquistadors conquered the Aztec and Inca and claimed their lands, encouraging Spain to carve out an empire in the Americas. Spain's success led countries such as France, the Netherlands, Sweden, and England to form their own colonies in North America.

The English Colonies

England founded thirteen colonies in North America, in three general regions, each with its own unique characteristics. The first permanent English settlement in North America was Jamestown, in what is now Virginia. Jamestown colonists came seeking wealth. Other colonists, such as the Pilgrims and the English Catholics who founded Maryland, came seeking religious freedom. All found many challenges and opportunities awaiting them in a new land.

The Southern Colonies

Virginia, Maryland, Georgia, and North and South Carolina made up the southern colonies. Like later colonists in New England, the early Virginia settlers relied on the aid of local Native Americans to survive the harsh conditions they faced. The southern economy depended upon growing cash crops such as tobacco and rice. The biggest farms were called plantations. At first indentured servants did much of the work on these plantations. By the 1700s, however, enslaved Africans had replaced indentured servants as the main source of labor. The southern colonies used harsh laws called slave codes to control and punish slaves.

The New England Colonies

New England consisted of Massachusetts, Connecticut, New Hampshire, and Rhode Island. Pilgrims and Puritans seeking religious freedom founded New England. They built a diverse economy based on shipping, fishing, farming, and manufacturing. Puritan families valued education

The Colonies, 1607–1765

April 6, 1607
English settlers found Jamestown, the first permanent English settlement in North America.

1607

1620 The Pilgrims arrive in New England to found the Plymouth Colony.

1630 Puritan colonists arrive in New England and found the Massachusetts Bay Colony.

Reconstruction of the Jamestown colony

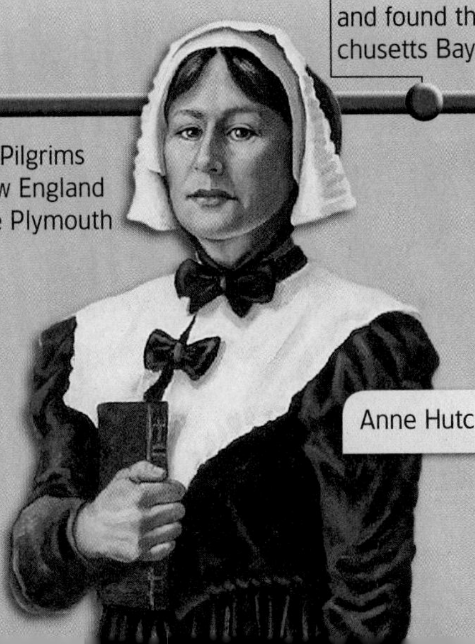

Anne Hutchinson

© Houghton Mifflin Harcourt Publishing Company • Image Credits: (bl), ©Prisma/SuperStock and built schools for their children. Politics and religion were closely connected, with only church members allowed to vote or hold office. The center of politics was the town meeting, where people met to discuss local issues. Conflict over religious beliefs led Puritan leaders to banish people like Anne Hutchinson and Roger Williams from Massachusetts.

The Middle Colonies

The middle colonies included New York, New Jersey, Pennsylvania, and Delaware. They combined qualities of the New England and southern colonies. Like New England, they had many towns and were centers of trade with Britain and the West Indies. Like the southern colonies, the middle colonies grew large amounts of crops, mainly wheat, barley, and oats. Indentured servants and, to a lesser degree, slaves did much of the labor.

Creating a Nation

Two shared events helped unite colonists living in very different areas. In the 1730s and 1740s, a Christian religious movement called the Great Awakening swept the colonies. It drew people from all walks of life to hear sermons about spiritual equality and social issues. In 1754 the French and Indian War began, pitting the British colonists against French colonists and their Indian allies. The British won the war in 1763. This victory encouraged colonists to settle farther west.

The Thirteen Colonies

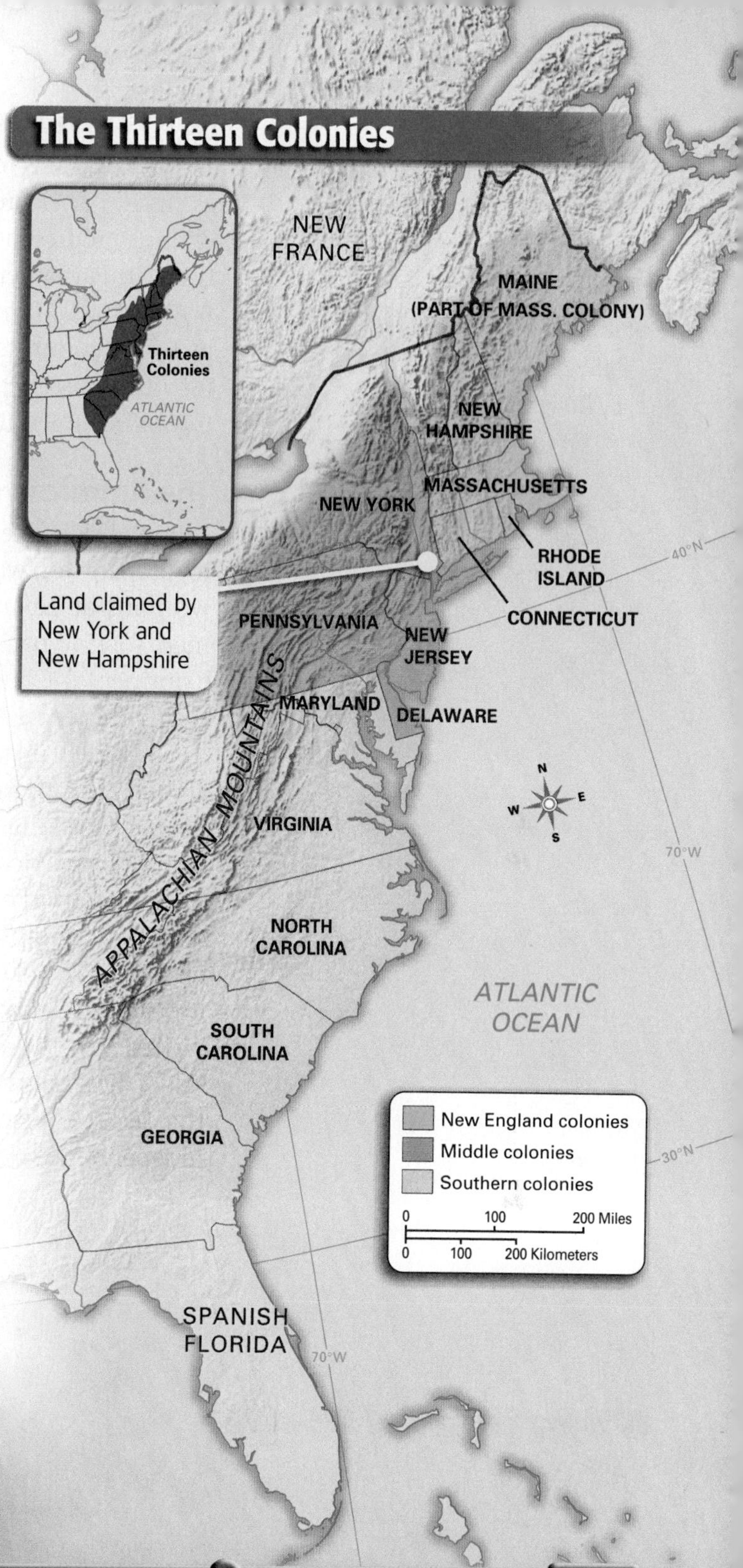
Thirteen Colonies
ATLANTIC OCEAN
NEW FRANCE
MAINE (PART OF MASS. COLONY)
NEW HAMPSHIRE
MASSACHUSETTS
NEW YORK
RHODE ISLAND
CONNECTICUT
Land claimed by New York and New Hampshire
PENNSYLVANIA
NEW JERSEY
MARYLAND
DELAWARE
APPALACHIAN MOUNTAINS
VIRGINIA
NORTH CAROLINA
SOUTH CAROLINA
GEORGIA
SPANISH FLORIDA
ATLANTIC OCEAN
New England colonies
Middle colonies
Southern colonies
0 100 200 Miles
0 100 200 Kilometers
40°N
30°N
70°W
N
S
E
W

1647 The General Court of Massachusetts orders the creation of public schools.

1664 The English capture the Dutch colony of New Amsterdam, renaming it New York.

1690s The Salem witch trials take place in Massachusetts.

1765

Peter Stuyvesant was forced to surrender New Amsterdam to the English in 1664.

© Houghton Mifflin Harcourt Publishing Company • Image Credits: (b), © SuperStock

KEY FACTS

- **1775** The "shot heard 'round the world" begins the Revolutionary War at the Battle of Concord.
- **1776** The Declaration of Independence is approved by Congress on July 4.

Road to War

To pay for the war, Parliament passed new taxes on colonial goods such as sugar, paper products, and tea. Many colonists saw this as "taxation without representation," because they had no officials representing them in Parliament. They responded by boycotting, or refusing to buy, British goods. Tensions rose. When British troops fired on a Boston mob in 1770, colonists were outraged. When colonists dumped British tea into the Boston Harbor in 1773, Parliament was furious. Soon British troops occupied Boston and closed its harbor.

The American Revolution

Colonial delegates met at the First Continental Congress and decided to prepare for war. When British troops tried to destroy a supply of weapons at Lexington and Concord, Massachusetts, colonial minutemen fought back, beginning the Revolutionary War. At the Second Continental Congress, delegates put George Washington in charge of the Continental Army.

A widely read pamphlet by Thomas Paine called *Common Sense* argued that the colonies should declare independence, and that the people, not kings, should make the laws. On July 4, 1776, the United States of America was born when the Continental Congress approved the Declaration of Independence.

The Patriots, or supporters of independence, lacked a well-trained army, but they knew the land on which they fought. They had few victories until defeating the British in the Battle of Saratoga. This win convinced France and Spain to become their allies. After a brutal winter at Valley Forge and a shift to fighting in the South, the Patriots finally won the decisive victory at Yorktown in 1781. Great Britain recognized U.S. independence in the Treaty of Paris of 1783.

A New Nation, 1765–1787

1776 George Washington and his troops crossed the partially frozen Delaware River on the night of December 25, 1776. This daring act led to a key Patriot victory at the Battle of Trenton.

1765

1765 The Stamp Act taxes newspapers, licenses, and other colonial paper products.

Tax stamp

1770 The Boston Massacre occurs when British soldiers fire on a crowd of colonists, killing five men.

1773 The Boston Tea Party takes place when colonists protest the Tea Act by dumping British tea into Boston Harbor.

Boston Massacre

© Houghton Mifflin Harcourt Publishing Company • Image Credits: (c), © SuperStock; (br), © Bettmann/CORBIS; (bl), ©Everett Collection/SuperStock

A New Nation

Reading Focus *As you read, identify the problems of the young nation and the steps taken to strengthen it.* The new United States needed a government to lead it. American political ideas were shaped by European and colonial models. English examples included Magna Carta and the English Bill of Rights. Magna Carta had made the king subject to law, while the Bill of Rights gave Parliament greater power. Enlightenment philosophers also influenced American political ideas. John Locke claimed that rulers and their people were bound by a social contract. Baron de Montesquieu called for the separation of government powers. Americans also had their own models of self-government, such as town meetings, the Mayflower Compact, and the principles set forth in the Declaration of Independence.

KEY FACTS

- **1639** The people of Connecticut create the first written constitution in the English colonies.
- **1689** The English Bill of Rights is created.

Forming a Government

The Second Continental Congress drafted the Articles of Confederation, the first national constitution. The Articles created a Congress with limited powers. There was no executive branch or judicial system. To organize western settlement, Congress passed the Northwest Ordinance of 1787, creating the Northwest Territory. The law allowed new territories to join the Union as equal states.

National Challenges

The weakness of the new Congress caused many problems, especially with the economy. Great Britain and Spain cut American merchants off from trade and made them pay high taxes on imports and exports. Trade laws also varied from state to state, hurting businesses. In an effort to pay high war debts, some states printed too much paper money. This money soon became worthless, causing inflation. When poor farmers in Massachusetts faced high taxes, they joined Shays's Rebellion against the state courts. Although the rebellion failed, to many people it was a sign that a change in the government was needed.

Daniel Shays, at the top of the steps, blocks the courthouse in Massachusetts. By shutting down the courts, farmers hoped to stop the government from selling their land.

1781 The Articles of Confederation are ratified, establishing the first national government of the United States.

1781 Washington defeats Cornwallis at the Battle of Yorktown.

1783 The Treaty of Paris of 1783 ends the Revolutionary War and recognizes the independence of the United States.

1787 Shays's Rebellion ends in Massachusetts.

1787

Battle of Yorktown

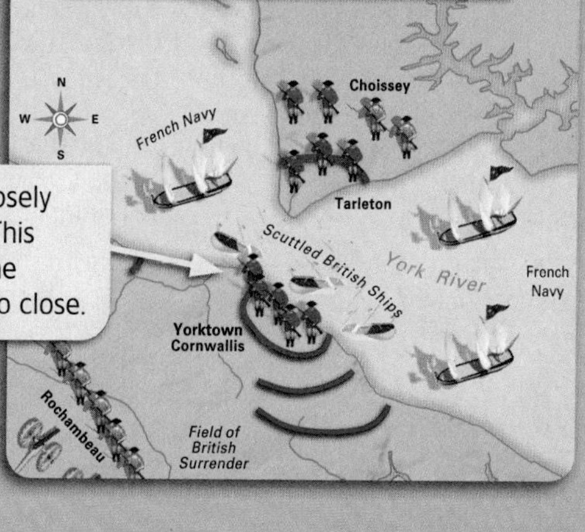
N
W
E
S
French Navy
Choissey
Tarleton
Scuttled British Ships
York River
French Navy
Yorktown
Cornwallis
Rochambeau
Field of British Surrender

The British scuttled, or purposely sank, dozens of their ships. This formed a barrier that kept the French ships from coming too close.

© Houghton Mifflin Harcourt Publishing Company • Image Credits: (b), The Granger Collection, New York

KEY FACTS

- **May 1787** The Constitutional Convention begins in Philadelphia.

Strengths of the Constitution
most power held by national government
three branches of government
executive branch led by president
legislative branch has many powers
firm system of checks and balances

Weaknesses of the Articles of Confederation
• most power held by states
• one branch of government
• legislative branch has few powers
• no executive branch
• no judicial system
• no system of checks and balances

The Constitutional Convention

The states held a Constitutional Convention in 1787 to improve the Articles of Confederation. Instead of rewriting the Articles, however, the convention drafted a new document. Delegates included Benjamin Franklin, Alexander Hamilton, James Madison, and George Washington. The delegates debated many issues. The Great Compromise created a two-house Congress where each state has an equal voice in the Senate and larger states have more representation in the House of Representatives. The Three-Fifths Compromise counted three-fifths of the slave population when determining representation. These compromises settled disputes between large and small states and northern and southern states. Opponents of the new Constitution, called Antifederalists, objected to the plan for a stronger central government. Supporters of the Constitution, called Federalists, won the public debate by convincing people that the new government would not only provide security but also protect their rights.

The Constitution

The system of government established by the Constitution is called federalism. Under federalism powers are divided between the states and the federal, or national, government. States keep control over many issues, such as local government and local laws. The power of the federal government is divided among three branches. The legislative branch, or Congress, passes laws. The executive branch, made up of the president and many departments, makes sure the laws are carried out. The judicial branch, consisting of the national courts, interprets laws and punishes criminals. A system of checks and balances keeps any one branch from becoming too

Creating the Constitution, 1787–1800

Alexander Hamilton, John Jay, and James Madison authored the *Federalist Papers.*

1787

1787 Delaware becomes the first state to ratify the Constitution.

1788 The *Federalist Papers* supporting the Constitution are collected and published.

1789 Congress passes the Judiciary Act of 1789, setting up the federal court system.

1791 Officials choose the site of the nation's future capital, which becomes Washington, D.C.

1791 The first 10 amendments to the Constitution, known as the Bill of Rights, are ratified.

This painting shows the signing of the Constitution on September 17, 1787.

© Houghton Mifflin Harcourt Publishing Company • Image Credits: (c), The Granger Collection, New York; (bl), Hall of Representatives, Washington, DC/ Bridgeman Art Library; (cl), (cr), © Stock Montage/Getty Images powerful. For example, the president can veto a law passed by Congress. The Constitution also allows the people to ratify amendments that change the document to adjust to changing times. Citizens have not only rights but also responsibilities under federalism. Fulfilling these duties helps the system work fairly and effectively for all Americans.

KEY FACTS

- **1788** The Constitution goes into effect after New Hampshire becomes the ninth state to ratify it.
- **1789** George Washington is elected as the first president of the United States.
- **1791** Congress establishes the first Bank of the United States.

Washington's Presidency

General George Washington was elected as the first U.S. president. Congress created executive departments to help the president run the country, and Washington set up a cabinet to help advise him. Secretary of State Thomas Jefferson and Secretary of the Treasury Alexander Hamilton disagreed on many important issues, including the size and purpose of government, financing the government, and interpreting the Constitution. Their disagreements helped shape the young nation.

Foreign and domestic conflicts disrupted the peace during Washington's administration. The United States tried to remain neutral in European conflicts, but the U.S. Army did go to war with Native American forces in the Northwest Territory. The government faced angry farmers when Congress passed a tax on American whiskey. Washington led an army to end the so-called Whiskey Rebellion.

Washington decided not to run for reelection in 1796 after two terms in office. In his farewell address, Washington advised future leaders to maintain U.S. neutrality in foreign affairs and to avoid the dangers of political parties. Political divisions between followers of Jefferson and Hamilton contributed to the growth of political parties, however.

George Washington

1794 Angry farmers begin the Whiskey Rebellion against the federal government.

1796 George Washington gives his Farewell Address to the country after two terms in office.

1800

A tax collector is tarred and feathered during the Whiskey Rebellion.

© Houghton Mifflin Harcourt Publishing Company • Image Credits: (l), The Granger Collection, New York

KEY FACTS

- **1803** The United States purchases Louisiana from France.
- **1804** The Lewis and Clark expedition sets out to explore the Louisiana Purchase.
- **1812** The U.S. Congress declares war on Great Britain.

The New Republic

Reading Focus *As you read, notice how the young republic was different from the nation you live in today.* Federalist John Adams defeated Democratic-Republican Thomas Jefferson in the 1796 presidential election. During Adams's term, the United States nearly went to war with France. When Democratic-Republicans who supported France criticized the Federalists for their actions toward France, Congress passed the Alien and Sedition Acts. These laws limited freedom of speech and the press. Jefferson and others called these acts unconstitutional.

The American Republic

The election of 1800 pitted Adams and Jefferson against each other again. Jefferson won the election after a bitter campaign. This victory marked the first peaceful change of power from one political party to another in U.S. history.

Jefferson's Era

During Jefferson's presidency the Supreme Court increased its power with the case *Marbury* v. *Madison.* Chief Justice John Marshall's ruling established the power of judicial review, which allows the Court to declare an act of Congress unconstitutional. One of Jefferson's biggest achievements as president was agreeing to the Louisiana Purchase, which nearly doubled the size of the United States. He then sent the Lewis and Clark expedition to explore this vast new territory.

War and Peace

Jefferson tried unsuccessfully to protect American neutrality with France and Great Britain. Both countries captured U.S. ships trading with the enemy. Efforts to ban trade with these countries only hurt Americans. The British also supported Native Americans who opposed American settlement in the West. As a result, President James Madison called for war against Britain. During the War of 1812, neither side gained any territory.

The New Republic, 1800–1840

1800

1801 Thomas Jefferson is elected president of the United States.

1803 Chief Justice John Marshall establishes the principle of judicial review in the case *Marbury* v. *Madison*.

1806 Lewis and Clark return home after reaching the Pacific Ocean.

1814 Great Britain and the United States sign the Treaty of Ghent, ending the War of 1812.

Thomas Jefferson

Meriwether Lewis and William Clark

© Houghton Mifflin Harcourt Publishing Company • Image Credits: (l), © Bettmann/CORBIS

Growing Nationalism

A positive outcome of the war was that it boosted American patriotism and confidence. President James Monroe issued the Monroe Doctrine, warning Europeans not to interfere in the Western Hemisphere. Political conflict declined from 1815 to 1825, called the Era of Good Feelings. States built new roads and canals—like the Erie Canal—to link regions together. Writers such as Washington Irving and painters like the members of the Hudson River school created new American styles of art. Yet one threat to unity remained. Northern and southern states disagreed about whether to let slavery expand westward. The Missouri Compromise of 1820 tried to keep the balance between the number of slave and free states. It was only a temporary solution, however.

KEY FACTS

- **1820** The Missouri Compromise settles a conflict between the free and slave states.
- **1823** President James Monroe issues the Monroe Doctrine.
- **1825** The Erie Canal is completed.

The Age of Jackson

By 1828 many states had passed laws increasing suffrage for white men. This led to an era of a rise in popular politics, which became known as Jacksonian Democracy, after politician Andrew Jackson. Jackson's defeat in 1824 led his supporters to create the Democratic Party. Many saw his victory in the 1828 presidential election as a win for the common people.

Jackson faced a major crisis when South Carolina threatened to leave the Union if Congress did not lower taxes on imports. Jackson opposed the view that states could reject, or nullify, laws of Congress and the crisis ended. Jackson did not always support federal authority, however. He opposed the Second Bank of the United States because he felt it favored the rich. The Supreme Court had declared the Bank to be constitutional in *McCulloch* v. *Maryland*. Still, Jackson was able to kill public support for the Bank. After he left office, the loss of the Bank helped cause the economic depression called the Panic of 1837. This crisis hurt the Democratic Party and helped the Whig Party win the presidential election of 1840.

1819 The Supreme Court rules in *McCulloch* v. *Maryland* that the Bank of the United States is constitutional.

c. 1824 Supporters of Andrew Jackson found the Democratic Party.

1832 South Carolina starts the Nullification Crisis by declaring federal tariffs null and void.

1834 The Whig Party is formed to oppose Jackson.

1840

Jackson is shown fighting a monster representing the national bank in this cartoon.

Andrew Jackson

© Houghton Mifflin Harcourt Publishing Company • Image Credits: (bc), The Granger Collection, New York

KEY FACTS

- **1830** Congress passes the Indian Removal Act.
- **1845** Writer John O'Sullivan coins the term *manifest destiny.*
- **January 1848** Gold is discovered at Sutter's Mill in California.

The Nation Expands

Reading Focus *As you read, identify differences between the North and the South.* As America's population grew, settlers looked for more territory. In 1830 Congress passed the Indian Removal Act with the support of President Jackson. This law allowed the removal of Native Americans living east of the Mississippi to western land known as Indian Territory. Groups such as the Cherokee protested the law. Not even a Supreme Court ruling in their favor could save them, however. In 1838 several thousand Cherokee died on the march west known as the Trail of Tears.

Manifest Destiny

Indian removal did not stop more Americans from pushing even farther westward. Fur trappers were some of the first Americans to reach the Rockies. Later, thousands of pioneers followed the 2,000-mile-long Oregon Trail to the Pacific Northwest. Thousands more settled in the Mexican province of Texas. The Mexican government grew worried that these Americans were disobeying Mexican laws. When Mexico banned further American settlement, tempers flared. In 1836 Texas rebelled against Mexico and won its independence.

Many Americans began to believe that America had a manifest destiny, or obvious fate, to settle all the way to the Pacific Ocean. Soon there were calls to annex Texas and Oregon. President James K. Polk gained Oregon peacefully by treaty with Great Britain. But the conflict over Texas led to the Mexican-American War. The overwhelming U.S. victory in that war led Mexico to grant huge pieces of land to the United States. This so-called Mexican Cession included California and most of the present-day American Southwest.

The Nation Expands, 1830–1850

1830

1836 Texas wins independence from Mexico.

1830 American Peter Cooper builds the locomotive called *Tom Thumb.*

1938 During the Trail of Tears, thousands of Cherokee died from disease, starvation, and harsh weather. They were forced to walk hundreds of miles to their new land in the West. Other Native Americans were also moved, with similar results.

© Houghton Mifflin Harcourt Publishing Company • Image Credits: (cr), Stockbyte/Getty Images

The discovery of gold in California brought a rush of miners from all over the world. These included some of the first Chinese immigrants to America. California's population and economy boomed as a result of this Gold Rush. By 1850 California had become the 31st state.

The Industrial North

As pioneers headed West, new industries grew in the Northeast. The first American factories used water-powered machines to make cloth. Inventor Eli Whitney later came up with the idea of interchangeable parts, which helped make mass production and less expensive goods possible. Factories employed men, women, and children to run the machinery. Workers toiled long hours in difficult conditions, often for little pay. Labor reform efforts had little success. Some workers formed unions and used strikes to demand better treatment.

The Transportation Revolution

Steamboats and steam-powered trains made transportation faster and cheaper than ever before. By 1860 the United States had nearly 30,000 miles of railroads and hundreds of steamboats. Communication also improved with the invention of the telegraph, which carried messages across wires. These changes helped fuel economic growth.

Immigration and City Life

Steam power also allowed factories to move from the countryside to the cities. City populations boomed, thanks to new jobs and the arrival of several million immigrants. Most of these people came from Ireland and Germany, fleeing famine or political troubles. Many immigrants faced prejudice from other Americans. Industry and city growth helped create a new middle class of managers and skilled workers. The downsides of city growth were overcrowding, crime, disease, and the threat of fires.

KEY FACTS

- **1793** The first U.S. textile mill opens in Pawtucket, Rhode Island.
- **1798** Eli Whitney proposes to mass produce muskets using interchangeable parts.
- **1807** Robert Fulton successfully sails the first full-sized steamboat, the *Clermont*.
- **1814** Francis Lowell opens his first mill in Waltham, Massachusetts.

The Cherokee during the Trail of Tears

1846 The United States declares war on Mexico.

1848 The United States and Mexico sign the Treaty of Guadalupe Hidalgo, ending the Mexican-American War.

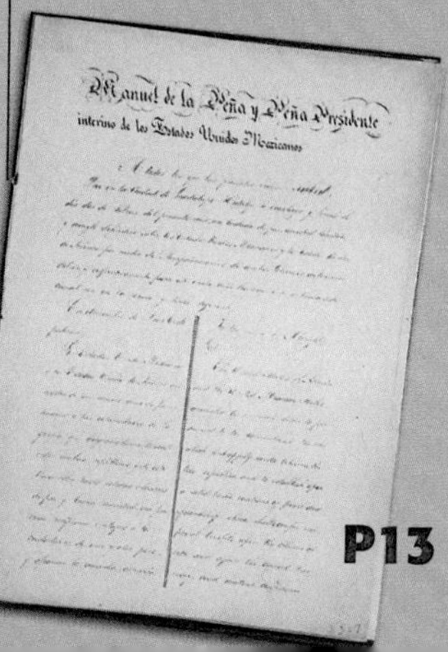

1849 Thousands of "forty-niners" come to California in search of gold.

1850

© Houghton Mifflin Harcourt Publishing Company • Image Credits: (br), National Archives (NARA); (bl), © SuperStock; (cr), Collection of Matthew Isenburg

KEY FACTS

- **1793** Eli Whitney patents the cotton gin.
- **1790s to early 1800s** The Second Great Awakening sweeps the nation.
- **1848** The first public meeting on women's rights in the United States is held in Seneca Falls, New York.

The Agricultural South

Compared to the North, the South had less industry and fewer big cities. As a result, fewer immigrants settled in the region. Instead, the South remained rural and agricultural, relying on cash crops for its wealth.

The Cotton Boom

The first southern cash crops were tobacco, rice, and indigo. Eli Whitney's invention of the cotton gin in 1793 made cotton the South's biggest crop. The gin quickly removed seeds from cotton fibers. The demand for cotton boomed as textile mills in the American North and in Great Britain grew. The South became a major player in world trade and was sometimes called the Cotton Kingdom.

The Slave System

Cotton brought wealth but also increased the demand for slave labor to grow and process the crop. Only about one-third of white southerners had slaves. Yeomen farmers and poor whites owned few or no slaves, but most defended the slave system. Many slaves lived on the small number of large plantations owned by wealthy planters. On big plantations most slaves worked in the fields, while some had specific skilled jobs like carpentry. Slaves' living conditions were poor and the punishments they faced harsh. Slave codes limited slaves' right to travel and banned them from schools. Still, enslaved people kept alive African customs and expressed themselves through folktales and spirituals. Some slaves even led rebellions, though these were rare and severely punished.

American Society, 1830–1855

1830

1831 Nat Turner leads an unsuccessful slave rebellion in Virginia.

1833 William Lloyd Garrison helps found the American Anti-Slavery Society.

An illustration of Nat Turner's rebellion

1840 The United States produces more than half of the world's cotton.

© Houghton Mifflin Harcourt Publishing Company • Image Credits: (bl), North Wind Picture Archives

New Movements in Society

Some Americans formed the abolitionist movement to oppose slavery. Former slaves Frederick Douglass and Sojourner Truth were two leading abolitionists. Abolitionists used speeches and newspapers to spread their antislavery messages. They based many speeches and articles on the ideas of equality found in the Declaration of Independence. Abolitionists fought against laws that protected slavery, including laws that made it illegal to help runaway slaves.

Abolition was just one of the many reform movements that arose in the United States. The religious revival called the Second Great Awakening triggered a wave of reform efforts. Some people supported the temperance movement, which tried to stop alcohol abuse. They blamed alcohol for problems of society such as crime and poverty. Others called for prison and education reform, such as better treatment for prisoners and more public schools for children. Reformers helped spread education to African Americans and women by opening schools that would accept them.

Women who took part in the abolition movement, like Elizabeth Cady Stanton, began to demand more rights for women as well. Stanton and other reformers called for women's suffrage, or the right to vote. Some claimed that women did not have an obligation to follow the laws of a nation that did not let them vote. These were just the first steps toward gaining equal rights for many Americans.

Harriet Tubman

1849 Harriet Tubman escapes slavery and soon begins leading fugitive slaves to freedom through the Underground Railroad.

1855

1855 The photograph above of the 1855 class at Oberlin College shows the slow integration of African Americans into previously white colleges.

© Houghton Mifflin Harcourt Publishing Company • Image Credits: (bl), Library of Congress Prints and Photographs Division, Washington, D.C.; (cr), Courtesy of Oberlin Archives

KEY FACTS

- **1852** Harriet Beecher Stowe publishes *Uncle Tom's Cabin.*
- **1854** Congress passes the Kansas-Nebraska Act.
- **1857** The Supreme Court issues the *Dred Scott* decision.
- **1861** Seven southern states leave the Union and form the Confederacy.

The Nation Breaks Apart

Reading Focus *As you read, list the sequence of events leading to the Civil War.* By 1850 the North and South had grown apart in many ways. The regions had different economies, different societies, and different goals. People in one region knew fairly little about their fellow citizens in another part of the country. As both regions pushed westward, their differences led to conflict.

Deepening Divisions

Many northerners did not want slavery to spread to the West. Some opposed it for moral reasons, while others felt it would take jobs from white workers. After the Mexican-American War, Representative David Wilmot said that slavery should be banned in the new lands gained by the United States. Southerners strongly opposed this idea. In the North, the Free-Soil Party arose to oppose the spread of slavery.

Failed Compromises

The addition of California as a state threatened to upset the political balance between slave and free states in the Union. An unequal balance would affect the political make up of the Senate. The North already had an edge in the House of Representatives. Henry Clay offered the Compromise of 1850 to keep the peace. California joined the Union as a free state, but other territories in the Southwest would be allowed to choose whether to allow slavery. The Kansas-Nebraska Act later applied the same approach by allowing new territories in the Midwest to support or oppose slavery. Neither of these compromises kept the peace for long.

Bleeding Kansas

The Compromise of 1850 introduced a law called the Fugitive Slave Act. This made it easier to capture runaway slaves hiding in the North. The law angered many northerners. Those opposed to slavery were equally upset

The Nation Breaks Apart, 1850–1860

1850 California enters the Union as a free state.

1854 The Republican Party is formed to oppose the spread of slavery.

1850

1854 The Kansas-Nebraska Act is passed, organizing the territories of Kansas and Nebraska.

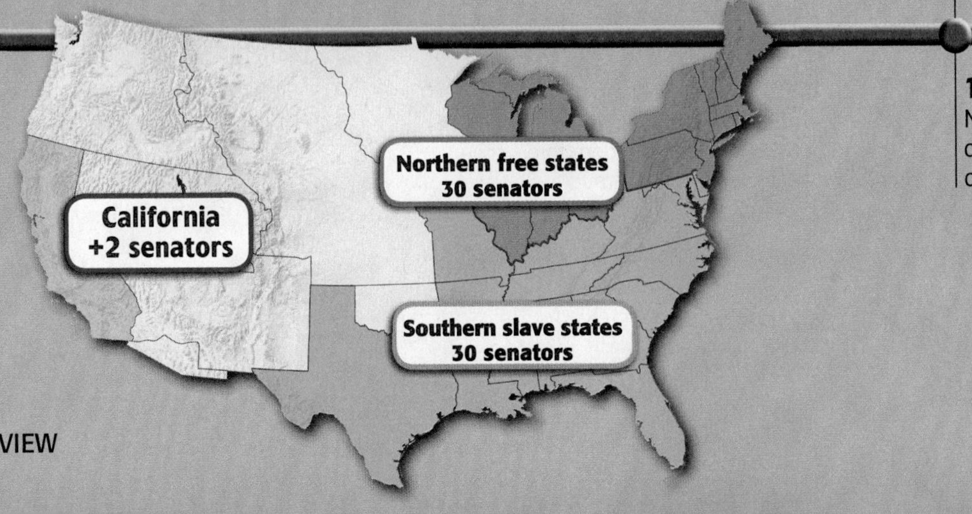

Northern free states
30 senators
California
+2 senators
Southern slave states
30 senators

© Houghton Mifflin Harcourt Publishing Company

when the Kansas-Nebraska Act opened the door to the spread of slavery in the Midwest. The Missouri Compromise had once banned slavery in that region. Harriet Beecher Stowe's popular antislavery novel *Uncle Tom's Cabin* fanned these flames by upsetting many southerners. So when the Kansas Territory was opened, pro- and antislavery settlers rushed in. Each side was determined to control the territory. The result was a series of attacks and killings by both groups that shocked the nation.

Prelude to War

Northerners received another shock with the Supreme Court's ruling in the *Dred Scott* case. The Court ruled that African Americans could not be U.S. citizens and that Congress could not ban slavery in any of the territories. This decision boosted support for the new Republican Party, which opposed the spread of slavery to the West.

Abolitionist John Brown stunned the South when he attacked Harpers Ferry, Virginia, trying to start a slave rebellion. Many northerners called Brown a hero. The election of 1860 took place in this bitter atmosphere. Republican Abraham Lincoln won the election without winning a single electoral vote from the South, upsetting southern leaders. They feared that Lincoln would ban slavery. Such a move would destroy the South's economy and change its society. South Carolina, Mississippi, Florida, Alabama, Georgia, Louisiana, and Texas responded to Lincoln's win by withdrawing from the Union. They formed the Confederate States of America, or the Confederacy. Lincoln insisted that the Confederate states could not simply leave the Union or keep the federal property within their borders. The stage was set for a terrible conflict pitting North against South.

SUMMARY AND PREVIEW America had moved from a collection of loose-knit colonies to an independent, united country, to a nation divided over issues such as slavery. Now the nation faced the terrible prospect of a civil war that would threaten its very existence.

Abraham Lincoln

Stephen Douglas

1858 Republican Abraham Lincoln and Democrat Stephen Douglas hold the Lincoln-Douglas debates in Illinois over the issue of slavery.

1859 Abolitionist John Brown leads a raid on Harpers Ferry.

1860 Abraham Lincoln wins the U.S. presidential election.

1860

Lincoln ran for U.S. Senate in Illinois against Douglas in 1858. The two men debated seven times at various locations around the state. Lincoln lost the election but gained national recognition.

© Houghton Mifflin Harcourt Publishing Company • Image Credits: (bl), Library of Congress Prints and Photographs Division, Washington, D.C. (LC-DIG-ppmsca-19204); (br), Library of Congress Prints and Photographs Division, Washington, D.C. (LC-DIG-cwpbh-00882)

UNIT 1

1861–1877

The Nation Breaks Apart

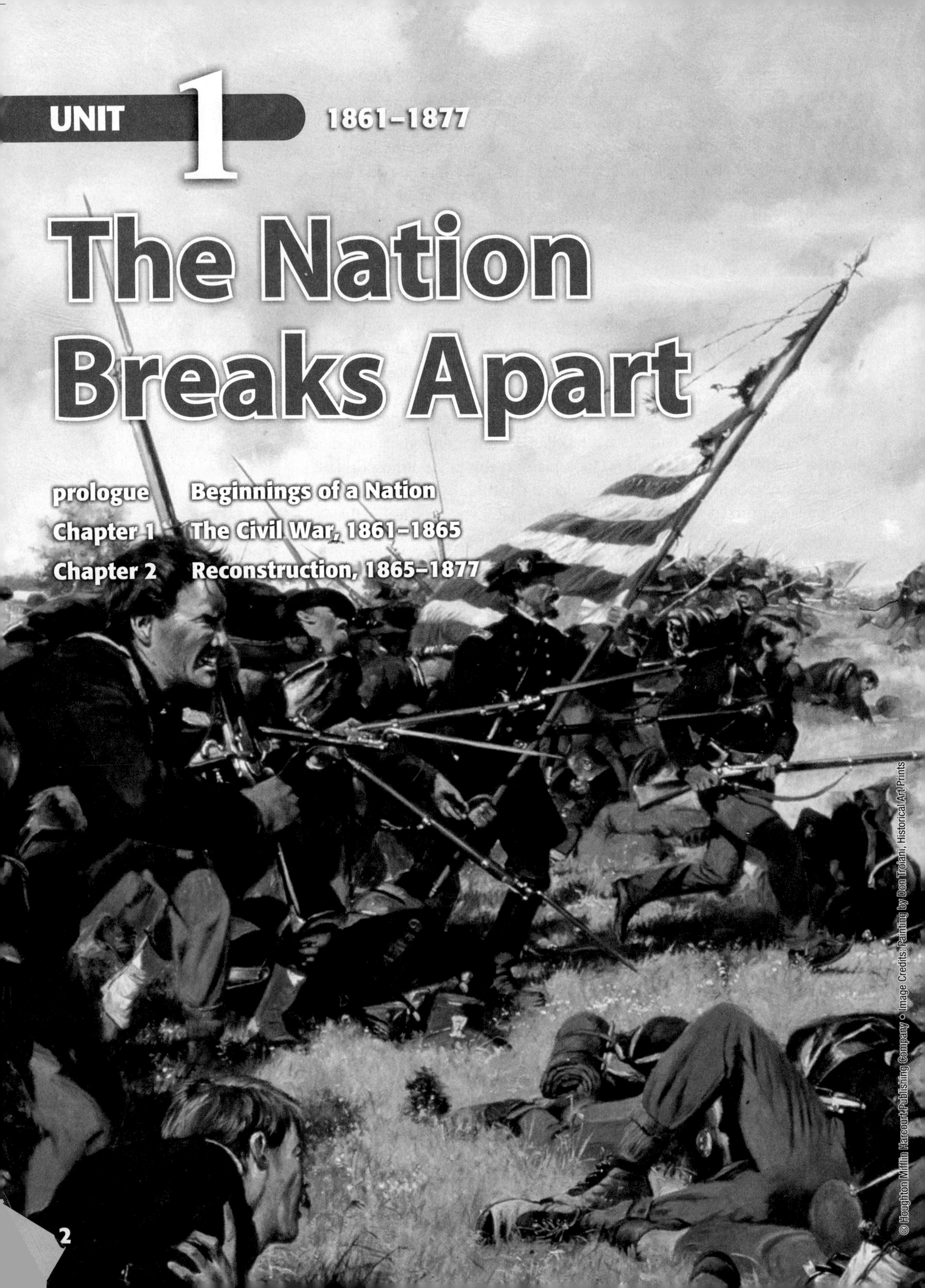

© Houghton Mifflin Harcourt Publishing Company • Image Credits: Painting by Don Troiani, Historical Art Prints

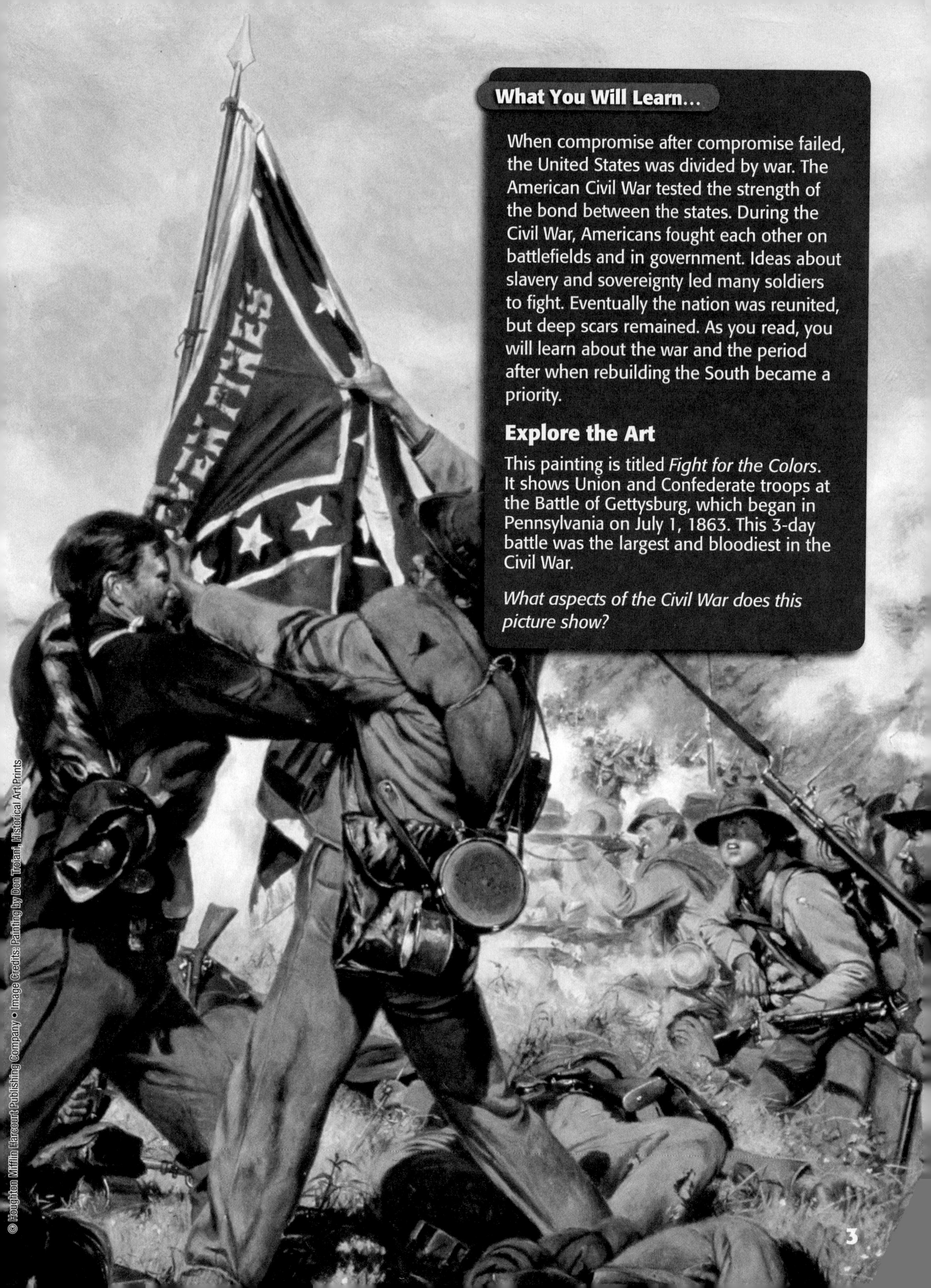

What You Will Learn...

When compromise after compromise failed, the United States was divided by war. The American Civil War tested the strength of the bond between the states. During the Civil War, Americans fought each other on battlefields and in government. Ideas about slavery and sovereignty led many soldiers to fight. Eventually the nation was reunited, but deep scars remained. As you read, you will learn about the war and the period after when rebuilding the South became a priority.

Explore the Art

This painting is titled *Fight for the Colors*. It shows Union and Confederate troops at the Battle of Gettysburg, which began in Pennsylvania on July 1, 1863. This 3-day battle was the largest and bloodiest in the Civil War.

What aspects of the Civil War does this picture show?

© Houghton Mifflin Harcourt Publishing Company • Image Credits: Painting by Don Troiani, Historical Art Prints

CHAPTER 1 1861–1865

The Civil War

Essential Question In what ways did the Civil War transform the nation?

ALABAMA COURSE OF STUDY

Identifying key Northern and Southern Civil War personalities, including Abraham Lincoln, Jefferson Davis, Ulysses S. Grant, Robert E. Lee, Thomas Jonathan "Stonewall" Jackson, and William Tecumseh Sherman .

Focus on Writing

Writing a Newspaper Article For most of this nation's history, newspapers have been an important way for citizens to learn about what is happening in the United States. In this chapter you will read about the main events of the Civil War. Then you will choose one of these events and write a newspaper article about it.

United States

1861 Confederate guns open fire on Fort Sumter on April 12. Confederates win the first battle of the Civil War on July 21 at Bull Run in Virginia.

1861

World

1861 Great Britain and France decide to buy cotton from Egypt instead of from the Confederacy.

Image Credits: (t), Library of Congress Prints & Photographs Division, Brady Civil War Photo Collection, Washington, D.C. (LC-B8171-7514)

© Houghton Mifflin Harcourt Publishing Company

Among those who marched off to war were these drummer boys of the Union army.

HISTORY Emancipation Proclamation

hmhsocialstudies.com VIDEO

1862 The *Monitor* fights the *Virginia* on March 9.

1863 The Emancipation Proclamation is issued on January 1.

1865 General Robert E. Lee surrenders to General Ulysses S. Grant on April 9.

1862 | 1863 | 1864 | 1865

1862 An imperial decree expels foreigners from Japan.

1864 With the support of French troops, Archduke Maximilian of Austria becomes emperor of Mexico.

1864 The Taiping Rebellion in China ends after the capture of Nanjing in July.

Image Credits: (t), Library of Congress Prints & Photographs Division, Brady Civil War Photo Collection, Washington, D.C. (LC-B8171-7514); (cr), ©SuperStock; (cl), ©SuperStock; (b), ©Hulton-Deutsch Collection/Corbis

© Houghton Mifflin Harcourt Publishing Company

Reading Social Studies

Economics | Geography | **Politics** | **Society and Culture** | Science and Technology

Focus on Themes As you read this chapter about the Civil War, you will see that this was a time in our history dominated by two major concerns: **politics** and **society and culture**. You will not only read about the political decisions made during this war, but also you will see how the war affected all of American society. You will read about the causes and the key events during the war and the many consequences of this war. This chapter tells of one of the most important events in our history.

Supporting Facts and Details

Focus on Reading Main ideas and big ideas are just that, ideas. How do we know what those ideas really mean?

Understanding Ideas and Their Support A main idea or big idea may be a kind of summary statement, or it may be a statement of the author's opinion. Either way, a good reader looks to see what support—facts and various kinds of details—the writer provides. If the writer doesn't provide good support, the ideas may not be trustworthy.

Notice how the passage below uses facts and details to support the main idea.

Civil War armies fought in the ancient battlefield formation that produced massive casualties. Endless rows of troops fired directly at one another, with cannonballs landing amid them. When the order was given, soldiers would attach bayonets to their guns and rush toward their enemy. Men died to gain every inch of ground. . .

Despite the huge battlefield losses, the biggest killer in the Civil War was not the fighting. It was diseases such as typhoid, pneumonia, and tuberculosis. Nearly twice as many soldiers died of illnesses as died in combat.

The main idea is stated first.

These sentences provide details about the challenges soldiers faced.

The writer concludes with some facts as support.

Writers support propositions with . . .

1. **Facts and statistics**—statements that can be proved; facts in number form
2. **Examples**—specific instances that illustrate the facts
3. **Anecdotes**—brief stories that help explain the facts
4. **Definitions**—explanation of unusual terms or words
5. **Comments from the experts or eyewitnesses**—statements from reliable sources

© Houghton Mifflin Harcourt Publishing Company

You Try It!

As you read the following passage, look for the writer's main idea and support.

> In February 1862, Grant led an assault force into Tennessee. With help from navy gunboats, Grant's Army of the Tennessee took two outposts on key rivers in the west. On February 6, he captured Fort Henry on the Tennessee River. Several days later he took Fort Donelson on the Cumberland River.
>
> Fort Donelson's commander asked for the terms of surrender. Grant replied, "No terms except an unconditional and immediate surrender can be accepted." The fort surrendered. The North gave a new name to Grant's initials: "Unconditional Surrender" Grant.

After you read the passage, answer the following questions.

1. Which sentence best states the writer's main idea?
  - **a.** The fort surrendered.
  - **b.** In February 1862, Grant led an assault force into Tennessee.
  - **c.** Fort Donelson's commander asked for the terms of surrender.

2. Which method of support is not used to support the main idea?
  - **a.** facts
  - **b.** comments from experts or eyewitnesses
  - **c.** anecdotes

3. Which sentence in this passage provides a comment from an expert or eyewitness?

As you read this chapter, pay attention to the details that the writers have chosen to support their main ideas.

Key Terms and People

Chapter 1

Section 1
Fort Sumter
border states
Winfield Scott
cotton diplomacy

Section 2
Thomas "Stonewall" Jackson
First Battle of Bull Run
George B. McClellan
Robert E. Lee
Seven Days' Battles
Second Battle of Bull Run
Battle of Antietam
ironclads

Section 3
Ulysses S. Grant
Battle of Shiloh
David Farragut
Siege of Vicksburg

Section 4
emancipation
Emancipation Proclamation
contrabands
54th Massachusetts Infantry
Copperheads
habeas corpus
Clara Barton

Section 5
Battle of Gettysburg
George Pickett
Pickett's Charge
Gettysburg Address
Wilderness Campaign
William Tecumseh Sherman
total war
Appomattox Courthouse

Academic Vocabulary

In this chapter, you will learn the following academic words:

innovation
execute

© Houghton Mifflin Harcourt Publishing Company

SECTION 1

The War Begins

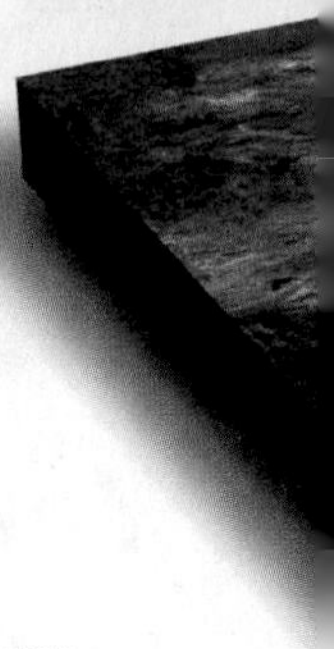

What You Will Learn...

Main Ideas

1. Following the outbreak of war at Fort Sumter, Americans chose sides.
2. The Union and the Confederacy prepared for war.

The Big Idea

Civil war broke out between the North and the South in 1861.

Key Terms and People

Fort Sumter
border states
Winfield Scott
cotton diplomacy

hmhsocialstudies.com
TAKING NOTES

Use the graphic organizer online to take notes on how Americans chose sides in the Civil War and how each side prepared for the war.

If YOU were there...

You are a college student in Charleston in early 1861. Seven southern states have left the Union and formed their own government. All-out war seems unavoidable. Your friends have begun to volunteer for either the Union or the Confederate forces. You are torn between loyalty to your home state and to the United States.

Would you join the Union or the Confederate army?

BUILDING BACKGROUND The divisions within the United States reached a breaking point with the election of Abraham Lincoln in 1860. Several southern states angrily left the Union to form a new confederation. In border states such as Virginia and Kentucky, people were divided. The question now was whether the United States could survive as a disunified country.

Americans Choose Sides

Furious at Lincoln's election and fearing a federal invasion, seven southern states had seceded. The new commander in chief tried desperately to save the Union.

In his inaugural address, Lincoln promised not to end slavery where it existed. The federal government "will not assail [attack] you. You can have no conflict without being yourselves the aggressors," he said, trying to calm southerners' fears. However, Lincoln also stated his intention to preserve the Union. He believed that saving the Union would help to save democracy. If the Union and its government failed, then monarchs could say that people were unable to rule themselves. As a result, Lincoln refused to recognize secession, declaring the Union to be "unbroken."

In fact, after decades of painful compromises, the Union was badly broken. From the lower South, a battle cry was arising, born out of fear, rage—and excitement. Confederate officials began seizing branches of the federal mint, arsenals, and military outposts. In a last-ditch effort to avoid war between the states, Secretary of State Seward suggested a united effort of threatening war against Spain and France for interfering in Mexico and the Caribbean. In the highly charged atmosphere, it would take only a spark to unleash the heat of war.

© Houghton Mifflin Harcourt Publishing Company

History Close-up

Fort Sumter

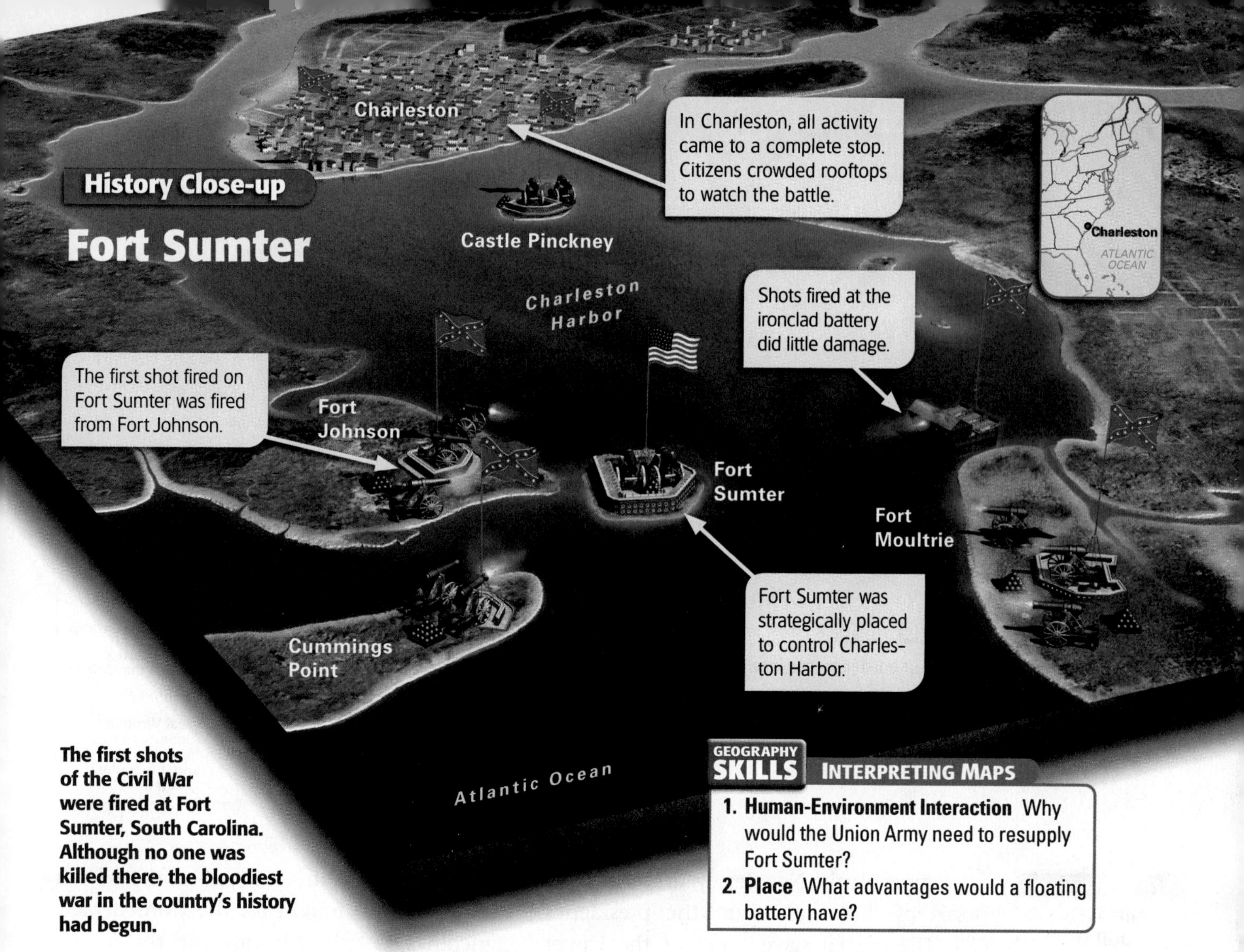
Charleston
In Charleston, all activity came to a complete stop. Citizens crowded rooftops to watch the battle.
Castle Pinckney
Charleston Harbor
Shots fired at the ironclad battery did little damage.
Charleston
ATLANTIC OCEAN
The first shot fired on Fort Sumter was fired from Fort Johnson.
Fort Johnson
Fort Sumter
Fort Moultrie
Fort Sumter was strategically placed to control Charleston Harbor.
Cummings Point
Atlantic Ocean

The first shots of the Civil War were fired at Fort Sumter, South Carolina. Although no one was killed there, the bloodiest war in the country's history had begun.

GEOGRAPHY SKILLS **INTERPRETING MAPS**

1. **Human-Environment Interaction** Why would the Union Army need to resupply Fort Sumter?
2. **Place** What advantages would a floating battery have?

In 1861, that spark occurred at **Fort Sumter**, a federal outpost in Charleston, South Carolina, that was attacked by Confederate troops, beginning the Civil War. Determined to seize the fortress—which controlled the entrance to Charleston harbor—the Confederates ringed the harbor with heavy guns. Instead of surrendering the fort, Lincoln decided to send in ships to provide badly needed supplies to defend the fort. Confederate officials demanded that the federal troops evacuate. The fort's commander, Major Robert Anderson, refused.

Before sunrise on April 12, 1861, Confederate guns opened fire on Fort Sumter. A witness wrote that the first shots brought "every soldier in the harbor to his feet, and every man, woman, and child in the city of Charleston from their beds." The Civil War had begun.

The fort, although massive, stood little chance. Its heavy guns faced the Atlantic Ocean, not the shore. After 34 hours of cannon blasts, Fort Sumter surrendered. "The last ray of hope for preserving the Union has expired at the assault upon Fort Sumter . . ." Lincoln wrote.

Reaction to Lincoln's Call

The fall of Fort Sumter stunned the North. Lincoln declared the South to be in a state of rebellion and asked state governors for 75,000 militiamen to put down the rebellion. States now had to choose: Would they secede, or would they stay in the Union? Democratic Senator Stephen Douglas, speaking in support of Lincoln's call for troops, declared, "There can be no neutrals in this war, *only patriots—or traitors.*"

North Versus South

QUICK FACTS

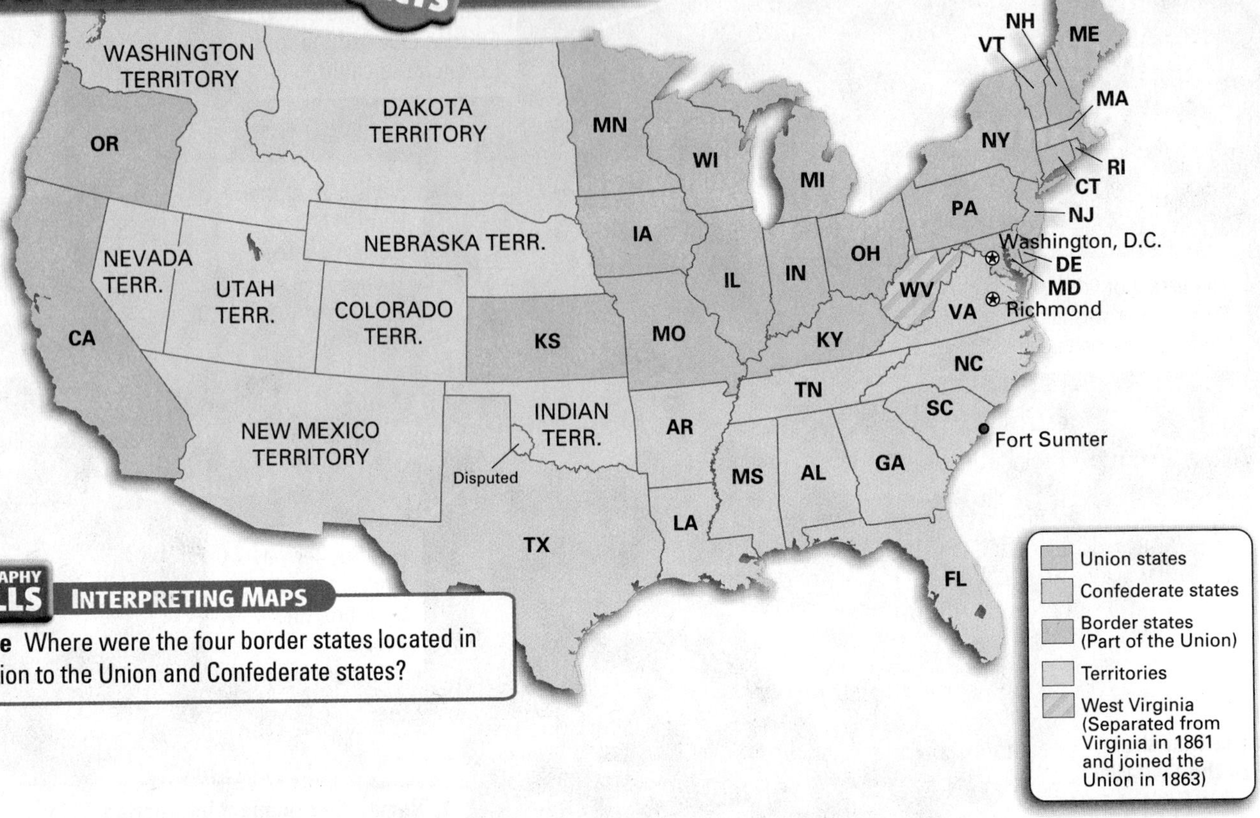

GEOGRAPHY SKILLS **INTERPRETING MAPS**

Place Where were the four border states located in relation to the Union and Confederate states?

hmhsocialstudies.com

ANIMATED GEOGRAPHY

States Choose Sides 1861

Pennsylvania, New Jersey, and the states north of them rallied to the president's call. The crucial slave states of the Upper South—North Carolina, Tennessee, Virginia, and Arkansas—seceded. They provided soldiers and supplies to the South. Mary Boykin Chesnut, whose husband became a Confederate congressman, wrote in her diary:

> "I did not know that one could live in such days of excitement...Everybody tells you half of something, and then rushes off...to hear the last news."
>
> —Mary Boykin Chesnut, quoted in *Mary Chesnut's Civil War*, edited by C. Vann Woodward

Wedged between the North and the South were the key **border states** of Delaware, Kentucky, Maryland, and Missouri—slave states that did not join the Confederacy. Kentucky and Missouri controlled parts of important rivers. Maryland separated the Union capital, Washington, D.C., from the North.

People in the border states were deeply divided on the war. The president's own wife, Mary Todd Lincoln, had four brothers from Kentucky who fought for the Confederacy. Lincoln sent federal troops into the border states to help keep them in the Union. He also sent soldiers into western Virginia, where Union loyalties were strong. West Virginia set up its own state government in 1863.

Northern Resources

Numbers tell an important story about the Civil War. Consider the North's advantages. It could draw soldiers and workers from a population of 22 million. The South had only 5.5 million people to draw from. One of the greatest advantages in the North was the region's network of roads, canals, and railroads. Some 22,000 miles of railroad track could move soldiers and supplies throughout the North. The South had only about 9,000 miles of track.

In the North, the Civil War stimulated economic growth. To supply the military, the production of coal, iron, wheat, and wool increased. Also, the export of corn, wheat, beef, and pork to Europe doubled. In the South, the export of resources decreased because of the Union blockade.

Finally, the Union had money. It had a more developed economy, banking system, and a currency called greenbacks. The South had to start printing its own Confederate dollars. Some states printed their own money, too. This led to financial chaos.

Taking advantage of the Union's strengths, General **Winfield Scott** developed a two-part strategy: (1) destroy the South's economy with a naval blockade of southern ports; (2) gain control of the Mississippi River to divide the South. Other leaders urged an attack on Richmond, Virginia, the Confederate capital.

Southern Resources

The Confederacy had advantages as well. With its strong military tradition, the South put many brilliant officers into battle. Southern farms provided food for its armies. The South's best advantage, however, was strategic. It needed only to defend itself until the North grew tired of fighting.

The North had to invade and control the South. To accomplish this, the Union army had to travel huge distances. For example, the distance from northern Virginia to central Georgia is about the length of Scotland and England combined. Because of distances such as this, the North had to maintain long supply lines.

In addition, wilderness covered much of the South. Armies found this land difficult to cross. Also, in Virginia, many of the rivers ran from east to west. Because of this, they formed a natural defense against an army that attacked from the north to the south. As a result, Northern generals were often forced to attack Confederate troops from the side rather than from the front. Furthermore, because southerners fought mostly on their home soil, they were often familiar with the area.

The South hoped to wear down the North and to capture Washington, D.C. Confederate president Jefferson Davis also tried to win foreign allies through **cotton diplomacy**. This was the idea that Great Britain would support the Confederacy because it needed the South's raw cotton to supply its booming textile industry. Cotton diplomacy did not work as the South had hoped. Britain had large supplies of cotton, and it got more from India and Egypt.

READING CHECK **Comparing** What advantages did the North and South have leading up to the war?

Resources of the North and South

QUICK FACTS

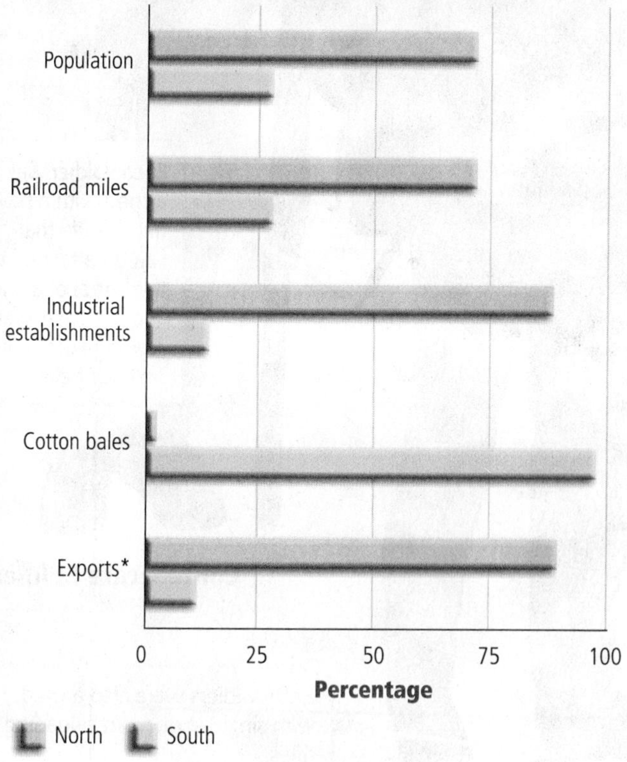

*Southern exports do not include Tennessee, Arkansas, and Mississippi.

ANALYSIS SKILL **ANALYZING VISUALS**

1. Do you think the North or the South could maintain better supply lines for their troops? Explain.
2. Do you think the North or the South could provide more weapons for their troops? Explain.

Union and Confederate Soldiers

Early in the war, uniforms differed greatly, especially in the Confederate army. Uniforms became simpler and more standard as the war dragged on.

The soldiers carried food, extra ammunition, and other items in their haversacks.
Each soldier was armed with a bayonet, a knife that can be attached to the barrel of a rifle. The bayonets were stored in scabbards on their belts.
Confederate Soldier
Both soldiers were also armed with single-shot, muzzle-loading rifles.
Union Soldier

ANALYSIS SKILL **ANALYZING VISUALS**

How are the Union and Confederate uniforms and equipment similar and different?

Preparing for War

The North and the South now rushed to war. Neither side was prepared for the tragedy to come.

Volunteer Armies

Volunteer militias had sparked the revolution that created the United States. Now they would battle for its future. At the start of the war, the Union army had only 16,000 soldiers. Within months that number had swelled to a half million. Southern men rose up to defend their land and their ways of life. Virginian Thomas Webber came to fight "against the invading foe [enemy] who now pollute the sacred soil of my beloved native state." When Union soldiers asked one captured rebel why he was fighting, he replied, "I'm fighting because you're down here."

Helping the Troops

Civilians on both sides helped those in uniform. They raised money, provided aid for soldiers and their families, and ran emergency hospitals. Dr. Elizabeth Blackwell, the first woman to receive a license to practice medicine, organized a group that pressured President Lincoln to form the U.S. Sanitary Commission in June 1861. The Sanitary, as it was called, was run by clergyman Henry Bellows. Tens of thousands of volunteers worked with the U.S. Sanitary Commission to send bandages, medicines, and food to Union army camps and hospitals. Some 3,000 women served as nurses in the Union army.

Training the Soldiers

Both the Union and Confederate armies faced shortages of clothing, food, and even rifles. Most troops lacked standard uniforms and simply wore their own clothes. Eventually, each side chose a color for their uniforms. The Union chose blue. The Confederates wore gray.

© Houghton Mifflin Harcourt Publishing Company

The problem with volunteers was that many of them had no idea how to fight. Schoolteachers, farmers, and laborers all had to learn the combat basics of marching, shooting, and using bayonets.

In a letter to a friend, a Union soldier described life in the training camp.

> "We have been wading through mud knee deep all winter... For the last two weeks we have been drilled almost to death. Squad drill from 6 to 7 A.M. Company drill from 9 to 11 A.M. Battalion Drill from 2 to 4 1/2 P.M. Dress Parade from 5 to 5 1/2 P.M. and non-commissioned officers' school from 7 to 8 in the evening. If we don't soon become a well drilled Regiment, we ought to."
>
> —David R. P. Shoemaker, 1862

With visions of glory and action, many young soldiers were eager to fight. They would not have to wait long.

Discipline and drill were used to turn raw volunteers into an efficient fighting machine. During a battle, the success or failure of a regiment often depended on its discipline—how well it responded to orders.

Volunteers also learned how to use rifles. Eventually, soldiers were expected to be able to load, aim, and fire their rifles three times in one minute. The quality of the weapons provided varied greatly. Most soldiers favored the Springfield and Enfield rifles for their accuracy. On the other hand, soldiers often complained about their Austrian and Belgian rifles. A soldier remarked, "I don't believe one could hit the broadside of a barn with them."

The Union army provided the infantry with two-person tents. However, soldiers often discarded these tents in favor of more portable ones. The Confederate army did not usually issue tents. Instead, Confederates often used tents that were captured from the Union army.

READING CHECK **Summarizing** How did soldiers and civilians prepare for war?

SUMMARY As citizens chose sides in the Civil War, civilians and soldiers alike became involved in the war effort.

Section 1 Assessment

hmhsocialstudies.com ONLINE QUIZ

Reviewing Ideas, Terms, and People

1. a. **Identify** What event triggered the war between the Union and the Confederacy?
   b. **Contrast** How did the Union's strategy differ from that of the Confederacy?
   c. **Evaluate** Which side do you believe was better prepared for war? Explain your answer.
2. a. **Describe** How did women take part in the war?
   b. **Summarize** In what ways were the armies of the North and South unprepared for war?
   c. **Elaborate** Why did men volunteer to fight in the war?

Critical Thinking

3. **Comparing and Contrasting** Review your notes on the preparations for war by the North and the South. Then copy the graphic organizer shown below and use it to show the strengths and weaknesses of each side in the war.

	Union	Confederacy
Strengths		
Weaknesses		

Focus on Writing

4. **Taking Notes on the War's Beginning** As you read this section, take notes on the crisis at Fort Sumter and on the recruiting and training of the armies. Be sure to answer the following questions: Who? Where? When? Why? and How?

SECTION 2

The War in the East

What You Will Learn...

Main Ideas

1. Union and Confederate forces fought for control of the war in Virginia.
2. The Battle of Antietam gave the North a slight advantage.
3. The Confederacy attempted to break the Union naval blockade.

The Big Idea

Confederate and Union forces faced off in Virginia and at sea.

Key Terms and People

Thomas "Stonewall" Jackson
First Battle of Bull Run
George B. McClellan
Robert E. Lee
Seven Days' Battles
Second Battle of Bull Run
Battle of Antietam
ironclads

hmhsocialstudies.com
TAKING NOTES

Use the graphic organizer online to take notes on the battles in the East and at sea and the winners of each.

If YOU were there...

You live in Washington, D.C., in July 1861. You and your friends are on your way to Manassas, near Washington, to watch the battle there. Everyone expects a quick Union victory. Your wagon is loaded with food for a picnic, and people are in a holiday mood. You see some members of Congress riding toward Manassas, too. Maybe this battle will end the war!

Why would you want to watch this battle?

BUILDING BACKGROUND The shots fired at Fort Sumter made the war a reality. Neither the North nor the South was really prepared. Each side had some advantages—more industry and railroads in the North, a military tradition in the South. The war in the East centered in the region around the two capitals: Washington, D.C., and Richmond, Virginia.

War in Virginia

The troops that met in the first major battle of the Civil War found that it was no picnic. In July 1861, Lincoln ordered General Irvin McDowell to lead his 35,000-man army from the Union capital, Washington, to the Confederate capital, Richmond. The soldiers were barely trained. McDowell complained that they "stopped every moment to pick blackberries or get water; they would not keep in the ranks." The first day's march covered only five miles.

Bull Run/Manassas

McDowell's army was headed to Manassas, Virginia, an important railroad junction. If McDowell could seize Manassas, he would control the best route to the Confederate capital. Some 22,000 Confederate troops under the command of General Pierre G. T. Beauregard were waiting for McDowell and his troops along a creek called Bull Run. For two days, Union troops tried to find a way around the Confederates. During that time, Beauregard requested assistance, and

© Houghton Mifflin Harcourt Publishing Company

General Joseph E. Johnston headed toward Manassas with another 10,000 Confederate troops. By July 21, 1861, they had all arrived.

That morning, Union troops managed to cross the creek and drive back the left side of the Confederate line. Yet one unit held firmly in place.

"There is Jackson standing like a stone wall!" cried one southern officer. "Rally behind the Virginians!" At that moment, General **Thomas "Stonewall" Jackson** earned his famous nickname.

A steady stream of Virginia volunteers arrived to counter the attack. The Confederates surged forward, letting out their terrifying "rebel yell." One eyewitness described the awful scene.

> "There is smoke, dust, wild talking, shouting; hissings, howlings, explosions. It is a new, strange, unanticipated experience to the soldiers of both armies, far different from what they thought it would be."
>
> —Charles Coffin, quoted in *Voices of the Civil War* by Richard Wheeler

The battle raged through the day, with rebel soldiers still arriving. Finally, the weary Union troops gave out. They tried to make an orderly retreat back across the creek, but the roads were clogged with the fancy carriages of panicked spectators. The Union army scattered in the chaos.

The Confederates lacked the strength to push north and capture Washington, D.C. But clearly, the rebels had won the day. The **First Battle of Bull Run** was the first major battle of the Civil War, and the Confederates' victory. The battle is also known as the First Battle of Manassas. It shattered the North's hopes of winning the war quickly.

More Battles in Virginia

The shock at Bull Run persuaded Lincoln of the need for a better-trained army. He put his hopes in General **George B. McClellan**. The general assembled a highly disciplined force of 100,000 soldiers called the Army of the Potomac. The careful McClellan spent months training. However, because he overestimated the size of the Confederate army, McClellan hesitated to attack. Lincoln grew impatient. Finally, in the spring of 1862, McClellan launched an effort to capture Richmond called the "Peninsular Campaign." Instead of marching south for a direct assault, McClellan slowly brought his force through the peninsula between the James and York rivers. More time slipped away.

The South feared that McClellan would receive reinforcements from Washington. To prevent this, Stonewall Jackson launched an attack toward Washington. Although the attack was pushed back, it prevented the Union from sending reinforcements to McClellan.

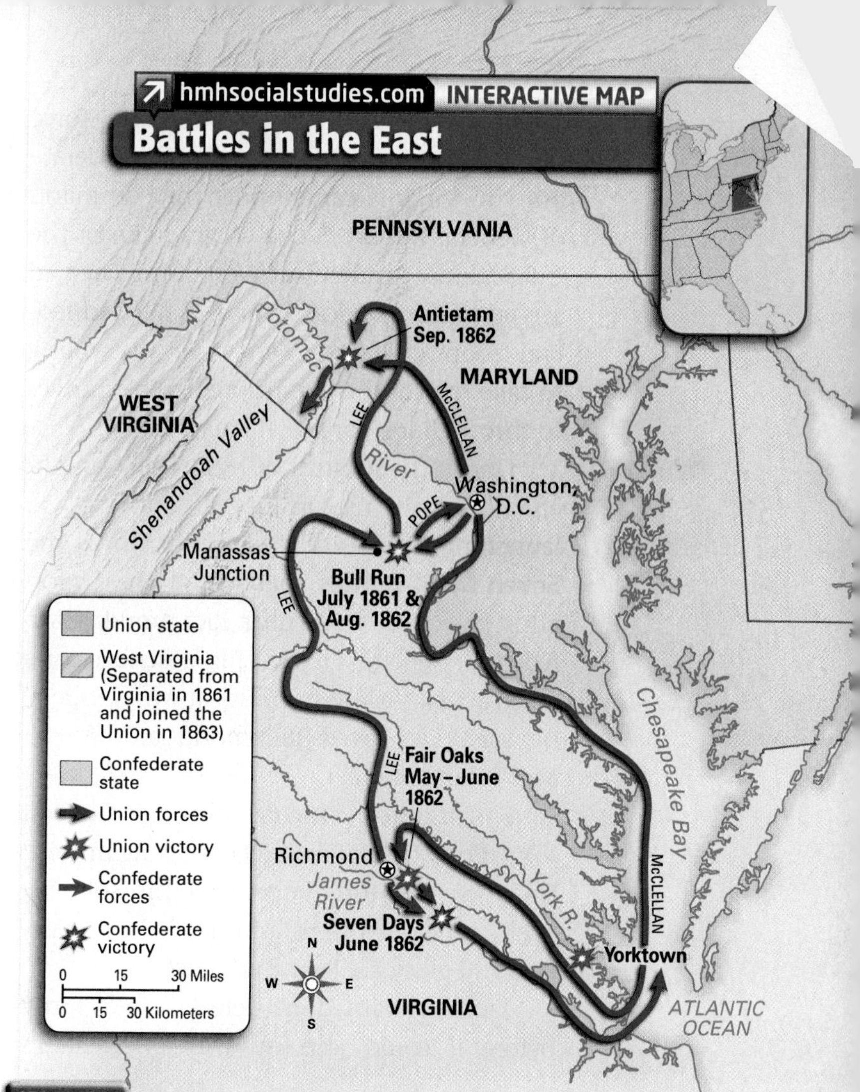

GEOGRAPHY SKILLS **INTERPRETING MAPS**

1. **Location** Which battle was fought in Maryland?
2. **Human-Environment Interaction** How did geography influence the movement of forces?

THE IMPACT TODAY

Many Americans continue to be fascinated by the Civil War. Some history buffs regularly stage re-enactments of famous battles, complete with uniforms, guns, and bayonets.

© Houghton Mifflin Harcourt Publishing Company

In June 1862, with McClellan's force poised outside Richmond, the Confederate army in Virginia came under the command of General **Robert E. Lee**. A graduate of the U.S. Military Academy at West Point, Lee had served in the Mexican War and had led federal troops at Harpers Ferry. Lee was willing to take risks and make unpredictable moves to throw Union forces off balance.

During the summer of 1862, Lee strengthened his positions. On June 26, he attacked, launching a series of clashes known as the **Seven Days' Battles** that forced the Union army to retreat from near Richmond. Confederate General D. H. Hill described one failed attack. "It was not war—it was murder," he said. Lee saved Richmond and forced McClellan to retreat.

A frustrated Lincoln ordered General John Pope to march directly on Richmond from Washington. Pope told his soldiers, "Let us look before us and not behind. Success and glory are in the advance."

Jackson wanted to defeat Pope's army before it could join up with McClellan's larger Army of the Potomac. Jackson's troops met Pope's Union forces on the battlefield in August in 1862. The three-day battle became known as the **Second Battle of Bull Run**, or the Second Battle of Manassas.

The first day's fighting was savage. Captain George Fairfield of the 7th Wisconsin regiment later recalled, "What a slaughter! No one appeared to know the object of the fight, and there we stood for one hour, the men falling all around." The fighting ended in a stalemate.

On the second day, Pope found Jackson's troops along an unfinished railroad grade. Pope hurled his men against the Confederates. But the attacks were pushed back with heavy casualties on both sides.

On the third day, the Confederates crushed the Union army's assault and forced it to retreat in defeat. The Confederates had won a major victory, and General Robert E. Lee decided it was time to take the war to the North.

READING CHECK **Sequencing** List in order the events that forced Union troops out of Virginia.

Eyewitness at Antietam

© Houghton Mifflin Harcourt Publishing Company • Image Credits: (b) National Park Service

Battle of Antietam

Confederate leaders hoped to follow up Lee's successes in Virginia with a major victory on northern soil. On September 4, 1862, some 40,000 Confederate soldiers began crossing into Maryland. General Robert E. Lee decided to divide his army. He sent about half of his troops, under the command of Stonewall Jackson, to Harpers Ferry. There they defeated a Union force and captured the town. Meanwhile, Lee arrived in the town of Frederick and issued a Proclamation to the People of Maryland, urging them to join the Confederates. However, his words would not be enough to convince Marylanders to abandon the Union. Union soldiers, however, found a copy of Lee's battle plan, which had been left at an abandoned Confederate camp. General McClellan learned that Lee had divided his army in order to attack Harpers Ferry. However, McClellan hesitated to attack. As a result, the Confederates had time to reunite.

BIOGRAPHY

Robert E. Lee

(1807–1870)

Robert E. Lee was born into a wealthy Virginia family in 1807. Lee fought in the Mexican-American War, helping to capture Veracruz. When the Civil War began, President Lincoln asked Lee to lead the Union army. Lee declined and resigned from the U.S. Army to become a general in the Confederate army.

Drawing Conclusions How did Lee's choice reflect the division of the states?

The two armies met along Antietam Creek in Maryland on September 17, 1862. The battle lasted for hours. By the end of the day, the Union had suffered more than 12,000 casualties. The Confederates endured more than 13,000 casualties. Union officer A. H. Nickerson later recalled, "It seemed that everybody near me was killed." The **Battle of Antietam,** also known as the Battle of Sharpsburg, was the bloodiest single-day battle of the Civil War—and of U.S. history. More soldiers were killed and wounded at the Battle of Antietam than the deaths of all Americans in the American Revolution, War of 1812, and Mexican-American War combined.

During the battle, McClellan kept four divisions of soldiers in reserve and refused to use them to attack Lee's devastated army. McClellan was convinced that Lee was massing reserves for a counterattack. Those reserves did not exist. Despite this blunder, Antietam was an important victory. Lee's northward advance had been stopped.

READING CHECK **Analyzing** Why was the Battle of Antietam significant?

James Hope was a professional artist who joined the Union army. Too sick to fight at Antietam, Hope was reassigned to work as a scout and a mapmaker. He sketched scenes from the battle as it happened and later used his sketches to make paintings like this one. This scene is of early morning on the battlefield. This painting doesn't represent a particular moment, but is meant to show a series of events.

ANALYSIS SKILL **ANALYZING VISUALS**

How is this painting different from modern war reporting?

Primary Source

POLITICAL CARTOON

Anaconda Plan

This cartoon shows visually the North's plan to cut off supplies to the South through naval blockades, a strategy called the Anaconda Plan.

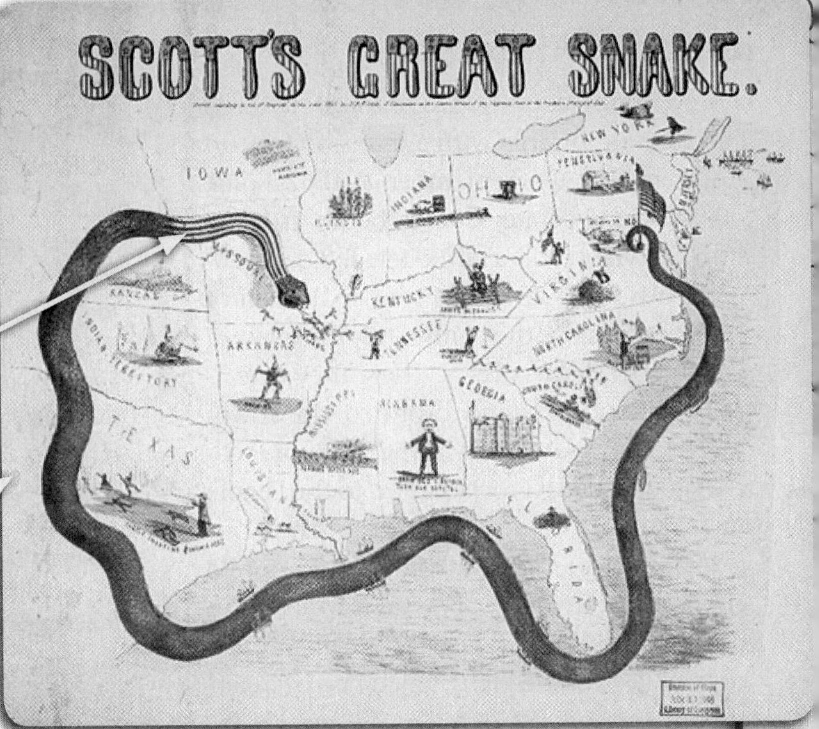

Why is the snake's head red, white, and blue?

How does the cartoonist show what the snake represents?

ANALYSIS SKILL **ANALYZING PRIMARY SOURCES**

Why do you think the plan was called the Anaconda Plan?

Breaking the Union's Blockade

While the two armies fought for control of the land, the Union navy controlled the sea. The North had most of the U.S. Navy's small fleet, and many experienced naval officers had remained loyal to the Union. The North also had enough industry to build more ships. The Confederacy turned to British companies for new ships.

ACADEMIC VOCABULARY
innovation a new idea or way of doing something

The Union's Naval Strategy

The Union navy quickly mobilized to set up a blockade of southern ports. The blockade largely prevented the South from selling or receiving goods, and it seriously damaged the southern economy.

The blockade was hard to maintain because the Union navy had to patrol thousands of miles of coastline from Virginia to Texas. The South used small, fast ships to outrun the larger Union warships. Most of these blockade runners traveled to the Bahamas or Nassau to buy supplies for the Confederacy. These ships, however, could not make up for the South's loss of trade. The Union blockade reduced the number of ships entering southern ports from 6,000 to 800 per year.

Clash of the Ironclads

Hoping to take away the Union's advantage at sea, the Confederacy turned to a new type of warship—**ironclads**, or ships heavily armored with iron. The British government neglected to stop these ships from being delivered, in violation of its pledge of neutrality. The Confederates had captured a Union steamship, the *Merrimack*, and turned it into an ironclad, renamed the *Virginia*. One Union sailor described the innovation as "a huge half-submerged crocodile." In early March 1862, the ironclad sailed into Hampton Roads, Virginia, an important waterway guarded by Union ships. Before nightfall, the *Virginia* easily sank two of the Union's wooden warships, while it received minor damage.

© Houghton Mifflin Harcourt Publishing Company • Image Credits: (t) Library of Congress Geography and Map Division Washington D.C.

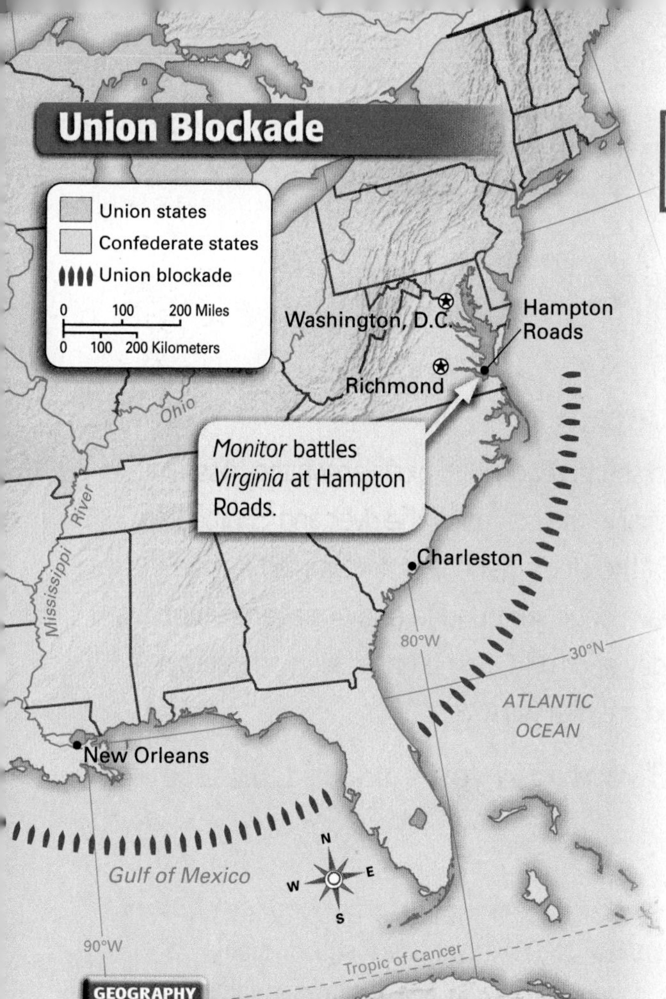
Union Blockade
Union states
Confederate states
Union blockade
0 100 200 Miles
0 100 200 Kilometers
Washington, D.C.
Hampton Roads
Richmond
Ohio
Monitor battles Virginia at Hampton Roads.
River
Mississippi
Charleston
80°W
30°N
ATLANTIC OCEAN
New Orleans
Gulf of Mexico
N
E
W
S
90°W
Tropic of Cancer

GEOGRAPHY SKILLS **INTERPRETING MAPS**

Location What major port cities in the South were affected by the blockade?

The Union navy had already built its own ironclad, the *Monitor*, designed by Swedish-born engineer John Ericsson. Ericsson's ship had unusual new features, such as a revolving gun tower. One Confederate soldier called the *Monitor* "a tin can on a shingle!" Although small, the *Monitor* carried powerful guns and had thick plating.

When the *Virginia* returned to Hampton Roads later that month, the *Monitor* was waiting. After several hours of fighting, neither ship was seriously damaged, but the *Monitor* forced the *Virginia* to withdraw. This success saved the Union fleet and continued the blockade. The clash of the ironclads also signaled a revolution in naval warfare. The days of wooden warships powered by wind and sails were drawing to a close.

THE IMPACT TODAY

The *Monitor* sank in North Carolina in the winter of 1862. The shipwreck was located by scientists in 1973, and remains of the ship are part of the exhibit at the USS *Monitor* Center, which opened in 2007.

READING CHECK **Evaluating** How effective was the Union blockade?

SUMMARY The early battles of the Civil War were centered in the East.

Section 2 Assessment

hmhsocialstudies.com
ONLINE QUIZ

Reviewing Ideas, Terms, and People

1. a. **Identify** List the early battles in the East and the outcome of each battle.
   b. **Elaborate** Why do you think the Union lost the **First Battle of Bull Run**?
2. a. **Describe** What costly mistake did the Confederacy make before the **Battle of Antietam**?
   b. **Analyze** What was the outcome of the Battle of Antietam, and what effect did it have on both the North and the South?
   c. **Elaborate** Why do you think General **George B. McClellan** did not finish off General **Robert E. Lee**'s troops when he had the chance?
3. a. **Describe** What was the Union's strategy in the war at sea?
   b. **Draw Conclusions** Why were **ironclads** more successful than older, wooden ships?

Critical Thinking

4. **Supporting a Point of View** Review your notes on the battles in the East and at sea. Then copy the graphic organizer below and use it to show which three conflicts you think were the most significant and why.

Most Significant	Why

Focus on Writing

5. **Taking Notes on the War in the East** As you read this section, take notes on the First Battle of Bull Run, the Seven Days' Battles, the Second Battle of Bull Run, and the Battle of Antietam. Be sure to answer the following questions: Who? Where? When? Why? and How?

© Houghton Mifflin Harcourt Publishing Company

SECTION 3

The War in the West

What You Will Learn...

Main Ideas

1. Union strategy in the West centered on control of the Mississippi River.
2. Confederate and Union troops struggled for dominance in the Far West.

The Big Idea

Fighting in the Civil War spread to the western United States.

Key Terms and People

Ulysses S. Grant
Battle of Shiloh
David Farragut
Siege of Vicksburg

hmhsocialstudies.com
TAKING NOTES

Use the graphic organizer online to take notes on Civil War battles in the West.

If YOU were there...

You live in the city of Vicksburg, set on high bluffs above the Mississippi River. Vicksburg is vital to the control of the river, and Confederate defenses are strong. But the Union general is determined to take the town. For weeks, you have been surrounded and besieged. Cannon shells burst overhead, day and night. Some have fallen on nearby homes. Supplies of food are running low.

How would you survive this siege?

BUILDING BACKGROUND The Civil War was fought on many fronts, all across the continent and even at sea. In the East, fighting was at first concentrated in Virginia. In the West, cities and forts along the Mississippi River were the main target of Union forces. Northern control of the river would cut off the western states of the Confederacy.

Union Strategy in the West

While Lincoln fumed over the cautious, hesitant General McClellan, he had no such problems with **Ulysses S. Grant**. Bold and restless, Grant grew impatient when he was asked to lead defensive maneuvers. He wanted to be on the attack. As a commander of forces in the Union's western campaign, he would get his wish.

The western campaign focused on taking control of the Mississippi River. This strategy would cut off the eastern part of the Confederacy from sources of food production in Arkansas, Louisiana, and Texas. From bases on the Mississippi, the Union army could attack southern communication and transportation networks.

In February 1862, Grant led an assault force into Tennessee. With help from navy gunboats, Grant's Army of the Tennessee took two outposts on key rivers in the west. On February 6, he captured Fort Henry on the Tennessee River. Several days later he took Fort Donelson on the Cumberland River.

Fort Donelson's commander asked for the terms of surrender. Grant replied, "No terms except an unconditional and immediate

© Houghton Mifflin Harcourt Publishing Company

hmhsocialstudies.com INTERACTIVE MAP

The War in the West

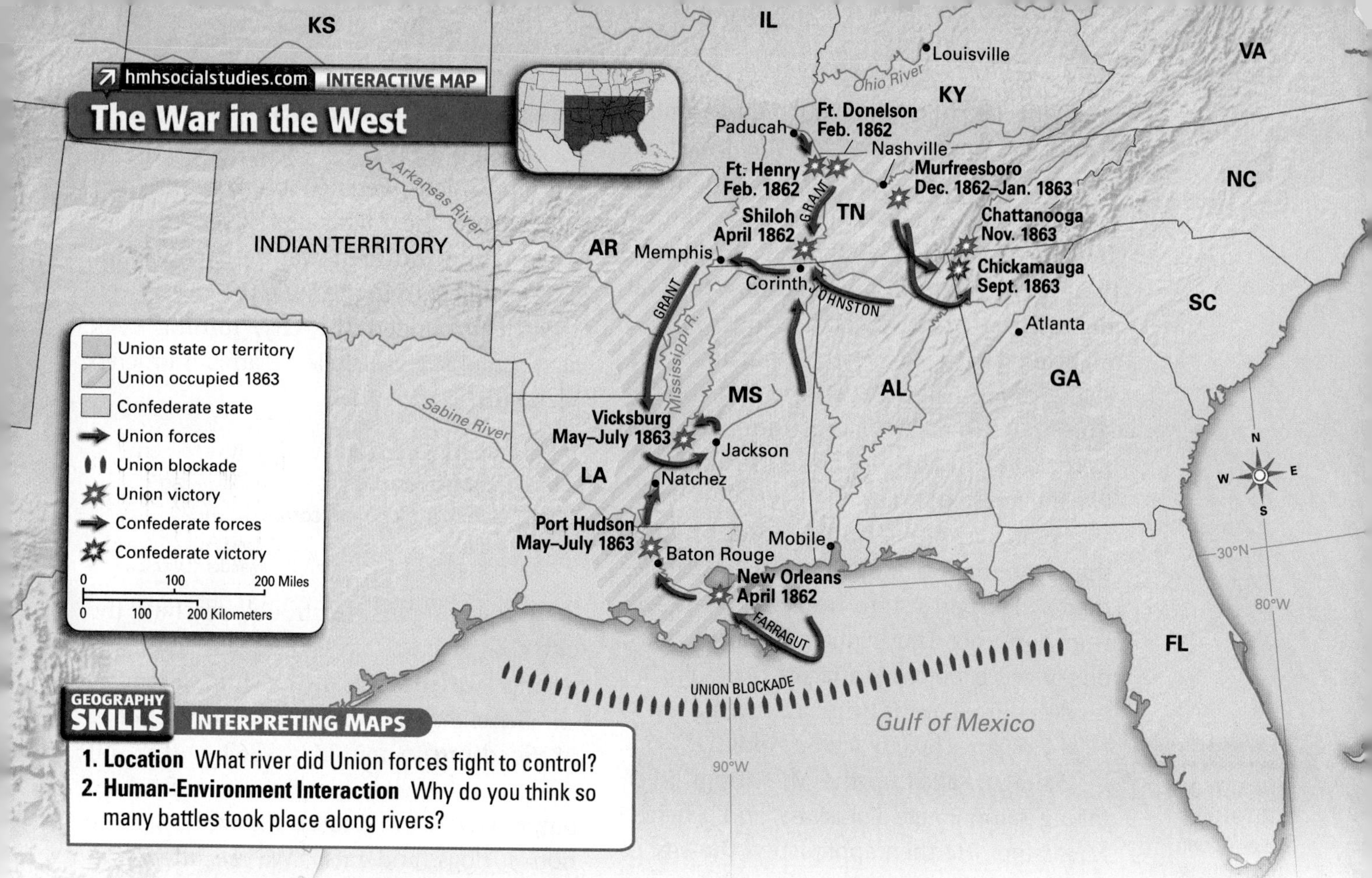
KS
IL
VA
Louisville
Ohio River
KY
Ft. Donelson
Feb. 1862
Paducah
Nashville
Ft. Henry
Feb. 1862
Murfreesboro
Dec. 1862–Jan. 1863
NC
Arkansas River
GRANT
Shiloh
April 1862
TN
Chattanooga
Nov. 1863
INDIAN TERRITORY
AR
Memphis
Chickamauga
Sept. 1863
Corinth
JOHNSTON
SC
Atlanta
GRANT
Mississippi R.
Union state or territory
Union occupied 1863
Confederate state
Union forces
Union blockade
Union victory
Confederate forces
Confederate victory
0 100 200 Miles
0 100 200 Kilometers
MS
AL
GA
Sabine River
Vicksburg
May–July 1863
Jackson
LA
Natchez
N
W
E
S
Port Hudson
May–July 1863
Baton Rouge
Mobile
New Orleans
April 1862
30°N
80°W
FARRAGUT
FL
UNION BLOCKADE
Gulf of Mexico
90°W

GEOGRAPHY SKILLS **INTERPRETING MAPS**

1. **Location** What river did Union forces fight to control?
2. **Human-Environment Interaction** Why do you think so many battles took place along rivers?

surrender can be accepted." The fort surrendered. The North gave a new name to Grant's initials: "Unconditional Surrender" Grant.

Advancing south in Tennessee, General Grant paused near Shiloh Church to await the arrival of the Army of the Ohio. Grant knew that the large rebel army of General A. S. Johnston was nearby in Corinth, Mississippi, but he did not expect an attack. Instead of setting up defenses, he worked on drilling his new recruits.

In the early morning of April 6, 1862, the rebels sprang on Grant's sleepy camp. This began the **Battle of Shiloh**, in which the Union army gained greater control of the Mississippi River valley.

During the bloody two-day battle, each side gained and lost ground. Johnston was killed on the first day. The arrival of the Ohio force helped Grant regain territory and push the enemy back into Mississippi. The armies finally gave out, each with about 10,000 casualties. Both sides claimed victory, but, in fact, the victor was Grant.

The Fall of New Orleans

As Grant battled his way down the Mississippi, the Union navy prepared to blast its way upriver to meet him. The first obstacle was the port of New Orleans, the largest city in the Confederacy and the gateway to the Mississippi River.

BIOGRAPHY

David Farragut

(1801–1870)

David Farragut was born in Tennessee to a Spanish father and an American mother. At age seven Farragut was adopted by a family friend who agreed to train the young boy for the navy. Farragut received his first navy position—midshipman at large—at age nine and commanded his first vessel at 12. He spent the rest of his life in the U.S. Navy. Farragut led key attacks on the southern ports of Vicksburg and New Orleans.

Drawing Inferences How did Farragut help the war effort of the North?

© Houghton Mifflin Harcourt Publishing Company

With 18 ships and 700 men, Admiral **David Farragut** approached the two forts that guarded the entrance to New Orleans from the Gulf of Mexico. Unable to destroy the forts, Farragut decided to race past them.

The risky operation would take place at night. Farragut had his wooden ships wrapped in heavy chains to protect them like ironclads. Sailors slapped Mississippi mud on the ships' hulls to make them hard to see. Trees were tied to the masts to make the ships look like the forested shore.

Before dawn on April 24, 1862, the warships made their daring dash. The Confederates fired at Farragut's ships from the shore and from gunboats. They launched burning rafts, one of which scorched Farragut's own ship. But his fleet slipped by the twin forts and made it to New Orleans. The city fell on April 29.

Farragut sailed up the Mississippi River, taking Baton Rouge, Louisiana, and Natchez, Mississippi. He then approached the city of Vicksburg, Mississippi.

hmhsocialstudies.com
ANIMATED HISTORY
Naval Action at Vicksburg

The Siege of Vicksburg

Vicksburg's geography made invasion all but impossible. Perched on 200-foot-high cliffs above the Mississippi River, the city could rain down firepower on enemy ships or on soldiers trying to scale the cliffs. Deep gorges surrounded the city, turning back land assaults. Nevertheless, Farragut ordered Vicksburg to surrender.

> "Mississippians don't know, and refuse to learn, how to surrender . . . If Commodore Farragut . . . can teach them, let [him] come and try."
>
> —Colonel James L. Autry, military commander of Vicksburg

Farragut's guns had trouble reaching the city above. It was up to General Grant. His solution was to starve the city into surrender.

General Grant's troops began the **Siege of Vicksburg** in mid-May 1863, cutting off the city and shelling it repeatedly. As food ran out, residents and soldiers survived by eating horses, dogs, and rats. "We are utterly cut off from the world, surrounded by a circle of fire," wrote one woman. "People do nothing

Primary Source

SPEECH

Response to Farragut

The mayor of New Orleans considered the surrender of the city to the Union navy:

> "We yield to physical force alone and maintain allegiance to the Confederate States; beyond this, a due respect for our dignity, our rights and the flag of our country does not, I think, permit us to go."
>
> **–Mayor John T. Monroe,**
> quoted in *Confederate Military History, Vol. 10*

ANALYSIS SKILL ANALYZING PRIMARY SOURCES

How does Monroe's statement reveal his attitude about surrender?

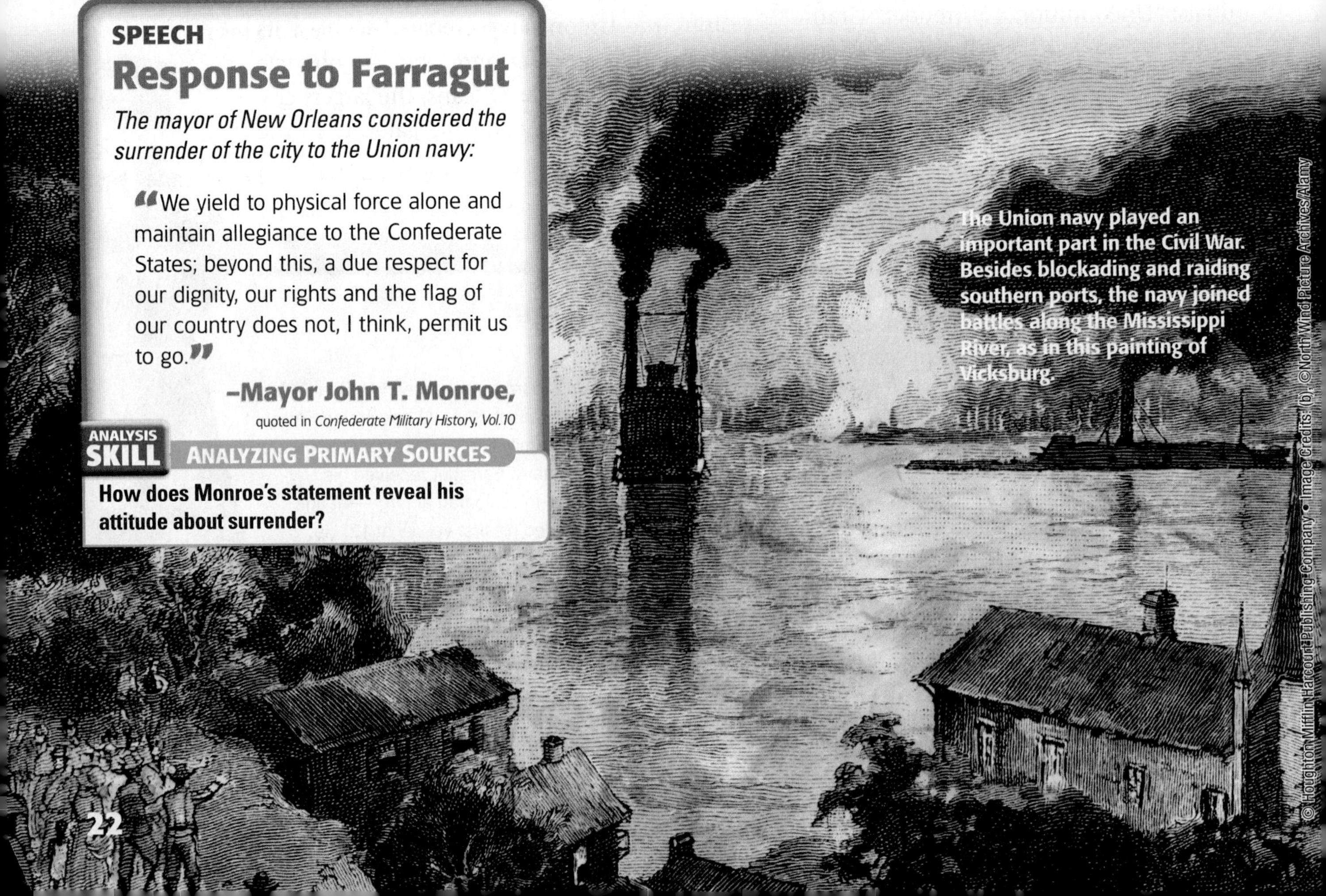

The Union navy played an important part in the Civil War. Besides blockading and raiding southern ports, the navy joined battles along the Mississippi River, as in this painting of Vicksburg.

© Houghton Mifflin Harcourt Publishing Company • Image Credits: (b) ©North Wind Picture Archives/Alamy but eat what they can get, sleep when they can, and dodge the shells."

The Confederate soldiers were also sick and hungry. In late June a group of soldiers sent their commander a warning.

> "The army is now ripe for mutiny [rebellion], unless it can be fed. If you can't feed us, you'd better surrender us, horrible as the idea is."
>
> —Confederate soldiers at Vicksburg to General John C. Pemberton, 1863

On July 4, Pemberton surrendered. Grant immediately sent food to the soldiers and civilians. He later claimed that "the fate of the Confederacy was sealed when Vicksburg fell."

READING CHECK **Summarizing** How did the Union gain control of the Mississippi River?

Struggle for the Far West

Early on in the war, the Union halted several attempts by Confederate armies to control lands west of the Mississippi. In August 1861, a Union detachment from Colorado turned back a Confederate force at Glorieta Pass. Union volunteers also defeated rebel forces at Arizona's Pichaco Pass.

Confederate attempts to take the border state of Missouri also collapsed. Failing to seize the federal arsenal at St. Louis in mid-1861, the rebels fell back to Pea Ridge in northwest Arkansas. There, in March 1862, they attacked again, aided by some 800 Cherokee. The Indians hoped the Confederates would give them greater freedom. In addition, slavery was legal in Indian Territory, and some Native Americans who were slaveholders supported the Confederacy. Despite being outnumbered, Union forces won the Battle of Pea Ridge. The Union defense of Missouri held.

Pro-Confederate forces remained active in the region throughout the war. They attacked Union forts and raided towns in Missouri and Kansas, forcing Union commanders to keep valuable troops stationed in the area.

READING CHECK **Analyzing** What was the importance of the fighting in the Far West?

SUMMARY The North and the South continued their struggle with battles in the West. A number of key battles took place in the Western theater, and several important Union leaders emerged from these battles. One, Ulysses S. Grant, would soon become even more important to the Union army.

Section 3 Assessment

hmhsocialstudies.com ONLINE QUIZ

Reviewing Ideas, Terms, and People

1. a. **Identify** What role did **Ulysses S. Grant** play in the war in the West?
   b. **Explain** Why was the **Battle of Shiloh** important?
   c. **Elaborate** Do you think President Lincoln would have approved of Grant's actions in the West? Why or why not?
2. a. **Describe** How did the Union take New Orleans, and why was it an important victory?
   b. **Draw Conclusions** How were civilians affected by the **Siege of Vicksburg**?
   c. **Predict** What might be some possible results of the Union victory at Vicksburg?

Critical Thinking

3. **Identifying Cause and Effect** Review your notes on Union strategy in the West. Then copy this graphic organizer and use it to show the causes and effects of each battle.

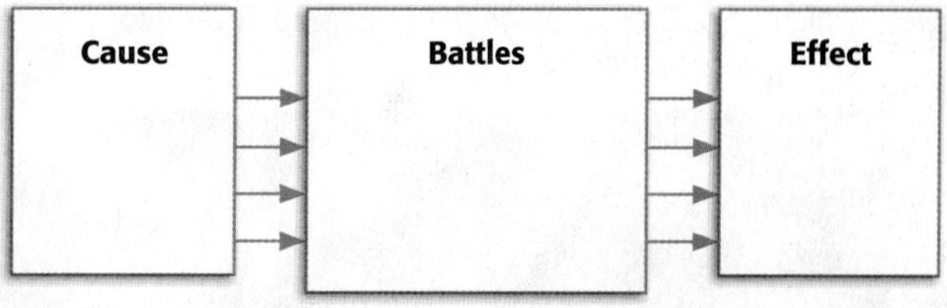

FOCUS ON WRITING

4. **Taking Notes on the War in the West** As you read this section, take notes on the fight for the Mississippi River and the Siege of Vicksburg. Be sure to answer the following questions: Who? Where? When? Why? and How?

© Houghton Mifflin Harcourt Publishing Company

The Vicksburg Strategy

"Vicksburg is the key!"
President Abraham Lincoln declared. "The war can never be brought to a close until that key is in our pocket." Vicksburg was so important because of its location on the Mississippi River, a vital trade route and supply line. Union ships couldn't get past the Confederate guns mounted on the high bluffs of Vicksburg. Capturing Vicksburg would give the Union control of the Mississippi, stealing a vital supply line and splitting the Confederacy in two. The task fell to General Ulysses S. Grant.

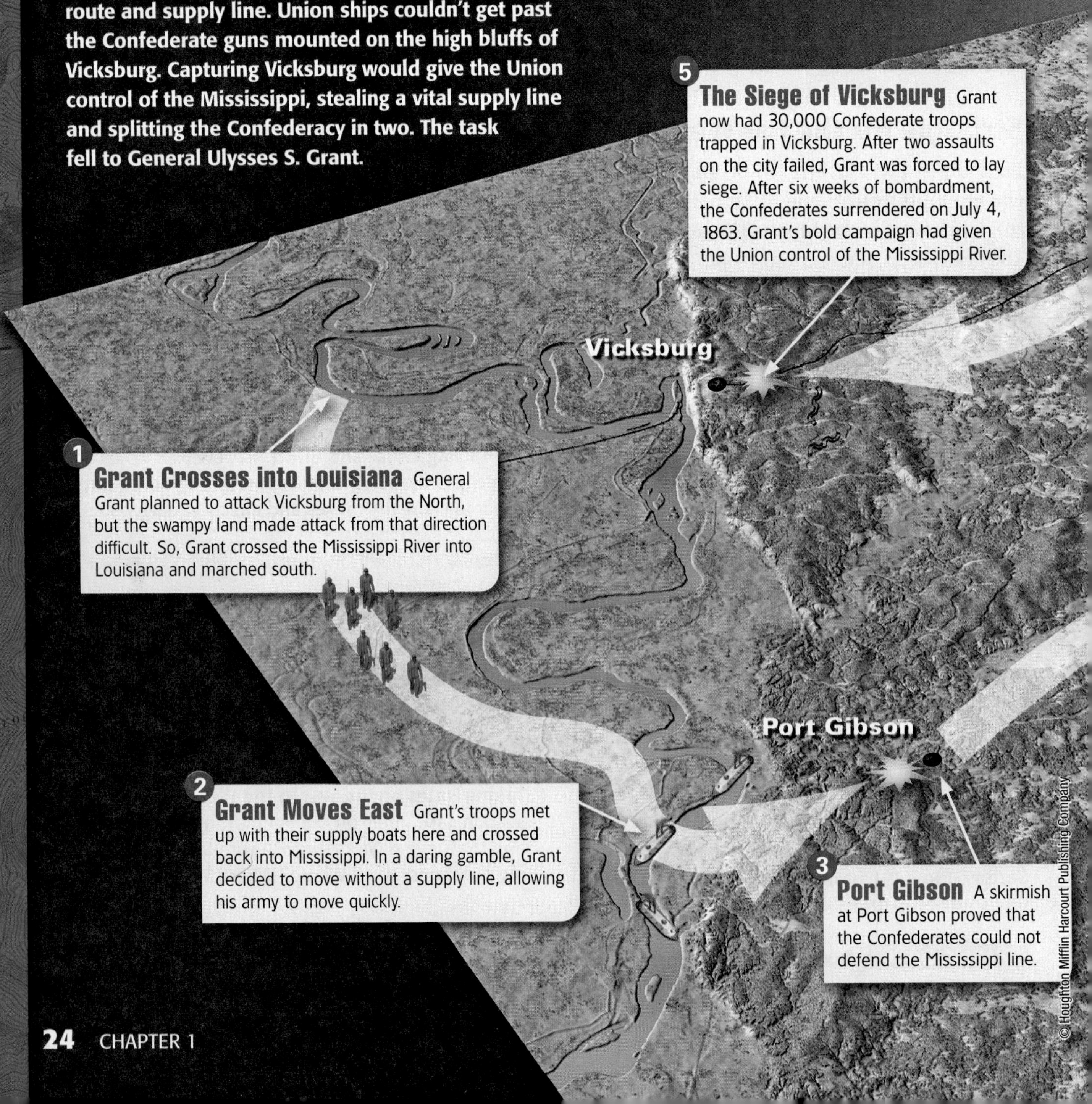

1 **Grant Crosses into Louisiana** General Grant planned to attack Vicksburg from the North, but the swampy land made attack from that direction difficult. So, Grant crossed the Mississippi River into Louisiana and marched south.

2 **Grant Moves East** Grant's troops met up with their supply boats here and crossed back into Mississippi. In a daring gamble, Grant decided to move without a supply line, allowing his army to move quickly.

3 **Port Gibson** A skirmish at Port Gibson proved that the Confederates could not defend the Mississippi line.

5 **The Siege of Vicksburg** Grant now had 30,000 Confederate troops trapped in Vicksburg. After two assaults on the city failed, Grant was forced to lay siege. After six weeks of bombardment, the Confederates surrendered on July 4, 1863. Grant's bold campaign had given the Union control of the Mississippi River.

© Houghton Mifflin Harcourt Publishing Company

Missouri
Kentucky
Virginia
North Carolina
Arkansas
Tennessee
South Carolina
Mississippi River
Alabama
Georgia
VICKSBURG
Mississippi
Louisiana
GULF OF MEXICO
UNION CONTROL
CONFEDERATE CONTROL

Ironclads

Union ironclads were vital to the Vicksburg campaign. These gunboats protected Grant's troops when they crossed the Mississippi. Later, they bombarded Vicksburg during the siege of the city.

Jackson

4 **The Battle of Jackson** Grant defeated a Confederate army at Jackson and then moved on to Vicksburg. This prevented Confederate forces from reinforcing Vicksburg.

BIOGRAPHY

Ulysses S. Grant
(1822–1885)

Ulysses S. Grant was born in April 1822 in New York. Grant attended West Point and fought in the Mexican-American War. He resigned in 1854 and worked at various jobs in farming, real estate, and retail. When the Civil War started, he joined the Union army and was quickly promoted to general. After the Civil War, Grant rode a wave of popularity to become president of the United States.

GEOGRAPHY SKILLS INTERPRETING MAPS

1. **Location** Why was Vicksburg's location so important?
2. **Place** What natural features made Vicksburg difficult to attack?

© Houghton Mifflin Harcourt Publishing Company

Image Credits: (t), Naval Historical Center

SECTION 4

Daily Life during the War

What You Will Learn...

Main Ideas

1. The Emancipation Proclamation freed slaves in Confederate states.
2. African Americans participated in the war in a variety of ways.
3. President Lincoln faced opposition to the war.
4. Life was difficult for soldiers and civilians alike.

The Big Idea

The lives of many Americans were affected by the Civil War.

Key Terms and People

emancipation
Emancipation Proclamation
contrabands
54th Massachusetts Infantry
Copperheads
habeas corpus
Clara Barton

hmhsocialstudies.com
TAKING NOTES

Use the graphic organizer online to take notes on the effects of the Civil War on the lives of African Americans, soldiers, and women and children.

If YOU were there...

You live in Maryland in 1864. Your father and brothers are in the Union army, and you want to do your part in the war. You hear that a woman in Washington, D.C., is supplying medicines and caring for wounded soldiers on the battlefield. She is looking for volunteers. You know the work will be dangerous, for you'll be in the line of fire. You might be shot or even killed.

Would you join the nurses on the battlefield?

BUILDING BACKGROUND The Civil War touched almost all Americans. Some 3 million men fought in the two armies. Thousands of other men and women worked behind the lines, providing food, supplies, medical care, and other necessary services. Civilians could not escape the effects of war, as the fighting destroyed farms, homes, and cities.

Emancipation Proclamation

© Houghton Mifflin Harcourt Publishing Company
○ Image Credits: (b), SuperStock

Emancipation Proclamation

At the heart of the nation's bloody struggle were millions of enslaved African Americans. Abolitionists urged President Lincoln to free them.

In an 1858 speech, Lincoln declared, "There is no reason in the world why the negro is not entitled to all the natural rights numerated in the Declaration of Independence—the right to life, liberty, and the pursuit of happiness." Yet as president, Lincoln found **emancipation**, or the freeing of slaves, to be a difficult issue. He did not believe he had the constitutional power. He also worried about the effects of emancipation.

Lincoln Issues the Proclamation

Northerners had a range of opinions about abolishing slavery.

- The Democratic Party, which included many laborers, opposed emancipation. Laborers feared that freed slaves would come north and take their jobs at lower wages.
- Abolitionists argued that the war was pointless if it did not win freedom for African Americans. They warned that the Union would remain divided until the problem was resolved.

The painting at left shows Lincoln and his cabinet after the signing of the Emancipation Proclamation. Above is a photo of former slaves who were freed by the proclamation.

How do you think the Emancipation Proclamation would affect the Civil War?

© Houghton Mifflin Harcourt Publishing Company • Image Credits: (b), South Carolina Historical Society

Emancipation Proclamation

GEOGRAPHY SKILLS INTERPRETING MAPS

Place In which places was slavery still legal after the Emancipation Proclamation?

- Lincoln worried about losing support for the war. Previous wartime Confiscation Acts that had attempted to free the slaves had been unpopular in the border states.
- Others, including Secretary of War Edwin Stanton, agreed with Lincoln that the use of slave labor was helping the Confederacy make war. Therefore, as commander in chief, the president could free the slaves in all rebellious states. Freed African Americans could then be recruited into the Union army.

For several weeks in 1862, Lincoln worked intensely, thinking, writing, and rewriting. He finally wrote the **Emancipation Proclamation**, the order to free the Confederate slaves. The proclamation declared that:

> "... all persons held as slaves within any State or designated part of a State the people whereof shall then be in rebellion against the United States shall be then, thenceforward, and forever free."
>
> —Emancipation Proclamation, 1862

The Emancipation Proclamation was a military order that freed slaves only in areas

New Soldiers

NOW IN CAMP AT READVILLE!
54th REGIMENT!
MASS. VOLUNTEERS, composed of men of
AFRICAN DESCENT
Col. ROBERT G. SHAW.
Colored Men, Rally 'Round the Flag of Freedom!
BOUNTY $100!
AT THE EXPIRATION OF THE TERM OF SERVICE.
Pay, $13 a Month!
Good Food & Clothing!
State Aid to Families!
RECRUITING OFFICE,
COR. CAMBRIDGE & NORTH RUSSELL STS.,
BOSTON.
Lieut. J. W. M. APPLETON, Recruiting Officer.

African American soldiers, such as the 54th Massachusetts Infantry and Company E of the 4th U.S. Colored Infantry, shown here, fought proudly and bravely in the Civil War. At right is a flyer used to recruit African American soldiers.

VIDEO
54th Regiment HISTORY
hmhsocialstudies.com

controlled by the Confederacy. In fact, the proclamation had little immediate effect. It was impossible for the federal government to enforce the proclamation in the areas where it actually applied—the states in rebellion that were not under federal control. The proclamation did not stop slavery in the border states, where the federal government would have had the power to enforce it. The words written in the Emancipation Proclamation were powerful, but the impact of the document was more symbolic than real. It defined what the Union was fighting against, and discouraged Britain from aiding the Confederacy.

Lincoln wanted to be in a strong position in the war before announcing his plan. The Battle of Antietam gave him the victory he needed. He issued the Emancipation Proclamation on September 22, 1862. The proclamation went into effect on January 1, 1863.

Reaction to the Proclamation

New Year's Eve, December 31, 1862: In "night watch" meetings at many African American churches, worshippers prayed, sang, and gave thanks. When the clocks struck midnight, millions were free. Abolitionists rejoiced. Frederick Douglass called January 1, 1863, "the great day which is to determine the destiny not only of the American Republic, but that of the American Continent."

William Lloyd Garrison was quick to note, however, that "slavery, as a system" continued to exist in the loyal slave states. Yet where slavery remained, the proclamation encouraged many enslaved Africans to escape when the Union troops came near. They flocked to the Union camps and followed them for protection. The loss of slaves crippled the South's ability to wage war.

READING CHECK **Finding Main Ideas** How did northerners view the Emancipation Proclamation?

© Houghton Mifflin Harcourt Publishing Company • Image Credits: (t), Library of Congress Prints & Photographs Division, Washington, D.C.; (inset), Courtesy of the Massachusetts Historical Society

Primary Source

LETTER

June 23, 1863

Joseph E. Williams, an African American soldier and recruiter from Pennsylvania, wrote this letter describing why African Americans fought for the Union.

"We are now determined to hold every step which has been offered to us as citizens of the United States for our elevation [benefit], which represent justice, the purity, the truth, and aspiration [hope] of heaven. We must learn deeply to realize the duty, the moral and political necessity for the benefit of our race...Every consideration of honor, of interest, and of duty to God and man, requires that we should be true to our trust."

—quoted in *A Grand Army of Black Men*, edited by Edwin S. Redkey

ANALYSIS SKILL ANALYZING PRIMARY SOURCES

Why did Williams think being soldiers was so important for African Americans?

African Americans Participate in the War

As the war casualties climbed, the Union needed even more troops. African Americans were ready to volunteer. Not all white northerners were ready to accept them, but eventually they had to. Frederick Douglass believed that military service would help African Americans gain rights.

"Once let the black man get upon his person the brass letters, U.S.; . . . and a musket on his shoulder and bullets in his pocket, and there is no power on earth which can deny that he has earned the right to citizenship."

—Frederick Douglass, quoted in *The Life and Writings of Frederick Douglass, Vol. 3*

Congress began allowing the army to sign up African American volunteers as laborers in July 1862. The War Department also gave **contrabands**, or escaped slaves, the right to join the Union army in South Carolina. Free African Americans in Louisiana and Kansas also formed their own units in the Union army. By the spring of 1863, African American army units were proving themselves in combat. They took part in a Union attack on Port Hudson, Louisiana, in May.

One unit stood out above the others. The **54th Massachusetts Infantry** consisted mostly of free African Americans. In July 1863 this regiment led a heroic charge on South Carolina's Fort Wagner. The 54th took heavy fire and suffered huge casualties in the failed operation. About half the regiment was killed, wounded, or captured. Edward L. Pierce, a correspondent for the *New York Tribune,* wrote, "The Fifty-fourth did well and nobly...They moved up as gallantly as any troops could, and with their enthusiasm they deserved a better fate." The bravery of the 54th regiment made it the most celebrated African American unit of the war.

About 180,000 African Americans served with the Union army. They received $10 a month, while white soldiers got $13. They were usually led by white officers, some from abolitionist families.

African Americans faced special horrors on the battlefield. Confederates often killed their black captives or sold them into slavery. In the 1864 election, Lincoln suggested rewarding African American soldiers by giving them the right to vote.

READING CHECK **Analyzing Information**
How did African Americans support the Union?

© Houghton Mifflin Harcourt Publishing Company

Growing Opposition

The deepening shadows in Lincoln's face reflected the huge responsibilities he carried. Besides running the war, he had to deal with growing tensions in the North.

Copperheads

As the months rolled on and the number of dead continued to increase, a group of northern Democrats began speaking out against the war. Led by U.S. Representative Clement L. Vallandigham of Ohio, they called themselves Peace Democrats. Their enemies called them Copperheads, comparing them to a poisonous snake. The name stuck.

Many **Copperheads** were midwesterners that sympathized with the South and opposed abolition. They believed the war was not necessary and called for its end. Vallandigham asked what the war had gained, and then said, "Let the dead at Fredericksburg and Vicksburg answer."

Lincoln saw the Copperheads as a threat to support of the war effort. To silence them, he suspended the right of habeas corpus. **Habeas corpus** is a constitutional protection against unlawful imprisonment. Ignoring this protection, Union officials jailed their enemies, including some Copperheads, without evidence or trial. Lincoln's action greatly angered Democrats and some Republicans.

Northern Draft

In March 1863, war critics erupted again when Congress approved a draft, or forced military service. For $300, men were allowed to buy their way out of military service. For an unskilled laborer, however, that was nearly a year's wages. Critics of the draft called the Civil War a "rich man's war and a poor man's fight."

In July 1863, riots broke out when African Americans were brought into New York City to replace striking Irish dock workers. The city happened to be holding a war draft at the same time. The two events enraged rioters, who attacked African Americans and draft offices. More than 100 people died.

In this tense situation, the northern Democrats nominated former General George McClellan for president in 1864. They called

Infantry Family

While wealthy civilians could avoid military service, poorer men were drafted to serve in the Union army. This member of the 31st Pennsylvania Infantry brought his family along with him. His wife probably helped the soldier with many daily chores such as cooking and laundry.

Why would soldiers bring their families to live with them in camp?

© Houghton Mifflin Harcourt Publishing Company • Image Credits: (b) ©Bettmann/Corbis

for an immediate end to the war. Lincoln defeated McClellan in the popular vote, winning by about 400,000 votes out of 4 million cast. The electoral vote was not even close. Lincoln won 212 to 21.

READING CHECK **Identifying Cause and Effect** Who opposed the war, and how did Lincoln respond to the conflict?

Life for Soldiers and Civilians

Young, fresh recruits in both armies were generally eager to fight. Experienced troops, however, knew better.

On the Battlefield

Civil War armies fought in the ancient battlefield formation that produced massive casualties. Endless rows of troops fired directly at one another, with cannonballs landing amid them. When the order was given, soldiers would attach bayonets to their guns and rush toward their enemy. Men died to gain every inch of ground.

Doctors and nurses in the field saved many lives. Yet they had no medicines to stop infections that developed after soldiers were wounded. Many soldiers endured the horror of having infected legs and arms amputated without painkillers. Infections from minor injuries caused many deaths.

Despite the huge battlefield losses, the biggest killer in the Civil War was not the fighting. It was diseases such as typhoid, pneumonia, and tuberculosis. Nearly twice as many soldiers died of illnesses as died in combat.

Prisoners of War

Military prisoners on both sides lived in unimaginable misery. In prison camps, such as Andersonville, Georgia, and Elmira, New York, soldiers were packed into camps designed to hold only a fraction of their number. Soldiers had little shelter, food, or clothing. Starvation and disease killed thousands of prisoners.

LINKING TO TODAY

Battlefield Communications

The drummer was an essential member of every Civil War unit. Drummers served army commanders by drumming specific beats that directed troop movements during battle. Different beats were used to order troops to prepare to attack, to fire, to cease fire, and to signal a truce. Drummers had to stay near their commanders to hear orders. This meant that the drummers—some as young as nine years old—often saw deadly combat conditions.

The Civil War gave birth to the Signal Corps, the army unit devoted to communications. Today battlefield communications are primarily electronic. Radio, e-mail, facsimile, and telephone messages, often relayed by satellites, enable orders and other information to be transmitted nearly instantaneously all over the globe.

Drum Corps of 61st New York Infantry

Modern battlefield communications

ANALYSIS SKILL **ANALYZING INFORMATION**

Why is communication so important on the battlefield?

© Houghton Mifflin Harcourt Publishing Company • Image Credits: (b), ©Reuters/Kai Pfaffenbach/Corbis; (t), Library of Congress Prints & Photographs Division, Washington, D.C. (LC-DIG-cwpb-4019)

Life as a Civilian

Clara Barton founded the American Red Cross.

The war effort involved all levels of society. Women as well as people too young or too old for military service worked in factories and on farms. Economy in the North boomed as production and prices soared. The lack of workers caused wages to rise by 43 percent between 1860 and 1865.

THE IMPACT TODAY

Providing assistance to victims of war is still part of the American Red Cross's mission today. In addition, the American Red Cross aids victims of natural disasters, provides services to the needy, supports military members and their families, and collects and distributes lifesaving blood.

Women were the backbone of civilian life. On the farms, women and children performed the daily chores usually done by men. One visitor to Iowa in 1862 reported that he "met more women . . . at work in the fields than men." Southern women also managed farms and plantations.

One woman brought strength and comfort to countless wounded Union soldiers. Volunteer **Clara Barton** organized the collection of medicine and supplies for delivery to the battlefield. At the field hospitals, the "angel of the battlefield" soothed the wounded and dying and assisted doctors as bullets flew around her. Barton's work formed the basis for the future American Red Cross.

In the South, Sally Louisa Tompkins established a small hospital in Richmond, Virginia. By the end of the war, it had grown into a major army hospital. Jefferson Davis recognized her value to the war effort by making her a captain in the Confederate army.

READING CHECK **Analyzing** How did women help the war effort on both sides?

SUMMARY Many lives were changed by the war.

Section 4 Assessment

hmhsocialstudies.com
ONLINE QUIZ

Reviewing Ideas, Terms, and People

1. a. **Recall** Why did some Americans want to end slavery?
   b. **Contrast** How did reactions to the **Emancipation Proclamation** differ?
   c. **Elaborate** Do you think that the **emancipation** of slaves should have extended to the border states? Explain your answer.
2. a. **Recall** Why did some northerners want to recruit African Americans into the Union army?
   b. **Contrast** In what ways did African American soldiers face more difficulties than white soldiers did?
3. a. **Identify** Who were **Copperheads**, and why did they oppose the war?
   b. **Evaluate** Should President Lincoln have suspended the right to **habeas corpus**? Why?
4. a. **Describe** What were conditions like in military camps?
   b. **Draw Conclusions** How did the war change life on the home front?

Critical Thinking

5. **Identifying Effects** Review your notes. Then copy the graphic organizer below. Use it to summarize the reasons for the Emancipation Proclamation, its main points, and its effects on different people.

Reasons for the Emancipation Proclamation
↓
Main points of the Proclamation
↓
Effect on People's Lives
↓

Focus on Writing

6. **Taking Notes on Life During the War** As you read this section, take notes on the emancipation of the slaves, African American soldiers, and women who provided medical care for soldiers. Answer the following questions: Who? Where? When? Why? and How?

© Houghton Mifflin Harcourt Publishing Company • Image Credits: (t) American Antiquarian Society

BIOGRAPHY

Abraham Lincoln

What would you do to save the struggling Union?

When did he live? 1809–1865

Where did he live? Abraham Lincoln was born in a log cabin to a poor family in Kentucky. Growing up in Kentucky and Illinois, Lincoln went to school for less than a year. He taught himself law and settled in Springfield, where he practiced law and politics. As president he lived in Washington, D.C. There, at age 56, his life was cut short by an assassin, John Wilkes Booth.

What did he do? The issue of slavery defined Lincoln's political career. He was not an abolitionist, but he strongly opposed extending slavery into the territories. In a series of famous debates against Senator Stephen Douglas of Illinois, Lincoln championed his views on slavery and made a brilliant defense of democracy and the Union. As president, Lincoln led the nation through the Civil War.

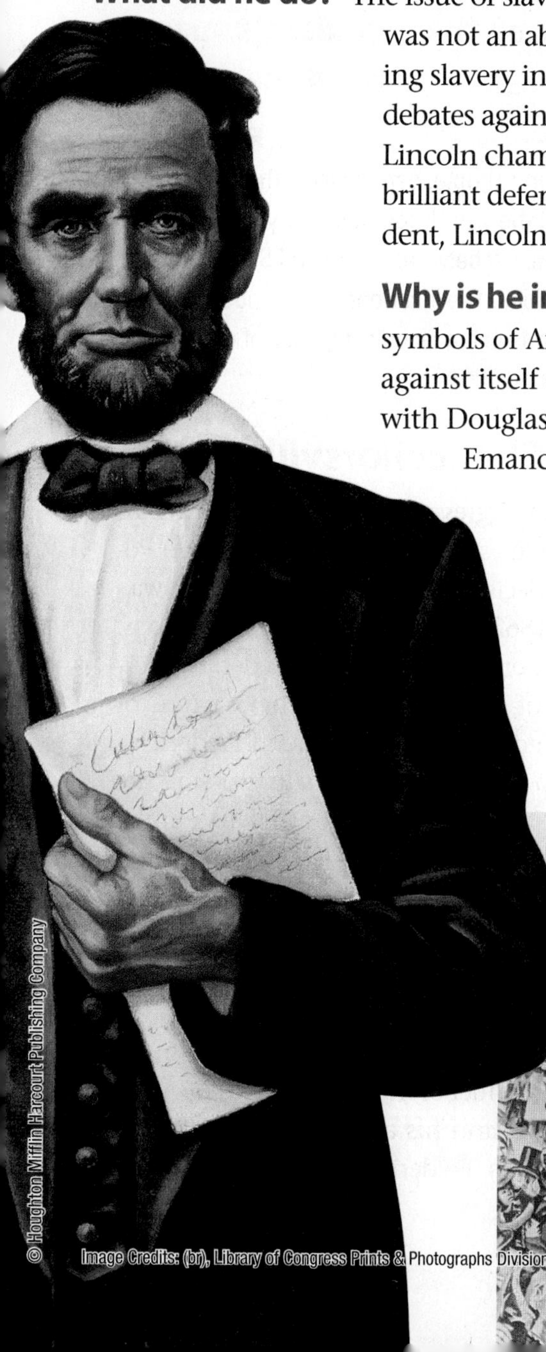

Why is he important? Lincoln is one of the great symbols of American democracy. "A house divided against itself cannot stand," he declared in a debate with Douglas. In 1863 Lincoln issued the Emancipation Proclamation. His address to commemorate the bloody battlefield at Gettysburg is widely considered to be one of the best political speeches in American history.

Summarizing Why is Lincoln such an important figure in American history?

KEY EVENTS

- **1834** Elected to the Illinois legislature
- **1842** Marries Mary Todd
- **1858** Holds series of famous debates with U.S. Senator Stephen Douglas
- **1860** Elected president on November 6
- **1863** Issues the Emancipation Proclamation on January 1
- **1863** Gives the Gettysburg Address on November 19
- **1865** Gives second inaugural address on March 4
- **1865** Shot on April 14; dies the next day

Lincoln's address at the dedication of the Gettysburg National Cemetery.

© Houghton Mifflin Harcourt Publishing Company

Image Credits: (br), Library of Congress Prints & Photographs Division, Washington, D.C.

SECTION 5

The Tide of War Turns

What You Will Learn...

Main Ideas

1. The Union tried to divide the Confederate Army at Fredericksburg, but the attempt failed.
2. The Battle of Gettysburg in 1863 was a major turning point in the war.
3. During 1864, Union campaigns in the East and South dealt crippling blows to the Confederacy.
4. Union troops forced the South to surrender in 1865, ending the Civil War.

The Big Idea

Union victories in 1863, 1864, and 1865 ended the Civil War.

Key Terms and People

Battle of Gettysburg
George Pickett
Pickett's Charge
Gettysburg Address
Wilderness Campaign
William Tecumseh Sherman
total war
Appomattox Courthouse

hmhsocialstudies.com
TAKING NOTES

Use the graphic organizer online to take notes on the events that led to the end of the Civil War.

If YOU were there...

You live in southern Pennsylvania in 1863, near a battlefield where thousands died. Now people have come from miles around to dedicate a cemetery here. You are near the front of the crowd. The first speaker impresses everyone with two hours of dramatic words and gestures. Then President Lincoln speaks—just a few minutes of simple words. Many people are disappointed.

Why do you think the president's speech was so short?

BUILDING BACKGROUND Many people, especially in the North, had expected a quick victory, but the war dragged on for years. The balance of victories seemed to seesaw between North and South, and both sides suffered terrible casualties. The last Confederate push into the North ended at Gettysburg in one of the bloodiest battles of the war.

Fredericksburg and Chancellorsville

Frustrated by McClellan's lack of aggression, Lincoln replaced him with General Ambrose E. Burnside as leader of the Army of the Potomac. Burnside favored a swift, decisive attack on Richmond by way of Fredericksburg. In November 1862, he set out with 120,000 troops.

Burnside's tactics surprised General Lee. The Confederate commander had divided his force of 78,000 men. Neither section of the Confederate army was in a good position to defend Fredericksburg. However, Burnside's army experienced delays in crossing the Rappahannock River. These delays allowed Lee's army to reunite and entrench themselves around Fredericksburg. Finally, the Union army crossed the Rappahannock and launched a series of charges. These attacks had heavy casualties and failed to break the Confederate line. Eventually, after suffering about 12,600 casualties, Burnside ordered a retreat. The Confederates had about 5,300 casualties.

Soon Burnside stepped down from his position. Lincoln made General Joseph Hooker the commander of the Army of the Potomac. At the end of April 1863, Hooker and his army of about 138,000 men launched a frontal attack on Fredericksburg. Then Hooker

© Houghton Mifflin Harcourt Publishing Company

ordered about 115,000 of his troops to split off and approach the Confederate's flank, or side. Hooker's strategy seemed about to work. But for some reason he hesitated and had his flanking troops take a defensive position at Chancellorsville. This town was located a few miles west of Fredericksburg.

The following day, Lee used most of his army (about 60,000 men) to attack Hooker's troops at Chancellorsville. Stonewall Jackson led an attack on Hooker's flank while Lee commanded an assault on the Union front. The Union army was almost cut in two. They managed to form a defensive line, which they held for three days. Then Hooker ordered a retreat.

Lee's army won a major victory. But this victory had severe casualties. During the battle, Lee's trusted general, Stonewall Jackson, was accidentally shot by his own troops. He died a few days later.

READING CHECK **Comparing** What did generals McClellan, Burnside, and Hooker have in common?

Battle of Gettysburg

General Lee launched more attacks within Union territory. As before, his goal was to break the North's will to fight. He also hoped that a victory would convince other nations to recognize the Confederacy.

First Day

In early June 1863, Lee cut across northern Maryland into southern Pennsylvania. His forces gathered west of a small town called Gettysburg. Lee was unaware that Union soldiers were encamped closer to town. He had been suffering from lack of enemy information for three days because his cavalry chief "Jeb" Stuart was not performing his duties. Stuart and his cavalry had gone off on their own raiding party, disobeying Lee's orders.

Another Confederate raiding party went to Gettysburg for boots and other supplies. There, Lee's troops ran right into Union general George G. Meade's cavalry, triggering the **Battle of Gettysburg**, a key battle that finally turned the tide against the Confederates. The battle began on July 1, 1863, when the

Three Days at Gettysburg

Gettysburg was the largest and bloodiest battle of the Civil War. In three days, more than 51,000 soldiers were killed, wounded, captured, or went missing. It was an important victory for the Union, and it stopped Lee's plan of invading the North.

Artillery played a key role in the Battle of Gettysburg on July 1, 1863.

Day One: July 1, 1863

© Houghton Mifflin Harcourt Publishing Company

Confederate raiding party and the Union forces began exchanging fire. The larger Confederate forces began to push the Union troops back through Gettysburg.

The Union soldiers regrouped along the high ground of Cemetery Ridge and Culp's Hill. General Lee wanted to prevent the Union forces from entrenching themselves. He therefore ordered General Ewell to attack immediately. However, Ewell hesitated and thereby gave the Federals time to establish an excellent defensive position.

In fact, Confederate General James Longstreet thought that the Union position was almost impossible to overrun. Instead of attacking, he felt that the Confederate army should move east, take a strong defensive position themselves, and wait for the Union forces to attack them. However, General Lee was not convinced. He believed that his troops were invincible.

The Confederates camped at Seminary Ridge, which ran parallel to the Union forces. Both camps called for their main forces to reinforce them and prepare for combat the next day.

Second Day

On July 2, Lee ordered an attack on the left side of the Union line. Lee knew that he could win the battle if his troops captured Little Round Top from the Union forces. From this hill, Lee's troops could easily fire down on the line of Union forces. Union forces and Confederate troops fought viciously for control of Little Round Top. The fighting was particularly fierce on the south side of the hill. There the 20th Maine led by Colonel Joshua Chamberlain battled the 15th Alabama led by Colonel William Oates. Later, when describing the conflict, Oates said, "The blood stood in puddles in some places in the rocks." Eventually, the Union forced the Confederates to pull back from Little Round Top.

Then the Confederates attacked Cemetery Hill and Culp's Hill. The fighting lasted until nightfall. The assault on Cemetery Hill was unsuccessful. The Confederates did manage to take a few trenches on Culp's Hill. Even so, the Union forces still held a strong defensive position by the day's end.

Three Days at Gettysburg (continued)

Day Two: July 2, 1863, 10 a.m.

Union soldiers desperately defended Little Round Top from a fierce Confederate charge.

© Houghton Mifflin Harcourt Publishing Company

Pickett's Charge

On the third day of battle, Longstreet again tried to convince Lee not to attack. But Lee thought that the Union forces were severely battered and ready to break. Because of this, he planned to attack the center of the Union line on Cemetery Ridge. Such a tactic, he felt, would not be expected. Indeed, General Meade left only about 5,750 troops to defend the center.

For over an hour, the Confederates shelled Cemetery Ridge with cannon fire. For a while, the Union cannons fired back. Then they slacked off. The Confederates assumed that they had seriously damaged the Union artillery. In reality, the Confederate barrage did little damage.

The task of charging the Union center fell to three divisions of Confederate soldiers. General **George Pickett** commanded the largest unit. In late afternoon, nearly 15,000 men took part in **Pickett's Charge**. For one mile, the Confederates marched slowly up toward Cemetery Ridge. Showered with cannon and rifle fire, they suffered severe losses. But eventually, some of them almost reached their destination. Then Union reinforcements added to the barrage on the rebels. Soon the

hmhsocialstudies.com INTERACTIVE MAP

Pickett's Charge, July 3, 1863

General George Pickett led his troops across Emmitsburg Road to attack the Union position. He lost more than half of his men in the 50-minute battle.

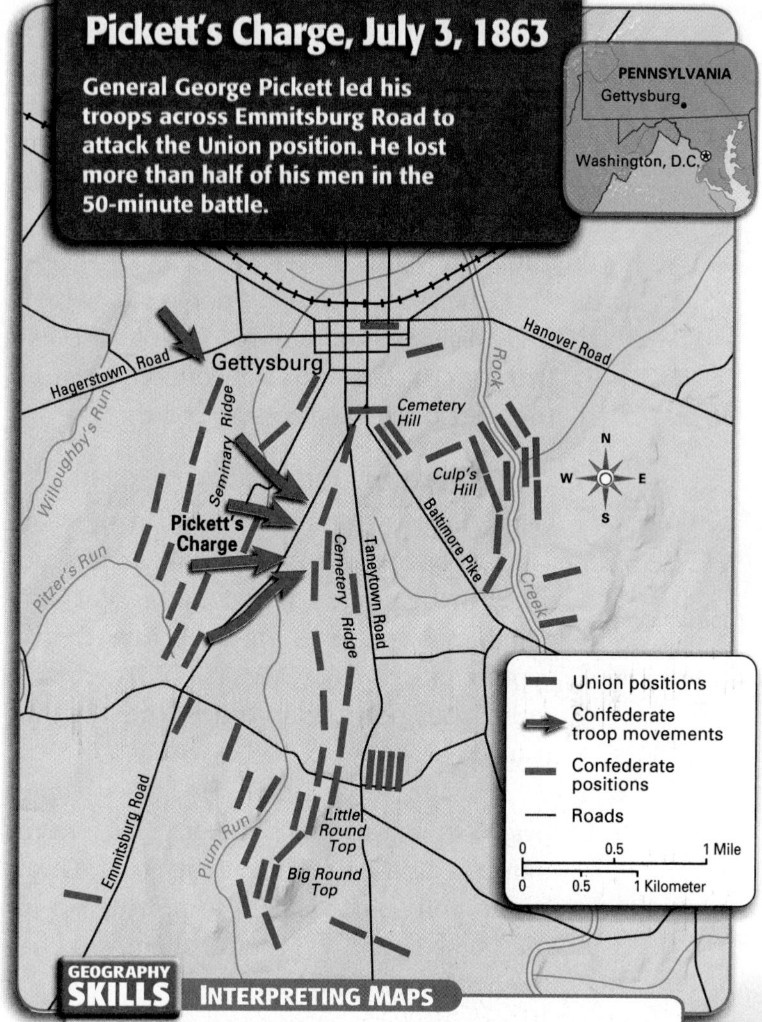
PENNSYLVANIA
Gettysburg
Washington, D.C.
Gettysburg
Hagerstown Road
Hanover Road
Rock Creek
Willoughby's Run
Seminary Ridge
Cemetery Hill
Culp's Hill
Baltimore Pike
Pickett's Charge
Pitzer's Run
Cemetery Ridge
Taneytown Road
Emmitsburg Road
Plum Run
Little Round Top
Big Round Top
N
S
E
W
Union positions
Confederate troop movements
Confederate positions
Roads
0
0.5
1 Mile
0
0.5
1 Kilometer

GEOGRAPHY SKILLS INTERPRETING MAPS

1. **Human-Environment Interaction** How do you think geography affected Pickett's Charge?
2. **Movement** In which direction did Pickett's soldiers charge?

Pickett's Charge

Pickett's Charge proved a disaster for the Confederate attackers. Fewer than half of them survived.

Day Three: July 3, 1863, 3 p.m.

© Houghton Mifflin Harcourt Publishing Company

Confederates retreated, leaving about 7,500 casualties on the field of battle. Distressed by this defeat, General Lee rode among the survivors and told them, "It is all my fault."

On the fourth day, Lee began to retreat to Virginia. In all, nearly 75,000 Confederate soldiers and 90,000 Union troops had fought during the Battle of Gettysburg.

General Meade decided not to follow Lee's army. This decision angered Lincoln. He felt that Meade had missed an opportunity to crush the Confederates and possibly end the war.

Aftermath of Gettysburg

Focus on Reading
The first sentence of the paragraph to the right is a main idea. The rest of this paragraph supports the idea.

Gettysburg was a turning point in the war. Lee's troops would never again launch an attack in the North. The Union victory at Gettysburg took place on the day before Grant's capture of Vicksburg, Mississippi. These victories made northerners believe that the war could be won.

In addition, the Union win at Gettysburg helped to end the South's search for foreign influence in the war. After Gettysburg, Great Britain and France refused to provide aid to the Confederacy. The South's attempt at cotton diplomacy failed.

The Gettysburg Address

HISTORY
VIDEO
Gettysburg Address
hmhsocialstudies.com

On November 19, 1863, at the dedicating ceremony of the Gettysburg battlefield cemetery, President Lincoln gave a speech called the **Gettysburg Address**, in which he praised the bravery of Union soldiers and renewed his commitment to winning the Civil War. This short but moving speech is one of the most famous in American history. In one of its frequently quoted lines, Lincoln referenced the Declaration of Independence and its ideals of liberty, equality, and democracy. He reminded listeners that the war was being fought for those reasons.

Lincoln rededicated himself to winning the war and preserving the Union. A difficult road still lay ahead.

Academic Vocabulary
execute to perform, carry out

READING CHECK **Analyzing** Why was Gettysburg a turning point?

Union Campaigns Cripple the Confederacy

Lincoln had been impressed with General Grant's successes in capturing Vicksburg. He transferred Grant to the East and gave him command of the Union army. In early 1864, Grant forced Lee to fight a series of battles in Virginia that stretched Confederate soldiers and supplies to their limits.

Wilderness Campaign in the East

From May through June, the armies fought in northern and central Virginia. Union troops launched the **Wilderness Campaign**—a series of battles designed to capture the Confederate capital at Richmond, Virginia. The first battle took place in early May, in woods about 50 miles outside of Richmond. Grant then ordered General Meade to Spotsylvania, where the fighting raged for five days.

Over the next month, Union soldiers moved the Confederate troops back toward Richmond. However, Grant experienced his worst defeat at the Battle of Cold Harbor in early June, just 10 miles northeast of Richmond. In only a few hours the Union army suffered 7,000 casualties. The battle delayed Grant's plans to take the Confederate capital.

Union forces had suffered twice as many casualties as the Confederates had, yet Grant continued his strategy. He knew he would be getting additional soldiers, and Lee could not. Grant slowly but surely advanced his troops through Virginia. He told another officer, "I propose to fight it out on this line if it takes all summer."

After Cold Harbor, General Grant moved south of Richmond. He had hoped to take control of the key railroad junction at Petersburg, Virginia. Lee's army, however, formed a solid defense, and Grant could not execute his attack. Grant was winning the war, but he still had not captured Richmond. Facing re-election, Lincoln was especially discouraged by this failure.

© Houghton Mifflin Harcourt Publishing Company

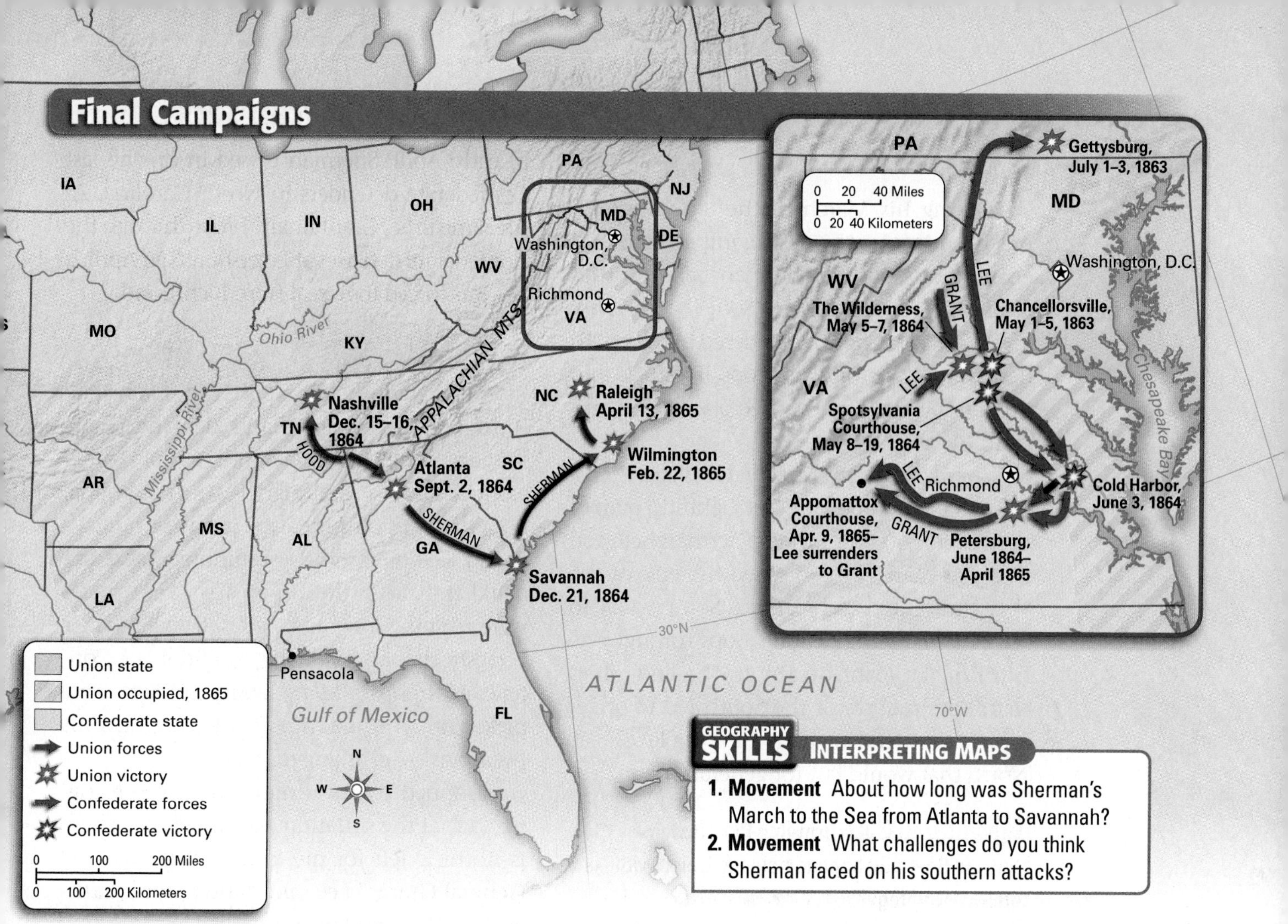
Final Campaigns
IA
IL
IN
OH
PA
NJ
MD
DE
Washington, D.C.
WV
Richmond
VA
MO
KY
Ohio River
APPALACHIAN MTS.
Mississippi River
TN
Nashville
Dec. 15–16, 1864
HOOD
Atlanta
Sept. 2, 1864
SC
NC
Raleigh
April 13, 1865
Wilmington
Feb. 22, 1865
SHERMAN
AR
MS
AL
GA
Savannah
Dec. 21, 1864
LA
30°N
Pensacola
Gulf of Mexico
FL
ATLANTIC OCEAN
70°W
N
S
E
W
Union state
Union occupied, 1865
Confederate state
Union forces
Union victory
Confederate forces
Confederate victory
0 100 200 Miles
0 100 200 Kilometers
PA
Gettysburg,
July 1–3, 1863
MD
0 20 40 Miles
0 20 40 Kilometers
Washington, D.C.
WV
The Wilderness,
May 5–7, 1864
GRANT
LEE
Chancellorsville,
May 1–5, 1863
VA
Spotsylvania
Courthouse,
May 8–19, 1864
Chesapeake Bay
Richmond
Cold Harbor,
June 3, 1864
Appomattox
Courthouse,
Apr. 9, 1865–
Lee surrenders
to Grant
Petersburg,
June 1864–
April 1865

GEOGRAPHY SKILLS INTERPRETING MAPS

1. **Movement** About how long was Sherman's March to the Sea from Atlanta to Savannah?
2. **Movement** What challenges do you think Sherman faced on his southern attacks?

Sherman Strikes the South

Lincoln needed a victory for the Union army to help him win re-election in 1864. The bold campaign of General **William Tecumseh Sherman** provided this key victory. Sherman carried out the Union plan to destroy southern railroads and industries.

In the spring of 1864, Sherman marched south from Tennessee with 100,000 troops. His goal was to take Atlanta, Georgia, and knock out an important railroad link. From May through August, Sherman's army moved steadily through the Appalachian Mountains toward Atlanta. Several times, Sherman avoided defenses set up by Confederate general Joseph Johnston.

In July, Sherman was within sight of Atlanta. Confederate president Jefferson Davis gave General John Hood command of Confederate forces in the region. Hood repeatedly attacked Sherman in a final attempt to save Atlanta, but the Union troops proved stronger. The Confederate troops retreated as Sherman held Atlanta under siege.

Atlanta fell to Sherman's troops on September 2, 1864. Much of the city was destroyed by artillery and fire. Sherman ordered the residents who still remained to leave. Responding to his critics, Sherman later wrote, "War is war, and not popularity-seeking." The loss of Atlanta cost the South an important railroad link and its center of industry.

Many people in the North had been upset with the length of the war. However, the capture of Atlanta showed that progress was being made in defeating the South. This success helped to convince Union voters to re-elect Lincoln in a landslide.

Sherman did not wait long to begin his next campaign. His goal was the port city of Savannah, Georgia. In mid-November 1864,

© Houghton Mifflin Harcourt Publishing Company

Sherman left Atlanta with a force of about 60,000 men. He said he would "make Georgia howl!"

During his March to the Sea, Sherman practiced **total war**—destroying civilian and economic resources. Sherman believed that total war would ruin the South's economy and its ability to fight. He ordered his troops to destroy railways, bridges, crops, livestock, and other resources. They burned plantations and freed slaves.

Sherman's army reached Savannah on December 10, 1864. They left behind a path of destruction 60 miles wide. Sherman believed that this march would speed the end of the war. He wanted to break the South's will to fight by marching Union troops through the heart of the Confederacy. In the end, Sherman's destruction of the South led to anger and resentment toward the people of the North that would last for generations.

READING CHECK **Drawing Conclusions**
How did Sherman hope to help the Union with his total-war strategy?

QUICK FACTS

Causes and Effects of the Civil War

Causes
- Disagreement over the institution of slavery
- Economic differences
- Political differences

Effects
- Slavery ends
- 620,000 Americans killed
- Military districts created
- Southern economy in ruins

ANALYSIS SKILL **INTERPRETING CHARTS**
How important was slavery to the Civil War?

The South Surrenders

In early April, Sherman closed in on the last Confederate defenders in North Carolina. At the same time, Grant finally broke through the Confederate defenses at Petersburg. On April 2, Lee was forced to retreat from Richmond.

Fighting Ends

By the second week of April 1865, Grant had surrounded Lee's army and demanded the soldiers' surrender. Lee hoped to join other Confederates in fighting in North Carolina, but Grant cut off his escape just west of Richmond. Lee tried some last-minute attacks but could not break the Union line. Lee's forces were running low on supplies. General James Longstreet told about the condition of Confederate troops. "Many weary soldiers were picked up . . . some with, many without, arms [weapons],—all asking for food."

Trapped by the Union army, Lee recognized that the situation was hopeless. "There is nothing left for me to do but go and see General Grant," Lee said, "and I would rather die a thousand deaths."

On April 9, 1865, the Union and Confederate leaders met at a home in the small town of **Appomattox Courthouse** where Lee surrendered to Grant, thus ending the Civil War.

During the meeting, Grant assured Lee that his troops would be fed and allowed to keep their horses, and they would not be tried for treason. Then Lee signed the surrender documents. The long, bloody war had finally ended. Grant later wrote that he found the scene at Appomattox Courthouse more tragic than joyful.

> "I felt . . . sad and depressed at the downfall of a foe [enemy] who had fought so long and valiantly [bravely], and had suffered so much for a cause, though that cause was, I believe, one of the worst for which a people ever fought."
>
> —Ulysses S. Grant, *Battle Cry of Freedom*

© Houghton Mifflin Harcourt Publishing Company

Surrender at Appomattox

Union general Grant rose to shake hands with Confederate general Lee after the surrender. Grant allowed Lee to keep his sword and Lee's men to keep their horses.

Was it important for Grant and Lee to shake hands? Why or why not?

As General Lee returned to his troops, General Grant stopped Union forces from cheering their victory. "The war is over," Grant said with relief. "The rebels are our countrymen again."

The Effects of the War

The Civil War had deep and long-lasting effects. Almost 620,000 Americans lost their lives during the four years of fighting.

The defeat of the South ended slavery there. The majority of former slaves, however, had no homes or jobs. The southern economy was in ruins.

A tremendous amount of hostility remained, even after the fighting had ceased. The war was over, but the question remained: How could the United States be united once more?

READING CHECK **Predicting** What problems might the Union face following the Civil War?

SUMMARY After four long years of battles, the Civil War ended with General Lee's surrender at Appomattox Courthouse.

Section 5 Assessment

hmhsocialstudies.com ONLINE QUIZ

Reviewing Ideas, Terms, and People

1. a. **Identify** What Confederate general died from his wounds at Chancellorsville?
   b. **Draw Conclusions** Why was the Union army defeated at Chancellorsville?
2. a. **Identify** What was the **Gettysburg Address**?
   b. **Analyze** Why was geography important to the outcome of the Battle of Gettysburg?
3. a. **Recall** What was the purpose of the **Wilderness Campaign**?
   b. **Draw Conclusions** In what way was the capture of Atlanta an important victory for President Lincoln?
4. a. **Identify** What events led to Lee's surrender at **Appomattox Courthouse**?
   b. **Summarize** What problems did the South face at the end of the war?

Critical Thinking

5. **Supporting a Point of View** Review your notes on the end of the Civil War. Then copy the graphic organizer below. Use it to show the three events in this section that you think contributed most to the end of the Civil War and explain why.

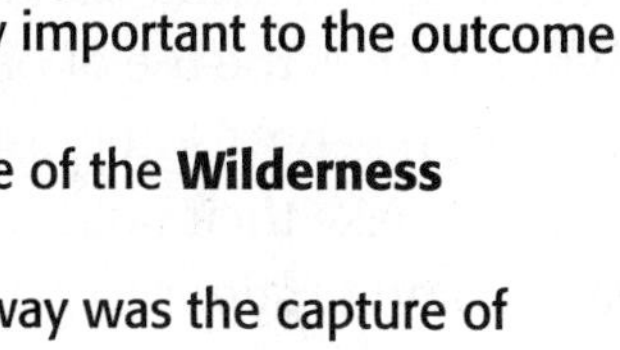

Focus on Writing

6. **Taking Notes on the End of the War** As you read this section, take notes on the Battle of Gettysburg, the Wilderness Campaign, the fall of Atlanta, and the South's surrender. Be sure to answer the following questions: Who? Where? When? Why? and How?

© Houghton Mifflin Harcourt Publishing Company • Image Credits: (t), ©SuperStock

Interpreting Political Cartoons

Define the Skill

Political cartoons are drawings that express views on important issues. They have been used throughout history to influence public opinion. The ability to interpret political cartoons will help you understand issues and people's attitudes about them.

Learn the Skill

Political cartoons use both words and images to convey their message. They often contain caricatures or symbolism. A caricature is a drawing that exaggerates the features of a person or object. Symbolism is the use of one thing to represent something else. Cartoonists use these techniques to help make their point clear. They also use titles, labels, and captions to get their message across.

Use these steps to interpret political cartoons.

1. Read any title, labels, and caption to identify the cartoon's general topic.
2. Identify the people and objects. Determine if they are exaggerated and, if so, why. Identify any symbols and analyze their meaning.
3. Draw conclusions about the message the cartoonist is trying to convey.

The following cartoon was published in the North in 1863. The cartoonist has used symbols to make his point. Lady Liberty, representing the Union, is being threatened by the Copperheads. The cartoonist has expressed his opinion of these people by drawing them as the poisonous snake for which they were named. This cartoon clearly supports the Union's continuing to fight the war.

Practice the Skill

Apply the guidelines to interpret the cartoon below and answer the questions that follow.

1. What do the two men on either side of Lincoln represent?
2. What message do you think the artist was trying to convey?

TAXES
LINCOLN'S TWO DIFFICULTIES.
LIN. "WHAT? NO MONEY! NO MEN!"

Chapter 1 Chapter Review

History's Impact
▶ video series
Review the video to answer the closing question:
How do you think the age of a country relates to its citizens' national pride?

Visual Summary

Use the visual summary below to help you review the main ideas of the chapter.

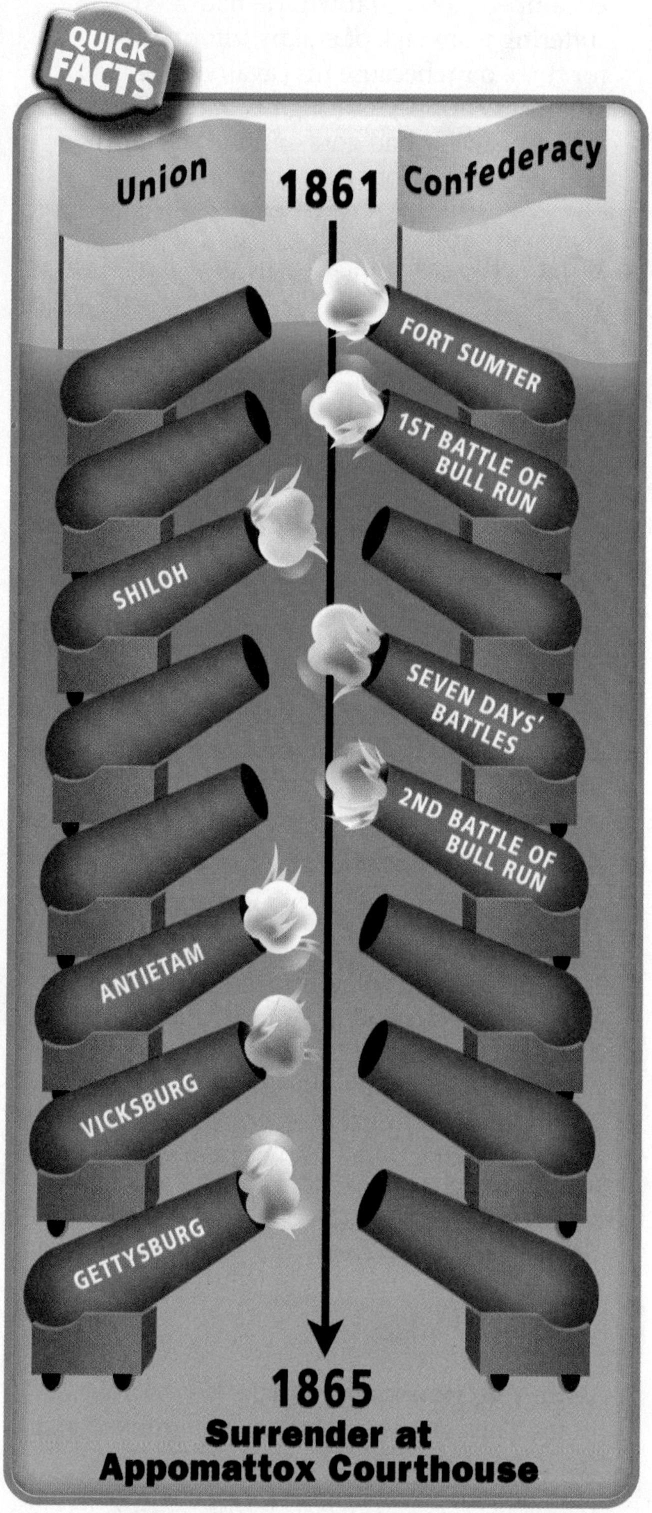
QUICK FACTS
Union
1861
Confederacy
FORT SUMTER
1ST BATTLE OF BULL RUN
SHILOH
SEVEN DAYS' BATTLES
2ND BATTLE OF BULL RUN
ANTIETAM
VICKSBURG
GETTYSBURG
1865
Surrender at Appomattox Courthouse

Reviewing Vocabulary, Terms, and People

Match the numbered definitions with the correct terms from the list below.

a. contrabands
b. cotton diplomacy
c. Second Battle of Bull Run
d. Siege of Vicksburg
e. Thomas "Stonewall" Jackson

1. Attack by Union general Ulysses S. Grant that gave the North control of the Mississippi River
2. Confederate general who held off Union attacks and helped the South win the First Battle of Bull Run
3. Important Confederate victory in which General Robert E. Lee defeated Union troops and pushed into Union territory for the first time
4. Southern strategy of using cotton exports to gain Britain's support in the Civil War
5. Term given to escaped slaves from the South

Comprehension and Critical Thinking

SECTION 1

6. **a. Identify** When and where did fighting in the U.S. Civil War begin?
   b. Analyze How did civilians help the war effort in both the North and the South?
   c. Elaborate Why do you think the border states chose to remain in the Union despite their support of slavery?

SECTION 2

7. **a. Identify** What was the first major battle of the war? What was the outcome of the battle?
   b. Analyze What was the Union army hoping to accomplish when it marched into Virginia at the start of the war?
   c. Evaluate Was the Union's naval blockade of the South successful? Why or why not?

SECTION 3

8. **a. Identify** Which side did the Cherokee support in the fighting at Pea Ridge? Why?

   b. Draw Conclusions What progress did Union leaders make in the war in the West?

   c. Evaluate Which victory in the West was most valuable to the Union? Why?

SECTION 4

9. **a. Describe** What responsibilities did women take on during the war?

   b. Analyze What opposition to the war did President Lincoln face, and how did he deal with that opposition?

   c. Predict What might be some possible problems that the newly freed slaves in the South might face?

SECTION 5

10. **a. Recall** When and where did the war finally end?

    b. Compare and Contrast How were the efforts of Generals Grant and Sherman at the end of the war similar and different?

    c. Elaborate What do you think led to the South's defeat in the Civil War? Explain.

Social Studies Skills 21st CENTURY

Interpreting Political Cartoons *Use the Social Studies Skills taught in this chapter to answer the question about the political cartoon below.*

11. What do you think the artist is saying about politicians with this cartoon?

Reading Skills 21st CENTURY

Supporting Facts and Details *Use the Reading Skills taught in this chapter to answer the question about the reading selection below.*

> Lee was unaware that Union soldiers were encamped closer to town. He had been suffering from lack of enemy information for three days because his cavalry chief "Jeb" Stuart was not performing his duties. Stuart and his cavalry had gone off on their own raiding party, disobeying Lee's orders.

12. What is the main idea of the above reading selection?

    a. "Jeb" Stuart was not performing his duties.

    b. Stuart and his cavalry had gone off on their own.

    c. Stuart and his cavalry disobeyed Lee's orders.

    d. Lee was suffering from a lack of enemy information.

Reviewing Themes

13. **Society and Culture** What effects did the Civil War have on American society?

14. **Politics** What political difficulties did the Emancipation Proclamation cause for President Lincoln?

Using the Internet 21st CENTURY

15. **Activity: Writing a Poem** Soldiers in the Civil War came from all walks of life. Despite hoping for glory and adventure, many encountered dangerous and uncomfortable conditions. Through your online textbook, learn more about Civil War soldiers. After viewing photographs and reading letters, write a poem describing the life of a soldier. Your poem should reflect on the soldier's emotions and experiences.

    hmhsocialstudies.com

FOCUS ON WRITING

16. **Write Your Newspaper Article** Review your notes. Then choose the subject you think would make the best newspaper article. Write an attention-grabbing headline. Then write your article, giving as many facts as possible.

© Houghton Mifflin Harcourt Publishing Company • Image Credits: (b) The Granger Collection, New York

CHAPTER 1

Standardized Test Practice

DIRECTIONS: Read each question and write the letter of the best response.

1 Use the map below to answer the following question.

The place where two major battles of the Civil War were fought is indicated on the map by which letter?

A W

B X

C Y

D Z

2 The Battle of Gettysburg was an important battle of the Civil War because

A it was an overwhelming Confederate victory.

B the Union army's advance on the Confederate capital was stopped.

C it ended Lee's hopes of advancing into northern territory.

D it enabled the Union to control the Mississippi River.

3 Overall command of Confederate forces in Virginia during most of the Civil War was held by

A Jefferson Davis.

B William Tecumseh Sherman.

C Thomas "Stonewall" Jackson.

D Robert E. Lee.

4 Which of Lincoln's speeches and writings praised the efforts of Union soldiers?

A the Emancipation Proclamation

B the first inaugural address (1861)

C the second inaugural address (1865)

D the Gettysburg Address

5 The tactics that Sherman used against Confederate armies in the South were based on what strategy?

A cutting off troops from their officers

B a naval blockade of southern ports

C destroying the South's resources and economy

D hit-and-run attacks on major southern cities

6 In the War of 1812 the British navy blockaded American seaports in the hope that the U.S. economy would suffer and the United States would surrender. Which Civil War strategy was similar?

A Scott's plan to destroy the southern economy

B Sherman's March to the Sea

C General Ulysses S. Grant's capture of Vicksburg

D Admiral David Farragut's defeat of New Orleans

7 Read the following quote from Grant about Lee's surrender and use it to answer the question below.

> "What General Lee's feelings were I do not know. He was a man of much dignity, without expression on his face. It was impossible to say whether he felt inwardly glad that the end had finally come, or felt sad over the result, and was too manly to show it. Whatever his feelings, they were entirely hidden from me."
>
> –Ulysses S. Grant, adapted from *Personal Memoirs of U.S. Grant, Vol. 2*

Document-Based Question What is your opinion about what Lee might have been feeling during his surrender?

© Houghton Mifflin Harcourt Publishing Company

HISTORY

MULTIMEDIA CONNECTIONS

DAYS OF DARKNESS: THE GETTYSBURG CIVILIANS

Gettysburg, Pennsylvania, was a sleepy agricultural town of about 2,400 residents when the Civil War arrived on its doorstep in the early summer of 1863. Many of the town's men were elsewhere, either fighting in the war or guarding their livestock in the countryside. This left mostly women and children to endure the battle. For three terrifying days they hid in basements or in tightly shuttered houses. Even after the battle finally ended the horrors continued, as the Gettysburg civilians emerged to find a scene of unimaginable death and destruction.

Explore some of the personal stories and recollections of the Gettysburg civilians online. You can find a wealth of information, video clips, primary sources, activities, and more at hmhsocialstudies.com.

© Houghton Mifflin Harcourt Publishing Company • Image Credits: ©Bettmann/Corbis

"I had scarcely reached the front door, when, on looking up the street, I saw some of the men on horseback . . .

What a horrible sight! . . .

I was fully persuaded that the Rebels had actually come at last. What they would do with us was a fearful question to my young mind . . ."

— Tillie Pierce, age 15

A Young Woman's Account

Read the document to witness the arrival of Confederate troops through the eyes of a Gettysburg teenager.

© Houghton Mifflin Harcourt Publishing Company • Image Credits: ©Bettmann/Corbis

CLICK THROUGH INTER/ACTIVITIES

hmhsocialstudies.com

A Citizen-Soldier

Watch the video to meet John Burns, the man who would come to be called the "Citizen Hero of Gettysburg."

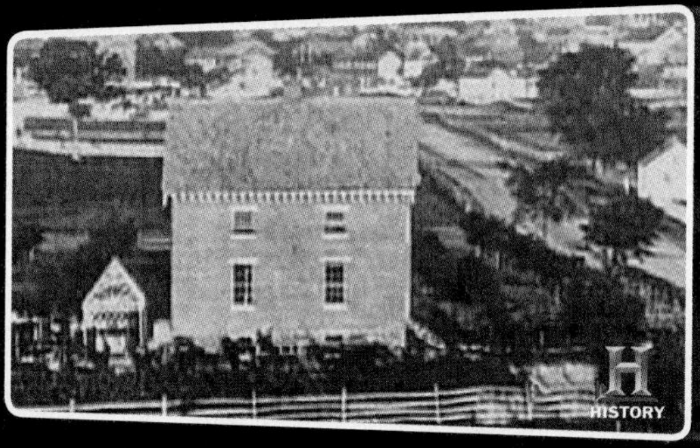

A Family's Story

Watch the video to discover the story of courage and commitment exhibited by one Gettysburg family.

The National Cemetery

Watch the video to learn about the Soldiers' National Cemetery and the speech President Lincoln gave there.

CHAPTER 2 1865–1877

Reconstruction

Essential Question How did a deeply divided nation move forward after the Civil War?

ALABAMA COURSE OF STUDY

1 Explain the impact of industrialization, urbanization, communication, and cultural changes on life in the United States from the late nineteenth century to World War I.

Focus on Writing

Job History When the Civil War ended, it was time to rebuild. People were ready to get back to work. But life had changed for many people and would continue to change. As you read this chapter, think about jobs people may have had during Reconstruction.

UNITED STATES

1865
Abraham Lincoln is assassinated.

1865

1865
Black Jamaicans rebel against the wealthy planter class.

WORLD

Image Credits: (t), ©Paul Rocheleau; (b), ©Kean Collection/Getty Images

© Houghton Mifflin Harcourt Publishing Company

HISTORY Lincoln's Legacy

hmhsocialstudies.com VIDEO

The ruins of this Virginia plantation stand as a bleak reminder of the changes brought to the South by the Civil War.

1868
President Andrew Johnson is impeached and almost removed from office.

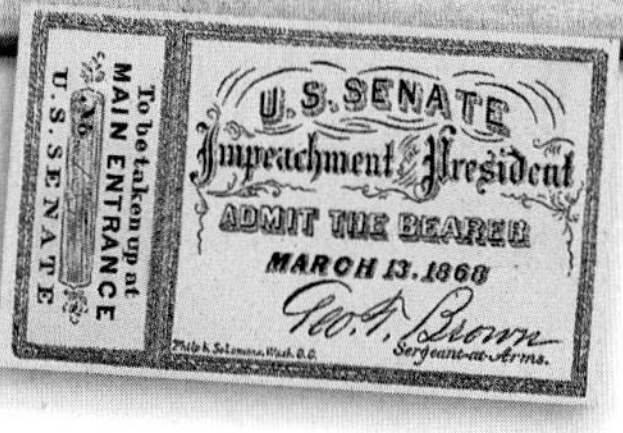

To be taken up at
MAIN ENTRANCE
U.S. SENATE
U.S. SENATE
Impeachment of the President
ADMIT THE BEARER
MARCH 13, 1868
Sergeant-at-Arms.

1870
Hiram Revels becomes the first African American to serve in the U.S. Senate.

1877
The Compromise of 1877 ends Reconstruction.

1870 — 1875 — 1880

1868
The Meiji dynasty returns to power in Japan.

1869
The Suez Canal opens, linking the Mediterranean and Red seas.

1871
Otto von Bismarck and Wilhelm I unite Germany.

Image Credits: (t), ©Paul Rocheleau; (cl), The Granger Collection, New York; (cr), Herbert F. Johnson Museum of Art, Cornell University; (bl), ©Michael Maslan Historic Photographs/Corbis

© Houghton Mifflin Harcourt Publishing Company

Reading Social Studies

Focus on Themes In this chapter you will read about the time immediately after the Civil War. You will see how the government tried to rebuild the South and will learn about how life changed for African Americans after slavery was declared illegal. You will read about the **political** conflicts that emerged as southern leadership worked to gain control of Reconstruction efforts. Throughout the chapter, you will read how the **culture** of the South changed after the War.

Analyzing Historical Information

Focus on Reading History books are full of information. As you read, you are confronted with names, dates, places, terms, and descriptions on every page. You don't want to have to deal with anything unimportant or untrue.

Identifying Relevant and Essential Information Information in a history book should be relevant to the topic you're studying. It should also be essential to understanding the topic and be verifiable. Anything else distracts from the material you are studying.

The first passage below includes several pieces of irrelevant and nonessential information. In the second, this information has been removed. Note how much easier the revised passage is to comprehend.

First Passage

President Abraham Lincoln, who was very tall, wanted to reunite the nation as quickly and painlessly as possible. He had proposed a plan for readmitting the southern states even before the war ended, which happened on a Sunday. Called the Ten Percent Plan, it offered southerners amnesty, or official pardon, for all illegal acts supporting the rebellion. Today a group called Amnesty International works to protect the rights of prisoners. Lincoln's plan certainly would have worked if it would have been implemented.

Lincoln's appearance and the day on which the war ended are not essential facts.

Amnesty International is not relevant to this topic.

There is no way to prove the accuracy of the last sentence.

Revised Passage

President Abraham Lincoln wanted to reunite the nation as quickly and painlessly as possible. He had proposed a plan for readmitting the southern states even before the war ended. Called the Ten Percent Plan, it offered southerners amnesty, or official pardon, for all illegal acts supporting the rebellion.

© Houghton Mifflin Harcourt Publishing Company

You Try It!

As you read the following passage, look for irrelevant, nonessential, or unverifiable information.

The Freedmen's Bureau

In 1865 Congress established the Freedmen's Bureau, an agency providing relief for freedpeople and certain poor people in the South. The Bureau had a difficult job. It may have been one of the most difficult jobs ever. At its high point, about 900 agents served the entire South. All 900 people could fit into one hotel ballroom today. Bureau commissioner Oliver O. Howard eventually decided to use the Bureau's limited budget to distribute food to the poor and to provide education and legal help for freedpeople. One common food in the South at that time was salted meat. The Bureau also helped African American war veterans. Today the Department of Veterans' Affairs assists American war veterans.

After you read the passage, answer the following questions.

1. Which sentence in this passage is unverifiable and should be cut?
2. Find two sentences in this passage that are irrelevant to the discussion of the Freedmen's Bureau. What makes those sentences irrelevant?
3. Look at the last sentence of the passage. Do you think this sentence is essential to the discussion? Why or why not?

As you read this chapter, ask yourself what makes the information you are reading essential to a study of Reconstruction.

Key Terms and People

Chapter 2

Section 1

Reconstruction
Ten Percent Plan
Thirteenth Amendment
Freedmen's Bureau
Andrew Johnson

Section 2

Black Codes
Radical Republicans
Civil Rights Act of 1866
Fourteenth Amendment
Reconstruction Acts
impeachment
Fifteenth Amendment

Section 3

Hiram Revels
Ku Klux Klan
Compromise of 1877
poll tax
segregation
Jim Crow laws
Plessy v. *Ferguson*
sharecropping

Academic Vocabulary

Success in school is related to knowing academic vocabulary—the words that are frequently used in school assignments and discussions. In this chapter, you will learn the following academic words:

procedure
principle

© Houghton Mifflin Harcourt Publishing Company

SECTION 1

Rebuilding the South

What You Will Learn...

Main Ideas

1. President Lincoln and Congress differed in their views as Reconstruction began.
2. The end of the Civil War meant freedom for African Americans in the South.
3. President Johnson's plan began the process of Reconstruction.

The Big Idea

The nation faced many problems in rebuilding the Union.

Key Terms and People

Reconstruction
Ten Percent Plan
Thirteenth Amendment
Freedmen's Bureau
Andrew Johnson

hmhsocialstudies.com
TAKING NOTES

Use the graphic organizer online to take notes on the different ways the U.S. government attempted to reconstruct the South after the Civil War.

If YOU were there...

You are a young soldier who has been fighting in the Civil War for many months. Now that the war is over, you are on your way home. During your journey, you pass plantation manor homes, houses, and barns that have been burned down. No one is doing spring planting in the fields. As you near your family's farm, you see that fences and sheds have been destroyed. You wonder what is left of your home and family.

What would you think your future on the farm would be like?

BUILDING BACKGROUND When the Civil War ended, much of the South lay in ruins. Like the young soldier above, many people returned to destroyed homes and farms. Harvests of corn, cotton, rice, and other crops fell far below normal. Many farm animals had been killed or were roaming free. These were some of the challenges in restoring the nation.

Reconstruction Begins

After the Civil War ended in 1865, the U.S. government faced the problem of dealing with the defeated southern states. The challenges of **Reconstruction**, the process of readmitting the former Confederate states to the Union, lasted from 1865 to 1877.

© Houghton Mifflin Harcourt Publishing Company • Image Credits: (b), National Archives (NARA)

Damaged South

Tired southern soldiers returned home to find that the world they had known before the war was gone. Cities, towns, and farms had been ruined. Because of high food prices and widespread crop failures, many southerners faced starvation. The Confederate money held by most southerners was now worthless. Banks failed, and merchants had gone bankrupt because people could not pay their debts.

Former Confederate general Braxton Bragg was one of many southerners who faced economic hardship. He found that "*all, all* was lost, except my debts." In South Carolina, Mary Boykin Chesnut wrote in her diary about the isolation she experienced after the war. "We are shut in here . . . All RR's [railroads] destroyed—bridges gone. We are cut off from the world."

Lincoln's Plan

President Abraham Lincoln wanted to reunite the nation as quickly and painlessly as possible. He had proposed a plan for readmitting the southern states even before the war ended. Called the **Ten Percent Plan**, it offered southerners amnesty, or official pardon, for all illegal acts supporting the rebellion. To receive amnesty, southerners had to do two things. They had to swear an oath of loyalty to the United States. They also had to agree that slavery was illegal. Once 10 percent of voters in a state made these pledges, they could form a new government. The state then could be readmitted to the Union.

Louisiana quickly elected a new state legislature under the Ten Percent Plan. Other southern states that had been occupied by Union troops soon followed Louisiana back into the United States.

Wade-Davis Bill

Some politicians argued that Congress, not the president, should control the southern states' return to the Union. They believed that Congress had the power to admit new states. Also, many Republican members of Congress thought the Ten Percent Plan did not go far enough. A senator from Michigan expressed their views.

> "The people of the North are not such fools as to . . . turn around and say to the traitors, 'all you have to do [to return] is . . . take an oath that henceforth you will be true to the Government.'"
>
> –Senator Jacob Howard, quoted in *Reconstruction: America's Unfinished Revolution, 1863–1877,* by Eric Foner

Two Republicans—Senator Benjamin Wade and Representative Henry Davis—had an alternative to Lincoln's plan. Following **procedures** of the Wade-Davis bill, a state had to meet two conditions before it could rejoin the Union. First, it had to ban slavery. Second, a majority of adult males in the state had to take the loyalty oath.

ACADEMIC VOCABULARY
procedure a series of steps taken to accomplish a task

War destroyed Richmond, Virginia, once the capital of the Confederacy.

© Houghton Mifflin Harcourt Publishing Company • Image Credits: (b), National Archives (NARA)

Under the Wade-Davis bill, only southerners who swore that they had never supported the Confederacy could vote or hold office. In general, the bill was much stricter than the Ten Percent Plan. Its provisions would make it harder for southern states to rejoin the Union quickly.

President Lincoln therefore refused to sign the bill into law. He thought that few southern states would agree to meet its requirements. He believed that his plan would help restore order more quickly.

READING CHECK **Contrasting** How was the Ten Percent Plan different from the Wade-Davis bill?

Freedom for African Americans

One thing Republicans agreed on was abolishing slavery. The Emancipation Proclamation had freed slaves only in areas that had not been occupied by Union forces, not in the border states. Many people feared that the federal courts might someday declare the proclamation unconstitutional.

Slavery Ends

On January 31, 1865, at President Lincoln's urging, Congress proposed the **Thirteenth Amendment**. This amendment made slavery illegal throughout the United States.

© Houghton Mifflin Harcourt Publishing Company • Image Credits: (t), Library of Congress Prints & Photographs Division, Washington, D.C.

The freedpeople at left have packed their household belongings and are leaving Richmond. Many people traveled in search of relatives. Others placed newspaper advertisements looking for long-lost relatives. For other freedpeople, like the couple above, freedom brought the right to marry.

In what ways did former slaves react to freedom?

The amendment was ratified and took effect on December 18, 1865. When abolitionist William Lloyd Garrison heard the news, he declared that his work was now finished. He called for the American Anti-Slavery Society to break up. Not all abolitionists agreed that their work was done, however. Frederick Douglass insisted that "slavery is not abolished until the black man has the ballot [vote]."

Freedom brought important changes to newly freed slaves. Many couples held ceremonies to legalize marriages that had not been recognized under slavery. Many freedpeople searched for relatives who had been sold away from their families years earlier. Others placed newspaper ads seeking information about their children. Many women began to work at home instead of in the fields. Still others adopted children of dead relatives to keep families together. Church members established voluntary associations and mutual-aid societies to help those in need.

Now that they could travel without a pass, many freedpeople moved from mostly white counties to places with more African Americans. Other freedpeople traveled simply to test their new freedom of movement. A South Carolina woman explained this need. "I must go, if I stay here I'll never know I'm free."

For most former slaves, freedom to travel was just the first step on a long road toward equal rights and new ways of life. Adults took new last names and began to insist on being called Mr. or Mrs. as a sign of respect, rather than by their first names or by nicknames. Freedpeople began to demand the same economic and political rights as white citizens. Henry Adams, a former slave, argued that "if I cannot do like a white man I am not free."

Forty Acres to Farm?

Many former slaves wanted their own land to farm. Near the end of the Civil War, Union general William Tecumseh Sherman had issued an order to break up plantations in coastal South Carolina and Georgia. He wanted to divide the land into 40-acre plots and give them to former slaves as compensation for their forced labor before the war.

Many white planters refused to surrender their land. Some freedpeople pointed out that it was only fair that they receive some of this land because their labor had made the plantations prosper. In the end, the U.S. government returned the land to its original owners. At this time, many freedpeople were unsure about where they would live, what kind of work they would do, and what rights they had. Freedoms that were theirs by law were difficult to enforce.

© Houghton Mifflin Harcourt Publishing Company • Image Credits: (t), Library of Congress Prints & Photographs Division, Washington, D.C.; (t), University of Texas at El Paso Library, Special Collections Department, Ada Tharp Photograph Collection

Freedmen's Bureau

In 1865 Congress established the **Freedmen's Bureau**, an agency providing relief for freedpeople and certain poor people in the South. The Bureau had a difficult job. At its high point, about 900 agents served the entire South. Bureau commissioner Oliver O. Howard eventually decided to use the Bureau's limited budget to distribute food to the poor and to provide education and legal help for freedpeople. The Bureau also helped African American war veterans.

The Freedmen's Bureau played an important role in establishing more schools in the South. Laws against educating slaves meant that most freedpeople had never learned to read or write. Before the war ended, however, northern groups, such as the American Missionary Association, began providing books and teachers to African Americans. The teachers were mostly women who were committed to helping freedpeople. One teacher said of her students, "I never before saw children so eager to learn . . . It is wonderful how [they] . . . can have so great a desire for knowledge, and such a capacity for attaining [reaching] it."

After the war, some freedpeople organized their own education efforts. For example, Freedmen's Bureau agents found that some African Americans had opened schools in abandoned buildings. Many white southerners continued to believe that African Americans should not be educated. Despite opposition, by 1869 more than 150,000 African American students were attending more than 3,000 schools. The Freedmen's Bureau also helped establish a number of universities for African Americans, including Howard and Fisk universities.

Students quickly filled the new classrooms. Working adults attended classes in the evening. African Americans hoped that education would help them to understand and protect their rights and to enable them to find better jobs. Both black and white southerners benefited from the effort to provide greater access to education in the South.

READING CHECK **Analyzing** How did the Freedmen's Bureau help reform education in the South?

Helping the Freedpeople

Congress created the Freedmen's Bureau to help freedpeople and poor southerners recover from the Civil War. The Bureau assisted people by:

- **providing supplies and medical services**
- **establishing schools**
- **supervising contracts between freedpeople and employers**
- **taking care of lands abandoned or captured during the war**

What role did the Freedmen's Bureau play during Reconstruction?

© Houghton Mifflin Harcourt Publishing Company • Image Credits: (b), ©Corbis

President Johnson's Reconstruction Plan

While the Freedmen's Bureau was helping African Americans, the issue of how the South would politically rejoin the Union remained unresolved. Soon, however, a tragic event ended Lincoln's dream of peacefully reuniting the country.

A New President

On the evening of April 14, 1865, President Lincoln and his wife attended a play at Ford's Theater in Washington, D.C. During the play, John Wilkes Booth, a southerner who opposed Lincoln's policies, sneaked into the president's theater box and shot him. Lincoln was rushed to a boardinghouse across the street, where he died early the next morning. Vice President **Andrew Johnson** was sworn into office quickly. Reconstruction had now become his responsibility. He would have to win the trust of a nation shocked at its leader's death.

Johnson's plan for bringing southern states back into the Union was similar to Lincoln's plan. However, he decided that wealthy southerners and former Confederate officials would need a presidential pardon to receive amnesty. Johnson shocked Radical Republicans by eventually pardoning more than 7,000 people by 1866.

New State Governments

Johnson was a Democrat whom Republicans had put on the ticket in 1864 to appeal to the border states. A former slaveholder, he was a stubborn man who would soon face a hostile Congress.

Johnson offered a mild program for setting up new southern state governments. First, he appointed a temporary governor for each state. Then he required that the states revise their constitutions. Next, voters elected state and federal representatives. The new state government had to declare that secession was illegal. It also had to ratify the Thirteenth Amendment and refuse to pay Confederate debts.

By the end of 1865, all the southern states except Texas had created new governments. Johnson approved them all and declared that the United States was restored. Newly elected representatives came to Washington from each reconstructed southern state. However, Republicans complained that many new representatives had been leaders of the Confederacy. Congress therefore refused to readmit the southern states into the Union. Clearly, the nation was still divided.

READING CHECK **Summarizing** What was President Johnson's plan for Reconstruction?

SUMMARY In this section you learned about early plans for Reconstruction.

Section 1 Assessment

hmhsocialstudies.com ONLINE QUIZ

Reviewing Ideas, Terms, and People

1. a. **Identify** What does **Reconstruction** mean?
   b. **Summarize** What was President Lincoln's plan for Reconstruction?
2. a. **Recall** What is the **Thirteenth Amendment**?
   b. **Elaborate** In your opinion, what was the most important accomplishment of the **Freedmen's Bureau**? Explain.
3. a. **Recall** Why was President Lincoln killed?
   b. **Analyze** Why did some Americans oppose President Johnson's Reconstruction plan?

Critical Thinking

4. **Summarizing** Review your notes on Reconstruction. Then copy the graphic organizer below and use it to show how African Americans were affected by the end of the war.

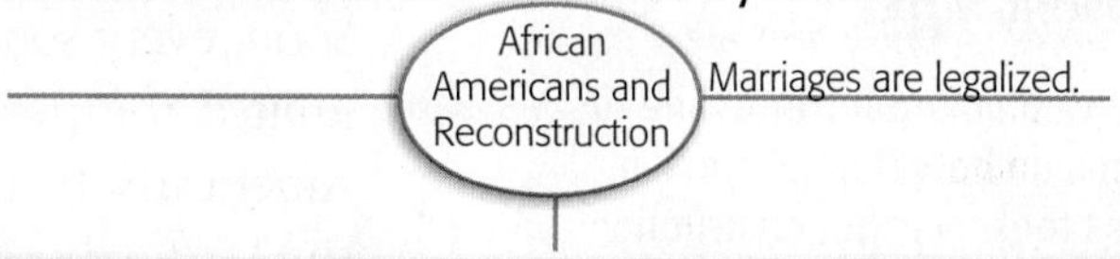

African Americans and Reconstruction
Marriages are legalized.

FOCUS ON WRITING

5. **Considering Historical Context** Many people planned to continue doing what they had done before the war. Others planned to start a new life. How do you think events and conditions you just read about might have affected their plans?

© Houghton Mifflin Harcourt Publishing Company

SECTION 2

The Fight over Reconstruction

What You Will Learn...

Main Ideas

1. Black Codes led to opposition to President Johnson's plan for Reconstruction.
2. The Fourteenth Amendment ensured citizenship for African Americans.
3. Radical Republicans in Congress took charge of Reconstruction.
4. The Fifteenth Amendment gave African Americans the right to vote.

The Big Idea

The return to power of the pre-war southern leadership led Republicans in Congress to take control of Reconstruction.

Key Terms and People

Black Codes
Radical Republicans
Civil Rights Act of 1866
Fourteenth Amendment
Reconstruction Acts
impeachment
Fifteenth Amendment

hmhsocialstudies.com
TAKING NOTES

Use the graphic organizer online to take notes on how Republicans in Congress took over Reconstruction and how they changed Reconstruction policies.

If YOU were there...

A member of Congress, you belong to the same political party as the president. But you strongly disagree with his ideas about Reconstruction and civil rights for African Americans. Now some of the president's opponents are trying to remove him from office. You do not think he is a good president. On the other hand, you think removing him would be bad for the unity of the country.

Will you vote to remove the president?

BUILDING BACKGROUND Americans were bitterly divided about what should happen in the South during Reconstruction. They disagreed about ending racial inequality and guaranteeing civil rights for African Americans. These conflicts split political parties. They led to showdowns between Congress and the president. Political fights even threatened the president's job.

Opposition to President Johnson

In 1866 Congress continued to debate the rules for restoring the Union. Meanwhile, new state legislatures approved by President Johnson had already begun passing laws to deny African Americans' civil rights. "This is a white man's government, and intended for white men only," declared Governor Benjamin F. Perry of South Carolina.

Black Codes

Soon, every southern state passed **Black Codes**, or laws that greatly limited the freedom of African Americans. They required African Americans to sign work contracts, creating working conditions similar to those under slavery. In most southern states, any African Americans who could not prove they were employed could be arrested. Their punishment might be one year of work without pay. African Americans were also prevented from owning guns. In addition, they were not allowed to rent property except in cities.

The Black Codes alarmed many Americans. As one Civil War veteran asked, "If you call this freedom, what do you call slavery?"

© Houghton Mifflin Harcourt Publishing Company

African Americans organized to oppose the codes. One group sent a petition to officials in South Carolina.

> “We simply ask . . . that the same laws which govern *white men* shall govern *black men* . . . that, in short, we be dealt with as others are—in equity [equality] and justice.”
>
> —Petition from an African American convention held in South Carolina, quoted in *There Is a River: The Black Struggle for Freedom in America* by Vincent Harding

Radical Republicans

The Black Codes angered many Republicans. They thought the South was returning to its old ways. Most Republicans were moderates who wanted the South to have loyal state governments. They also believed that African Americans should have rights as citizens. They hoped that the government would not have to force the South to follow federal laws.

Radical Republicans, on the other hand, took a harsher stance. They wanted the federal government to force change in the South. Like the moderates, they thought the Black Codes were cruel and unjust. The Radicals, however, wanted the federal government to be much more involved in Reconstruction. They feared that too many southern leaders remained loyal to the former Confederacy and would not enforce the new laws. Thaddeus Stevens

Primary Source

POLITICAL CARTOON

Supporting Radical Republican Ideas

Republicans were outraged to see former Confederates return to power as leaders of the Democratic Party. This 1868 political cartoon shows former Confederates Raphael Semmes and Nathan Bedford Forrest. Semmes was a Confederate admiral who had captured 62 Union merchant ships during the Civil War. Forrest was a cavalry officer known for brutality who later founded the Ku Klux Klan.

LEADERS' OF THE DEMOCRATIC PARTY.
THE PIRATE SEMMES.
THE BUTCHER FORREST.
“Captain Semmes ordered the captains of both ships on board the Alabama, examined their papers, and allowing them to take a small quantity of clothing, burned their ships, and sent them adrift in their boats without any water or provisions.”—Report of the burning of the American ships Sonora and Highlander, near Singapore, East Indies.
“Forrest says: ‘No quarter! no quarter! Kill 'em! kill 'en! damn 'em!’ That's Forrest's orders, not to leave one alive.”—May's Official Report.

How do the actions of the people in these illustrations support the artist's point of view?

How do events in the background of these illustrations support the artist's point of view?

ANALYSIS SKILL ANALYZING PRIMARY SOURCES

Why do you think that the men are shown in their Confederate uniforms?

© Houghton Mifflin Harcourt Publishing Company • Image Credits: (b), Library of Congress Prints & Photographs Division, Washington, D.C.

Primary Source

POINTS OF VIEW

Johnson vs. Stevens

President Andrew Johnson argued that the South should not be placed under military control.

"Military governments . . . established for an indefinite period, would have divided the people into the vanquishers and the vanquished, and would have envenomed [made poisonous] hatred rather than have restored affection."

—Andrew Johnson

Thaddeus Stevens believed that Congress had the power to treat the South as conquered territory.

"The future condition of the conquered power depends on the will of the conqueror. They must come in as new states or remain as conquered provinces. Congress . . . is the only power that can act in the matter."

—Thaddeus Stevens

ANALYSIS SKILL IDENTIFYING POINTS OF VIEW

How did Johnson's and Stevens's views on the South differ?

of Pennsylvania and Charles Sumner of Massachusetts were the leaders of the Radical Republicans.

A harsh critic of President Johnson, Stevens was known for his honesty and sharp tongue. He wanted economic and political justice for both African Americans and poor white southerners. Sumner had been a strong opponent of slavery before the Civil War. He continued to argue tirelessly for African Americans' civil rights, including the right to vote and the right to fair laws.

Both Stevens and Sumner believed that President Johnson's Reconstruction plan was a failure. Although the Radicals did not control Congress, they began to gain support among moderates when President Johnson ignored criticism of the Black Codes. Stevens believed the federal government could not allow racial inequality to survive.

ACADEMIC VOCABULARY
principle basic belief, rule, or law

READING CHECK **Comparing and Contrasting** How were Radical Republicans and moderate Republicans similar and different?

Fourteenth Amendment

Urged on by the Radicals in 1866, Congress proposed a new bill. It would give the Freedmen's Bureau more powers. The law would allow the Freedmen's Bureau to use military courts to try people accused of violating African Americans' rights. The bill's supporters hoped that these courts would be fairer than local courts in the South.

Johnson versus Congress

Surprising many members of Congress, Johnson vetoed the Freedmen's Bureau Bill. He insisted that Congress could not pass any new laws until the southern states were represented in Congress. Johnson also argued that the Freedmen's Bureau was unconstitutional.

Republicans responded with the **Civil Rights Act of 1866**. This act provided African Americans with the same legal rights as white Americans. President Johnson once again used his veto power. He argued that the act gave too much power to the federal government. He also rejected the principle of equal

© Houghton Mifflin Harcourt Publishing Company • Image Credits: (r), ©Corbis; (l), Library of Congress Prints & Photographs Division, Washington, D.C.

rights for African Americans. Congress, however, overrode Johnson's veto.

Many Republicans worried about what would happen when the southern states were readmitted. Fearing that the Civil Rights Act might be overturned, the Republicans proposed the **Fourteenth Amendment** in the summer of 1866. The Fourteenth Amendment included the following provisions.

1. It defined all people born or naturalized within the United States, except Native Americans, as citizens.
2. It guaranteed citizens the equal protection of the laws.
3. It said that states could not "deprive any person of life, liberty, or property, without due process of law."
4. It banned many former Confederate officials from holding state or federal offices.
5. It made state laws subject to federal court review.
6. It gave Congress the power to pass any laws needed to enforce it.

1866 Elections

President Johnson and most Democrats opposed the Fourteenth Amendment. As a result, civil rights for African Americans became a key issue in the 1866 congressional elections. To help the Democrats, Johnson traveled around the country defending his Reconstruction plan. Johnson's speaking tour was a disaster. It did little to win votes for the Democratic Party. Johnson even got into arguments with people in the audiences of some of his speaking engagements.

Two major riots in the South also hurt Johnson's campaign. On May 1, 1866, a dispute in Memphis, Tennessee, took place between local police and black Union soldiers. The dispute turned into a three-day wave of violence against African Americans. About three months later, another riot took place during a political demonstration in New Orleans. During that dispute, 34 African Americans and three white Republicans were killed.

READING CHECK **Summarizing** What issue did the Fourteenth Amendment address, and how did it affect the congressional elections of 1866?

Congress Takes Control of Reconstruction

The 1866 elections gave the Republican Party a commanding two-thirds majority in both the House and the Senate. This majority gave the Republicans the power to override any presidential veto. In addition, the Republicans became united as the moderates joined with the Radicals. Together, they called for a new form of Reconstruction.

Reconstruction Acts

In March 1867, Congress passed the first of several **Reconstruction Acts**. These laws divided the South into five districts. A U.S. military commander controlled each district.

hmhsocialstudies.com
ANIMATED GEOGRAPHY
The Southern Military Districts 1867

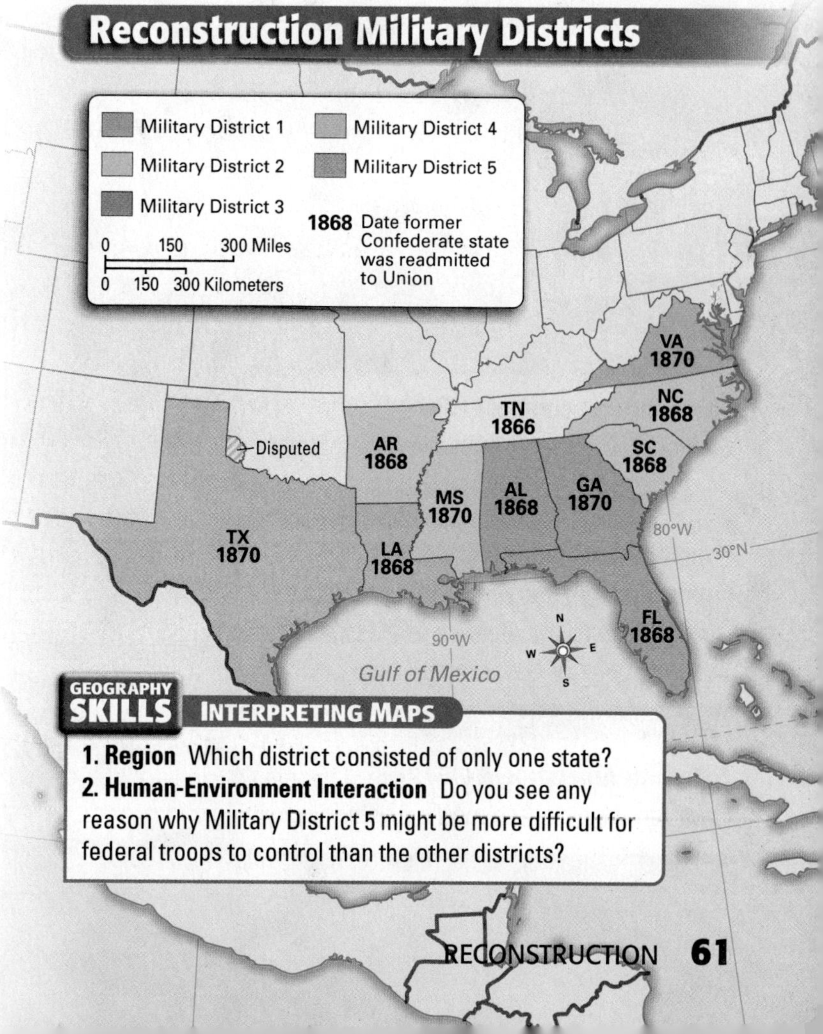

Reconstruction Military Districts
Military District 1
Military District 2
Military District 3
Military District 4
Military District 5
1868 Date former Confederate state was readmitted to Union
0 150 300 Miles
0 150 300 Kilometers
VA 1870
NC 1868
TN 1866
SC 1868
GA 1870
AL 1868
MS 1870
AR 1868
LA 1868
TX 1870
FL 1868
Disputed
80°W
30°N
90°W
Gulf of Mexico
N
S
E
W

GEOGRAPHY SKILLS **INTERPRETING MAPS**

1. **Region** Which district consisted of only one state?
2. **Human-Environment Interaction** Do you see any reason why Military District 5 might be more difficult for federal troops to control than the other districts?

© Houghton Mifflin Harcourt Publishing Company

The military would remain in control of the South until the southern states rejoined the Union. To be readmitted, a state had to write a new state constitution supporting the Fourteenth Amendment. Finally, the state had to give African American men the right to vote.

Thaddeus Stevens was one of the new Reconstruction Acts' most enthusiastic supporters. He spoke in Congress to defend the acts.

> "Have not loyal blacks quite as good a right to choose rulers and make laws as rebel whites? Every man, no matter what his race or color . . . has an equal right to justice, honesty, and fair play with every other man; and the law should secure him those rights."
>
> –Thaddeus Stevens, quoted in *Sources of the American Republic*, edited by Marvin Meyers et al.

President on Trial

President Johnson strongly disagreed with Stevens. He argued that African Americans did not deserve the same treatment as white people. The Reconstruction Acts, he said, used "powers not granted to the federal government or any one of its branches." Knowing that Johnson did not support its Reconstruction policies, Congress passed a law limiting his power. This law prevented the president from removing cabinet officials without Senate approval. Johnson quickly broke the law by firing Edwin Stanton, the secretary of war.

For the first time in United States history, the House of Representatives responded by voting to impeach the president. **Impeachment** is the process used by a legislative body to bring charges of wrongdoing against a public official. The next step, under Article I of the Constitution, was a trial in the Senate. A two-thirds majority was required to find Johnson guilty and remove him from office.

Although Johnson was unpopular with Republicans, some of them believed he was being judged unfairly. Others did not trust the president pro tempore of the Senate, Benjamin Wade. He would become president if Johnson were removed from office. By a single vote, Senate Republicans failed to convict Johnson. Even so, the trial weakened his power as president.

Election of 1868

Johnson did not run for another term in 1868. The Democrats chose

The Reconstruction Amendments

QUICK FACTS

Thirteenth Amendment (1865)
Banned slavery throughout the United States

Fourteenth Amendment (1868)
Overturned the *Dred Scott* case by granting citizenship to all people born in the United States (except for Native Americans)

Fifteenth Amendment (1870)
Gave African American men the right to vote

This Reconstruction-era painting shows African American men voting after passage of the Fifteenth Amendment.

What right did the Fifteenth Amendment protect?

© Houghton Mifflin Harcourt Publishing Company • Image Credits: (b), ©North Wind / North Wind Picture Archives — All rights reserved.

former New York governor Horatio Seymour as their presidential candidate. The Republicans chose Ulysses S. Grant. As a war hero, Grant appealed to many northern voters. He had no political experience but supported the congressional Reconstruction plan. He ran under the slogan "Let Us Have Peace."

Shortly after Grant was nominated, Congress readmitted seven southern states—Alabama, Arkansas, Florida, Georgia, Louisiana, North Carolina, and South Carolina. (Tennessee had already been readmitted in 1866.) Under the terms of readmission, these seven states approved the Fourteenth Amendment. They also agreed to let African American men vote. However, white southerners used violence to try to keep African Americans away from the polls.

Despite such tactics, hundreds of thousands of African Americans voted for Grant and the "party of Lincoln." The *New Orleans Tribune* reported that many former slaves "see clearly enough that the Republican party [is] their political life boat." African American votes helped Grant to win a narrow victory.

READING CHECK **Analyzing** To what voters did Grant appeal in the presidential election of 1868?

Fifteenth Amendment

After Grant's victory, Congressional Republicans wanted to protect their Reconstruction plan. They worried that the southern states might try to keep black voters from the polls in future elections. Also, some Radical Republicans argued that it was not fair that many northern states still had laws preventing African Americans from voting. After all, every southern state was required to grant suffrage to African American men.

In 1869 Congress proposed the **Fifteenth Amendment**, which gave African American men the right to vote. Abolitionist William Lloyd Garrison praised what he saw as "this wonderful, quiet, sudden transformation of four millions of human beings from . . . the auction block to the ballot-box." The amendment went into effect in 1870 as one of the last Reconstruction laws passed at the federal level.

The Fifteenth Amendment did not please every reformer, however. Many women were angry because the amendment did not also grant them the right to vote.

THE IMPACT TODAY

The Voting Rights Act of 1965 enforces and expands the voting protections of the Fifteenth Amendment.

READING CHECK **Finding Main Ideas** How did Radical Republicans take control of Reconstruction?

SUMMARY In this section you learned that Congress took control of Reconstruction and took steps to protect the rights of African Americans.

Section 2 Assessment

hmhsocialstudies.com ONLINE QUIZ

Reviewing Ideas, Terms, and People

1. a. **Describe** What were **Black Codes**?
   b. **Make Inferences** Why did Republicans think Johnson's Reconstruction plan was a failure?
2. a. **Recall** What was the **Civil Rights Act of 1866**?
   b. **Summarize** Why was the **Fourteenth Amendment** important?
3. a. **Recall** Why was President Johnson impeached?
   b. **Evaluate** Which element of the **Reconstruction Acts** do you believe was most important? Why?
4. a. **Recall** What does the **Fifteenth Amendment** state?
   b. **Elaborate** Do you think that women should have been included in the Fifteenth Amendment? Explain.

Critical Thinking

5. **Identify** Review your notes on the issues that led Republicans to take over Reconstruction. Then copy the graphic organizer below and use it to identify the main provisions of the Fourteenth Amendment and their effects.

Provisions	Effects

FOCUS ON WRITING

6. **Recognizing Cause-and-Effect Relationships** As you have read in this section, social and political unrest continued long after the war ended. How could this unrest cause people to leave their jobs? What new jobs might they find?

© Houghton Mifflin Harcourt Publishing Company

SECTION 3

Reconstruction in the South

What You Will Learn...

Main Ideas

1. Reconstruction governments helped reform the South.
2. The Ku Klux Klan was organized as African Americans moved into positions of power.
3. As Reconstruction ended, the rights of African Americans were restricted.
4. Southern business leaders relied on industry to rebuild the South.

The Big Idea

As Reconstruction ended, African Americans faced new hurdles and the South attempted to rebuild.

Key Terms and People

Hiram Revels
Ku Klux Klan
Compromise of 1877
poll tax
segregation
Jim Crow laws
Plessy v. *Ferguson*
sharecropping

hmhsocialstudies.com
TAKING NOTES

Use the graphic organizer online to take notes on the South's efforts to rebuild and the effects of those efforts on African Americans.

If YOU were there...

You live on a farm in the South in the 1870s. Times are hard because you do not own your farm. Instead, you and your family work in a landowner's cotton fields. You never seem to earn enough to buy land of your own. Some of your neighbors have decided to give up farming and move to the city. Others are going to work in the textile mills. But you have always been a farmer.

Will you decide to change your way of life?

BUILDING BACKGROUND Reconstruction affected politics and economics in the South. Republican and Democratic politicians fought over policies and programs. New state governments began reforms, but later leaders ended many of them. Some parts of the southern economy improved. However, many farmers, like the family above, went through hard times.

Reconstruction Governments

After Grant became president in 1869, the Republicans seemed stronger than ever. They controlled most southern governments, partly because of the support of African American voters. However, most of the Republican officeholders were unpopular with white southerners.

Carpetbaggers and Scalawags

Some of these office-holders were northern-born Republicans who had moved to the South after the war. Many white southerners called them carpetbaggers. Supposedly, they had rushed there carrying all their possessions in bags made from carpeting. Many southerners resented these northerners, accusing them—often unfairly—of trying to profit from Reconstruction.

Southern Democrats cared even less for white southern Republicans. They referred to them as scalawags, or greedy rascals. Democrats believed that these southerners had betrayed the South by

© Houghton Mifflin Harcourt Publishing Company

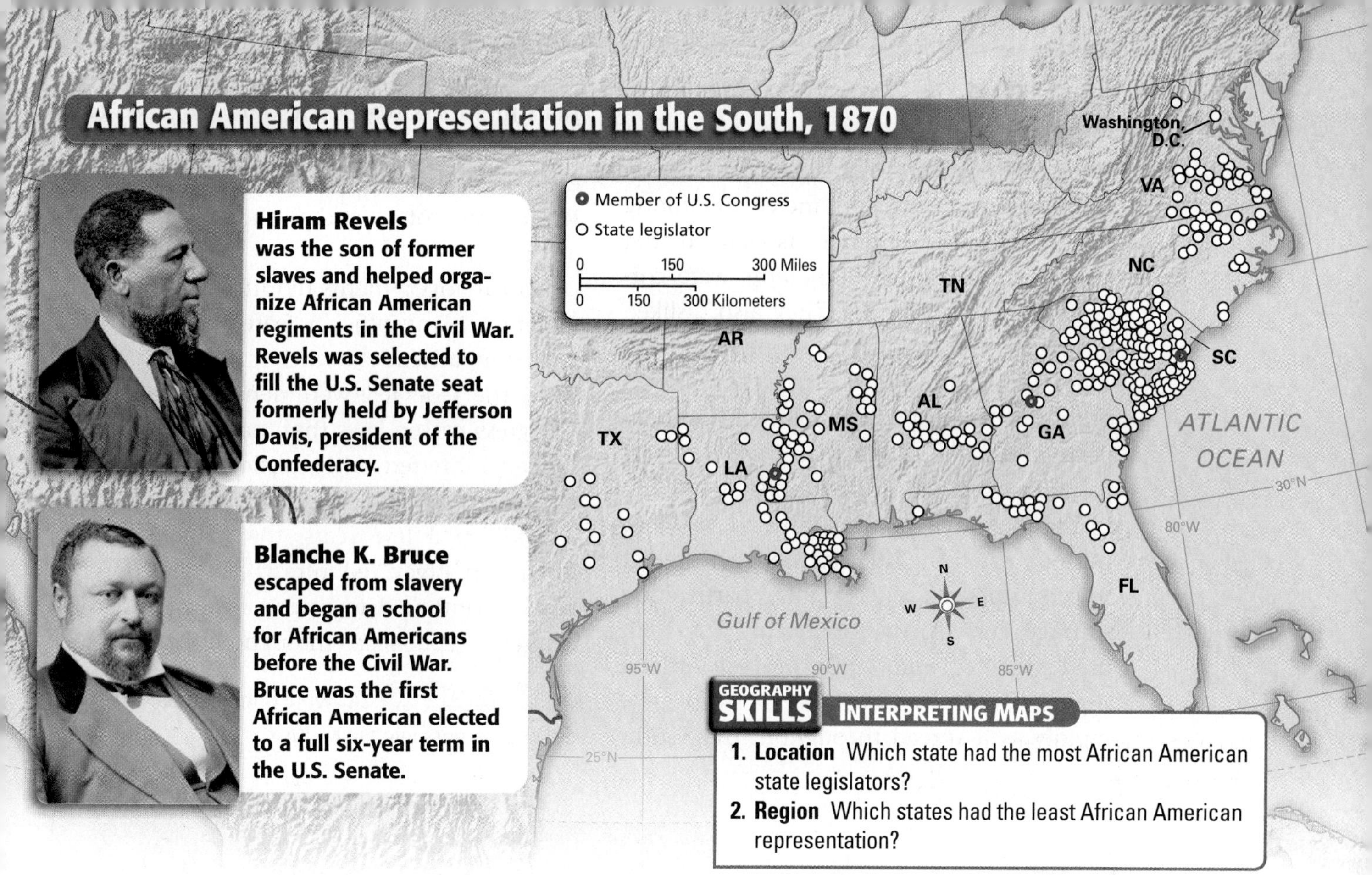
African American Representation in the South, 1870
Member of U.S. Congress
State legislator
0 150 300 Miles
0 150 300 Kilometers
Washington, D.C.
VA
NC
TN
SC
AR
AL
MS
GA
TX
LA
ATLANTIC OCEAN
Gulf of Mexico
FL
N
E
S
W
30°N
80°W
95°W
90°W
85°W
25°N

Hiram Revels was the son of former slaves and helped organize African American regiments in the Civil War. Revels was selected to fill the U.S. Senate seat formerly held by Jefferson Davis, president of the Confederacy.

Blanche K. Bruce escaped from slavery and began a school for African Americans before the Civil War. Bruce was the first African American elected to a full six-year term in the U.S. Senate.

GEOGRAPHY SKILLS **INTERPRETING MAPS**

1. **Location** Which state had the most African American state legislators?
2. **Region** Which states had the least African American representation?

voting for the Republican Party. Many southern Republicans were small farmers who had supported the Union during the war. Others, like Mississippi governor James Alcorn, were former members of the Whig Party. They preferred to become Republicans rather than join the Democrats.

African American Leaders

African Americans were the largest group of southern Republican voters. During Reconstruction, more than 600 African Americans won election to state legislatures. Some 16 of these politicians were elected to Congress. Other African Americans held local offices in counties throughout the South.

African American politicians came from many backgrounds. **Hiram Revels** was born free in North Carolina and went to college in Illinois. He became a Methodist minister and served as a chaplain in the Union army. In 1870 Revels became the first African American in the U.S. Senate. He took over the seat previously held by Confederate president Jefferson Davis. Unlike Revels, Blanche K. Bruce grew up in slavery in Virginia. Bruce became an important Republican in Mississippi and served one term as a U.S. senator.

State Governments Change Direction

Reconstruction governments provided money for many new programs and organizations in the South. They helped to establish some of the first state-funded public school systems in the South. They also built new hospitals, prisons, and orphanages and passed laws prohibiting discrimination against African Americans.

Southern states under Republican control spent large amounts of money. They aided the construction of railroads, bridges, and public buildings. These improvements were intended to help the southern economy recover from the war. To get the money for these projects, the Reconstruction governments raised taxes and issued bonds.

READING CHECK **Summarizing** What reforms did Reconstruction state governments carry out?

FOCUS ON READING
How does the heading of this section tell you about what you will learn?

© Houghton Mifflin Harcourt Publishing Company • Image Credits: (b), (t), Library of Congress Prints & Photographs Division, Washington, D.C.

Ku Klux Klan

As more African Americans took office, resistance to Reconstruction increased among white southerners. Democrats claimed that the Reconstruction governments were corrupt, illegal, and unjust. They also disliked having federal soldiers stationed in their states. Many white southerners disapproved of African American officeholders. One Democrat noted, "'A white man's government' [is] the most popular rallying cry we have." In 1866 a group of white southerners in Tennessee created the **Ku Klux Klan**. This secret society opposed civil rights, particularly suffrage, for African Americans. The Klan used violence and terror against African Americans. The group's membership grew rapidly as it spread throughout the South. Klan members wore robes and disguises to hide their identities. They attacked—and even murdered—African Americans, white Republican voters, and public officials, usually at night.

Local governments did little to stop the violence. Many officials feared the Klan or were sympathetic to its activities. In 1870 and 1871 the federal government took action. Congress passed laws that made it a federal crime to interfere with elections or to deny citizens equal protection under the law.

Within a few years, the Klan was no longer an organized threat. But groups of whites continued to assault African Americans and Republicans throughout the 1870s.

READING CHECK **Drawing Conclusions** Why did southerners join the Ku Klux Klan?

The Ku Klux Klan

Members of the Ku Klux Klan often attacked under cover of darkness to hide their identities. This klansman, shown on the left, even disguised his horse.

Why do you think Klan members disguised themselves?

© Houghton Mifflin Harcourt Publishing Company • Image Credits: (l), The Granger Collection, New York; (r), ©Bettmann/Corbis

Reconstruction Ends

The violence of the Ku Klux Klan was not the only challenge to Reconstruction. Republicans slowly lost control of southern state governments to the Democratic Party. The General Amnesty Act of 1872 allowed former Confederates, except those who had held high ranks, to serve in public office. Many of these former Confederates, most of whom were Democrats, were soon elected to southern governments.

The Republican Party also began losing its power in the North. Although President Grant was re-elected in 1872, financial and political scandals in his administration upset voters. In his first term, a gold-buying scheme in which Grant's cousin took a leading role led to a brief crisis on the stock market called Black Friday. During his second term, his personal secretary was involved in the Whiskey Ring scandal, in which whiskey distillers and public officials worked together to steal liquor taxes from the federal government. Furthermore, people blamed Republican policies for the Panic of 1873.

Panic of 1873

This severe economic downturn began in September 1873 when Jay Cooke and Company, a major investor in railroads and the largest financier of the Union's Civil War effort, declared bankruptcy. The company had lied about the value of land along the side of the Northern Pacific Railroad that it owned and was trying to sell. When the truth leaked out, the company failed.

The failure of such an important business sent panic through the stock market, and investors began selling shares of stock more rapidly than people wanted to buy them. Companies had to buy their shares back from the investors. Soon, 89 of the nation's 364 railroads had failed as well. The failure of almost 18,000 other businesses followed within two years, leaving the nation in an economic crisis. By 1876 unemployment had risen to 14 percent, with an estimated 2 million people out of work. The high unemployment rate set off numerous strikes and protests around the nation, many involving railroad workers. In 1874 the Democrats gained control of the House of Representatives. Northerners were becoming less concerned about southern racism and more concerned about their financial well-being.

Election of 1876

Republicans could tell that northern support for Reconstruction was fading. Voters' attention was shifting to economic problems. In 1874 the Republican Party lost control of the House of Representatives to the Democrats. The Republicans in Congress managed to pass one last civil rights law. The Civil Rights Act of 1875 guaranteed African Americans equal rights in public places, such as theaters and public transportation. But as Americans became increasingly worried about economic problems and government corruption, the Republican Party began to abandon Reconstruction.

Republicans selected Ohio governor Rutherford B. Hayes as their 1876 presidential candidate. He believed in ending federal support of the Reconstruction governments. The Democrats nominated New York governor Samuel J. Tilden. During the election, Democrats in the South again used violence at the polls to keep Republican voters away.

The election between Hayes and Tilden was close. Tilden appeared to have won. Republicans challenged the electoral votes in Oregon and three southern states. A special commission of members of Congress and Supreme Court justices was appointed to settle the issue.

The commission narrowly decided to give all the disputed votes to Hayes. Hayes thus won the presidency by one electoral vote. In the **Compromise of 1877**, the Democrats agreed to accept Hayes's victory. In return, they wanted all remaining federal troops removed from the South. They also asked for funding for internal improvements in the South and

© Houghton Mifflin Harcourt Publishing Company

Supreme Court Decisions

Plessy v. *Ferguson* (1896)

Background of the Case In 1892, Homer Plessy took a seat in the "whites only" car of a train in Louisiana. He was arrested, put on trial, and convicted of violating Louisiana's segregation law. Plessy argued that the Louisiana law violated the Thirteenth Amendment and denied him the equal protection of the law as guaranteed.

The Court's Ruling

The Court ruled that the Louisiana "separate-but-equal" law was constitutional.

The Court's Reasoning

The Court stated that the Thirteenth and Fourteenth Amendments did not apply. The Court decided that the case had nothing to do with the abolition of slavery mentioned in the Thirteenth Amendment. The justices also ruled that the Fourteenth Amendment was not designed to eliminate social barriers to equality between the races, only political barriers.

Justice John Marshall Harlan disagreed with the Court's ruling. In a dissenting opinion, he wrote that "in respect of civil rights, all citizens are equal before the law."

Why It Matters

Plessy was important because it approved the idea of separate-but-equal facilities for people based on race. The doctrine of separate-but-equal led to segregation in trains, buses, schools, restaurants, and many other social institutions.

The separate-but-equal doctrine led to unequal treatment of minority groups for decades. It was finally struck down by another Supreme Court ruling, *Brown* v. *Board of Education,* in 1954.

ANALYSIS SKILL **ANALYZING INFORMATION**

1. **Why did the Court reject Plessy's arguments?**
2. **Why was *Plessy* v. *Ferguson* an important Supreme Court case?**

the appointment of a southern Democrat to the president's cabinet. Shortly after he took office in 1877, President Hayes removed the last of the federal troops from the South.

Redeemers

Gradually, Democrats regained control of state governments in the South. In each state, they moved quickly to get rid of the Reconstruction reforms.

Democrats who brought their party back to power in the South were called Redeemers. They came from a variety of backgrounds. For instance, U.S. senator John T. Morgan of Alabama was a former general in the Confederate army. Newspaper editor Henry Grady of Georgia was interested in promoting southern industry.

Redeemers wanted to reduce the size of state government and limit the rights of African Americans. They lowered state budgets and got rid of a variety of social programs. The Redeemers cut property taxes and cut public funding for schools. They also succeeded in limiting African Americans' civil rights.

African Americans' Rights Restricted

Redeemers set up the poll tax in an effort to deny the vote to African Americans. The **poll tax** was a special tax people had to pay before they could vote.

Some states also targeted African American voters by requiring them to pass a literacy test. A so-called grandfather clause written into law affected men whose fathers or grandfathers could vote before 1867. In those cases, a voter did not have to pay a poll tax or pass a literacy test. As a result, almost every white man could escape the voting restrictions.

Redeemer governments also introduced legal **segregation**, the forced separation of whites and African Americans in public places. **Jim Crow laws**—laws that enforced segregation—became common in southern states in the 1880s.

African Americans challenged Jim Crow laws in court. In 1883, however, the U.S. Supreme Court ruled that the Civil Rights Act of 1875 was unconstitutional. The Court

© Houghton Mifflin Harcourt Publishing Company • Image Credits: (t) Getty Images also ruled that the Fourteenth Amendment applied only to the actions of state governments. This ruling allowed private individuals and businesses to practice segregation.

Plessy v. *Ferguson*

In 1896 the U.S. Supreme Court returned to the issue of segregation. When Homer Plessy, an African American, refused to leave the whites-only Louisiana train car he was riding on, he was arrested and accused of breaking a state law requiring separate cars for blacks and whites. Plessy sued the railroad company and lost. His lawyers argued that the law violated his right to equal treatment under the Fourteenth Amendment. He then appealed to the U.S. Supreme Court. The Supreme Court ruled against Plessy in ***Plessy* v. *Ferguson***. Segregation was allowed, said the Court, if "separate-but-equal" facilities were provided. Among the justices, only John Marshall Harlan disagreed with the Court's decision. He explained his disagreement in a dissenting opinion:

> "In the eye of the law, there is in the country no superior, dominant [controlling], ruling class of citizens . . . Our constitution is color-blind, and neither knows nor tolerates classes among citizens. In respect of civil rights, all citizens are equal before the law."
>
> —John Marshall Harlan, quoted in *Plessy v. Ferguson: A Brief History with Documents,* edited by Brook Thomas

Despite Harlan's view, segregation became widespread across the country. African Americans were forced to use separate public schools, libraries, and parks. When they existed, these facilities were usually of poorer quality than those created for whites. In practice, these so-called separate-but-equal facilities were separate and unequal.

Farming in the South

Few African Americans in the South could afford to buy or even rent farms. Moving to the West also was costly. Many African Americans therefore remained on plantations. Others tried to make a living in the cities.

African Americans who stayed on plantations often became part of a system known as **sharecropping**, or sharing the crop. Landowners provided the land, tools, and supplies, and sharecroppers provided the labor. At harvest time, the sharecropper usually had to give most of the crop to the landowner. Whatever remained belonged to the sharecropper. Many sharecroppers hoped to save enough money from selling their share of the crops to one day be able to buy a farm. Unfortunately, only a few ever achieved this dream.

Instead, most sharecroppers lived in a cycle of debt. When they needed food, clothing, or supplies, most families had to buy goods on credit because they had little cash.

Hopes Raised and Denied

QUICK FACTS

Slavery

- No rights
- Forced labor
- No freedom of movement without permission
- Family members sold away from one another
- No representation in government

Freedom

- Slavery banned
- Free to work for wages
- Could move and live anywhere
- Many families reunited
- Could serve in political office

Rights Denied

- Sharecropping system put in place
- Ability to vote and hold office restricted
- White leadership regained control of southern state governments

© Houghton Mifflin Harcourt Publishing Company

The New South

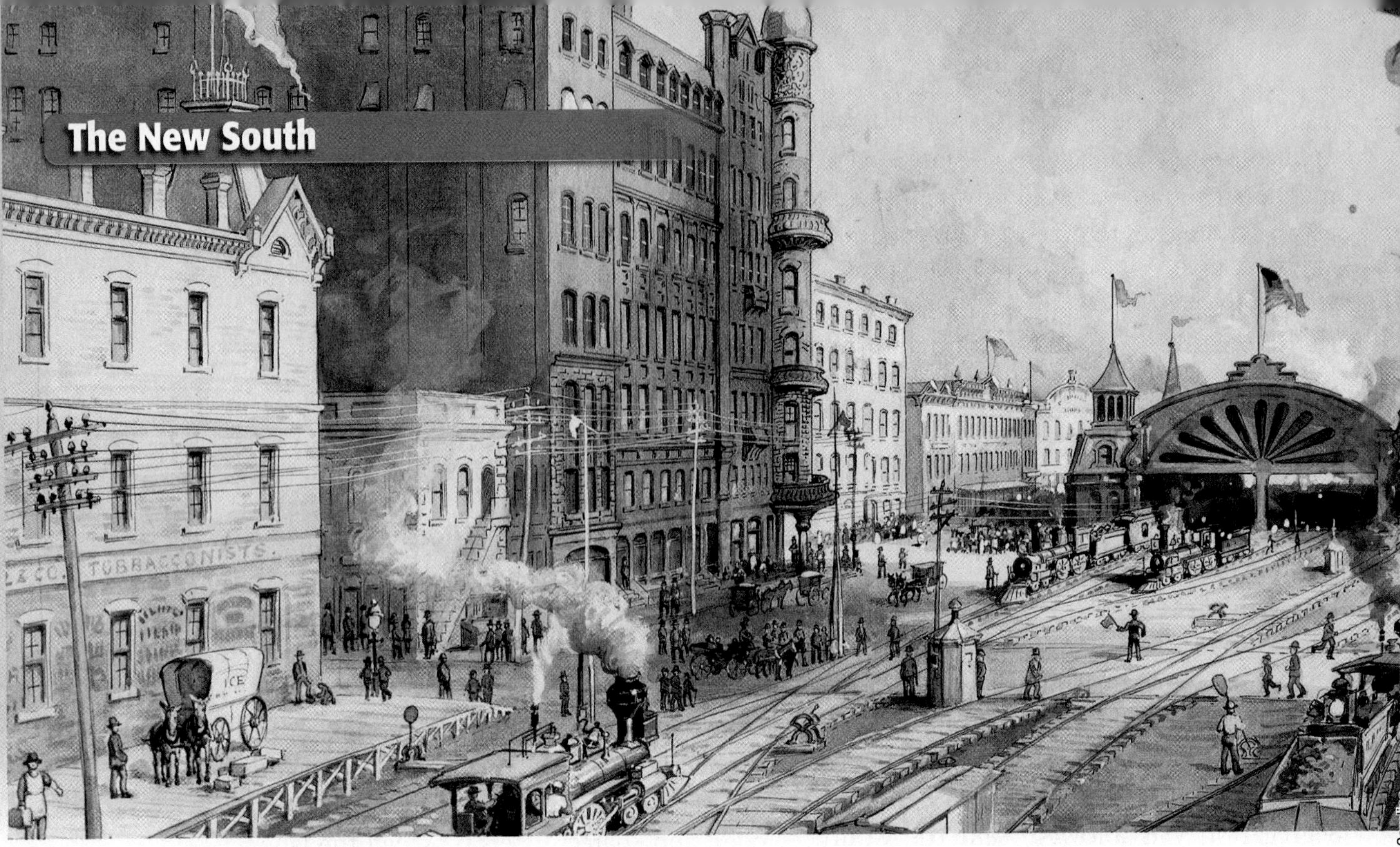

When sharecroppers sold their crops, they hoped to be able to pay off these debts. However, bad weather, poor harvests, or low crop prices often made this dream impossible.

Sharecroppers usually grew cotton, one of the South's most important cash crops. When too many farmers planted cotton, however, the supply became excessive. As a result, the price per bale of cotton dropped. Many farmers understood the drawbacks of planting cotton. However, farmers felt pressure from banks and others to keep raising cotton. A southern farmer explained why so many sharecroppers depended on cotton:

> "Cotton is the thing to get credit on in this country . . . You can always sell cotton . . . [Y]ou load up your wagon with wheat or corn . . . and I doubt some days whether you could sell it."
>
> –Anonymous farmer quoted in *The Promise of the New South,* by Edward L. Ayers

READING CHECK **Finding Main Ideas** How were African Americans' rights restricted?

Rebuilding Southern Industry

The southern economy suffered through cycles of good and bad years as cotton prices went up and down. Some business leaders hoped industry would strengthen the southern economy and create a New South.

Southern Industry

Henry Grady, an Atlanta newspaper editor, was a leader of the New South movement. "The new South presents . . . a diversified [varied] industry that meets the complex needs of this complex age," he wrote. Grady and his supporters felt that with its cheap and abundant labor, the South could build factories and provide a workforce for them.

The most successful industrial development in the South involved textile production. Businesspeople built textile mills in many small towns to produce cotton fabric. Many people from rural areas came to work in the mills, but African Americans were not allowed to work in most of them.

© Houghton Mifflin Harcourt Publishing Company • Image Credits: (t) Courtesy of The Charleston Renaissance Gallery, Robert M. Hicklin, Jr. Inc., Charleston, South Carolina

"The New South...is stirred with the breath of a new life."

—Henry Grady

Atlanta rebuilt quickly after the war, becoming a leading railroad and industrial center. Newspaper editor Henry Grady gave stirring speeches about the need for industry in the South. He became one of the best-known spokesmen of the "New South."

Why might Grady point to Atlanta as a model for economic change?

Southern Mill Life

Work in the cotton mills appealed to farm families who had trouble making ends meet. As one mill worker explained, "It was a necessity to move and get a job, rather than depend on the farm." Recruiters sent out by the mills promised good wages and steady work.

Entire families often worked in the same cotton mill. Mills employed large numbers of women and children. Many children started working at about the age of 12. Some children started working at an even earlier age. Women did most of the spinning and were valued workers. However, few women had the opportunity to advance within the company.

Many mill workers were proud of the skills they used, but they did not enjoy their work. One unhappy worker described it as "the same thing over and over again . . . The more you do, the more they want done." Workers often labored 12 hours a day, six days a week. Cotton dust and lint filled the air, causing asthma and an illness known as brown-lung disease. Fast-moving machinery caused injuries and even deaths. Despite the long hours and dangerous working conditions, wages remained low. However, mill work did offer an alternative to farming.

READING CHECK **Finding Main Ideas** What did southern business leaders hope industry would do?

SUMMARY In this section you learned about the end of Recon-struction.

Section 3 Assessment

hmhsocialstudies.com ONLINE QUIZ

Reviewing Ideas, Terms, and People

1. a. **Identify** Who were some prominent African American leaders during Reconstruction?
   b. **Evaluate** What do you think was the most important change made by Reconstruction state governments? Explain your answer.
2. a. **Recall** For what reasons did some local governments not stop the **Ku Klux Klan**?
   b. **Draw Conclusions** How did the Ku Klux Klan's use of terror interfere with elections in the South?
3. a. **Recall** How did Reconstruction come to an end?
   b. **Explain** What was the relationship between **Jim Crow laws** and **segregation**?
4. a. **Identify** Who was Henry Grady, and why was he important?
   b. **Predict** What are some possible results of the rise of the "New South"?

Critical Thinking

5. **Identifying Causes and Effects** Review your notes on Reconstruction governments. Then copy the graphic organizer below and use it to show why Reconstruction ended, as well as the results of its end.

Causes	→	Effect/Cause End of Reconstruction	→	Effects

Focus on Writing

6. **Relating Historical Change to Individual Choice** Despite the difficulties of Reconstruction, the Freedmen's Bureau and plans to bring industry to the "New South" did create new jobs. What might have led people to leave their jobs for new ones?

© Houghton Mifflin Harcourt Publishing Company • Image Credits: (t), ©Bettmann/Corbis

Social Studies Skills

Analysis | Critical Thinking | Civic Participation | Study

21ST CENTURY

Chance, Oversight, and Error in History

Understand the Skill

Sometimes, history can seem very routine. One event leads to others which, in turn, lead to still others. You learn to look for cause-and-effect relationships among events. You learn how point of view and bias can influence decisions and actions. These approaches to the study of history imply that the events of the past are orderly and predictable.

In fact, many of the events of the past *are* orderly and predictable! They may seem even more so since they're over and done with, and we know how things turned out. Yet, predictable patterns of behavior *do* exist throughout history. Recognizing them is one of the great values and rewards of studying the past. As the philosopher George Santayana once famously said, "Those who cannot remember the past are condemned to repeat it."

At its most basic level, however, history is people, and people are "human." They make mistakes. Unexpected things happen to them, both good things and bad. This is the unpredictable element of history. The current phrase "stuff happens" is just as true of the past as it is today. Mistakes, oversights, and just plain "dumb luck" have shaped the course of history—and have helped to make the study of it so exciting.

Learn the Skill

California merchant John Sutter decided to build a sawmill along a nearby American river in 1848. He planned to sell the lumber it produced to settlers who were moving into the area. Sutter put James W. Marshall to work building the mill. To install the large water wheel that would power the saw, Marshall first had to deepen the river bed next to the mill. During his digging, he noticed some shiny bits of yellow metal in the water. The result of this accidental find was the California gold rush, which sent thousands of Americans to California, and speeded settlement of the West.

In 1863 the army of Confederate General Robert E. Lee invaded Maryland. The Civil War had been going well for the South. Lee hoped a southern victory on Union soil would convince the British to aid the South in the war. However, a Confederate officer forgot his cigars as his unit left its camp in the Maryland countryside. Wrapped around the cigars was a copy of Lee's battle plans. When a Union soldier came upon the abandoned camp, he spotted the cigars. This chance discovery enabled the Union army to defeat Lee at the Battle of Antietam. The Union victory helped keep the British out of the war. More important, it allowed President Lincoln to issue the Emancipation Proclamation and begin the process of ending slavery in the United States.

Practice the Skill

In April 1865 President Lincoln was assassinated while attending the theater in Washington, D.C. Bodyguard John Parker was stationed outside the door of the president's box. However, Parker left his post to find a seat from which he could watch the play. This allowed the killer to enter the box and shoot the unprotected president.

Write an essay about how this chance event altered the course of history. How might Reconstruction, North–South relations, and African Americans' struggle for equality have been different had Lincoln lived?

CHAPTER 2

Chapter Review

History's Impact
▶ **video series**
Review the video to answer the closing question:
Name three ways the Thirteenth, Fourteenth, and Fifteenth Amendments are related.

Visual Summary

QUICK FACTS

Use the visual summary below to help you review the main ideas of the chapter.

Reform During Reconstruction, the Freedmen's Bureau opened schools for former slaves and performed other services to help the poorest southerners.

Dispute Differing ideas about how to govern the South led to conflicts between African Americans and white southerners, as well as between Republicans and Democrats.

Division After the Compromise of 1877 ended Reconstruction, segregation laws were enacted by southern governments and upheld by the U.S. Supreme Court.

Reviewing Vocabulary, Terms, and People

Complete each sentence by filling in the blank with the correct term or person from the chapter.

1. _______________ were laws that allowed racial segregation in public places.

2. The Radical Republicans were led by _______, a member of Congress from Pennsylvania.

3. The period from 1865 to 1877 that focused on reuniting the nation is known as _______.

4. Following the Civil War, many African Americans in the South made a living by participating in the __________ system.

5. After opposing Congress, Andrew Johnson became the first president to face _____ proceedings.

6. The _____ Amendment made slavery in the United States illegal.

7. In 1870 ________ became the first African American to serve in the U.S. Senate.

Comprehension and Critical Thinking

SECTION 1

8. a. Describe How did the lives of African Americans change after the Civil War?

b. Compare and Contrast How was President Johnson's Reconstruction plan similar and different from President Lincoln's Ten Percent Plan?

c. Evaluate Which of the three Reconstruction plans that were originally proposed do you think would have been the most successful? Why?

SECTION 2

9. a. Identify Who were the Radical Republicans, and how did they change Reconstruction?

b. Analyze How did the debate over the Fourteenth Amendment affect the election of 1866?

c. Elaborate Do you think Congress was right to impeach President Andrew Johnson? Explain.

SECTION 3

10. a. Describe What reforms did Reconstruction governments in the South support?

b. Draw Conclusions In what ways did southern governments attempt to reverse the accomplishments of Reconstruction?

c. Evaluate Do you think the South was successful or unsuccessful in its rebuilding efforts? Explain your answer.

Reviewing Themes

11. Politics Explain the political struggles that took place during Reconstruction.

12. Society and Culture How were the lives of ordinary southerners affected in the years after Reconstruction?

Using the Internet

21ST CENTURY

13. Activity: Drawing Conclusions A challenge for anyone trying to understand Reconstruction is drawing conclusions from primary and secondary sources from the time period. Through your online textbook, rate the credibility of the sources provided. Make sure you explain whether the source is a primary or secondary source, whether you think the source is credible or is not, and the reasons for your thoughts.

hmhsocialstudies.com

Reading Skills

21ST CENTURY

Analyzing Historical Information *Use the Reading Skills taught in this chapter to answer the question about the reading selection below.*

> Radical Republicans, on the other hand, took a harsher stance. They wanted the federal government to force change in the South. Like the moderates, they thought the Black Codes were cruel and unjust.

14. Which of the following is relevant information for the passage above?

a. Thaddeus Stevens was a Radical Republican.

b. Andrew Johnson was a Democrat.

c. Radical Republicans wanted the federal government to make major changes in the South.

d. Radical Republicans were eventually removed from power.

Social Studies Skills

21ST CENTURY

Chance, Oversight, and Error in History *Use the Social Studies Skills taught in this chapter to answer the question about the reading selection below.*

> Johnson's speaking tour was a disaster. It did little to win votes for the Democratic Party. Johnson even got into arguments with people in the audiences of some of his speaking engagements.

15. Which of the following is an example of chance, oversight, or error that affected history?

a. Johnson got into arguments with audiences.

b. The tour was a disaster.

c. The tour did not win votes.

d. Johnson spoke for the Democratic Party.

Focus on Writing

16. Writing a Job History Review your notes about the changing job scene during Reconstruction. Put yourself in the shoes of a person living then. It could be anyone—a returning soldier, a shopkeeper, a schoolteacher, or a politician. What jobs would that person seek? Why would he or she leave one job for another?

Write a brief job history for that person during Reconstruction. Include at least four jobs. Make each job description two to four sentences long. End each one with a sentence or two about why the person left that job. Add one sentence explaining why he or she took the next job. Be sure to include specific historical details.

CHAPTER 2

Standardized Test Practice

DIRECTIONS: Read each question and write the letter of the best response.

1 Use the map below to answer the following question.

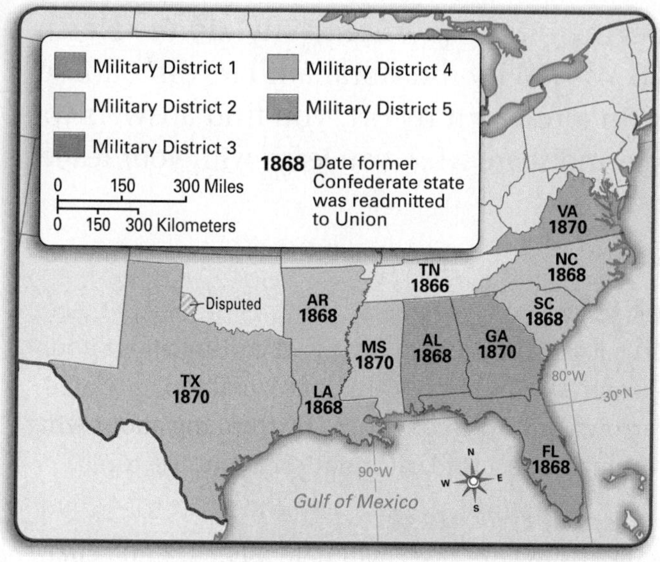

Military District 1
Military District 2
Military District 3
Military District 4
Military District 5
1868 Date former Confederate state was readmitted to Union
0 150 300 Miles
0 150 300 Kilometers
VA 1870
NC 1868
TN 1866
SC 1868
AR 1868
Disputed
GA 1870
MS 1870
AL 1868
TX 1870
LA 1868
80°W
30°N
FL 1868
90°W
N
W
E
S
Gulf of Mexico

Which military district contained the largest number of states?

A Military District 2

B Military District 3

C Military District 4

D Military District 5

2 What can you infer from the map information?

A South Carolina was difficult to reconstruct.

B The largest number of troops was in Military District 1.

C Military District 5 was the last district to end Reconstruction.

D Tennessee was readmitted to the Union before the other southern states.

3 The quickest approach to reuniting the nation was proposed by the

A Ten Percent Plan.

B Wade-Davis Bill.

C Civil Rights Act of 1866.

D Compromise of 1877.

4 What development convinced Republicans in Congress to take control of Reconstruction from the president?

A President Abraham Lincoln was assassinated by a southern sympathizer.

B President Andrew Johnson vetoed the Wade-Davis bill.

C Southern states began passing Black Codes to restrict African Americans' freedoms.

D White southern women refused to support the Fifteenth Amendment.

5 Which of the following limited opportunities for African Americans in the South after Reconstruction ended?

A Ten Percent plan

B Radical Republicans

C Jim Crow laws

D carpetbaggers

6 Examine the following passage from a northern schoolteacher's letter home and then use it to answer the question.

> "Wishing to work where there was the most need—there are so many places where nothing has been done for the freedmen, and where they are sorely persecuted—we came here. A schoolhouse built by the soldiers had just been destroyed by the citizens. The feeling is intensely bitter against anything northern. The affairs of the [Freedmen's] Bureau have been very much mismanaged in Columbus, and our government has been disgraced by the troops who were stationed here."
>
> –Sarah Chase, from *Dear Ones at Home*

Document-Based Question What were some of the problems facing the Freedmen's Bureau in the South?

© Houghton Mifflin Harcourt Publishing Company

21ST CENTURY

Assignment

Collect information and write an informative report on a topic related to the Civil War.

A Social Studies Report

All research begins with a question. Why did the North win the Civil War? Why did Abraham Lincoln choose Ulysses S. Grant? In a research report, you find answers to questions like these and share what you learn with your reader.

TIP **Narrowing the Task** The key to a successful research report is picking a topic that is broad enough that you can find information, but narrow enough that you can cover it in detail. To narrow a subject, focus on one aspect of the larger subject. Then think about whether that one aspect can be broken down into smaller parts. Here's an example of how to narrow a topic:
Too Broad: Civil War Leaders
Less Broad: Civil War Generals
Narrower: Robert E. Lee's Role in the Civil War

1. Prewrite

Choosing a Subject

Since you will spend a lot of time researching and writing about your topic, pick one that interests you. First, think of several topics related to the Civil War. Narrow your list to one topic by thinking about what interests you and where you can find information about the topic.

Developing a Research Question

A guiding question related to your topic will help focus your research. For example, here is a research question for the topic "Robert E. Lee's Role in the Civil War": *How did Lee's decision to turn down the leadership of the Union army affect the Civil War?* The answer to this question becomes the thesis, or the big idea of your report.

Finding Historical Information

Use at least three sources of historical information besides your textbook. Good sources include

- books, maps, magazines, newspapers
- television programs, movies, Internet sites, CD-ROMs.

For each source, write down the kinds of information shown below. When taking notes, put a circled number next to each source.

Encyclopedia article
① "Title of Article." Name of Encyclopedia. Edition or year published.
Book
② Author. Title. City of Publication: Publisher, year published.
Magazine or newspaper article
③ Author. "Title of Article." Publication name. Date: page number(s).
Internet site
④ Author (if known). "Document title." Web site. Date of electronic publication. Date information was accessed <url>.

Taking Notes

As you read the source material, take thorough notes on facts, statistics, comparisons, and quotations. Take special care to spell names correctly and to record dates and facts accurately. If you use a direct quotation from a source, copy it word for word and enclose it in quotation marks. Along with each note, include the number of its source and its page number.

Organizing Your Ideas and Information

Informative research reports are usually organized in one of these ways:

- Chronological order (the order in which events occurred)
- Order of importance
- Causes (actions or situations that make something else happen) and effects (what happened as a result of something else).

Use one of these orders to organize your notes in an outline. Here is a partial outline for a paper on Robert E. Lee.

The Thesis/Big Idea: Robert E. Lee's decision to decline the leadership of the Union army had serious consequences for the path of the Civil War.

I. Lee's Military Expertise
   A. Achievements at the U.S. Military Academy
   B. Achievements during the Mexican War
II. Lee's Personality and Character
   A. Intelligence and strength
   B. Honesty and fairness
   C. Daring and courage
III. Lee's Military Victories
   A. Battle of Fredericksburg
   B. Battle of Chancellorsville

TIP Seeing Different Viewpoints Consult a variety of sources, including those with different points of view on the topic. Reading sources with different opinions will give you a more complete picture of your subject. For example, reading articles about Robert E. Lee written by a southern writer as well as a northern writer may give you a more balanced view of Lee.

TIP Recording Others' Ideas You will be taking three types of notes.
Paraphrases Restatements of all the ideas in your own words.
Summaries Brief restatements of only the most important parts.
Direct quotations The writer's exact words inside quotation marks.

2. Write

You can use this framework to help you write your first draft.

A Writer's Framework

Introduction
- Start with a quote or an interesting historical detail to grab your reader's attention.
- State the main idea of your report.
- Provide any historical background readers need to understand your main idea.

Body
- Present your information under at least three main ideas, using logical order.
- Write at least one paragraph for each of these main ideas.
- Add supporting details, facts, or examples to each paragraph.

Conclusion
- Restate your main idea, using slightly different words.
- Include a general comment about your topic.
- You might comment on how the historical information in your report relates to later historical events.

Studying a Model

Here is a model of a research report. Study it to see how one student developed a paper. The first and the concluding paragraphs are shown in full. The paragraphs in the body of the paper are summarized.

INTRODUCTORY PARAGRAPH

Attention grabber

Statement of thesis

"I cannot raise my hand against my birthplace, my home, my children." With these words, Robert E. Lee changed the course of the Civil War. Abraham Lincoln had turned to Lee as his first choice for commander of the Union army. However, Lee turned Lincoln down, choosing instead to side with his home state of Virginia and take command of the Confederate army. Lee's decision to turn Lincoln down weakened the North and strengthened the Confederates, turning what might have been an easy victory for the North into a long, costly war.

BODY PARAGRAPHS

In the first part of the body, the student points out that Lee graduated from the U.S. Military Academy at West Point, served in the Mexican War, and was a member of the Union army. She goes on to explain that he would have been a strong leader for the North, and his absence made the North weaker.

In the middle of the report, the writer discusses Lee's personality and character. She includes information about the strength of character he showed while in the military academy and while leading the Confederate army. She discusses and gives examples of his intelligence, his daring, his courage, and his honesty.

In the last part of the body of the report, the student provides examples of Lee leading the outnumbered Confederate army to a series of victories. The student provides details of the battles of Fredericksburg and Chancellorsville and explains how a lesser general than Lee may have lost both battles.

CONCLUDING PARAGRAPH

Summary of main points

Restatement of big idea

Lee's brilliant and resourceful leadership bedeviled a series of Union generals. He won battles that most generals would have lost. If Lee had used these skills to lead the larger and more powerful Union army, the Civil War might have ended in months instead of years.

3. Evaluate and Revise

Evaluating and Revising Your Draft

Evaluate your first draft by carefully reading it twice. Ask the questions below to decide which parts of your first draft should be revised.

Evaluation Questions for an Informative Report

- Does the introduction attract the readers' interest and state the big idea/thesis of your report?
- Does the body of your report have at least three paragraphs that develop your big idea? Is the main idea in each paragraph clearly stated?
- Have you included enough information to support each of your main ideas? Are all facts, details, and examples accurate? Are all of them clearly related to the main ideas they support?
- Is the report clearly organized? Does it use chronological order, order of importance, or cause and effect?
- Does the conclusion restate the big idea of your report? Does it end with a general comment about the importance or significance of your topic?
- Have you included at least three sources in your bibliography? Have you included all the sources you used and not any you did not use?

TIP **Organizing Your Time** By creating a schedule and following it, you can avoid that panicky moment when the due date is near and you haven't even started your research. To create your schedule and manage your time, include these six steps.

1 Develop a question and research your topic (10% of your total time).
2 Research and take notes (25%).
3 Write your main idea statement and create an outline (15%).
4 Write a first draft (25%).
5 Evaluate and revise your first draft (15%).
6 Proofread and publish your report (10%).

4. Proofread and Publish

Proofreading

To improve your report before sharing it, check the following:

- The spelling and capitalization of all proper names for people, places, things, and events.
- Punctuation marks around any direct quotation.
- Your list of sources (Works Cited or Bibliography) against a guide to writing research papers. Make sure you follow the examples in the guide when punctuating and capitalizing your source listings.

Publishing

Choose one or more of these ideas to publish your report.

- Share your report with your classmates by turning it into an informative speech.
- Submit your report to an online discussion group that focuses on the Civil War and ask for feedback.
- With your classmates, create a magazine that includes reports on several different topics or post the reports on your school Web site.

5. Practice and Apply

Use the steps and strategies outlined in this workshop to research and write an informative report on the Civil War.

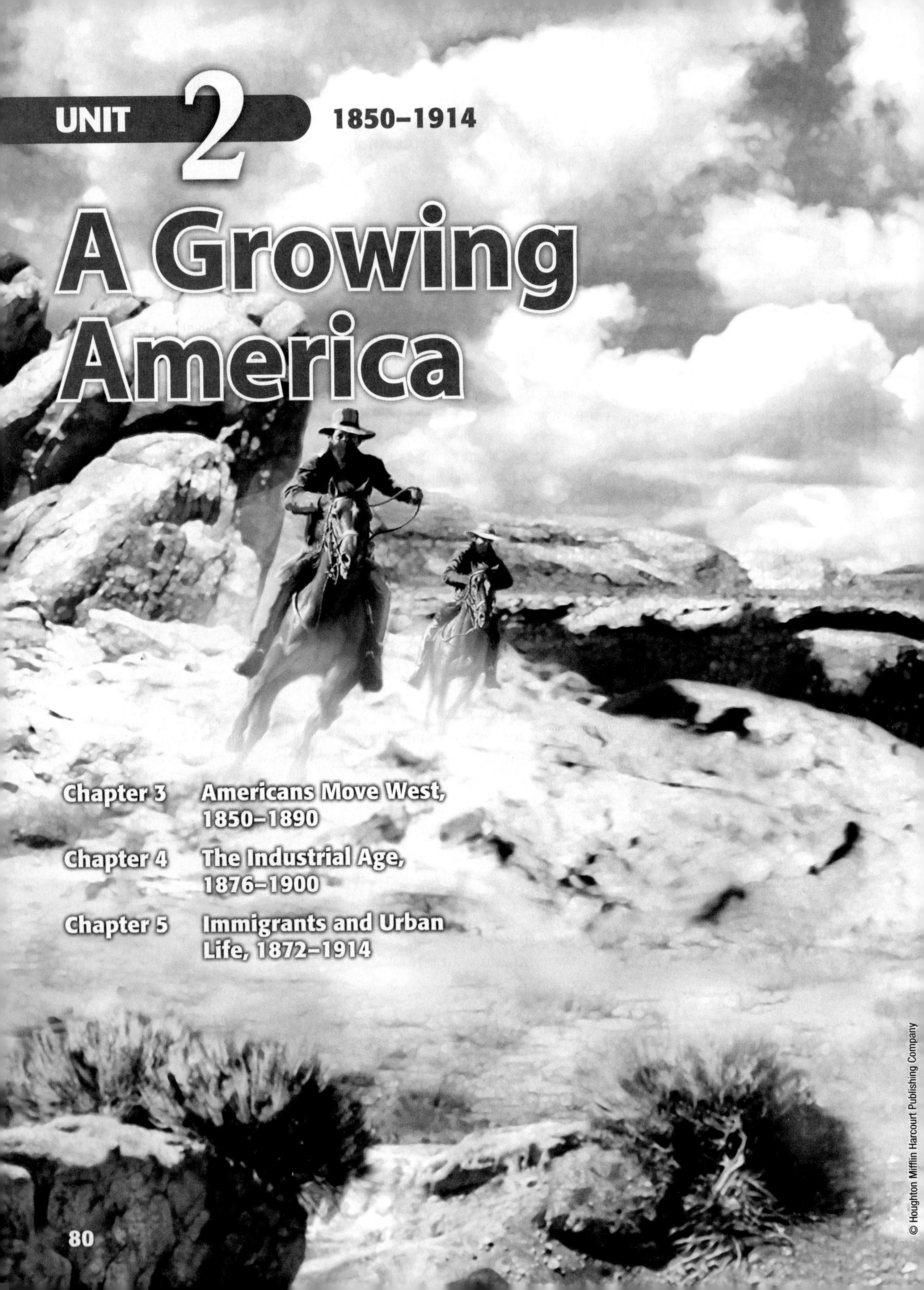

UNIT 2 1850–1914

A Growing America

© Houghton Mifflin Harcourt Publishing Company

What You Will Learn...

After the American Civil War, the United States began a process of building a new economy and political structure. Events in the rest of the world began affecting the nation more noticeably.

During this period of expansion, the U.S. population spread across the continent. New immigrants and new technology began to change life in many parts of the country, especially in cities. As you read, you will learn about changes in the United States that helped the country increase its size, wealth, and power.

Explore the Art

In this picture, a teenage Buffalo Bill Cody flees from bandits on his Pony Express route. How does this picture show the importance of communication in the expansion of the United States?

© Houghton Mifflin Harcourt Publishing Company

CHAPTER 3 1850–1890

Americans Move West

Essential Question What changes occurred in the American West during the late 1800s?

ALABAMA COURSE OF STUDY

1 Explain the impact of industrialization, urbanization, communication, and cultural changes on life in the United States from the late nineteenth century to World War I.

Focus on Writing

Writing a Letter Before telephones and e-mail, one way to communicate with people far away was by letter. In this chapter, you will read about the settlement of the West by European Americans. Suppose you were an Irish immigrant working on a railroad that crossed the Great Plains. What might you have seen or experienced? After you read the chapter, you will write a letter to your sister in Ireland telling her about your experiences.

Wagon trains carried hundreds of thousa
of settlers across the Great Plains.

UNITED STATES

1860 The Pony Express begins delivering mail between East and West.

1850 | 1860

1855 Paris holds a World's Fair.

WORLD

Image Credits: (c), ©James L. Amos/Corbis; (b), Courtesy Wells Fargo Bank

© Houghton Mifflin Harcourt Publishing Company

HISTORY Railroads That Tamed the West

hmhsocialstudies.com VIDEO

10 MILES
OF
TRACK, LAID
IN ONE DAY.
APRIL 28TH 1869

1864 French scientist Louis Pasteur invents the purification process of pasteurization.

1869 The first transcontinental railroad is completed.

1870

1874 Gold is discovered in the Black Hills of the Dakotas.

1879 Thousands of African Americans migrate from the South to Kansas.

1880

ORIENT-EXPRESS
PARIS - VIENNE - CONSTANTINOPLE

1883 The Orient Express railway makes its first run from Paris to Istanbul.

1888 Brazil abolishes slavery.

1890 The Massacre at Wounded Knee occurs.

1890

Image Credits: (c), ©James L. Amos/Corbis; (br), The Granger Collection, New York; (cr), ©Corbis; (cl), Southern Pacific Lines/Courtesy of Picture Research Consultants, Inc.; (bl), ©The Gallery Collection/Corbis

© Houghton Mifflin Harcourt Publishing Company

Reading Social Studies

Economics | **Geography** | Politics | Society and Culture | Science and Technology

Focus on Themes In this chapter you will follow the development of the United States from the mid-1800s through the 1890s. You will learn that California was admitted to the Union in 1850. You will find out about the struggles that people faced as the movement West continued and people settled the Great Plains. You will learn about the **technological** advancements made during this time as well as the difficult **geographical** obstacles miners and ranchers faced in the West.

Understanding through Questioning

Focus on Reading When newspaper reporters want to get to the heart of a story, they ask certain questions: who, what, when, where, why, and how. When you are reading a history book, you can use the same questions to get to the heart of what happened in the past.

Hypothetical Questions You can also use questions to dig deeper than what is in the text. You can ask hypothetical, or what if, questions. These questions ask what might have happened had events occurred differently. Sometimes asking such questions can help history come alive.

In 1862 Congress passed two important land grant acts that helped open the West to settlers. The Homestead Act gave government-owned land to small farmers. Any adult who was a U.S. citizen or planned to become one could receive 160 acres of land. In exchange, homesteaders promised to live on the land for five years. The Morrill Act granted more than 17 million acres of federal land to the states.

Who?
Congress

Where?
the West

How?
Congress gave land to anyone who agreed to settle on it for five years.

What?
encouraged new settlement

When?
1862

Why?
Perhaps Congress feared what would happen to western lands if they remained unsettled by U.S. citizens.

What if?
If Congress had not passed these laws, U.S. citizens might not have moved West. The United States might not have grown as quickly as it did.

© Houghton Mifflin Harcourt Publishing Company

21st Century

You Try It!

Read the following passage and then answer the questions below.

Building Communities

Women were an important force in the settlement of the frontier. They joined in the hard work of farming and ranching and helped build communities out of the widely spaced farms and small towns. Their role in founding communities facilitated a strong voice in public affairs. Wyoming women, for example, were granted the vote in the new state's constitution, which was approved in 1869. Annie Bidwell, one of the founders of Chico, California, used her influence to support a variety of moral and social causes such as women's suffrage and temperance.

Answer these questions based on the passage you just read.

1. Who is this passage about?
2. What did they do?
3. When did they do this?
4. How do you think they accomplished it?
5. Why do you think they were able to accomplish so much?
6. How can knowing this information help you understand the past?
7. What if women in the West had been given more rights? Fewer rights? How might the West have been different?

As you read this chapter, ask questions like *who, what, when, where, why, how,* and *what if* to help you analyze what you are reading.

Key Terms and People

Chapter 3

Section 1
frontier
Comstock Lode
boomtowns
Cattle Kingdom
cattle drive
Chisholm Trail
Pony Express
transcontinental railroad

Section 2
Treaty of Fort Laramie
reservations
Crazy Horse
Treaty of Medicine Lodge
buffalo soldiers
George Armstrong Custer
Sitting Bull
Battle of the Little Bighorn
Massacre at Wounded Knee
Long Walk
Geronimo
Ghost Dance
Sarah Winnemucca
Dawes General Allotment Act

Section 3
Homestead Act
Morrill Act
Exodusters
sodbusters
dry farming
Annie Bidwell
National Grange
deflation
William Jennings Bryan
Populist Party

Academic Vocabulary

In this chapter, you will learn the following academic words:

establish
facilitate

© Houghton Mifflin Harcourt Publishing Company

SECTION 1

Miners, Ranchers, and Railroads

What You Will Learn...

Main Ideas

1. A mining boom brought growth to the West.
2. The demand for cattle created a short-lived Cattle Kingdom on the Great Plains.
3. East and West were connected by the transcontinental railroad.

The Big Idea

As more settlers moved West, mining, ranching, and railroads soon transformed the western landscape.

Key Terms

frontier
Comstock Lode
boomtowns
Cattle Kingdom
cattle drive
Chisholm Trail
Pony Express
transcontinental railroad

hmhsocialstudies.com
TAKING NOTES

Use the graphic organizer online to take notes on the kinds of economic opportunities that people found in the West.

If YOU were there...

You are a cowboy in Texas in 1875. You love life on the open range, the quiet nights, and the freedom. You even like the hard work of the long cattle drives to Kansas. But you know that times are changing. Homesteaders are moving in and fencing off their lands. Some of the older cowboys say it's time to settle down and buy a small ranch. You hope that they're not right.

What would make you give up a cowboy's life?

BUILDING BACKGROUND In the years following the Civil War, the U.S. population grew rapidly. Settlements in the West increased. More discoveries of gold and silver attracted adventurers, while the open range drew others. Thousands of former Civil War soldiers also joined the move West.

Mining Boom Brings Growth

During the years surrounding the War, most Americans had thought of the Great Plains and other western lands as the Great American Desert. In the years following the Civil War, Americans witnessed the rapid growth of the U.S. population and the spread of settlements throughout the West. With the admission of the state of California to the Union in 1850, the western boundary of the American **frontier**—an undeveloped area—had reached the Pacific Ocean.

The frontier changed dramatically as more and more people moved westward. Settlers built homes, fenced off land, and laid out ranches and farms. Miners, ranchers, and farmers remade the landscape of the West as they adapted to their new surroundings. The geography of the West was further changed by the development and expansion of a large and successful railroad industry that moved the West's natural resources to eastern markets. Gold and silver were the most valuable natural resources, and mining companies used the growing railroad network to bring these precious metals to the East.

© Houghton Mifflin Harcourt Publishing Company

Causes and Effects of Westward Expansion

QUICK FACTS

Causes
- New land for settlers and ranchers
- Mineral resources
- Businesses to support settlers, ranchers, and miners
- Immigration

Effects
- New towns
- Railroads across the continent
- Cattle Kingdom

ANALYSIS SKILL INTERPRETING CHARTS

What three economic activities attracted people to the West?

Posters like this one were designed to persuade people to move West.

Big Business

Most of the precious metals were located in western Nevada. In 1859 miner Henry Comstock discovered a huge deposit of gold and silver in Nevada that became called the **Comstock Lode**. The deposit was incredibly rich and deep. In just the first year after its discovery, the Comstock Lode lured thousands of California miners to Nevada. Over the next 20 years, the Comstock Lode produced more than $500 million worth of gold and silver.

Expensive equipment was needed to remove the silver and gold that were trapped within quartz rock. Larger mining companies bought up land claims from miners who could not afford this machinery. As a result, mining became a big business in the West.

As companies dug bigger and deeper mines, the work became more dangerous. Miners had to use unsafe equipment, such as elevator platforms without protective walls. They worked in dark tunnels and breathed hot, stuffy air. They suffered from lung disease caused by dusty air. Miners often were injured or killed by poorly planned explosions or by cave-ins. Fire was also a great danger. Mining was therefore one of the most dangerous jobs in the country. In the West, worries about safety and pay led miners to form several unions in the 1860s.

Settlers

People from all over the world came to work in the western mines. Some miners came from the eastern United States. Others emigrated from Europe, Central and South America, and Asia. Many Mexican immigrants and Mexican Americans were experienced miners. They were skilled in assaying, or testing, the contents of valuable ore. One newspaper reporter wrote, "Here were congregated the most varied elements of humanity . . . belonging to almost every nationality and every status of life."

© Houghton Mifflin Harcourt Publishing Company • Image Credits: (tr), California, Cornucopia of the World, published by Rand McNally & Co., c.1870 (colour litho), American School, (19th century)/©Collection of the New-York Historical Society, USA/The Bridgeman Art Library International

New Towns

Mining booms also produced **boomtowns**, communities that grew suddenly when a mine opened. They disappeared just as quickly when the mine closed. Most boomtowns had general stores, saloons, and boardinghouses.

Few women or families lived in boomtowns. "I was never so lonely and homesick in all my life," wrote one young woman. Women washed, cooked, made clothes, and chopped wood. They also raised families, **established** schools, and wrote for newspapers. Their work helped turn some mining camps into successful, permanent towns.

ACADEMIC VOCABULARY
establish to set up or create

READING CHECK **Summarizing** What risks did miners face?

The Cattle Kingdom

The cattle industry was another area of rapid growth. Following the Civil War, a growing economy and population created a greater demand for beef in the East. Cattle worth $3 to $6 each in Texas could be sold for $38 each in Kansas. In New York, they could be sold for $80 each. The most popular breed of cattle was the longhorn. The longhorn spread quickly throughout western Texas. Because these animals needed very little water and could survive harsh weather, they were well-suited to the dry, desert-like environment of western Texas. But how could Texas ranchers move the longhorns to eastern markets?

In 1867 businessman Joseph McCoy discovered a solution. He built pens for cattle in the small town of Abilene, Kansas. The Kansas

Myth and Reality in the Wild West

No episode in American history has given rise to as many myths as the Wild West. Writers of dime novels, popular in the East, helped created the myths in the years after the Civil War. Even today, popular books, television shows, and movies continue to portray the West in ways that are more myth than reality.

Myth: The cowboy was a free-spirited individual.

Reality: Most cowboys were employees. Many joined labor unions and even went on strike.

Myth: Western cowtowns were wild places where cowboys had gunfights, and there was little law and order.

Reality: Most were orderly cities with active law enforcement. Showdowns rarely, if ever, occurred.

Myth: Almost all cowboys were Anglo Americans.

Reality: About 25 percent of cowboys were African Americans, and 12 percent were Hispanic.

© Houghton Mifflin Harcourt Publishing Company • Image Credits: (l), Denver Public Library, Western History Collection; (r), The Granger Collection, New York

Pacific Railroad line went through Abilene. As a result, cattle could be shipped by rail from there. Soon, countless Texas ranchers were making the trip north to Abilene to sell their herds of cattle.

Around the same time, cattle ranching began to expand in the Midwest. The Great Plains from Texas to Canada, where many ranchers raised cattle in the late 1800s, became known as the **Cattle Kingdom**. Ranchers grazed huge herds on public land called the open range. The land had once been occupied by Plains Indians and buffalo herds.

Importance of Cowboys

The workers who took care of the ranchers' cattle were known as cowhands or cowboys. They borrowed many techniques and tools from vaqueros (bah-KER-ohs), Mexican ranch hands who cared for cattle and horses. From vaqueros came the western saddle and the lariat—a rope used for lassoing cattle. The cowboys also borrowed the vaqueros' broad felt hat. However, they changed it into the familiar high-peaked cowboy hat.

One of the cowboy's most important and dangerous duties was the **cattle drive**. On these long journeys, cowboys herded cattle to the market or to the northern Plains for grazing. The trips usually lasted several months and covered hundreds of miles. The **Chisholm Trail**, which ran from San Antonio, Texas, to the cattle town of Abilene, Kansas, was one of the earliest and most popular routes for cattle drives. It was blazed, or marked, by Texas cowboy Jesse Chisholm in the late 1860s.

At times, rowdy cowboys made life in cattle towns rough and violent. There were rarely shoot-outs in the street, but there was often disorderly behavior. Law officials such as Wyatt Earp became famous for keeping the peace in cattle towns.

hmhsocialstudies.com
ANIMATED GEOGRAPHY
Cattle Drive Trails

Marshal Wyatt Earp

Deadwood, South Dakota

© Houghton Mifflin Harcourt Publishing Company • Image Credits: (r), The Granger Collection, New York; (inset), ©Bettmann/Corbis

End of the Open Range

As the cattle business boomed, ranchers faced more competition for use of the open range. Farmers began to buy range land on the Great Plains where cattle had once grazed. Small ranchers also began competing with large ranchers for land. Then in 1874, the invention of barbed wire allowed westerners to fence off large amounts of land cheaply. The competition between farmers, large ranchers, and small ranchers increased. This competition led to range wars, or fights for access to land.

FOCUS ON READING
Ask yourself questions about the information in this paragraph to help you understand the competition between farmers and ranchers.

Making matters worse, in 1885 and 1886, disaster struck the Cattle Kingdom. The huge cattle herds on the Plains had eaten most of the prairie grass. Unusually severe winters in both years made the ranching situation even worse. Thousands of cattle died, and many ranchers were ruined financially. The Cattle Kingdom had come to an end.

READING CHECK **Drawing Conclusions**
Why did the Cattle Kingdom come to an end?

The Transcontinental Railroad

As more Americans began moving West, the need to send goods and information between the East and West increased. Americans searched for ways to improve communication and travel across the country.

In 1860 a system of messengers on horseback called the **Pony Express** began to carry messages west. The messengers carried mail between relay stations on a route about 2,000 miles long. However, telegraph lines, which sent messages faster, quickly put the Pony Express out of business.

Some Americans wanted to build a **transcontinental railroad**—a railroad that would cross the continent and connect the East to the West. The federal government, therefore, passed the Pacific Railway Acts in 1862 and in 1864. These acts gave railroad companies loans and large land grants that could be sold to pay for construction costs. Congress had granted more than 131 million acres of public land to railroad companies. In exchange, the government asked the railroads to carry U.S. mail and troops at a lower cost. Many railroad companies were inspired to begin laying miles of tracks.

Great Race

Two companies, the Central Pacific and the Union Pacific, led the race to complete the transcontinental railroad. In February 1863, the Central Pacific began building east from Sacramento, California. At the end of the year, the Union Pacific started building west from Omaha, Nebraska.

The Union Pacific hired thousands of railroad workers, particularly Irish immigrants. Chinese immigrants made up some 85 percent of the Central Pacific workforce. The railroad's part-owner Leland Stanford praised them, but he paid them less than other laborers. Chinese crews also were given the most dangerous tasks and had to work longer hours than other railroad laborers. They took the job, however, because the $30 a month

Routes West, 1870

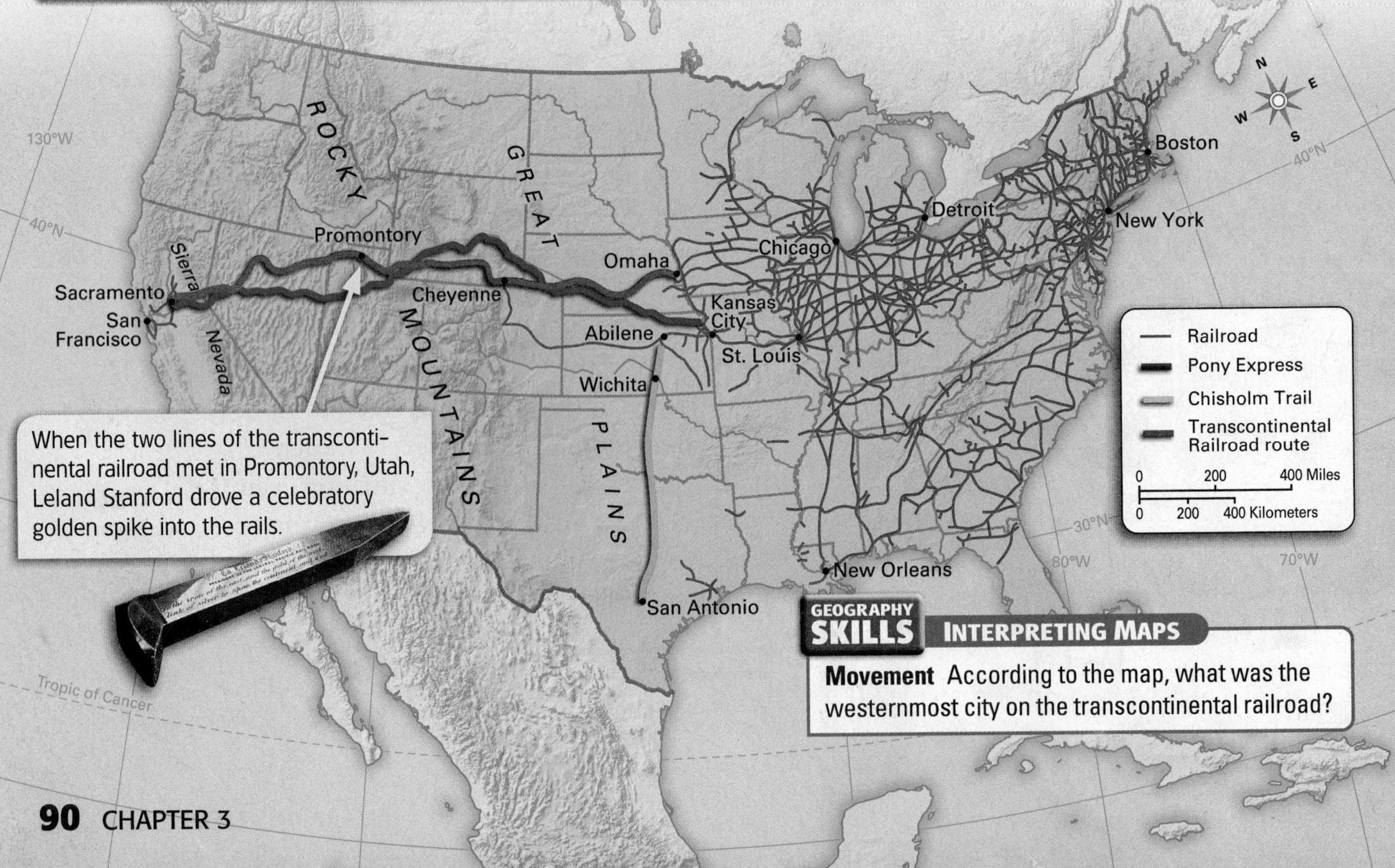

When the two lines of the transcontinental railroad met in Promontory, Utah, Leland Stanford drove a celebratory golden spike into the rails.

GEOGRAPHY SKILLS **INTERPRETING MAPS**

Movement According to the map, what was the westernmost city on the transcontinental railroad?

© Houghton Mifflin Harcourt Publishing Company • Image Credits: (inset), ©James L. Amos/Corbis that the Central Pacific paid was as much as 10 times what they could earn in China.

Railroad companies faced many geographic challenges. For example, workers for Central Pacific struggled to cross the Sierra Nevada mountain range in California. Breaking apart its rock formations required setting carefully controlled explosions using large amounts of blasting powder and the explosive nitroglycerin. And in the winter of 1866, snowdrifts more than 60 feet high trapped and killed dozens of workers. Faced with these obstacles, the Central Pacific took four years to lay the first 115 miles of track.

Meanwhile, Union Pacific workers faced harsh weather on the Great Plains. In addition, the company pressured them to work at a rapid pace—at times laying 250 miles of track in six months.

For both railroad companies, providing food and supplies for workers was vital. This job became more difficult in remote areas. The railroad companies consequently often relied on local resources. Professional hunters, such as William "Buffalo Bill" Cody, shot thousands of buffalo to feed Union Pacific workers.

Golden Spike

Congress required the two completed rail lines to connect at Promontory, Utah. On May 10, 1869, a golden spike was used to connect the railroad tie joining the two tracks. Alexander Toponce witnessed the event.

> "Governor Stanford, president of the Central Pacific, took the sledge [hammer], and the first time he struck he missed the spike and hit the rail. What a howl went up! Irish, Chinese, Mexicans, and everybody yelled with delight. 'He missed it' . . . Then Stanford tried it again and tapped the spike."
>
> —Alexander Toponce, quoted in *A Treasury of Railroad Folklore*, edited by B. A. Botkin and Alvin F. Harlo

The railroad companies were not finished, though. Following completion of the transcontinental railroad, companies continued building railroads until the West was crisscrossed with rail lines.

The Central Pacific and Union Pacific connected their tracks at Promontory, Utah, in 1869, completing the transcontinental railroad.

© Houghton Mifflin Harcourt Publishing Company • Image Credits: (b) ©Bettmann/Corbis

QUICK FACTS

Effects of the Transcontinental Railroad

- Increased settlement of the West
- Increased business activity and East-West trade
- Helped make the railroad industry one of the most powerful in the country

Results of the Railroad

The transcontinental railroad increased both economic growth and the population in the West. Railroad companies provided better transportation for people and goods. They also sold land to settlers, which encouraged people to move West.

THE IMPACT TODAY

Today's businesses ship goods across the country using railroads, the interstate highway system, and airplanes.

New railroads helped businesses. Western timber companies, miners, ranchers, and farmers shipped wood, metals, meat, and grain east by railroad. In exchange, eastern businesses shipped manufactured goods to the West. As trade between regions increased, the idea that the U.S. economy was interdependent became more widespread. Even perceptions of time became more formal as railroad schedules began to unite areas that had before existed under different times. Four continental time zones were established in 1883.

Railroad companies encouraged people to put their money into the railroad business, which they did—sometimes unwisely. Railroad speculation and the collapse of railroad owner Jay Cooke's banking firm helped start the Panic of 1873. By the 1880s, many small western railroads were deeply in debt. Despite such setbacks, Americans remained interested in railroad investments. By 1890 there were about 164,000 more miles of track in operation than in 1865. Railroads had become one of the biggest industries in the United States.

READING CHECK **Finding Main Ideas** How did the railroad affect the development of the West?

SUMMARY In this section you learned about the increased settlement of the West.

Section 1 Assessment

hmhsocialstudies.com ONLINE QUIZ

Reviewing Ideas, Terms, and People

1. **a. Recall** Why did Americans move West in the years following the Civil War?
   b. Draw Conclusions What effect did the discovery of the **Comstock Lode** have on the West?
   c. Evaluate Do you think women were important to the success of mining towns? Why or why not?
2. **a. Recall** What led to the cattle boom in the West?
   b. Analyze Why was there competition between ranchers and farmers to settle in the Great Plains?
   c. Evaluate What played the biggest role in ending the **Cattle Kingdom**? Why?
3. **a. Recall** When and where did the Union Pacific and Central Pacific lines meet?
   b. Make Generalizations How do you think the **transcontinental railroad** improved people's lives?

Critical Thinking

4. **Comparing** Review your notes about opportunities in the West. Then use a graphic organizer like the one below to list the effects of these opportunities.

Opportunity	Effect

Focus on Writing

5. **Taking Notes on Mining, Ranching, and the Railroads** As you read this section, take notes on how mining, ranching, and railroads changed the West. How might a railroad worker feel about these changes?

© Houghton Mifflin Harcourt Publishing Company • Image Credits: (t), The Granger Collection, New York

Wars for the West

SECTION 2

If YOU were there...

You are a member of the Sioux nation, living in Dakota Territory in 1875. These lands are sacred to your people, and the U.S. government has promised them to you. But now gold has been found here, and the government has ordered you to give up your land. Some Sioux leaders want to fight. Others say that it is of no use, that the soldiers will win.

Would you fight to keep your lands? Why?

BUILDING BACKGROUND Miners, ranchers, and farmers all moved West in the years after the Civil War. The arrival of settlers and the U.S. army to the Great Plains meant the end of the way of life of the Indians who lived there. The coming of the railroad began this destruction, with the killing of thousands of buffalo. Treaties were made but did not protect Indian lands from settlers.

Settlers Encounter the Plains Indians

As miners and settlers began crossing the Great Plains in the mid-1800s, they pressured the federal government for more access to western lands. To protect these travelers, U.S. officials sent agents to negotiate treaties with the Plains Indians.

The Plains Indians lived in the Great Plains, which stretch north into Canada and south into Texas. Indian groups such as the Apache and the Comanche lived in and around Texas and

The Plains Indians depended on two animals—the horse and the buffalo.

What You Will Learn...

Main Ideas

1. As settlers moved to the Great Plains, they encountered the Plains Indians.
2. The U.S. Army and Native Americans fought in the northern plains, the Southwest, and the Far West.
3. Despite efforts to reform U.S. policy toward Native Americans, conflict continued.

The Big Idea

Native Americans and the U.S. government came into conflict over land in the West.

Key Terms and People

Treaty of Fort Laramie
reservations
Crazy Horse
Treaty of Medicine Lodge
buffalo soldiers
George Armstrong Custer
Sitting Bull
Battle of the Little Bighorn
Massacre at Wounded Knee
Long Walk
Geronimo
Ghost Dance
Sarah Winnemucca
Dawes General Allotment Act

hmhsocialstudies.com TAKING NOTES

Use the graphic organizer online to take notes on the major events in Native Americans' loss of land rights.

© Houghton Mifflin Harcourt Publishing Company • Image Credits: (b), SuperStock what is now Oklahoma. The Cheyenne and the Arapaho lived in different regions across the central Plains. The Pawnee lived in parts of Nebraska. To the north were the Sioux. These groups spoke many different languages. However, they used a common sign language to communicate and they shared a similar lifestyle.

Hunting Buffalo

For survival, Plains Indians depended on two animals—the horse and the buffalo. The Spanish brought horses to America in the 1500s. Plains Indians learned to ride horses, and hunters used them to follow buffalo herds year-round. While on horseback, most Plains Indian hunters used a short bow and arrows to shoot buffalo from close range.

Plains Indians used buffalo for food, shelter, clothing, utensils, and tools. Women dried buffalo meat to make jerky. They made tepees and clothing from buffalo hides, and cups and tools from buffalo horns. As one Sioux explained, "When our people killed a buffalo, all of the animal was utilized [used] in some manner; nothing was wasted." The Plains Indians prospered. By 1850, some 75,000 Native Americans lived on the Plains.

Struggle to Keep Land

Miners and settlers were also increasing in numbers—and they wanted Indians' land. The U.S. government tried to avoid disputes by negotiating the **Treaty of Fort Laramie**, the first major treaty between the U.S. government and Plains Indians. Two years later, several southern Plains nations signed a treaty at Fort Atkinson in Nebraska. These treaties recognized Indian claims to most of the Great Plains. They also allowed the United States to build forts and roads and to travel across Indian homelands. The U.S. government promised to pay for any damages to Indian lands.

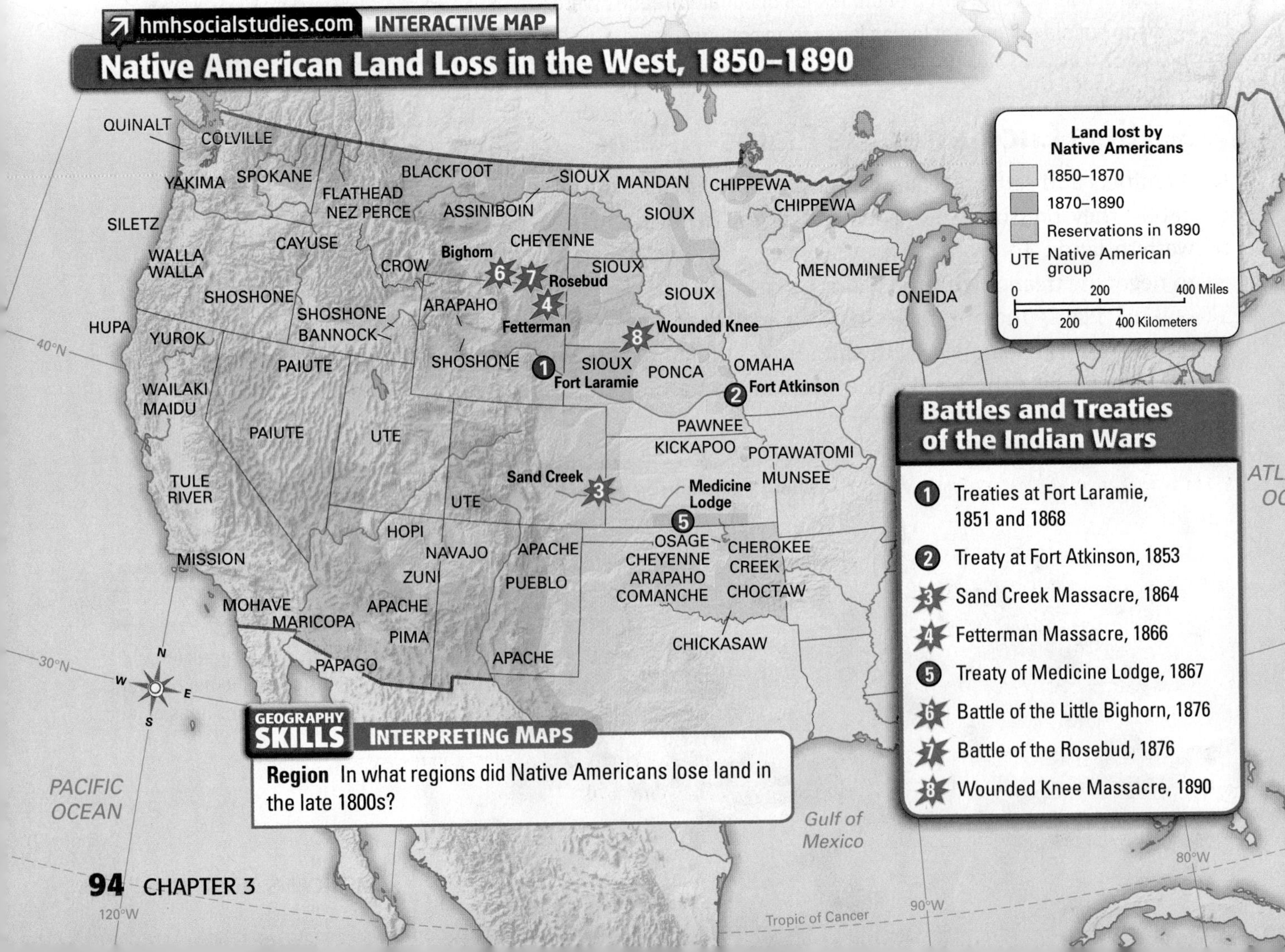

GEOGRAPHY SKILLS INTERPRETING MAPS

Region In what regions did Native Americans lose land in the late 1800s?

© Houghton Mifflin Harcourt Publishing Company

LINKING TO TODAY

Tribal Councils

Native Americans have long held tribal councils to make decisions on behalf of the group. Today this tradition of Native American government continues. There are more than 500 tribal governments in the United States. Tribal governments provide a wide range of services, including law enforcement, health care, and education. Here, a member of the Blackfoot Tribal Council addresses the Montana state legislature.

ANALYSIS SKILL ANALYZING INFORMATION

What types of services do tribal governments provide?

The treaties did not keep the peace for long. In 1858 the discovery of gold in what is now Colorado brought thousands of miners to the West. They soon clashed with the Cheyenne and the Arapaho. In 1861 the U.S. government negotiated new treaties with Plains Indians. These treaties created **reservations**, areas of federal land set aside for Native Americans. The government expected Indians to stay on the reservations, which made hunting buffalo almost impossible.

Pioneers and miners continued to cross the Great Plains. Many miners used the Bozeman Trail. To protect them, the U.S. Army built forts along the trail, which ran through favored Sioux hunting grounds. The Sioux responded with war. In late 1866, **Crazy Horse** and a group of Sioux ambushed and killed 81 cavalry troops.

In 1868, under the Second Treaty of Fort Laramie, the government agreed to close the Bozeman Trail, abandon the forts, and provide reservation land to the Sioux.

The U.S. government also negotiated for southern Plains Indians to move off their land. In the 1867 **Treaty of Medicine Lodge**, most southern Plains Indians agreed to live on reservations. However, many Indians did not want to give up their hunting grounds. Fighting soon broke out between the Comanche and Texans. The U.S. Army and the Texas Rangers were unable to defeat the Comanche, so they cut off the Comanche's access to food and water. In 1875 the last of the Comanche war leaders surrendered.

READING CHECK **Summarizing** What was the federal policy toward the Plains Indians in the 1860s and 1870s?

© Houghton Mifflin Harcourt Publishing Company • Image Credits: (t), ©George Lane/AP/Wide World Photos

Two Views of a Historic Battle

The Native Americans are shown surrounding a small force of U.S. soldiers.
General Custer is shown standing among his men as he fires.

CONNECT TO THE ARTS

Art historians have identified about 1,000 paintings of the Battle of the Little Bighorn. The painting on this page was painted in 1899. The painting on the next page is one of the many colored-pencil drawings of the battle done by Amos Bad Heart Buffalo, who based his drawing on memories from Sioux warriors who participated in the battle.

How do these paintings show the influences of different cultures?

Fighting on the Plains

In the northern Plains, Southwest, and Far West, Native Americans continued to resist being moved to and confined on reservations. The U.S. government sent troops, including African American cavalry, whom the Indians called **buffalo soldiers**, into the area to force the Indians to leave.

Battles on the Northern Plains

As fighting on the southern Plains came to an end, new trouble started in the north. In 1874 Lieutenant Colonel **George Armstrong Custer**'s soldiers discovered gold in the Black Hills of the Dakotas. **Sitting Bull**, a leader of the Lakota Sioux, protested U.S. demands for the land.

HISTORY

VIDEO
Sitting Bull: Chief of the Lakota Nation

hmhsocialstudies.com

"What treaty that the whites have kept has the red man broken? Not one. What treaty that the white man ever made with us have they kept? Not one."

—Sitting Bull, quoted in *Touch the Earth* by T. C. McLuhan

Other Sioux leaders listened to Sitting Bull and refused to give up land. Fighting soon broke out between the army and the Sioux.

On June 25, 1876, Custer's scouts found a Sioux camp along the Little Bighorn River in Montana Territory. Leading 264 of his soldiers, Custer raced ahead without waiting for any supporting forces. In the **Battle of the Little Bighorn**, Sioux forces led by Crazy Horse and Sitting Bull surrounded and defeated Custer and his troops. Newspapers called the battle "Custer's Last Stand" because his entire command was killed. It was the worst defeat the U.S. Army suffered in the West. The Battle of the Little Bighorn was also the Sioux's last major victory.

In 1881 Sitting Bull and a few followers returned from Canada where they had moved. They had run out of food during the hard winter. They joined the Sioux on Standing Rock Reservation in Dakota Territory.

© Houghton Mifflin Harcourt Publishing Company • Image Credits: (t), ©Bettmann/Corbis

The U.S. Army is shown on horseback in this painting.
These horses have been captured by the Native Americans.

Almost a decade later, in 1890, while following orders to arrest Sitting Bull, reservation police killed him. Many Sioux left the reservations in protest. Later that year, the U.S. Army shot and killed about 150 Sioux near Wounded Knee Creek in South Dakota. This **Massacre at Wounded Knee** was the last major incident on the Great Plains.

Southwest

The Navajo lived in what became Arizona and New Mexico. In 1863 the Navajo refused to settle on a reservation. In response, U.S. troops made raids on the Navajo's fields, homes, and livestock.

When the Navajo ran out of food and shelter, they started surrendering to the U.S. Army. In 1864 the army led Navajo captives on the **Long Walk**. On this 300-mile march the Navajo were forced to walk across the desert to a reservation in Bosque Redondo, New Mexico. Along the way, countless Navajo died.

Far West

The United States had promised to let the peaceful Nez Percé keep their land in Oregon. Within a few years, however, the government ordered the Nez Percé to a reservation in what is now Idaho. Before leaving, a few angry Nez Percé killed some local settlers and tried to escape to Canada. Near the border, U.S. troops overtook them and sent them to a reservation in what is now Oklahoma.

Final Battles

By the 1880s, most Native Americans had stopped fighting. The Apache of the Southwest, however, continued to battle the U.S. Army. A Chiricahua Apache named **Geronimo** and his band of raiders avoided capture for many years. In September 1886 Geronimo surrendered, ending the Apache armed resistance.

READING CHECK **Contrasting** How did the Apache resistance differ from that of the Navajo?

© Houghton Mifflin Harcourt Publishing Company • Image Credits: (tl), ©Bettmann/Corbis; (tr), ©Stapleton Collection/Corbis

Conflict Continues

By the 1870s, many Native Americans lived on reservations, where land was usually not useful for farming or buffalo hunting. Many Indians were starving.

A Paiute Indian named Wovoka began a religious movement, the **Ghost Dance**, that predicted the arrival of paradise for Native Americans. In this paradise, the buffalo herds would return and the settlers would disappear.

U.S. officials did not understand the meaning of the Ghost Dance. They feared it would lead to rebellion, so they tried to end the movement, which had spread to other groups, including the Sioux. After the massacre in 1890 at Wounded Knee, the Ghost Dance movement gradually died out.

In the late 1870s, a Paiute Indian named **Sarah Winnemucca** called for reform. She gave lectures on problems of the reservation system. Writer Helen Hunt Jackson published a book that pushed for reform of U.S. Indian policy in 1881.

Sarah Winnemucca spoke out for the fair treatment of her people.

Some reformers believed that Native Americans should adopt the ways of white people. The **Dawes General Allotment Act** of 1887 tried to lessen traditional influences on Indian society by making land ownership private rather than shared. The act also promised—but failed to deliver—U.S. citizenship to Native Americans. After breaking up reservation land, the government sold the acreage remaining. The Act took about two-thirds of Indian land.

READING CHECK **Evaluating** How did reformers try to influence Native Americans' lives?

SUMMARY In this section you read about conflict in the settlement of the West.

Section 2 Assessment

hmhsocialstudies.com
ONLINE QUIZ

Reviewing Ideas, Terms, and People

1. a. **Describe** What animals did Plains Indians depend on, and how did they use those animals?
   b. **Analyze** How did U.S. policy toward the Plains Indians change in the late 1850s?
   c. **Elaborate** Would you have agreed to move to a **reservation**? Why or why not?
2. a. **Describe** What events led to the **Battle of the Little Bighorn**?
   b. **Elaborate** Why do you think most Indian groups eventually stopped resisting the United States?
3. a. **Describe** How did the **Dawes General Allotment Act** affect American Indians?
   b. **Predict** What effect do you think the **Massacre at Wounded Knee** would have on relations between Plains Indians and the United States?

Critical Thinking

4. **Identifying Cause and Effect** Review your notes about Native American land losses. Organize the events in a time line like the one below.

1851 1864 1867 1887

Focus on Writing

5. **Reading about the Wars for the West** As you read this section, take notes on the wars between the U.S. government and the Plains Indians. How might a railroad worker have experienced these conflicts?

© Houghton Mifflin Harcourt Publishing Company • Image Credits: (t), The Granger Collection, New York

BIOGRAPHY

Chief Joseph

What would you do to protect your home and your ways of life?

When did he live? 1840–1904

Where did he live? Chief Joseph lived in the Wallowa Valley, the Nez Percé homeland, in present-day Oregon.

What did he do? Chief Joseph led his people in an effort to hold on to the Nez Percé homeland and to avoid war with the United States. For years, Joseph and a band of Nez Percé refused to move as white settlers moved into the valley. Finally, after being threatened with attack, Joseph gave in. An army led by General Oliver Otis Howard eventually chased the Nez Percé across Idaho, Wyoming, and Montana. They were sent to a reservation in what is now Oklahoma, where many died.

Why is he so important? Chief Joseph's surrender speech earned him a place in American history. The band of 700 people, including only 200 warriors, made a courageous three-month, 1,400-mile trek, hoping to cross into Canada for protection. Exhausted, hungry, and freezing, Joseph's people collapsed just short of the Canadian border. In later years, the chief spoke about what had happened.

Cause and Effect What brought suffering to Chief Joseph and his people?

Chief Joseph of the Nez Percé nation tried to protect his people from the advancement of white settlers.

© Houghton Mifflin Harcourt Publishing Company

Speech

"I am tired of fighting. Our chiefs are killed . . . The old men are all dead . . . It is cold, and we have no blankets. The little children are freezing to death. My people, some of them, have run away to the hills, and have no blankets, no food. No one knows where they are—perhaps freezing to death. I want to have time to look for my children, and see how many of them I can find. Maybe I shall find them among the dead. Hear me, my chiefs! I am tired. My heart is sick and sad. From where the sun now stands I will fight no more forever."

—Chief Joseph of the Nez Percé, surrender speech, October 5, 1877

SECTION 3

Farming and Populism

What You Will Learn...

Main Ideas

1. Many Americans started new lives on the Great Plains.
2. Economic challenges led to the creation of farmers' political groups.
3. By the 1890s, the western frontier had come to an end.

The Big Idea

Settlers on the Great Plains created new communities and unique political groups.

Key Terms and People

Homestead Act
Morrill Act
Exodusters
sodbusters
dry farming
Annie Bidwell
National Grange
deflation
William Jennings Bryan
Populist Party

hmhsocialstudies.com
TAKING NOTES

Use the graphic organizer online to take notes on the reasons for the rise of populism.

If YOU were there...

You are a female schoolteacher in Wisconsin in 1880. You live and teach in a small town, but you grew up on a farm and are used to hard work. Now you are thinking about moving West to claim free land from the government. You could teach in a school there, too. You think it would be an exciting adventure, but your family is horrified that a single woman would move West on her own.

Would you decide to become a homesteader?

BUILDING BACKGROUND By the 1870s and 1880s, the Great Plains had been "tamed" and made more welcoming to settlers. The end of the open cattle range was coming, and the Indian wars were nearly over. The government moved to encourage permanent settlements in the West by offering land to homesteaders.

New Lives on the Plains

In 1862 Congress passed two important land grant acts that helped open the West to settlers. The **Homestead Act** gave government-owned land to small farmers. Any adult who was a U.S. citizen or planned to become one could receive 160 acres of land. In exchange, homesteaders promised to live on the land for five years. The **Morrill Act** granted more than 17 million acres of federal land to the states. The act required each state to sell this land and to use the money to build colleges to teach agriculture and engineering.

Settling the Plains

People from all over the country moved West. Many farming families moved from areas where farmland was becoming scarce or expensive, such as New England. Many single women moved West. The Homestead Act granted land to unmarried women, which was unusual for the time.

The promise of land and a life free of discrimination also drew a large group of African Americans West. In 1879 some

© Houghton Mifflin Harcourt Publishing Company

20,000 to 40,000 southern African Americans moved to Kansas. Known as **Exodusters**, these southerners made a mass exodus, or departure, from the South. A number of black communities soon developed.

Western homesteads also were attractive to immigrants. Norwegian, Swedish, Danish, German, and Czech immigrants formed many small communities on the Great Plains.

Farming the Plains

Plains farmers had many unique challenges. The seasons were extreme. Weather could be extreme. Also, the root-filled sod, or dirt, beneath the Plains grass was very tough. The hard work of breaking up the sod earned Plains farmers the nickname **sodbusters**.

In the 1890s western Plains farmers began **dry farming**, a new method of farming that shifted the focus away from water-dependent crops such as corn. Instead, farmers grew more hardy crops like red wheat. In addition, by the 1880s mechanical farming was becoming common. By using machinery, farmers could work much more quickly on large fields with fewer workers. Farmers shipped their harvest east by train. From there, crops were shipped overseas. The Great Plains soon became known as the breadbasket of the world.

Primary Source

LETTER

Letter from the Plains, 1863

In a letter to her family in Norway, immigrant Gro Svendsen describes her new life as a farmer on the plains of Iowa.

"I remember I used to wonder when I heard that it would be impossible to keep the milk here as we did at home. Now I have learned that it is indeed impossible because of the heat here in the summertime . . . It's difficult, too, to preserve the butter. One must pour brine [salt water] over it or salt it.

The thunderstorms are so violent that one might think it was the end of the world . . . Quite often the lightning strikes down both cattle and people, damages property, and splinters sturdy oak trees into many pieces."

—quoted in *Sources in American History*

ANALYSIS SKILL **ANALYZING PRIMARY SOURCES**

What might be some of the differences between Norway and Svendsen's new home in Iowa?

Pioneers like this family often lived in houses made of sod because there were few trees for lumber on the Plains.

© Houghton Mifflin Harcourt Publishing Company • Image Credits: (b) Western History Collections, University of Oklahoma

Building Communities

Women were an important force in the settlement of the frontier. They joined in the hard work of farming and ranching and helped build communities out of the widely spaced farms and small towns. Their role in founding communities **facilitated** a strong voice in public affairs. Wyoming women, for example, were granted the vote in the new state's constitution, which was approved in 1869. **Annie Bidwell**, one of the founders of Chico, California, used her influence to support a variety of moral and social causes such as women's suffrage and temperance.

ACADEMIC VOCABULARY
facilitate to make easier

Many early settlers found life on their remote farms to be extremely difficult. Farmers formed communities so that they could assist one another in times of need. One of the first things that many pioneer communities did was establish a local church and school.

Children helped with many chores around the farm. Author Laura Ingalls Wilder was one of four children in a pioneer family. Wilder's books about settlers' lives on the prairie are still popular today.

READING CHECK **Comparing and Contrasting** How were settlers' lives alike and different from their lives in the East?

Farmers' Political Groups

From 1860 to 1900, the U.S. population more than doubled. To feed this growing population, the number of farms tripled. With modern machines, farmers in 1900 could harvest a bushel of wheat almost 20 times faster than they could in 1830.

Farm Incomes Fall

The combination of more farms and greater productivity, however, led to overproduction. Overproduction resulted in lower prices for crops. As their incomes decreased, many farmers found it difficult to pay bills. Farmers who could not make their mortgage payments lost their farms and homes. Many of these homeless farmers became tenant farmers who worked land owned by others. By 1880 one-fourth of all farms were rented by tenants, and the number continued to grow.

The National Grange

Many farmers blamed businesspeople—wholesalers, brokers, grain buyers, and especially railroad owners—for making money at their expense. As economic conditions worsened, farmers began to follow the example of other workers. They formed associations to protect and help their interests.

Time Line

Farming and the Rise of Populism

1862 President Lincoln signs the bill that authorizes the transcontinental railroad.

1867 The National Grange is founded.

1879 Exodusters move to Kansas.

© Houghton Mifflin Harcourt Publishing Company • Image Credits: (br), Nebraska State Historical Society; (tr), Elias Carr Papers, East Carolina Manuscript Collection, J.Y. Joyner Library, East Carolina University, Greenville, NC. Photo

One such organization was founded by Oliver Hudson Kelley, who toured the South in 1866 for the U.S. Department of Agriculture. Kelley saw firsthand how the country's farmers suffered. Afterward, Kelley and several government clerks formed the National Grange of the Patrons of Husbandry in 1867. The **National Grange** was a social and educational organization for farmers. (*Grange* is an old word for granary.) Local chapters were quickly founded, and membership grew rapidly.

The Grange campaigned for political candidates who supported farmers' goals. The organization also called for laws that regulated rates charged by railroads. The U.S. Supreme Court ruled in 1877 that the government could regulate railroads because they affected the public interest. In 1886 the Court said that the federal government could only regulate companies doing business across state lines. Rate regulation for railroad lines within states fell to the state governments.

In February 1887 Congress passed the Interstate Commerce Act, providing national regulations over trade between states and creating the Interstate Commerce Commission to ensure fair railroad rates. However, the commission lacked power to enforce its regulations.

Agricultural Supply and Demand

CONNECT TO ECONOMICS

Supply **is the amount of a good that is available.**
Demand **is the amount of a good that people want to buy.**
When supply exceeds demand, prices fall.

What happened to the price of wheat as the supply increased?

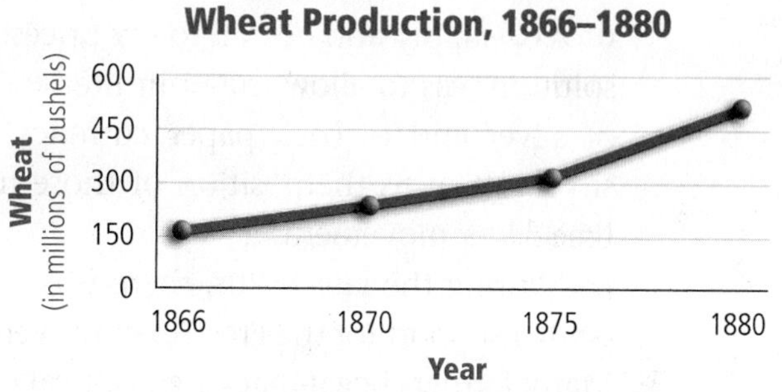

Wheat Production, 1866–1880
Wheat (in millions of bushels)
600
450
300
150
0
1866
1870
1875
1880
Year

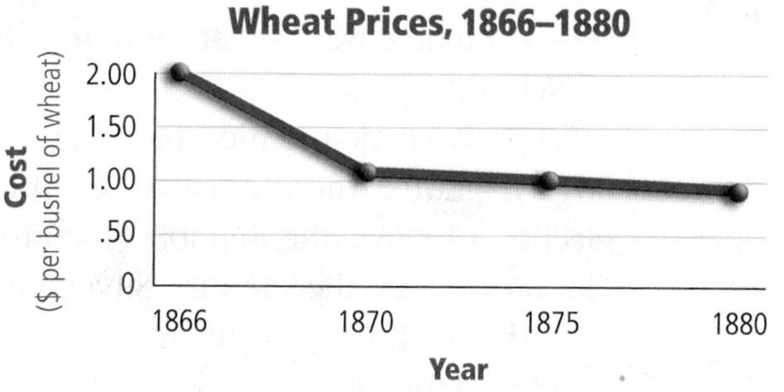

Wheat Prices, 1866–1880
Cost ($ per bushel of wheat)
2.00
1.50
1.00
.50
0
1866
1870
1875
1880
Year

W. McKINLEY.

1887 The Interstate Commerce Commission is formed to regulate railroad prices.

1892 The national Populist Party is formed.

1896 The Populist Party backs William Jennings Bryan as the Democratic presidential candidate.

ANALYSIS SKILL **READING TIME LINES**

How many years after the authorization of the transcontinental railroad was the Interstate Commerce Commission created?

© Houghton Mifflin Harcourt Publishing Company • Image Credits: (l), The Granger Collection, New York; (br), Janice L. and David J. Frent Collection of Political Americana

Free Silver Debate

Money issues also caused problems for farmers. Many farmers hoped that help would come from new laws affecting the money supply.

Since 1873 the United States had been on the gold standard, meaning that all paper money had to be backed by gold in the treasury. As a result, the money supply grow more slowly than the nation's population and led to **deflation**—a decrease in the money supply and overall lower prices. One solution was to allow the unlimited coining of silver and to back paper currency with silver. This was the position of those in the Free Silver movement.

During the late 1870s, there was a great deal of support for the Free Silver movement. Many farmers began backing political candidates who favored free silver coinage. One such candidate was **William Jennings Bryan** of Nebraska.

The two major political parties, however, largely ignored the money issue. After the election of 1888, the Republican-controlled Congress passed the Sherman Silver Purchase Act. The act increased the amount of silver purchased for coinage. However, this did not help farmers as much as they had hoped.

BIOGRAPHY

William Jennings Bryan

1860–1925

William Jennings Bryan was born in Illinois but moved to Nebraska when he finished law school. He was elected Nebraska's first Democratic Congress member in 1890. Through his political campaigns and work as a newspaper editor, he became one of the best-known supporters of Populist ideas. After a dramatic speech at the 1896 Democratic National Convention, Bryan was nominated for the presidency. He was the youngest presidential candidate up to that time. Although he lost the election, he continued to be an influential speaker.

Making Inferences Why was Bryan's support of Populist ideas important?

Populist Party

To have greater power, many farmers organized to elect candidates that would help them. These political organizations became known as the Farmers' Alliances.

In the 1890 elections the Alliances were a strong political force. State and local wins raised farmers' political hopes. At a conference in Cincinnati, Ohio, in 1891, Alliance leaders met with labor and reform groups. Then, at a convention in St. Louis in February 1892, the Alliances formed a new national political party.

The new party was called the **Populist Party**, and it called for the government to own railroads and telephone and telegraph systems. It also favored the "free and unlimited coinage of silver." To gain the votes of workers, the Populists backed an eight-hour workday and limits on immigration.

The concerns of the Populists were soon put in the national spotlight. During the Panic of 1893, the U.S. economy experienced a crisis that some critics blamed on the shortage of gold. The failure of several major railroad companies also contributed to the economic problems.

The Panic of 1893 led more people to back the Populist call for economic reform. In 1896 the Republicans nominated William McKinley for president. McKinley was firmly against free coinage of silver. The Democrats nominated William Jennings Bryan, who favored free coinage.

The Populists had to decide between running their own candidate, and thus splitting the silver vote, or supporting Bryan. They decided to support Bryan. The Republicans had a well-financed campaign, and they won the election. McKinley's victory in 1896 marked the end of both the Populist Party and the Farmers' Alliances.

READING CHECK **Summarizing** Why did farmers, laborers, and reformers join to form the Populist Party?

Guthrie, Oklahoma

Oklahoma Land Rush

- The rush began at noon on April 22, 1889.
- Some witnesses said they could feel the ground shake as 50,000 people raced to claim land.
- Single women and widows could claim land on an equal basis with men.
- Many settlers were dismayed to find some people had claimed land before the rush legally began. These people were called sooners.

End of the Frontier

By 1870 only small portions of the Great Plains remained unsettled. For most of the next two decades, this land remained open range.

In March 1889, government officials announced that homesteaders could file claims on land in what is now the state of Oklahoma. This land had belonged to Creek and Seminole Indians. Within a month, about 50,000 people rushed to Oklahoma to stake their claims.

In all, settlers claimed more than 11 million acres of former Indian land in the famous Oklahoma land rush. This huge wave of pioneers was the last chapter of the westward movement. By the early 1890s, the frontier had ceased to exist in the United States.

READING CHECK **Finding Main Ideas** What event signaled the closing of the frontier?

SUMMARY In this section you read about the challenges settlers faced.

Section 3 Assessment

hmhsocialstudies.com ONLINE QUIZ

Reviewing Ideas, Terms, and People

1. a. **Describe** What groups settled in the Great Plains?
   b. **Explain** How did the U.S. government make lands available to western settlers?
   c. **Elaborate** Would you have chosen to settle on the frontier? Why or why not?
2. a. **Recall** What was the goal of the **National Grange**?
   b. **Make Inferences** Why did the **Populist Party** want the government to own railroads and telegraph and telephone systems?
   c. **Evaluate** Do you think farmers were successful in bringing about economic and political change? Explain.
3. a. **Recall** What was the Oklahoma land rush?
   b. **Explain** Why did the frontier cease to exist in the United States?

Critical Thinking

4. **Comparing and Contrasting** Look back over your notes about the rise of populism. Use them to explain why Populists sought the changes they did in a chart like the one below.

Change sought	Reason why

Focus on Writing

5. **Farming the Great Plains** As you read this section, take notes on the growth of farming on the Great Plains. How did farmers interact with the railroads? What changes might have been apparent to a railroad worker?

Social Studies Skills

Analysis | Critical Thinking | Civic Participation | **Study**

Comparing Migration Maps

Define the Skill

One of the best ways of using geography to learn history is by comparing maps. This skill allows you to see changes over time. It also helps you see relationships between one factor, such as population growth, and another factor, such as transportation routes or economic activities in an area.

Learn the Skill

Follow these steps to compare information on maps.

1. Apply basic map skills by reading the title and studying the legend and symbols for each map.
2. Note the date of each map and the area it covers. Maps compared for changes over time should include the same areas. Those used to look for relationships should have similar dates.
3. Note similarities or differences. Closely examine and compare each map's patterns and symbols.
4. Apply critical thinking skills. Make generalizations and draw conclusions about the relationships you find.

Practice the Skill

Use the maps below to answer the following questions.

1. What present-day state was unsettled by Americans in 1850 and almost completely settled in 1890?
2. Which other two present-day states show the most settlement by Americans from 1850 to 1890?
3. Why do you think the West coast was settled before the interior of the United States?
4. According to the maps, how might rivers have shaped the settlement of the West?

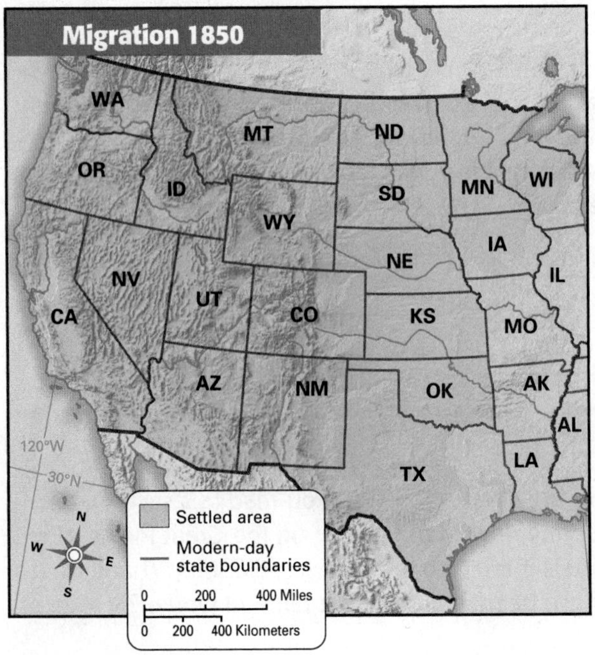

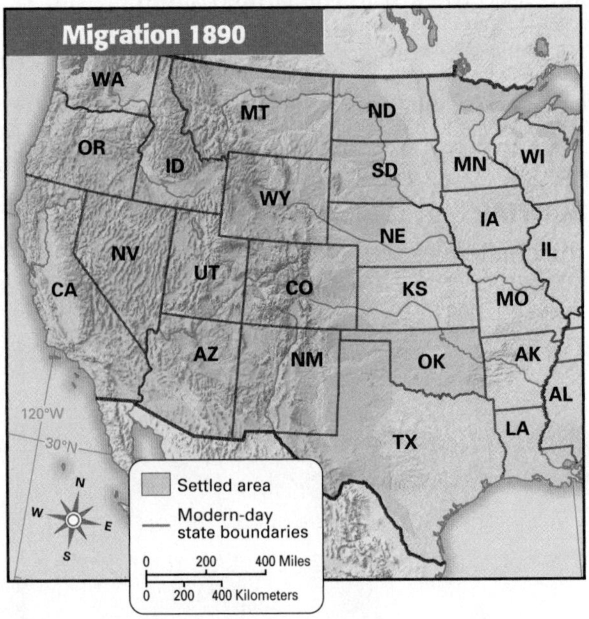

Chapter Review

History's Impact
▶ **video series**
Review the video to answer the closing question:
How was a cowboy's job essential to the American economy?

Visual Summary

QUICK FACTS

Use the visual summary below to help you review the main ideas of the chapter.

As settlers moved West, they came into conflict with American Indians. The U.S. government defeated Indian resistance and moved many tribes to reservations.

The completion of the transcontinental railroad in 1869 opened the West to more settlement. Gold and silver strikes also drew people hoping to get rich.

The railroads helped make the rise of the Cattle Kingdom possible. Cowboys drove huge herds of cattle from ranches to railway stations to be shipped to the East.

Farmers settled the Great Plains in large numbers. They overcame many hardships to make the Plains the breadbasket of America.

Reviewing Vocabulary, Terms, and People

1. Who was the leader of the 7th Cavalry in the Battle of the Little Bighorn?

a. Cyrus McCormick
b. Leland Stanford
c. William Jennings Bryan
d. George Armstrong Custer

2. What act gave millions of acres of federal lands to the states, which were to sell them and use those funds to build agricultural and engineering colleges?

a. Morrill Act
b. Sherman Act
c. Pacific Railway Act
d. Interstate Commerce Act

3. Which frontier woman was instrumental in supporting reform efforts in the West?

a. Sarah Winnemucca
b. Laura Ingalls Wilder
c. Annie Bidwell
d. Lucretia Mott

Comprehension and Critical Thinking

SECTION 1

4. a. Recall Why were many Americans eager to move to the western frontier?

b. Analyze How did railroads and ranching change the landscape of the West?

c. Elaborate In your opinion, which made the greatest changes to the West—mining, ranching, or railroads? Explain your answer.

SECTION 2

5. a. Describe What was life like for the Plains Indians before and after the arrival of large numbers of American settlers?

b. Draw Conclusions Why did the spread of the Ghost Dance movement cause concern for U.S. officials?

c. Elaborate What do you think about the reservation system established by the United States?

SECTION 3

6. a. **Identify** What political organizations did western farmers create? Why did farmers create these organizations?

   b. **Analyze** How did women participate in the settling of the American frontier?

   c. **Predict** How might the end of the frontier in the United States affect the nation?

Reviewing Themes

7. **Geography** What geographic obstacles did miners, ranchers, and railroad workers face in the West?
8. **Science and Technology** What types of technology did farmers on the Great Plains use, and how did it benefit them?

Using the Internet

9. **Activity: Creating a Presentation** Our view of the settlement of the West is heavily influenced by popular culture. Writers, painters, and illustrators provided a steady flow of words and images that sensationalized life in the American West. Later, film makers and television producers also contributed to the myth of the Wild West. "When legend becomes fact," said one actor in the classic western movie *The Man Who Shot Liberty Valance,* "print the legend." How does legend affect our view of this part of our history? Through the activities found in the online book, analyze the myths and realities of the West and the ways in which they shaped our view of that time period. Then create a visual display or PowerPoint presentation to present your research.

hmhsocialstudies.com

Reading Skills

Understanding Through Questioning *Use the Reading Skills taught in this chapter to answer the question about the reading selection below.*

> For survival, Plains Indians depended on two animals—the horse and the buffalo. The Spanish brought horses to America in the 1500s. Plains Indians learned to ride horses, and hunters used them to follow buffalo herds year-round.

10. Write two or three questions you have about the information in the passage above. Remember to use the five W's—Who? What? When? Where? and Why?

Social Studies Skills

Comparing Migration Maps *Use the Social Studies Skills taught in this chapter to answer the questions about the map below.*

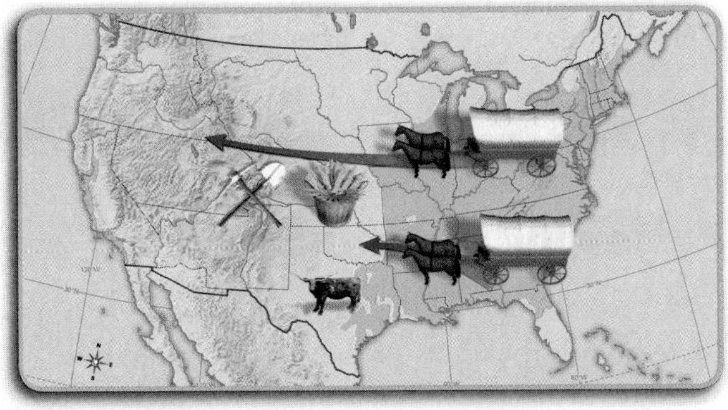

11. According to the map above, for what reasons did settlers migrate to the West?

   a. for mining, ranching, and farming

   b. for jobs in manufacturing

   c. for the homes in the major cities there

   d. for the fishing industry

Focus on Writing

12. **Writing Your Letter** Review your notes. Then write a letter to your sister back in Ireland about your experiences on the Great Plains. Describe all the changes you have seen. Use colorful language and precise details to make your sister feel as though she were there.

© Houghton Mifflin Harcourt Publishing Company • Image Credits: (b) Sam Dudgeon/HMH

Standardized Test Practice

DIRECTIONS: Read each question and write the letter of the best response.

1

- Government ownership of railroads
- Free and unlimited coinage of silver
- An eight-hour day for industrial workers
- Strict limits on foreign immigration
- Election of officials who will help farmers

Which of the following intended to accomplish the changes listed above in American society?

A the Morrill Act
B the Populist Party
C the National Grange
D the Homestead Act

2 The goal of many reformers who wanted to help Native Americans in the late 1800s was to

A get Indians to adopt the ways of white people.
B return to Indians all the land that had been taken from them.
C relocate all the nations to create an American Indian state in Oklahoma.
D negotiate treaties to bring peace to the frontier.

3 What played the *most* important part in the growth of the West's population and economy between 1865 and 1900?

A the mining industry
B the Cattle Kingdom
C the Populist Party
D the railroad

4 In general, the policy of the United States government toward Native Americans in the West was to

A send the army to track them down and engage them in battle.
B move them onto reservations and open their homelands to white settlers.
C kill all the buffalo so that they could not continue their traditional way of life.
D drive them into Canada or Mexico to settle.

5 The biggest problem facing western farmers in the late 1800s was

A a scarcity of good, cheap land to farm.
B their lack of organization to achieve change.
C overproduction and low crop prices.
D the threat of attacks by Native Americans.

6 Read the following speech from Comanche chief Ten Bears and use it to answer the question below.

> "You said that you wanted to put us upon a reservation, to build us houses and make us medicine lodges [places of religious practice]. I do not want them. I was born upon the prairie, where the wind blew free and there was nothing to break the light of the sun. I was born where there were no enclosures and where everything drew a free breath. I want to die there and not within walls."
>
> —Ten Bears, quoted in *Eyewitnesses and Others*

Document-Based Question Why does Ten Bears not want to move to a reservation?

© Houghton Mifflin Harcourt Publishing Company

CHAPTER 4 1876–1900

The Industrial Age

Essential Question How did technological advances change people's lives and affect businesses?

ALABAMA COURSE OF STUDY

1 Explain the impact of industrialization, urbanization, communication, and cultural changes on life in the United States from the late nineteenth century to World War I.

4 Identify cultural and economic developments in the United States from 1900 through the 1930s.

- Identifying contributions of turn-of-the-century inventors.
- Identifying notable persons of the early 1900s.

Focus on Writing

A Business Plan You are an inventor in the late 1800s, and you want to start a business to sell your new inventions. Write a business plan for investors that will encourage them to lend you money to start your business. As you read this chapter, gather information about the new business practices that you can use to run your business. Then write your plan. Include information about what you will sell, how you will make it, and how you can avoid conflicts with the workers who make your product.

United States

1879 Thomas Edison invents the first lightbulb.

1870

World

1876 German engineer Nikolaus A. Otto perfects a gasoline-powered engine.

Image Credits: (c), Picture Research Consultants, Inc.

© Houghton Mifflin Harcourt Publishing Company

HISTORY
Great Minds in Business: Andrew Carnegie
hmhsocialstudies.com VIDEO

Technological advances changed city life in the United States.

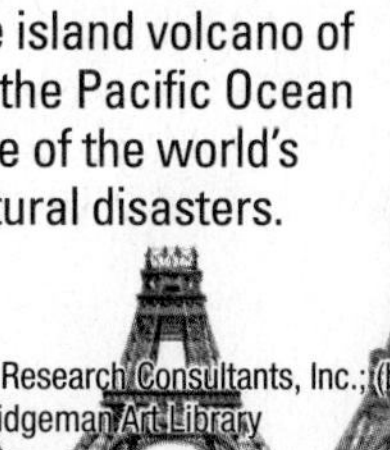

1886 The American Federation of Labor is formed on December 8.

1890 Congress passes the Sherman Antitrust Act.

1892 On June 29 the Homestead strike begins. Carnegie Steel Company refuses to negotiate with the union.

1880 — 1890 — 1900

1883 The island volcano of Krakatau in the Pacific Ocean erupts in one of the world's greatest natural disasters.

1889 The Eiffel Tower is built in Paris.

1898 French scientists Pi… and Mari… discov…

Image Credits: (c), Picture Research Consultants, Inc.; (bl), ©Bettmann/Corbis; (cl), George Meany Memorial Archives; (br), Archives Larousse, Paris, France/Bridgeman Art Library

© Houghton Mifflin Harcourt Publishing Company

Reading Social Studies

Economics | Geography | Politics | **Society and Culture** | Science and Technology

Focus on Themes In this chapter, you will read about the advancements in transportation and communication made during what is called the Second Industrial Revolution. You will learn about the rise of powerful corporations. You will also read about the workers who organized in the late 1800s and will see what happened as unions began demanding better treatment for workers. Throughout the chapter, you will see how **society** was affected by the changing **economy**.

Organization of Facts and Information

Focus on Reading How are clothes organized in a department store? How are files arranged in a file cabinet? Clear organization helps us find the product we need, and it also helps us find facts and information.

Understanding Structural Patterns Writers use structural patterns to organize information in sentences or paragraphs. What's a structural pattern? It's simply a way of organizing information. Learning to recognize those patterns will make it easier for you to read and understand social studies texts.

Patterns of Organization

Pattern	Clue Words	Graphic Organizer
Cause-effect shows how one thing leads to another.	as a result, therefore, because, this led to	Cause → Effect; Cause → Effect → Effect; Cause → Effect
Chronological order shows the sequence of events or actions.	after, before, first, then, not long after, finally	First → Next → Last
Comparison-contrast points out similarities and/or differences.	although, but, however, on the other hand, similarly, also	Differences; Similarities
Listing presents information in categories such as size, location, or importance.	also, most important, for example, in fact	**Category** • Fact • Fact • Fact

To use text structure to improve your understanding, follow these steps:

1. Look for the main idea of the passage you are reading.
2. Then look for clues that signal a specific pattern.
3. Look for other important ideas and think about how the ideas connect. Is there any obvious pattern?
4. Use a graphic organizer to map the relationships among the facts and details.

© Houghton Mifflin Harcourt Publishing Company

You Try It!

As you read each set of sentences, ask yourself what structural pattern the writer used to organize the information.

Recognizing Structural Patterns

(A) Great advances in communication technologies took place in the late 1800s. By 1861, telegraph wires connected the East and West coasts. Five years later, a telegraph cable on the floor of the Atlantic Ocean connected the United States and Great Britain.

(B) Many business leaders justified their business methods through their belief in social Darwinism . . . Other business leaders, however, believed that the rich had a duty to aid the poor.

(C) During the late 1800s, several factors led to a decline in the quality of working conditions. Machines run by unskilled workers were eliminating the jobs of many skilled craftspeople. These low-paid workers could be replaced easily.

After you read the passages, answer the questions below:

1. Reread passage A. What structural pattern did the writer use to organize this information? How can you tell?
2. Reread passage B. What structural pattern did the writer use to organize this information? How can you tell? Why do you think the writer chose this pattern?
3. Reread passage C. What structural pattern did the writer use to organize this information? How can you tell? Why do you think the writer chose this pattern?

As you read this chapter, think about the organization of the ideas. Ask yourself why the writer chose to organize the information in this way.

Key Terms and People

Chapter 4

Section 1

Second Industrial Revolution
Bessemer process
Thomas Edison
patents
Alexander Graham Bell
Henry Ford
Wilbur and Orville Wright

Section 2

corporations
Andrew Carnegie
vertical integration
John D. Rockefeller
horizontal integration
trust
Leland Stanford
social Darwinism
monopoly
Sherman Antitrust Act

Section 3

Frederick W. Taylor
Knights of Labor
Terence V. Powderly
American Federation of Labor
Samuel Gompers
collective bargaining
Mary Harris Jones
Haymarket Riot
Homestead strike
Pullman strike

Academic Vocabulary

In this chapter, you will learn the following academic words:

implement
acquire

SECTION 1

The Second Industrial Revolution

What You Will Learn...

Main Ideas

1. Breakthroughs in steel processing led to a boom in railroad construction.
2. Advances in the use of oil and electricity improved communications and transportation.
3. A rush of inventions changed Americans' lives.

The Big Idea

The Second Industrial Revolution led to new sources of power and advances in transportation and communication.

Key Terms and People

Second Industrial Revolution
Bessemer process
Thomas Edison
patents
Alexander Graham Bell
Henry Ford
Wilbur and Orville Wright

hmhsocialstudies.com
TAKING NOTES

Use the graphic organizer online to take notes on the inventors of the Second Industrial Revolution.

go to 360

If YOU were there...

You live in a small town but are visiting an aunt in the city in the 1890s. You are amazed when your aunt pushes a button on the wall to turn on electric lights. At home you still use kerosene lamps. You hear a clatter outside and see an electric streetcar traveling down the street. You are shocked when a telephone rings, and your aunt speaks to someone miles away!

Which of these inventions would you find most amazing?

BUILDING BACKGROUND The first Industrial Revolution in America began in the early 1800s. It changed the way products were made, from handwork to machines. It moved the workplace from cottages to factories. Later, it brought advances in transportation and communication. The Second Industrial Revolution built on these changes, introducing new technology and new sources of power.

© Houghton Mifflin Harcourt Publishing Company; Image Credits: (b) Library of Congress Prints & Photographs Division, Washington, D.C.

Breakthroughs in Steel Processing

Technological advances were important to the **Second Industrial Revolution**, a period of rapid growth in U.S. manufacturing in the late 1800s. By the mid-1890s, the United States had become the world's industrial leader.

The Steel Industry

Some of the most important advances in technology happened in the steel industry. Steel is iron that has been made stronger by heat and the addition of other metals. In the mid-1850s Henry Bessemer invented the **Bessemer process**, a way to manufacture steel quickly and cheaply by blasting hot air through melted iron to quickly remove impurities. Before, turning several tons of iron ore into steel took a day or more. The Bessemer process took only 10 to 20 minutes.

The Bessemer process helped increase steel production. U.S. mills had produced 77,000 tons of steel in 1870. By 1879 production had risen to more than 1 million tons in one year.

Riding the Rails

As steel dropped in price, so did the cost of building railroads. Companies built thousands of miles of new steel track. The design of elegant passenger and sleeping cars improved passenger service. Manufacturers and farmers sent products to market faster than ever by rail in newly invented refrigerated shipping cars. Cities where major rail lines crossed, such as Chicago, grew rapidly. Railroads also increased western growth by offering free tickets to settlers. Finally, as rail travel and shipping increased, railroads and related industries began employing more people.

QUICK FACTS

Factors Affecting Industrial Growth

- Greater ability to use natural resources
- A growing population
- Transportation advances
- Rising immigration
- Inventions and innovations
- Increasing business investment
- Government policies assisting business, such as protective tariffs

READING CHECK **Identifying Cause and Effect** How did steel processing change in the 1850s, and how did this affect the United States?

Homestead Steel Mill

Steel mills like this one in Homestead, Pennsylvania, were the center of the new steel industry that led to advancements in rail travel. Workers used the Bessemer process to make steel more quickly.

How do you think mills like this one affected the surrounding area?

© Houghton Mifflin Harcourt Publishing Company • Image Credits: (b), Library of Congress Prints & Photographs Division, Washington, D.C.

Time Line

The Spirit of Innovation

1850 — **1860**

1852 Elisha Otis invents the elevator safety brake, making elevators safe for people.

1854 Henry Bessemer patents a method for making cast steel.

SAFE FOR ONLY 25 MEN AT ONE TIME. DO NOT WALK CLOSE TOGETHER NOR RUN. JUMP. OR TROT. BREAK STEP!
W.A.Roebling Engr in Chief
FACTORY

1869 John Roebling begins work on the Brooklyn Bridge.

Use of Oil and Electricity

The Second Industrial Revolution was characterized by dramatic developments in the use and distribution of oil and electricity. These power sources fueled other changes.

Oil as a Power Source

An important technological breakthrough in the late 1800s was the use of petroleum, or oil, as a power source. People had known about oil for many years but had discovered few ways to use it. However, in the 1850s, chemists invented a way to convert crude, or unprocessed, oil into a fuel called kerosene. Kerosene could be used for cooking, heating, and lighting. Suddenly there was a demand for oil.

FOCUS ON READING
How does this paragraph show the cause and effect structure?

As demand grew, people began searching for a reliable source for oil. In 1859 Edwin L. Drake proved that it was possible to pump crude oil from the ground. Soon, wildcatters, or oil prospectors, drilled for oil in Ohio, Pennsylvania, and West Virginia. Oil became a big business as these states began producing millions of barrels per year. Oil companies built refineries to turn the crude oil into finished products like kerosene. One oil company supervisor referred to oil workers as "men who are supplying light for the world."

Electricity Spreads

In addition to kerosene, electricity became a critical source of light and power during the Second Industrial Revolution. The possible uses of electricity interested inventors like **Thomas Edison**. His research center in Menlo Park, New Jersey, was called an invention factory. Edison explained his practical approach to science.

> "I do not regard myself as a pure scientist, as so many persons have insisted that I am. I do not search for the laws of nature . . . for the purpose of learning truth. I am only a professional inventor . . . with the object [goal] of inventing that which will have commercial utility [use]."
>
> —Thomas Edison, quoted in *American Made*, by Harold C. Livesay

Edison eventually held more than 1,000 **patents**, exclusive rights to make or sell inventions. Patents allowed inventors to protect their inventions from being manufactured by others.

In 1878 Edison announced that he would soon invent a practical electric light. By the end of 1879 Edison and his team of inventors had created the electric lightbulb. The public was excited. However, Edison had a problem. At the time, few homes or businesses could get electricity. Edison therefore built a power plant that began supplying electricity to dozens of New York City buildings in

© Houghton Mifflin Harcourt Publishing Company • Image Credits: (tr) Museum of the City of New York/Getty Images

1872 Elijah McCoy receives the patent for his device that oiled machine engines.

1876 Alexander Graham Bell invents the telephone.

1879 Thomas Edison creates a durable electric lightbulb.

1887 Harriet Strong receives a patent for her advances in dam and reservoir construction.

1893 J. Frank and Charles Duryea successfully test their first gasoline-powered automobile.

1870 — 1880 — 1890

September 1882. The *New York Times* reported that with electric lighting in the newspaper offices, "it seemed almost like writing by daylight." However, Edison's equipment could not send electricity over long distances. As a result, his power company, Edison Electric, provided electricity mainly to central cities.

In the late 1880s, George Westinghouse built a power system that could send electricity across many miles. As Edison and Westinghouse competed, the use of electricity spread rapidly in the nation's cities. After a while, electricity soon lit homes and businesses and powered city factories. Electricity also was used to power streetcars in cities across the nation.

READING CHECK **Drawing Conclusions**
Why did people begin to pump oil from the ground?

Rush of Inventions

In the late 1800s, inventors focused on finding solutions to practical problems. Communication and transportation took the lead.

Advances in Communication

Great advances in communication technologies took place in the late 1800s. By 1861, telegraph wires connected the East and West coasts. Five years later, a telegraph cable on the floor of the Atlantic Ocean connected the United States and Great Britain.

However, the telegraph carried only written messages and was difficult for untrained people to use. These problems were solved in March 1876, when inventor **Alexander Graham Bell** patented the telephone. Bell was a Scottish-born speech teacher who studied the science of sound. He called the telephone a "talking telegraph."

Telephone companies raced to lay thousands of miles of phone lines. By 1880 there were about 55,000 telephones in the United States, and by 1900 there were almost 1.5 million.

THE IMPACT TODAY

AT&T Corporation is a direct descendant of Bell's original company. AT&T pioneered the use of telephone cables across the oceans, satellite communications, and a radar system for the U.S. Defense Department.

Automobiles and Planes

In 1876 a German engineer invented an engine powered by gasoline, another fuel made from oil. In 1893 Charles and J. Frank Duryea used a gasoline engine to build the first practical motorcar in the United States. By the early 1900s, thousands of cars were being built in the United States.

At first, only the wealthy could buy these early cars. **Henry Ford** introduced the Model T in 1908. Ford was the first to implement the moving assembly line in manufacturing, a process that greatly reduced the cost of building a product, thus making cars more affordable.

HISTORY

VIDEO
Henry Ford: Taking the Low Road
hmhsocialstudies.com

ACADEMIC VOCABULARY
implement
to put in place

© Houghton Mifflin Harcourt Publishing Company • Image Credits: (cr), Whittier Historical Society Museum, Whittier California; (r), ©Hulton Archive/Getty Images; (l), ©Bettmann/Corbis; (tl), ©Schomburg Center for Research in Black Culture/NYPL/Photo Researchers, Inc.

Time Line

The Spirit of Innovation

1893 George Ferris displays the first Ferris wheel at the World's Columbian Exposition in Chicago.

1900

1903 Orville Wright makes the first flight in a motorized airplane.

ANALYSIS SKILL **READING TIME LINES**

When was the telephone invented?

HISTORY

VIDEO
The Wright Brothers Controversy

hmhsocialstudies.com

New engine technology helped make another breakthrough in transportation possible—air flight. Brothers **Wilbur and Orville Wright** built a lightweight airplane that used a small, gas-powered engine. In Kitty Hawk, North Carolina, Orville Wright made the first piloted flight in a gas-powered plane on December 17, 1903. This invention would change the way that many Americans traveled in the future and would increase the demand for oil production.

READING CHECK **Comparing** What new inventions excited the public in the 1800s, and how were they used?

SUMMARY The Second Industrial Revolution led to advances in energy sources, communication, and transportation.

Section 1 Assessment

hmhsocialstudies.com
ONLINE QUIZ

Reviewing Ideas, Terms, and People

1. a. **Describe** What was the **Bessemer process**?
   b. **Summarize** How did improvements to railroads affect the economy and transportation in the United States?
   c. **Elaborate** What do you think was the most important effect of the Bessemer process? Why?
2. a. **Identify** What is kerosene, and for what could it be used?
   b. **Explain** What problem did **Thomas Edison** face regarding the use of electricity, and how did he solve it?
3. a. **Recall** What contribution did **Wilbur and Orville Wright** make to transportation?
   b. **Draw Conclusions** How did **Alexander Graham Bell**'s invention improve life in the United States?
   c. **Elaborate** Why do you think there was a rush of inventions in the late 1800s?

Critical Thinking

4. **Analyzing** Look over your notes on inventors. Use them to complete a table like the one below about inventors and their inventions.

Inventor	Invention

Focus on Writing

5. **Information on a Product** In your notes, list what kinds of new products became available at this time. What do you think would be a good thing to make and sell during the late 1800s?

© Houghton Mifflin Harcourt Publishing Company • Image Credits: (l), ©Corbis; (r), Library of Congress Prints & Photographs Division, Washington, D.C.

Big Business

SECTION 2

If YOU were there...

It is 1895, and your town is home to a large corporation. The company's founder and owner, a wealthy man, lives in a mansion on a hill. He is a fair employer but not especially generous. Many townspeople work in his factory. You and other town leaders feel that he should contribute more to local charities and community organizations.

How could this business leader help the town more?

BUILDING BACKGROUND Advanced technology along with the use of oil and electric power helped American businesses grow. Soon the shape of the American economy changed. Some companies grew so large that they began to dominate entire industries.

What You Will Learn...

Main Ideas

1. The rise of corporations and powerful business leaders led to the dominance of big business in the United States.
2. People and the government began to question the methods of big business.

The Big Idea

The growth of big business in the late 1800s led to the creation of monopolies.

Key Terms and People

corporations
Andrew Carnegie
vertical integration
John D. Rockefeller
horizontal integration
trust
Leland Stanford
social Darwinism
monopoly
Sherman Antitrust Act

hmhsocialstudies.com
TAKING NOTES

Use the graphic organizer online to take notes on the new business practices you learn about while reading the chapter.

Dominance of Big Business

In the late 1800s many entrepreneurs formed their businesses as **corporations**, or businesses that sell portions of ownership called stock shares. The leaders of these corporations were some of the most widely respected members of American society in the late 1800s. Political leaders praised prosperous businesspeople as examples of American hard work, talent, and success.

New sales techniques like those taught by John H. Patterson helped change business practices.

© Houghton Mifflin Harcourt Publishing Company • Image Credits: (b) The NCR Archive at Dayton History

Corporations Generate Wealth

↗ hmhsocialstudies.com
ANIMATED GEOGRAPHY AND HISTORY
Industrial Growth 1860–1900

Successful corporations reward not only the people who found them but also investors who hold stock. Stockholders in a corporation typically get a percentage of profits based on the amount of stock they own. Although stockholders actually own the corporation, they do not run its day-to-day business. Instead, they elect a board of directors that chooses the corporation's main leaders, such as the president.

Corporations provided several important advantages over earlier business forms. Stockholders in a corporation are not responsible for business debts. If a corporation fails financially, the stockholders lose only the money that they invested. Stockholders are also usually free to sell their stock to whomever they want, whenever they want. As a result, corporations encouraged more investment in businesses. By 1900 more than 100 million shares per year were being traded on the New York Stock Exchange.

ACADEMIC VOCABULARY
acquire to get

Business Leaders

Countless business leaders became wealthy, powerful, and famous because of the business boom. **Andrew Carnegie** was one of the most admired businesspeople of the time. Born in Scotland, Carnegie came to the United States as a poor immigrant. As a teenager he took a job with a railroad company and quickly worked his way up to the position of railroad superintendent.

In 1873 he focused his efforts on steelmaking. Carnegie expanded his business by buying out competitors when steel prices were low. By 1901 Carnegie's mills were producing more steel than all of Great Britain's mills combined. Carnegie's businesses succeeded largely through **vertical integration**, or ownership of businesses involved in each step of a manufacturing process. For example, to lower production costs, Carnegie acquired the iron ore mines, coalfields, and railroads needed to supply and support his steel mills.

John D. Rockefeller was also successful in consolidating, or combining, businesses. By age 21, while a partner in a wholesale business, he decided to start an oil-refining company. In only 10 years Rockefeller's Standard Oil Company was the country's largest oil refiner. Like Carnegie, Rockefeller used

The Rise of Investing

Investors purchased stock in corporations in record numbers in the late 1800s. They received stock certificates, like the one shown here, to document their part ownership in corporations. Corporations used the money raised by selling stocks to expand. Standard Oil Company financed the building of this refinery in Richmond, California, by selling stock.

Why did investors buy stock?

© Houghton Mifflin Harcourt Publishing Company • Image Credits: (l), ©Corbis; (inset), ©INTERFOTO/Alamy

Primary Source

POLITICAL CARTOON

Trusts

The wealth and size of trusts such as Standard Oil made many Americans fear the influence of business leaders over government.

What do you think the smokestacks on the Capitol building represent?

What does the position of the White House suggest?

ANALYSIS SKILL **ANALYZING PRIMARY SOURCES**

How does the cartoonist show Rockefeller's power?

vertical integration. For example, the company controlled most of the pipelines it used.

Rockefeller's company also developed **horizontal integration**, or owning all businesses in a certain field. By 1880 Rockefeller's companies controlled about 90 percent of the oil refining business in the United States. Rockefeller also formed a **trust**, a legal arrangement grouping together a number of companies under a single board of directors. To earn more money, trusts often tried to get rid of competition and to control production.

Leland Stanford was another important business leader of the late 1800s. He made a fortune selling equipment to miners. While governor of California, he became one of the founders of the state's Central Pacific railroad. Stanford also founded Stanford University.

Late in life, Stanford argued that industries should be owned and managed cooperatively by workers. He believed this would be the fulfillment of democracy.

READING CHECK **Comparing and Contrasting** Why did Andrew Carnegie use vertical integration?

Questioning the Methods of Big Business

By the late 1800s, people and the government were becoming uncomfortable with child labor, low wages, and poor working conditions. They began to view big business as a problem.

Social Darwinism

Many business leaders justified their business methods through their belief in **social Darwinism**, a view of society based on scientist Charles Darwin's theory of natural selection. Social Darwinists thought that Darwin's "survival of the fittest" theory decided which human beings would succeed in business and in life in general.

Other business leaders, however, believed that the rich had a duty to aid the poor. These leaders tried to help the less fortunate through philanthropy, or giving money to charities. Carnegie, Rockefeller, Stanford, and other business leaders gave away large sums. Carnegie gave away more than $350 million to charities, about $60 million of which went to

HISTORY

VIDEO
John D. Rockefeller: The Standard Oil Trust

hmhsocialstudies.com

© Houghton Mifflin Harcourt Publishing Company • Image Credits: (t), Snark/Art Resource, NY fund public libraries to expand access to books. By the late 1800s, various charities had received millions of dollars from philanthropists.

The Antitrust Movement

Critics of big business said that many business leaders earned their fortunes through unfair business practices. These criticisms grew stronger in the 1880s as corporations became more powerful. Large corporations often used their size and strength to drive smaller competitors out of business. Carnegie and Rockefeller, for example, pressured railroads to charge their companies lower shipping rates. Powerful trusts also arranged to sell goods and services below market value. Smaller competitors went out of business trying to match those prices. Then the trusts raised prices again.

Some people became concerned when a trust gained a **monopoly**, or total ownership of a product or service. Critics argued that monopolies reduced necessary competition. They believed competition in a free market economy kept prices low and the quality of goods and services high.

Some Americans also worried about the political power of wealthy trusts. Many citizens and small businesses wanted the government to help control monopolies and trusts. People who favored trusts responded that trusts were more efficient and gave the consumer dependable products or services.

Many members of Congress favored big business. However, elected officials could not ignore the concerns of voters. In July 1890 Congress passed the **Sherman Antitrust Act**, a law that made it illegal to create monopolies or trusts that restrained trade. It stated that any "attempt to monopolize . . . any part of the trade or commerce among the several States" was a crime. However, the act did not clearly define a trust in legal terms. The antitrust laws were therefore difficult to enforce. Corporations and trusts kept growing in size and power.

READING CHECK **Analyzing** How did concerns about trusts lead to the Sherman Antitrust Act?

SUMMARY In the late 1800s some corporations became monopolies that dominated industries such as oil.

Section 2 Assessment

hmhsocialstudies.com
ONLINE QUIZ

Reviewing Ideas, Terms, and People

1. a. **Identify** What are **horizontal** and **vertical integration**?
   b. **Explain** What are the benefits of investing in **corporations**?
   c. **Evaluate** What do you think about the business methods of **Carnegie**, **Rockefeller**, and **Stanford**?
2. a. **Describe** What is **social Darwinism**?
   b. **Summarize** What concerns did critics of big business have regarding **trusts**?
   c. **Evaluate** Was the **Sherman Antitrust Act** successful? Why or why not?

Critical Thinking

3. **Contrasting** Look back over your notes about new business practices. Find examples of the new business practices. Use them to complete a graphic organizer like the one below.

New Practices	Example

Focus on Writing

4. **Gathering Information on Business** Look back over your notes and determine what new practices helped businesses expand during this time. Which practices could you use to start your business? Where would you try to sell your product?

© Houghton Mifflin Harcourt Publishing Company

BIOGRAPHY

VIDEO
HISTORY
Great Minds in Business: Andrew Carnegie
hmhsocialstudies.com

Andrew Carnegie, John D. Rockefeller, and Leland Stanford

How would you go about building an industry?

Andrew Carnegie (1835–1919) Born in Scotland, Carnegie rose to become a multimillionaire in the steel industry. He brought new technologies to his steel mills and made them extremely efficient. In 1901 he sold Carnegie Steel Company for $250 million, making him the richest man in the world.

John D. Rockefeller (1839–1937) Rockefeller got his start in the oil business in Cleveland, Ohio. Rockefeller's Standard Oil Company quickly bought out its competitors throughout the United States. To better control oil production and delivery, Rockefeller also bought railroad rights, terminals, and pipelines.

Leland Stanford (1825–1893) Leland Stanford was born to a New York farming family that sent him to excellent private schools. After practicing law in Wisconsin, he made his career in California. Stanford was instrumental in building the western section of the transcontinental railroad. He then plunged into politics, serving one term as governor. His political connections helped him obtain huge state land grants and other benefits for his railroad companies. As president of Central Pacific and Southern Pacific, he oversaw the laying of thousands of miles of track throughout the West.

Why are they so important? Carnegie, Rockefeller, and Stanford helped make America the world's greatest industrial power by the end of the 1800s. They built giant industries that made goods cheaply by keeping workers' wages low. They also engaged in ruthless business practices to defeat their competition and create monopolies. The Sherman Antitrust Act was passed in reaction to the Standard Oil monopoly. Later in life, all three men became philanthropists, people devoted to charity work. Rockefeller's philanthropies gave out $500 million in his lifetime. Carnegie spent $350 million, funding educational grants, concert halls, and nearly 3,000 public libraries. Stanford founded Stanford University in 1884.

Finding Main Ideas
Why are these three men important figures in U.S. history?

© Houghton Mifflin Harcourt Publishing Company

SECTION 3

Industrial Workers

What You Will Learn...

Main Ideas

1. The desire to maximize profits and become more efficient led to poor working conditions.
2. Workers began to organize and demand improvements in working conditions and pay.
3. Labor strikes often turned violent and failed to accomplish their goals.

The Big Idea

Changes in the workplace led to a rise in labor unions and workers' strikes.

Key Terms and People

Frederick W. Taylor
Knights of Labor
Terence V. Powderly
American Federation of Labor
Samuel Gompers
collective bargaining
Mary Harris Jones
Haymarket Riot
Homestead strike
Pullman strike

hmhsocialstudies.com
TAKING NOTES

Use the graphic organizer online to take notes about the problems workers faced in the new economy.

If YOU were there...

You run a button machine in a clothing factory in the 1890s. You work from 7:00 in the morning until 6:00 at night, every day except Sunday. Your only break is 15 minutes for lunch. Now you hear about a movement to start a workers' union to bargain with your employer. Union members will ask for an eight-hour workday. But you think your employer might fire you if you join.

Would you join the union?

BUILDING BACKGROUND The rise of corporations and the establishment of monopolies gave big business a great deal of power. An antitrust movement arose to try to limit the power of trusts. Workers themselves began to organize and take action against bad working conditions and other problems.

Maximizing Profits and Efficiency

During the late 1800s, several factors led to a decline in the quality of working conditions. Machines run by unskilled workers were eliminating the jobs of many skilled craftspeople. These low-paid workers could be replaced easily. Factories began to focus on specialization, or workers repeating a single step again and again. Specialization brought costs down and caused production to rise. But it also made workers tired, bored, and more likely to be injured. Specialization allowed for Henry Ford's idea of a moving assembly line to speed production. Ford's use of the moving assembly line allowed automobiles to be made more quickly and cheaply. Automobiles soon became available to a wider segment of the population than ever before.

In 1909 **Frederick W. Taylor**, an efficiency engineer, published a popular book called *The Principles of Scientific Management.* He encouraged managers to view workers as interchangeable parts of the production process. In factories, managers influenced by Taylor paid less attention to working conditions. Injuries increased, and as conditions grew worse, workers looked for ways to bring about change.

READING CHECK **Identifying Cause and Effect** Why did companies begin to use scientific management, and how did it affect workers?

© Houghton Mifflin Harcourt Publishing Company

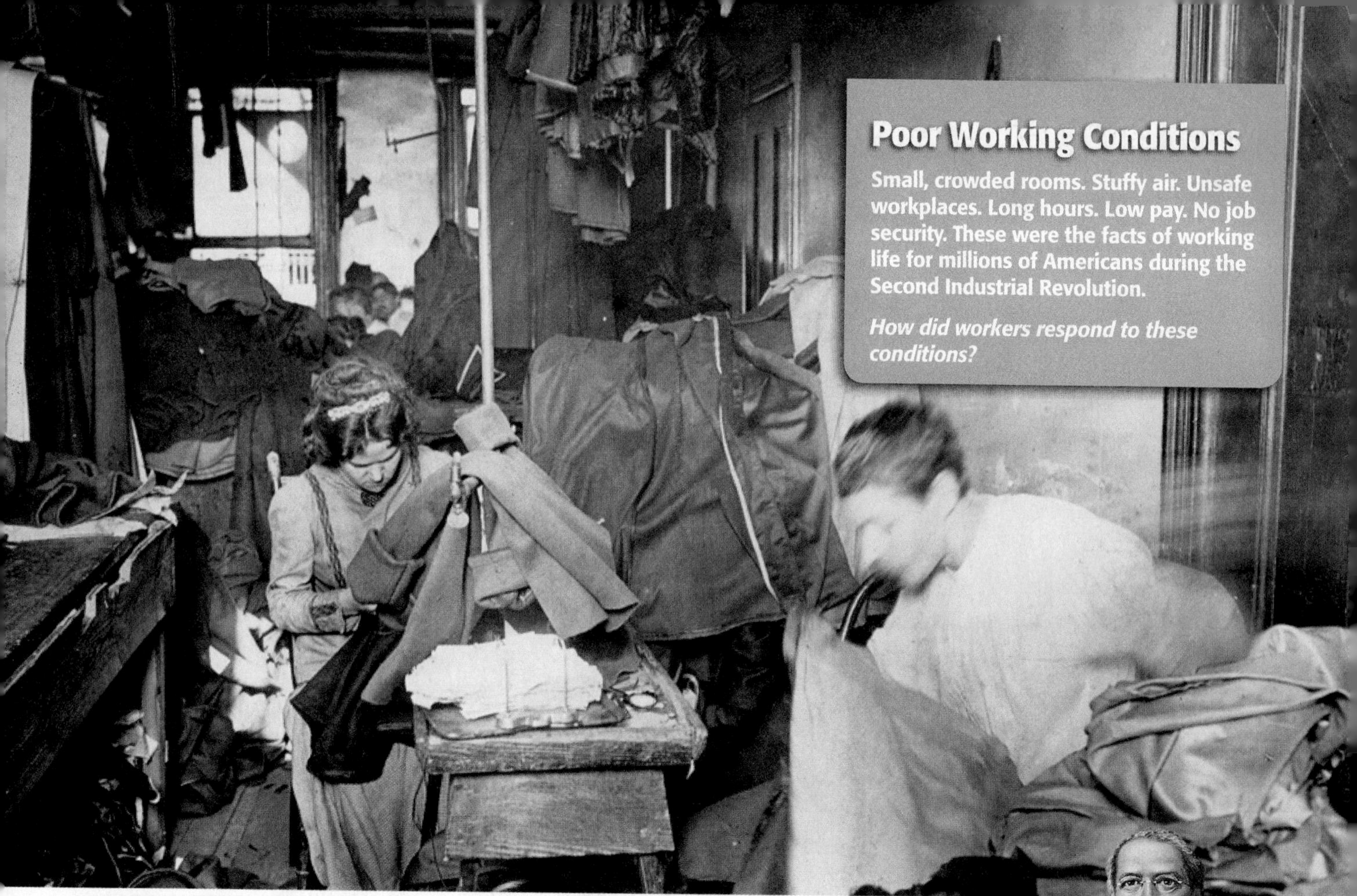

Poor Working Conditions

Small, crowded rooms. Stuffy air. Unsafe workplaces. Long hours. Low pay. No job security. These were the facts of working life for millions of Americans during the Second Industrial Revolution.

How did workers respond to these conditions?

Workers Organize

Workers formed labor unions to get better wages and working conditions for all workers in a factory or industry. The first national labor union, the **Knights of Labor**, was founded in the 1870s. It pushed for an eight-hour workday, equal pay for equal work, and an end to child labor. Union members also wanted the government to regulate trusts. Unlike most unions at the time, the Knights included both skilled and unskilled workers. The Knights of Labor was originally organized much like a secret society. In 1879 **Terence V. Powderly** became leader of the Knights. He ended all secrecy, creating the first truly national labor union in the United States.

Another early labor union was the **American Federation of Labor (AFL),** led by **Samuel Gompers.** Unlike the Knights, the American Federation of Labor organized individual national unions, such as the mineworkers' and steelworkers' unions. The AFL

BIOGRAPHY

Samuel Gompers

1850–1924

Samuel Gompers was a young Jewish immigrant born in London. He came to the United States with his parents in 1863 at age 13. He worked as a cigar maker and joined a local union, eventually becoming its president. The Cigarmakers Union was reorganized and later joined the American Federation of Labor. Gompers became the AFL's first president and remained so, except for the year 1895, until his death. He campaigned for basic trade-union rights, such as the right to picket and to organize boycotts and strikes. His efforts on behalf of workers helped organized labor to gain respect.

Summarizing How did Samuel Gompers help the labor-union movement?

© Houghton Mifflin Harcourt Publishing Company • Image Credits: (t), Brown Brothers

hmhsocialstudies.com INTERACTIVE MAP

Major Labor Strikes, Late 1800s

1 **Haymarket Riot** In May 1886 the Haymarket Riot erupted between protesters and police in Chicago. It resulted in the decline of the Knights of Labor.

2 **Homestead Strike** In 1892 a strike occurred at Carnegie Steel Company in Homestead, Pennsylvania. The resulting fight left workers and Pinkerton guards dead.

3 **Colorado Miners' Strike** In the summer of 1893, gold miners at Cripple Creek, Colorado, went on strike for higher wages and a shorter workday.

4 **Pullman Strike** The Pullman strike of 1894 began with workers who made Pullman train cars. It soon spread to workers who worked on trains pulling the sleeper cars.

5 **California Railroad Strike** In 1894 railroad workers in Oakland went on strike in the Bay Area's first major strike. Supporting Chicago Pullman workers, they halted passenger, freight, and mail trains for months.

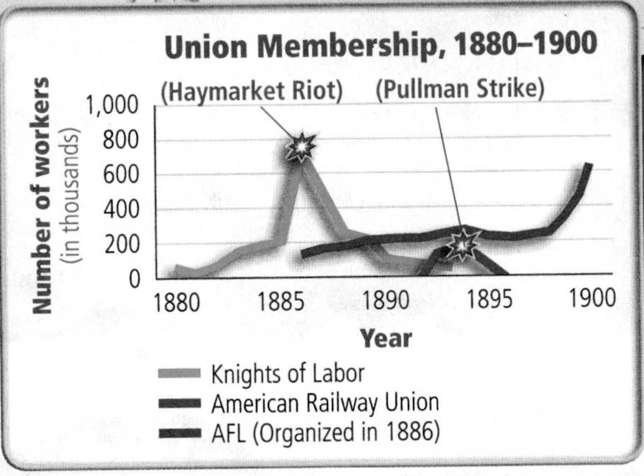

ANALYSIS SKILL **ANALYZING INFORMATION**

How did conflicts between striking workers and authorities affect union membership?

also limited its membership to skilled workers. This gave the union great bargaining power but left out most workers. The AFL tried to get better wages, hours, and working conditions for laborers. By 1890 the AFL's membership was larger than that of the Knights. With **collective bargaining** —all workers acting collectively, or together—workers had a much greater chance of success in negotiating with management. Most employers opposed collective bargaining. One company president said, "I shall never give in. I would rather go out of business."

THE IMPACT TODAY

In 1955 the AFL merged with the Congress of Industrial Organizations to become the AFL-CIO. Today the organization has more than 10 million members.

Many women took active roles in unions. For example, **Mary Harris Jones**, an Irish immigrant, worked for better conditions for miners. A fiery speaker, she organized strikes and helped educate workers.

READING CHECK **Contrasting** How did the Knights of Labor and the AFL differ?

Labor Strikes

By the late 1800s, other unions were gaining strength. Major workers' strikes swept the country and included miners in Colorado, steel workers in Pennsylvania, and railroad workers in Illinois and California. The first major labor strike began in 1886 in Chicago.

In May 1886, thousands of union members in Chicago went on strike because they wanted an eight-hour workday. Two strikers were killed in a fight with police. The next night, workers met at Haymarket Square to protest the killings. In what became known as the **Haymarket Riot**, someone threw a bomb that wounded many police officers and killed eight. The police fired into the crowd, killing several people and wounding 100 others.

© Houghton Mifflin Harcourt Publishing Company

Eight people, some of whom were not at the riot, were arrested and convicted of conspiracy. One of them had a Knights of Labor membership card. Though Knights leadership had not supported the strike, several local chapters had. Membership in the Knights fell quickly.

Sometimes, business owners succeeded in breaking up unions. In 1892 a violent strike called the **Homestead strike** took place at Andrew Carnegie's Homestead steel factory in Pennsylvania. Union members there protested a plan to buy new machinery and cut jobs. The company refused to negotiate with the union and locked workers out of the plant, hiring strike breakers to perform their jobs. The workers responded by seizing control of the plant. Gunfire erupted on July 6, when Pinkerton detectives hired by the company tried to enter the plant. A fierce battle raged for 14 hours, leaving 16 people dead. The governor called out the state militia to restore order. Continuing for four more months, the union was eventually defeated.

Another major strike happened at George Pullman's Pullman Palace Car Company in the company town of Pullman, Illinois. Most of the company workers lived there, paying high rents. During a financial depression that began in 1893, Pullman laid off about half of the workers and cut pay for those that were left, without lowering their rents. On May 11, 1894, workers began the **Pullman strike**, which stopped traffic on many railroad lines until federal courts ordered the workers to return to their jobs. President Grover Cleveland sent federal troops to Chicago to stop the strike. Such defeats seriously damaged the labor movement for years.

READING CHECK **Analyzing** What were the effects of early major strikes on workers?

SUMMARY Workers formed unions to fight for better conditions and to keep their jobs.

Section 3 Assessment

hmhsocialstudies.com
ONLINE QUIZ

Reviewing Ideas, Terms, and People

1. a. **Recall** Why did conditions in factories begin to decline?
   b. **Draw Conclusions** How were workers affected by specialization and scientific management?
   c. **Evaluate** Do you think scientific management made businesses more successful? Explain.
2. a. **Identify** What role did **Mary Harris Jones** play in the labor movement?
   b. **Analyze** Why did workers demand **collective bargaining**, and why did business owners oppose it?
   c. **Elaborate** Do you think the demands made by labor unions were reasonable? Explain your answer.
3. a. **Describe** What major labor strikes took place in the late 1800s?
   b. **Evaluate** Do you think President Cleveland was right to use federal troops to end the **Pullman strike**? Explain.

Critical Thinking

4. **Analyzing** Review your notes about the problems workers faced. Use them to complete a table like the one below about how workers tried to solve the problems they faced.

Problem	Solution

FOCUS ON WRITING

5. **Taking Notes on Working Conditions** In your notebook, list some reasons why industrial workers were unhappy with working conditions. Can you think of ways to run your business so that you can avoid the problem of strikes?

© Houghton Mifflin Harcourt Publishing Company

Analyzing Costs and Benefits

Define the Skill

Everything you do has both costs and benefits connected to it. *Benefits* are things that you gain from something. *Costs* are what you give up to obtain benefits. For example, if you buy a video game, the benefits of your action include the game itself and the enjoyment of playing it. The most clear cost is what you pay for the game. However, there are other costs that do not involve money. One is the time you spend playing the game. This is a cost because you give up something else, such as doing your homework or watching a TV show, when you choose to play the game.

The ability to analyze costs and benefits is a valuable life skill as well as a useful tool in the study of history. Weighing an action's benefits against its costs can help you decide whether or not to take it.

Learn the Skill

Analyzing the costs and benefits of historical events will help you to better understand and evaluate them. Follow these guidelines to do a cost-benefit analysis of an action or decision in history.

1. First determine what the action or decision was trying to accomplish. This step is needed in order to determine which of its effects were benefits and which were costs.
2. Then look for the positive or successful results of the action or decision. These are its benefits.
3. Consider the negative or unsuccessful effects of the action or decision. Also think about what positive things would have happened if it had *not* occurred. All these things are its costs.
4. Making a chart of the costs and benefits can be useful. By comparing the list of benefits to the list of costs you can better understand the action or decision and evaluate it.

For example, you learned in this chapter about the Second Industrial Revolution and its effects on the American economy. A cost-benefit analysis of the changes in American businesses might produce a chart like this one:

Benefits	Costs
New inventions made life easier.	New business methods ran smaller companies out of business.
Communication became easier with new technologies.	Workers received lower wages.
Efficient management reduced costs of products.	Strikes resulted in violence and deaths.
Workers began to organize for better conditions.	

Based on this chart, one might conclude that the Second Industrial Revolution was beneficial to the nation's economy.

Practice the Skill

Among the changes that occurred in the early 1900s was an increase in specialization and efficiency in the workplace. Use information from the chapter and the guidelines above to do a cost-benefit analysis of this development. Then write a paragraph explaining whether or not it was a wise one.

© Houghton Mifflin Harcourt Publishing Company

CHAPTER 4

Chapter Review

History's Impact
▶ *video series*
Review the video to answer the closing question:
What advantages and disadvantages did the assembly line create? Do you think assembly lines still exist today?

Visual Summary

QUICK FACTS

Use the visual summary below to help you review the main ideas of the chapter.

Inventions
- Bessemer process
- Lightbulb
- Automobile

Big Business
- Growth of corporations
- Wealthy business owners
- Antitrust movements

Labor Movement
- Knights of Labor
- American Federation of Labor
- Haymarket Riot
- Homestead Strike

Reviewing Vocabulary, Terms, and People

Identify the descriptions below with the correct term or person from the chapter.

1. Labor organization that represented both skilled and unskilled laborers and was the first national labor union in the United States

2. Inventor who patented the telephone in 1876

3. A way of making steel quickly and cheaply by blasting hot air through melted iron to quickly remove waste

4. A system of business in which one company owns businesses in each step of the manufacturing process

5. Powerful business leader who helped to found the Central Pacific Railroad

6. Union speaker who worked to better the lives of mine workers

7. A method of negotiating for better wages or working conditions in which all workers act together to ensure a better chance for success

Comprehension and Critical Thinking

SECTION 1

8. a. ***Identify*** What was the Second Industrial Revolution?

b. ***Draw Conclusions*** Why were advances in transportation and communication important to the Second Industrial Revolution?

c. ***Elaborate*** Which invention do you think had the greatest effect on people's lives in the late 1800s? Explain your answer.

SECTION 2

9. a. ***Recall*** What criticisms were made of business leaders and trusts?

b. ***Analyze*** How did the rise of corporations and powerful business leaders lead to the growth of big business?

c. ***Evaluate*** Do you think the growth of big business helped or hurt ordinary Americans? Explain your answer.

© Houghton Mifflin Harcourt Publishing Company

SECTION 3

10. *a. Recall* What led to poor working conditions in factories during the Second Industrial Revolution?

b. Make Inferences Why did labor unions have a better chance of improving working conditions than laborers did on their own?

c. Evaluate Did the strikes of the 1880s and 1890s hurt or help the labor movement in the long run? Explain your answer.

Reviewing Themes

11. *Economics* How did the rise of big business affect consumers in the United States?

12. *Society and Culture* What changes in society were brought about by the organization of labor?

Using the Internet

13. *Activity: Creating a Time Line* Technology in some sense has been part of human history since we began to write history. All tools are, in a sense, technology. In this chapter you read about new scientific discoveries that had positive and negative effects. Using the activities available through the online textbook, choose one technological innovation mentioned in the chapter and trace its development to the present day. Create an illustrated time line to present your research.

hmhsocialstudies.com

Reading Skills

Organization of Facts and Information *Use the Reading Skills taught in this chapter to answer the question about the reading selection below.*

> Corporations provided several important advantages over earlier business forms. Stockholders in a corporation are not responsible for business debts. If a corporation fails financially, the stockholders lose only the money that they invested. Stockholders are also usually free to sell their stock to whomever they want, whenever they want.

14. By which structural pattern is the above passage organized?

a. Listing

b. Cause-effect

c. Chronological order

d. Comparison-contrast

Social Studies Skills

Analyzing Costs and Benefits *Use the Social Studies Skills taught in this chapter to answer the question below.*

15. Write two costs and two benefits of the Pullman strike from the point of view of the workers who participated.

Focus on Writing

16. *Writing Your Business Plan* Collect your notes and determine a good product to sell during the late 1800s. Decide which business practices you would use and which you would not. Write two to three paragraphs in which you explain why your product would sell, which business practices you can use to make your product, and how to avoid conflicts with workers. Remember to explain to the investors why your plan will work.

© Houghton Mifflin Harcourt Publishing Company

CHAPTER 4 Standardized Test Practice

DIRECTIONS: Read each question and write the letter of the best response. Use the map below to answer question 1.

1

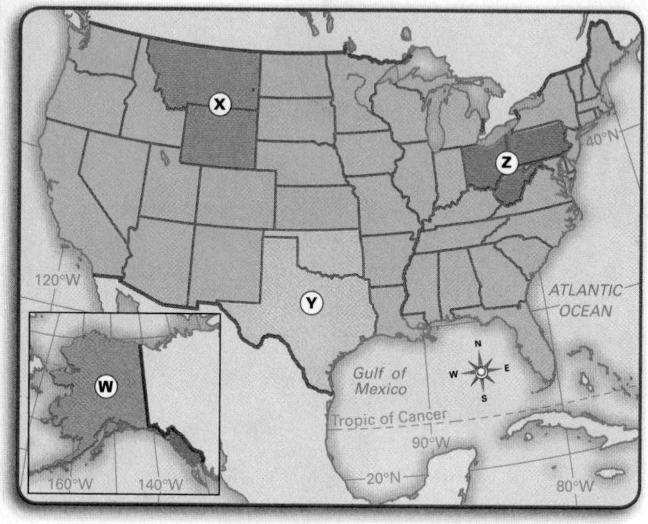

Which area on the map provided the petroleum for the oil-refining industry that arose in the United States in the mid- to late 1800s?

A the area labeled W
B the area labeled X
C the area labeled Y
D the area labeled Z

2 The person *most* responsible for making the steel industry a big business in the United States is

A John D. Rockefeller.
B Andrew Carnegie.
C Henry Bessemer.
D Leland Stanford.

3 The exclusive right to make or sell an invention or product is called

A a corporation.
B a patent.
C vertical integration.
D a trust.

4 The development of corporations in America was helped by

A suburbs.
B vertical integration.
C the Sherman Antitrust Act.
D social Darwinism.

5 Which of the following was an inventor of the late 1800s?

A Andrew Carnegie
B Thomas Edison
C Leland Stanford
D John D. Rockefeller

6 One cause of labor strikes in the late 1800s was that workers sought

A shorter workdays.
B vertical integration.
C social Darwinism.
D lower wages.

7 Read the following excerpt from the 1889 book *Recent Economic Changes* and use it to answer the question below.

> "Machinery is now recognized as essential to cheap production. Nobody can produce effectively and economically without it, and what was formerly known as domestic manfacture is now almost obsolete. But machinery is one of the most expensive of all products, and its extensive purchase and use require an amount of capital far beyond the capacity [ability] of the ordinary individual to furnish."
>
> —David Wells, quoted in *Voices of the American Past*

Document-Based Question How might the large amounts of money needed for machinery affect the future of business?

© Houghton Mifflin Harcourt Publishing Company

Henry Ford

Henry Ford was a brilliant inventor and industrialist and founder of the Ford Motor Company. He helped bring about a time of rapid growth and progress that forever changed how people worked and lived. Henry Ford grew up on his family's farm near Dearborn, Michigan. As a child, he disliked life on the farm. He found the clicks and whirs of machinery much more exciting. When Ford was 16, he went to nearby Detroit to work in a machine shop. From there, he turned his ideas for how to make affordable and well-built cars into one of the world's largest automobile companies.

Explore the amazing life and career of Henry Ford online. You can find a wealth of information, video clips, primary sources, activities, and more at hmhsocialstudies.com.

© Houghton Mifflin Harcourt Publishing Company • Image Credits: (t), ©Underwood & Underwood/Corbis

"My 'gasoline buggy' was the first and for a long time the only automobile in Detroit. It was considered . . . a nuisance, for it made a racket and it scared horses."

— Henry Ford

My Life and Work

Read the document to learn more about Henry Ford's life and career in his own words.

CLICK THROUGH

INTER/ACTIVITIES

hmhsocialstudies.com

Big Plans

Watch the video to learn more about Henry Ford's early career.

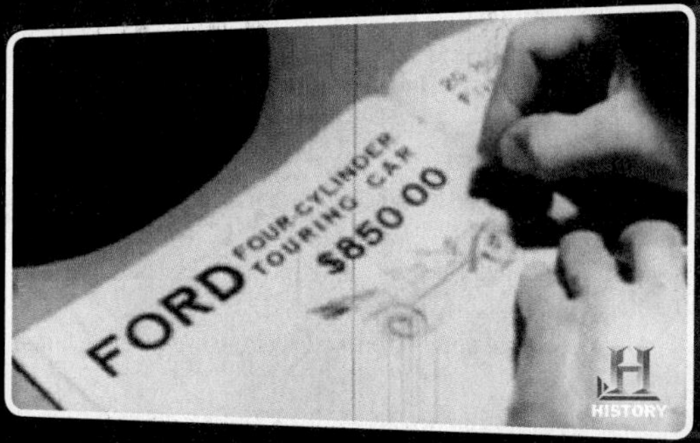

Taking the Low Road

Watch the video to explore Henry Ford's vision for his car company.

The Assembly Line

Watch the video to see how Henry Ford used the assembly line to produce cars more efficiently and cheaply.

© Houghton Mifflin Harcourt Publishing Company • Image Credits: (c), ©Underwood & Underwood/Corbis

CHAPTER 5 1872–1914

Immigrants and Urban Life

Essential Question How did immigration during the late 1800s affect the United States?

ALABAMA COURSE OF STUDY

1 Explain the impact of industrialization, urbanization, communication, and cultural changes on life in the United States from the late nineteenth century to World War I.

2 Describe reform movements and changing social conditions during the Progressive Era in the United States.

- Relating countries of origin and experiences of new immigrants to life in the United States.
- Identifying social reforms of the Progressive movement, including efforts by Jane Adams, Clara Barton, and Julia Tutwiler.

4 Identify cultural and economic developments in the United States from 1900 through the 1930s.

- Describing the emergence of the modern woman during the early 1900s.
- Identifying notable persons of the early 1900s.

Focus on Writing

A Memo You are a writer at a television network, and you have an idea for a TV drama series set in the late 1800s. Draft a memo telling your boss about your story idea. As you read this chapter, gather information about the people, places, and events of this time period. Tell about the cast of characters, the setting, and the basic plot of your series.

UNITED STATES

1873 Olmsted designs the U.S. Capitol grounds.

1876 The Centennial Exposition opens in Philadelphia.

1870

WORLD

1878 Electric streetlights are introduced in London.

© Houghton Mifflin Harcourt Publishing Company

Image Credits: (t), ©Bettmann/Corbis

HISTORY

Arrival at Ellis Island

hmhsocialstudies.com VIDEO

These immigrants to the United States entered through Ellis Island

1886 Workers complete the Statue of Liberty.

1889 Jane Addams founds Hull House in Chicago.

1893 The Ferris Wheel is introduced at the 1893 Columbian Exposition in Chicago.

1880 — 1890 — 1900 — 1910

1886 Impressionists' exhibit opens in Paris.

1891 Construction begins on Russia's Trans-Siberian Railroad.

1901 The first Nobel Prizes are awarded in Stockholm, Sweden.

© Houghton Mifflin Harcourt Publishing Company

Image Credits: (t), ©Bettmann/Corbis; (br), ©Ted Spiegel/Corbis; (cr), ©Corbis; (cl), ©Joseph Sohm, Chromosohm, Inc./Corbis

Reading Social Studies

Economics | Geography | Politics | **Society and Culture** | Science and Technology

Focus on Themes In this chapter, you will read about the changes in **society and culture** in the late 1800s. Among these changes was an increase in immigration. New immigrants to America found a society full of **economic** opportunities and hardships. Immigration and technology combined to change the way of life in cities.

Understanding Historical Fact versus Historical Fiction

Focus on Reading When you read a book like *The Red Badge of Courage* or see a movie about World War II, do you ever wonder how much is fiction and how much is fact?

Distinguishing Fact from Fiction Historical fiction gives readers a chance to meet real historical people and real historical events in the framework of a made-up story. Some of what you read in historical fiction could be verified in an encyclopedia, but other parts existed only in the author's mind until he or she put it on paper. As a good reader of history, you should know the difference between facts, which can be proved or verified, and fiction.

Notice how one reader determined which details could be verified or proved.

> That was a <u>*woman filling her pail by the hydrant*</u> you just bumped against. The <u>*sinks are in the hallway,*</u> that all the tenants may have access—and all be poisoned alike by their summer stenches. Hear the pump squeak! It is the lullaby of tenement house babes. In summer, when <u>*a thousand thirsty throats pant for a cooling drink in this block,*</u> it is worked in vain ...
>
> — From *How the Other Half Lives*, by Jacob Riis

The woman filling her pail isn't a fact I can check. He's just using her as an example of what women did.

We could probably check city records to see whether the buildings really had sinks in the hallways.

The writer is generalizing here. We probably can't prove 1,000 thirsty throats. We could find out whether the city's water pumps actually went dry in the summer. That's verifiable.

You Try It!

The following passage is from *Bread Givers* by Anzia Yezierska, a young Jewish immigrant to New York. After you read it, answer the questions below.

> Mashah [Anzia's sister] came home with stories that in rich people's homes they had silver knives and forks, separate, for each person. And new-ironed tablecloths and napkins every time they ate on them. And rich people had marble bathtubs in their own houses, with running hot and cold water all day and night long so they could take a bath any time they felt like it, instead of having to stand on a line before the public bath-house, as we had to do when we wanted a bath for the holidays. But these millionaire things were so far over our heads that they were like fairy tales.
>
> That time when Mashah had work hemming towels in an uptown house, she came home with another new-rich idea, another money-spending thing, which she said she had to have. She told us that by those Americans, everybody in the family had a toothbrush and a separate towel for himself.
>
> —Anzia Yezierska, *Bread Givers*

1. Which facts from the paragraph above can be confirmed?
2. What sources might you check to confirm some of these facts?
3. List two things from the passage that could not be confirmed.
4. Why are these two things not able to be confirmed?

As you read this Chapter, notice which facts you could easily confirm.

Key Terms and People

Chapter 5

Section 1
old immigrants
new immigrants
steerage
benevolent societies
tenements
sweatshops
Chinese Exclusion Act

Section 2
mass transit
suburbs
mass culture
Joseph Pulitzer
William Randolph Hearst
department stores
Frederick Law Olmsted

Section 3
Jacob Riis
settlement houses
Jane Addams
Hull House
Florence Kelley

Academic Vocabulary
advocate
factor

SECTION 1

A New Wave of Immigration

What You Will Learn...

Main Ideas

1. U.S. immigration patterns changed during the late 1800s as new immigrants arrived from Europe, Asia, and Mexico.
2. Immigrants worked hard to adjust to life in the United States.
3. Some Americans opposed immigration and worked to restrict it.

The Big Idea

A new wave of immigration in the late 1800s brought large numbers of immigrants to the United States.

Key Terms and People

old immigrants
new immigrants
steerage
benevolent societies
tenements
sweatshops
Chinese Exclusion Act

hmhsocialstudies.com
TAKING NOTES

Use the graphic organizer online to take notes on the benefits and challenges immigrants found.

If YOU were there...

You live with your family on a small farm in Italy in the 1890s. You want to earn some money to help your parents, but there are not many jobs nearby. You have heard that jobs are easy to find in the booming factories of the United States. But you speak no English and know no one in America.

Would you travel to the United States in search of new opportunities?

BUILDING BACKGROUND From its beginnings, America has attracted people from many parts of the world. They came for many reasons, including land, religious freedom, and the chance to start new lives. In the late 1800s, jobs created by the rapid growth of the U.S. economy drew millions of new immigrants.

Changing Patterns of Immigration

Millions of immigrants came to the United States from northern Europe in the mid-1800s. They came mainly from Great Britain, Germany, Ireland, and the countries of Scandinavia. Except for the Irish, who were Roman Catholics, most were Protestants. Many were skilled workers. Others settled in rural areas and became farmers. By the late 1800s immigrants from northern Europe were known as **old immigrants**. A newer and larger wave of immigration—from different parts of the world—was arriving in the United States.

New Immigrants

During the 1880s more than 5 million immigrants arrived in the United States—about the same number of people as had arrived during the six decades from 1800 to 1860 combined. The majority of these **new immigrants** were from southern and eastern Europe. Thousands of Czechs, Greeks, Hungarians, Italians, Poles, Russians, and Slovaks came to the United States to find new opportunities and better lives. A young woman from Russia spoke for many of her fellow immigrants when she said she hoped "for all manner of miracles in a strange, wonderful land!"

New immigrants came from many different cultural and religious backgrounds. They included Orthodox Christians, Roman Catholics, and Jews. Some were escaping political or religious persecution. They were eager for the job opportunities created by the U.S. industrial boom of the late 1800s.

Arriving in a New Land

Immigrants usually faced a difficult journey by ship to America. Most traveled in **steerage**—an area below a ship's deck where steering mechanisms were located. Steerage tickets were inexpensive, but the cabins were hot, cramped, and foul-smelling. Many passengers were seasick for the entire journey. Some even died of diseases contracted along the way.

Once in the United States, new arrivals were processed through government-run immigration centers. The busiest center on the East Coast was Ellis Island, which opened in New York Harbor in 1892. The first immigrant processed through Ellis Island was Annie Moore Schayer, a 14 year old from Ireland. Over the next 40 years, millions of European immigrants came through Ellis Island.

At immigration centers officials interviewed and examined immigrants to decide whether to let them enter the country. People with contagious diseases or legal problems could be turned away. "There was this terrible anxiety that one of us might be rejected," remembered one immigrant traveling with his family. "And if one of us was, what would the rest of the family do?" This rarely happened, however. Less than 2 percent of the people who arrived at Ellis Island were not allowed into the country.

On the West Coast, many Chinese immigrants entered the United States through Angel Island, which opened near San Francisco in 1910. Because laws limited immigration from China, only people whose fathers were U.S. citizens were allowed into the country. Chinese immigrants were often kept at Angel Island for weeks or months while officials investigated their families.

Mexican immigrants also came to the United States in large numbers in the late 1800s. The main processing center for immigrants from Mexico was in El Paso, Texas. Most settled in the Southwest. They found work in construction, steel mills, and mines, and on large commercial farms.

Primary Source

AUTOBIOGRAPHY

An Immigrant's Story

Mary Antin and her family were Jewish. They moved from Russia to Boston in the 1890s to find religious freedom. Here, Antin writes about their journey.

What do you think *fugitive* means here?

For sixteen days the ship was our world ... [It] pitched and rolled so that people were thrown from their berths [beds] ... All this while the seasickness lasted. Then came happy hours on deck, with fugitive sunshine, birds atop the crested waves, band music and dancing and fun ... And so suffering, fearing, brooding [worrying], rejoicing, we crept nearer and nearer to the coveted [wished for] shore, until, on a glorious May morning, six weeks after our departure from Polotzk our eyes beheld the Promised Land [the United States].

—Mary Antin, *The Promised Land*

Antin describes a mix of emotions.

ANALYSIS SKILL ANALYZING PRIMARY SOURCES

Why do you think Antin was both "fearing" and "rejoicing" during her trip?

READING CHECK **Contrasting** How was the experience of immigrants at Ellis Island different from that of immigrants at Angel Island?

HISTORY

VIDEO
Angel Island: Ellis Island of the West

hmhsocialstudies.com

hmhsocialstudies.com

ANIMATED HISTORY
Ellis Island

Coming to America

ASIA
NORTH AMERICA
SOUTH AMERICA
PACIFIC OCEAN
San Francisco
El Paso
New York City
40°N
Equator
160°W

In this photo, Japanese men and Chinese women leave the detention center on Angel Island in San Francisco Bay. Angel Island was the processing center for many immigrants from Asia.

Augustin and Maria Lozano and their two children are shown after moving from Mexico to California. Many Mexican immigrants moved into the Southwest.

HISTORY

VIDEO
Italians in America: Old World, New Land

hmhsocialstudies.com

Focus on Reading
How could you verify the facts in this paragraph?

Adjusting to a New Life

Once they entered the United States, immigrants began the hard work of adjusting to life in a new country. They needed to find homes and jobs. They had to learn a new language and get used to new customs. This was all part of building a new life.

Immigrant Neighborhoods

Many immigrants moved into neighborhoods with others from the same country. In these neighborhoods, they could speak their native language and eat foods that reminded them of home. Immigrants could also practice the customs that their families had passed down from generation to generation. An Italian immigrant remembered that in his new neighborhood, "cheeses from Italy, sausage, salamis were all hanging in the window."

In their newly adopted neighborhoods, many immigrant groups published newspapers in their own languages. They founded schools, clubs, and places of worship to help preserve their customs. In New York City, for example, Jewish immigrants founded a theater that gave performances in Yiddish—the language spoken by Jews from central and eastern Europe.

Immigrants often opened local shops and small neighborhood banks. Business owners helped new arrivals by offering credit and giving small loans. Such aid was important for newcomers because there were few commercial banks in immigrant neighborhoods. In 1904 Italian immigrant Amadeo Peter Giannini started the Bank of Italy in San Francisco. This bank later grew and became the Bank of America.

EUROPE
AFRICA
80°E

Swedish immigrant Swan August Swanson followed his father to Wisconsin to help with the family farm. Like many new Americans, he married within the immigrant community.

The son of Italian immigrants, Amadeo Peter Giannini founded the Bank of Italy in San Francisco in 1904. Due to his guidance and perseverance, it became the largest privately owned bank in the world.

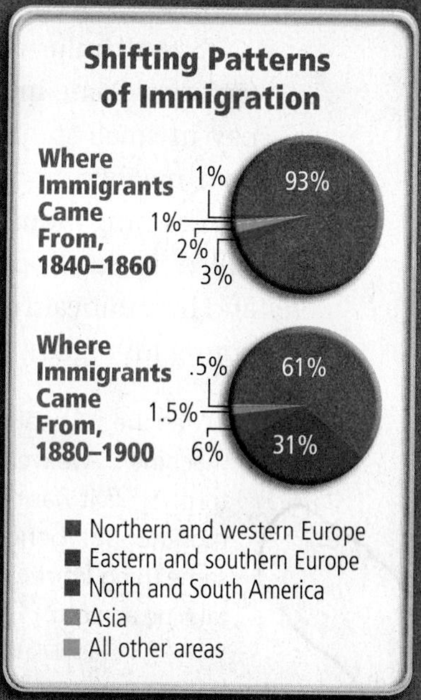
Shifting Patterns of Immigration
Where Immigrants Came From, 1840–1860
1%
1%
2%
3%
93%
Where Immigrants Came From, 1880–1900
.5%
1.5%
6%
61%
31%
Northern and western Europe
Eastern and southern Europe
North and South America
Asia
All other areas

During the late 1800s the places people came from began to change. The charts above show the percentages of people who moved from different places. The total number of immigrants reached a peak in the 1880s, when about 5 million people came to the United States.

By how much did the percentage of immigrants from northern and western Europe change from 1840 to 1900?

Some immigrant communities formed **benevolent societies**. These aid organizations offered immigrants help in cases of sickness, unemployment, or death. At that time, few national government agencies provided such aid.

Even with neighborhood support, however, immigrants often found city life difficult. Many immigrants lived in **tenements**—poorly built, overcrowded apartment buildings. One young woman in New York City described the difference between her hopes and reality in the new land:

> "[I dreamed] of the golden stairs leading to the top of the American palace where father was supposed to live. [I] went 'home' to . . . an ugly old tenement in the heart of the Lower East Side. There were stairs to climb but they were not golden."
>
> – Miriam Shomer Zusner, *Yesterday: A Memoir of a Russian Jewish Family*

Immigrants worked hard to adjust to their new country. Children often learned American customs more quickly than their parents. In public schools immigrant children learned English from McGuffey's Readers—illustrated textbooks that taught reading and writing.

Finding Work

Many new immigrants had worked on farms in their homelands. Few could afford to buy land in the United States, however. Instead, they found jobs in cities, where most of the country's manufacturing took place.

Having come from rural areas, few new immigrants were skilled in modern manufacturing or industrial work. They often had no choice but to take low-paying, unskilled jobs in garment factories, steel mills, or construction. Long hours were common.

Not all industrial labor took place in large factories. Some immigrants worked for little pay in small shops or mills located in their own neighborhoods. Often associated with the clothing industry, these workplaces were called **sweatshops** because of long hours and hot, unhealthy working conditions. One young immigrant worker remembered:

> "When the shirtwaists were finished at the machine ... we were given scissors to cut the threads off. It wasn't heavy work, but it was monotonous [boring], because you did the same thing from seven-thirty in the morning till nine at night."
>
> – Pauline Newman, quoted in *American Mosaic: The Immigrant Experience in the Words of Those Who Lived It*, by Joan Morrison and Charlotte Fox Zabusky

Immigrants with skills that were in demand sometimes found work outside factories and sweatshops. For example, some immigrants worked as bakers, carpenters, masons, or skilled machinists. Others saved or borrowed money to open small businesses such as laundries, barbershops, or street vending carts. New immigrants often opened the same types of businesses in which other immigrants from the same country were already succeeding. They worked hard for long hours to become successful themselves.

READING CHECK **Summarizing** How did new immigrants help themselves and others to try to make successful lives in the United States?

LINKING TO TODAY

Asian Americans Today

Today, almost 15 million people in the United States are of Asian origin. They account for about 5 percent of the U.S. population—or about 1 in 20 Americans. Asian Americans trace their roots to various countries, including China, India, the Philippines, and, like this family, Vietnam. Most Asian Americans live in the West. California has by far the largest Asian American population of any state.

ANALYSIS SKILL **ANALYZING INFORMATION**

Why have so many people moved to the United States?

(t) ©A. Ramey/PhotoEdit; (b) Library of Congress Prints & Photographs Division, Arnold Genthe Collections, Washington, D.C.

Opposition to Immigration

Some Americans welcomed new immigrants. Many business leaders, for example, wanted immigrant workers who were willing to work for low pay. In general, however, anti-immigrant feelings grew along with the rise in immigration in the late 1800s. Some labor unions opposed immigration because their members believed immigrants would take jobs away from native-born Americans.

Other Americans called nativists also feared that too many new immigrants were being allowed into the country. Many nativists held racial and ethnic prejudices. They thought that the new immigrants would not learn American customs, which might harm American society.

Some nativists were violent toward immigrants. Others advocated laws to stop or limit immigration. For example, in 1880 about 105,000 Chinese immigrants lived in the United States. Two years later, Congress passed the **Chinese Exclusion Act**, banning Chinese people from immigrating to the United States for 10 years. This law marked the first time a nationality was banned from entering the country. Although the law violated treaties with China, Congress continued to renew the law for decades to come. In 1892 another law was passed restricting convicts, immigrants with certain diseases, and those likely to need public assistance from entering the country.

Despite such opposition immigrants continued to arrive in large numbers. They worked for low pay in factories and built buildings, highways, and railroads. Their labor helped power the continuing industrial growth of the late 1800s and early 1900s. Although they did not always achieve their dreams as quickly as they had hoped, most immigrants were still confident about the future for themselves and their families in the United States. A Jewish immigrant from Russia named Abraham Hyman expressed this idea, saying, "Your feeling is that a better time is coming, if not for yourself, for your families, for your children."

ACADEMIC VOCABULARY

advocate to plead in favor of

READING CHECK **Analyzing** Why did nativists oppose immigration?

SUMMARY Immigrants helped build the nation's economy and cities, but they met resistance from some native-born Americans.

Section 1 Assessment

hmhsocialstudies.com ONLINE QUIZ

Reviewing Ideas, Terms, and People

1. a. **Identify** What was Ellis Island?
   b. **Contrast** What differences existed between the **old immigrants** and the **new immigrants**?
2. a. **Identify** What job opportunities were available to new immigrants?
   b. **Summarize** How did immigrants attempt to adapt to their new lives in the United States?
   c. **Elaborate** Why do you think many immigrants tolerated difficult living and working conditions?
3. a. **Recall** What was the purpose of the **Chinese Exclusion Act**?
   b. **Explain** Why did some labor unions oppose immigration?
   c. **Predict** How might the growing opposition to immigration lead to problems in the United States?

Critical Thinking

4. **Categorizing** Review your notes on the benefits and challenges new U.S. immigrants faced. Then use the following graphic organizer to categorize the challenges into different areas of life.

Education:
Work:
Challenges faced by new immigrants
Culture:
Living Conditions:

FOCUS ON WRITING

5. **Writing about Immigrants and Their Lives** Make a list of potential characters for your TV series, and be sure to include new immigrants. Take notes about what life was like for them.

© Houghton Mifflin Harcourt Publishing Company

SECTION 2

The Growth of Cities

What You Will Learn...

Main Ideas

1. Both immigrants and native-born Americans moved to growing urban areas in record numbers in the late 1800s and early 1900s.
2. New technology and ideas helped cities change and adapt to rapid population growth.

The Big Idea

American cities experienced dramatic expansion and change in the late 1800s.

Key Terms and People

mass transit
suburbs
mass culture
Joseph Pulitzer
William Randolph Hearst
department stores
Frederick Law Olmsted

hmhsocialstudies.com
TAKING NOTES

Use the graphic organizer online to take notes on the causes of the growth of cities.

If YOU were there...

The year is 1905 and you have just come to the city of Chicago from the small town where you grew up. People rush past as you stop to stare up at the skyscrapers. Elevated trains roar overhead, and electric streetcars clatter along streets already crowded with pushcarts and horse-drawn wagons.

Will you stay and look for work in this big city?

BUILDING BACKGROUND Industrial growth and a new wave of immigration swelled the populations of American cities in the late 1800s. Cities changed quickly to accommodate so many new people, offering urban residents excitement and new kinds of entertainment.

Growth of Urban Areas

In 1850 New York City was the only U.S. city with a population of more than 500,000. By 1900 New York City, Chicago, Philadelphia, St. Louis, Boston, and Baltimore all had more than half a million residents. More than 35 U.S. cities had populations greater than 100,000. About 40 percent of Americans now lived in urban areas.

As you have read, new immigrants were responsible for a lot of this urban growth. So were families from rural areas in the United States. As farm equipment replaced workers in the countryside, large numbers of rural residents moved to the cities in search of work. African Americans from the rural South also began moving to northern cities in the 1890s. They hoped to escape discrimination and find better educational and economic opportunities. Cities such as Chicago; Cleveland, Ohio; Detroit, Michigan; and New York saw large increases in their African American populations during the late 1800s and early 1900s.

Perhaps the most dramatic example of urban growth was the rise of Chicago. The city's population exploded from 30,000 in 1850 to 1.7 million in 1900. Chicago passed St. Louis as the

© Houghton Mifflin Harcourt Publishing Company

Primary Source

POSTCARD

Chicago, 1900

Postcards like this one were one way people shared the experience of visiting or living in a big city like Chicago. This scene shows a bustling street corner at which modern transportation like streetcars mingle with horse-drawn carts.

Streetcars move large numbers of people through the crowded cities.

Population Growth of Chicago, 1870–1900

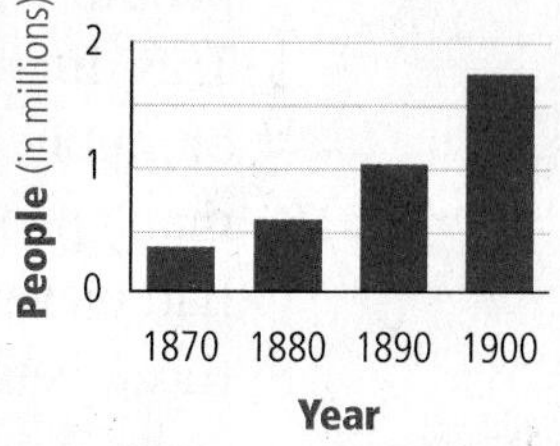

ANALYSIS SKILL ANALYZING PRIMARY SOURCES

What changes does this picture show taking place in cities at the time?

biggest city in the Midwest. Along with the large numbers of African Americans moving to the city, many of Chicago's new residents were immigrants from southern and eastern Europe. In 1900 immigrants and their children made up three quarters of Chicago's population.

Chicago's location was another factor in its rapid growth. Many of the new railroad lines connecting the East and West coasts ran through Chicago. This put Chicago at the heart of the nation's trade in lumber, grain, and meat. Thousands of new Chicago residents found work in the city's huge slaughterhouses and meatpacking plants. Here, meat from the West and Midwest was packed into refrigerated train cars and shipped to the growing cities of the East, where it could be sold in shops to customers.

READING CHECK **Identifying Cause and Effect**

What factors led to massive population growth in urban areas during the late 1800s and early 1900s?

Changing Cities

American cities such as Chicago were ill-prepared for the rapid urban growth of the late 1800s and early 1900s. Where was everyone going to live? How were people going to get from home to work on crowded city streets? Several new technologies helped cities meet these challenges. These technologies forever changed the look and function of U.S. cities.

ACADEMIC VOCABULARY

factor cause

Building Skyscrapers

With so many people moving to urban areas, cities quickly ran out of building space in downtown areas. One solution would be to build taller buildings. Typical city buildings in the mid-1800s were only five stories tall, but taller structures were impossible to construct because the building materials available were either too weak or too heavy.

This changed with the rise of the American steel industry in the late 1800s.

© Houghton Mifflin Harcourt Publishing Company • Image Credits: (t) Lake County (IL) Museum/Curt Teich Postcard Archives

THE IMPACT TODAY

Skyscrapers today use much of the same technology that was developed in the late 1800s—steel skeletons and elevators. Chicago's Willis Tower, with 110 stories, is one of the tallest buildings in the world.

Mills began producing tons of strong and inexpensive steel. Soon, architects such as Louis Sullivan of Chicago began designing multistory buildings called skyscrapers. Architects used steel beams to make sturdy frames that could support the weight of tall buildings. This allowed builders to use limited city space more efficiently.

The safety elevator, patented by Elisha Otis in the 1850s, helped make skyscrapers practical. Previous elevators had been unsafe because they would crash to the ground if the elevator cable snapped. Otis's safety elevator included a device to hold the elevator in place if the cable broke.

Getting Around

Taller buildings made it possible for more people to live and work in city centers. This increased the need for **mass transit**, or public transportation designed to move many people. By the late 1860s New York City had elevated trains running on tracks above the streets. Chicago followed in the 1890s.

Some cities built underground railroads, known as subways. In 1897 the first subway in the United States opened in Boston. In 1904 the first line of the New York City subway system began operation. Cable cars and electric trolleys also became common. These streetcars cheaply and quickly carried people in the cities to and from work.

Many Americans who could afford it moved to **suburbs**, residential neighborhoods outside of downtown areas that had begun springing up before the Civil War. Mass transit networks made such moves possible. People could live in the suburbs and take trolleys, subways, or trains into the cities.

New Ideas

In the late 1800s the United States also began to develop forms of **mass culture**, or leisure and cultural activities shared by many people. One factor contributing to mass culture was a boom in publishing. The invention of the Linotype, an automatic typesetting machine, greatly reduced the time and cost of printing. In 1850

Frederick Law Olmsted

CONNECT TO THE ARTS

Frederick Law Olmsted designed Central Park to serve as a place where New York City residents could relax, exercise, and enjoy nature. Olmsted included areas for horseback riding, ice-skating, boating, and baseball. The Children's District was designed as a place where parents could bring children to stay cool in the summer.

Why do you think a city dweller might be attracted to Central Park?

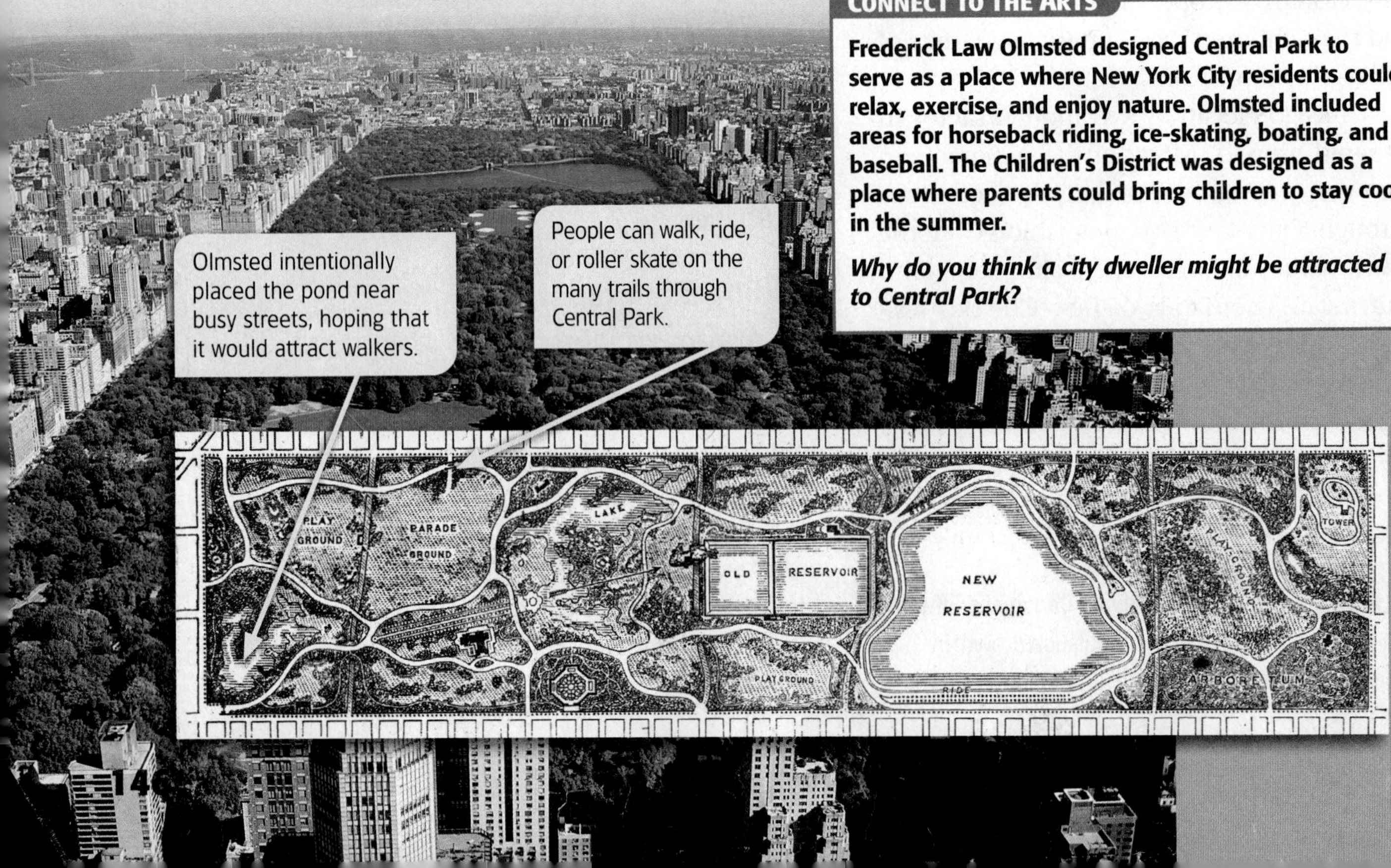

Olmsted intentionally placed the pond near busy streets, hoping that it would attract walkers.
People can walk, ride, or roller skate on the many trails through Central Park.
PLAY GROUND
PARADE GROUND
LAKE
OLD
RESERVOIR
NEW RESERVOIR
PLAY GROUND
RIDE
TOWER
ARBORETUM

© Houghton Mifflin Harcourt Publishing Company • Image Credits: (b) ©David Ball/Corbis; (bc) The Granger Collection, New York there were fewer than 300 daily newspapers in the country. Because of the use of Linotype machines, by 1900 there were more than 2,000 newspapers.

Big cities often had many newspapers, so publishers had to compete for readers. In 1896 **Joseph Pulitzer** added a color comic to his *New York World* newspaper. More people started buying Pulitzer's paper. **William Randolph Hearst**, publisher of the *New York Journal*, saw that comics helped sell newspapers. So he added a color comic strip to the *Journal*. Soon, newspapers across the country were adding comic strips.

Mass culture affected how people shopped as well. Giant retail shops, or **department stores**, appeared in some cities during the late 1800s. One of the earliest was Marshall Field in Chicago, which offered low prices and large quantities of products. It also was the first department store to offer its customers a restaurant where they could eat while shopping. Newspaper advertising was used to bring in customers. The public was also attracted by fancy window displays.

World fairs were another example of mass culture. Fairs brought merchants together, which sometimes resulted in new ideas and products. At the 1904 St. Louis World's Fair, for example, a Syrian food vendor began making cones for a nearby ice cream vendor who had run out of dishes. Ice cream cones became popular throughout the country.

The demand for public entertainment also led to the creation of amusement parks, such as New York's Coney Island. The inexpensive entry tickets made Coney Island a favorite destination for children and families. For a nickel, visitors could ride a new invention called the Switchback Railway—the country's first roller coaster.

As cities grew, people became aware of the need for open public space. Landscape architect **Frederick Law Olmsted** became nationally famous. He designed Central Park in New York City, as well as many state and national parks. Some of his other well-known projects include Prospect Park in Brooklyn, New York, and the U.S. Capitol grounds, which he worked on between 1874 and 1895.

READING CHECK **Summarizing** What forms of mass culture were available in urban areas?

SUMMARY Immigration and new technology helped cities grow in the late 1800s.

Section 2 Assessment

hmhsocialstudies.com
ONLINE QUIZ

Reviewing Ideas, Terms, and People

1. **a. Identify** What groups of people began moving to cities in the late 1800s?
   b. Explain Why did African Americans begin to move to northern cities in the 1890s?
   c. Predict Do you think cities such as Chicago continued to grow in the 1900s? Why or why not?
2. **a. Define** What is **mass transit**? What made mass transit necessary?
   b. Explain How did new inventions make it possible for people to build skyscrapers?
   c. Evaluate Which improvement to urban living do you think had the greatest impact on people's lives? Explain your answer.

Critical Thinking

3. **Identifying Cause and Effect** Review your notes on the causes for the growth of cities. Then copy the following graphic organizer and use it to identify the effects of city growth. You may need to add more circles.

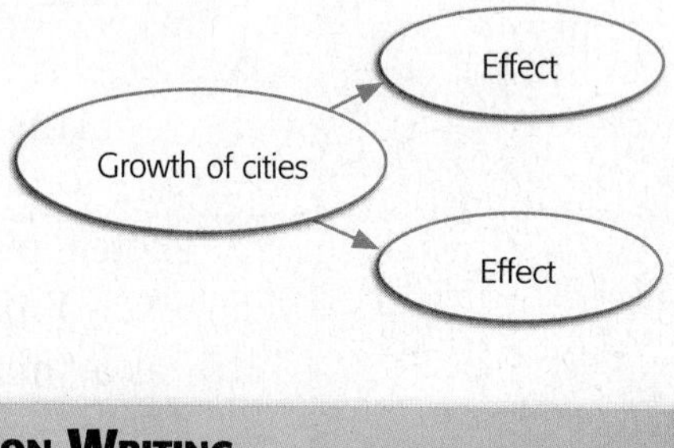

Focus on Writing

4. **Describing Setting** A city like those you have read about could serve as the setting of your TV series. How could you describe the city?

© Houghton Mifflin Harcourt Publishing Company

SECTION 3

City Life

What You Will Learn...

Main Ideas

1. Crowded urban areas faced a variety of social problems.
2. People worked to improve the quality of life in U.S. cities.

The Big Idea

The rapid growth of cities in the late 1800s created both challenges and opportunities.

Key Terms and People

Jacob Riis
settlement houses
Jane Addams
Hull House
Florence Kelley

hmhsocialstudies.com
TAKING NOTES

Use the graphic organizer online to take notes on problems facing city residents.

If YOU were there...

You live in a fast-growing city in 1895. When you walk the streets, you meet families that are packed into run-down apartments in crowded, filthy neighborhoods. You meet immigrants who want to study English but have no money for classes. You are determined to help these city residents improve their lives.

What would you do to help improve life in your city?

BUILDING BACKGROUND Despite the new public parks, skyscrapers, and mass transit systems, many cities were not ready for the rapid population growth that began taking place in the late 1800s. Overcrowding and poor living conditions forced people to search for solutions to these problems.

Urban Problems

In the late 1800s and early 1900s, shortages of affordable housing forced many poor families to squeeze into tiny tenement apartments, which were frequently unsafe and unsanitary. Journalist and photographer **Jacob Riis** became famous for exposing the horrible conditions in New York City tenements. Riis wrote about one typical tenement family:

> "There were nine in the family: husband, wife, an aged grandmother, and six children... All nine lived in two rooms, one about ten feet square that served as parlor, bedroom, and eating-room, the other a small hall-room made into a kitchen."
>
> — Jacob Riis, *How the Other Half Lives*

This kind of overcrowding caused sanitation problems. Most cities did not have a good system for collecting trash, so garbage often piled up outside apartment buildings. An article in the *New York Tribune* described the garbage in front of one tenement as a "mass of air poisoning, death-breeding filth, reeking in the fierce sunshine."

Unsafe conditions were also common in tenements. Before 1900 most cities did not have laws requiring landlords to fix their tenements or to maintain safety standards. A fire on one floor could easily spread, and fire escapes were often blocked or broken.

© Houghton Mifflin Harcourt Publishing Company

Tenement Life

QUICK FACTS

Causes
- Overcrowding
- Unsafe buildings
- Unsanitary conditions
- Scarce running water
- Poor ventilation

Effects
- Diseases such as tuberculosis and cholera
- High child death rates
- Fire
- Crime

Tenement rooms had few or no windows to let in fresh air and sunshine. Comfort was also scarce, with so many people crowded into such small spaces. Running water and indoor plumbing were also scarce. So was clean water—cities often dumped garbage into local rivers that were used for drinking water.

Disease-causing bacteria grew easily in these conditions. Diseases such as cholera, typhoid, influenza, and tuberculosis spread quickly in crowded neighborhoods. Children were the most vulnerable to these diseases. For example, babies born in Chicago in 1870 had only a 50 percent chance of living to the age of five.

Air pollution was also a serious problem in many growing cities. This was a time when many business leaders were building huge oil refineries, steel mills, and other factories. The steel mills of Andrew Carnegie, for example, helped make Pittsburgh the nation's steelmaking center in the late 1800s. Steel mills brought jobs and wealth to Pittsburgh, but they also caused some of the nation's worst air pollution. "Every street appears to end in a huge, black cloud," said one writer. "Pittsburgh is smoke, smoke, smoke—everywhere smoke." The air was so polluted at times that the city had to turn on outdoor lighting during the day.

The work of many city governments slowly helped to lessen some of these urban problems. By the late 1800s new sewage and water purification systems improved city sanitation. Many major cities also were hiring full-time firefighters and police officers. Police officers in cities were typically placed in one neighborhood. They knew the local residents and were frequently involved in local activities. They could spot local problems and, in many cases, provide help to immigrants.

THE IMPACT TODAY

Like many industrial cities, Pittsburgh has made great progress in cleaning its air and water. Today, Pittsburgh is ranked as one of the cleanest American cities.

READING CHECK **Summarizing** What challenges did many city residents face in the late 1800s?

© Houghton Mifflin Harcourt Publishing Company • Image Credits: (tr), The Granger Collection, New York

Improving City Life

Jacob Riis hoped his book *How the Other Half Lives* would shock many Americans—and it did. A reformer named Lawrence Veiller helped lead the effort to improve conditions in tenements. Describing the effects of tenement living on children, he wrote:

> "A child living its early years in dark rooms, without sunlight or fresh air, does not grow up to be a normal, healthy person ... It is not of such material that strong nations are made."
>
> – Lawrence Veiller, quoted in *Readings in American History, Vol. 2*

Veiller worked with an organization called the Charity Organization Society (COS) to get changes made to New York laws. In 1900 he and the COS sponsored an exhibit of photographs and maps graphically showing the conditions of New York tenements. More than 10,000 people visited the exhibit, and they were shocked by what they saw. The work of Veiller and the COS helped to get the 1901 New York State Tenement House Act passed. This law required new buildings to have better ventilation and running water. The act became a model for housing reform in other states.

Because there was little government aid available in the 1800s, private organizations generally took on the task of helping the urban poor. Some individuals set up **settlement houses**, or neighborhood centers in poor areas that offered education, recreation, and social activities.

Settlement houses were staffed by professionals and volunteers. Many were educated women who came from wealthy families. In 1886 Charles B. Stover and Stanton Coit established the first settlement house in the United States. It was called Neighborhood Guild and was located on the Lower East Side in New York City. In 1889 **Jane Addams** and Ellen Gates Starr moved into a run-down building in a poor Chicago neighborhood and turned it into **Hull House**, the most famous settlement house of the period.

The Hull House staff focused on the needs of immigrant families, and by 1893 Hull House was serving 2,000 people a week. It provided services such as English classes, day care, and cooking and sewing classes. Children and adults came to take part in club meetings, art classes, plays, and sports.

Jane Addams and the staff at Hull House also worked for reforms. They studied the problems facing immigrants and poor city dwellers, then searched for ways to improve conditions. **Florence Kelley** was one important reformer at Hull House. She visited sweatshops and wrote about the problems there. Her work helped convince lawmakers to take action. Illinois passed a law in 1893 to limit working hours for women and to prevent child labor.

Kelley became the state's chief factory inspector and helped enforce the law. Although she believed more reforms were needed, she did report some improvements:

Hull House

Neighborhood children attended kindergarten at Hull House. Their parents typically had low-paying jobs, and many were children of immigrants. Children like these had few other options for education.

How did Hull House try to improve the lives of children?

© Houghton Mifflin Harcourt Publishing Company • Image Credits: (bl), Wallace Kirkland/Time & Life Pictures/Getty Images

"Previous to the passage of the factory law of 1893, it was the rule of [a candy] factory to work the children . . . from 7 A.M. to 9 P.M., with twenty minutes for lunch, and no supper, a working week of eighty-two hours . . . Since the enactment of the factory law, their working week has consisted of six days of eight hours each, a reduction of thirty-four hours a week."

– Florence Kelley and Alzina P. Stevens, from *Hull House Maps and Papers*

As Hull House gained recognition, the settlement house movement spread to other cities. Most settlement houses continued to provide programs and services for city dwellers through the early 1900s. Some, such as Germantown Settlement in Pennsylvania, remain active today.

READING CHECK **Drawing Conclusions** How did Hull House help improve city life?

SUMMARY Reformers in the late 1800s worked to solve urban problems.

BIOGRAPHY

Jane Addams

1860–1935

Jane Addams was born in Cedarville, Illinois. Like many upper-class women of the era, she received a college education but found few jobs open to her. In 1888, on a visit to England with classmate Ellen Gates Starr, she visited a London settlement house. On their return to the United States, Addams and Starr opened a settlement house in Chicago. They started a kindergarten and a public playground. Addams also became involved in housing safety and sanitation issues, factory inspection, and immigrants' rights. In 1931 she shared the Nobel Peace Prize for her work with the Women's International League for Peace and Freedom.

Summarizing How did Jane Addams try to improve the lives of workers?

Section 3 Assessment

hmhsocialstudies.com ONLINE QUIZ

Reviewing Ideas, Terms, and People

1. a. **Describe** What were conditions like in tenements?
   b. **Summarize** What problems resulted from the rapid growth of cities?
   c. **Draw Conclusions** Why do you think people lived in tenements?
2. a. **Define** What is a **settlement house**?
   b. **Explain** How did settlement houses help city dwellers?
   c. **Evaluate** Do you think settlement houses were successful? Why or why not?

Critical Thinking

3. **Categorizing** Review your notes on urban problems. Then copy the chart to the right onto your own sheet of paper and use it to identify the responses to those problems.

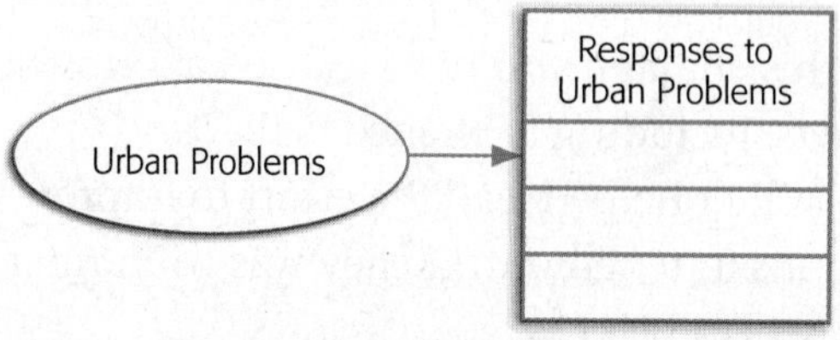

FOCUS ON WRITING

4. **Writing about Urban Problems** Finding solutions to problems is an important part of the plot of many stories. Take notes on scenes you could include in your TV series in which characters deal with the problems of urban life.

© Houghton Mifflin Harcourt Publishing Company

Making Comparisons

Define the Skill

Understanding similarities is important when studying history. Comparing two or more people, things, events, or ideas highlights the similarities between them. Making comparisons can help clarify larger historical issues. This is true when comparing different time periods or when comparing different things from the same time period. Making comparisons is important in identifying historical connections.

Learn the Skill

When you encounter similar people, things, events, or ideas in history, use the following guidelines to make comparisons.

1. Identify who or what you are going to compare.
2. Look for similarities between them. Find examples of what makes them alike. Note any differences as well.
3. Use comparison words such as "like," "both," and "similar" to point out similarities.

In this chapter, you have learned about several reformers, including Lawrence Veiller and Florence Kelley. Veiller helped lead the effort to improve conditions in tenements. Kelley was a reformer who worked at Hull House.

Lawrence Veiller and Florence Kelley were alike in many ways. Although Veiller focused on tenements and Kelley concentrated on factory work, both were concerned with problems that affected children. Both did research about their issues. Both then wrote about the poor conditions they found.

Both Veiller and Kelley worked successfully for laws that would improve those conditions. Kelley's work helped convince Illinois lawmakers to pass a law to limit child labor. Similarly, Veiller helped to get the 1901 New York State Tenement House Act passed.

Practice the Skill

Review the chapter to find two people, things, events, or ideas that are similar. Then apply the guidelines to answer the following questions.

1. Which people, events, or ideas will you compare? Why is each of them important?
2. How are they alike? How are they different?

© Houghton Mifflin Harcourt Publishing Company

CHAPTER 5

Chapter Review

History's Impact

▶ **video series**

Review the video to answer the closing question:

Why do you think the United States had stricter immigration regulations for Asian immigrants?

Visual Summary

QUICK FACTS

Use the visual summary below to help you review the main ideas of the chapter.

People Arrived

- New immigrants, mostly from southern and eastern Europe
- Came for new opportunities and better lives
- Mostly found jobs in cities
- Faced opposition from some Americans

Cities Grew

- Massive urban growth
- New technologies emerged—skyscrapers and mass transit
- New urban culture

Problems Developed

- Overcrowded tenements
- Unsanitary conditions

Reviewing Vocabulary, Terms, and People

Identify the descriptions below with the correct term or person from the chapter.

1. Public transportation systems built to move many people and ease traffic in crowded cities
2. Founded Hull House with Ellen Gates Starr in 1889
3. Organizations created by immigrants to help each other in times of sickness, unemployment, or other troubles
4. Law banning Chinese people from moving to the United States
5. Neighborhood centers in poor urban areas that offered education, recreation, and social activities
6. Landscape architect who designed New York City's Central Park
7. Small shops or mills where immigrants worked for long hours in hot, unhealthy conditions

Comprehension and Critical Thinking

SECTION 1

8. a. Identify From what parts of the world did the wave of new immigrants come?

b. Analyze In what ways did immigration patterns in the United States change in the late 1800s?

c. Elaborate In your opinion, were the difficulties that immigrants faced worth the benefits of life in the United States? Explain.

SECTION 2

9. a. Recall Why did U.S. cities experience such rapid growth in the late 1800s?

b. Analyze How did new technologies help cities deal with population growth?

c. Elaborate Would you have preferred to live in a city or in a suburb? Why?

© Houghton Mifflin Harcourt Publishing Company

SECTION 3

10. a. **Recall** What were conditions like in tenements in the late 1800s?

    b. **Make Inferences** Why did rapid population growth cause problems in cities?

    c. **Elaborate** Why do you think the settlement house movement grew in the late 1800s and early 1900s?

Reviewing Themes

11. **Economics** What role did economics play in the growth of cities?
12. **Society and Culture** How did the lives of city dwellers change with the rise of mass culture?

Reading Skills

Understanding Historical Fact versus Historical Fiction *Use the Reading Skills taught in this chapter to answer the question about the reading selection below.*

> Mass culture affected how people shopped as well. Giant retail shops, or department stores, appeared in some cities during the late 1800s. One of the earliest was Marshall Field in Chicago, which offered low prices and large quantities of products. It also was the first department store to offer its customers a restaurant where they could eat while shopping. Newspaper advertising was used to bring in customers. The public was also attracted by fancy window displays.

13. Which facts above can be verified? Where would you look to verify them?

Social Studies Skills

Making Comparisons *Use the Social Studies Skills taught in this chapter to answer the question below.*

14. Choose two reforms that were discussed in this chapter. Make a comparison between the two.

Using the Internet

15. **Activity: Investigating Culture** Mass culture developed in the late 1800s and early 1900s as a result of new and broader forms of communication taking root. Using the online textbook, explore some of the early influences on mass culture. Then research the ways in which modern culture is influenced by the media, the Internet, and other forms of mass communication. How does today's society experience mass culture? Create a visual display or computer-based presentation that compares mass culture then and now.

hmhsocialstudies.com

Focus on Writing

16. **Writing Your Memo** Look back over your notes about the people, places, and events of the late 1800s. Decide which of these you will include in your television drama series. Then draft a one- to two-paragraph memo to your boss describing the series. Remember to describe the basic plot, setting, and characters.

© Houghton Mifflin Harcourt Publishing Company • Image Credits: (b), HMH Photo

CHAPTER 5

Standardized Test Practice

DIRECTIONS: Read each question and write the letter of the best response.

1 Which of the following is associated with providing a better life for urban immigrants in the late 1800s and early 1900s?

A the department store
B the suburb
C the tenement
D the settlement house

2 Immigrants to the United States in the late 1800s and early 1900s came *mainly* from

A southern and eastern Europe.
B Japan, China, and the rest of Asia.
C Mexico and Central America.
D northern and western Europe.

3 Ellis Island and Angel Island were both

A locations of settlement houses.
B immigration processing centers.
C centers of shipping and industry.
D amusement parks.

4 Which of the following is an example of mass culture?

A newspaper comics
B immigrant neighborhoods
C Yiddish-language theaters
D subways

5 The *main* goal of Hull House was to

A provide jobs for wealthy women.
B pass the Tenement House Act of 1901.
C help poor immigrants.
D oppose the Chinese Exclusion Act.

6 Anti-immigrant feeling resulted in

A benevolent societies.
B the Chinese Exclusion Act.
C tenements.
D the Tenement House Act.

7 Which of the following groups moved from the southern United States to the North in large numbers during the 1890s?

A Chinese immigrants
B Mexican Americans
C African Americans
D Irish immigrants

8 Read this 1896 newspaper article describing poor conditions faced by many people and use it to answer the question below.

> "lack of family privacy … lack of light and air, and of sanitary accommodations, insuring a large death rate, and danger from fire … [These places are] infested with vermin [insects] and infected with disease germs, they are a disgrace to humanity and a menace, not only to the health of the unfortunate residents therein, but to the health of the whole community."
>
> —*The New York Times*, 1896

Document-Based Question Based on this description, to what was this article most likely referring?

Ellis Island

For most European immigrants, Ellis Island was the first stop. Between 1892 and 1954, the immigration station processed over 12 million immigrants. These immigrants went through an inspection before they were allowed to enter the United States. Those with serious health problems were sent home, as were those who did not meet various legal requirements. Others were sent home because they exceeded immigration quotas. However, if immigrants could clear these hurdles, they were free to enter the United States and begin their new lives.

Go online to explore some of the personal stories and recollections of immigrants who made the journey to America and passed through Ellis Island. You can find a wealth of information, video clips, primary sources, activities, and more at hmhsocialstudies.com.

© Houghton Mifflin Harcourt Publishing Company • Image Credits: (c) Illustration by Nick Rotundo/Bizzy Productions, Inc.

1. Doctors examined immigrants as they headed upstairs to the Great Hall.
2. Lines were long, but the inspection often lasted only a few minutes.
3. Immigrants who passed the inspection could exchange money, send mail or telegrams, or buy train tickets.
4. Immigrants then met relatives or loved ones.
5. Immigrants who had to stay overnight were assigned to dormitories.

© Houghton Mifflin Harcourt Publishing Company • Image Credits: (c) Illustration by Nick Rotundo/Bizzy Productions, Inc.

CLICK THROUGH INTERACTIVITIES

hmhsocialstudies.com

The Golden Door

Watch the video to see how and why immigrants traveled to the United States.

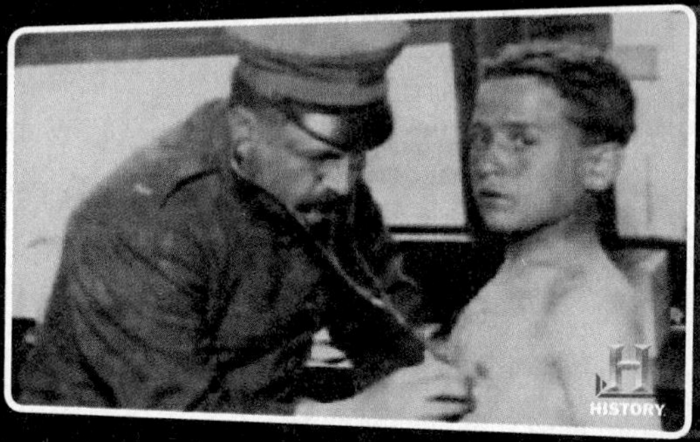

Examination

Watch the video to see the physical examination that immigrants experienced at Ellis Island.

Quotas

Watch the video to see how immigration quotas affected immigrants trying to come to the United States.

21st CENTURY

Assignment

Write a persuasive essay either for or against one of these statements.

1. New laws should have limited immigration in the late 1800s.
2. The government should have done more to improve conditions in tenements.

TIP Using Order of Importance

How do you know whether to start or end with your most important or most convincing reason? If you are worried about getting your readers to read your entire paper, you might try to catch their attention by starting with the most convincing reason. If you are concerned that your readers remember one point after they finish reading, you may want to place that point, or reason, at the end of your paper.

Persuasion and History

You have probably heard people disagree about current political events—perhaps a new law or a government leader. People also disagree about events of the past. When we disagree about historical events, those of the past or those of the present, we can use persuasive arguments to convince others to agree with our opinion.

1. Prewrite

Stating Your Opinion

Persuasion starts with an opinion or a position on a topic. Choose one of the statements in the assignment and decide on your opinion, either for or against. Write your opinion in a statement: it will be the big idea of your persuasive paper. For example, here is an opinion statement about the first topic:

The government should not have limited immigration in the late 1800s.

Building and Organizing a Logical Argument

A strong persuasive essay includes a logical argument, sound reasoning, and proof in support of an opinion. Reasons tell *why* you have an opinion. Proof, or evidence, includes facts, examples, or expert opinions.

- **Opinion:** *Reformers' work improved Americans' lives.*
- **Reason:** *Reforms improved life in cities.*
- **Evidence:** *Lawrence Veiller influenced the passage of the 1901 New York State Tenement House Act.*

Persuasive writing is usually organized by order of importance.

2. Write

Here is a framework to help you write your first draft.

A Writer's Framework

Introduction	Body	Conclusion
■ Start with an interesting opener, such as a quotation or a surprising fact. ■ Include your opinion statement, or big idea, for the paper.	■ Present one reason and its supporting evidence in each body paragraph. ■ Address your reasons by order of importance.	■ Restate your opinion in different words. ■ Summarize your reasons. ■ Make a connection to a current event.

© Houghton Mifflin Harcourt Publishing Company

3. Evaluate and Revise

Evaluating

Use these questions to discover ways to improve your draft.

Evaluation Questions for a Persuasive Essay

- Does your introduction include a clear statement of your opinion on the topic?
- Do you present your reasons by order of importance in the body paragraphs?
- Do you provide at least three reasons to support your opinion?
- Do you include facts, examples, or expert opinions to support each reason?
- Do you restate your opinion in different words in your conclusion?
- Does your conclusion include a summary of the reasons that support your opinion?

TIP **Fact vs. Opinion** Knowing the difference between a fact and an opinion is important for both writers and readers of persuasive essays.

- **Facts** are statements that can be proven true or false. *Jane Addams founded Hull House in 1889.*
- **Opinions** are statements of personal belief and cannot be proven. *Jane Addams was the greatest American woman of her time.*

Revising

Your essay will be more forceful if you write in the active voice.

Passive voice: *New parks were designed by Frederick Law Olmsted.*

Active voice: *Frederick Law Olmsted designed new parks.*

Active voice is more forceful, and often clearer, because it makes a stronger connection between the action and the actor. However, we may use passive voice because we do not know, or do not want to say, who the actor is or was.

Example: *New parks were designed in the late 1800s.*

4. Proofread and Publish

Proofreading

If you are writing your paper on a computer, you should use the spell-check feature to look for spelling errors. However, the spell-check feature will not help much if you have used the wrong word. Here are some examples to look for: *their/they're, its/it's, accept/except, affect/effect, advice/advise, altar/alter, capitol/capital.* When you spot one of these words in your paper, check your dictionary to make sure you have used the correct word.

Publishing

Share your essay with a classmate who took an opinion opposed to yours. Review each other's reasons. Can one of you persuade the other?

5. Practice and Apply

Use the steps and strategies in this workshop to write a persuasive essay.

© Houghton Mifflin Harcourt Publishing Company

UNIT 3 1867–1920

The Beginning of Modern America

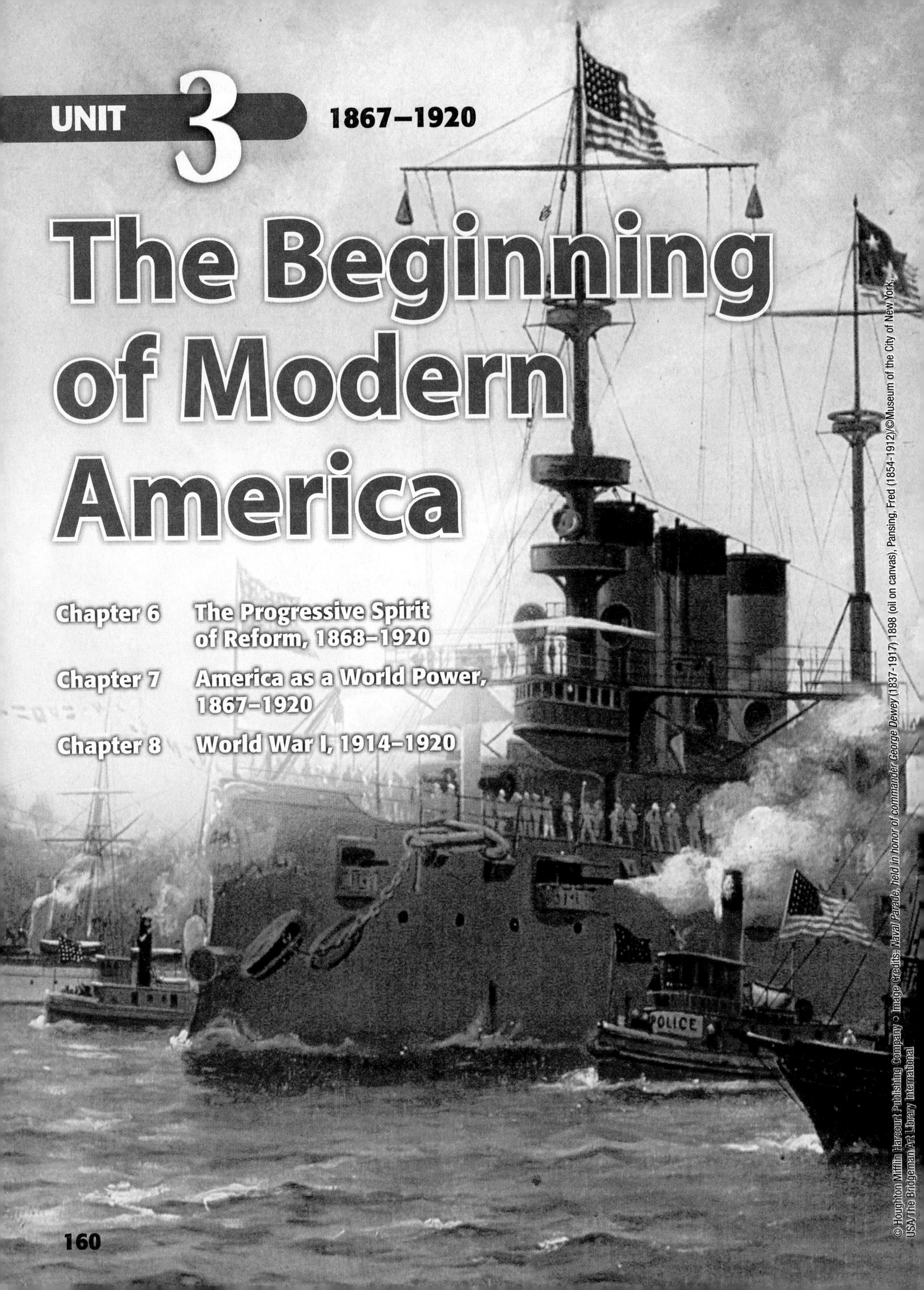

© Houghton Mifflin Harcourt Publishing Company • Image Credits: *Naval Parade, held in honor of commander George Dewey* (1837-1917) 1898 (oil on canvas), Pansing, Fred (1854-1912)/©Museum of the City of New York, USA/The Bridgeman Art Library International

What You Will Learn...

As cities in the United States became more prosperous, people began to examine the inequalities in American society. A progressive spirit emerged that led to changes in American culture. The United States also began to expand its influence overseas.

Presidents were called upon to deal with many domestic and foreign challenges, including two wars that changed the landscape of international politics. During the Spanish-American War, the United States acquired overseas territories. During World War I, Americans fought in Europe for the first time.

Explore the Art

This painting shows the Great White Fleet, a group of U.S. ships that toured the world from 1907 to 1909. How might a tour of American ships affect foreign views of the United States?

© Houghton Mifflin Harcourt Publishing Company • Image Credits: *Naval Parade, held in honor of commander George Dewey* (1837-1917) 1898 (oil on canvas), Pansing, Fred (1854-1912)/©Museum of the City of New York, USA/The Bridgeman Art Library International

CHAPTER 6 1868–1920

The Progressive Spirit of Reform

Essential Question How did Americans benefit from Progressive reforms?

ALABAMA COURSE OF STUDY

1 Explain the impact of industrialization, urbanization, communication, and cultural changes on life in the United States from the late nineteenth century to World War I.

2 Describe reform movements and changing social conditions during the Progressive Era in the United States.

- Identifying workplace reforms, including the eight-hour workday, child labor laws, and workers' compensation laws.
- Identifying political reforms of Progressive movement leaders, including Theodore Roosevelt and the establishment of the national park system.
- Identifying social reforms of the Progressive movement, including efforts by Jane Adams, Clara Barton, and Julia Tutwiler.
- Recognizing goals of the early civil rights movement and the purpose of the National Association for the Advancement of Colored People (NAACP).
- Explaining Progressive movement provisions of the Sixteenth, Seventeenth, Eighteenth, Nineteenth, and Twenty-first Amendments to the Constitution of the United States.

4 Identify cultural and economic developments in the United States from 1900 through the 1930s.

- Describing the emergence of the modern woman during the early 1900s.
- Identifying notable persons of the early 1900s.

Focus on Speaking

Campaign Promises In this chapter you will read about the political corruption of the Gilded Age and the reform movements that followed. Serious problems face the nation, and you must convince voters that you should be the one to tackle those problems. Create and present a list of campaign promises that you would make if you were a politician running for office in the United States in the late 1800s or early 1900s.

UNITED STATES

1868 Ulysses S. Grant is elected president.

1865 — 1870

1871 The British Parliament legalizes labor unions.

WORLD

© Houghton Mifflin Harcourt Publishing Company

Image Credits: (t), ©Bettmann/Corbis

The reform movements of the late 1800s and early 1900s were led by ordinary citizens, such as these women calling for their right to vote.

HISTORY Teddy Roosevelt vs. Corporate America

hmhsocialstudies.com VIDEO

1881 Charles Guiteau, a frustrated federal job seeker, assassinates President James A. Garfield.

1888 Brazil officially ends slavery.

1901 President William McKinley is assassinated, and Vice President Theodore Roosevelt becomes president.

1912 The British luxury liner *Titanic* sinks after hitting an iceberg during its first voyage. About 1,500 passengers die.

1917 Mexico adopts a new constitution.

1920 Congress declares the Nineteenth Amendment ratified, giving women the right to vote.

1880 1890 1900 1910 1920

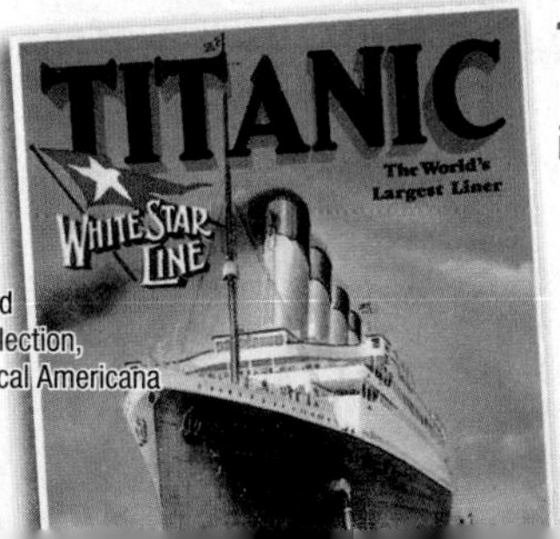

Image Credits: (t), ©Bettmann/Corbis; (cr), Janice L. and David J. Frent Collection of Political Americana; (b), The Granger Collection, New York; (cl), Janice L. and David J. Frent Collection of Political Americana

© Houghton Mifflin Harcourt Publishing Company

Reading Social Studies

Economics | Geography | **Politics** | **Society and Culture** | Science and Technology

Focus on Themes In this chapter, you will read about the corrupt **politics** of the Gilded Age, a time marked by attempts at reform. You will learn how **society and culture** reacted and responded to the problems of corruption and inequality. Finally, you will read about several presidents of the early 1900s who supported ideas and initiatives that promoted social reform.

Evaluating Sources

Focus on Reading Historical texts and current history books are good sources of information about the past. However, some sources can be more reliable than others to learn the truth.

Evaluating Texts Sometimes people write texts with a specific purpose or viewpoint in mind. Determining what the author's goal was in writing a passage can help you evaluate whether to believe all of the text, or merely some of it. Knowing which parts you can believe and which you cannot will help you understand what really happened in history.

Notice how one reader evaluated the source below.

> The man, therefore, who as the owner of newspapers, would corrupt public opinion is the most dangerous enemy of the State. We may talk about the perils incident [dangers attached] to the concentration of wealth, about the perils flowing from a disregard of fiduciary [financial] responsibility, about abuses of privilege, about exploiting the government for private advantage; but all of these menaces, great as they are, are nothing compared with a deliberate, persistent, artful, purchased endeavor to [change and direct] the public judgment.
>
> –*Harper's Weekly*, October 20, 1906, quoted in *Yellow Journalism* by W. Joseph Campbell

The author is using strong words to describe his viewpoint. Maybe he isn't being as objective as he should be.

The article lists several ideas that the author seems to think are bad. Are these things really bad? Can that help me determine the author's viewpoint?

This magazine was widely read when the article appeared. I think that makes the article a good source for some viewpoints of the time.

© Houghton Mifflin Harcourt Publishing Company

You Try It!

Read the passage below and evaluate whether you would use it as a source for a paper.

> Space is no intervention now between communication. [N]ot only do the wires of copper bind the world together in closer communication, but with the telephone it is possible to converse [talk] with friends a thousand miles away, hearing distinctly every word and recognizing the individual voice. Closer acquaintance has thus wrought [created] vast changes in public opinions and policies. The entire civilized world has been drawn more closely together, old ideas and prejudices have been wiped out.
>
> –*Cincinnati Times-Star,* January 1, 1900, quoted in *Yellow Journalism* by W. Joseph Campbell

1. What viewpoint of new technology is the author taking in this article? How can you tell?
2. Do you believe that the telephone brought about "changes in public opinions and policies"? Why or why not? Why might the author say this?
3. Can you trust the author when he says that "old ideas and prejudices have been wiped out"? Why or why not? Why might the author say this?
4. Did this article appear in a well-known newspaper? Does this make it more trustworthy or less?
5. Would you use this article as a source for writing a paper about how new inventions affected life in the early 1900s? Explain your answer.

As you read this chapter, evaluate the primary sources for their usefulness in understanding history.

Key Terms and People

Chapter 6

Section 1

political machines
Progressives
muckrakers
Seventeenth Amendment
recall
initiative
referendum
Robert M. La Follette

Section 2

Triangle Shirtwaist Fire
workers' compensation laws
capitalism
socialism
William "Big Bill" Haywood
Industrial Workers of the World

Section 3

Eighteenth Amendment
National American Woman Suffrage Association
Alice Paul
Nineteenth Amendment
Booker T. Washington
Ida B. Wells
W. E. B. Du Bois
National Association for the Advancement of Colored People

Section 4

Theodore Roosevelt
Pure Food and Drug Act
conservation
William Howard Taft
Progressive Party
Woodrow Wilson
Sixteenth Amendment

Academic Vocabulary

In this chapter you will learn the following academic words:

motive
various

© Houghton Mifflin Harcourt Publishing Company

SECTION 1

The Gilded Age and the Progressive Movement

What You Will Learn...

Main Ideas

1. Political corruption was common during the Gilded Age.
2. Progressives pushed for reforms to improve living conditions.
3. Progressive reforms expanded the voting power of citizens.

The Big Idea

From the late 1800s through the early 1900s, the Progressive movement addressed problems in American society.

Key Terms and People

political machines
Progressives
muckrakers
Seventeenth Amendment
recall
initiative
referendum
Robert M. La Follette

hmhsocialstudies.com
TAKING NOTES

Use the graphic organizer online to take notes on progressive reforms and the problems they addressed.

If YOU were there...

You live in a big-city neighborhood in the 1890s. You and your brother are both looking for jobs. You know that the man down the street is the "ward boss." He can always get city jobs for his friends and neighbors. But in return you'll have to promise to vote the way he tells you to in the upcoming election.

Would you ask the ward boss for a job? Why or why not?

BUILDING BACKGROUND The late 1800s were a time of contrasts in American life. Great wealth created through business ventures existed alongside poverty and the difficulties of tenement life. In politics, money led to corruption and dishonesty. Reacting to these conditions, reformers worked to improve many areas of American life.

Political Corruption

The late 1800s in the United States are often called the Gilded Age. The term came from a novel by that name. *The Gilded Age* highlights the inequality between wealthy business owners, who profited from the Industrial Revolution, and workers, who often labored under terrible conditions for little pay. Many people began to believe that the government should help fix this inequality. The first step was to get rid of corruption in politics.

Political Machines

In the late 1800s city and county politics were dominated by **political machines**—powerful organizations that used both legal and illegal methods to get their candidates elected to public office. For example, members of political machines sometimes stuffed ballot boxes with extra votes for their candidates. They also paid people to vote a certain way and then bribed vote counters. Through such actions, political machines could control local governments.

© Houghton Mifflin Harcourt Publishing Company

Primary Source

POLITICAL CARTOON

The Tammany Ring

This political cartoon shows a ring of corrupt politicians known as Tammany Hall. The cartoonist shows how each person blames the one next to him for the corruption in government. As a result of political machines like Tammany Hall, many Americans began demanding political reforms.

The men have labels on their backs that show they represent different interests.

The Granger Collection, New York

ANALYSIS SKILL ANALYZING PRIMARY SOURCES

Why are the men shown standing in a circle?

Political machines were run by leaders called bosses. The machine's boss frequently traded favors for votes. For example, the boss might hand out city jobs to unqualified people or allow an illegal business to operate. The bosses drew much of their support from immigrants. They became popular among poor families because of the services they provided, including jobs and social services such as a fire brigade. A Boston politician said that the role of the machine boss was "to be . . . somebody that any bloke [man] can come to . . . and get help."

New York City's political machine, Tammany Hall, was one of the most notorious. After winning city elections in 1888, members of Tammany Hall rewarded their supporters with about 12,000 jobs. As boss of Tammany Hall, William Marcy Tweed may have stolen up to $200 million from the city. One man remembered how Tammany Hall stayed in power by intimidating voters:

> "Father used to say, 'They know how you're voting. You can't fool them.' He was a Republican at heart, but he had to vote Democratic in order that they didn't find out and make it difficult for him."
>
> —Henry Fenner, quoted in *You Must Remember This*, edited by Jeff Kisseloff

Cleaning Up Political Corruption

Corruption was also a problem in the federal government. Many people thought that the corruption extended to the presidential administration of Ulysses S. Grant. During Grant's second term, federal officials were jailed for taking bribes from whiskey makers in exchange for allowing them to avoid paying taxes. Another scandal involved members of Congress who had taken bribes to allow the Union Pacific Railway to receive government funds. These scandals and others caused many Americans to question the honesty of national leaders.

In response, Americans began calling for changes in the civil service, the government job system. They disliked the spoils system, the practice of giving jobs to the winning candidates' supporters. Thomas Jefferson was the first to reward supporters with jobs. After his administration, each time a new party took power, it replaced many government officials. Many new employees were unqualified and untrained.

By the late 1800s government corruption was so widespread that reformers demanded that only qualified people be given government jobs. In response, President Rutherford B. Hayes

Gilded Age Presidents

QUICK FACTS

Rutherford B. Hayes
Republican
In office: 1877–1881
Hayes promised to reform the government with "thorough, radical, and complete" changes.

James A. Garfield
Republican
In office: 1881
Garfield attempted reforms before he was assassinated.

Chester A. Arthur
Republican
In office: 1881–1885
Arthur supported a system for awarding federal jobs based on merit, not party loyalty.

Grover Cleveland
Democrat
In office: 1885–1889, 1893–1897
Cleveland was known for his honesty and for getting involved in the day-to-day details of government.

Benjamin Harrison
Republican
In office: 1889–1893
Harrison supported the Sherman Antitrust Act, which regulated business monopolies.

William McKinley
Republican
In office: 1897–1901
McKinley avoided scandals and helped win public trust in the government.

THE IMPACT TODAY

Tests are still required for many federal jobs, including secretarial positions, air traffic control, and law enforcement.

made minor reforms, such as firing a powerful member of the New York Republican political machine. President James A. Garfield also attempted reforms. But on July 2, 1881, Garfield was attacked and shot twice by a mentally unstable federal job seeker named Charles Guiteau. The president later died from his wounds, and Vice President Chester A. Arthur became president.

Arthur continued the push for reforms by backing the Pendleton Civil Service Act, which was passed in 1883. This law set up a merit system for awarding federal jobs. Under the Pendleton Act, more than 10 percent of government job applicants had to pass an exam before they could be hired. It was a start to reforming other government practices.

READING CHECK **Analyzing** What factors led to civil-service reform?

Progressives Push for Reforms

A group of reformers known as **Progressives** were also working to improve society in the late 1800s. Progressives tried to solve problems caused by rapid industrial and urban growth. Their goals were to eliminate the causes of problems such as crime, disease, and poverty. They fought for reforms ranging from better working conditions to education programs in poor neighborhoods.

Muckrakers at Work

Some journalists urged Progressives to action by writing stories that vividly described problems in U.S. society. These journalists were nicknamed **muckrakers** because they "raked up" and exposed the muck, or filth, of society. Muckrakers wrote about troubling issues such as child labor, racial discrimination, slum housing, and corruption in business and politics.

In 1902 and 1903 Lincoln Steffens wrote a series of articles in *McClure's Magazine* exposing corruption in city government. In one article, he described how government officials in St. Louis, Missouri, used their positions to earn extra money illegally:

> "Men empowered to issue peddlers' licenses and permits to citizens who wished to erect awnings or use a portion of the sidewalk for storage purposes charged an amount in excess of the prices stipulated [set] by law, and pocketed the difference."
>
> —Lincoln Steffens, *The Shame of the Cities*

Primary Source

PHOTOGRAPH

The Other Half

In 1890 Jacob Riis published How the Other Half Lives. *The book was a collection of photographs of residents and workers in New York City tenement buildings, including families and immigrants. The conditions of life that Riis showed in his photographs, like this one, shocked many wealthier Americans.*

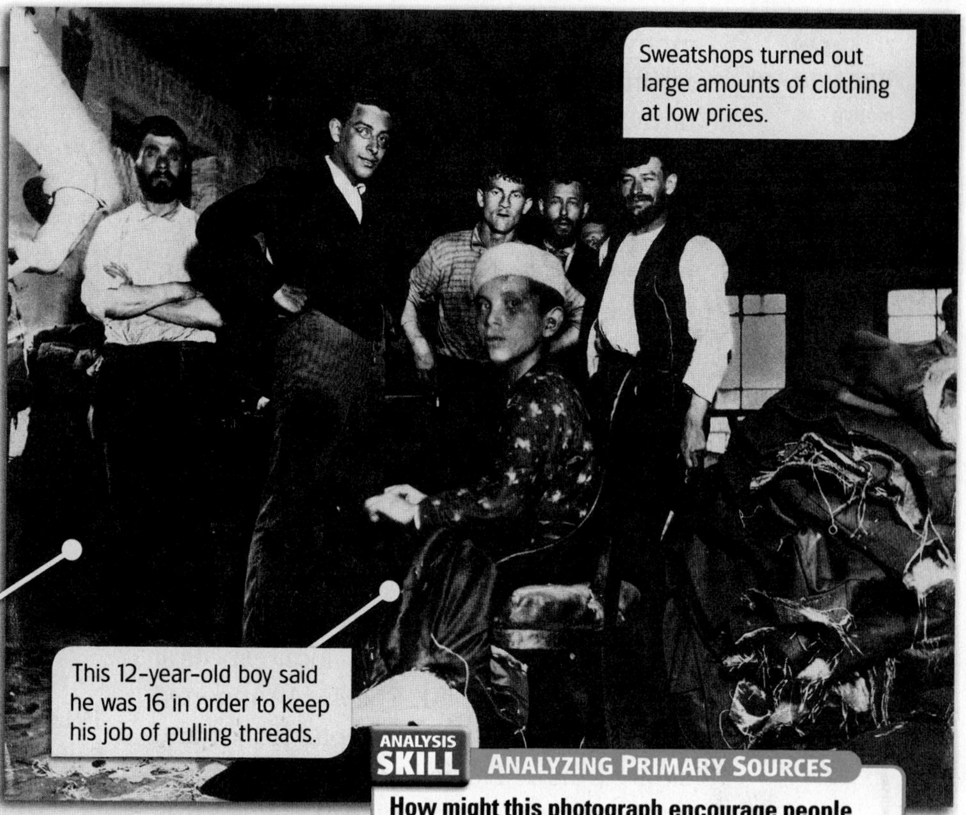

Sweatshops turned out large amounts of clothing at low prices.
Sweatshops were located in tenements to avoid the labor laws that affected factories. Workers crowded into the small, stuffy spaces.
This 12-year-old boy said he was 16 in order to keep his job of pulling threads.

ANALYSIS SKILL **ANALYZING PRIMARY SOURCES**

How might this photograph encourage people to become reformers?

Another muckraker, Ida B. Tarbell, wrote articles criticizing the unfair business practices of the Standard Oil Company. Upton Sinclair exposed unsanitary practices in the meat-processing industry in his novel *The Jungle*.

Although such writing angered many politicians and business leaders, it also helped to unite Progressives. Muckrakers influenced voters, causing them to pressure politicians into backing reforms.

Reform Successes

A major goal of Progressive reformers was to help the urban poor. You have read about the work of housing reformers, which led to the 1901 New York State Tenement House Act. Other Progressives started settlement houses similar to Jane Addams's Hull House. People usually started settlement houses in poor areas in order to improve education, housing, and sanitation there.

The movement for urban reform also led to new professions, such as city planning and civil engineering. City planners helped design safer building codes and opened new public parks. Civil engineers improved transportation by paving streets and building bridges. Sanitation engineers tried to solve problems concerning pollution, waste disposal, and impure water supplies. Death rates dropped dramatically in areas where planners and engineers addressed these problems.

Progressives also believed that improving education would lead to a better society. In response to their demands for reform, states passed laws requiring all children to attend school. Some Progressives started kindergarten programs to help young city children learn basic social skills. In 1873 reformer Susan Blow opened the first American public kindergarten in St. Louis. By 1898 more than 4,000 kindergartens had opened in the United States.

Philosopher John Dewey was a key supporter of early childhood education. His

ACADEMIC VOCABULARY

motive a reason for doing something

motive was to help children learn problem-solving skills, not just memorize facts. This, he thought, would help them in everyday life. Dewey's teaching methods became a model for progressive education across the country.

Progressives also worked to improve the education of medical professionals. In the late 1800s the United States lacked a ready supply of well-trained and professionally organized doctors. Researchers knew the causes of diseases such as pneumonia and tuberculosis. However, there were few medical organizations that could help spread this knowledge.

Under the leadership of Joseph McCormack, the American Medical Association (AMA) brought together local medical or-ganizations in 1901. The AMA supported laws designed to protect public health and showed how Progressives could organize to help improve society. Other organizations followed the AMA's lead.

READING CHECK **Finding Main Ideas** How did progressive reforms improve society?

BIOGRAPHY

Robert M. La Follette

1855–1925

Born in rural Wisconsin, Robert M. La Follette began his political career at a young age. He was elected to the U.S. House of Representatives in 1884, becoming the youngest member of Congress. He soon earned the nickname "Fighting Bob" for his energetic speaking style and his active support for progressive reforms.

After serving as Wisconsin's governor and as U.S. senator, La Follette ran for president as the Progressive Party candidate in 1924. He won his home state and received about 16 percent of the popular vote.

Drawing Conclusions Why might La Follette have been proud of the nickname "Fighting Bob"?

Expansion of Voting Power

Some Progressives worked to change state and local governments in order to reduce the power of political machines. In many places, reformers replaced corrupt ballots that listed only one party's candidates with government-prepared ballots that listed all candidates. Under pressure from reformers, many states adopted secret ballots, a measure that ensured the privacy of every voter.

Voting Reforms

Reformers also hoped to expand voting power. For example, they favored the **Seventeenth Amendment**, which allowed Americans to vote directly for U.S. senators. Before the constitutional amendment was passed in 1913, state legislatures had elected senators. Reformers also favored the direct primary, in which voters choose candidates for public office directly. Previously, party leaders had selected which candidates would run for office.

Other reform measures allowed voters to take action against corrupt politicians. Some states and cities gave unhappy voters the right to sign a petition asking for a special vote. The purpose of that vote was to **recall**, or remove, an official before the end of his or her term. If enough voters signed the petition, the vote took place. The official could then be removed from office if there was a majority of recall votes.

In California, Oregon, and states in the Midwest, Progressives worked on reforms to give voters direct influence over new laws. A procedure called the **initiative** allowed voters to propose a new law by collecting signatures on a petition. If enough signatures were collected, the proposed law was voted on at the next election. Another measure, called the **referendum**, permitted voters to approve or reject a law that had already been proposed or passed by a government body. This process gave voters a chance to overrule laws that they opposed.

Government Reforms

In addition to working for greater voter participation, Progressives attempted to change the way city government operated. Some reformers wanted city government to be run like a business. As a result of their efforts, several cities changed to council-manager governments. Under this system, voters elect a city council. The council then appoints a professional manager to run the city. Other business-minded reformers supported the commission form of government. Under this system, the city is headed by a group of elected officials. Each official manages a major city agency, such as housing or transportation.

One of the leaders of the effort to reform state government was Wisconsin's Republican governor **Robert M. La Follette**. La Follette decreased the power of political machines and used university professors and other experts to help write new laws and work in state agencies. He also made available to the public information on how politicians voted. That way, voters would know if leaders had kept their campaign promises. Called the Wisconsin Idea, La Follette's plan became a model for progressive reforms in other states.

Expanding Democracy QUICK FACTS

Direct Primaries	Voters choose candidates.
Recall	Voters can remove an official from office.
Initiatives	Voters can propose laws by petition.
Referendum	Voters can overrule a law.
17th Amendment	Senators are elected directly by voters.

READING CHECK **Evaluating** How did Progressives work to change voting procedures?

SUMMARY Progressives worked to reform government and improve city life.

Section 1 Assessment

hmhsocialstudies.com ONLINE QUIZ

Reviewing Ideas, Terms, and People

1. a. **Recall** What was the main goal of **political machines** during the Gilded Age?
   b. **Draw Conclusions** Why do you think some immigrants supported political machines?
   c. **Predict** Do you think the system of testing created by the Pendleton Civil Service Act would work to reduce corruption in the spoils system? Why or why not?
2. a. **Identify** Who were **muckrakers**, and what effect did they have on reform?
   b. **Explain** How did **Progressives** try to improve education?
   c. **Evaluate** Which progressive reform do you think was most important? Why?
3. a. **Describe** What new ideas and practices were introduced to give voters more power?
   b. **Draw Conclusions** How did progressive reforms limit the power of political machines?

Critical Thinking

4. **Categorizing** Review your notes on the problems that progressive reforms addressed. Then copy the chart below and use it to categorize the various progressive reforms.

Progressive Reforms		
Social	Political	Urban

Focus on Speaking

5. **Addressing Political and Social Problems** How would you address the problems of political corruption and urban growth during the late 1800s? Jot down notes about campaign promises you might make to assure voters that you would make the necessary reforms.

Reform Literature

from *How the Other Half Lives*

by Jacob Riis (1849–1914)

About the Reading How the Other Half Lives *describes the tenement houses where immigrants lived in New York City. Its author, Jacob Riis, was a newspaper reporter. His nonfiction book made Americans aware of the extremes of poverty suffered by working people. Riis believed that every human being deserved a decent, safe place to live.* How the Other Half Lives *led to reforms and new laws that improved housing conditions.*

AS YOU READ **Look for details that help you see, hear, and smell Cherry Street.**

Cherry Street. Be a little careful, please! ❶ The hall is dark and you might stumble over the children pitching pennies back there. Not that it would hurt them; kicks and cuffs are their daily diet. They have little else. Here where the hall turns and dives into utter darkness is a step, and another, another. A flight of stairs. You can feel your way, if you cannot see it. Close? Yes! What would you have? All the fresh air that ever enters these stairs comes from the hall door that is forever slamming, and from the windows of dark bedrooms that in turn receive from the stairs their sole supply of the elements God meant to be free . . . That was a woman filling her pail by the hydrant you just bumped against. The sinks are in the hallway, that all the tenants may have access—and all be poisoned alike by their summer stenches. Hear the pump squeak! It is the lullaby of tenement house babes. In summer, when a thousand thirsty throats pant for a cooling drink in this block, it is worked in vain . . . ❷

The sea of a mighty population, held in galling fetters, heaves uneasily in the tenements . . . If it rise once more, no human power may avail to check it. The gap between the classes in which it surges, unseen, unsuspected by the thoughtless, is widening day by day . . . I know of but one bridge that will carry us over safe, a bridge founded upon justice and built of human hearts.

GUIDED READING

WORD HELP

cuffs punches
utter complete
close stuffy
sole only
access right to use
stenches bad smells
in vain without success
galling causing pain; irritating
fetters chains
heaves rises and falls
avail help

❶ ***The writer wants you to imagine that he is taking you on a tour of the building. Why do you think he chooses this way to describe the place?***

❷ ***Find one detail that appeals to each sense: sight, sound, smell, taste, and touch. How would you sum up, in one sentence, the place that Riis describes?***

from *The Jungle*

by Upton Sinclair (1878–1968)

About the Reading The Jungle *focused the nation's attention on immigrant workers in the meatpacking industry. Upton Sinclair's novel showed bosses forcing human beings to live and work like animals. He also described, in shocking detail, how meat was handled. Sinclair published his book in 1906. Later that same year, the U.S. government passed the Pure Food and Drug Act and the Meat Inspection Act. Many Americans even gave up eating meat for a while.*

AS YOU READ **Look for details that create one overwhelming effect.**

There was never the least attention paid to what was cut up for sausage; there would come back from Europe old sausage that had been rejected, and that was mouldy and white—it would be dosed with borax and glycerine, and dumped into hoppers, and made over again for home consumption. There would be meat that had tumbled out on the floor, in the dirt and sawdust, where the workers had tramped and spit uncounted billions of consumption germs. ❶ There would be meat stored in great piles in rooms and the water from leaky roofs would drip over it, and thousands of rats would race about on it. It was too dark in these storage places to see well, but a man would run his hand over these piles of meat and sweep off handfuls of the dried dung of rats. ❷ These rats were nuisances, and the packers would put poisoned bread out for them; they would die, and then rats, bread, and meat would go into the hoppers together . . . ❸ There was no place for the men to wash their hands before they ate their dinner, and so they made a practice of washing them in the water that was to be ladled into the sausage. ❹

GUIDED READING

WORD HELP

borax white powder used in manufacturing and cleaning
glycerine sweet, sticky liquid
hoppers containers
consumption eating or drinking
consumption tuberculosis, a lung disease that was fatal at that time
ladled added with a large spoon

❶ ***What overall effect or mood does Sinclair create?***

❷ ***Based on the details in this passage, what were the packers most concerned about?***

❸ ***Why do you think rats were considered nuisances?***

❹ ***Find details that reveal how one improvement in working conditions might have resulted in healthier sausage.***

CONNECTING LITERATURE TO HISTORY

1. **Identify Cause and Effect** Jacob Riis and Upton Sinclair were both muckraking journalists. Why do you think so much muck existed in the tenements and in the meatpacking business? Why had people ignored those conditions for so long?
2. **Identify Cause and Effect** Both Riis and Sinclair believed that improving conditions for immigrants would benefit all of society. Explain how one specific change in the tenements might have a favorable effect on everyone. Then explain how one specific change in meat handling might affect everyone.
3. **Compare and Contrast** Both *How the Other Half Lives* and *The Jungle* inspired Progressives to work for reform. Which work do you think had the greater effect on its readers? Use details from each passage to explain your answer.

SECTION 2

Reforming the Workplace

What You Will Learn...

Main Ideas

1. Reformers attempted to improve conditions for child laborers.
2. Unions and reformers took steps to improve safety in the workplace and to limit working hours.

The Big Idea

In the early 1900s, Progressives and other reformers focused on improving conditions for American workers.

Key Terms and People

Triangle Shirtwaist Fire
workers' compensation laws
capitalism
socialism
William "Big Bill" Haywood
Industrial Workers of the World

hmhsocialstudies.com
TAKING NOTES

Use the graphic organizer online to take notes on important labor problems and the workers they affected.

If YOU were there...

You have been working in a hat factory since 1900, when you were eight years old. Now you are experienced enough to run one of the sewing machines. You don't earn as much as older workers, but your family needs every penny you bring home. Still, the long hours make you very tired. One day you hear that people are trying to stop children from doing factory work. They think that children should be at school or playing.

Would you be for or against this social reform? Why?

BUILDING BACKGROUND Since the Second Industrial Revolution, more and more people were working long hours in difficult conditions. With adult workers earning low wages, many children had to work full time to help support their families. Progressive reformers began to focus on these problems.

Improving Conditions for Children

In the early 1900s a reformer named Marie Van Vorst took a series of jobs in factories and clothing mills around the country. She wanted to investigate working conditions for children by living and working alongside them. In a South Carolina textile mill, Van Vorst met children as young as seven years old. She described working with one young child:

> "Through the looms I catch sight of ... my landlord's little child. She is seven; so small that they have a box for her to stand on ... I can see only her fingers as they clutch at the flying spools."
>
> – Marie Van Vorst, quoted in *A History of Women in America*, edited by Carol Hymowitz

This girl—and other children like her—provided cheap labor for manufacturers. Some children were paid as little as 40 cents per day. Marie Van Vorst helped focus attention on the problem of child labor. Eliminating the problems of child labor became a major issue for Progressives and other reformers.

Children at Work

Children did many jobs in the late 1800s. Boys sold newspapers and shined shoes on the streets. Girls often cooked or cleaned for boarders staying with their families. Girls also worked at home with their mothers, sewing clothes or making handicrafts.

Like the child Van Vorst encountered, many children worked in industry. In 1900 more than 1.75 million children age 15 and under worked in factories, mines, and mills, earning very low wages.

Calls for Reform

As reporters published shocking accounts of working conditions for children, more people became aware of the problem. Progressives began to call for new reforms. You have read about Florence Kelley's work against child labor in Illinois. Kelley also served as a board member of the National Consumers' League, the major lobbying group for women's and children's labor issues. A lobbying group works to influence legislators in favor of a cause.

During the early 1900s, reformers finally succeeded in getting some laws passed to ease the conditions of child laborers. In 1912 the state of Massachusetts passed the first minimum wage law, and a commission was created to establish rates for child workers.

In 1916 and 1919 Congress passed federal child labor laws. The laws banned products made with child labor from being shipped from one state to another. The Supreme Court, however, ruled that the laws were unconstitutional. The Court argued that the laws went beyond the federal government's legal power to regulate interstate commerce.

In any case, laws alone could not end child labor. Some parents ignored child labor laws so that their children could continue contributing to the family income. Children were often instructed to lie about their age to government inspectors and tell them they were older than they really were.

Focus on Reading
What do you think the author's goal is in this paragraph?

READING CHECK **Finding Main Ideas** How did reformers try to improve child labor conditions?

Child Labor

Young children did much of the work in the American factories of the late 1800s. They were paid less than adult workers.

Why did some parents want their children to work?

History Close-up

Working Conditions for Children, Early 1900s

This illustration shows some of the jobs that children did in glass factories in the early 1900s. You can see that there were many ways for young workers to be injured on the job.

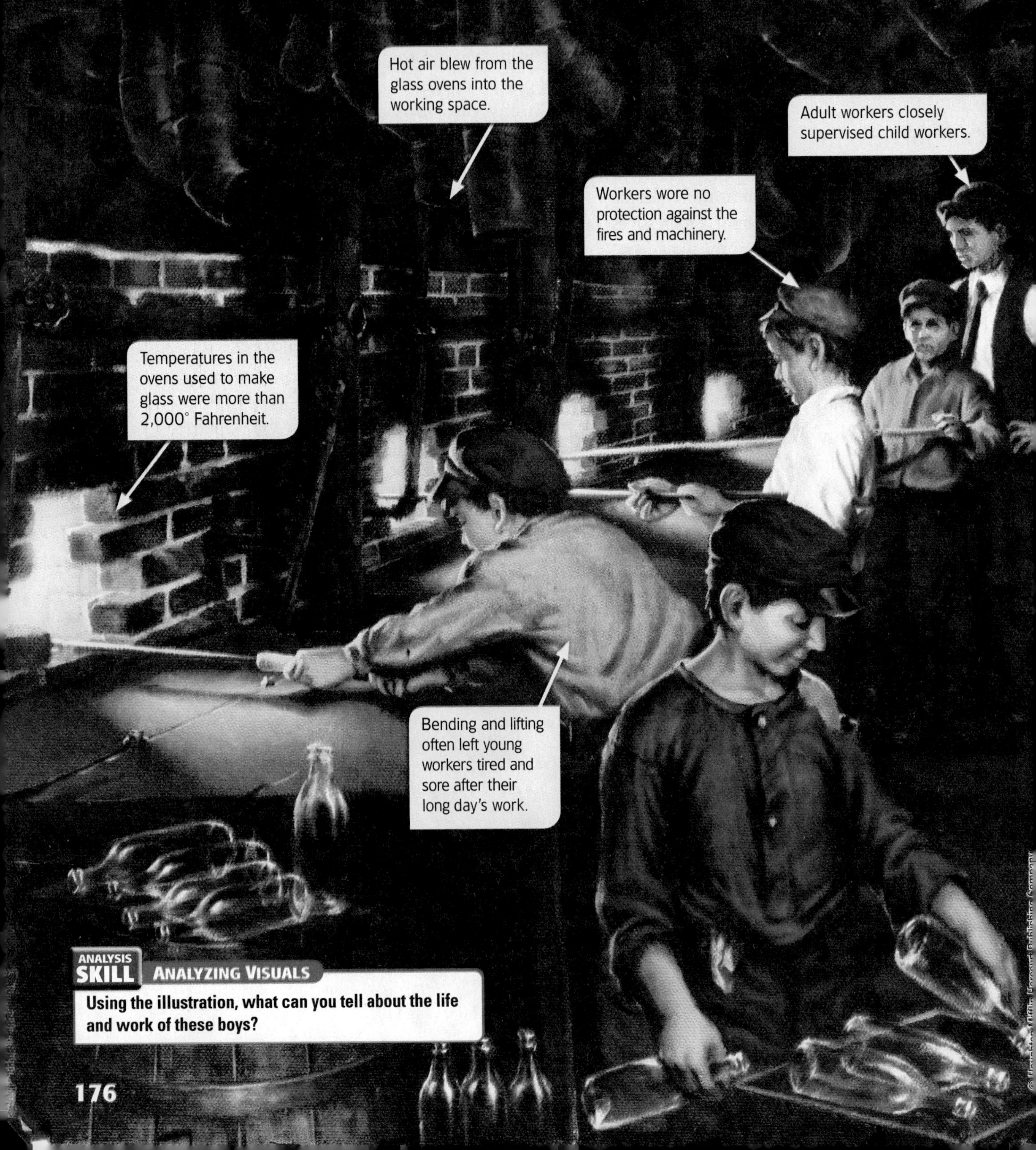

Hot air blew from the glass ovens into the working space.
Adult workers closely supervised child workers.
Workers wore no protection against the fires and machinery.
Temperatures in the ovens used to make glass were more than 2,000° Fahrenheit.
Bending and lifting often left young workers tired and sore after their long day's work.

ANALYSIS SKILL ANALYZING VISUALS

Using the illustration, what can you tell about the life and work of these boys?

© Houghton Mifflin Harcourt Publishing Company

Safety and Working Conditions

Child labor reform was only part of the progressive effort to help American workers. Many Progressives also favored laws to ensure workers' safety, limit working hours, and protect workers' rights.

Workplace Safety

Workplace accidents were common in the 1800s and early 1900s. In 1900 some 35,000 people were killed in industrial accidents. About 500,000 suffered injuries. One child described how her sister was injured using a machine in a string factory. "You see you mustn't talk or look off a minute," she explained. "My sister was like me. She forgot and talked, and just that minute her finger was off, and she didn't even cry till she picked it up."

Accidents like this were not big news in the early 1900s, but in 1911 a much greater workplace tragedy shocked the nation. It took place at the Triangle Shirtwaist Company, a New York City clothing factory that employed mostly Jewish and Italian teenage immigrant women. On the afternoon of March 25, a fire started on the eighth floor of the factory. Workers tried to escape, but factory owners had locked the exit doors—to reduce theft of materials, they said.

By the time firefighters brought the fire under control, 146 workers had died. At a memorial service for the victims, union leader Rose Schneiderman called for action. "It is up to the working people to save themselves," she said. The **Triangle Shirtwaist Fire** and similar accidents led to the passage of laws improving factory safety standards.

Labor leaders and reformers also fought for **workers' compensation laws**, which guaranteed a portion of lost wages to workers injured on the job. In 1902 Maryland became the first state to pass such a law. However, new laws were not always strictly enforced. Working conditions remained poor in many places.

Primary Source

TRIAL TRANSCRIPT

Triangle Shirtwaist Fire

Ethel Monick was one of the teenage factory workers at the Triangle Shirtwaist Company. In the trial that followed the disaster, she described her experience in the fire. Rose Freedman, pictured, was the longest-living survivor of the fire. She died in 2001.

I seen the fire and then I seen all the girls rushing down to the place to escape. So I tried to go through the Greene Street door, and there were quick girls there and I seen I can't get out there, so I went to the elevator, and then I heard the elevator fall down, so I ran through to the Washington Place side . . . I tried the door and I could not open it, so I thought I was not strong enough to open it, so I hollered girls here is a door, and they all rushed over and they tried to open it, but it was locked and they hollered "the door is locked and we can't open it!"

—Testimony of Ethel Monick, age 16

ANALYSIS SKILL — ANALYZING PRIMARY SOURCES

According to Monick, what is the feeling in the factory?

The Courts and Labor

Not everyone supported the new workplace regulations. Some business leaders believed that the economy should operate without any government interference. They went to court to block new labor laws.

One important case began in New York in 1897, after the state passed a law limiting bakers to a 10-hour workday. Joseph Lochner, a bakery owner, challenged the law. The case eventually went to the U.S. Supreme Court in 1905. In *Lochner* v. *New York*, the Court ruled that states could not restrict the rights of employers and workers to enter into any type of labor agreement. The New York law was declared unconstitutional.

The Supreme Court did uphold some limits on working hours for women and children. In the 1908 *Muller* v. *Oregon* case, the Court upheld laws restricting women's work hours. The justices stated that such laws protected women's health, which was of public concern.

Labor Organizations

Labor unions were also a strong force for improving working conditions. Union membership rose from about 800,000 in 1900 to about 5 million in 1920. Led by Samuel Gompers, the American Federation of Labor (AFL) remained one of the strongest labor unions. The AFL focused on better working conditions and pay for skilled workers. Gompers supported the American system of **capitalism**, an economic system in which private businesses run most industries and competition determines the price of goods.

Some union members, however, believed in **socialism**—a system in which the government owns and operates a country's means of production. Socialists, led by Eugene V. Debs, hoped that the government would protect workers.

In 1905 a group of socialists and union leaders founded a union that welcomed immigrants, women, African Americans, and others not welcome in the AFL. Led by **William "Big Bill" Haywood**, this socialist union was called the **Industrial Workers of the World** (IWW). Its goal was to organize all workers into one large union that would overthrow capitalism. Staging strikes across the country, the IWW frightened many Americans with its aggressive tactics. Strong opposition led to its decline by 1920.

READING CHECK **Analyzing** How did reforms change the workplace?

SUMMARY Progressive reformers fought to improve working conditions.

Section 2 Assessment

hmhsocialstudies.com
ONLINE QUIZ

Reviewing Ideas, Terms, and People

1. **a. Recall** What jobs did child laborers often hold?
   b. Explain Why did businesses employ children in factories?
   c. Elaborate Why do you think reformers began to demand improvements to child labor conditions?
2. **a. Identify** What events led to the movement to improve workplace safety?
   b. Make Inferences Why did the **Industrial Workers of the World** frighten some people?
   c. Predict What conflicts might arise between supporters of **capitalism** and **socialism**?

Critical Thinking

3. **Analyzing** Review your notes on labor reforms and workers. Then copy the graphic organizer shown below. Use it to give specific examples of how Progressives tried to reform child labor, women's labor, and workplace conditions.

Labor Reform
- Child labor:
- Women's labor:
- Workplace conditions:

Focus on Speaking

4. **Addressing Problems in the Workplace** How would you address problems in the workplace? Make notes on campaign promises you might make to assure voters that you would address issues of child labor and workplace safety.

The Rights of Women and Minorities

SECTION 3

If YOU were there...

You are a member of the graduating class of 1912 from an excellent women's college. You have always been interested in science, especially biology. You would like to be a doctor, but you know that medical schools accept very few women. One career path for you is to go into social work. Yet that's not what you really want to do.

How would you want to use your education?

BUILDING BACKGROUND The Progressives had a wide variety of goals. Besides attacking social problems such as child labor, they worked to reform government and make it more democratic. Changes in women's education affected the movement, as college-educated women often became leaders in working for reforms.

Women Fight for Temperance and Voting Rights

New educational opportunities drew more women into the Progressive movement. In the late 1800s, women began attending women's colleges, such as Smith College in Massachusetts and Vassar College in New York, in record numbers. In 1870 only about 20 percent of college students were women. By 1910 that number had doubled. The goal of female students was "to develop as fully as may be the powers of womanhood," said Sophia Smith, founder of Smith College.

Many women graduates entered fields such as social work and teaching. They found it much harder to enter professions such as law and medicine, which were dominated by men. Denied access to such professions, women often put their education to use by becoming active in reform. Women's clubs campaigned for causes such as temperance, women's suffrage, child welfare, and political reform.

What You Will Learn...

Main Ideas

1. Women fought for temperance and the right to vote.
2. African American reformers challenged discrimination and called for equality.
3. Progressive reforms failed to benefit all minorities.

The Big Idea

The Progressive movement made advances for the rights of women and some minorities.

Key Terms and People

Eighteenth Amendment
National American Woman Suffrage Association
Alice Paul
Nineteenth Amendment
Booker T. Washington
Ida B. Wells
W. E. B. Du Bois
National Association for the Advancement of Colored People

hmhsocialstudies.com
TAKING NOTES

Use the graphic organizer online to take notes on the causes supported by different groups of progressive reformers.

© Houghton Mifflin Harcourt Publishing Company

The Temperance Movement

In the mid-1800s many of these reformers blamed social problems such as family violence and criminal behavior on a number of factors, including urbanization and immigration. They also blamed problems on alcohol consumption. As a result, many groups took up the cause of temperance, or avoidance of alcohol.

In 1874, reformers from many different backgrounds formed the Woman's Christian Temperance Union (WCTU), which fought for adoption of local and state laws restricting the sale of alcohol. Under the leadership of Frances Willard, the organization started 10,000 branches. More than 1,000 saloons were forced to shut down as a result of temperance supporters' efforts.

One especially radical temperance fighter chose more aggressive methods to fight for her cause. In the 1890s Carry Nation became famous for storming into saloons with a hatchet and smashing liquor bottles. Nation described destroying a Kansas saloon with bricks and rocks:

> "I threw as hard, and as fast as I could, smashing mirrors and bottles and glasses and it was astonishing how quickly this was done."
>
> —Carry Nation, quoted in *Witnessing America: The Library of Congress Book of Firsthand Accounts of Life in America, 1600–1900*

In 1919 many years of temperance efforts led to the passage of the **Eighteenth Amendment**, banning the production, sale, and transportation of alcoholic beverages throughout the United States.

The Right to Vote

Women reformers also fought for suffrage, or the right to vote. Many people at this time opposed giving women the vote. Political bosses, for instance, worried about the anti-corruption efforts of women. Some business leaders worried that women voters would support minimum wage and child labor laws. Other people believed that women should only be homemakers and mothers and not politically active citizens.

In spite of such opposition, the women's suffrage movement began to gain national support in the 1890s. Elizabeth Cady Stanton and Susan B. Anthony founded the **National American Woman Suffrage Association** (NAWSA) in 1890 to promote the cause of women's suffrage. That same year, women

hmhsocialstudies.com
ANIMATED GEOGRAPHY AND HISTORY
Woman Suffrage 1919

Time Line

The Nineteenth Amendment

Women had been seeking the right to vote since 1776. Finally, in 1920 they achieved success with the passage of the Nineteenth Amendment.

1919

- **May 21, 1919** The House of Representatives passes the Nineteenth Amendment by a vote of 304 to 89.
- **June 4, 1919** The Senate passes the Nineteenth Amendment by a vote of 56 to 25.
- **June 10, 1919** Illinois, Michigan, and Wisconsin become the first states to ratify the Nineteenth Amendment.

© Houghton Mifflin Harcourt Publishing Company • Image Credits: (b) ©Bettmann/Corbis

won the right to vote in Wyoming. Colorado, Idaho, and Utah followed.

Carrie Chapman Catt became president of the NAWSA in 1900. Catt mobilized more than 1 million volunteers for the movement. She argued that women should have a voice in creating laws that affected them. "We women demand an equal voice," she said. "We shall accept nothing less."

Some women believed that NAWSA did not go far enough. In 1913 **Alice Paul** founded what would become the National Woman's Party (NWP). The NWP used parades, public demonstrations, picketing, hunger strikes, and other means to draw attention to the suffrage cause. Paul even organized picketing in front of the White House. Paul and other NWP leaders were jailed for their actions.

Suffragists finally succeeded in gaining the vote. In 1919 the U.S. Congress passed the **Nineteenth Amendment**, granting American women the right to vote. The Nineteenth Amendment was ratified by the states the following year, making it law.

READING CHECK **Analyzing** How did reformers draw attention to the temperance and women's suffrage movements?

African Americans Challenge Discrimination

White reformers often overlooked issues such as racial discrimination and segregation. African American reformers took the lead in addressing these problems.

One of the most important African American leaders was **Booker T. Washington**. Born into slavery, he became a respected educator while in his twenties. Washington's strategy was not to fight discrimination directly. Instead, he encouraged African Americans to improve their educational and economic well-being. This, he believed, would eventually lead to the end of discrimination.

Other African Americans spoke out more directly against discrimination. Journalist **Ida B. Wells** wrote articles about the unequal education available to African American children. In her Memphis newspaper *Free Speech,* Wells also drew attention to the lynching of African Americans. During lynchings people were murdered by mobs instead of receiving a trial after being accused of a crime, or even for breaking social codes. More than 3,000 African Americans were lynched between 1885 and 1915.

Although death threats forced Wells to move to the North, she continued campaigning against lynching. In 1900 she wrote:

> "Our country's national crime is *lynching* ... In fact, for all kinds of offenses—and, for no offenses—from murders to misdemeanors, men and women are put to death without judge or jury."
>
> —Ida B. Wells, from her article "Lynch Law in America"

1920

August 26, 1920 The secretary of state officially declares the Nineteenth Amendment ratified by three-fourths of the states, making it law.

1921

August 18, 1920 Tennessee becomes the thirty-sixth state to ratify the Nineteenth Amendment.

November 2, 1920 The first national election in which all women can vote is held.

© Houghton Mifflin Harcourt Publishing Company • Image Credits: (bl) ©Bettmann/Corbis; (br) Library of Congress Prints & Photographs Division, Washington, D.C.

Like Wells, **W. E. B. Du Bois** took a direct approach to fighting racial injustice. Born in Massachusetts, Du Bois was a college graduate who earned a doctorate from Harvard University. As part of his research, he studied and publicized cases of racial prejudice. Du Bois believed that African Americans should protest unjust treatment and demand equal rights.

In 1909 Du Bois and other reformers founded the **National Association for the Advancement of Colored People** (NAACP), an organization that called for economic and educational equality for African Americans. The NAACP attacked discrimination by using the courts. In 1915 it won the important case of *Guinn* v. *United States,* which made grandfather clauses illegal. These laws were used in the South to keep African Americans from voting. Grandfather clauses imposed strict qualifications on voters unless their grandfathers had been allowed to vote. Many white voters met this requirement and were therefore automatically permitted to vote in elections. However, most African Americans' grandfathers had been enslaved and could not vote.

THE IMPACT TODAY

The NAACP has grown tremendously since 1909. Today the organization has about 2,200 branches and 500,000 members.

Another important organization, the National Urban League, was formed in 1911 by Dr. George Edmund Haynes. This organization aided many African Americans moving from the South by helping them find jobs and housing in northern cities. The League addressed many of the same problems faced by other Progressives, such as health, sanitation, and education.

READING CHECK **Finding Main Ideas** What was the purpose of the NAACP?

Primary Source

POINTS OF VIEW

Fighting Discrimination

Booker T. Washington and W. E. B. Du Bois had very different views on how African Americans should handle discrimination.

"Our greatest danger is that in the great leap from slavery to freedom we may overlook the fact that the masses of us are to live by the productions of our hands, and fail to keep in mind that we shall prosper in proportion as we learn to dignify and glorify common labour and put brains and skill into the common occupations of life . . . It is at the bottom of life we must begin, and not at the top."

—Booker T. Washington

"Is it possible, and probable, that nine millions of men can make effective progress in economic lines if they are deprived of political rights, made a servile caste,* and allowed only the most meager chance for developing their exceptional men? If history and reason give any distinct answer to these questions, it is an emphatic No."

*lower social rank

—W. E. B. Du Bois

ANALYSIS SKILL **ANALYZING POINTS OF VIEW**

Finding Main Ideas What is the primary difference between the views of Washington and Du Bois?

© Houghton Mifflin Harcourt Publishing Company

Failures of Reform

Other minority groups felt left behind by the Progressive movement. Although some reformers tried to aid such groups, the aim of many was to encourage other ethnicities to adopt the ways of European society. The Society of American Indians, formed in 1911, was one such attempt. Started by Native American doctors Carlos Montezuma and Charles Eastman, the society believed that integration into white society would end Native American poverty. Many Native Americans, however, wanted to preserve their traditional culture. They resisted the movement toward adopting white culture.

Immigrant groups from non-European countries also formed groups to help support their members. Chinese immigrants, for example, organized neighborhood associations in the communities in which they lived. District associations, cultural groups, churches, and temples provided public services that white reformers ignored. Such groups provided the money for building San Francisco's Chinese hospital in 1925. Chinese immigration dropped, however, due in part to anti-Chinese riots that occurred in some western towns and cities.

While fewer Chinese immigrants came to the United States, the number of Mexican immigrants increased. The northern and southern borders between the United States and its neighbors were fairly easy to cross in this period. Many Mexican immigrants moved to the South and Southwest, where they became an important part of the societies and economies of these regions. Many Mexican immigrants found jobs in the mining and railroad industries. Others began farms or became migrant workers. Progressive labor laws and factory reforms did nothing to improve the poor living and working conditions of migrant farm workers.

READING CHECK **Summarizing** What were the limitations of progressive reforms?

SUMMARY Many U.S. citizens worked for progressive reforms.

Section 3 Assessment

hmhsocialstudies.com
ONLINE QUIZ

Reviewing Ideas, Terms, and People

1. a. **Identify** What did the **Eighteenth** and **Nineteenth Amendments** accomplish?
   b. **Summarize** How did **Alice Paul** and the National Woman's Party try to draw attention to the issue of women's suffrage?
2. a. **Identify** What role did **Ida B. Wells** play in reform efforts for African Americans?
   b. **Contrast** How did **Booker T. Washington** differ from other African American leaders?
   c. **Evaluate** Do you think the **National Association for the Advancement of Colored People** was successful in fighting discrimination? Explain.
3. a. **Describe** What discrimination did Chinese Americans face?
   b. **Summarize** How were some minority groups overlooked by the Progressive movement?

Critical Thinking

4. **Analyzing** Review your notes on Progressives' causes. Then copy the diagram shown and use it to identify the progressive reforms introduced by the temperance movement, the women's suffrage movement, and African Americans.

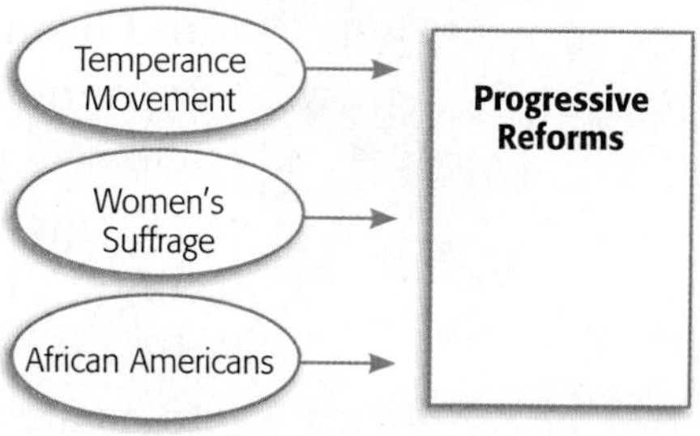

FOCUS ON SPEAKING

5. **Addressing the Rights of Women and Minorities** Review this section's material on education for women, women's suffrage, temperance, racial discrimination, and segregation. As a politician, what promises would you make regarding these issues? Think about how you would make your ideas acceptable to the American public. Would you be willing to compromise your ideals?

© Houghton Mifflin Harcourt Publishing Company

Case Study

Progressive Era Reforms

Women supported many of the efforts to reform society during the Progressive Era. Many of them fought for women's suffrage in order to vote for Progressive candidates and laws.

Improving Work and Society

In the late 1800s and early 1900s, Progressives focused on two broad areas of reform: improving working conditions for men, women, and children, and reforming society to help improve people's lives. The Progressive Era reforms that resulted from these efforts can still be felt today.

Labor leaders had long campaigned for the rights of adult male workers. For example, they fought for fairer pay and the right to organize and form unions. Eventually the movement demanded greater protections for women and children workers as well. One area of reform was the length of the workday. In the mid- to late-1800s, workers gradually shifted from demanding a ten-hour workday to an eight-hour one. By the beginning of the 1900s, an eight-hour workday was becoming more common, and today it is typical.

Reforming society was another area of focus for Progressives. They fought to help the poor, create safer and healthier cities, ban alcohol, improve education, and expand voting rights—all with the goal of creating a better society. Many of these reformers were women. Jane Addams, for example, worked tirelessly to improve living conditions for Chicago's poor. Clara Barton helped to found the International Red Cross. Later, in 1881, she worked to create the American branch, suggesting that the group could help with humanitarian aid, disaster relief, and wartime needs. In Alabama, Julia Tutwiler worked to reform the state's education and prison systems.

One legacy of these Progressive Era reforms can be found in the U.S. Constitution, which includes several important amendments ratified during this time. The Sixteenth Amendment granted Congress the power to tax individual incomes, which Progressives supported as a way to more fairly pay for government programs. The Seventeenth Amendment

© Houghton Mifflin Harcourt Publishing Company • Image Credits: (l) ©Library of Congress Prints & Photographs Division gave voters, rather than state legislators, the power to directly elect their U.S. Senators. The Eighteenth Amendment banned the sale of alcohol, though it was later repealed with the passage of the Twenty-first Amendment. Finally, the Nineteenth Amendment guaranteed women the right to vote. It was the crowning achievement of the women's suffrage movement and a major milestone in the spread of Progressive reforms.

Case Study Assessment

1. What are three examples of workplace reforms resulting from the Progressive Era?
2. Name two Progressive reformers and identify the social reforms for which each is known.
3. **Activity** Find and read the full text of the Sixteenth, Seventeenth, Eighteenth, Nineteenth, and Twenty-first Amendments. Analyze each amendment. Then explain which parts of each amendment reflect Progressive values.

BIOGRAPHY

Julia Tutwiler

1841–1916

Julia Tutwiler was born in Tuscaloosa, Alabama, where her father was a professor at the recently founded University of Alabama. Tutwiler's father valued education and sent Julia to study Latin, Greek, art, music, and other subjects in both America and Europe. Julia became an incredibly accomplished writer, educator, and advocate for Progressive reforms. By 1880, she had organized the Tuscaloosa Benevolent Association (TBA), a women's group that worked to reform prison conditions in Alabama. In 1892 she helped open the University of Alabama to women. Tutwiler also taught, led other civic organizations and schools, and helped set up a standard teacher-certification system for Alabama. Her poem "Alabama" even provided the lyrics for the official state song.

Finding the Main Idea What contributions did Julia Tutwiler make to Alabama society?

Progressives worked to reform the educational system. Many public high schools were built during the time period. Children began attending school more than they had in the past, and they attended to a later age.

© Houghton Mifflin Harcourt Publishing Company • Image Credits: (bkgd) ©Library of Congress Prints & Photographs Division; (tr) ©Birmingham, Ala. Public Library Archives

SECTION 4

The Progressive Presidents

What You Will Learn...

Main Ideas

1. Theodore Roosevelt's progressive reforms tried to balance the interests of business, consumers, and laborers.
2. William Howard Taft angered Progressives with his cautious reforms, while Woodrow Wilson enacted far-reaching banking and antitrust reforms.

The Big Idea

American presidents in the early 1900s did a great deal to promote progressive reforms.

Key Terms and People

Theodore Roosevelt
Pure Food and Drug Act
conservation
William Howard Taft
Progressive Party
Woodrow Wilson
Sixteenth Amendment

hmhsocialstudies.com
TAKING NOTES

Use the graphic organizer online to take notes on the achievements of each of the progressive presidents.

If YOU were there...

It is 1912 and you're voting in your first presidential election. This election is unusual—there are three major candidates. One is the popular former president Theodore Roosevelt, who is running as a third-party candidate. He thinks the Republican candidate will not make enough progressive reforms. But the Democratic candidate is a progressive reformer too.

How will you decide which candidate to support?

BUILDING BACKGROUND Political corruption was one early target of the progressive reformers. Some politicians who joined them believed that government—local, state, and national—should play an active role in improving society and people's lives.

Roosevelt's Progressive Reforms

During a summer tour after his second inauguration in 1901, President William McKinley met a friendly crowd in Buffalo, New York. Suddenly, anarchist Leon Czolgosz stepped forward and shot the president. A little more than a week later, McKinley died. Vice President **Theodore Roosevelt** took office.

Roosevelt's Square Deal

Roosevelt believed that the interests of businesspeople, laborers, and consumers should be balanced for the public good. He called this policy the Square Deal. He put the policy to the test in 1902 when faced by a coal miners' strike. Roosevelt knew the strike might leave the country without heating fuel for the coming winter. He threatened to take over the mines unless managers and strikers agreed to arbitration—a formal process to settle disputes. He felt this was the only fair way to protect Americans.

> "The labor unions shall have a square deal, and the corporations shall have a square deal, and in addition all private citizens shall have a square deal."
>
> —President Theodore Roosevelt, quoted in *The Presidency of Theodore Roosevelt*, by Lewis L. Gould

© Houghton Mifflin Harcourt Publishing Company

The National Park System

In 1872 Yellowstone National Park, located mostly in Wyoming, became the first national park in the United States—and the world. Today there are 58 national parks in the United States and its territories. They are managed by the National Park Service (NPS), an agency of the federal government. In addition to the national parks, the NPS administers 334 other park areas, including monuments, battlefields, and seashores. Together these areas make up the National Park System.

President Theodore Roosevelt and conservationist John Muir in Yosemite National Park in California

Cathedral Rocks, Yosemite National Park

Regulating Big Business

Roosevelt made regulating big business a top goal of his administration. Muckrakers helped build support for this regulation. The public was shocked, for instance, after reading Upton Sinclair's description of the meatpacking industry in *The Jungle*. Roosevelt opened an investigation and later convinced Congress to pass a meat inspection law.

In 1906 Congress passed the **Pure Food and Drug Act**. This law prohibited the manufacture, sale, and transport of mislabeled or contaminated food and drugs. Roosevelt also was the first president to successfully use the 1890 Sherman Antitrust Act to break up a monopoly. He persuaded Congress to regulate railroad shipping rates. The public largely supported this expansion of federal regulatory powers.

Conservation

Roosevelt's love of the outdoors inspired him to join other Progressives in supporting **conservation**, or the protection of nature and its resources. Roosevelt was the first president to consider conservation an important national priority.

People believed in conservation for various reasons. Preservationists such as John Muir thought that nature should be left untouched so that people could enjoy its beauty:

> "Thousands of tired, nerve-shaken, over-civilized people are beginning to find out that going to the mountains is going home; that wildness is a necessity; and that mountain parks and reservations are useful not only as fountains of timber and irrigating rivers, but as fountains of life."
>
> —John Muir, *Our National Parks*

Other conservationists wanted to make sure the nation used its natural resources efficiently. Gifford Pinchot, the first head of the newly created Forest Service, valued forests for the resources they provided to build "prosperous homes." The disagreement between the two ideals of conservation eventually widened.

While Roosevelt was in office, the Forest Service gained control of nearly 150 million acres of public land. Roosevelt doubled the number of national parks, created 18 national monuments, and started 51 bird sanctuaries.

READING CHECK **Summarizing** What reforms did Roosevelt support?

HISTORY
VIDEO
Teddy Roosevelt's Acts and Legacy
hmhsocialstudies.com

© Houghton Mifflin Harcourt Publishing Company • Image Credits: (tr), ©W. Perry Conway/Corbis; (tc), ©Bettmann/Corbis

Reforms of Taft and Wilson

Theodore Roosevelt hoped that his secretary of war, **William Howard Taft**, would take his place as president in 1908. Like Roosevelt, Taft favored business regulation and opposed socialism. With Roosevelt's assistance, Taft defeated William Jennings Bryan in the election of 1908.

Taft Angers Progressives

Despite their friendship, Roosevelt and Taft held different ideas about how a president should act. Taft thought Roosevelt had claimed more power than a president was constitutionally allowed.

As president, therefore, Taft chose to move cautiously toward reform and regulation. This upset Roosevelt and various Progressives, who supported stricter regulation of big business. Although Taft's administration started twice as many antitrust lawsuits as Roosevelt's had, Progressives were not satisfied.

ACADEMIC VOCABULARY
various
of many types

Taft angered Progressives further by signing the Payne-Aldrich Tariff of 1909. This tariff reduced some rates on imported goods, but it raised others. Progressives wanted all tariffs to be lowered, in order to lower prices for consumers.

Furious with Taft, Roosevelt decided to run for president again in 1912. After Taft won the Republican nomination, Roosevelt and his followers formed the **Progressive Party**. It was nicknamed the Bull Moose Party because Roosevelt said he was "as strong as a bull moose." The split between Taft and Roosevelt divided the Republican vote, and Democratic candidate **Woodrow Wilson** won the electoral vote by a wide margin.

Wilson's Reforms

In his inaugural address, Wilson spoke of the terrible social conditions under which many working-class Americans lived. "We have been proud of our industrial achievements," he said, "but we have not hitherto [yet] stopped thoughtfully enough to count the human cost." Passing reform legislation was Wilson's top goal. He pushed for two measures soon after taking office: tariff revision and banking reform.

Wilson backed the Underwood Tariff Act of 1913, which lowered tariffs. The act also introduced a version of the modern

The Election of 1912

	Electoral Vote	Popular Vote
Wilson (Democrat)	435	6,286,214
T. Roosevelt (Progressive)	88	4,126,020
Taft (Republican)	8	3,483,922

*California cast 11 electoral votes for Roosevelt and 2 for Wilson.

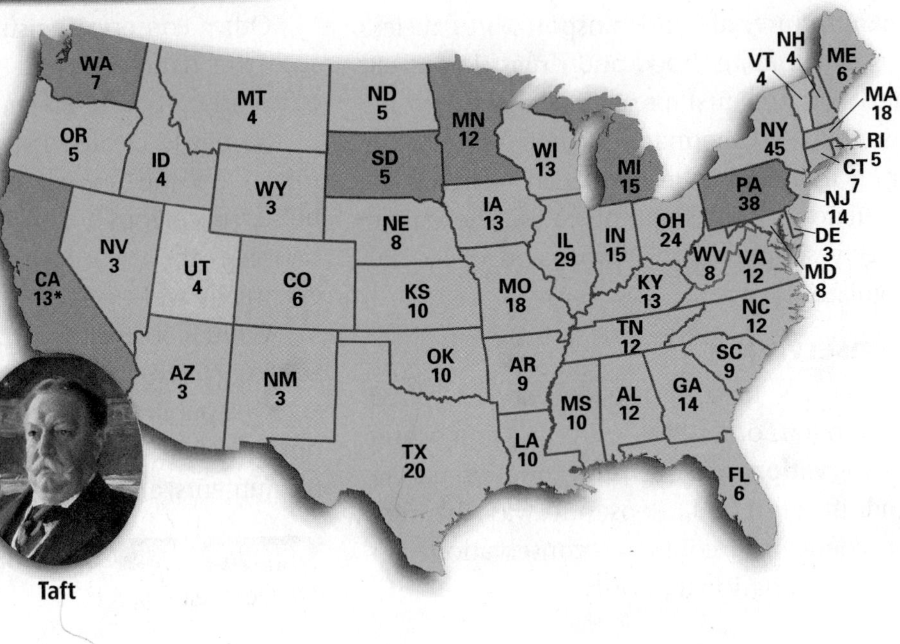

Wilson Roosevelt Taft

© Houghton Mifflin Harcourt Publishing Company • Image Credits: (all), White House Collection, copyright White House Historical Association

The Progressive Amendments, 1909–1920

QUICK FACTS

Number	Description	Proposed by Congress	Ratified by States
16th	Federal income tax	1909	1913
17th	Senators elected by people rather than state legislatures	1912	1913
18th	Manufacture, sale, and transport of alcohol prohibited	1917	1919
19th	Women's suffrage	1919	1920

income tax. The new tax was made possible in 1913 by the ratification of the **Sixteenth Amendment**. This amendment allows the federal government to impose direct taxes on citizens' incomes.

President Wilson next addressed banking reform with the 1913 Federal Reserve Act. This law created a national banking system called the Federal Reserve to regulate the economy.

Wilson also pushed for laws to regulate big business. The Clayton Antitrust Act of 1914 strengthened federal laws against monopolies. The Federal Trade Commission, created in 1914, had the power to investigate and punish unfair trade practices. Wilson's success in guiding reform programs through Congress helped him to win re-election in 1916.

READING CHECK **Analyzing** Why did Wilson win the election of 1912?

SUMMARY The progressive presidents tried to change American society for the better.

Section 4 Assessment

hmhsocialstudies.com
ONLINE QUIZ

Reviewing Ideas, Terms, and People

1. a. **Describe** How did **Theodore Roosevelt** support progressive reforms?
   b. **Analyze** Why did many Americans support **conservation**?
   c. **Evaluate** Do you think Roosevelt's reforms benefited the nation? Why or why not?
2. a. **Identify** What was the **Progressive Party**? Why was it created?
   b. **Compare and Contrast** How were the administrations of **William Howard Taft** and Roosevelt similar, and how were they different?
   c. **Evaluate** Which president do you think had the biggest influence on progressive reform—Roosevelt, Taft, or **Woodrow Wilson**? Explain your choice.

Critical Thinking

3. **Comparing and Contrasting** Review your notes on the progressive presidents. Then copy the diagram below and use it to compare and contrast the reforms of the progressive presidents.

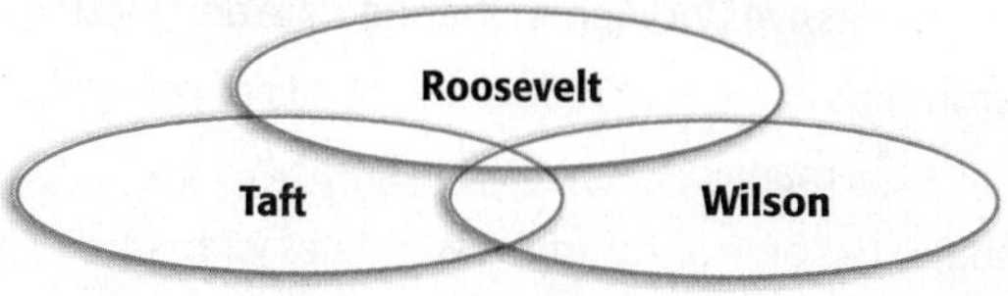

FOCUS ON SPEAKING

4. **The Ideas of Roosevelt, Taft, and Wilson** Do you agree or disagree with Presidents Roosevelt, Taft, and Wilson? Take notes on any of their ideas that you would include in your campaign promises.

© Houghton Mifflin Harcourt Publishing Company

Short- and Long-term Causal Relationships

Define the Skill

Most historical events are the result of other events. When something happens as a result of other things that occur, it is an effect of those things. Some events take place soon after the things that cause them. Such events are called *short-term effects*. In contrast, *long-term effects* can occur years, decades, or even hundreds of years after the events that caused them. Being able to recognize short-term and long-term cause-and-effect relationships will help you to better understand historical events.

Learn the Skill

Clue words can sometimes reveal a cause-and-effect relationship between events. Often, however, such language clues may not be present. Therefore, when you study history, you should always look for other clues that might explain why an action or event occurred.

Short-term effects are usually fairly easy to identify. In historical writing they are often closely linked to the event that caused them. For example, consider this passage.

> "Some Progressives worked to change state and local governments in order to reduce the power of political machines. In many places, reformers replaced corrupt ballots that listed only one party's candidates with government-prepared ballots that listed all candidates. Under pressure from reformers, many states adopted secret ballots, giving every voter a private vote."

This passage contains no clue words. Yet it is clear that cause-and-effect relationships exist. The power of political machines created corrupt voting practices. Reformers wanted to change this. One effect of this situation was the government-prepared ballot, and another was the secret ballot.

Recognizing long-term causal relationships is often more difficult. Since long-term effects take place well after the event that caused them, they may not be discussed at the same time as their cause. This is why you should always question why an event occurred as you learn about it. For example, in 1971 Congress passed the first federal law to protect the health and safety of all workers. This law was a long-term result of efforts begun years earlier by the progressives you read about in this chapter.

Many long-term effects result from major forces running through history that make things happen. They include economics, science and technology, expansion, conflict and cooperation among people, cultural clashes and differences, and moral and religious issues. Ask yourself if one of these forces is involved in the event being studied. If so, the event may have long-term effects that you should be on the lookout for when studying later events.

Practice and Apply the Skill

Review the information in this chapter and answer these questions to practice recognizing short- and long-term causal relationships.

1. All packaged food today must have its contents listed on the container. This requirement is a long-term effect of what progressive reform?
2. Write a paragraph explaining the effects of the muckrakers on the news media today.

© Houghton Mifflin Harcourt Publishing Company

CHAPTER 6

Chapter Review

History's Impact
▶ **video series**
Review the video to answer the closing question:
How did the rights of women in individual states play a role in the women's suffrage movement?

Visual Summary

QUICK FACTS

Use the visual summary below to help you review the main ideas of the chapter.

Progressives hoped to improve society through reform. Their goals included

- Temperance
- Women's suffrage
- Big business regulation
- Conservation
- Tariff and banking reform

Reviewing Vocabulary, Terms, and People

Complete each sentence by filling in the blank with the correct term or person from the chapter.

1. Some Americans supported a _________ system, which proposed government ownership of the country's means of production.
2. Republican _________ began a program to reform state politics in Wisconsin.
3. The _________ granted women in the United States the right to vote.
4. The _________ prohibited the manufacture, sale, and transport of mislabeled or contaminated food and drugs.
5. During the Gilded Age, _________ often dominated local politics and used corruption to get their candidates elected.
6. _________ were journalists who wrote about troubling issues such as child labor, tenement housing, and political corruption.

Comprehension and Critical Thinking

SECTION 1

7. a. **Describe** What tactics did bosses and political machines use to gain control of local governments?

   b. **Analyze** What changes did Progressives make to city life?

   c. **Elaborate** Which progressive reform do you think had the greatest effect on Americans?

SECTION 2

8. a. **Identify** What reforms were made to improve working conditions, and who was affected by these reforms?

   b. **Contrast** What are the differences between capitalism and socialism?

   c. **Elaborate** If you were a business owner, would you have supported the progressive workplace reforms? Explain your answer.

© Houghton Mifflin Harcourt Publishing Company

SECTION 3

9. a. **Recall** What minority groups were overlooked by progressive reform efforts?

   b. **Analyze** How did women's involvement in the Progressive movement lead to constitutional change?

   c. **Elaborate** Do you agree with Booker T. Washington's approach to improving life for African Americans? Explain your answer.

SECTION 4

10. a. **Describe** How did William Howard Taft disappoint Progressives?

    b. **Compare** In what ways were the reforms of Presidents Roosevelt, Taft, and Wilson similar?

    c. **Elaborate** Would you have supported Wilson's progressive reforms? Explain your answer.

Reviewing Themes

11. **Politics** What role did political machines play in local politics during the Gilded Age?
12. **Society and Culture** How were children affected by the movement for workplace reforms?

Reading Skills 21ST CENTURY

Evaluating Sources *Use the Reading Skills taught in this chapter to answer the question about the reading selection below.*

> The next day Rose went to town [Chicago] alone. The wind had veered [turned] to the south, the dust blew, and the whole terrifying panorama [view] of life in the street seemed some way blurred together, and forms of men and animals were like figures in tapestry. The grind and clang and clatter and hiss and howl of the traffic was all about her . . .
>
> —Hamlin Garland, from his novel *Rose of Dutcher's Coolly*, 1895

13. Is this a good source for understanding the experiences of Chicago in the late 1800s? Why or why not?

Social Studies Skills 21ST CENTURY

Short- and Long-Term Causal Relationships *Use the Social Studies Skills taught in this chapter to answer the question about the reading selection below.*

> Despite their friendship, Roosevelt and Taft held different ideas about how a president should act. Taft thought Roosevelt had claimed more power than a president was constitutionally allowed.
>
> As president, therefore, Taft chose to move cautiously toward reform and regulation.

14. According to the passage above, what was a long-term cause of Taft's cautious reforms?

Using the Internet 21ST CENTURY

15. **Activity: Researching Progressives** Rapid industrial and urban growth in the United States during the late 1800s resulted in a number of problems. Progressives worked to address these problems in many ways, including efforts to clean up political corruption, improve working conditions, and enact social reforms. Through your online textbook, explore the lives of some of the leaders of the Progressive movement. Then write a profile of a Progressive leader that outlines his or her life and impact on American reform.

hmhsocialstudies.com

FOCUS ON SPEAKING

16. **Share Your Campaign Promises** Review your notes about possible campaign promises. Which promises will be most helpful in getting you elected? Look at your promises to see whether they focus on issues important to voters. Then write a speech including your campaign promises that you can deliver to your class.

© Houghton Mifflin Harcourt Publishing Company

CHAPTER 6

Standardized Test Practice

DIRECTIONS: Read each question and write the letter of the best response.

1

The people in this photograph would probably have been *most* interested in which of the following reforms?

A secret ballots

B the Pure Food and Drug Act

C child labor laws

D elimination of political machines

2 **One direct result of immigration and urban growth was the rise of**

A political machines.

B the civil-service system.

C the spoils system.

D primary elections.

3 **What was the *main* idea behind the creation of the civil-service system in the late 1800s?**

A Government jobs should be awarded to people who support the party in power.

B Government workers should be required to support the elected officials who hire them.

C Government employees should be qualified to do the jobs for which they were hired.

D Government jobs should not be filled with employees who serve in those jobs for life.

4 **The Nineteenth Amendment to the Constitution increased democracy in the United States by**

A granting women the right to vote.

B allowing the people of each state to elect their senators.

C establishing direct primary elections.

D enabling voters to remove elected officials from office before the end of their terms.

5 **Earlier in the book you learned how Frederick Douglass wrote and spoke against slavery and unfair treatment of African Americans. What later reformer also spoke out for equal rights for African Americans?**

A John Dewey

B W. E. B. Du Bois

C William Howard Taft

D Upton Sinclair

6 **Read the following excerpt from an interview with a boss at Tammany Hall and use it to answer the question below.**

> There's only one way to hold a district: you must study human nature and act accordin' . . . To learn real human nature you have to go among the people, see them and be seen. I know every man, woman, and child in the Fifteenth District, except them that's been born this summer—and I know some of them, too. I know what they like and what they don't like, what they are strong at and what they are weak in, and I reach them by approachin' at the right side.
>
> —George Washington Plunkitt, quoted in *Eyewitnesses and Others*

Document-Based Question How did Plunkitt say he kept his position in the political machine?

© Houghton Mifflin Harcourt Publishing Company

Image Credits: (t), Library of Congress Prints & Photographs Division, Washington, D.C.

CHAPTER 7 1867–1920

America as a World Power

Essential Question How did America's growing power affect its relationships with other nations?

ALABAMA COURSE OF STUDY

3 Identify causes and consequences of World War I and reasons for United States' entry into the war.

4 Identify cultural and economic developments in the United States from 1900 through the 1930s.

- Identifying notable persons of the early 1900s.

Focus on Writing

A List of Pros and Cons In the last half of the 1800s, the United States became more involved in international affairs. As you read this chapter, you will analyze the nation's new role and use the results of your analysis to guide U.S. policy in the future. In order to analyze the advantages and disadvantages of an aggressive foreign policy, you will need to create a list of the pros and cons of U.S. involvement with other nations in the late 1800s and early 1900s. As you create your list, note which items are facts and which are opinions—either yours or someone else's.

UNITED STATES

1867 The United States buys Alaska.

1867

WORLD

1868 Japan begins a time of modernization known as the Meiji Restoration.

© Houghton Mifflin Harcourt Publishing Company

Image Credits: (b), ©Charles Sleicher; (t), ©Bettmann/Corbis

HISTORY Panama Canal Locks

hmhsocialstudies.com VIDEO

Through a combination of economic strength, military might, and aggressive foreign policy, the United States made its presence known in many parts of the world. One such place was Panama, where the United States built the Panama Canal, shown here.

1880 — **1890** — **1900** — **1910** — **1920**

1885 The Indian National Congress is formed in British-controlled India.

1890 Congress passes the McKinley Tariff, which gives a subsidy to U.S. sugar producers.

1895 Cubans rebel against Spanish rule.

1898 The United States wins the Spanish-American War, gaining the Philippine Islands and Puerto Rico.

1900 The Boxer Rebellion erupts in China.

1903 Panama declares itself an independent nation.

1910 The Mexican Revolution begins.

1914 The Panama Canal officially opens.

Image Credits: (t), ©Bettmann/Corbis; (c), Denver Public Library, Western History Collection; (bl), Press Information Bureau of India

© Houghton Mifflin Harcourt Publishing Company

Reading Social Studies

Economics | **Geography** | **Politics** | Society and Culture | Science and Technology

Focus on Themes In this chapter, you will learn about how the physical **geography** of the United States changed as it acquired overseas territories. You will also read about how national and international **politics** affected foreign policy and brought new responsibilities to the government of the United States.

Comparing Historical Texts

Focus on Reading A good way to learn what people in the past thought is to read what they wrote. However, most documents will only tell you one side of the story. By comparing writings by different people, you can learn a great deal about various sides of a historical issue or debate.

Comparing Texts When you compare historical texts, you should consider two things: who wrote the documents and what the documents were meant to achieve. To do this, you need to find the writers' main point or points.

Document 1

"We have cherished the policy of non-interference with affairs of foreign governments wisely inaugurated [begun] by Washington, keeping ourselves free from entanglement, either as allies or foes, content to leave undisturbed with them the settlement of their own domestic concerns."

–President William McKinley, First Inaugural Address, 1897

Document 2

"Therefore, Mr. President, here is a war with terrible characteristics flagrant [obvious] at our very doors [in Cuba]. We have the power to bring it to an end. I believe that the whole American people would welcome steps in that direction."

–Senator Henry Cabot Lodge, Speech in Congress, 1896

Document 1	Document 2
Writer	
President William McKinley	Senator Henry Cabot Lodge
Main point	
The United States should not involve itself in the affairs of other countries.	The United States should go to war in Cuba.
Both Sides of the Issue	
Americans were torn over the war in Cuba. Some thought the United States should remain uninvolved as it always had. Others thought it was time for a change in foreign policy.	

© Houghton Mifflin Harcourt Publishing Company

You Try It!

Read the following passages, both taken from presidential addresses to Congress. As you read, look for the main point each president makes in his address.

Foreign Policy

In treating of our foreign policy and of the attitude that this great Nation should assume in the world at large, it is absolutely necessary to consider the Army and the Navy, and the Congress, through which the thought of the Nation finds its expression, should keep ever vividly in mind the fundamental fact that it is impossible to treat our foreign policy, whether this policy takes shape in the effort to secure justice for others or justice for ourselves, save as conditioned upon the attitude we are willing to take toward our Army, and especially toward our Navy.

—President Theodore Roosevelt, Message to Congress, 1904

The diplomacy of the present administration has sought to respond to modern ideas of commercial intercourse [involvement]. This policy has been characterized as substituting dollars for bullets. It is one that appeals alike to idealistic humanitarian sentiments [feelings], to the dictates [rules] of sound policy and strategy, and to legitimate [make real] commercial aims.

—President William Howard Taft, Message to Congress, 1912

After you read the passages, answer the following questions.

1. What was the main point Roosevelt made in his address?
2. What was the main point Taft made in his address?
3. How can a comparison of Roosevelt's and Taft's addresses to Congress help you understand the issues that shaped U.S. foreign policy in the early 1900s?

Key Terms and People

Chapter 7

Section 1
imperialism
isolationism
William H. Seward
Liliuokalani
spheres of influence
Open Door Policy
Boxer Rebellion

Section 2
yellow journalism
Teller Amendment
Emilio Aguinaldo
Anti-Imperialist League
Platt Amendment

Section 3
Panama Canal
Roosevelt Corollary
dollar diplomacy
Mexican Revolution
John J. Pershing
Francisco "Pancho" Villa

Academic Vocabulary

In this chapter, you will learn the following academic words:

process
role

As you read this chapter, organize your notes to help you point out the similarities and differences among events or policies.

© Houghton Mifflin Harcourt Publishing Company

SECTION 1

The United States Gains Overseas Territories

What You Will Learn...

Main Ideas

1. The United States ended its policy of isolationism.
2. Hawaii became a U.S. territory in 1898.
3. The United States sought trade with Japan and China.

The Big Idea

In the last half of the 1800s, the United States joined the race for control of overseas territories.

Key Terms and People

imperialism
isolationism
William H. Seward
Liliuokalani
spheres of influence
Open Door Policy
Boxer Rebellion

hmhsocialstudies.com
TAKING NOTES

Use the graphic organizer online to take notes on examples of U.S. expansion.

If YOU were there...

You are a Hawaiian living on Maui, one of the Hawaiian Islands, in 1890. Your parents work in a sugar mill owned by American planters. Although the mill supplies jobs, you don't trust the sugar planters. They have already made your king sign a treaty that gives them a lot of power in the islands. You are afraid they will take over the government.

What would you do if the planters took over your islands?

BUILDING BACKGROUND In the mid-1800s, most Americans had little interest in being involved with the rest of the world diplomatically. The Civil War and Reconstruction kept their focus on challenges at home. In the meantime, though, European nations were busily acquiring overseas territories. The United States would soon join them.

End of Isolation

In the 1800s powerful Western nations were busy building naval bases to protect their shipping routes around the world. This was an aspect of **imperialism**—building an empire by founding colonies or conquering other nations. Between 1870 and 1914, Europeans extended their colonial empires until they controlled most of Africa and Southeast Asia.

Roots of Imperialism

Several forces drove this wave of European imperialism. Countries wanted sources of raw materials—such as copper, rubber, and tin—to fuel industrial growth. Businesspeople wanted new markets for their manufactured goods. And many

Europeans saw colonies as a source of power and national pride.

In contrast, the United States followed a limited policy of **isolationism**—avoiding involvement in the affairs of other countries. In 1789 President George Washington had warned Americans "to steer clear of permanent alliances" with other countries. American leaders tried to follow this advice by staying out of overseas conflicts.

By the late 1800s, however, some Americans believed the United States needed to expand to keep its economy strong. In his 1890 book *The Influence of Sea Power upon History,* Alfred T. Mahan argued that the United States needed a strong navy to protect its economic interests. Mahan also explained that a strong navy needed overseas bases and coaling stations—places for ships to take on coal for fuel.

Seward's Folly

In 1867 the United States greatly expanded its North American territory when Secretary of State **William H. Seward** arranged the purchase of Alaska from Russia for $7.2 million. Some people thought Alaska was a frozen wasteland, calling the deal "Seward's Folly" [foolish act]. But Seward had purchased an area more than twice the size of Texas for two cents an acre. And as he had hoped, Alaska became a source of valuable natural resources such as fur, timber, and minerals. Gold was found in Alaska in the 1890s, bringing miners and settlers to the area.

Based on Seward's belief that the United States "must continue to move on westward," the nation also annexed the Midway Islands in 1867. The islands' location about halfway between the U.S. West Coast and Japan made Midway an excellent coaling station for the U.S. Navy.

The United States wanted the island group of Samoa for similar reasons. The United States and Germany agreed to divide Samoa in 1899.

THE IMPACT TODAY

Today the United States has hundreds of military bases in foreign countries.

READING CHECK **Analyzing** Why did U.S. leaders end isolationist policies in the late 1800s?

U.S. Territories in the Pacific, 1856–1899

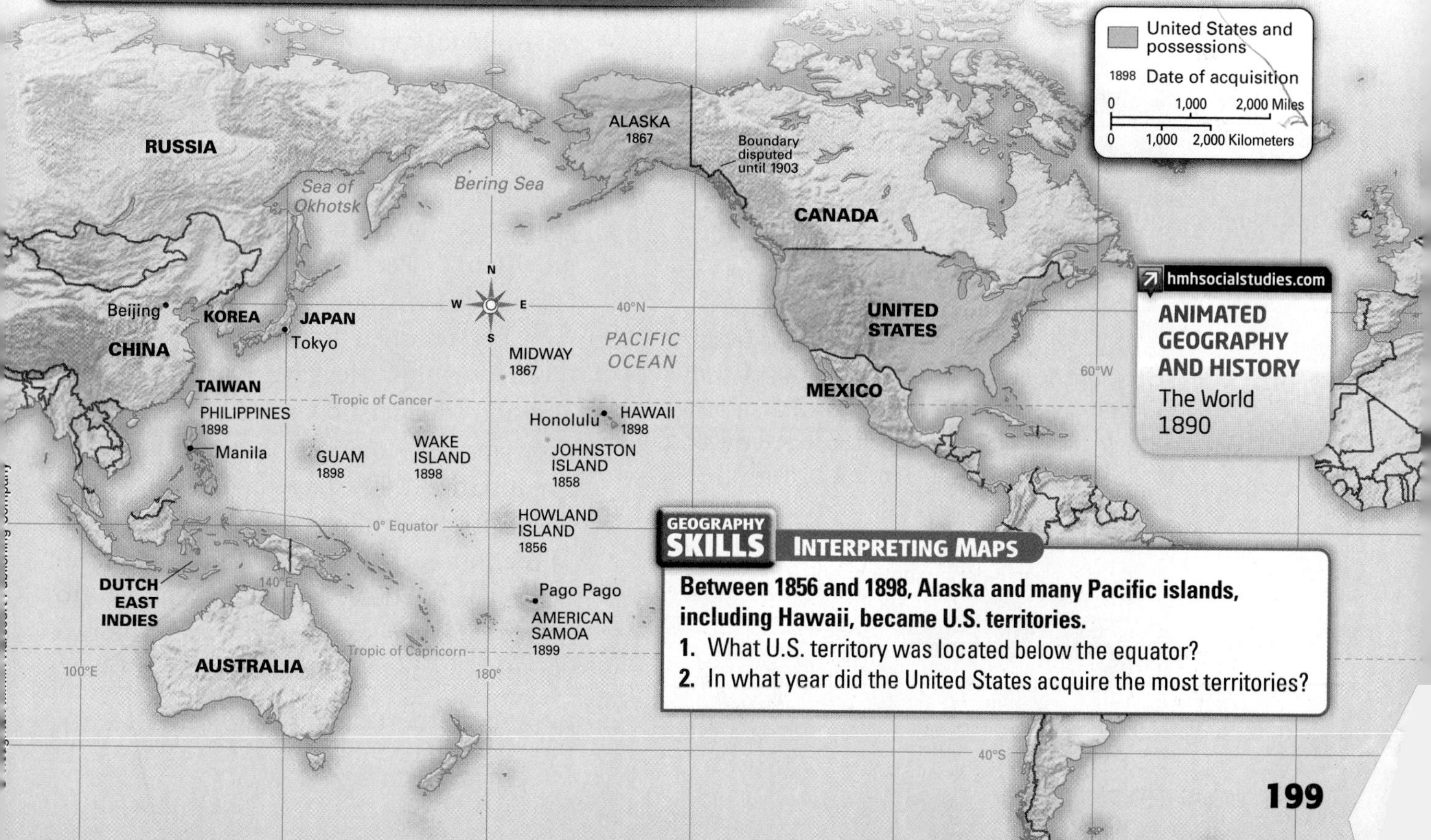

United States and possessions
1898 Date of acquisition
0 1,000 2,000 Miles
0 1,000 2,000 Kilometers
RUSSIA
ALASKA 1867
Boundary disputed until 1903
Sea of Okhotsk
Bering Sea
CANADA
UNITED STATES
MEXICO
Beijing
KOREA
JAPAN
Tokyo
CHINA
TAIWAN
PHILIPPINES 1898
Manila
GUAM 1898
WAKE ISLAND 1898
MIDWAY 1867
PACIFIC OCEAN
Honolulu
HAWAII 1898
JOHNSTON ISLAND 1858
HOWLAND ISLAND 1856
Pago Pago
AMERICAN SAMOA 1899
DUTCH EAST INDIES
AUSTRALIA
40°N
Tropic of Cancer
0° Equator
Tropic of Capricorn
100°E
140°E
180°
60°W
40°S

hmhsocialstudies.com

ANIMATED GEOGRAPHY AND HISTORY

The World 1890

GEOGRAPHY SKILLS **INTERPRETING MAPS**

Between 1856 and 1898, Alaska and many Pacific islands, including Hawaii, became U.S. territories.

1. What U.S. territory was located below the equator?
2. In what year did the United States acquire the most territories?

Hawaii Becomes a Territory

Even more appealing than Samoa were the Hawaiian Islands. Hawaiians first saw Europeans in 1778. Trading and whaling ships in the Pacific soon began stopping in Hawaii. In the early 1800s American missionaries came and attempted to convert Hawaiians to Christianity. Missionaries opened businesses and raised crops, such as sugarcane. Some Americans became rich sugar planters.

By the 1840s most shops and shipyards in Hawaii were owned by Americans. Sugar became a leading export of the Hawaiian economy. An 1875 treaty allowed Hawaiian sugar to be shipped duty-free to the United States. (A duty is a tax on imported items.) This agreement helped the Hawaiian sugar industry prosper.

THE IMPACT TODAY

Sugarcane is Hawaii's most valuable crop, but acreage and production have declined in recent years. Only two functioning sugarcane farms remain in the state.

The planters used their power to force the Hawaiian king to sign a new constitution in 1887. It became known as the Bayonet Constitution because the king was forced to sign it at gunpoint. The constitution granted more power to the planter-controlled legislature. Many Hawaiians feared the foreigners' increase in power.

BIOGRAPHY

Liliuokalani

(1838–1917)

Born in Honolulu, Queen Liliuokalani was proud of Hawaiian traditions. Even after being driven from power in 1883, she continued speaking out on behalf of native-born Hawaiians. In 1887 she traveled to Washington, D.C., meeting with President Grover Cleveland to argue against the annexation of Hawaii by the United States. Until her death, Liliuokalani served as a symbol of Hawaiian pride and a reminder of the islands' history as an independent nation.

Drawing Conclusions Why do you think Liliuokalani was a symbol of Hawaiian pride?

In 1891 the king died, and his sister, **Liliuokalani** (li-LEE-uh-woh-kuh-LAHN-ee), became queen. She proposed a new constitution that would return power to the monarchy. The planters revolted. John L. Stevens, U.S. minister to Hawaii, called 150 marines ashore to support the revolt, and it succeeded without a battle. The planters formed a new government. Congress voted to annex the Hawaiian Islands in 1898.

READING CHECK **Identifying Cause and Effect** What effect did the growing power of the planters have on the Hawaiian monarchy?

United States Seeks Trade with Japan and China

Economic interest also drew the United States to Japan and China. The United States wanted to open and secure trade markets in both Asian countries.

Opening Trade with Japan

By the mid-1800s European powers had formed strong trade ties with most East Asian countries. However, the island nation of Japan had isolated itself from the rest of the world for hundreds of years.

The United States wanted to open up trade with Japan before Europeans arrived. President Millard Fillmore sent Commodore Matthew Perry to Japan to secure "friendship, commerce, [and] a supply of coal and provisions." Perry attempted a peaceful alliance in 1853, but he was not successful.

Perry returned to Japan in 1854 with seven warships. He gave Japanese leaders gifts and tried to show some of the benefits that Japanese-American trade would have. For instance, Perry presented them with a telegraph transmitter and a model train. This effort—and the presence of U.S. naval power—persuaded Japanese officials to open trade with the United States. The two countries signed a trade agreement in 1858.

Perry Arrives in Japan

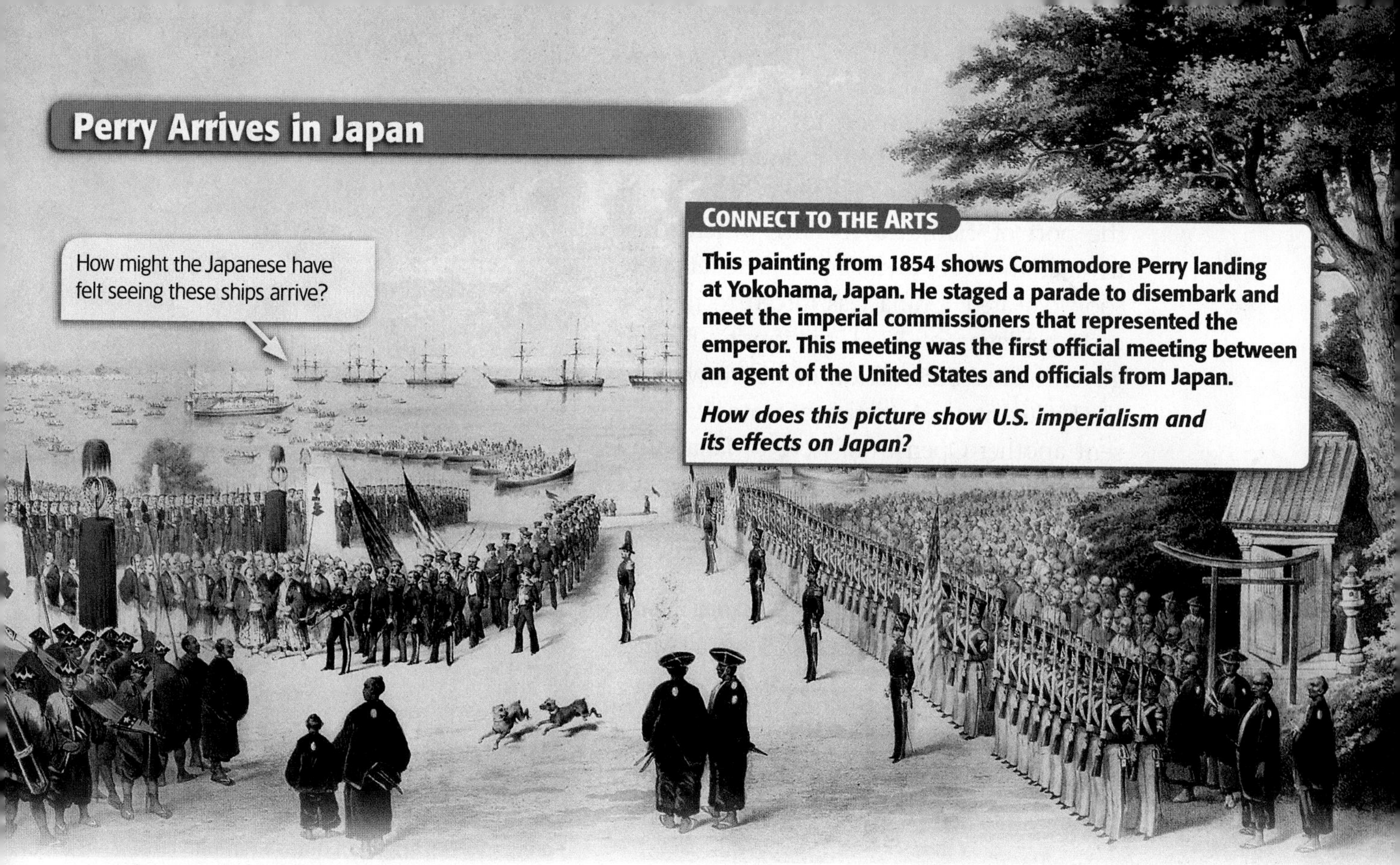
How might the Japanese have felt seeing these ships arrive?

CONNECT TO THE ARTS

This painting from 1854 shows Commodore Perry landing at Yokohama, Japan. He staged a parade to disembark and meet the imperial commissioners that represented the emperor. This meeting was the first official meeting between an agent of the United States and officials from Japan.

How does this picture show U.S. imperialism and its effects on Japan?

Some Japanese leaders welcomed trade with the United States. In 1868 people who favored the industrialization process came to power in Japan, beginning a 40-year period of modernization. By the 1890s Japan was becoming a major imperial power. It defeated China in the Sino-Japanese War from 1894 to 1895. As a result, Japan gained new territory and enjoyed the same trading privileges in China as European countries. In 1904 Japan attacked Russian forces stationed in China. President Theodore Roosevelt helped to negotiate a peace treaty to end the Russo-Japanese War a year later. Japan gained control of Korea, a lease on Port Arthur in China, and other rights. Japan had become a world power.

Foreign Powers in China

After Japan defeated China, other countries took advantage of China's weakness by seizing **spheres of influence**—areas where foreign nations controlled resources. Germany, Great Britain, France, Japan, and Russia all took control of areas within China.

Some U.S. leaders feared that the United States would be closed out of Chinese markets. In 1899 Secretary of State John Hay sent notes to Japan and many European countries announcing the **Open Door Policy**. This policy stated that all nations should have equal access to trade in China. The policy was neither rejected nor accepted by European powers and Japan but made U.S. intentions clear.

Meanwhile, many Chinese resented the power and control held by foreign nations. This hostility sparked the **Boxer Rebellion**. The Boxers were Chinese nationalists who were angered by foreign involvement in China. In their language, the group was called the Fists of Righteous Harmony. Westerners called them Boxers because they used a clenched fist as their symbol. Although officially denounced, they were secretly supported by the Chinese government.

In June 1900 the Boxers took to the streets of Beijing, China's capital, and laid siege to the walled settlement where foreigners lived. They killed more than 200 people.

ACADEMIC VOCABULARY

process a series of steps by which a task is accomplished

The siege continued for two months. Foreign military forces, including United States Marines, fought their way from the port of Tianjin to Beijing, where they invaded the Forbidden City. The Boxers were soon defeated. China was forced to make a cash payment of $333 million to foreign governments, $25 million of which went to the United States. Secretary of State Hay then sent another Open Door note to Japan and the European nations. The Open Door Policy remained in effect until World War II again closed China's borders to foreign influence.

READING CHECK **Identifying Cause and Effect** What factors led to the Boxer Rebellion, and what was the result?

SUMMARY The United States greatly expanded its territory and influence in the Pacific.

Foreign forces engage Chinese nationalists in battle at Tianjin, China, in this illustration of China's Boxer Rebellion.

Section 1 Assessment

hmhsocialstudies.com
ONLINE QUIZ

Reviewing Ideas, Terms, and People

1. a. **Describe** What policy had the United States followed regarding other countries before the late 1800s?
   b. **Analyze** Why did the United States expand to Alaska and to islands in the Pacific?
   c. **Evaluate** Do you think **William H. Seward**'s purchase of Alaska was a good decision? Explain.
2. a. **Recall** What became Hawaii's leading export?
   b. **Sequence** What events led to Hawaii's annexation as a U.S. territory?
   c. **Elaborate** What do you think about the planters' revolt against Queen **Liliuokalani**?
3. a. **Describe** How did the United States persuade Japanese leaders to sign a trade treaty?
   b. **Contrast** How was the U.S. experience establishing trade with China different from U.S. attempts to open trade with Japan?
   c. **Evaluate** Do you think Japan made the right decision in agreeing to open trade with the United States? Explain your answer.

Critical Thinking

4. **Generalizing** Review your notes on the areas or trade rights gained by the United States. Then use the chart below to identify the benefits of these areas and trade rights.

American Expansion

Areas or Trade Rights Gained	Benefits for United States

FOCUS ON WRITING

5. **Identifying Pros and Cons of U.S. Involvement Overseas** What did the United States gain from its involvement in these areas of the world? What were the disadvantages? As you read this section, identify pros and cons to add to your list.

The Spanish-American War

SECTION 2

If YOU were there...

You live in New York City in 1898. Newspaper headlines are screaming about the start of war in Cuba. You hear that Theodore Roosevelt wants volunteers for a cavalry troop called the Rough Riders. You know how to ride a horse, and you've admired Roosevelt ever since he was New York's police commissioner. You know it will be dangerous, but it also sounds like a great adventure.

Would you join the Rough Riders? Why?

BUILDING BACKGROUND While the United States, Japan, and several European powers were gaining colonies, Spain's empire was declining. By the late 1800s Spain's once-extensive American empire was reduced to two island colonies—Cuba and Puerto Rico. Eager for independence, some Cubans revolted against Spanish rule. Many Americans sympathized with Cuba's fight for independence.

War with Spain

You read earlier that newspaper publishers Joseph Pulitzer and William Randolph Hearst were in a fierce competition for readers. In the late 1890s their newspapers published stories from Cuba, where Cuban rebels were fighting for independence from Spain. To attract readers, Pulitzer and Hearst printed sensational, often exaggerated news stories. This technique is called **yellow journalism**. Vivid stories about Spanish brutality in Cuba convinced many Americans that the U.S. military should support the Cuban rebels.

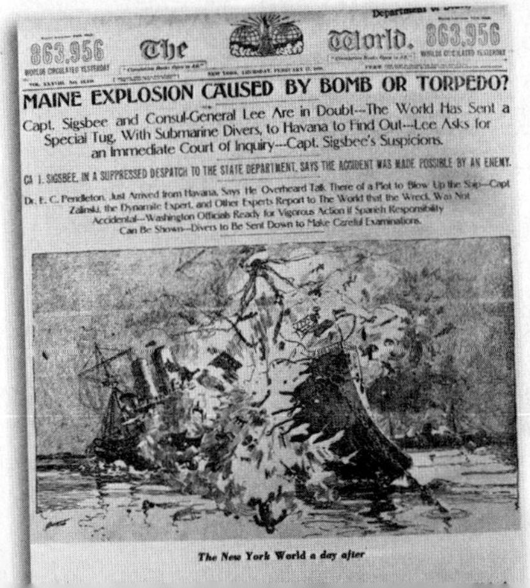

863,956 The World. 863,956

MAINE EXPLOSION CAUSED BY BOMB OR TORPEDO?

Capt. Sigsbee and Consul-General Lee Are in Doubt--The World Has Sent a Special Tug, With Submarine Divers, to Havana to Find Out--Lee Asks for an Immediate Court of Inquiry--Capt. Sigsbee's Suspicions.

CAPT. SIGSBEE, IN A SUPPRESSED DESPATCH TO THE STATE DEPARTMENT, SAYS THE ACCIDENT WAS MADE POSSIBLE BY AN ENEMY.

Dr. E. C. Pendleton, Just Arrived from Havana, Says He Overheard Talk There of a Plot to Blow Up the Ship--Capt. Zalinski, the Dynamite Expert, and Other Experts Report to The World that the Wreck Was Not Accidental--Washington Officials Ready for Vigorous Action if Spanish Responsibility Can Be Shown--Divers to Be Sent Down to Make Careful Examinations.

The New York World a day after

Newspapers such as this one encouraged Americans to seek war with Spain.

What You Will Learn...

Main Ideas

1. In 1898 the United States went to war with Spain in the Spanish-American War.
2. The United States gained territories in the Caribbean and Pacific.

The Big Idea

The United States expanded into new parts of the world as a result of the Spanish-American War.

Key Terms and People

yellow journalism
Teller Amendment
Emilio Aguinaldo
Anti-Imperialist League
Platt Amendment

hmhsocialstudies.com
TAKING NOTES

Use the graphic organizer online to take notes on the results of the Spanish-American War.

Despite growing support for military action in Cuba, President Grover Cleveland was opposed to U.S. involvement. In 1896 William McKinley, a supporter of Cuban independence, was elected president. Several events soon led to war.

In February 1898 Hearst's newspaper published a letter written by the Spanish minister to the United States, Enrique Dupuy de Lôme. In it, de Lôme called McKinley "weak and a bidder for the admiration of the crowd." Many Americans were outraged.

In January 1898, even before de Lôme's letter became public, the United States sent the battleship USS *Maine* to Havana Harbor. The *Maine*'s mission was to protect U.S. citizens and economic interests in Cuba. On February 15 the *Maine* exploded and sank, with a loss of 266 men. Although the cause of the explosion was unclear, the American press immediately blamed Spain. "Remember the *Maine*!" became a rallying cry for angry Americans.

President McKinley requested $50 million to prepare for war. Congress approved the money. Although Cuba was not a U.S. territory, Congress issued a resolution on April 20 declaring Cuba independent and demanding that Spain leave the island within three days. Attached to the resolution was the **Teller Amendment**, which stated that the United States had no interest in taking control of Cuba. In response to the resolution, Spain declared war on the United States. The next day, Congress passed, and McKinley signed, a declaration of war against Spain.

"Remember the *Maine*!"

Most of the men aboard the USS *Maine* were sleeping when a terrible explosion demolished the forward third of the ship at 9:40 P.M. on February 15, 1898. The rest of the ship sank quickly. Some 266 men were killed.

Who did the United States blame for the explosion?

Prints & Photographs Division, Washington, D.C.; (b) ©Bettmann/Corbis

War in the Philippines

While attention was focused on Cuba, the U.S. Navy won a quick victory nearly halfway around the world in the Philippines, a Spanish colony in the Pacific. Filipinos, like Cubans, were rebelling against Spanish rule.

As soon as the Spanish-American War began, American commodore George Dewey raced to the Philippines with four large warships and two small gunboats. On May 1, ignoring reports that mines beneath the water barred his way, he sailed into Manila Bay and destroyed the Spanish Pacific fleet stationed there. Dewey's forces sank or captured 10 ships. The Spanish lost 381 lives, but none of Dewey's men were killed.

Dewey had defeated the Spanish, but he did not have enough troops to occupy and secure the Philippines. Troops eventually arrived, and on August 13, U.S. troops and Filipino rebels led by **Emilio Aguinaldo** (ahg-ee-NAHL-doh) took control of the Philippine capital, Manila.

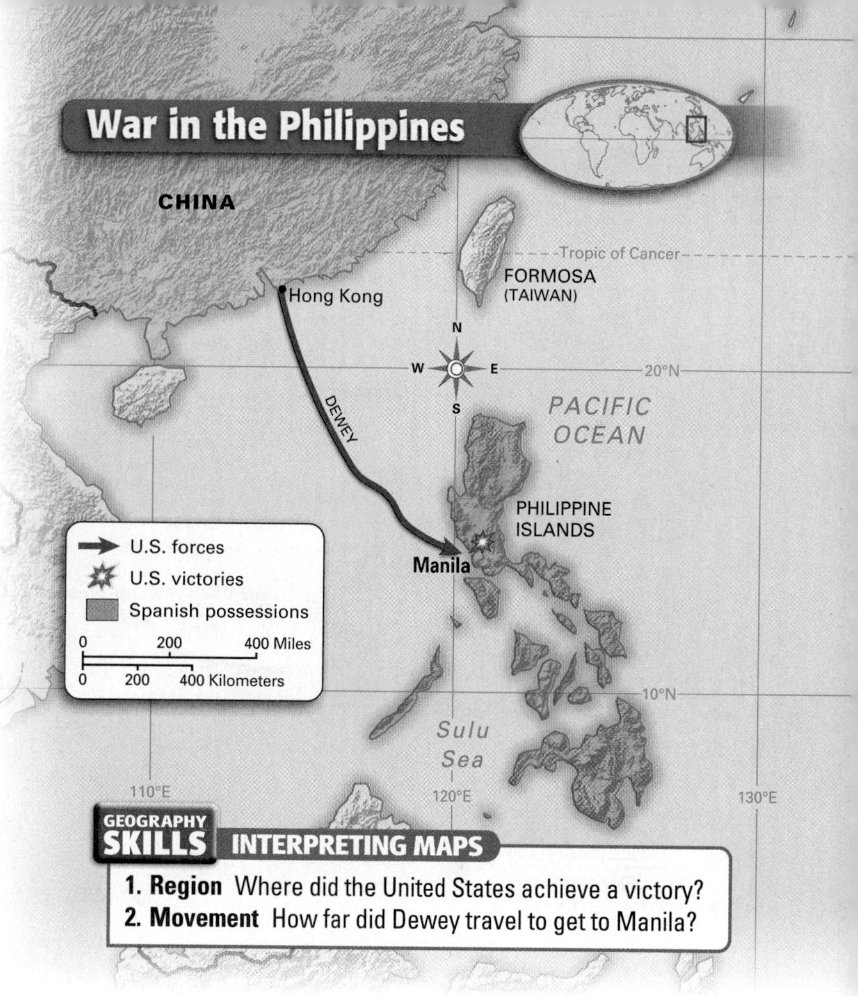
War in the Philippines
CHINA
Hong Kong
FORMOSA
(TAIWAN)
Tropic of Cancer
N
W
E
S
20°N
PACIFIC
OCEAN
DEWEY
PHILIPPINE
ISLANDS
Manila
U.S. forces
U.S. victories
Spanish possessions
0 200 400 Miles
0 200 400 Kilometers
10°N
Sulu
Sea
110°E
120°E
130°E

GEOGRAPHY SKILLS **INTERPRETING MAPS**

1. **Region** Where did the United States achieve a victory?
2. **Movement** How far did Dewey travel to get to Manila?

War in the Caribbean

In contrast to the navy, the U.S. Army was unprepared for war. At the start of the conflict, the entire U.S. Army had only 28,000 soldiers. New volunteers quickly raised that figure to more than 280,000. The army did not have enough rifles or bullets for these soldiers. It did not even have appropriate clothing for the troops. Many soldiers received warm woolen uniforms to wear in Cuba's tropical heat.

The soldiers faced harsh living conditions in Cuba. They ate canned meat that one general called "embalmed beef," and many were stricken with yellow fever and other deadly diseases. More than 2,000 Americans died from diseases they contracted in Cuba. Fewer than 400 were killed in battle.

The most colorful group of soldiers was the Rough Riders. Second in command of this group was Lieutenant Colonel Theodore Roosevelt. Roosevelt had organized the Rough Riders to fight in Cuba. Volunteers included Native Americans, college athletes, cowboys, miners, and ranchers. Newspaper stories of their heroism earned the Rough Riders Americans' admiration. Four privates of the African American 10th Cavalry, who served with the Rough Riders, received the Congressional Medal of Honor.

Landing on June 22, 1898, the U.S. troops captured the hills around the main Spanish forces at Santiago. At the village of El Caney on July 1, some 7,000 U.S. soldiers, aided by Cuban rebels, overwhelmed about 600 Spanish defenders.

The main U.S. force then attacked and captured San Juan Hill. The Rough Riders and the African American 9th and 10th cavalries captured nearby Kettle Hill. The many accounts of the battle became popular with the American public back home. A journalist on the scene described the soldiers' charge:

FOCUS ON READING

How might accounts of the war written by these various soldiers have been different?

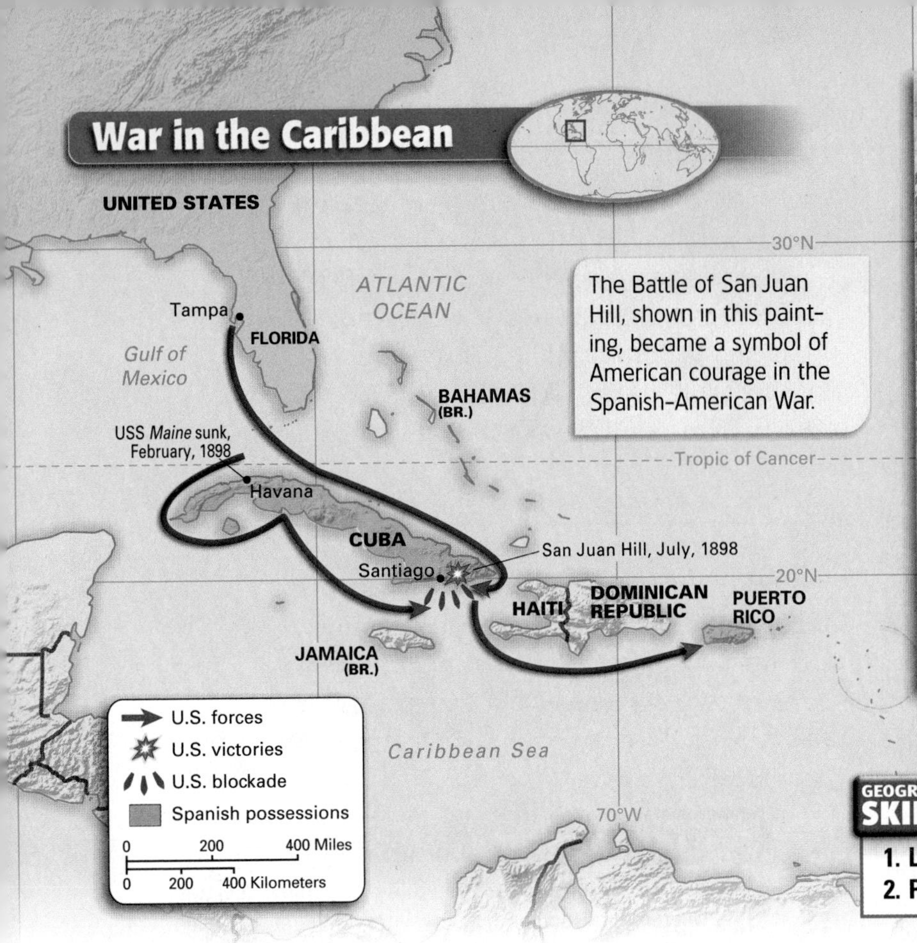
War in the Caribbean
UNITED STATES
ATLANTIC OCEAN
30°N
Tampa
FLORIDA
Gulf of Mexico
BAHAMAS (BR.)
USS Maine sunk, February, 1898
Tropic of Cancer
Havana
CUBA
Santiago
San Juan Hill, July, 1898
20°N
HAITI
DOMINICAN REPUBLIC
PUERTO RICO
JAMAICA (BR.)
U.S. forces
U.S. victories
U.S. blockade
Spanish possessions
0 200 400 Miles
0 200 400 Kilometers
Caribbean Sea
70°W

The Battle of San Juan Hill, shown in this painting, became a symbol of American courage in the Spanish-American War.

GEOGRAPHY SKILLS **INTERPRETING MAPS**

1. **Location** About how far is Havana from Tampa?
2. **Place** When was the victory at San Juan Hill?

> "It was a miracle of self-sacrifice, a triumph of bulldog courage . . . The fire of the Spanish riflemen . . . doubled and trebled [tripled] in fierceness, the crests of the hills crackled and burst in amazed roars and rippled with waves of tiny flame. But the blue line [of United States soldiers] crept steadily up and on."
>
> —Richard Harding Davis, quoted in *The American Reader*, edited by Paul M. Angle

On July 3 the commander of the Spanish fleet decided to try breaking through the U.S. blockade. Though every Spanish ship was destroyed in the battle, American forces suffered only two casualties. Santiago surrendered two weeks later. President McKinley began peace negotiations with Spain, which was assured of defeat. A few days later, U.S. troops invaded Spanish-held Puerto Rico, which surrendered with little resistance. Spain signed a cease-fire agreement on August 12, 1898.

READING CHECK **Comparing** How was fighting in the Pacific and the Caribbean similar?

United States Gains Territories

The peace treaty placed Cuba, Guam, Puerto Rico, and the Philippines under U.S. control. In reaction, some Americans formed the **Anti-Imperialist League**, a group that opposed the treaty and the creation of an American colonial empire. They argued that the treaty threatened democracy because it denied self-government to the people living in the newly acquired territories. The Senate approved the peace treaty by a vote of 57 to 27—just one vote more than the two-thirds majority needed to ratify treaties.

Cuba

The Teller Amendment had declared that the United States would not annex Cuba. However, McKinley wanted to create stability and increase U.S. economic activity there, so he set up a military government. He appointed Leonard Wood, who had commanded the Rough Riders during the war, as governor.

Wood quickly began building schools and a sanitation system.

Even with the new sanitation system, disease remained a major problem. Dr. Walter Reed, head of the army's Yellow Fever Commission, was sent to Cuba in 1900 to help fight the disease. He and his volunteers conducted experiments, including allowing themselves to be bitten by infected insects. They soon proved that yellow fever was transmitted by mosquitoes. Getting rid of the standing water where mosquitoes lived helped health officials to control the disease.

Governor Wood also oversaw the writing of a Cuban constitution. The document included the **Platt Amendment**, which limited Cuba's right to make treaties and allowed the United States to intervene in Cuban affairs. It also required Cuba to sell or lease land to the United States. Cuban leaders compared the Platt Amendment to "handing over the keys to our house so that they [the Americans] can enter it at any time, whenever the desire seizes them." The Cubans reluctantly accepted the amendment, and U.S. troops withdrew. The amendment remained in force until 1934, and the U.S. government stayed actively involved in Cuban affairs until the late 1950s.

Puerto Rico

Like Cubans, Puerto Ricans had hoped for independence after the war. Instead, the U.S. government made the island a territory. On April 12, 1900, the Foraker Act established a civil government in Puerto Rico. It was headed by a governor and included a two-house legislature.

A debate over the new territory soon arose. People who lived in Puerto Rico were

LINKING TO TODAY

Puerto Ricans Today

Today more than 4 million Puerto Ricans live on the mainland United States. This is the second-largest Hispanic population in the country, behind people of Mexican descent. Puerto Ricans live throughout the United States, but about one-third live in New York State. Puerto Rican culture is very strong in New York—the National Puerto Rican Day Parade in New York City is one of the largest parades for any ethnic group in the city.

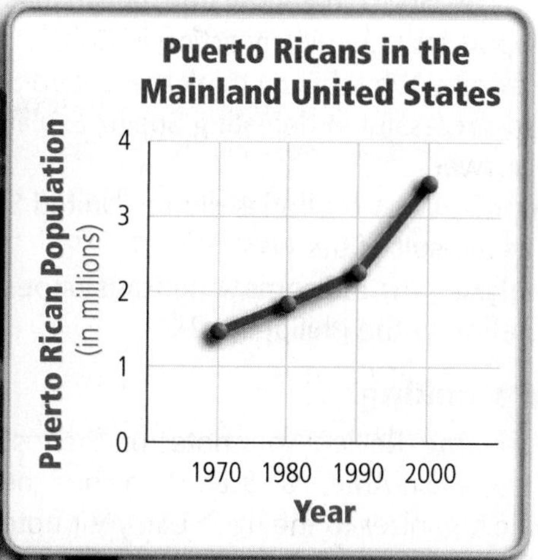

ANALYSIS SKILL ANALYZING INFORMATION

How are the people in the picture showing support for Puerto Rican culture?

considered citizens of the island but not of the United States. In 1917 the Jones Act gave Puerto Ricans U.S. citizenship and made both houses of the legislature elective. However, another 30 years passed before Puerto Ricans could elect their own governor. Today the island has its own constitution and elected officials but remains associated with the United States as what is known as a commonwealth.

The Philippines

Spain had surrendered the Philippines in return for a $20 million payment from the United States. Many Americans agreed with President McKinley, who said that the United States would benefit from the islands' naval and commercial value and that annexing the islands would keep Europeans from seizing them.

Filipino rebels, however, had expected to gain independence after the war. They had helped U.S. forces to capture Manila. When the United States decided instead to keep the islands, rebels led by Emilio Aguinaldo started a guerrilla war against the American forces. More than 4,200 U.S. soldiers and hundreds of thousands of Filipinos died before the conflict ended in 1902.

That same year, Congress passed the Philippine Government Act. It provided that an appointed governor and a two-house legislature would rule the Philippines. In 1946 the United States granted full independence to the Philippines.

READING CHECK **Summarizing** What areas did the United States control as a result of the war?

SUMMARY The United States fought a war with Spain and gained new territories in the Pacific and Caribbean regions.

Section 2 Assessment

hmhsocialstudies.com
ONLINE QUIZ

Reviewing Ideas, Terms, and People

1. **a. Recall** What was the cause of the conflict between Cuba and Spain?
   b. Analyze How did **yellow journalism** affect public support for U.S. military action in Cuba?
   c. Elaborate Why do you think the United States was so successful in defeating Spain? Explain your answer.
2. **a. Identify** What territories did the United States gain as a result of the war?
   b. Analyze Why did some Americans oppose the annexation of the Philippines?

Critical Thinking

3. **Categorizing** Review your notes on the results of the Spanish-American War. Then copy the graphic organizer to the right. Use your notes to identify arguments for and against taking control of foreign territories.

Arguments for Imperialism		Arguments against Imperialism
	vs.	

Focus on Writing

4. **Identifying Pros and Cons of the Spanish-American War** As you read this section, add to your pros and cons list by identifying American losses and gains as a result of the Spanish-American War. What were the costs in human lives? What were the gains in territory? Can you identify any other losses and gains? For example, how did the United States handle the issues of self-rule involved in the war?

BIOGRAPHY

Theodore Roosevelt

VIDEO
Teddy Roosevelt and the Spanish American War
HISTORY
hmhsocialstudies.com

What would you do to reform your country and make it stronger?

When did he live? 1858–1919

Where did he live? Theodore Roosevelt was born into a wealthy family in New York City. He spent two years on a ranch in the Dakota Territory, where he became an avid hunter and conservationist. His political career then took him to Albany, New York, where he served as state governor, and Washington, D.C., where he served as vice president and president.

What did he do? Roosevelt became a national hero while leading the Rough Riders in the Spanish-American War. After serving less than a year as vice president, the 42-year-old Roosevelt became the youngest president in U.S. history when President William McKinley was killed in 1901. As president, Roosevelt fought for progressive reforms and set aside millions of acres as national parks and forests. Roosevelt's aggressive foreign policy expanded American power in the world.

Why is he so important? "I believe in a strong executive," Roosevelt once declared. "While president, I have been president, emphatically [forcefully]; I have used every ounce of power there was in the office." As this quote suggests, Roosevelt was a strong leader who set a precedent for a more active and powerful presidency.

Drawing Conclusions What characteristics made Theodore Roosevelt a successful leader?

KEY EVENTS

1882
Elected to the New York State Assembly at age 23

1898
Becomes a hero in the Spanish-American War; elected governor of New York

1900
Elected vice president

1901
Becomes president when McKinley is assassinated

1903
Gains Panama Canal Zone for the United States

1906
Visits Panama, becoming the first president to travel outside the country while in office

1919
Dies at home in New York

President Theodore Roosevelt and the Rough Riders

© Houghton Mifflin Harcourt Publishing Company

Image Credits: (br), ©Corbis

SECTION 3

The United States and Latin America

What You Will Learn...

Main Ideas

1. The United States built the Panama Canal in the early 1900s.
2. Theodore Roosevelt changed U.S. policy toward Latin America.
3. Presidents Taft and Wilson promoted U.S. interests in Latin America.

The Big Idea

The United States expanded its role in Latin America in the early 1900s.

Key Terms and People

Panama Canal
Roosevelt Corollary
dollar diplomacy
Mexican Revolution
John J. Pershing
Francisco "Pancho" Villa

hmhsocialstudies.com
TAKING NOTES

Use the graphic organizer online to take notes on U.S. policies toward Latin America.

If YOU were there...

You are an engineer, and you've been working on the Panama Canal for almost eight years. Your work crews used huge steam shovels to slice through a ridge of mountains and built a huge artificial lake. You planned a system to move ships through different water levels. Now your work is done. You can watch massive ships travel from the Atlantic to the Pacific.

Which part of the work on the canal was the most challenging?

BUILDING BACKGROUND When the Spanish-American War began in 1898, the U.S. battleship *Oregon* set out from Washington State to join the fighting in Cuba. The approximately 12,000-mile trip around the southern tip of South America took more than two months. This delay convinced many U.S. leaders that the United States needed to build a canal linking the Atlantic and Pacific oceans.

Building the Panama Canal

A canal across the narrow neck of Central America would link the Atlantic and Pacific oceans and cut some 8,000 miles off the voyage by ship from the West to the East coasts of the United States. It would also allow the U.S. Navy to link its Atlantic and Pacific naval fleets quickly.

Image Credits: (b) Library of Congress Prints & Photographs Division, Washington, D.C.

Revolution in Panama

No one was a stronger supporter of a Central American canal than President Theodore Roosevelt. Roosevelt knew that the best spot for the canal was the Isthmus of Panama, which at the time was part of the nation of Colombia. But he was unable to convince the Colombian senate to lease a strip of land across Panama to the United States.

Roosevelt considered other ways to gain control of the land. He learned that Panamanian revolutionaries were planning a revolt against Colombia. On November 2, 1903, a U.S. warship arrived outside Colón, Panama. The next day the revolt began. Blocked by the U.S. warship, Colombian forces could not reach Panama to stop the rebellion. Panama declared itself an independent country. The United States then recognized the new nation.

The new government of Panama supported the idea of a canal across its land. The United States agreed to pay Panama $10 million plus $250,000 a year for a 99-year lease on a 10-mile-wide strip of land across the isthmus.

Building the Canal

Canal construction began in 1904. The first obstacle to overcome was tropical disease. The canal route ran through 51 miles of forests and swamps filled with mosquitoes, many of which carried the deadly diseases malaria and yellow fever.

Dr. William C. Gorgas, who had helped Dr. Walter Reed stamp out yellow fever in Cuba, organized a successful effort to rid the canal route of disease-carrying mosquitoes. If Gorgas had not been successful, the canal's construction would have taken much longer. It also would have cost much more in terms of both lives and money.

Even with the reduced risk of disease, the work was very dangerous. Most of the canal had to be blasted out of solid rock with explosives. Workers used dozens of steam shovels to cut a narrow, eight-mile-long channel through the mountains of central Panama. Sometimes workers died when their shovels struck explosive charges. "The flesh of men flew in the air like birds every day," recalled one worker from the West Indies.

Some 6,000 lives were lost during the American construction of the **Panama Canal**. It was finally opened to ships on August 15, 1914, linking the Atlantic and Pacific oceans. An opening ceremony was held the next year. It had taken 10 years to complete, and the cost was $375 million. In the end, however, the world had its "highway between the oceans."

THE IMPACT TODAY

Today the Panama Canal Zone is threatened by deforestation and erosion because of heavy use. Decreased rainfall is also hurting the canal.

READING CHECK **Drawing Conclusions** Why did building the canal cost so many lives?

The massive Gatun Locks, shown here under construction in 1914, raise ships 85 feet onto Gatun Lake, an inland waterway on the Panama Canal.

↗ hmhsocialstudies.com INTERACTIVE MAP

The Panama Canal

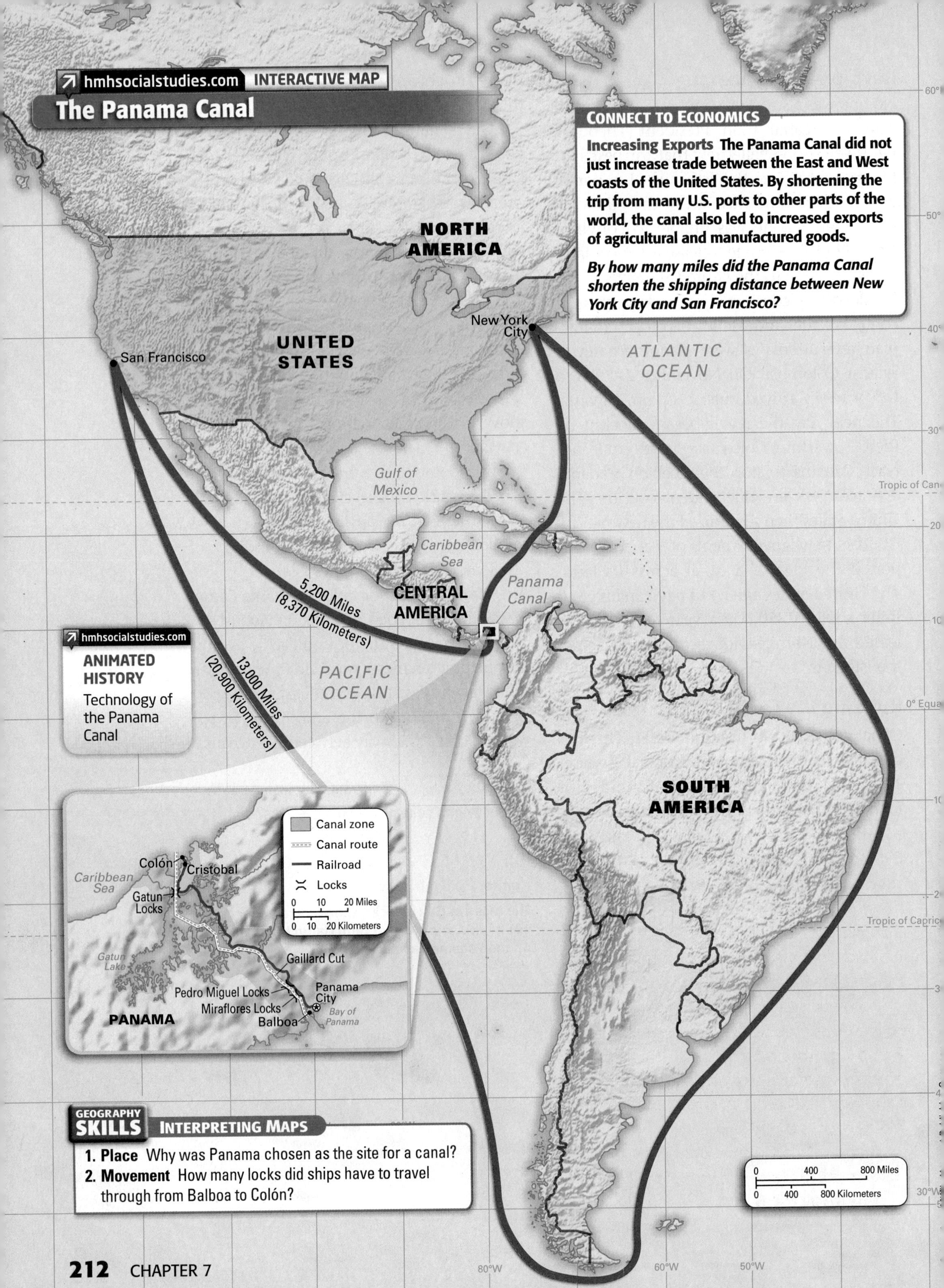
NORTH AMERICA
UNITED STATES
San Francisco
New York City
ATLANTIC OCEAN
Gulf of Mexico
Caribbean Sea
Panama Canal
CENTRAL AMERICA
PACIFIC OCEAN
SOUTH AMERICA
5,200 Miles (8,370 Kilometers)
13,000 Miles (20,900 Kilometers)
Tropic of Cancer
Tropic of Capricorn
0° Equator
80°W
60°W
50°W
0 400 800 Miles
0 400 800 Kilometers
Canal zone
Canal route
Railroad
Locks
0 10 20 Miles
0 10 20 Kilometers
Colón
Cristobal
Caribbean Sea
Gatun Locks
Gatun Lake
Gaillard Cut
Pedro Miguel Locks
Miraflores Locks
Balboa
Panama City
Bay of Panama
PANAMA

↗ hmhsocialstudies.com

ANIMATED HISTORY

Technology of the Panama Canal

Connect to Economics

Increasing Exports The Panama Canal did not just increase trade between the East and West coasts of the United States. By shortening the trip from many U.S. ports to other parts of the world, the canal also led to increased exports of agricultural and manufactured goods.

By how many miles did the Panama Canal shorten the shipping distance between New York City and San Francisco?

GEOGRAPHY SKILLS INTERPRETING MAPS

1. **Place** Why was Panama chosen as the site for a canal?
2. **Movement** How many locks did ships have to travel through from Balboa to Colón?

U.S. Policy Toward Latin America

As president, Theodore Roosevelt actively pursued progressive reforms at home. He also believed the United States should play a more active role in the Western Hemisphere. In 1900 Roosevelt said, "I have always been fond of the West African proverb: 'Speak softly and carry a big stick; you will go far.'" Roosevelt wanted everyone to know he would use a "big stick"—meaning U.S. military force—to protect U.S. interests in Latin America.

This was a change from the policies of previous presidents. In the 1823 Monroe Doctrine, President James Monroe had warned European nations not to interfere in the Western Hemisphere. And while the Monroe Doctrine became a major principle of U.S. foreign policy, the United States did not have the military strength to enforce it. By the time Roosevelt became president, however, this situation was changing. The United States was growing stronger and expanding its influence. The United States was becoming a world power.

How should the United States use its new power in Latin America? This question came up often in the early 1900s. European banks had made loans to a number of Latin American countries. Venezuela, for example, fell deeply in debt to British and German investors. Venezuela refused to repay these debts in 1902. A similar situation arose in the Caribbean nation of the Dominican Republic in 1904. European powers prepared to use military force to collect the debts.

Roosevelt insisted the countries must repay their debts. But he did not want to allow Europeans to intervene in Latin America. The presence of European forces there would violate the Monroe Doctrine and threaten U.S. power in the region.

Roosevelt knew that U.S. officials would have to force debtor nations to repay their loans in order to keep European nations from directly intervening in Latin America. In December 1904 he announced what became known as the **Roosevelt Corollary** to the Monroe Doctrine. This addition warned that in cases of "wrongdoing" by Latin American countries, the United States might exercise "international police power."

The Roosevelt Corollary asserted a new **role** for the United States as an "international police power" in the Western Hemisphere. Roosevelt actively enforced the corollary throughout the rest of his presidency.

ACADEMIC VOCABULARY
role assigned behavior

READING CHECK **Finding Main Ideas** Why did Roosevelt announce the Roosevelt Corollary?

Primary Source

POLITICAL CARTOON

Roosevelt's Imperialism

Theodore Roosevelt's foreign policy is shown visually in this cartoon. Roosevelt is the giant leading a group of ships that represent debt collection. The U.S. president is patrolling the Caribbean Sea and Latin American countries, trying to enforce the payment of debts to European countries.

What do you think this stick represents?

Why are these vessels warships?

ANALYSIS SKILL **ANALYZING PRIMARY SOURCES**

Analyzing How does the cartoonist portray the parts of the Roosevelt Corollary?

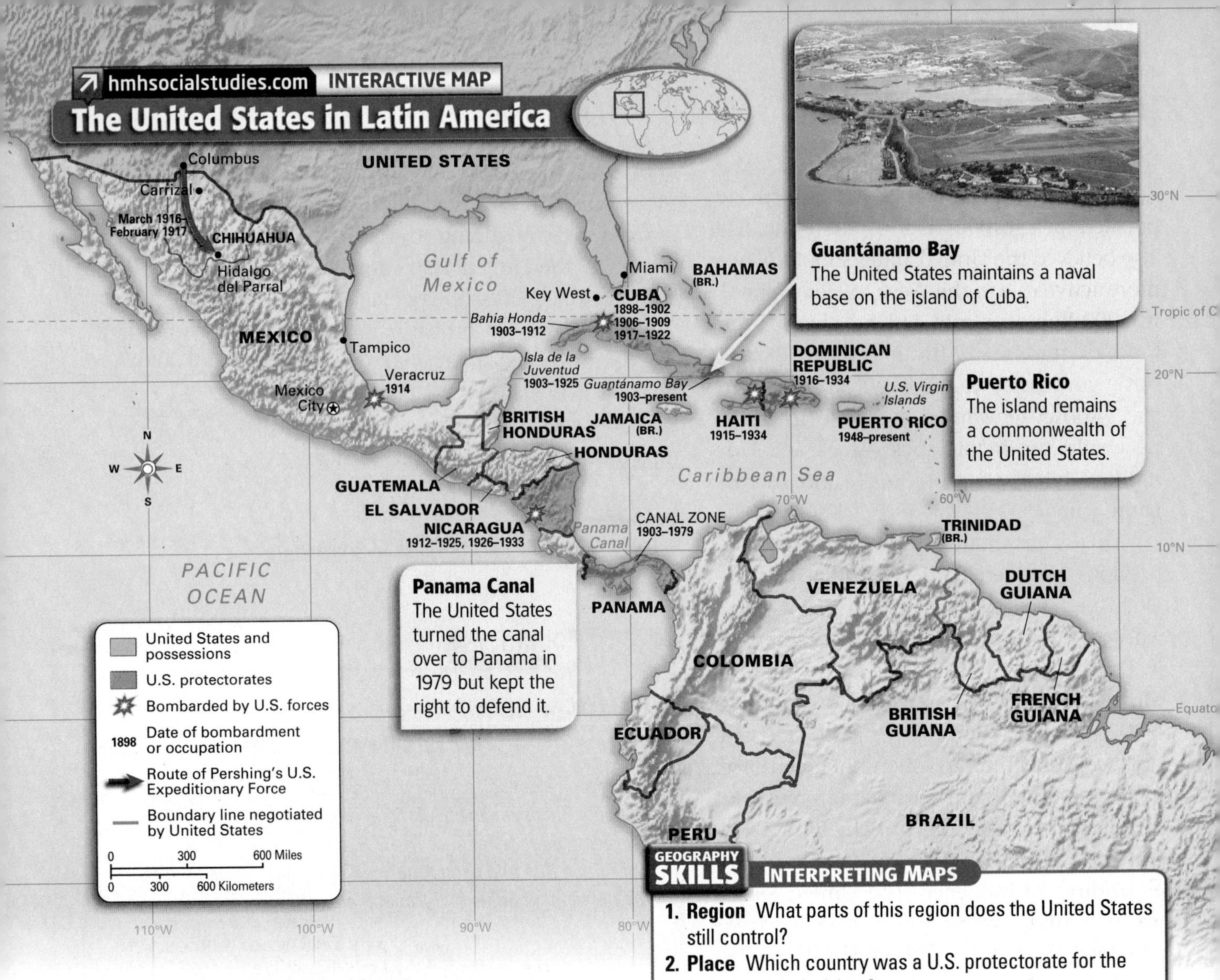
hmhsocialstudies.com INTERACTIVE MAP
The United States in Latin America
UNITED STATES
Columbus
Carrizal
March 1916–February 1917
CHIHUAHUA
Hidalgo del Parral
MEXICO
Tampico
Veracruz 1914
Mexico City
Gulf of Mexico
Miami
Key West
BAHAMAS (BR.)
CUBA 1898–1902 1906–1909 1917–1922
Bahia Honda 1903–1912
Isla de la Juventud 1903–1925
Guantánamo Bay 1903–present
Guantánamo Bay
The United States maintains a naval base on the island of Cuba.
DOMINICAN REPUBLIC 1916–1934
HAITI 1915–1934
U.S. Virgin Islands
PUERTO RICO 1948–present
Puerto Rico
The island remains a commonwealth of the United States.
BRITISH HONDURAS
JAMAICA (BR.)
HONDURAS
GUATEMALA
EL SALVADOR
NICARAGUA 1912–1925, 1926–1933
Caribbean Sea
Panama Canal
CANAL ZONE 1903–1979
TRINIDAD (BR.)
PANAMA
VENEZUELA
DUTCH GUIANA
BRITISH GUIANA
FRENCH GUIANA
COLOMBIA
ECUADOR
PERU
BRAZIL
PACIFIC OCEAN
Panama Canal
The United States turned the canal over to Panama in 1979 but kept the right to defend it.
United States and possessions
U.S. protectorates
Bombarded by U.S. forces
1898 Date of bombardment or occupation
Route of Pershing's U.S. Expeditionary Force
Boundary line negotiated by United States
0 300 600 Miles
0 300 600 Kilometers
30°N
Tropic of C
20°N
10°N
Equato
110°W
100°W
90°W
80°W
70°W
60°W
N S E W

GEOGRAPHY SKILLS INTERPRETING MAPS

1. **Region** What parts of this region does the United States still control?
2. **Place** Which country was a U.S. protectorate for the longest period of time?

U.S. Interests in Latin America

William Howard Taft, who became president in 1909, also acted to protect U.S. interests in Latin America. Taft used a policy called **dollar diplomacy**—influencing governments through economic, not military, intervention.

President Taft described dollar diplomacy as "substituting dollars for bullets. It is . . . directed to the increase of American trade." He wanted to encourage stability and keep Europeans out of Latin America by expanding U.S. business interests there.

For example, in 1911 Nicaragua failed to repay a loan from British investors. American bankers lent Nicaragua $1.5 billion in return for control of the National Bank of Nicaragua and the government-owned railway. When local anger over this deal led to revolt in Nicaragua, Taft sent U.S. Marines to protect American interests.

When President Woodrow Wilson took office in 1913, he rejected Taft's dollar diplomacy. He believed the United States had a moral obligation to promote democracy in Latin America. Like Roosevelt, Wilson was willing to use military force to protect U.S. interests in the region.

In 1910 many Mexicans revolted against the harsh rule of Mexican dictator Porfirio Díaz. This was the start of the **Mexican Revolution**, a long, violent struggle for power in Mexico. The war affected U.S. interests

© Houghton Mifflin Harcourt Publishing Company • Image Credits: (inset) ©Bettmann/Corbis

U.S. Foreign Policy QUICK FACTS

Departing from the example set by the nation's first president, George Washington, future presidents increased U.S. involvement around the world, particularly in Latin America.

Washington's Farewell Address
The United States will not become involved in European affairs.

Monroe Doctrine
The United States will defend its interests in the Western Hemisphere and keep European powers out.

Roosevelt Corollary
The United States will police wrongdoing by nations in the Western Hemisphere.

Taft's Dollar Diplomacy
The United States will use economic means to aid its interests in Latin America.

Wilson and Democracy
The United States will promote and protect democracy in the Western Hemisphere.

because Americans had invested more than $1 billion in Mexican land, mining, oil, and railways. American business leaders feared they would lose their investments.

In 1914 President Wilson learned that a German ship carrying weapons was headed to the port of Veracruz, Mexico. To keep the weapons from reaching the rebels, Wilson ordered the navy to seize Veracruz. Wilson acted again in 1916, sending General **John J. Pershing** and 15,000 U.S. soldiers into Mexico. Pershing's mission was to catch the rebel leader **Francisco "Pancho" Villa**, who had killed 17 Americans in New Mexico. Pershing failed to capture Villa, and Wilson recalled the troops.

In 1917 a new constitution began to bring order to Mexico. The violence caused more than 120,000 Mexicans to flee to the United States between 1905 and 1915.

READING CHECK **Summarizing** How did Wilson respond to events in Mexico?

SUMMARY The United States and Latin America established relationships through both conflicts and agreements.

Section 3 Assessment

hmhsocialstudies.com ONLINE QUIZ

Reviewing Ideas, Terms, and People

1. a. **Recall** Why did the United States want to build a canal?
   b. **Analyze** What challenges did the builders of the **Panama Canal** face, and how did they overcome them?
   c. **Elaborate** Defend or criticize the U.S. decision to support the revolution in Panama.
2. a. **Describe** What problem was causing conflict between European and Latin American nations?
   b. **Summarize** How and why did Theodore Roosevelt change U.S. policy toward Latin America?
3. a. **Recall** What did Woodrow Wilson believe was the United States's obligation to Latin America?
   b. **Compare and Contrast** How were the policies of Taft and Wilson toward Latin America similar, and how were they different?

Critical Thinking

4. **Categorizing** Review your notes on U.S. policies toward Latin America. Then copy the web diagram below. Use it to identify American policies toward Latin America.

Focus on Writing

5. **Identifying Pros and Cons of U.S. Intervention**
   What were the pros and cons of the construction of the Panama Canal and interventionist U.S. policies toward Latin America? Take notes for your list as you read this section.

© Houghton Mifflin Harcourt Publishing Company

America's Global Influence 1900

By 1900 most of the current boundaries of the United States had been established. But the world had become a much smaller place. American inventions were spreading, changing daily life in countries around the world. In addition, U.S. troops stationed in China were displaying the increasing importance of the United States in global affairs.

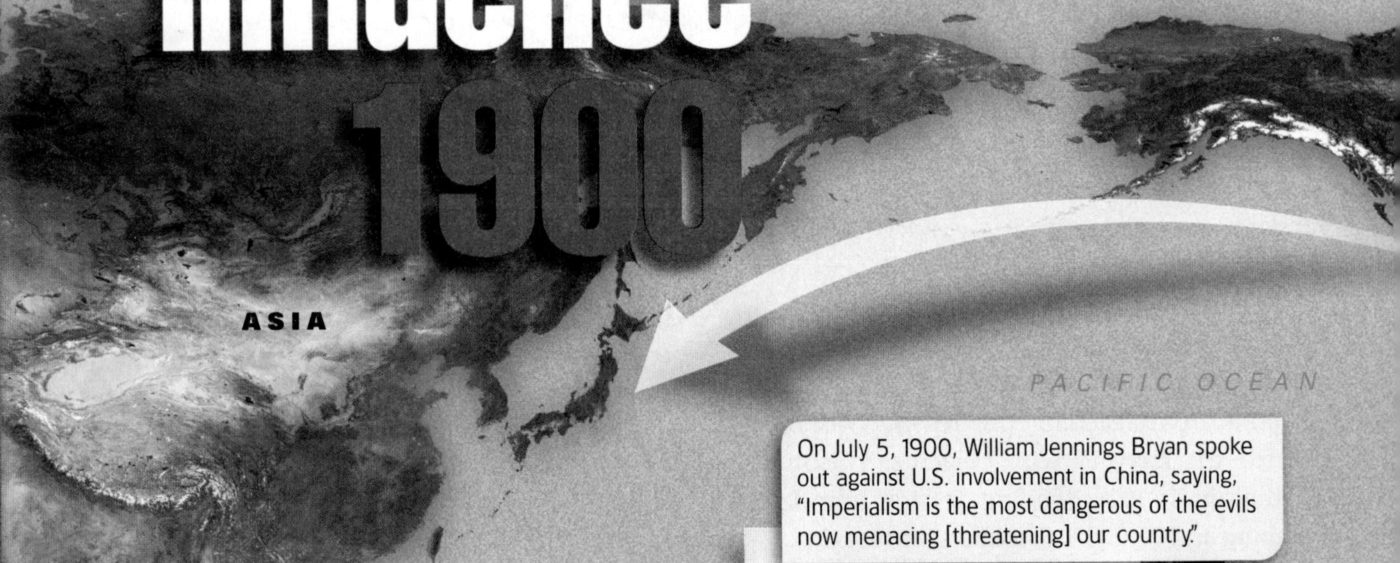
ASIA
PACIFIC OCEAN

On July 5, 1900, William Jennings Bryan spoke out against U.S. involvement in China, saying, "Imperialism is the most dangerous of the evils now menacing [threatening] our country."

Asia Before 1898, U.S. troops had never been sent outside the Western Hemisphere. But in 1900, some 5,000 troops were in Asia, fighting alongside European troops.

Image Credits: (c), (b), ©Bettmann/Corbis

© Houghton Mifflin Harcourt Publishing Company

Paris The Paris Exposition of 1900 showcased many U.S. inventions. One British writer claimed the exposition displayed "the Americanization of the world."

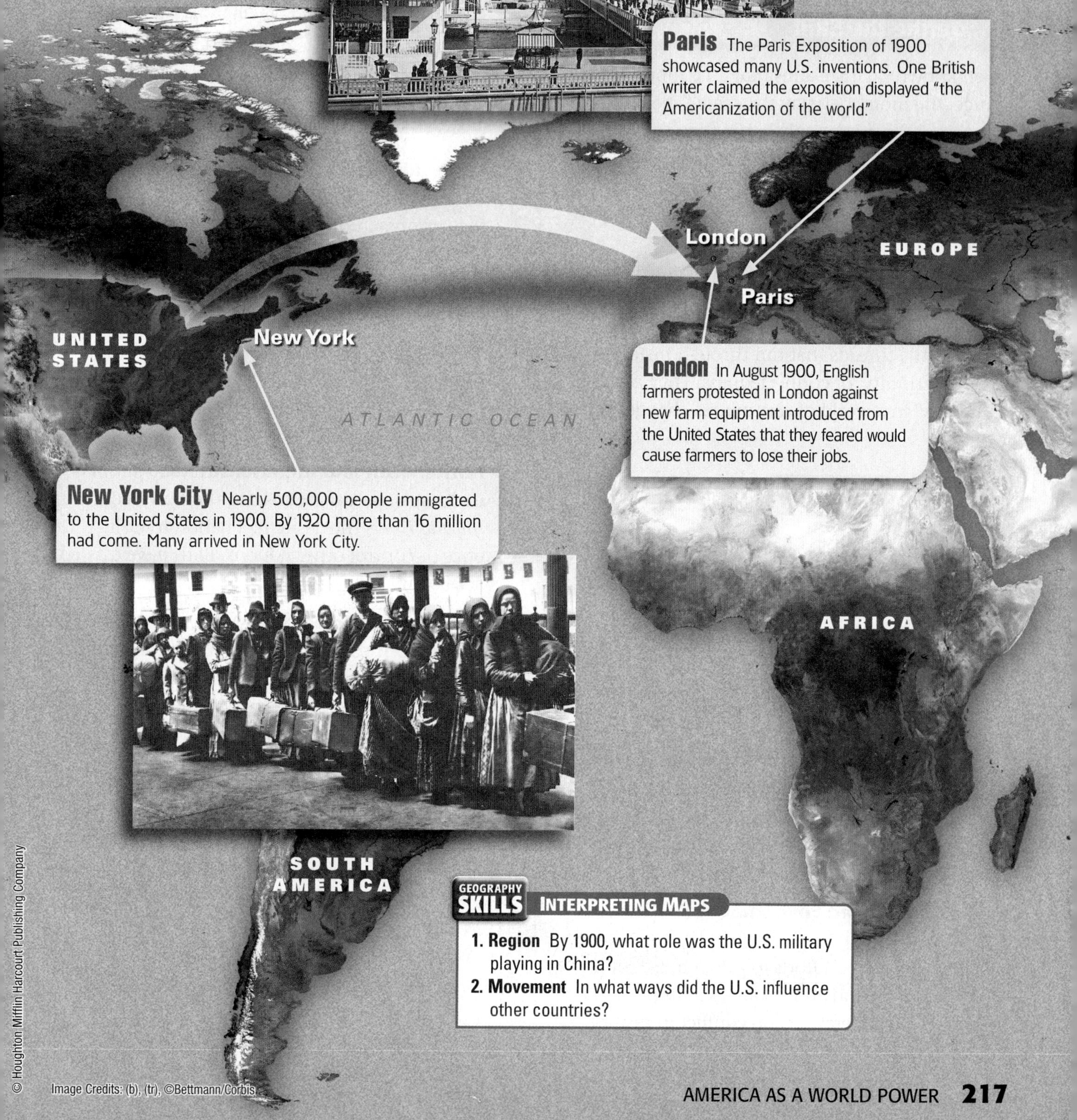
London
EUROPE
Paris
UNITED STATES
New York
ATLANTIC OCEAN
AFRICA
SOUTH AMERICA

London In August 1900, English farmers protested in London against new farm equipment introduced from the United States that they feared would cause farmers to lose their jobs.

New York City Nearly 500,000 people immigrated to the United States in 1900. By 1920 more than 16 million had come. Many arrived in New York City.

GEOGRAPHY SKILLS **INTERPRETING MAPS**

1. **Region** By 1900, what role was the U.S. military playing in China?
2. **Movement** In what ways did the U.S. influence other countries?

© Houghton Mifflin Harcourt Publishing Company

Image Credits: (b), (tr), ©Bettmann/Corbis

Social Studies Skills

Analysis | Critical Thinking | Civic Participation | Study

21ST CENTURY

Continuity and Change in History

Define the Skill

A well-known saying claims that "the more things change, the more they stay the same." Nowhere does this observation apply better than to the study of history. Any examination of the past will show many changes—nations expanding or shrinking, empires rising and falling, changes in leadership, or people on the move, for example.

The reasons for change have not changed, however. The same general forces have driven the actions of people and nations across time. These forces are the threads that run through history and give it continuity, or connectedness. They are the "sameness" in a world of continuous change.

Learn the Skill

You can find the causes of all events of the past in one or more of these major forces or themes that connect all history.

1. **Cooperation and Conflict** Throughout time, people and groups have worked together to achieve goals. They have also opposed others who stood in the way of their goals.
2. **Cultural Invention and Interaction** The values and ideas expressed in art, literature, customs, and religion have enriched the world. But the spread of cultures and their contact with other cultures have produced conflict as well.
3. **Geography and Environment** Physical environment and natural resources have shaped how people live. Efforts to gain, protect, or make good use of land and resources have been major causes of cooperation and conflict in history.
4. **Science and Technology** *Technology,* or the development and use of tools, has helped humans across time make better use of their environment. Science has changed their knowledge of the world, and changed their lives, too.
5. **Economic Opportunity and Development** From hunting and gathering to herding, farming, manufacturing, and trade, people have tried to make the most of their resources. The desire for a better life has also been a major reason people have moved from one place to another.
6. **The Impact of Individuals** Political, religious, military, business, and other leaders have been a major influence in history. The actions of many ordinary people have also shaped history
7. **Nationalism and Imperialism** *Nationalism* is the desire of a people to have their own country. *Imperialism* is the desire of a nation to influence or control other nations. Both have existed across time.
8. **Political and Social Systems** People have always been part of groups—families, villages, nations, or religious groups, for example. The groups to which people belong shape how they relate to others around them.

Practice the Skill

Check your understanding of continuity and change in history by answering the following questions.

1. What forces of history are illustrated by the events in this chapter? Explain with examples.
2. How do the events in this chapter show continuity with earlier periods in U.S. history?

© Houghton Mifflin Harcourt Publishing Company

CHAPTER 7

Chapter Review

History's Impact
▸ **video series**
Review the video to answer the closing question:
How would you characterize the current policy of the United States: isolationist or imperialist?

Visual Summary

QUICK FACTS

Use the visual summary below to help you review the main ideas of the chapter.

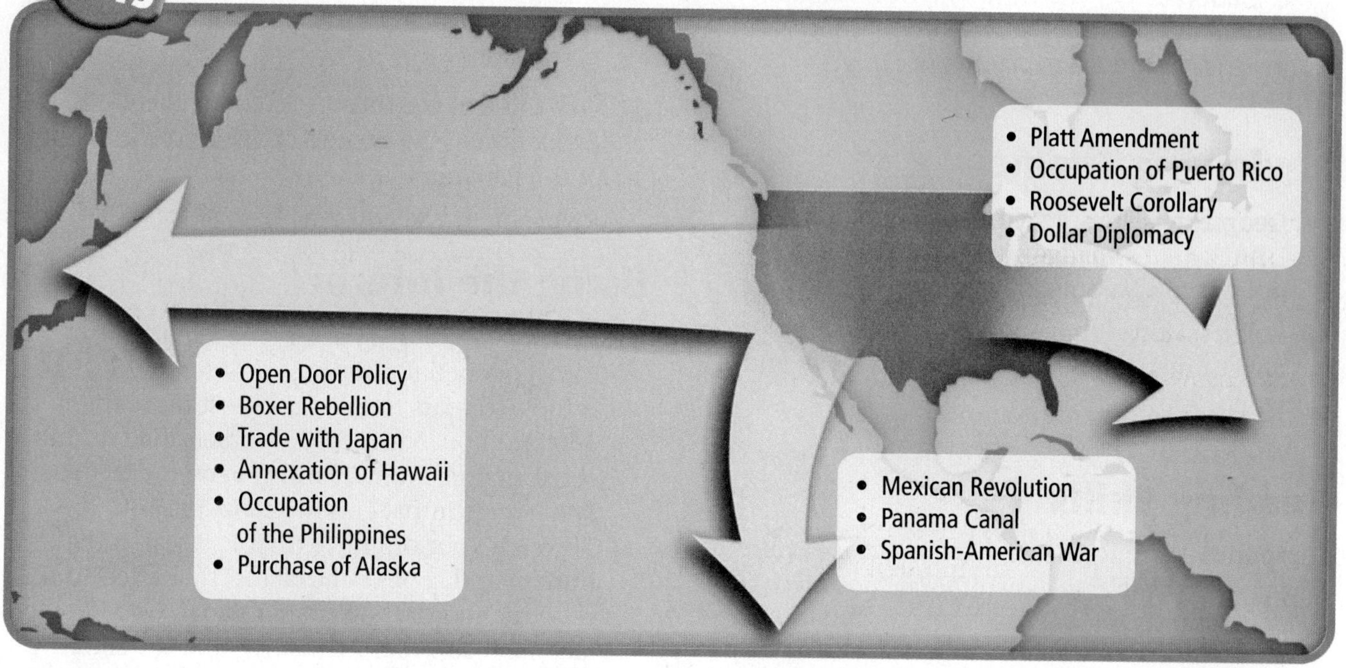

• Platt Amendment
• Occupation of Puerto Rico
• Roosevelt Corollary
• Dollar Diplomacy
• Open Door Policy
• Boxer Rebellion
• Trade with Japan
• Annexation of Hawaii
• Occupation of the Philippines
• Purchase of Alaska
• Mexican Revolution
• Panama Canal
• Spanish-American War

Reviewing Vocabulary, Terms, and People

1. In which of the following did the United States declare that it had no interest in taking control of Cuba?

a. Roosevelt Corollary **c.** Open Door Policy
b. Monroe Doctrine **d.** Teller Amendment

2. Which leader upset sugar planters in Hawaii by proposing a plan to return power to the monarchy?

a. Liliuokalani **c.** Millard Fillmore
b. John L. Stevens **d.** Woodrow Wilson

3. Which president supported Panama's revolt against Colombia in 1903?

a. Woodrow Wilson **c.** William Howard Taft
b. William McKinley **d.** Theodore Roosevelt

4. Who led U.S. forces into Mexico after attacks against U.S. citizens by Mexican rebels?

a. John Hay **c.** John J. Pershing
b. William H. Seward **d.** Theodore Roosevelt

Comprehension and Critical Thinking

SECTION 1

5. a. Identify Into what areas did the United States expand in the late 1800s?

b. Draw Conclusions How did the United States benefit from contact with foreign nations and territories?

c. Elaborate Which policy would you have supported—isolationism or imperialism? Explain your answer.

SECTION 2

6. a. Describe What events led the United States to declare war on Spain?

b. Analyze How did the United States benefit from the Spanish-American War?

c. Predict How might foreign countries view the actions of the United States in the Spanish-American War?

© Houghton Mifflin Harcourt Publishing Company

SECTION 3

7. **a. Identify** In what ways did the United States become involved in Latin American affairs?

   b. Draw Conclusions Why did the United States expand its role in Latin America in the early 1900s?

   c. Elaborate Do you think the United States should have been as actively involved in Latin America as it was? Explain your answer.

Reviewing Themes

8. **Geography** How did the geography of the United States change after the end of its policy of isolationism?
9. **Politics** How did the policy of imperialism affect American politics in the late 1800s and early 1900s?

Reading Skills 21ST CENTURY

Comparing Historical Texts *Use the Reading Skills taught in this chapter to answer the question about the reading selections below.*

A. "Sad to say, this most precious and sublime feature of the Yosemite National Park (Hetch Hetchy Valley), one of the greatest of all our natural resources for the uplifting joy and peace and health of the people, is in danger of being dammed and made into a reservoir to help supply San Francisco with water and light . . ."

—John Muir, *The Yosemite*, 1912

B. "As we all know, there is no use of water that is higher than the domestic use. Then, if there is, as the engineers tell us, no other source of supply that is anything like so reasonably available as this one; if this is the best, and, within reasonable limits of cost, the only means of supplying San Francisco with water, we come straight to the question of whether the advantage of leaving this valley in a state of nature is greater than the advantage of using it for the benefit of the city of San Francisco."

—Gifford Pinchot, address to Congress, 1913

10. How do the two men quoted above differ on the issue of building a dam in the Hetch Hetchy Valley?

Social Studies Skills 21ST CENTURY

Continuity and Change in History *Use the Social Studies Skills taught in this chapter to answer the question below.*

11. Pick three of the themes listed on page 712. Explain how the themes connect to the history of the Panama Canal.

Using the Internet 21ST CENTURY

12. **Activity: Creating a Poster** The Panama Canal opened for business on August 15, 1914. It took 10 years to build and cost more than $600 million. Some 6,000 workers died during construction. Human and geographic factors had a huge impact on the canal project. Through your online textbook, research the human and geographic factors that affected the construction of the Panama Canal. Geographic factors to consider include landforms, climate, and weather. Human factors to consider include technology, reasons for undertaking the project, and the hazards people faced. Create a poster that highlights the most important details of your research.

hmhsocialstudies.com

FOCUS ON WRITING

13. **Writing Your List of Pros and Cons** Review your notes and choose the pros and cons to include in your final list. Decide whether you want to include only facts, only opinions, or some of each. How can your analysis of history help guide U.S. foreign policy in the future? When you have finished your list, use it as the basis for a paragraph recommending either that the United States continue to involve itself in the affairs of other nations or that it pull back from such involvement.

© Houghton Mifflin Harcourt Publishing Company

CHAPTER 7

Standardized Test Practice

DIRECTIONS: Read each question and write the letter of the best response. Use the map below to answer question 1.

1

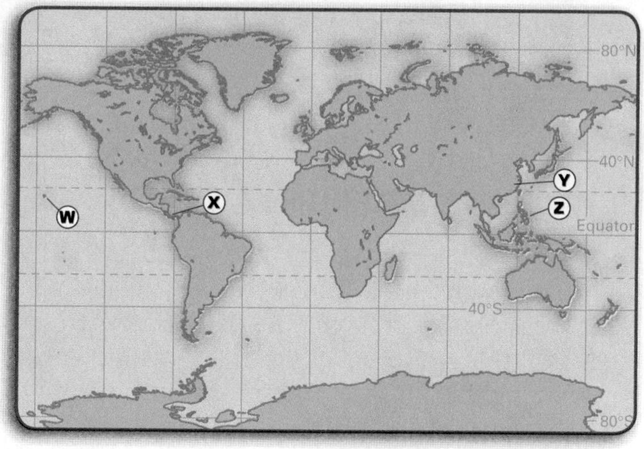

The only area in which the United States did not control territory in the late 1800s and early 1900s is shown on the map by which letter?

A W
B X
C Y
D Z

2 The practice of using U.S. businesses and economic aid to influence foreign governments and achieve U.S. goals in Latin America is known as

A imperialism.
B dollar diplomacy.
C isolationism.
D the big stick.

3 During the Mexican Revolution, President Wilson sent U.S. forces to Veracruz, Mexico. Which U.S. policy did this act best express?

A Roosevelt Corollary
B dollar diplomacy
C Teller Amendment
D isolationism

4 Which two nations did the United States hope to trade with rather than annex in the late 1800s?

A Hawaii and Japan
B Japan and China
C China and Cuba
D Cuba and Hawaii

5 How did American newspapers respond to the explosion of the USS *Maine* in Havana Harbor?

A They refused to report the story.
B They reported that the explosion was an accident.
C They blamed the explosion on Spain.
D They blamed the explosion on Cuban rebels.

6 In his book *The Influence of Sea Power upon History,* Alfred T. Mahan argued that the United States should

A avoid foreign conflicts.
B sell its naval bases.
C build a strong navy.
D remain isolationist.

7 Read the following passage from a letter from President Fillmore and use it to answer the question below.

> "I am desirous that our two countries should trade with each other, for the benefit of both Japan and the United States. We know that the ancient laws of your imperial majesty's government do not allow of foreign trade, except with the Chinese and the Dutch; but as the state of the world changes . . . it seems to be wise, from time to time, to make new laws."
>
> —Letter from U.S. President Millard Fillmore to Japan, 1852

Document-Based Question What is President Fillmore asking the Japanese to do?

© Houghton Mifflin Harcourt Publishing Company

CHAPTER 8 1914–1920

World War I

Essential Question How did World War I impact America and transform Europe?

ALABAMA COURSE OF STUDY

3 Identify causes and consequences of World War I and reasons for United States' entry into the war.
- Describing military and civilian roles in the United States during World War I.
- Explaining roles of important persons associated with World War I, including Woodrow Wilson and Archduke Franz Ferdinand.
- Analyzing technological advances of the World War I era for their impact on modern warfare.
- Locating on a map major countries involved in World War I and boundary changes after the war.
- Explaining the intensification of isolationism in the United States after World War I.
- Recognizing the strategic placement of military bases in Alabama.

4 Identify cultural and economic developments in the United States from 1900 through the 1930s.
- Describing the emergence of the modern woman during the early 1900s.

8 Describe how the United States' role in the Cold War influenced domestic and international events.
- Describing the origin and meaning of the Iron Curtain and communism.

Focus on Speaking

Persuasive Speech Before the United States entered World War I in 1917, Americans heatedly debated joining the fight. Many were torn between either helping Britain and France or remaining isolated from world conflict. In this chapter, you will read about U.S. involvement in World War I. Then you will make a speech presenting your point of view on whether the United States should have entered the war.

UNITED STATES

1914 President Wilson issues a proclamation of neutrality in the European war.

1914

WORLD

1914 Archduke Francis Ferdinand is assassinated.

Image Credits: (t), ©Bettmann/Corbis

© Houghton Mifflin Harcourt Publishing Company

HISTORY The Treaty of Versailles

hmhsocialstudies.com VIDEO

The photograph on this page shows the terrible conditions soldiers faced as they fought the enemy from their trench positions.

1916 Jeannette Rankin becomes the first woman elected to Congress.

I WANT YOU
FOR U.S. ARMY
NEAREST RECRUITING STATION

1917 The Selective Service Act is passed, introducing the draft.

1918 President Wilson announces the Fourteen Points.

1919 The U.S. Senate refuses to approve the Treaty of Versailles.

1916 — 1918 — 1920

1915 A German U-boat sinks the *Lusitania.*

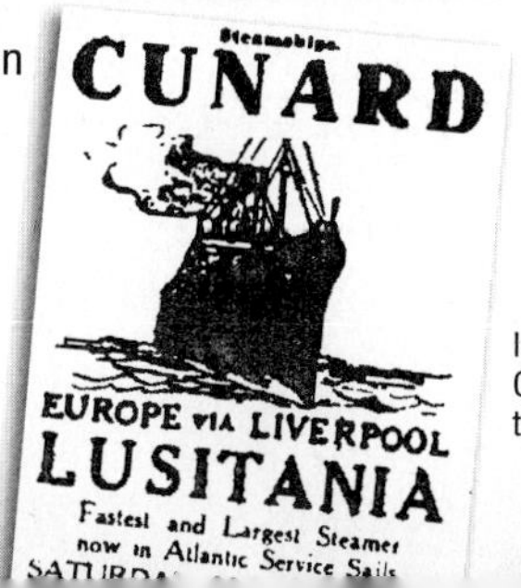
CUNARD
EUROPE VIA LIVERPOOL
LUSITANIA
Fastest and Largest Steamer
now in Atlantic Service Sails

1917 The United States declares war on Germany.

1918 Germany agrees to an armistice, ending World War I.

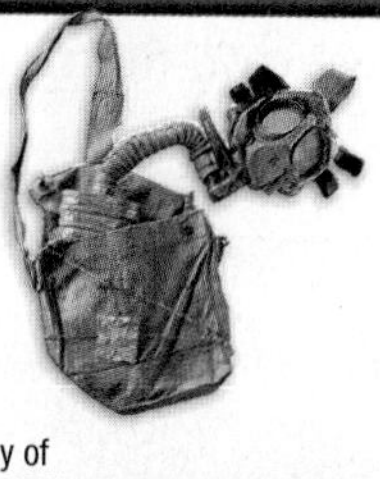

Image Credits: (t), ©Bettmann/Corbis; (bl), Stock Montage, Inc.; (br), Collection of Colonel Stuart S. Corning/Courtesy of Picture Research Consultants, Inc.; (cl), Courtesy of the Library of Congress Prints & Photographs Division, Washington, D.C. (LC-USZC4-3859)

© Houghton Mifflin Harcourt Publishing Company

Focus on Themes In this chapter, you will read about World War I and the changes it brought to the United States and the world. Many of the **political** tensions that led to the war were caused by the rise of nationalism in European countries. You will read about how the war devastated European **economies**, and how peace affected European countries.

Recognizing Fallacies in Reasoning

Focus on Reading As part of evaluating a historical argument, you can judge whether the reasoning is sound. A *fallacy* is a false or mistaken idea.

Recognizing Fallacies As you identify a main idea, judge its soundness. Look for cause-and-effect relationships that support the idea. Decide whether you think the argument is logical.

Notice how a reader explained the logical reasoning behind the main idea in the following paragraph.

Three main factors led to a shortage of labor in the United States during the war. First, American factories were working nonstop to produce weapons and supplies for the Allied forces. Factories needed new workers to meet this huge demand. Second, the war almost completely cut off immigration. As you know, immigrants had provided a steady source of labor to American industry. And third, many of the young men who would normally take factory jobs were off fighting in Europe.

If factories were working overtime, they would need more workers. This supports the main idea of a labor shortage.

If factories were used to having immigrants to hire, and there were fewer immigrants, it would make sense that there was a labor shortage.

Here's a third reason for a labor shortage: many men became soldiers. It makes sense that there was a labor shortage during the war.

You Try It!

The man who assassinated Archduke Francis Ferdinand was a Serb.

↓

All Serbians wanted war with Austria-Hungary.

Wilson wanted to establish the League of Nations

↓

because he thought it would help ensure peace.

Trench warfare was a new kind of warfare.

↓

Therefore, trench warfare was more horrible than any other kind of warfare.

1. Is the first conclusion reasonable? Why or why not? How can you tell?
2. Do you think the second conclusion is logical or illogical? What makes you think so?
3. Is the third conclusion a fallacy of reason? What reasonable conclusions can you draw from the statement?

Key Terms and People

Chapter 8

Section 1
militarism
Archduke Francis Ferdinand
mobilize
Central Powers
Allied Powers
trench warfare
stalemate
U-boats

Section 2
Lusitania
Zimmermann Note
Selective Service Act
Liberty bonds
National War Labor Board

Section 3
American Expeditionary Force
Communists
armistice

Section 4
League of Nations
reparations
Treaty of Versailles
Henry Cabot Lodge

Academic Vocabulary

In this chapter, you will learn the following academic words:

neutral
strategy

As you read this chapter, notice how the authors use logical reasoning to support their main ideas.

SECTION 1

The Road to War

What You Will Learn...

Main Ideas

1. Many factors contributed to the outbreak of World War I.
2. European nations suffered massive casualties in the war's early battles.

The Big Idea

In 1914 tensions in Europe exploded into the deadliest war the world had ever seen.

Key Terms and People

militarism
Archduke Francis Ferdinand
mobilize
Central Powers
Allied Powers
trench warfare
stalemate
U-boats

hmhsocialstudies.com
TAKING NOTES

Use the graphic organizer online to take notes on the major battles of the beginning of World War I.

If YOU were there...

You are walking past a newspaper stand when a headline catches your eye: "Austria-Hungary's Archduke Francis Ferdinand Assassinated in Sarajevo." Your first thought is, "Who's he?" You pick up the paper and read about the archduke and about the rising tensions in Europe related to his death. The article makes it sound like Europe is about to explode into war.

At this point, do you think the assassination will affect the United States? Why or why not?

BUILDING BACKGROUND European nations had not been involved in a major war in the region since the 1870s. Rising political tensions during the early 1900s threatened this peace, however, and nations began to build up their military forces. Even a small incident might trigger a major war.

Outbreak of War

Though Europe was at peace in the early 1900s, relations between European nations were not necessarily friendly. In fact, feelings of fear and distrust were growing among European powers such as Germany, France, Great Britain, Russia, and Austria-Hungary. This dangerous tension had several important causes.

Tensions in Europe

One cause of tension was the rise of nationalism in the 1800s. Nationalism is a strong sense of pride and loyalty to one's nation or culture. Nationalism inspired people who shared a language or culture to want to unite politically. In 1871, for example, Chancellor Otto von Bismarck and Kaiser Wilhelm I brought together several German states to form the nation of Germany.

While nationalism helped bring stability to Germany, it caused instability in other places. The empire of Austria-Hungary included people from many different cultural groups. One of these groups was the Slavs. Slavic nationalists wanted to break away from Austria-Hungary and join the independent Slavic country of Serbia on the

Balkan Peninsula. Leaders of Austria-Hungary reacted angrily, seeing this movement as a threat to their empire.

Another source of tension in Europe was imperialism. Britain's huge empire, stretching from Africa to Asia, brought it wealth and power. Eager to share in such benefits, other European powers competed for control of overseas territories. Fierce competition for territory took place within Europe as well. For example, Germany had taken the Alsace-Lorraine region from France in the Franco-Prussian War in 1871. France wanted it back.

In this competitive atmosphere, nations focused their resources on **militarism**—the aggressive strengthening of armed forces. European nations raced to build armies and navies that were larger than ever before.

As nations became more powerful, they sought to protect themselves by forming new alliances. Germany formed an alliance with Austria-Hungary in 1879. Each promised to defend the other in case of enemy attack. Concerned with Germany's growing power, France and Russia created their own alliance in 1893. Britain joined France and Russia in 1907.

The Spark

With so much hostility dividing the nations of Europe, a German general felt that "a European war is bound to come sooner or later." All that was needed was a spark to set Europe on fire. That spark flew from the Balkan province of Bosnia and Herzegovina.

Bosnia and Herzegovina had gained independence from Turkish rule in 1878. In 1908, however, Austria-Hungary annexed the province. Slavic nationalists resisted violently—they wanted the region to be part of Serbia.

On June 28, 1914, **Archduke Francis Ferdinand**, heir to the throne of Austria-Hungary, visited the province's capital of Sarajevo with his wife, Sophie. While riding through the streets, they were shot and killed by a 19-year-old Serb nationalist named Gavrilo Princip.

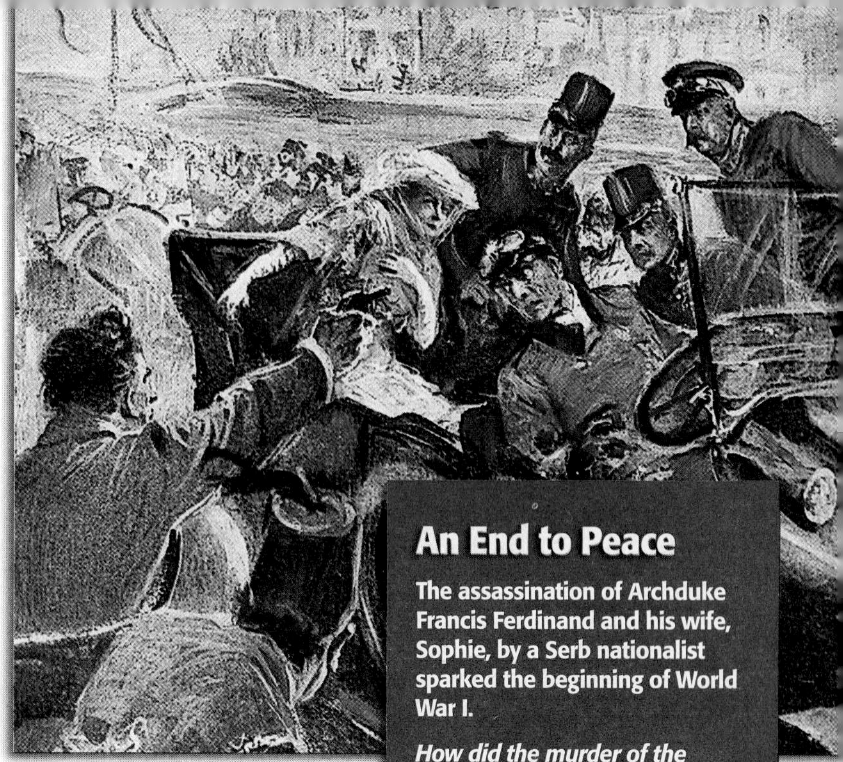

An End to Peace

The assassination of Archduke Francis Ferdinand and his wife, Sophie, by a Serb nationalist sparked the beginning of World War I.

How did the murder of the archduke bring war to Europe?

The assassination shattered Europe's fragile peace. Determined to crush Serbia and the Slavic nationalists, Austria-Hungary declared war on Serbia. Very quickly, other countries were pulled into the fighting. Russia had promised to support Serbia in case of war. It began to **mobilize**, or prepare its military for war. On August 1 Germany, Austria-Hungary's ally, declared war on Russia. Two days later, Germany also declared war on France, Russia's ally. To reach France quickly, the German army marched into Belgium on August 4. Britain, which had promised to support Belgium, then declared war on Germany.

As the fighting started, the alliance between Austria-Hungary and Germany came to be known as the **Central Powers**. Bulgaria and the Ottoman Empire later sided with the Central Powers. France, Russia, and Britain were known as the **Allied Powers**. Italy joined them in 1915. Over the next several years, soldiers from 30 nations and six continents would fight in what was then called the Great War. The conflict later became known as World War I.

READING CHECK **Identifying Cause and Effect**
How did nationalism contribute to political tensions in Europe?

© Houghton Mifflin Harcourt Publishing Company • Image Credits: (t) The Granger Collection, New York

Early Battles of the War

FOCUS ON READING
What mistake did the German leaders make in their reasoning?

Both sides expected the war to be over in a few months. German leaders planned to defeat France quickly, before Russia could join the fighting. But as the Germans marched toward France, they met fierce resistance from Belgian soldiers. This gave Britain and France time to mobilize their own troops.

The First Battle of the Marne

Belgian resistance slowed the German advance but could not stop it. On September 3 the German army was just 25 miles from Paris, the capital of France. The French army blocked the German advance at the Marne River, east of Paris. The First Battle of the Marne raged for several days before the Germans were pushed back.

By mid-September French and German troops faced each other along a long battle line called the western front. The western front stretched from the North Sea all the way to Switzerland. Meanwhile, the Russian and German armies were struggling back and forth along the eastern front, which reached from the Black Sea to the Baltic Sea. It quickly became clear that this war would be longer and deadlier than anyone had expected.

A New Kind of War

Part of what made World War I so long and deadly was a new technique called **trench warfare**—defending a position by fighting from the protection of deep ditches. When the French defeated the Germans in the First Battle of the Marne, the Germans did not retreat far. Instead, they dug trenches nearby. Opposite them, the French dug their own trenches. A 400-mile-long network of trenches soon stretched across the western front.

Soldiers fought in these cold, wet, and muddy ditches, sometimes for months at a time. The filthy trenches were perfect breeding

History Close-up

Trench Warfare

hmhsocialstudies.com
ANIMATED HISTORY
Trench Warfare

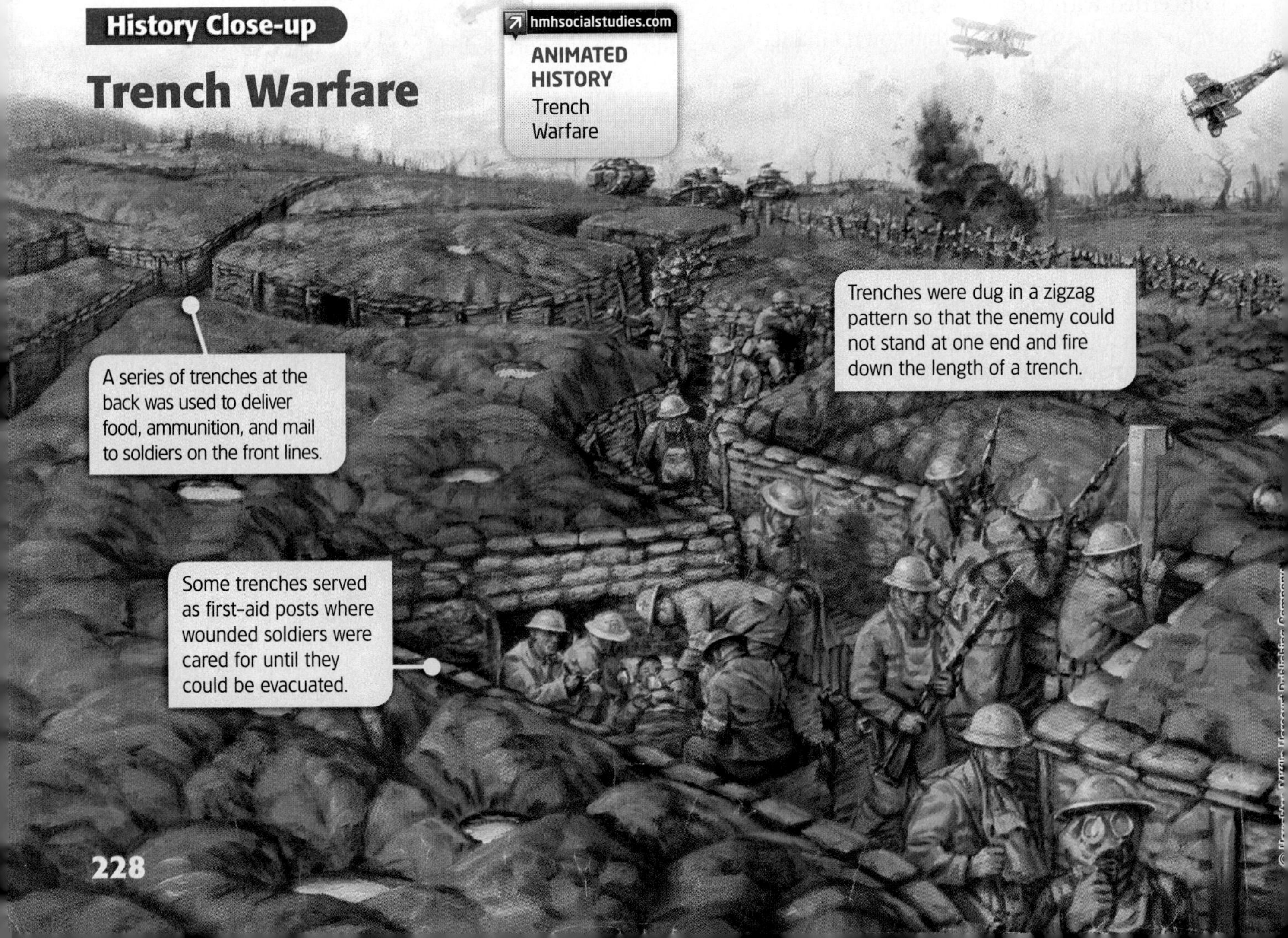

A series of trenches at the back was used to deliver food, ammunition, and mail to soldiers on the front lines.
Trenches were dug in a zigzag pattern so that the enemy could not stand at one end and fire down the length of a trench.
Some trenches served as first-aid posts where wounded soldiers were cared for until they could be evacuated.

grounds for germs, and soldiers on both sides died from disease. An American in the French army described life in the trenches:

> "The impossibility of the simplest kind of personal cleanliness makes vermin [bugs] a universal ill, against which there is no remedy. Cold, dirt, discomfort, are the ever present conditions, and the soldier's life comes to mean . . . the most misery that the human organism [body] can support."
>
> —Alan Seeger, *Letters and Diary of Alan Seeger*

The empty patch of ground between enemy trenches came to be known as "no-man's-land." This area was quickly stripped of trees and blasted full of holes by artillery shells. Anyone who ventured into no-man's-land was likely to be killed by enemy fire.

Another factor that made World War I deadlier than previous wars was the use of modern technology. New machine guns, for example, could fire 400 to 600 bullets a minute. Enormous artillery guns fired shells over the trenches, where they exploded and sent speeding scraps of metal onto the soldiers below. Other shells spread poisonous gases. If soldiers were not wearing gas masks, the gas destroyed their lungs, causing slow, painful deaths. Poisonous gases were originally banned but came into use by both sides by the end of the war.

Other new weapons included tanks and airplanes. Tanks are armored combat vehicles that can cause heavy damage but cannot be destroyed easily. Airplanes were used to fire down on soldiers in trenches and to gather information about enemy locations. Airplanes also battled each other in fights called "dogfights."

THE IMPACT TODAY

Many of the weapons first used in World War I, such as tanks and airplanes, are still used in warfare today. The use of poison gas, however, has been outlawed by international treaties.

Land and Sea Battles

After a year of vicious fighting, the war had become a **stalemate**—a situation in which neither side can win a decisive victory. Determined to break the stalemate, both sides launched massive attacks in 1916. In February 1916 the Germans attacked the French city of Verdun, at the southern end of the western front. That summer, the Allies staged an attack along the Somme River, in northeastern

Airplanes could scout enemy positions and drop bombs into trenches.
Because tanks were not damaged by either machine-gun or rifle fire, their use marked the beginning of the end for trench warfare.
No-man's land was the name given to the area between opposing trenches. It was usually about 250 yards wide and full of barbed wire and abandoned military equipment.

ANALYSIS SKILL **ANALYZING INFORMATION**

How does this picture help you understand why World War I was so deadly for soldiers?

German U-boats

Germany developed small submarines called U-boats as part of its war strategy. U-boats could strike Allied ships without being seen. They destroyed around 10 million tons of Allied and neutral ships and cargo from 1914 to 1918.

Why might U-boats have been so effective against the Allies?

France. Both battles raged for months, as the armies attacked and counterattacked.

ACADEMIC VOCABULARY
neutral unbiased, not favoring either side in a conflict

By the end of the year, the Germans had failed to take Verdun. At the Somme River, the Allies had advanced just seven miles. Almost nothing had changed on the western front. But nearly 1 million men had been killed at Verdun and the Somme River.

As the stalemate on land dragged on, sea battles in the Atlantic Ocean and the North Sea became even more important. The powerful British navy blockaded the ports of the Central Powers and laid explosive mines in the North Sea. These could blow a huge hole in a ship, sinking it in minutes. The tactic effectively stopped ships from reaching German ports with needed supplies.

The Germans responded by using submarines called **U-boats**. U-boats launched torpedoes against Allied supply ships, causing heavy losses. The Germans also attacked ships belonging to **neutral** countries they believed were helping the Allies. This would soon pull the United States into World War I.

READING CHECK **Categorizing** What new technologies did armies in World War I use?

SUMMARY World War I became a stalemate by 1916 as countries battled for control.

Section 1 Assessment

hmhsocialstudies.com
ONLINE QUIZ

Reviewing Ideas, Terms, and People

1. **a. Describe** What factors contributed to the outbreak of World War I?
   b. Contrast How did nationalism affect Germany and Austria-Hungary differently?
   c. Predict What might have happened if Russia had not honored its agreement to defend Serbia?
2. **a. Identify** What were the outcomes of the early battles of the war?
   b. Explain How did Belgian resistance affect the German war plan?
   c. Evaluate How successful was **trench warfare** as a strategy?

Critical Thinking

3. **Identifying Cause and Effect** Review your notes on the major battles of World War I. Then copy the graphic organizer below and use it to show the outcomes of these early battles and how they affected the war.

Battle	Outcome	Results

FOCUS ON SPEAKING

4. **Analyzing Rising Tensions** Start a list of ways that World War I might affect the United States. Was there sufficient reason for the United States to join the conflict at this time?

Americans Prepare for War

SECTION 2

If YOU were there...

Everywhere you go people are talking about the war in Europe. The United States has just joined the fighting on the side of the Allied Powers. Many young men you know are volunteering to fight. Women are signing up to drive ambulances or work as nurses. You know that the situation in Europe is dangerous, but you want to serve your country.

Will you volunteer for service in World War I?

BUILDING BACKGROUND When World War I began, the United States had a long history of avoiding involvement in European conflicts. Most Americans wanted the United States to remain neutral in this war as well. But as tensions with Germany increased, it became clear that distance from Europe would not keep Americans out of battle.

What You Will Learn...

Main Ideas

1. The United States entered the war after repeated crises with Germany.
2. The United States mobilized for war by training troops and stepping up production of supplies.
3. Labor shortages created new wartime opportunities for women and other Americans.

The Big Idea

After entering World War I in 1917, Americans began the massive effort of preparing for war.

Key Terms

Lusitania
Zimmermann Note
Selective Service Act
Liberty bonds
National War Labor Board

hmhsocialstudies.com
TAKING NOTES

Use the graphic organizer online to take notes on the new laws and government programs created to prepare for World War I.

The United States Enters World War I

Millions of Americans at this time were immigrants or children of immigrants. Many came from countries belonging to the Allied or Central Powers. They naturally sympathized with their former homelands. This did not change the fact that most Americans viewed World War I as a European conflict. They did not want American soldiers sent to the bloody battlefields of Europe. Shortly after World War I began, President Woodrow Wilson announced that the United States would remain neutral. Most Americans agreed that America should stay out of the war.

American Neutrality Threatened

Although the United States had a policy of neutrality, its merchants continued to trade with European nations. American ships carried supplies and war materials to the Allies. U.S. banks invested $2 billion in European war bonds, nearly all of it in Allied countries.

The Germans used U-boat attacks to try to stop supplies from reaching the Allies. Sometimes they attacked ships without warning. In May 1915 a German U-boat sank the ***Lusitania***, a British passenger liner. Nearly 1,200 people, including 128 Americans, were killed. The incident fueled anti-German feeling in the United States. Throughout the coming war, German Americans faced nativist attacks, including anti-German speeches, discrimination, and physical attacks.

Secretary of State William Jennings Bryan resigned over President Wilson's handling of the affair. Bryan thought that Wilson's protest note to the Germans was designed to bring the United States into the war.

In March 1916 a U-boat attacked the *Sussex*, a French passenger ship. Several of the 80 casualties were Americans. Wilson demanded that the Germans stop attacking nonmilitary ships. German leaders responded with the *Sussex* pledge, agreeing not to attack merchant ships without warning.

Congress Declares War

When Wilson ran for reelection in 1916, the promise to remain neutral helped him win the election. Nearly a year after the *Sussex* pledge, however, the Germans again began launching attacks on ships, including American vessels. In response, Wilson broke off diplomatic relations with Germany.

The United States stepped closer to war when Americans found out about the **Zimmermann Note**. This secret telegram to Mexico sent by the German foreign minister, Arthur Zimmermann, was decoded and then published by American newspapers in March 1917. In the note, Zimmermann proposed an alliance against the United States. He promised that Germany would help Mexico recapture areas that Mexico had lost during the Mexican-American War.

The American public was outraged by the telegram. President Wilson asked Congress to declare war on Germany. "The world must be made safe for democracy," he proclaimed. Congress declared war on April 6, 1917.

READING CHECK **Finding Main Ideas** What events challenged U.S. neutrality?

Primary Source

NEWSPAPER ARTICLE

Sinking of the *Lusitania*

In 1915 German U-boats sank the Lusitania, *an event that pushed the United States toward entry into World War I. Newspapers quickly spread news of the disaster.*

The accounts which have so far been received are fragmentary, and give no clear idea of the disaster. There is, however, no doubt that two torpedoes were fired without warning into the starboard side of the ship soon after 2 o'clock yesterday afternoon. There were conflicting accounts of the period during which the *Lusitania* remained afloat, but the Cunard Company states that she sunk 40 minutes after being struck.

—*The Register*, quoted in the *Times of London*

The ship was treated as an enemy warship.

The ship sank before enough rescue ships could arrive.

ANALYSIS SKILL **ANALYZING PRIMARY SOURCES**

How might this disaster draw the United States into war with Germany?

Supreme Court Decisions

Schenck v. *United States* (1919)

Background of the Case Charles Schenck was arrested for violating the Espionage Act. He had printed and distributed pamphlets urging resistance to the draft. Schenck argued that the First Amendment, which guarantees freedom of speech and freedom of the press, gave him the right to criticize the government.

The Court's Ruling
The Supreme Court ruled that the pamphlet was not protected by the First Amendment and that the Espionage Act was constitutional.

The Court's Reasoning
The Supreme Court decided that under certain circumstances, such as a state of war, Congress could limit free speech. The Court created a test to distinguish between protected and unprotected speech. Unprotected speech would have to present "a clear and present danger" to national security. For example, the First Amendment would not protect a person who created a panic by yelling "Fire!" in a crowded theater.

Why It Matters
Schenck v. *United States* was important because it was the first case in which the Supreme Court interpreted the First Amendment. The Court concluded that certain constitutional rights, such as free speech, could be limited under extraordinary conditions, such as war. Later rulings by the Court narrowed the test of "clear and present danger" to speech advocating violence. The nonviolent expression of ideas and opinions—however unpopular—was thereby protected.

ANALYSIS SKILL ANALYZING INFORMATION

1. According to the Supreme Court, when could free speech be limited?
2. How do you think this case affected other people who opposed the war?

Mobilizing for War

In order to persuade the public to support the war effort, President Wilson formed the Committee on Public Information (CPI). The CPI organized rallies and parades and published posters and pamphlets. Speakers known as "four-minute men" gave short patriotic speeches in movie theaters and churches.

The U.S. government's war effort also involved limiting some freedoms in the United States. The Espionage Act of 1917 and the Sedition Act of 1918 restricted free speech and allowed the government to arrest opponents of the war. Antiwar mail was prohibited and seized. About 900 opponents of the war were jailed for violating these laws. The Sedition Act was later repealed, but the Espionage Act is still in effect today.

To prepare the U.S. military, Congress passed the **Selective Service Act** in 1917. The act required men between the ages of 21 and 30 to register to be drafted. Almost 3 million Americans were drafted into service in World War I. A number of the draftees were African Americans. Altogether, about 400,000 African Americans served in the war. Their units were segregated from white forces and were commanded by white officers. Eventually, African Americans were trained as officers. During World War I, however, they were never placed in command of white troops.

Preparations for war were very expensive. Troops had to be trained, supplied, transported, and fed. Ships and airplanes had to be built and fueled. The government raised taxes and issued war bonds. Money from the sale of these **Liberty bonds** provided billions of dollars in loans to the Allies.

The government took other actions to supply the troops. The War Industries Board (WIB) oversaw the production and distribution of steel, copper, cement, and rubber. The Food Administration worked to increase food supplies for the troops. It guaranteed farmers high prices for their crops. To conserve food at home, citizens were encouraged to practice "meatless Mondays" and "wheatless Wednesdays." Many people also grew their own vegetables in "victory gardens" at home.

THE IMPACT TODAY
To conserve fuel used for lighting for the war effort, daylight saving time was first introduced in March 1918. The plan is still in effect today.

READING CHECK **Analyzing** How did the U.S. government gain public support for the war?

LINKING TO TODAY

Women on the Battlefield

The role of women in World War I was much like their roles in previous wars—providing support for male troops. Women drove ambulances and entered the battlefield as nurses and medics. Red Cross volunteers were often responsible for the first stage of treatment of the wounded. Today, women may also serve in the military as soldiers. They are not allowed to fight in ground combat, but they do serve as guards and pilots, and in the navy.

Red Cross volunteers in World War I

Soldier on duty in Iraq

ANALYSIS SKILL ANALYZING INFORMATION

How have wartime roles for women changed since World War I?

New Wartime Opportunities

Three main factors led to a shortage of labor in the United States during the war. First, American factories were working nonstop to produce weapons and supplies for the Allied forces. Factories needed new workers to meet this huge demand. Second, the war almost completely cut off immigration. As you know, immigrants had provided a steady source of labor to American industry. And third, many of the young men who would normally take factory jobs were off fighting in Europe.

Women's War Efforts

This labor shortage created new opportunities for many workers. American women took on new roles to help the war effort. Some 1 million women joined the U.S. workforce during the war years. For many, this was their first experience working outside the home.

Women also worked for the war effort in Europe. About 25,000 American women volunteered as nurses, telephone operators, signalers, typists, and interpreters in France. Women were not given jobs in combat, but they braved gunfire at the front lines as nurses and ambulance drivers. One female driver described her World War I experiences:

> "We had our first air-raid work last night. I was the night driver on duty . . . Some bombs fell very near just as I got to the [hospital] . . . when shrapnel [metal fragments] whizzed past my head and there was a tremendous crash close beside . . . Then an ambulance call came and I tore off."
>
> —Mrs. Guy Napier-Martin, quoted in *The Overseas War Record of the Winsor School, 1914–1919*

Other women, meanwhile, spoke out against U.S. participation in the war. Social reformer Jane Addams was against U.S. entry into the war. Jeannette Rankin of Montana, the first female member of Congress, was one of 50 House members to cast a vote against declaring war in 1917. "I want to stand by my country," she said, "but I cannot vote for war."

Labor and the War

Even with so many women joining the workforce, factories needed additional workers. New job opportunities encouraged Mexican Americans from the West and African Americans from the South to move to northern industrial cities.

Because labor was scarce, workers were in a good position to demand better wages and conditions. Union membership increased. More than 4 million unionized workers went on strike during the war. Because factory owners could not easily replace workers, they often agreed to demands.

President Wilson set up the **National War Labor Board** in April 1918. The board helped workers and management avoid strikes and reach agreements. The board settled more than 1,000 labor disputes. Its members were generally sympathetic to workers. They helped establish a minimum wage and limited work hours. They also required fair pay for women.

READING CHECK **Finding Main Ideas** How did war mobilization benefit American workers?

Patriotic Posters

Posters like this one encouraged American citizens to participate in the effort to provide weapons and food to soldiers fighting in World War I.

How does this poster inspire patriotism?

TEAMWORK WINS
UNITED STATES SHIPPING BOARD EMERGENCY FLEET CORPORATION

SUMMARY The war effort created new opportunities for women and other Americans.

Section 2 Assessment

hmhsocialstudies.com
ONLINE QUIZ

Reviewing Ideas, Terms, and People

1. a. **Explain** Why did the United States enter World War I?
   b. **Evaluate** Do you think the United States was right to stay neutral for so long? Why or why not?
2. a. **Explain** How did the United States prepare for war?
   b. **Recall** What was the purpose of the Committee on Public Information?
   c. **Summarize** How did the government exercise control over the economy during the war?
3. a. **Describe** How did women help the war effort abroad?
   b. **Predict** How do you think the end of the war affected labor unions? Explain your answer.

Critical Thinking

4. **Problem Solving** Review your notes on new laws and government programs during World War I. Then copy the graphic organizer below and use it to identify the challenges the United States faced when mobilizing for World War I. List which new laws, government programs, and other changes responded to those challenges.

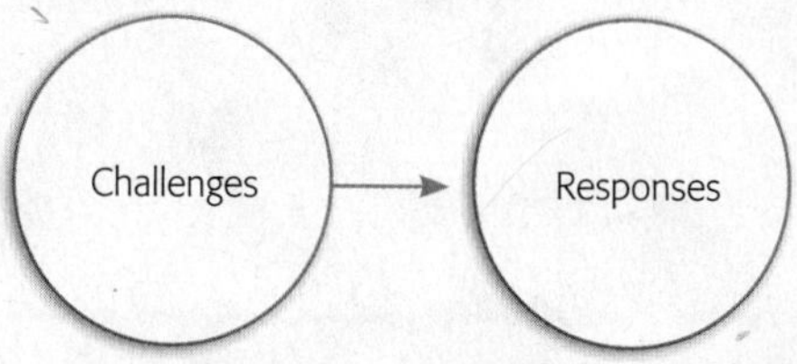

Challenges
Responses

Focus on Speaking

5. **Analyzing Wilson's Policies** Add to your list examples of causes of growing tension between Germany and the United States. What events led President Wilson to support war with Germany? Do you agree with his view? Why or why not?

Case Study

Alabama During World War I

The Alabama Home Front

In order to mobilize for World War I, the United States needed to train troops, build ships and airplanes, and make weapons and ammunition. Alabama played an important role in each of these efforts.

The U.S. government created posters to encourage people to support the war effort.

Training Camps

Immediately after the United States declared war, political leaders arranged for three training camps to be set up in Alabama. Infantry troops were trained at Camp Sheridan, near Montgomery, and Camp McClellan, near Anniston. Both of these camps were named in honor of prominent Union generals from the Civil War. The names were a reminder to southerners that the federal government was more powerful than the states. In addition, Alabama National Guard troops that had been sent to the Mexican border during Pancho Villa's rebellion had recently returned. They were called back into federal service almost immediately. Altogether, more than 70,000 Alabamians served in the military during the war.

Taylor Field, also at Montgomery, was a training center for army pilots. World War I marked the first time that airplanes were used in war, and Taylor Field was one of only a handful of locations where army pilots were trained. The field was near the site of the Wright brothers' civilian pilot training school, the first in the nation. During the war, the school was used as a repair center for army planes. Today the site is home to Maxwell Air Force Base.

© Houghton Mifflin Harcourt Publishing Company • Image Credits: (bl) Library of Congress Prints and Photographs Division Washington, D.C.

Ammunition Plants

The explosives and gunpowder used during World War I were manufactured using chemicals known as nitrates. But the United States was unable to produce enough of these chemicals for the war. In 1917 Woodrow Wilson selected Muscle Shoals, in northwest Alabama, as the site for new nitrate production facilities.

The first step was to build Wilson Dam on the Tennessee River. It would provide electricity for the nitrate plants. Before the dam was completed, however, the war was over. The facilities eventually produced nitrates anyway, to be used in making fertilizers.

The Port of Mobile

When the United States entered the war, it needed to expand its Merchant Navy to carry supplies and troops. Mobile was an ideal port to build new ships. The port was located along the Gulf Coast, making it less susceptible to attacks from German boats and submarines than ports along the Atlantic. Even though trade through the port had declined because of the war in Europe, the state had been improving the port's facilities. The Alabama Drydock and Shipbuilding Company had to install new machinery and hire more workers to build the ships ordered by the navy. Much like the nitrate factories at Muscle Shoals, however, the war ended before the ordered ships could be produced. Only one ship, the *Banago,* was completed before the armistice.

World War I Military Sites

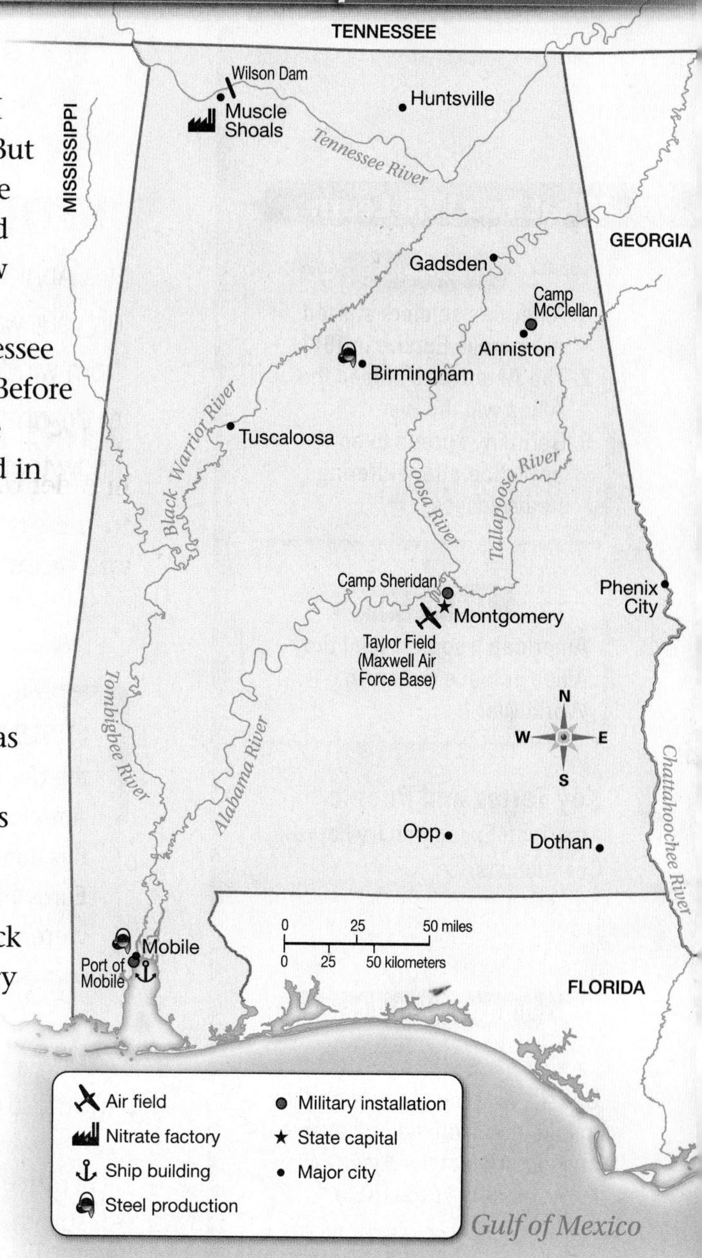

Case Study Assessment

1. Which World War I military facilities were located in Alabama?
2. Why was Alabama strategically located for shipping and shipbuilding?
3. **Activity** Alabamians in the Alabama National Guard were mustered into different regiments of federal troops. Research these different troops and their actions during the war. Then design a monument to one of these groups and the Alabamians who served in it.

GEOGRAPHY SKILLS **INTERPRETING MAPS**

Location Why was Maxwell Air Force Base located at Montgomery?

SECTION 3

Americans in World War I

What You Will Learn...

Main Ideas

1. American soldiers started to arrive in Europe in 1917.
2. The Americans helped the Allies win the war.
3. Germany agreed to an armistice after suffering heavy losses.

The Big Idea

American troops helped the Allies achieve victory in World War I.

Key Terms and People

American Expeditionary Force
Communists
armistice

hmhsocialstudies.com
TAKING NOTES

Use the graphic organizer online to take notes on the achievements and victories of the American Expeditionary Force (AEF).

If YOU were there...

It is April 1918. You are marching into Paris with your army unit on your way to the front lines. Women and children throw flowers from windows and balconies as you pass through the city. You want to do whatever it takes to defend this city and its residents. You know that defeating Germany will be difficult and very dangerous.

Do you think American forces can help the Allies win the war?

BUILDING BACKGROUND Preparations for war helped make the United States a strong military power. By 1918 nearly 5 million Americans were serving in the army, navy, and marine corps. While this huge armed force was being trained, however, the fighting in Europe was going badly for the Allies. French and British leaders were eager for help from America.

American Soldiers Arrive

By the time U.S. troops started to arrive in Europe in 1917, the Allies were dangerously near defeat. German forces were advancing in France, once again driving toward Paris. The German navy was destroying Allied ships at sea. And on the eastern front, the Russians were desperately struggling to hold back the Germans.

Joining the Fight

French and British generals called for immediate help on the front lines. They wanted the U.S. troops, known as the **American Expeditionary Force** (AEF), to join French and British units. But General John J. Pershing, leader of the American troops, insisted that the Americans join the fight as a separate force. He refused to have the AEF "scattered among the Allied forces where it will not be an American army at all."

Pershing also demanded that his troops be thoroughly trained for combat before rushing to the front lines. The AEF included many well-trained regular army and National Guard troops. But it also included a large number of inexperienced volunteers and draftees. Pershing gave the men three months of intense training in army discipline and trench warfare. He believed that taking the time to train his soldiers would help the Allies achieve victory.

Russia Leaves the War

While Pershing trained his troops, the Allies' position became even more dangerous. In November 1917 a group of Russians called the Bolsheviks overthrew the Russian government and seized power. The Bolsheviks were **Communists**—people who favor the equal distribution of wealth and the end of all forms of private property.

Led by Vladimir Lenin, the new Russian government faced a desperate situation. Around 8 million Russians had been killed or wounded during the war. Soldiers were deserting from the eastern front, and sailors were leaving naval bases. Food riots raged in the cities. The Russians could not keep fighting under these conditions. In March 1918 Russia signed the Treaty of Brest-Litovsk, a peace agreement with the Central Powers. A civil war then broke out in Russia between the Communists and forces loyal to the czar (ZAHR), Russia's emperor. The United States and other Allied countries sent aid to the czarist forces. Russia, however, one of the main Allied Powers, was out of World War I.

READING CHECK **Drawing Inferences** Why do you think General Pershing refused to put American troops in foreign units?

Winning the War

With Russia out of the fighting, German generals saw a chance to win the war. In the spring of 1918 Germany transferred many of its divisions of troops from the eastern front to the western front. Germany planned to smash the stalemate.

World War I U.S. Soldier

The appearance of the Springfield rifles fooled the Germans into thinking the Americans had machine guns.
Soldiers carried a pack called a haversack, which held food, personal items, and extra socks.
Gas masks were carried in a pouch around the neck.
A wool tunic was worn over a wool shirt and wool breeches.
A blanket could be carried at the bottom of the haversack with a special attachment.
Wool cloth strips called puttees were wrapped around the legs and tops of shoes for protection.

ANALYSIS SKILL **ANALYZING VISUALS**

How did clothing and supplies help a U.S. soldier in the battlefield?

The Final Battles

At the same time, American soldiers arrived. Even training had not prepared them for the realities of war. The troops lived on dried beef, hard biscuits, and canned emergency rations. The men shared the trenches with rats, lice, and sometimes the bodies of dead soldiers. A soldiers' song of the time described the situation:

> "Sing me to sleep where bullets fall,
> Let me forget the war and all;
> Damp is my dug-out [trench], cold my feet,
> Nothing but bully [canned meat] and biscuits
> to eat."
>
> —Quoted in *Great Push: An Episode of the Great War,* by Patrick MacGill

hmhsocialstudies.com INTERACTIVE MAP

World War I, 1914–1918

Allied Powers, 1916
Central Powers, 1916
Neutral Countries
Allied Powers troop movements
Central Powers troop movements
British naval blockade
Farthest Russian advance (1914)
Farthest Central Powers advance
Trench line, western front
Armistice line, Nov. 11, 1918
Allied victory
Central Powers victory
Undecided battle
German submarine activity
0 200 400 Miles
0 200 400 Kilometers
N
S
E
W
60°N
50°N
40°N
20°W
10°W
0°
10°E
ATLANTIC OCEAN
NORWAY
SWEDEN
GREAT BRITAIN
North Sea
DENMARK
Baltic Sea
RUSSIA
NETHERLANDS
Lusitania sunk May 1915
London
Ypres Oct.–Nov. 1914 Apr.–May 1915
Stebark Aug. 1914
Berlin
EASTERN FRONT DEC. 1917
English Channel
Sussex torpedoed March 1916
BELGIUM
GERMANY
Somme July–Nov. 1916
LUXEMBOURG
Paris
Battle of the Marne Sept. 1914, July 1918
Château-Thierry June 1918
Argonne Forest Sept.–Oct. 1918
Verdun Feb.–Dec. 1916
ALSACE-LORRAINE
WESTERN FRONT
Vienna
AUSTRIA-HUNGARY
Budapest
Bay of Biscay
SWITZERLAND
FRANCE
Kobarid Oct.–Nov. 1917
SERBIA
BOSNIA and HERZEGOVINA
Sarajevo
ROMANIA
PORTUGAL
SPAIN
Adriatic Sea
ITALY
BULGARIA
Bosporus
Rome
MONTENEGRO
BALKANS
ALBANIA
Constantinople
Dardanelles
Gallipoli April 1915–Jan. 1916
GREECE (Joined Allied Powers 1917)
OTTOMAN EMPIRE
Mediterranean Sea
Black Sea

GEOGRAPHY SKILLS — INTERPRETING MAPS

1. **Human-Environment Interaction** Why was the British naval blockade located where it was?
2. **Location** In which country were the most battles fought, according to this map?

On March 21, 1918, the Germans began blasting more than 6,000 heavy guns at Allied troops along the Somme River in northern France. German forces drove 40 miles into Allied lines before the advance stalled. Some 250,000 Germans had been killed or wounded. British and French casualties totaled 133,000.

The Germans then attacked farther south, advancing to the Marne River and pushing the French line back toward Paris. At this critical moment, General Pershing promised Allied commander Ferdinand Foch: "Infantry, artillery, aviation—all that we have . . . The American people would be proud to be engaged in the greatest battle of history." Two divisions of the AEF joined French forces.

The Germans were unprepared for the fresh energy and fighting skills of the Americans. The U.S. soldiers succeeded in stopping the German advance less than 50 miles from Paris. Then, at Belleau Wood, the Allies attacked and gradually drove the Germans back.

German generals became desperate. In July 1918 they launched their final offensive—one last attempt to cross the Marne River. Terrible losses on the German side stopped the German offensive and protected Paris from invasion. Although they suffered about 12,000 casualities, American troops had helped force a major turning point in the war.

Driving the Germans Back

Now the Allies drove toward victory. There were more than 1 million U.S. troops in France, and they played a key role in the later battles of the war. In September 1918 Allied forces attacked and defeated the Germans at the town of Saint-Mihiel on the border of France and Germany. Along the Meuse River and in the Argonne Forest, near the French-Belgian border, American and Allied troops again attacked German forces.

Among the many heroes of these battles was a young man from Tennessee named Alvin York. In October 1918 York killed 25 German gunners and captured 132 prisoners. His heroism earned him fame and many awards, including the Congressional Medal of Honor. His life story even became the basis for a popular movie in 1941.

Also among the brave American troops were the African American soldiers of the 369th Infantry. Known as the Harlem Hellfighters, the 369th spent more time in combat than any other American unit. Its members were the first to reach the Rhine River on the German border. France awarded them the prized Croix de Guerre (Cross of War) medal for their bravery.

The Allies were also winning the war at sea. Allied war planners used a new **strategy** called the convoy system to protect their ships. This meant that destroyers capable of sinking U-boats escorted and protected groups of Allied merchant ships.

ACADEMIC VOCABULARY

strategy a plan for fighting a battle or war

By November 1918, American soldiers were making rapid advances toward Germany. "For the first time the enemy lines were completely broken through," reported General Pershing.

READING CHECK **Sequencing** Identify significant events leading to the turning of the tide in the war.

Armistice

At home and on the battlefield, Germans were tired of war. Food was so scarce in Germany that more than 800 German civilians were dying of starvation every day. In Germany and other nations of the Central Powers, food riots and strikes occurred. Germany was also running out of soldiers. In addition to those killed or wounded in 1918, one quarter of Germany's fighting men had been captured by the Allies.

Germany's allies were also eager to end the war. Bulgaria and the Ottoman Empire quit the war in the fall of 1918. Austria-Hungary reached a peace agreement with the Allies on November 3. Seeing that his country was beaten, the German leader, Kaiser Wilhelm II, gave up his throne and fled to the Netherlands.

The 369th Infantry

The 369th Infantry spent 191 days in combat, longer than any other American force sent to Europe during World War I. Its members aided French forces at Château-Thierry and Belleau Wood, receiving the Croix de Guerre for their bravery. The "Harlem Hellfighters" became famous throughout Europe and America for their valor.

The Croix de Guerre was created by France in 1915 to reward bravery by members of the Allied armed forces—French citizens and foreigners alike.

The Germans then agreed to a cease-fire. The Allies demanded that Germany pull back from all its conquered territory. They insisted that Germany destroy its aircraft, tanks, and big guns, and surrender its U-boats. The Germans had no choice but to accept these demands to disarm. The **armistice**, or truce, went into effect on the 11th hour of the 11th day of the 11th month of 1918. "At eleven o'clock everything got so quiet that the silence was nearly unbearable," remembered an American soldier. Then the silence was broken with shouts like "I've lived through the war!"

READING CHECK **Analyzing** How did Allied troops break the stalemate with Germany?

SUMMARY America's entry into World War I helped the Allies achieve victory.

Section 3 Assessment

hmhsocialstudies.com
ONLINE QUIZ

Reviewing Ideas, Terms, and People

1. a. **Define** What was the **American Expeditionary Force**?
   b. **Analyze** How did the Russian Revolution change the course of the war?
   c. **Evaluate** Why did Russia leave the war?
2. a. **Analyze** How did U.S. troops make a difference in the final battles of the war?
   b. **Recall** How was the Second Battle of the Marne a turning point in the war?
3. a. **Describe** What was Germany required to surrender in the **armistice**?
   b. **Interpret** Were the terms of the armistice fair? Explain your answer.

Critical Thinking

4. **Categorizing** Review your notes on the victories of the American Expeditionary Force. Then copy the graphic organizer below and use it to list challenges the Allies faced from 1917 to 1918. List the Allies' achievements during the same time period.

Allied Challenges	
Allied Achievements	

FOCUS ON SPEAKING

5. **Analyzing the War's Effects on Soldiers** What examples from this section could you add to your list of how World War I events affected the United States? How did American soldiers contribute to the Allied war effort? What were conditions like for American soldiers? Do you think U.S. involvement was justified?

© Houghton Mifflin Harcourt Publishing Company • Image Credits: (t) ©Dorling Kindersley Ltd./Courtesy of Spink & Son Ltd, London; (c) ©Hulton/Getty Images

Establishing Peace

SECTION 4

If YOU were there...

Your older brother was drafted in 1917 and sent to fight on the western front in Europe. He has written home about the terrible conditions in the trenches and the horror of seeing men killed in battle. Now the war is over. You read in the newspaper that a peace treaty is being negotiated in Paris, France.

What do you hope the peace treaty will say?

BUILDING BACKGROUND After World War I, many questions about the future remained. Who would pay for the huge costs of the war? How should defeated powers' territories be divided? How could countries work together to avoid another world war? Leaders began discussing and debating these questions.

The Costs of War

While soldiers and civilians around the world celebrated the end of World War I in November 1918, the tragedy of war was never far from people's minds. When asked what the armistice meant, one British soldier simply said, "Time to bury the dead."

War Dead

The number of soldiers killed in World War I was beyond anything the world had ever experienced. About 5 million Allied soldiers and 3.5 million soldiers from the Central Powers died in combat. More than 20 million soldiers on both sides were wounded. The war devastated an entire generation of young men in many European nations. In France, for example, 90 percent of the healthy young men had served in World War I. More than 7 out of 10 of these men were killed or wounded. While the United States escaped this extreme level of devastation, American forces did suffer heavy losses. Some 116,000 U.S. troops died, and about 200,000 were wounded.

Financial Losses

Along with the shocking human losses, the war brought financial disaster to many parts of Europe. Factories and farms were left in ruins. "For mile after mile nothing was left," said one British visitor

What You Will Learn...

Main Ideas

1. The costs of war included millions of human lives as well as financial burdens.
2. President Woodrow Wilson and European leaders met to work out a peace agreement.
3. The U.S. Senate rejected the Treaty of Versailles.

The Big Idea

The United States and the victorious Allied Powers clashed over postwar plans.

Key Terms and People

League of Nations
reparations
Treaty of Versailles
Henry Cabot Lodge

hmhsocialstudies.com
TAKING NOTES

Use the graphic organizer online to take notes on the provisions of the Treaty of Versailles.

THE IMPACT TODAY

Today, vaccinations help prevent major outbreaks of the flu and other contagious diseases.

about the French countryside. "No building was habitable [livable] and no field fit for the plow." With farmers unable to raise crops, severe food shortages occurred.

The overall economic cost of the war was huge. Property worth $30 billion had been destroyed. The Allies had spent $145 billion on the war effort, and the Central Powers had spent $63 billion. France and Britain had borrowed large amounts of money to fight the war, and now they were deeply in debt to American banks. Germany was also in debt, and its people faced starvation.

The Influenza Epidemic

The world was in for another shock in 1918 when a worldwide epidemic of influenza, or flu, broke out. The virus was extremely contagious and deadly. Over the next two years, it spread around the world, killing approximately 30 million people—even more than the war itself.

The epidemic started in an army training camp in Kansas. Because the flu is transmitted through the air, it spread rapidly. American soldiers unknowingly spread the disease to other army camps, to American civilians, and eventually to soldiers and civilians in Europe. One American doctor said that seeing stacks of bodies at an army camp in Massachusetts "beats any sight they ever had in France after a battle." Half of the Americans who died during this period died from influenza.

The epidemic changed life everywhere in the United States. In Chicago, for example, the flu more than doubled the normal death rate in the fall of 1918. Many of those killed were young and strong. State and local governments took measures to prevent the spread of the disease. Kearney, Nebraska, imposed a quarantine, forbidding people who were ill from leaving their homes. Many cities banned public gatherings, including school classes. A man named Dan Tonkel remembered what life was like for children in his hometown of Goldsboro, North Carolina:

> "I felt like I was walking on eggshells. I was afraid to go out, to play with my playmates, my classmates, my neighbors . . . I remember I was actually afraid to breathe. People were afraid to talk to each other. It was like—don't breathe in my face, don't even look at me, because you might give me germs that will kill me."
>
> —Dan Tonkel, quoted in *Influenza 1918: The Worst Epidemic in American History,* by Lynette Lezzoni

Although there was no cure for the flu, people would try anything. One woman surrounded her daughter with raw onions. Another remembered, "We hung bags of . . . garlic about our necks. We smelled awful, but it was okay, because everyone smelled bad." By the time the influenza epidemic ended in 1919, it had killed 800,000 Americans at home and abroad.

READING CHECK **Finding Main Ideas** What made the influenza epidemic of 1918 so deadly?

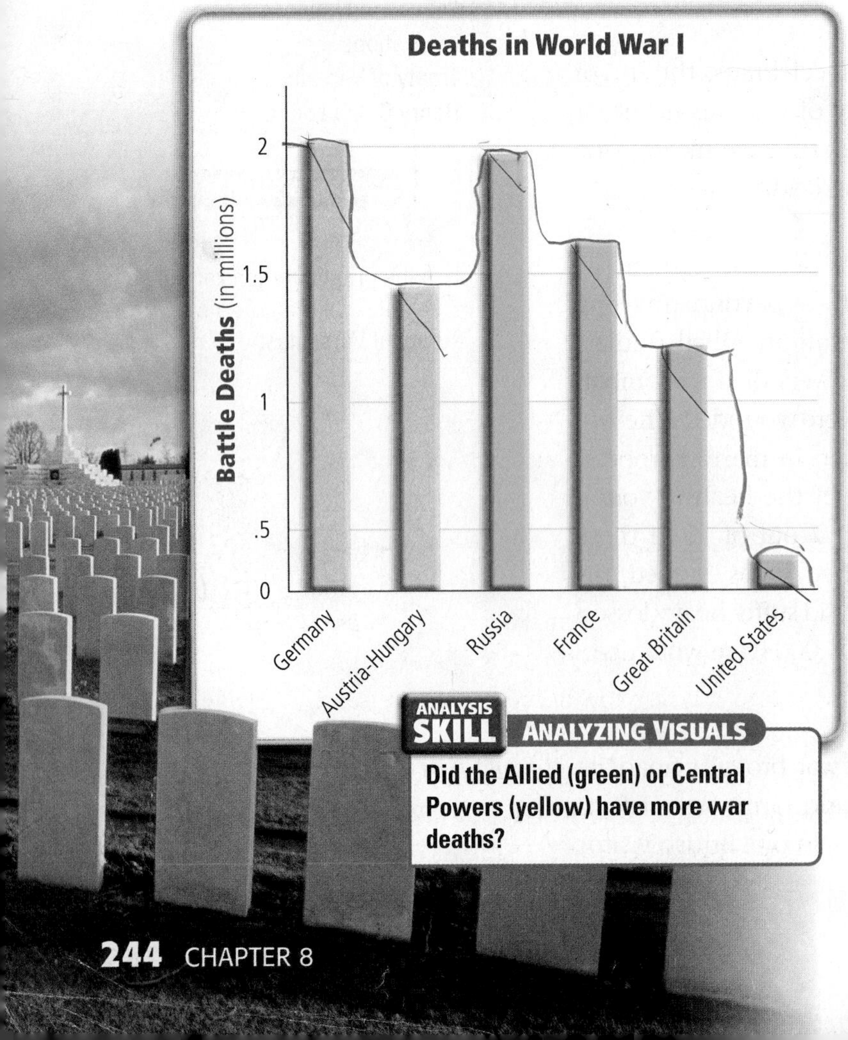

Memorials to soldiers killed in World War I, like this one at Somme, France, are located throughout Europe.

Deaths in World War I
Battle Deaths (in millions)
2
1.5
1
.5
0
Germany
Austria-Hungary
Russia
France
Great Britain
United States

ANALYSIS SKILL **ANALYZING VISUALS**

Did the Allied (green) or Central Powers (yellow) have more war deaths?

© Houghton Mifflin Harcourt Publishing Company • Image Credits: (bl) ©Michael St. Maur Sheil/Corbis

The Peace Agreement

Even before the United States entered World War I, President Woodrow Wilson began making plans for a peace agreement. He was determined to do everything possible to prevent another world war. On January 8, 1918, Wilson outlined his vision for the postwar world in a plan known as the Fourteen Points.

Wilson's Fourteen Points

Wilson's Fourteen Points were a list of specific proposals for postwar peace. Several of the points would settle national border disputes. Others called for military cutbacks, proposed lower tariffs, and banned secret agreements between nations. Another proposed settlements for colonial peoples who wished to be independent. This reflected Wilson's strong belief in self-determination—the right of people to choose their own political status. The final point called for the creation of an international assembly of nations called the **League of Nations**. The League's mission would be to work to settle international disputes and encourage democracy.

European leaders disagreed with Wilson's vision for the peace settlement, wanting it to clearly punish Germany for its role in the war. They wanted to prevent Germany from ever again becoming a world power.

The Treaty of Versailles

President Wilson traveled to Europe to attend the Paris Peace Conference, which was held at the palace of Versailles (ver-SY), outside of Paris. Wilson felt it was his duty to "play my full part in making good what [our soldiers] offered their lives to obtain."

The leaders, called the Big Four—President Wilson, British prime minister David Lloyd George, French premier Georges Clemenceau, and Italian prime minister Vittorio Orlando—took control of the conference. No representatives from Russia or the Central Powers attended.

BIOGRAPHY

Woodrow Wilson

1856–1924

Woodrow Wilson was born in Virginia in 1856. The terrible destruction he saw as a child during the Civil War would later influence his response to World War I. As president, he backed reforms such as child-labor restrictions and an eight-hour workday for railroad workers. Although he eventually abandoned American neutrality during World War I, Wilson was committed to world peace after the war. For his role in helping found the League of Nations, Wilson won the Nobel Peace Prize in 1919.

Making Inferences How did Wilson's childhood experiences affect his reaction to World War I?

Key Goals of the Fourteen Points

QUICK FACTS

- End secret alliances
- Encourage free shipping
- Remove barriers to trade
- Reduce armies and navies
- Resolve colonial claims
- Support the right of people to choose their own government
- Settle border disputes
- Establish the League of Nations

Many Allied leaders defended their own country's interests and insisted on severe punishment for Germany. They wanted Germany to accept complete blame for the war and pay for the damage it had caused. These **reparations**, or payments for war damages, were set at $33 billion. France and the other Allies also wanted to take control of large parts of German territory.

HISTORY

VIDEO
The Treaty of Versailles

hmhsocialstudies.com

Europe after World War I

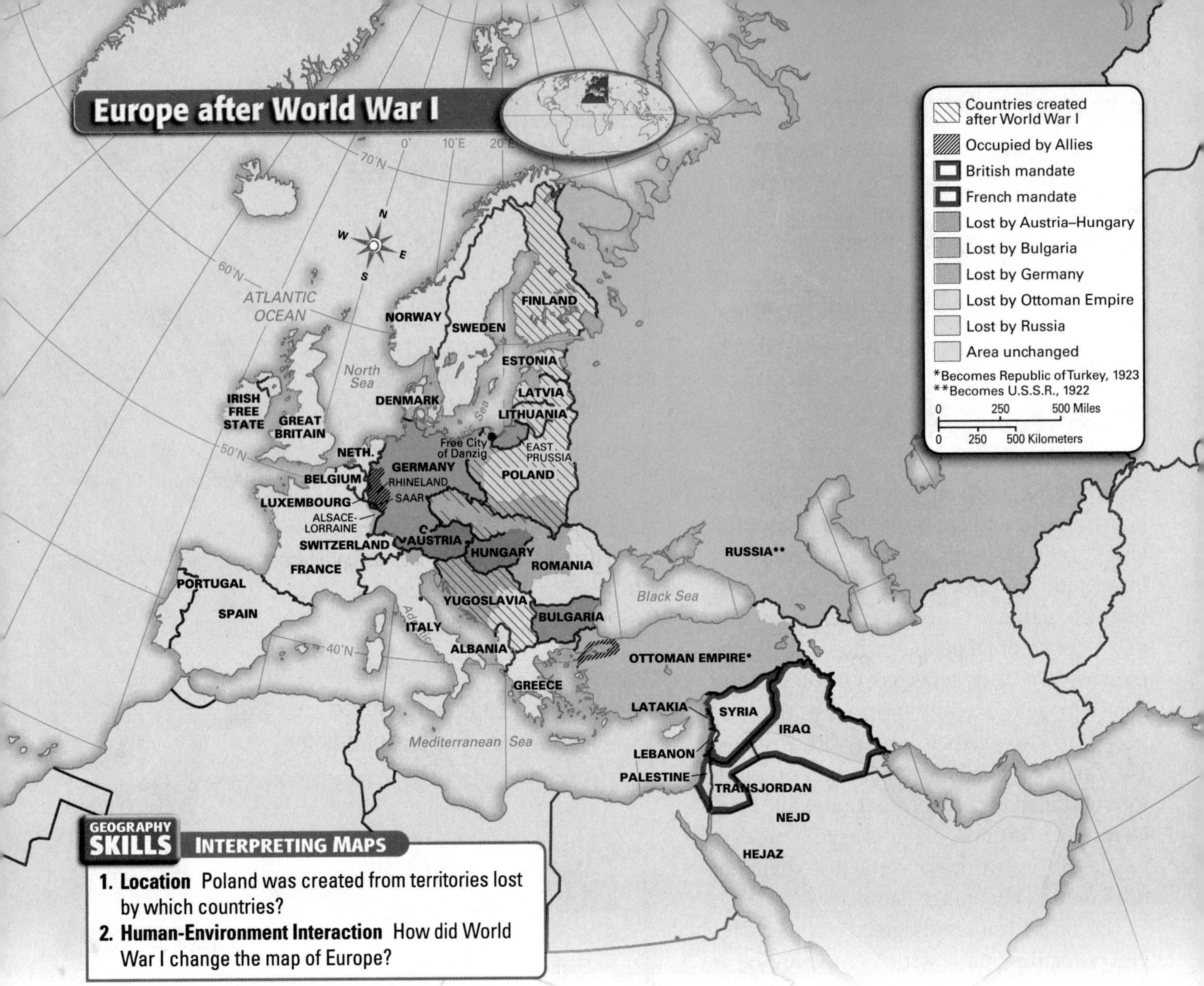

Europe after World War I
0°
10°E
20°E
70°N
60°N
50°N
40°N
N
S
E
W
ATLANTIC OCEAN
North Sea
Baltic Sea
Adriatic Sea
Black Sea
Mediterranean Sea
NORWAY
SWEDEN
FINLAND
ESTONIA
LATVIA
LITHUANIA
DENMARK
IRISH FREE STATE
GREAT BRITAIN
NETH.
BELGIUM
LUXEMBOURG
ALSACE-LORRAINE
GERMANY
RHINELAND
SAAR
Free City of Danzig
EAST PRUSSIA
POLAND
AUSTRIA
HUNGARY
SWITZERLAND
FRANCE
PORTUGAL
SPAIN
ITALY
YUGOSLAVIA
ROMANIA
BULGARIA
ALBANIA
GREECE
RUSSIA**
OTTOMAN EMPIRE*
LATAKIA
SYRIA
IRAQ
LEBANON
PALESTINE
TRANSJORDAN
NEJD
HEJAZ
Countries created after World War I
Occupied by Allies
British mandate
French mandate
Lost by Austria–Hungary
Lost by Bulgaria
Lost by Germany
Lost by Ottoman Empire
Lost by Russia
Area unchanged
*Becomes Republic of Turkey, 1923
**Becomes U.S.S.R., 1922
0 250 500 Miles
0 250 500 Kilometers

GEOGRAPHY SKILLS INTERPRETING MAPS

1. **Location** Poland was created from territories lost by which countries?
2. **Human-Environment Interaction** How did World War I change the map of Europe?

Wilson reluctantly agreed to the **Treaty of Versailles**, the peace settlement of World War I. In it, the League of Nations was established. Estonia, Finland, Latvia, Lithuania, Czechoslovakia, and Yugoslavia became inde-pendent countries. Poland was restored as a nation. The Central Powers turned over their colonies to the League of Nations, which assigned other European powers to rule. Though the Treaty of Versailles did not give Wilson everything he wanted, he hoped the League of Nations would solve remaining problems.

READING CHECK **Identifying Points of View** Why did Allied leaders object to Wilson's plan?

Versailles Treaty Rejected

The U.S. Constitution states that treaties must be ratified by at least two-thirds of the members of the Senate. Wilson knew he was going to have a hard time convincing some senators to vote to ratify the Versailles Treaty. Republican senator **Henry Cabot Lodge** declared: "No peace that satisfied Germany in any degree can ever satisfy us." Lodge wanted the winners to set the terms of the peace.

Republicans insisted on changes to the treaty before they would ratify it. Their main objection was the League of Nations' power to use military force. They were worried that as a member of the League, the United States

© Houghton Mifflin Harcourt Publishing Company

could be forced to send troops to war based on decisions made by the League of Nations. This, they argued, conflicted with Congress's constitutional power to declare war.

Wilson refused to compromise. He insisted that the treaty be ratified exactly as it was written. He traveled around the country, trying to convince the public to pressure Republican senators to vote for the treaty. Before he completed his tour, however, Wilson was weakened by a stroke.

Lodge announced that he was prepared to accept most of the treaty, though he still wanted to limit U.S. military commitment to the League of Nations. Wilson demanded that Democrats in the Senate refuse to change the treaty. When the vote was taken on November 19, 1919, neither the Democrats nor the Republicans would compromise. The Treaty of Versailles was defeated in the Senate.

It was a bitter disappointment for President Wilson. The United States signed separate peace treaties with Austria, Hungary, and Germany and never joined the League of Nations.

Causes and Effects of World War I

QUICK FACTS

Causes	Effects
• Nationalism • Militarism • Competition for territory • Alliance system in Europe	• U.S. entry into the war in 1917 • Millions of deaths and widespread destruction in Europe • Treaty of Versailles • Creation of several new nations • League of Nations

READING CHECK **Supporting a Point of View** Do you think Wilson should have compromised with Republicans in the Senate on the Treaty of Versailles? Why or why not?

SUMMARY World War I changed the world map and affected the lives of millions.

Section 4 Assessment

hmhsocialstudies.com
ONLINE QUIZ

Reviewing Ideas, Terms, and People

1. a. **Recall** Approximately how many soldiers were killed or wounded in World War I?
   b. **Draw Conclusions** How did the war affect the European economy?
   c. **Summarize** How did Americans try to fight the influenza epidemic of 1918?
2. a. **Define** What was the **League of Nations**?
   b. **Explain** How did the **Treaty of Versailles** change the map of Europe?
   c. **Elaborate** Which countries did not attend the Paris Peace Conference? How do you think this affected the outcome?
3. a. **Identify** Who was **Henry Cabot Lodge**?
   b. **Predict** How might Wilson have ensured that the U.S. Senate would ratify the Treaty of Versailles?

Critical Thinking

4. **Identifying Points of View** Review your notes on the Treaty of Versailles. Then copy the graphic organizer below and use it to compare the positions of Woodrow Wilson, Allied leaders, and Senate Republicans. Fill in the results of each person's or group's goals.

	Goals	Results
Woodrow Wilson		
Allied Leaders		
Senate Republicans		

Focus on Speaking

5. **Analyzing the Peace** Add to your list ways the United States was affected by World War I. How many American lives were lost? What were the results of the war? Do you think U.S. involvement in the war could have been avoided? Should the United States have joined the League of Nations?

© Houghton Mifflin Harcourt Publishing Company

Social Studies Skills

Analysis | Critical Thinking | Civic Participation | **Study**

21st Century

Using Visual Resources

Define the Skill

A major part of history is understanding the events and ideas of the past. Visual resources are often good sources of information about the past. Visual resources include paintings, drawings, cartoons, posters, and photographs. The symbols and images in these resources tell us about the ideas and values of a time period. They often provide different information and points of view than do written documents.

Learn the Skill

Visual resources can have special purposes. For example, the poster above was produced by the U.S. government to inspire patriotism and encourage support for the war effort. It uses symbols and images to suggest that all Americans can contribute to the war effort.

You know from reading the chapter that conserving food to provide supplies for troops was an important part of the war effort. This poster encourages Americans to can fruits and vegetables. The pictures show canned tomatoes and peas in glass jars.

The poster also shows the German kaiser in a jar. He cannot reach his sword, which is outside the jar. He is helpless. This suggests that, by canning fruit and vegetables, Americans can help defeat the German leader.

Practice the Skill

Study the World War I poster below. Like the poster above, it was produced by the U.S. government to encourage support for the war effort. Write a paragraph describing the poster. Your paragraph should include the specific purpose of the poster, the symbols it uses, and whether it conveys its message effectively. You can use the text above as a model.

© Houghton Mifflin Harcourt Publishing Company • Image Credits: (l), (r), Library of Congress Prints & Photographs Division, Washington, D.C.

CHAPTER 8

Chapter Review

History's Impact
▶ **video series**
Review the video to answer the closing question:
How did the U.S. entry into World War I affect the war's outcome and define the U.S. role in the global community?

Visual Summary

QUICK FACTS

Use the visual summary below to help you review the main ideas of the chapter.

The assassination of Archduke Francis Ferdinand threw Europe into a state of war.

Brutal fighting took place across Europe.

President Wilson thought a League of Nations would prevent future wars.

Reviewing Vocabulary, Terms, and People

Identify the descriptions below with the correct term or person from the chapter.

1. International assembly of nations designed to settle international disputes and encourage democracy

2. Strategy of defending a position by fighting from the protection of deep ditches

3. American fighting force trained and led by General John J. Pershing

4. Law that required men between the ages of 21 and 30 to register to be drafted into the armed forces

5. Senate leader who opposed the Treaty of Versailles

6. Truce between warring nations

7. Telegram from the German foreign minister proposing an alliance between Germany and Mexico against the United States

Comprehension and Critical Thinking

SECTION 1

8. a. Identify What event sparked World War I?

b. Explain How did tensions in Europe lead to war?

c. Draw Conclusions Why did the war in Europe become a stalemate?

SECTION 2

9. a. Recall What happened to the *Lusitania*? How did the American public react?

b. Analyze How did the country's mobilization for war affect American women?

c. Evaluate Do you think U.S. efforts to prepare for war were successful? Why or why not?

© Houghton Mifflin Harcourt Publishing Company

SECTION 3

10. a. Define How did the American Expeditionary Force prepare for war?

b. Contrast How was the Second Battle of the Marne different from the First Battle of the Marne?

c. Draw Conclusions Do you think the Allies would have won World War I without American help? Explain your answer.

SECTION 4

11. a. Recall Which nations' leaders dominated the Paris Peace Conference?

b. Summarize What were the main ideas of Wilson's Fourteen Points?

c. Predict How effective do you think the League of Nations was? Why?

Using the Internet

12. Activity: Researching the Technology of War World War I saw the introduction of many new technologies of warfare. The introduction of new weapons, like poison gas and machine guns, and combat vehicles, such as tanks and aircraft, made World War I deadlier than any previous war. Through your online textbook, research the new battlefield technologies in World War I. Then write three journal entries from the point of view of a soldier in the trenches. Your entries should describe what the soldier who experienced these technologies and inventions for the first time saw, felt, and thought. Remember to use facts from your research in your journal entries.

hmhsocialstudies.com

Reviewing Themes

13. Economics How did World War I affect the economy of the United States?

14. Politics What lasting political changes were brought about by World War I?

Social Studies Skills

Using Visual Resources *Use the Social Studies Skills taught in this chapter to answer the question below.*

15. What parts of the U.S. war effort are shown in this poster?

Reading Skills

Recognizing Fallacies in Reasoning *Use the Reading Skills taught in this chapter to answer the question about the reading selection below.*

> The number of soldiers killed in World War I was beyond anything the world had ever experienced. About 5 million Allied soldiers and 3.5 million soldiers from the Central Powers died in combat. More than 20 million soldiers on both sides were wounded.

16. Which of the following is an example of a false conclusion drawn from the selection above?

a. More soldiers were killed in World War I than in any war up to that point.

b. World War I devastated the European population.

c. Europe would never recover from World War I.

d. The number of soldiers wounded was more than two times the number of soldiers killed.

Focus on Speaking

17. Presenting Your Persuasive Speech Review your notes and form an opinion on whether the United States should have entered World War I. You will have about five minutes to present your point of view. Use note cards to organize your ideas. Begin by writing a one-sentence introduction clearly stating your opinion. Then write several sentences with details and examples from the chapter that support your point of view. Conclude your speech with a sentence that summarizes your ideas. Practice your speech and then present it to the class.

© Houghton Mifflin Harcourt Publishing Company • Image Credits: (t), ©K.J. Historical/Corbis

CHAPTER 8 Standardized Test Practice

DIRECTIONS: Read each question and write the letter of the best response.

1 Which of the following was made up of Germany, Austria-Hungary, the Ottoman Empire, and Bulgaria?

A Central Powers
B Allied Powers
C League of Nations
D Big Four

2 The Communist takeover of the Russian government caused

A the armistice to go into effect.
B a German victory at the Second Battle of the Marne.
C the United States to remain neutral.
D Russia to leave the war.

3 During the war, many African Americans

A gained equal rights because of their military service.
B served in segregated units in the military.
C were removed from jobs in war industries and the military.
D volunteered to serve in the military without pay.

4 One reason the United States entered World War I was Germany's violation of

A the Treaty of Versailles.
B the Zimmermann Note.
C the *Sussex* pledge.
D Wilson's Fourteen Points.

5 A major opponent of the Treaty of Versailles was

A Otto von Bismarck.
B Woodrow Wilson.
C Henry Cabot Lodge.
D John J. Pershing.

6 Which of the following technologies was important to warfare at sea during World War I?

A U-boats
B bayonets
C ironclads
D poison gas

7 Examine the fourth of Woodrow Wilson's Fourteen Points and use it to answer the question below:

> "Adequate guarantees given and taken that national armaments [weapons] will be reduced to the lowest point consistent with domestic safety."
>
> —Woodrow Wilson, Fourteen Points

Document-Based Question Why do you think Wilson wanted to reduce the amount of weapons in nations around the world?

© Houghton Mifflin Harcourt Publishing Company

Dear home: LETTERS FROM WWI

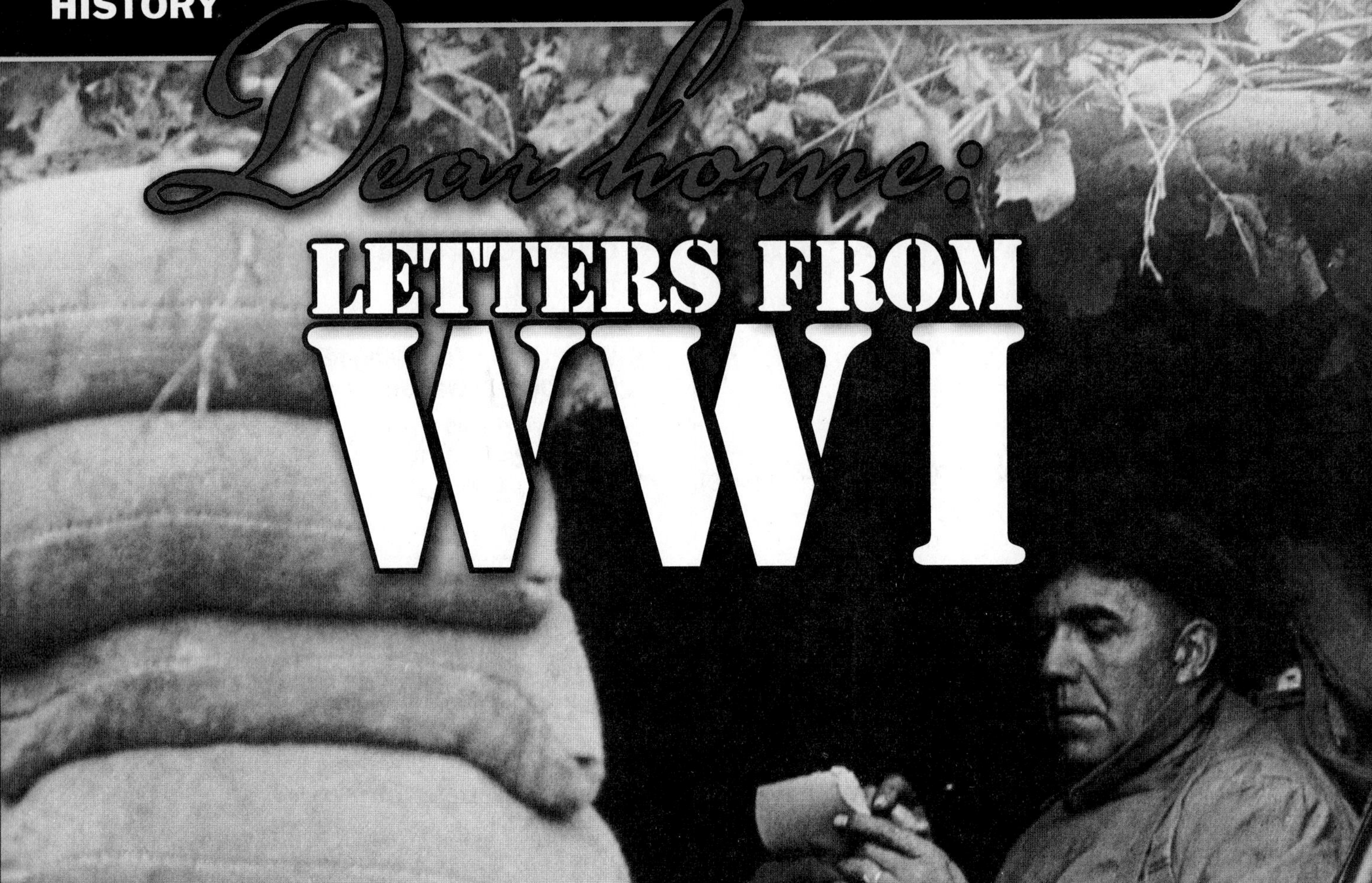

When U.S. troops arrived in Europe in 1917 to fight in World War I, the war had been dragging on for nearly three years. The American soldiers suddenly found themselves in the midst of chaos. Each day, they faced the threats of machine gun fire, poison gas, and aerial attacks. Still, the arrival of American reinforcements had sparked a new zeal among the Allies, who believed the new forces could finally turn the tide in their favor. The letters soldiers wrote to their families back home reveal the many emotions they felt on the battlefield: confusion about their surroundings, fear for their own safety, concern for friends and loved ones, and hope that the war would soon be over.

Explore World War I online through the eyes of the soldiers who fought in it. You can find a wealth of information, video clips, primary sources, activities, and more at hmhsocialstudies.com.

© Houghton Mifflin Harcourt Publishing Company • Image Credits: (c) ©Bettmann/Corbis

"I have been on every front in France. You cant imagine how torn up this country really is. Every where there are wire entanglements and trenches and dugouts. Even out of the war zone there are entanglements and dugouts to protect the civilians from air raids."

-Corp. Albert Smith, U.S. soldier

Letter from France

Read the document to learn about one soldier's observations of wartime life.

CLICK THROUGH

INTER/ACTIVITIES

hmhsocialstudies.com

Over There

Watch the video to learn about the experiences of American soldiers on the way to Europe and upon their arrival.

War on the Western Front

Watch the video to hear one soldier's vivid account of battle and its aftermath.

Surrender!

Watch the video to experience soldiers' reactions to the news that the war was finally over.

© Houghton Mifflin Harcourt Publishing Company • Image Credits: (c), ©Bettmann/Corbis

21st CENTURY

Assignment
Find a primary source from World War I and write an analysis of it.

Analyzing a Primary Source

Primary sources are often the best sources of information available to historians. Primary sources provide answers to questions about the past. They also provide a unique point of view from the past. Analyzing a primary source allows you to share that information.

TIP **Using the Internet** If you find a primary source on the Internet, make sure it is accurate. You should be able to identify the person or institution that runs the Web site and make sure that person or institution is trustworthy. The Web site should include basic information about the source, such as its author, when it was written, and where it first appeared. University and library Web sites are excellent places to find primary sources.

1. Prewrite

Locating Primary Sources

Many primary sources are available in libraries and on the Internet. Letters, diaries, autobiographies, memoirs, newspaper articles, public speeches, and legal documents are good examples of primary sources.

Reading the Primary Source

Take notes on these questions to better understand the document.

- Who wrote the document?
- What kind of document is it?
- When was it written? Where did it originally appear?
- What was the author's point of view? What was his or her experience during the war?
- Why did the author write the document?

As you read the primary source, take notes on these questions.

- Why is the document important? The answer to this question will be the main idea of your essay.
- What questions about World War I does it answer? Answering this question will help you write your body paragraphs.

2. Write

You can use this framework to help you write your first draft.

A Writer's Framework

Introduction	Body	Conclusion
■ Introduce your primary source and its main purpose. ■ Introduce the author of the source and include the date it was written. ■ State your main idea, explaining why this source is important.	■ Explain how the source answers at least two questions about World War I. ■ Include examples from the document.	■ Summarize the information in the source. ■ Restate why the document is important for historians.

© Houghton Mifflin Harcourt Publishing Company

3. Evaluate and Revise

Evaluating

Use these questions to discover ways to improve your paper.

Evaluation Questions for Analyzing a Primary Source

- Do you introduce your primary source with its main purpose?
- Do you introduce the author of the source and the document's date?
- Do you state a main idea explaining why this source is important?
- Do you explain how the source answers at least two questions about World War I?
- Do you include examples from the document?
- Do you summarize the information in the source?

Revising

Make sure each paragraph has a topic sentence at the beginning. Then check the information in the paragraph. It should all relate to the topic sentence. If it does not, there are several ways to fix the paragraph. First, you can remove unrelated information. If the information is related but not clearly explained, add a more detailed explanation. You can also change the topic sentence to include all the information in the paragraph.

TIP Using Pronouns Effectively

Use pronouns such as *he, she,* and *it* to replace frequently used nouns and proper nouns. This will help you vary your sentences. Make sure that the person or thing to which each pronoun refers is clear. If it is not, repeat the original noun or name.

EXAMPLE

Woodrow Wilson proposed a peace plan called the Fourteen Points. He wanted to make sure the postwar peace would last.

4. Proofread and Publish

Proofreading

Reread your paper carefully to make sure all the verbs are in the same tense. The past tense is usually best for history writing. Summaries of primary sources should also be in the past tense. A direct quotation from a primary source, however, should remain in its original tense.

Publishing

Share your paper with a classmate. Read each other's papers. Then write a one-paragraph summary of the new information you each learned.

5. Practice and Apply

Use the steps and strategies in this workshop to analyze your primary source.

© Houghton Mifflin Harcourt Publishing Company

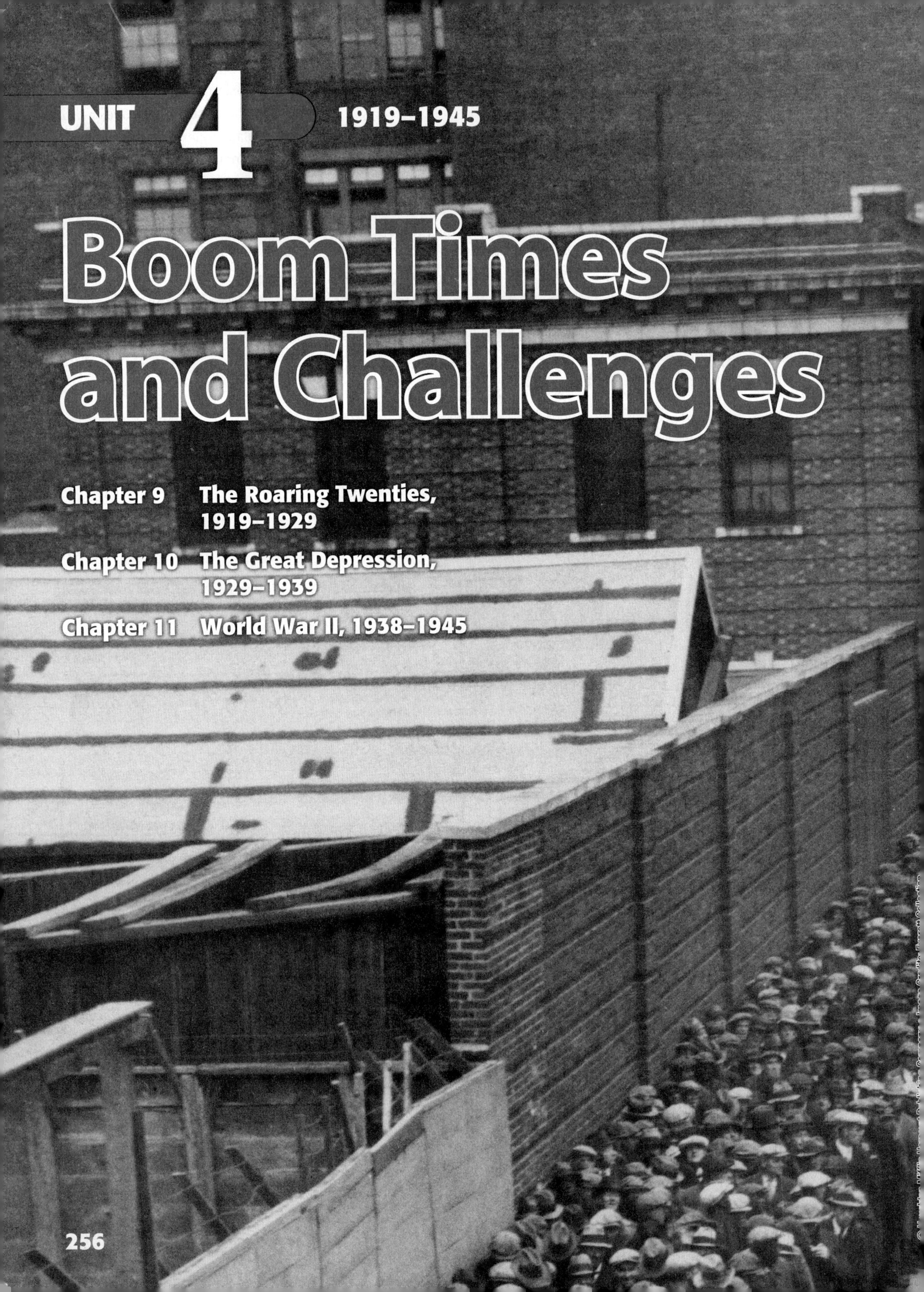

UNIT 4 1919–1945

Boom Times and Challenges

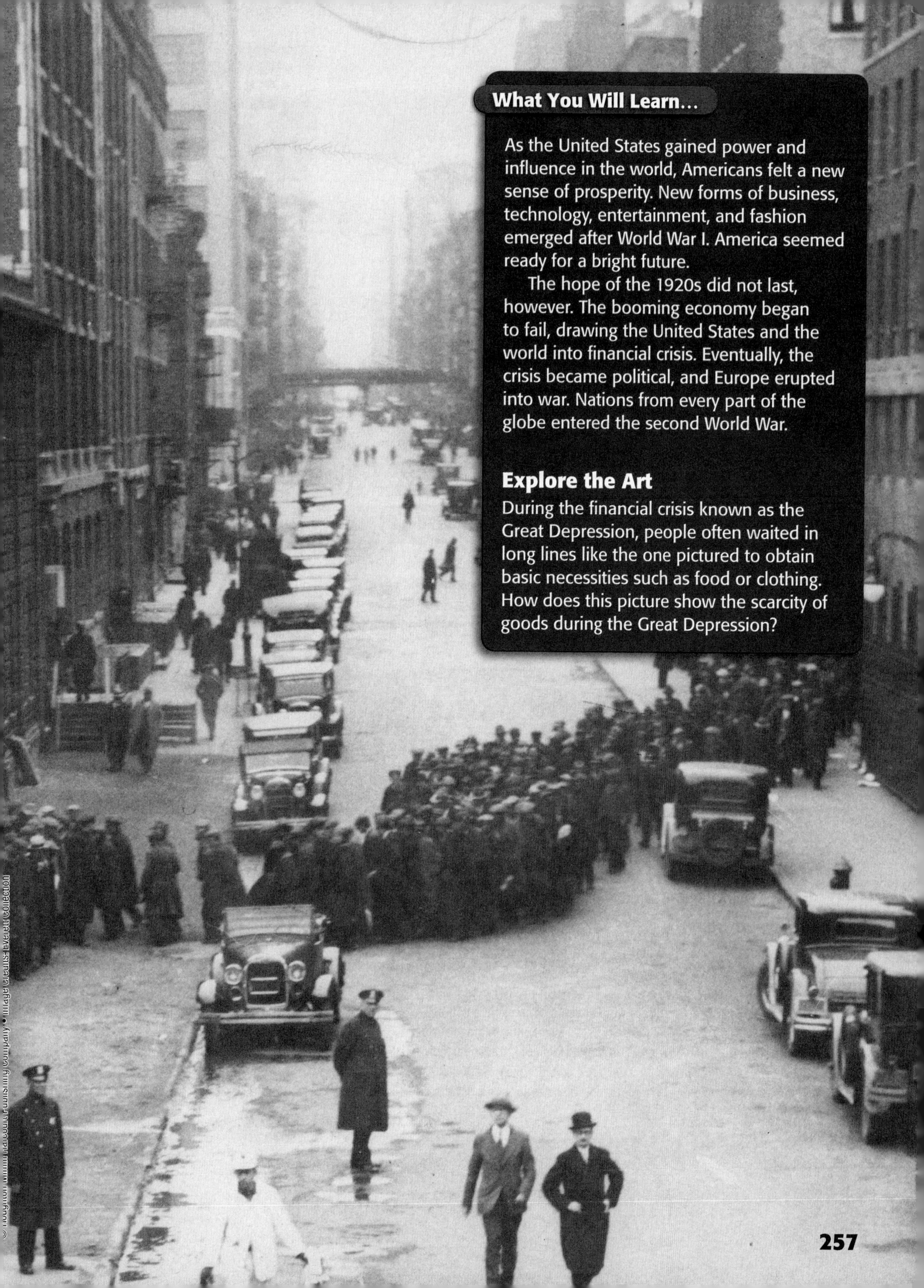

What You Will Learn...

As the United States gained power and influence in the world, Americans felt a new sense of prosperity. New forms of business, technology, entertainment, and fashion emerged after World War I. America seemed ready for a bright future.

The hope of the 1920s did not last, however. The booming economy began to fail, drawing the United States and the world into financial crisis. Eventually, the crisis became political, and Europe erupted into war. Nations from every part of the globe entered the second World War.

Explore the Art

During the financial crisis known as the Great Depression, people often waited in long lines like the one pictured to obtain basic necessities such as food or clothing. How does this picture show the scarcity of goods during the Great Depression?

© Houghton Mifflin Harcourt Publishing Company • Image Credits: Everett Collection

CHAPTER 9 1919–1929

The Roaring Twenties

Essential Question How did American society change during the Roaring Twenties?

ALABAMA COURSE OF STUDY

2 Describe reform movements and changing social conditions during the Progressive Era in the United States.

- Explaining Progressive movement provisions of the Sixteenth, Seventeenth, Eighteenth, Nineteenth, and Twenty-first Amendments to the Constitution of the United States.

3 Identify causes and consequences of World War I and reasons for United States' entry into the war.

- Explaining the intensification of isolationism in the United States after World War I.

4 Identify cultural and economic developments in the United States from 1900 through the 1930s.

- Describing the impact of various writers, musicians, and artists on American culture during the Harlem Renaissance and the Jazz Age.
- Identifying contributions of turn-of-the-century inventors.
- Describing the emergence of the modern woman during the early 1900s.
- Identifying notable persons of the early 1900s.
- Comparing results of the economic policies of the Warren G. Harding, Calvin Coolidge, and Herbert Hoover Administrations.

Focus on Writing

Radio Advertisement Radio stations began to air regular broadcasts in the 1920s. Radios linked Americans from coast to coast, allowing them to hear the same programs—and the same advertisements. In the 1920s Americans with means had new choices in entertainment, travel, fashion, and convenience. In this chapter, you will read about these new choices. You will then write a radio advertisement for a new product or form of entertainment of the 1920s.

United States

1920 Warren Harding wins the presidency in a landslide victory.

1920

World

1920 The League of Nations is established.

Image Credits: (t), *The Great White Way, Times Square*, 1925 (oil on canvas), Thain, Howard A. (1891-1959)/©New-York Historical Society, New York, USA/Bridgeman Art Library; (b), HMH Photo by Lance Schriner

© Houghton Mifflin Harcourt Publishing Company

HISTORY America Goes Dry with Prohibition

hmhsocialstudies.com VIDEO

People flocked to bustling city centers like New York City's Times Square.

1922 The tomb of King Tutankhamen is discovered.

1924 Native Americans are granted the right of U.S. citizenship.

1924 Joseph Stalin becomes dictator of Communist Russia.

1926 Ernest Hemingway publishes *The Sun Also Rises.*

1926 Prince Hirohito becomes emperor of Japan.

1928 Alexander Fleming discovers penicillin.

1929 Construction begins on the Empire State Building.

1922 | 1924 | 1926 | 1928 | 1930

Image Credits: (t), *The Great White Way, Times Square*, 1925 (oil on canvas), Thain, Howard A. (1891-1959)/©New-York Historical Society, New York, USA/Bridgeman Art Library; (c), The Granger Collection, New York; (bc), ©Bettmann/Corbis; (cr), Brown Brothers; (bl), Egyptian National Museum, Cairo, Egypt/SuperStock

© Houghton Mifflin Harcourt Publishing Company

Reading Social Studies

Economics | Geography | Politics | Society and Culture | Science and Technology

Focus on Themes In this chapter, you will learn about the decade of the 1920s, a period called the Roaring Twenties. During this time, many in **society** thought that the Great War would be the last major war and that the future was bright. Also during this time, **science and technology** made leaps forward that would make life easier for millions of Americans.

Synthesizing Information

Focus on Reading Learning about history means synthesizing, or combining, many different sources about the past. When you read this textbook, you are reading a synthesis of other sources, accounts, and ideas about history.

Synthesizing Once you have identified the subject you are studying, you should try to read as many different accounts of the story as you can. Be sure to investigate the author of a source to learn what his or her goals might be. Compare and contrast the different sources and evaluate which ones you believe. Finally, use all the various stories you have read to form your own interpretation of what happened in history.

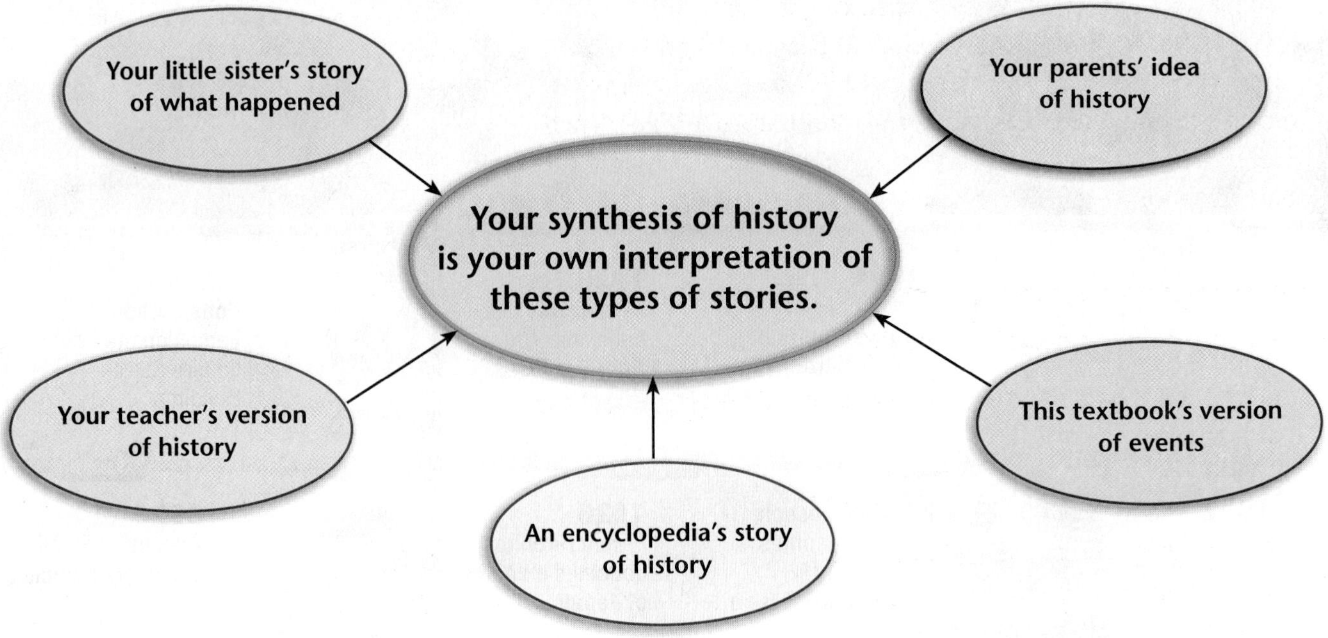

Your little sister's story of what happened
Your parents' idea of history
Your synthesis of history is your own interpretation of these types of stories.
Your teacher's version of history
This textbook's version of events
An encyclopedia's story of history

© Houghton Mifflin Harcourt Publishing Company

You Try It!

Read these varying accounts of the assassination of Archduke Francis Ferdinand and his wife, Sophie. Then write your own version of the story.

> "Two bullets fired on a Sarajevo street on a sunny June morning in 1914 set in motion a series of events that shaped the world we live in today. World War One, World War Two, the Cold War and its conclusion all trace their origins to the gunshots that interrupted that summer day."
>
> –Anonymous

> "As the car came abreast he stepped forward from the curb, drew his automatic pistol from his coat and fired two shots. The first struck the wife of the Archduke, the Archduchess Sofia, in the abdomen . . . She died instantly. The second bullet struck the Archduke close to the heart. He uttered only one word, 'Sofia'—a call to his stricken wife. Then his head fell back and he collapsed. He died almost instantly."
>
> –conspirator Borijove Jevtic

> "As I was pulling out my handkerchief to wipe the blood away from his mouth, the duchess cried out to him, 'In Heaven's name, what has happened to you?' At that she slid off the seat and lay on the floor of the car ... I had no idea that she too was hit and thought she had simply fainted with fright. Then I heard His Imperial Highness say, "Sopherl, Sopherl, don't die. Stay alive for the children!"
>
> –guard Count Franz von Harrach,
> quoted in "Assassination of an Archduke," *Eyewitness to History*

1. What differences do you notice between accounts?

2. Why might these different authors have a different view of the assassination?

3. How can you tell what each author's viewpoint is?

4. Write your own version of what might have happened. Use details that you believe from the sources above.

As you read this chapter, notice any differing views from different sources.

Key Terms and People

Chapter 9

Section 1
Warren G. Harding
Calvin Coolidge
Teapot Dome scandal
Kellogg-Briand Pact
Model T
moving assembly line
Herbert Hoover

Section 2
flappers
Red Scare
Twenty-first Amendment
fundamentalism
Scopes trial
Great Migration
Marcus Garvey

Section 3
talkie
Jazz Age
Harlem Renaissance
Langston Hughes
Lost Generation
expatriates
Georgia O'Keeffe

Academic Vocabulary

In this chapter, you will learn the following academic words:
incentive
traditional
innovation

© Houghton Mifflin Harcourt Publishing Company

SECTION 1

Boom Times

What You Will Learn...

Main Ideas

1. President Harding promised a return to peace and prosperity.
2. Calvin Coolidge supported a probusiness agenda.
3. American business boomed in the 1920s.
4. In 1928, Americans elected Herbert Hoover, hoping he would help good financial times continue.

The Big Idea

American industries boomed in the 1920s, changing many Americans' way of life.

Key Terms and People

Warren G. Harding
Calvin Coolidge
Teapot Dome scandal
Kellogg-Briand Pact
Model T
moving assembly line
Herbert Hoover

hmhsocialstudies.com
TAKING NOTES

Use the graphic organizer online to take notes on the presidents of the 1920s.

If YOU were there...

You have been working in a car factory for years, and now you have finally bought a car of your own—a shiny new 1920 Ford Model T. As you set out on your first drive, the car rattles and bounces over unpaved roads that were designed for horse-and-buggy travel. But you don't mind the rough ride. You now have the freedom to drive anywhere you want to go!

How will owning a car change your life?

BUILDING BACKGROUND The American economy boomed during World War I, as industries raced to produce weapons and supplies for the Allied armies. With more than 4 million men serving in the armed forces, there was a shortage of workers in American factories, and many people found jobs. When the war ended, however, conditions changed quickly, and the economy faced a difficult adjustment.

Return to Peace and Prosperity

The end of World War I had an immediate impact on the American economy. Because the government no longer needed war supplies, it canceled billions of dollars' worth of contracts with American factories. This meant that factories cut back on production at the very moment that millions of soldiers left the military and began looking for jobs. The result was a sharp rise in unemployment. Meanwhile, many people who did have jobs rushed to buy products they could not buy during the war. This caused prices to soar. Wages could not keep up with the rising prices, and thus workers could no longer afford to buy the goods they needed and wanted. Many went on strike for higher wages—more than 4 million in 1919 alone.

As the 1920 presidential election approached, the economic difficulties were bad news for the party in power, Woodrow Wilson's Democratic Party. Many voters blamed the Democrats for the hard times. Sensing the public's anger, the Republicans looked for a candidate who would offer new hope for American voters. They chose **Warren G. Harding**, a senator from Ohio. Harding picked Governor **Calvin Coolidge** of Massachusetts as his running mate.

© Houghton Mifflin Harcourt Publishing Company

Primary Source

POLITICAL CARTOON

Teapot Dome

During the Teapot Dome scandal, people began to question the judgment and honesty of government leaders. This cartoon, called "Juggernaut," was published in 1924 to show how harmful the scandal had been. A juggernaut is an indestructible force that crushes everything in its path.

How do the images in the cartoon illustrate the destructive force of the scandal?

ANALYSIS SKILL **ANALYZING PRIMARY SOURCES**

Why do you think the artist called this cartoon "Juggernaut"?

Harding based his campaign strategy on a promise to return the country to stability and prosperity, what he called "normalcy." His conservative policies contrasted with the reform-minded policies of the Progressive Era. Harding summed up his ideas in a campaign speech:

> "America's present need is not heroics, but healing; not nostrums [uncertain cures] but normalcy [normal times]; not revolution, but restoration."
>
> —Warren G. Harding, 1920

Democrats believed there was still support for Wilson's ideas for reform. They ran Ohio governor James M. Cox for president, and New York's Franklin D. Roosevelt for vice president. But Harding's promise of a return to normalcy captured the public's mood in 1920. Harding won a landslide victory with about 60 percent of the popular vote.

Harding worked quickly to help strengthen the economy. He put together a cabinet of experts who believed in reducing money owed by the government and limiting government involvement in the economy. Secretary of the Treasury Andrew Mellon pushed for tax cuts for wealthy Americans. Mellon believed that this policy would give the wealthy an <u>**incentive**</u> to invest in new businesses and create new jobs for other Americans. Mellon's opponents called this idea the trickle-down theory, arguing that money would only "trickle down" in small drops to less-well-off Americans.

While Harding was president, businesses did in fact bounce back from the postwar recession. The economy created new, better-paying jobs, leading to an economic boom that lasted for most of the decade.

Harding faced problems in other areas, however. He had appointed many of his trusted friends to high positions. Some of these men used their positions to gain wealth through illegal means. "I have no trouble with my enemies," Harding once said. "But my . . . friends . . . keep me walking the floor nights."

What came to be known as the the **Teapot Dome scandal** involved Secretary of the Interior Albert Fall, who accepted large sums of money and valuable gifts from private oil companies. In exchange, Fall allowed the companies to control government oil reserves in Elk Hills, California, and Teapot Dome, Wyoming. The U.S. Senate soon began investigating Fall, who was convicted of accepting bribes. He was the first cabinet member ever to be convicted of a crime for his actions while in office.

READING CHECK **Summarizing** What did Harding mean when he promised a return to normalcy?

HISTORY

VIDEO
Warren G. Harding

hmhsocialstudies.com

ACADEMIC VOCABULARY

incentive something that encourages people to behave a certain way

Coolidge's Probusiness Administration

Just before details of the Teapot Dome scandal became public, President Harding died of a heart attack. In August 1923 Vice President Calvin Coolidge took charge. Coolidge had a strong reputation as an honest and trustworthy leader. These qualities helped him restore confidence in the government.

Coolidge acted quickly to fire all officials who had been involved in the bribery scandals of Harding's administration. This helped him win the presidential election in 1924. He received nearly twice as many votes as the Democratic candidate, John W. Davis.

THE IMPACT TODAY

Countries still try to prevent wars with international agreements. More than 180 nations have signed the Treaty on the Non-Proliferation of Nuclear Weapons, an agreement to prevent the spread of nuclear weapons.

Coolidge proved to be even more pro-business than Harding had been. He once declared that "the business of America is business." He expanded the policies started under Harding, such as tax cuts for wealthier citizens. He also supported raising tariffs on foreign goods to decrease competition with domestic products. Despite higher tariffs, trade with other countries actually increased under Coolidge. This was mainly because many nations depended on trade with the United States to rebuild their economies after World War I. Not everyone profited from Coolidge's efforts, however. Coolidge vetoed congressional attempts to provide aid to farmers through the regulation of prices.

Like the United States, European nations wanted a return to prosperity. Europeans also wanted to avoid another devastating war. In 1928 the United States and 14 other nations signed the **Kellogg-Briand Pact**, an agreement that outlawed war. Eventually 62 nations accepted the pact. There was no way to enforce the pact, however. One U.S. senator complained that the treaty would be "as effective to keep down war as a carpet would be to smother an earthquake." Still, it was a sign that most countries wanted to prevent another global conflict.

READING CHECK **Comparing and Contrasting** How were Harding and Coolidge similar, and how were they different?

The Model T Assembly Line

CONNECT TO SCIENCE AND TECHNOLOGY

Early assembly lines involved workers moving down a line of parts. On a moving assembly line, workers along the line specialize in one or two simple assembly tasks that they perform as parts move past them. The moving assembly line greatly increases the efficiency of mass production.

These workers are building flywheel magnetos, a part of the ignition system of early engines.

Business Booms

The 1920s were years of rapid economic growth in the United States. Between 1921 and 1929, U.S. manufacturing nearly doubled. As jobs and wages increased, so did people's ability to buy new products. Some of these products changed the way Americans lived.

Ford's Model T

Today we think of cars as a major part of American life. In the early 1900s, though, cars were seen as luxury items that only the wealthy could afford. Henry Ford, an inventor and business leader from Detroit, helped to change this. Ford dreamed of building a car that most Americans could afford:

> "I will build a motor car for the great multitude [most of the people]. It will be large enough for the family but small enough for the individual to run and care for. It . . . will be so low in price that no man making a good salary will be unable to own one."
>
> —Henry Ford, quoted in *Daily Life in the United States, 1920–1940,* by David E. Kyvig

Ford achieved his goal by building a sturdy and reliable car called the **Model T**, nicknamed the Tin Lizzie. In 1908 the Model T sold for $850. By 1925 it cost just $290. Ford was able to make his car affordable by cutting costs of production. For example, every car looked the same. The Model T came only in black for many years.

To decrease the time it took to make the cars, Ford also began using a **moving assembly line**. This system used conveyer belts to move parts and partly assembled cars from one group of workers to another. The workers stood in one place and did a specialized job.

The chassis, or frame, and the engine are assembled on separate lines. Workers on a third line then attach them.

The assembled chassis is then connected to the body of the car.

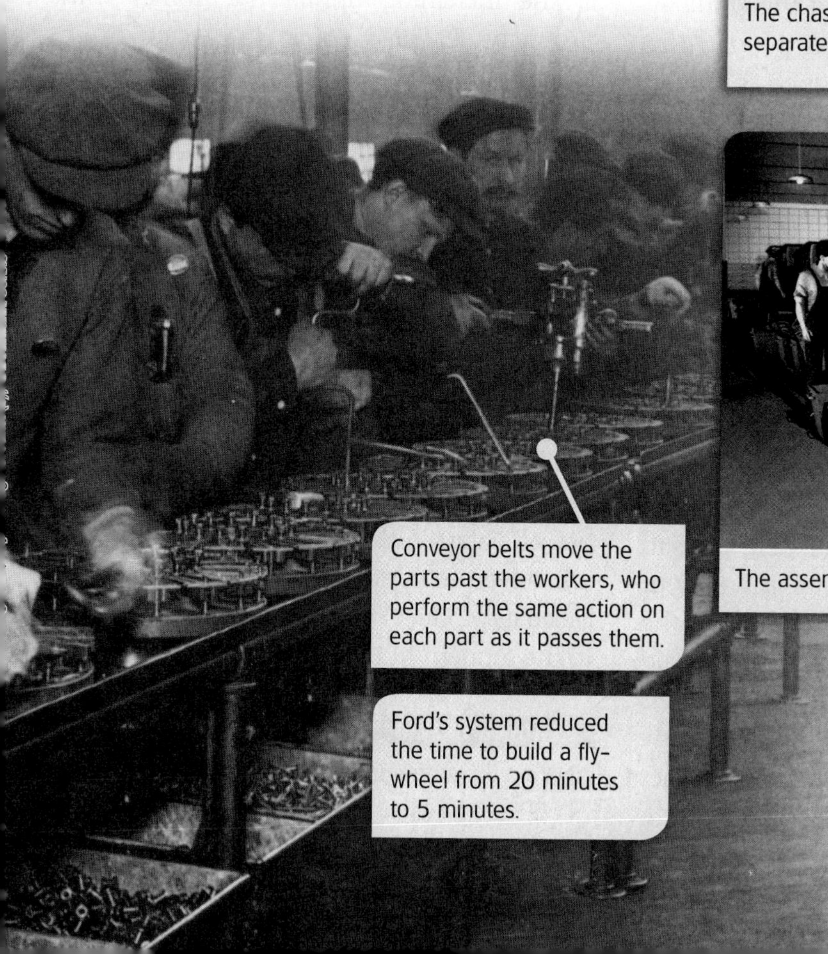

Conveyor belts move the parts past the workers, who perform the same action on each part as it passes them.

Ford's system reduced the time to build a flywheel from 20 minutes to 5 minutes.

ANALYSIS SKILL ANALYZING VISUALS

How does the moving assembly line reduce the time it takes to build a car?

The Model T

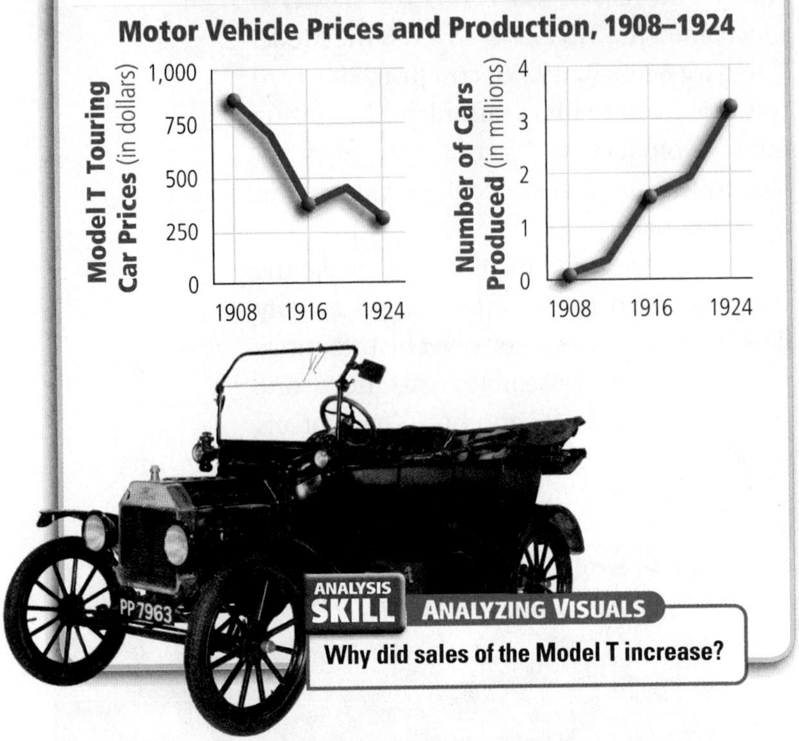

ANALYSIS SKILL ANALYZING VISUALS

Why did sales of the Model T increase?

In 1914 Ford raised the wages for his factory workers to $5 a day. This was good pay, compared with the $2 or $3 per day offered by many other factories. Ford believed the wage increase would keep his employees from quitting. He also lowered the workday to eight hours and employed people that other factories would not hire, such as African Americans and people with disabilities.

Even with the good wages, many workers had a hard time adjusting to the fast-paced and repetitive work on Ford's assembly line. One wife of an autoworker wrote to Ford saying, "My husband has come home and thrown himself down and won't eat his supper—so done out [tired]! . . . That $5 a day is a blessing—a bigger one than you know, but oh they earn it."

FOCUS ON READING
How is this paragraph an example of synthesized information?

To help make his cars more affordable, Ford allowed customers to buy cars using an installment plan. Most people were used to saving up for years to buy items. Installment plans let people pay a small amount of the cost every month until the entire car was paid for. Ford's competitors also allowed customers to pay with installment plans. For a slightly higher price than the Model T, companies such as General Motors offered cars in a variety of colors and with more power.

The automobile changed the way Americans lived. They could now go on long drives or take jobs farther away from where they lived. Cars gave people a sense of freedom and adventure. As *Motor Car* magazine told drivers, "You are your master, the road is ahead . . . your freedom is complete."

Growing Industries

The rise of the automobile affected the entire American economy. Millions of Americans found work making steel for car bodies, rubber for tires, or glass for windows. To improve road safety, the government spent millions of dollars paving highways and building new bridges. People opened roadside businesses to serve travelers, such as gas stations, restaurants, and motels. The rising number of cars also created a demand for car repair shops and car insurance.

Following Ford's example, other manufacturers began using assembly lines and allowing customers to pay on installment plans. Many companies also took advantage of the increasing number of homes with electricity. By 1929 about 85 percent of all Americans living in towns or cities had electricity. Companies responded by building new electrical appliances designed to make household chores easier, such as washing machines, vacuum cleaners, and refrigerators.

As companies competed to sell these new goods, the advertising industry boomed. Companies advertised in magazines and on the radio to convince people that their lives would be improved if they owned a certain product. Many advertisers targeted women, hoping to convince them that they needed the newest labor-saving products. For example, one advertisement for an electric dishwasher called its product "the greatest gift of electricity to the modern housewife."

READING CHECK **Identifying Cause and Effect** How did the automobile change society?

Hoover Elected

With the economy booming, public support for the Republican Party remained strong. When President Coolidge decided not to run for reelection in 1928, the party chose his secretary of commerce, **Herbert Hoover**, as its nominee. The Democrats nominated New York governor Alfred E. Smith.

Hoover told voters that he was the right choice to maintain economic prosperity. Hoover boldly claimed that "we in America today are nearer to the final triumph over poverty than ever before in the history of any land."

Smith's campaign focused mainly on issues facing city dwellers. This concerned some rural voters. Smith's religious faith also became an issue. He was the first Catholic to run for president. His opponents stirred up fears that Smith would be controlled by the pope and other church officials. In the end, Hoover won easily, gaining 58 percent of the popular vote.

READING CHECK **Drawing Conclusions** What helped Herbert Hoover win the presidency in 1928?

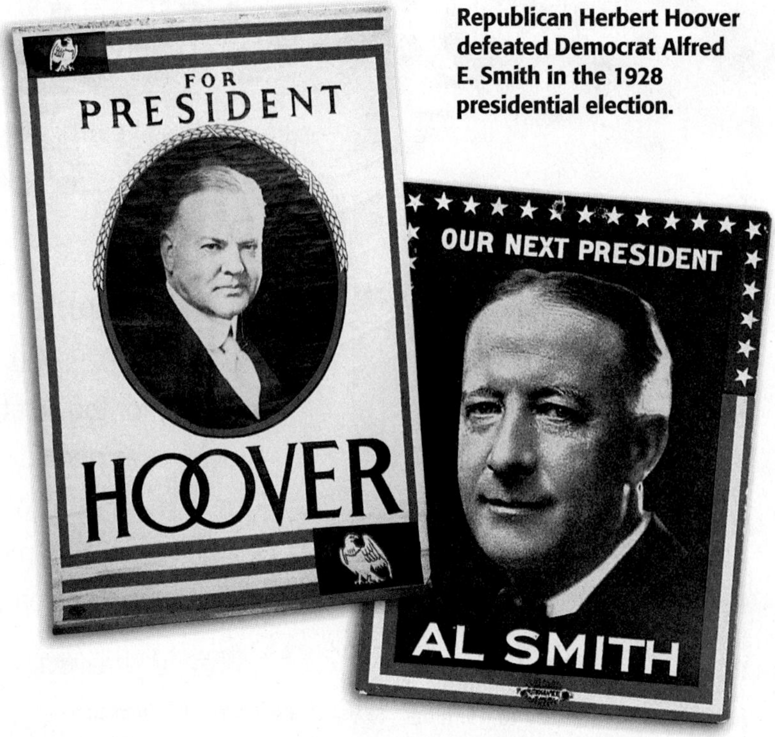

Republican Herbert Hoover defeated Democrat Alfred E. Smith in the 1928 presidential election.

SUMMARY In this section you learned about politics and the economy in the 1920s.

Section 1 Assessment

hmhsocialstudies.com
ONLINE QUIZ

Reviewing Ideas, Terms, and People

1. a. **Describe** What was the result of the 1920 presidential election, and why?
   b. **Summarize** What did the **Teapot Dome scandal** reveal about **Warren G. Harding**'s administration?
2. a. **Identify** Who succeeded Harding as president, and what were his main policies?
   b. **Analyze** What was the main weakness of the **Kellogg-Briand Pact**?
3. a. **Recall** Why did American businesses grow during the 1920s?
   b. **Explain** Why were Model T prices low?
4. a. **Recall** Why was **Herbert Hoover** elected?
   b. **Elaborate** Who would you have voted for in the 1928 election? Explain your answer.

Critical Thinking

5. **Summarizing** Review your notes on the presidents from the 1920s. Then copy the graphic organizer below and expand on your notes by summarizing the main ideas or achievements of each president.

President	Ideas/ Achievements

Focus on Writing

6. **Taking Notes on Consumer Goods** Make a list of new products people had access to in this decade, including cheaper automobiles and appliances for the home. Be sure to note how these products improved the lives of Americans. Use the information about advertising in this section to help you with ideas for your radio advertisement.

SECTION 2

Life during the 1920s

What You Will Learn...

Main Ideas

1. In the 1920s many young people found new independence in a changing society.
2. Postwar tensions occasionally led to fear and violence.
3. Competing ideals caused conflict between Americans with traditional beliefs and those with modern views.
4. Following the war, minority groups organized to demand their civil rights.

The Big Idea

Americans faced new opportunities, challenges, and fears as major changes swept the country in the 1920s.

Key Terms and People

flappers
Red Scare
Twenty-first Amendment
fundamentalism
Scopes trial
Great Migration
Marcus Garvey

hmhsocialstudies.com
TAKING NOTES

Use the graphic organizer online to take notes on changes that affected American life in the 1920s.

If YOU were there...

The year is 1925. You have just finished school and you are visiting a big city for the first time. You and your friends go to a club and watch young people dancing energetically to popular music. The women have short hair and wear makeup, trying to copy the glamorous style of movie stars. Some of your friends start talking about finding an apartment and looking for jobs in the city.

Would you want to move to a big city in 1925? Why?

BUILDING BACKGROUND The United States enjoyed nearly a decade of economic expansion during the 1920s. American society changed rapidly during this period. Although many people welcomed the new opportunities, others felt their traditional beliefs were being challenged. Conflicts between competing ideals and different groups of people ruffled the surface of America's peace and prosperity.

A Changing Society

The experience of living through World War I changed the way many young people saw the world around them. Young men returning from Europe had visited far-off countries and learned about other cultures. Many of them came home with a desire to continue expanding their horizons. The title of one popular song in 1919 asked, "How 'Ya Gonna Keep 'em Down on the Farm after They've Seen Paree [Paris]"?

Many young people moved away from farms and small towns to cities. By 1920, for the first time in American history, more than half of the country's population lived in urban areas. Young people took advantage of the economic opportunities of the 1920s to gain independence. In the past most young people had lived and worked at home until they got married. Now more young adults were experiencing a time of freedom before settling down. A new youth culture developed, which included going to parties and dance clubs, listening to popular music, and driving fast cars.

For many young Americans, access to education was an important part of this new independence. High school attendance doubled during the decade. The percentage of students going on to college was higher in the United States than in any other country. This included women, who were attending college in higher numbers than ever before.

The number of women in the workforce continued to grow as well. Women with college degrees worked as nurses, teachers, librarians, and social workers. Women were also finding new opportunities in politics. In 1925 Nellie Tayloe Ross (Wyoming) and Miriam "Ma" Ferguson (Texas) became the first women to serve as governors in the United States. Three years later, there were 145 women serving in state legislatures. Five women had won terms in the U.S. House of Representatives.

Women were still discouraged from pursuing fields such as medicine, law, and architecture, however. By the end of the 1920s, less than 5 percent of the country's doctors, lawyers, and architects were women. The percentage was small—but it was beginning to rise.

Some young women found other ways to express their freedom. Young women known as **flappers** cut their hair short and wore makeup and short dresses, openly challenging traditional ideas of how women were supposed to behave. Many older Americans considered this behavior scandalous. One 1920s writer expressed her admiration for flappers, saying:

> "I want my girl to do what she pleases, be what she pleases . . . I want [my daughter] to be a flapper, because flappers are brave."
>
> —Zelda Fitzgerald, quoted in *Zelda*, by Nancy Milford

Fashion magazines, Hollywood movies, and advertising helped promote these new images and ideas of youthful freedom.

READING CHECK **Generalizing** How did women in the 1920s express their independence?

Focus on Women

In 1923 suffrage leader Alice Paul introduced the Equal Rights Amendment to Congress, calling for equality of rights regardless of a person's gender. The U.S. Senate passed the amendment 49 years later, but it was never ratified by the states.

Bryn Mawr and other colleges provided education to women in new fields.

Bessie Coleman became the first African American woman to obtain her international pilot's license. She traveled the United States, performing stunts under the name "Brave Bessie."

Flappers challenged many of society's ideas about womanhood. They established new rules of speech, dress, and behavior.

ANALYSIS SKILL **ANALYZING VISUALS**

How do these images reflect new roles for women during the 1920s?

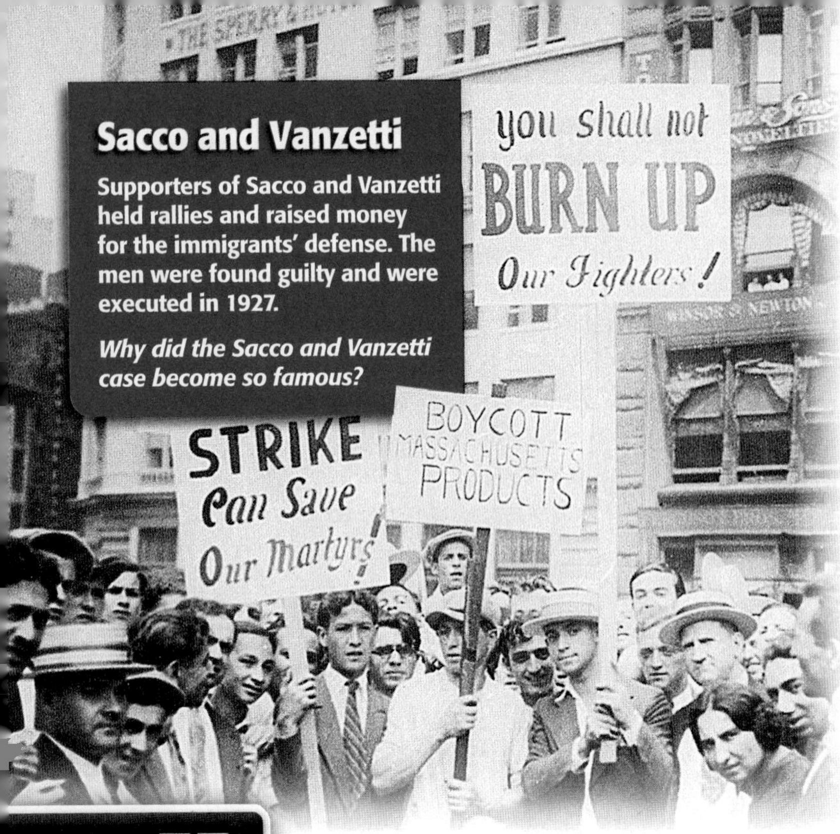
you shall not
BURN UP
Our Fighters!
STRIKE
Can Save
Our Martyrs
BOYCOTT
MASSACHUSETTS
PRODUCTS

Sacco and Vanzetti

Supporters of Sacco and Vanzetti held rallies and raised money for the immigrants' defense. The men were found guilty and were executed in 1927.

Why did the Sacco and Vanzetti case become so famous?

HISTORY

VIDEO
The True Story of Sacco and Vanzetti

hmhsocialstudies.com

Fear and Violence

Not all social changes during the 1920s were peaceful. You have read about the hard times that hit the U.S. economy after World War I—unemployment, inflation, and labor disputes that resulted in large strikes. These troubles worried many Americans. In this atmosphere, suspicion of foreigners and radicals, or people who believe in an extreme change in government, sometimes led to violence.

The Red Scare

After the Communists took power in Russia in 1917, many Americans began to fear Communist ideas. They worried that Communists would soon try to gain power in the United States. This fear increased when millions of American workers went on strike in 1919. Many Americans blamed Communists and radicals for the upheaval.

These attitudes led to a **Red Scare**, a time of fear of Communists, or Reds. The Red Scare began in April 1919, when U.S. postal workers found bombs hidden in several packages addressed to famous Americans. Officials never found out who sent the bombs, but they suspected members of the Communist Party.

In June a bomb exploded outside the home of Attorney General A. Mitchell Palmer. Palmer responded by organizing police raids to break up Communist and other groups. In what became known as the Palmer raids, government agents arrested thousands of suspected radicals, often without evidence. Palmer frightened the public by warning that radicals were planning a revolution.

The Red Scare led to one of the best-known criminal cases in American history. In 1920 police arrested Italian-born anarchists Nicola Sacco and Bartolomeo Vanzetti for the robbery and murder of a factory paymaster and his guard. (Anarchists are people opposed to organized government.) Though both men declared themselves innocent of the crime, Sacco and Vanzetti were found guilty. The American Civil Liberties Union (ACLU), founded in 1920 to defend people's civil rights, tried unsuccessfully to get the verdict overturned. Sacco and Vanzetti were convicted. They were executed in 1927.

Restricting Immigration

Some people thought the Sacco and Vanzetti case was influenced by a general fear of foreigners. Many recent immigrants were poor and did not speak English. Some Americans saw them as a threat to their jobs and culture. Immigrants "fill places that belong to the loyal wage-earning citizens of America," said Alabama senator James Thomas Heflin.

The government responded to these concerns with new laws. The Emergency Quota Act of 1921 limited the total number of immigrants allowed into the country. It also favored immigrants from western Europe. The National Origins Act of 1924 banned immigration from East Asia entirely and further reduced the number of immigrants allowed to enter the country. These laws caused a dramatic drop in immigration to the United States.

READING CHECK **Drawing Conclusions** Why were new immigration laws passed in the 1920s?

Competing Ideals

Fear of radical ideas and foreigners was part of a larger clash over ideals and values in America. Differences were growing between older, rural traditions and the beliefs and practices of modern urban society. Americans had very different ideas about what was best for the country's future.

Prohibition

An issue that highlighted this conflict was prohibition. The Eighteenth Amendment—which outlawed the manufacture, sale, and transportation of alcoholic beverages—went into effect in 1920. Support for prohibition was strongest in rural areas, while opposition was strongest in cities.

Government officials found it nearly impossible to enforce prohibition. Congress passed the Volstead Act, which set fines and punishments for disobeying prohibition. Even respectable citizens, however, broke the law. Many people found ways to make alcohol at home using household products. Others bought alcohol at speakeasies, or illegal bars.

Organized criminals called bootleggers quickly seized control of the illegal alcohol business. They made their own alcohol or smuggled it in from Canada or Mexico. Gangsters were able to avoid arrest by bribing local police and politicians. Competition between gangs often led to violent fighting. In Chicago gangster Al "Scarface" Capone gained control of the alcohol trade by murdering his rivals. By 1927 Capone was earning more than $60 million a year from his illegal businesses.

By the end of the decade, the nation was weary of the effects of prohibition. The law had reduced alcohol consumption but had not stopped Americans from drinking. Prohibition had also created new ways for criminals to grow rich. Without government supervision of alcohol production, much of the alcohol consumed in speakeasies was more dangerous than what had been produced before prohibition. Many people came to believe that it would be better to have a legal alcohol trade that could be monitored by the government. In 1933 state and federal governments responded with the **Twenty-first Amendment**, which ended prohibition.

THE IMPACT TODAY

The Twenty-first Amendment made the manufacture and sale of alcohol legal again, but laws today still regulate drinking. The National Minimum Drinking Age Act of 1984 raised the minimum drinking age from 18 to 21 in every state.

Primary Source

PHOTOGRAPH

Prohibition

Agents of federal and state governments tried to enforce the Eighteenth Amendment against great odds. They usually destroyed any liquor that they found. This photograph shows an illegal barrel of beer being broken with an axe. More illegal beer and liquor would soon turn up, however. Faced with a lack of public support and an impossible task of enforcing the ban on alcohol, prohibition was repealed with the Twenty-first Amendment in 1933.

ANALYSIS SKILL ANALYZING PRIMARY SOURCES

Why was enforcing prohibition such a hard task?

VIDEO
America Goes Dry with Prohibition
HISTORY
hmhsocialstudies.com

Academic Vocabulary
traditional customary, time-honored

Religious Ideals

Youth culture of the 1920s and prohibition's failure concerned many religious leaders. They saw these changes as movements away from **traditional** values. This led to a Protestant religious movement known as **fundamentalism**—characterized by the belief in a literal, or word-for-word, interpretation of the Bible. Popular preachers like Aimee Semple McPherson used the radio and modern marketing tools to draw followers. Fundamentalism was especially strong in rural areas and small towns, where people often blamed society's problems on the culture of urban areas.

Many fundamentalists believed that modern scientific theories, such as Charles Darwin's theory of evolution, conflicted with the teachings of the Bible. Darwin's theory states that species evolve over time by adapting to their environment. To fundamentalists, this contradicted the biblical account of how the world was made. They opposed the teaching of evolution in public schools. Many cities and states passed laws to prevent the teaching of evolution.

In May 1925 a Dayton, Tennessee, high school science teacher named John T. Scopes was put on trial for teaching evolution in what became known as the **Scopes trial**. National interest in the event was heightened by the fact that famous Americans represented each side. Criminal attorney Clarence Darrow led the ACLU defense team. Three-time presidential candidate William Jennings Bryan assisted the prosecution.

Over live radio, Darrow and Bryan attacked each other's ideas. After more than a week on trial, Scopes was convicted and fined $100 for breaking the law. The state supreme court later overturned his conviction, but the debate over evolution continued.

READING CHECK **Evaluating** What cultural conflict did the Scopes trial represent?

Primary Source

POINTS OF VIEW

The Scopes Trial

Although the focus of the Scopes trial was whether or not John Scopes had broken the law, prosecution witness William Jennings Bryan saw the conflict as one between science and faith.

"Science is a magnificent force, but it is not a teacher of morals. It can perfect machinery, but it adds no moral restraints to protect society from the misuse of the machine . . . The [Scopes] case has assumed the proportions of a battle-royal [a struggle involving many people] between unbelief that attempts to speak through so-called science and the defenders of the Christian faith."

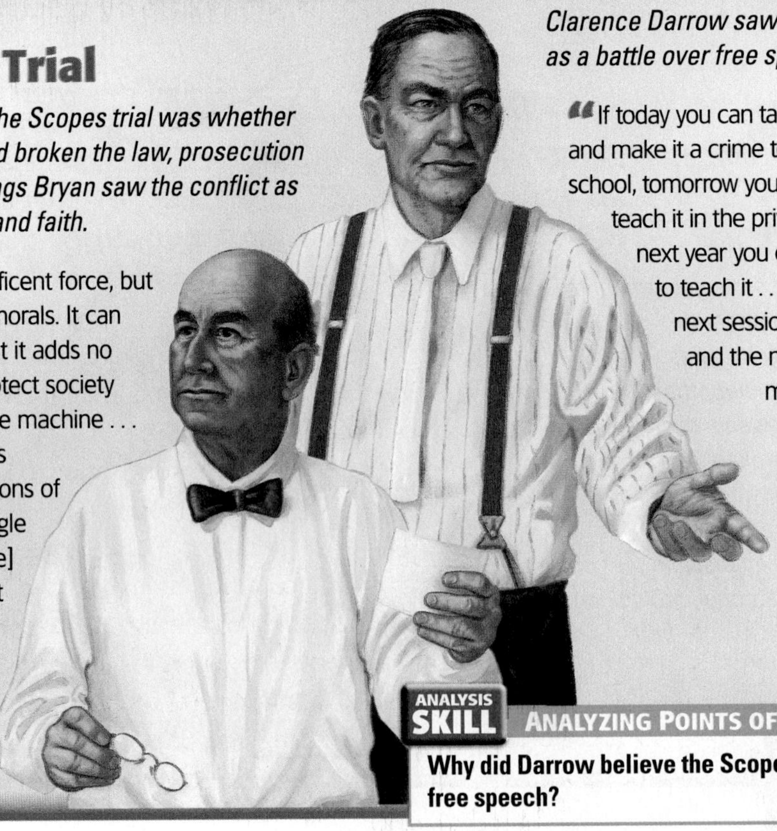

Clarence Darrow saw the conflict as a battle over free speech.

"If today you can take a thing like evolution and make it a crime to teach it in the public school, tomorrow you can make it a crime to teach it in the private schools, and the next year you can make it a crime to teach it . . . in the church. At the next session you may ban books and the newspapers. Soon you may set Catholic against Protestant and Protestant against Protestant, and try to foist [force] your own religion upon the minds of men."

ANALYSIS SKILL **ANALYZING POINTS OF VIEW**

Why did Darrow believe the Scopes trial was about free speech?

© Houghton Mifflin Harcourt Publishing Company

The Great Migration

CONNECT TO THE ARTS

From 1940 to 1941 artist Jacob Lawrence created a series of paintings that told the story of African Americans moving from the South to northern cities in search of jobs and equality. This is one of 60 paintings in the Migration Series. It shows African Americans about to begin their journey.

Where are the people in the painting going?

Minority Rights

During World War I large numbers of African Americans began leaving the South to take jobs in northern factories. This movement, called the **GreatMigration**, continued during the economic boom of the 1920s. While African Americans found jobs in the North, they did not escape racism.

Racial Tensions

The economic recession that followed the war led to increased racial tensions. Many white laborers feared the competition for jobs. Several race riots broke out in 1919, including one in Chicago that left 38 dead.

Racial tensions and fear of foreigners helped give rise to a new form of the Ku Klux Klan, the racist group that had terrorized African Americans during Reconstruction. The new Klan harassed Catholics, Jews, and immigrants, as well as African Americans. It also worked against urbanization, women's rights, and modern technology. By the mid-1920s the Klan had become an influential force in American politics, with more than 5 million members. Its influence then began to decline as news of financial corruption became public.

Protecting Rights

People who were the targets of the Klan's hatred found new ways to protect their rights. In 1922, for example, the NAACP began placing advertisements in newspapers that presented the harsh facts about the large number of lynchings taking place across the South.

Another way minorities attempted to protect their rights was to strengthen their culture. During the 1910s and 1920s, **Marcus Garvey** encouraged black people around the world to express pride in their culture. Garvey argued that black people should establish economic independence by building their own businesses and communities. These ideas were the basis of a movement known as black nationalism. The New York *Amsterdam News* praised Garvey's work, saying he "made black people proud of their race."

Hispanic Americans also organized to fight prejudice and promote civil rights. In 1929 Mexican American leaders met in Corpus Christi, Texas, to form the League of United Latin American Citizens (LULAC). This group worked to end unfair treatment such as segregation in schools and voting restrictions.

(r) © The Museum of Modern Art/Licensed by SCALA/Art Resource, NY.

BIOGRAPHY

Marcus Garvey

1887–1940

Marcus Garvey grew up in Jamaica and moved to the United States in 1916. A talented speaker, he quickly became one of the country's most famous and controversial black leaders. His newspaper *Negro World* promoted the idea of building an independent black economy. To encourage worldwide trade among black people, he created the Black Star Steamship Line. Some black leaders, including W. E. B. Du Bois, considered Garvey's ideas dangerous and extremist. After a series of legal problems related to his steamship company, Garvey was arrested in 1922 and was later deported.

Drawing Inferences How did Marcus Garvey try to help African Americans?

Most Native Americans lacked the legal protections of citizenship and the right to vote because they were not citizens of the United States. The fact that thousands of Native Americans had performed military service in World War I helped bring about change. In 1924 Congress passed the Indian Citizenship Act, granting citizenship to all Native Americans. However, the federal government also attempted to buy or take back some of the reservation lands. Native Americans successfully organized to stop these attempts, which were part of a larger effort to encourage Indians to adopt the culture of white Americans.

READING CHECK **Finding Main Ideas** How did minorities react to discrimination in the 1920s?

SUMMARY Americans saw many conflicts as their culture changed.

Section 2 Assessment

hmhsocialstudies.com
ONLINE QUIZ

Reviewing Ideas, Terms, and People

1. a. **Recall** How did **flappers** express their freedom?
   b. **Elaborate** How were young people of the 1920s more independent than their parents?
2. a. **Identify** What caused the **Red Scare,** and what was its result?
   b. **Explain** Describe the results of the immigration laws of the 1920s.
3. a. **Recall** What kinds of social conflicts developed during the 1920s?
   b. **Describe** What did the **Twenty-first Amendment** accomplish?
   c. **Analyze** How did **fundamentalism** influence the **Scopes trial**?
4. a. **Identify** How did minorities fight for their rights in the 1920s?
   b. **Define** What was the **Great Migration**?
   c. **Draw Conclusions** Why did **Marcus Garvey** call for black people to build their own businesses?

Critical Thinking

5. **Identifying Cause and Effect** Review your notes on social changes that took place in the 1920s. Then copy the graphic organizer below and use it to identify the causes and effects of several changes in American society.

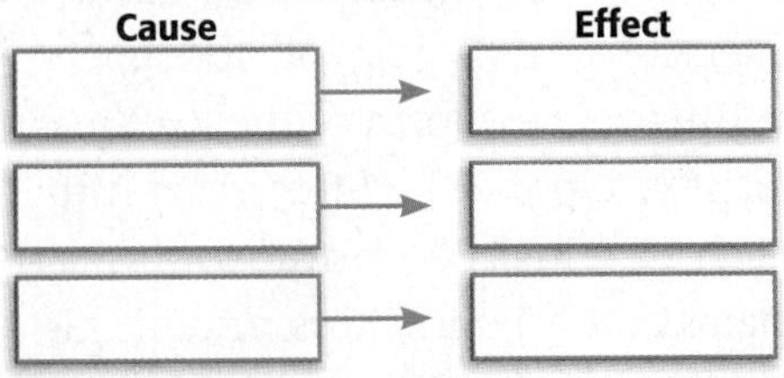

FOCUS ON WRITING

6. **Taking Notes on New Fashions** In the 1920s many women wore fashions that reflected their new independence. Look back at the example of flapper fashion on page 759. Think of how a radio advertisement could describe clothing like this to an audience that cannot see it.

The Jazz Age

SECTION 3

If YOU were there...

The year is 1924, and the New York Giants are playing the Washington Senators in the World Series. You just bought your first radio, and you are listening to an announcer describe the tense action as the seventh and deciding game goes into extra innings. You used to have to wait to read about the games in the newspaper. Now you can follow your favorite team pitch by pitch!

What other forms of entertainment could the radio bring to you?

BUILDING BACKGROUND You read earlier about the rise of mass culture in the United States in the late 1800s. Newspapers, department stores, and world's fairs allowed millions of Americans to share the same cultural activities. In the 1920s technologies such as radio broadcasts and movies helped the rise of mass culture continue.

A National Culture

On November 2, 1920, KDKA, the first commercial radio station, announced that Warren Harding had won the presidential election held that day. Just one year later, stations broadcast the action from the 1921 World Series. One newspaper writer predicted, "It might not be too long before farmers at the four corners of the Union may sit in their own houses and hear the president of the United States." Such an event seemed amazing to Americans in the early 1900s. But it quickly became a reality, as hundreds of radio stations began broadcasting all over the United States.

National radio networks, such as the National Broadcasting Company (NBC) and Columbia Broadcasting System (CBS), allowed people all over the country to listen to the same programs. People suddenly had access to music, news, weather reports, children's bedtime stories, sports broadcasts, and political speeches without leaving their homes. Business owners loved this technology because it allowed their advertisements to reach millions of listeners. Radio helped build a new national culture by allowing Americans everywhere to share common experiences.

What You Will Learn...

Main Ideas

1. Radio and movies linked the country in a national culture.
2. Jazz and blues music became popular nationwide.
3. Writers and artists introduced new styles and artistic ideas.

The Big Idea

Musicians, artists, actors, and writers contributed to American popular culture in the 1920s.

Key Terms and People

talkie
Jazz Age
Harlem Renaissance
Langston Hughes
Lost Generation
expatriates
Georgia O'Keeffe

hmhsocialstudies.com
TAKING NOTES

Use the graphic organizer online to take notes on examples of popular culture in the 1920s.

THE IMPACT TODAY

The Academy of Motion Picture Arts and Sciences has held the Oscar ceremony every year since 1929. It was first broadcast over the radio in 1930, and in 1953 the Academy Awards were first televised.

Movies also became a major national passion in the 1920s. Though early motion pictures had no sound, they opened a new world of exciting adventures for audiences. People packed theaters to see Westerns, romances, and stories about bootlegging gangsters. Movie fans were even more thrilled by the 1927 movie *The Jazz Singer*, in which actor Al Jolson shouted the line "You ain't heard nothin' yet!" This was the first **talkie**, or motion picture with sound.

The movies quickly became big business. By the end of the decade, Americans were buying 95 million movie tickets each week, an amazing figure considering that the U.S. population was only 123 million. Young movie fans copied hair and clothing styles of movie stars. Fans felt a personal connection to stars like Douglas Fairbanks, Charlie Chaplin, and Mary Pickford, who was known as "America's Sweetheart." Few fans at the time realized that Pickford was also a smart businesswoman. She was one of the highest paid actors in Hollywood and a founder of United Artists, one of the nation's most successful film companies.

HISTORY

VIDEO
Did You Know: Babe Ruth

hmhsocialstudies.com

Movie stars were not the only national heroes. Fans packed baseball stadiums to watch the great players of the 1920s, especially George Herman "Babe" Ruth. Ruth shattered home-run records, drawing thousands of new fans to the sport. Because baseball was segregated, African American players and business leaders started their own league. Negro League stars such as Satchel Paige and Josh Gibson are considered to be among the best baseball players in history.

Fans always loved to see athletes break records. In 1926 American swimmer Gertrude Ederle became the first woman to swim the English Channel between England and France, beating the men's world record by almost two hours.

Pilots also became national heroes in the 1920s. Charles Lindbergh dominated the national news in 1927 when he completed the first nonstop solo flight across the Atlantic Ocean, traveling from New York to Paris. A few years later, Amelia Earhart became the first woman to fly solo across the Atlantic.

New ideas like psychoanalysis became more popular. Developed by psychologist Sigmund Freud, psychoanalysis is a method for examining human behavior to find out why people behave the way they do.

READING CHECK **Summarizing** How did American culture change during the 1920s?

Time Line

Popular Culture of the 1920s

1920 Babe Ruth begins playing for the New York Yankees.

1920

1924 First Negro-League World Series is played.

Popular Music

With a booming economy and exciting forms of entertainment, the 1920s became known as the Roaring Twenties. An explosion in the popularity of jazz music gave the decade another nickname—the **Jazz Age**.

Jazz developed in New Orleans, where African American musicians blended spirituals with European harmonies and West African rhythms. When blacks moved north during the Great Migration, they brought their music with them.

As with many new forms of popular culture, jazz sparked arguments between older and younger generations. "When my grandmother found out that I was playing jazz music . . . she told me that I had disgraced the family," remembered "Jelly Roll" Morton, an early jazz composer. But young Americans loved the music and the wild, fast-paced dances that went along with it. Dance crazes sweeping the nation included the Charleston, the Toddle, and the Shimmy. New magazines arose that taught dance steps to subscribers.

Jazz musicians such as Louis Armstrong experimented with various sounds and rhythms to create a new kind of music. Armstrong, who played the trumpet, was known for his solo numbers. His method of stepping out from the band to perform a solo was an **innovation** that is still copied by musicians today. Another major figure of the Jazz Age was conductor and composer Edward "Duke" Ellington. His "big band" sound blended many instruments together in songs such as "Take the A Train." Ellington described the exciting life of Jazz Age musicians in New York City:

> "A lot of guys liked to play so much that in spite of being on a regular job, they'd still hire out to work matinees, or breakfast dances . . . Nobody went to bed at nights and round three or four in the mornings you'd find everyone making the rounds bringing their horns with them."
>
> —Duke Ellington, quoted in *Reminiscing in Tempo*, by Stuart Nicholson

Blues music, which came from the rural South of the Mississippi Delta, also gained national popularity in the 1920s. Blues began as an expression of the suffering of African Americans during slavery. One of the leading blues singers of the 1920s was Bessie Smith, nicknamed the Empress of the Blues. "She had music in her soul," said Louis Armstrong.

READING CHECK **Finding Main Ideas** Where did jazz originate, and what musical styles influenced it?

ACADEMIC VOCABULARY

innovation a new idea or way of doing something

hmhsocialstudies.com

ANIMATED GEOGRAPHY AND HISTORY

Personal Income in the U.S. 1927

1925 F. Scott Fitzgerald's *The Great Gatsby* is published.

1925 Louis Armstrong begins recording with his band, the Hot Five.

1926 Gertrude Ederle becomes the first woman to swim across the English Channel.

1926 NBC, the first national radio network, begins broadcasting.

1927 Charles Lindbergh completes the first non-stop solo flight across the Atlantic Ocean.

1927 *The Jazz Singer,* the first full-length talkie, is released.

1928

ANALYSIS SKILL **READING TIME LINES**

Which events reflected people's interest in breaking records?

The Granger Collection, New York

Writers and Artists

While musicians were creating new forms of music, writers and artists were also reshaping American culture. Many creative works of the 1920s are still admired today.

The Harlem Renaissance

Many of the African Americans who came north in the Great Migration built a thriving community in the Harlem neighborhood of New York City. This community became the center of the **Harlem Renaissance**, a period of African American artistic accomplishment.

Primary Source

POEM

"I, Too"

In one of his most celebrated poems, Langston Hughes expressed both pride in being African American and faith in the American dream.

"I, Too

I, too, sing America.
I am the darker brother.
They send me to eat in the kitchen
When company comes,
But I laugh,
And eat well,
And grow strong.

Tomorrow,
I'll be at the table
When company comes.
Nobody'll dare
Say to me,
'Eat in the kitchen,'
Then.

Besides,
They'll see how beautiful I am
And be ashamed—
I, too, am America."

ANALYSIS SKILL ANALYZING PRIMARY SOURCES

Analyzing Who do you think Hughes is referring to when he speaks of "they"?

Harlem Renaissance writers included **Langston Hughes** and Claude McKay. Hughes produced poems, plays, and novels about African American life. His works often incorporated African American slang and jazz rhythms. McKay was a poet and activist who spoke out against racial discrimination and called on African Americans to stand up against lynchings and other violence.

Another important writer of the Harlem Renaissance was Zora Neale Hurston. Her novels, such as *Their Eyes Were Watching God,* reflected the experiences of African American women.

The Lost Generation

Other Americans also wrote of their experiences living in the United States and in places around the world. Soon after he graduated from high school in Illinois, Ernest Hemingway volunteered as an ambulance driver in World War I. Hemingway called the war "the most colossal, murderous, mismanaged butchery that had ever taken place on earth." He began writing short stories and novels, and soon he gained fame for his powerful and direct writing style. Hemingway was among a group of young American writers who expressed feelings of disillusionment in the American society that they felt denied them a voice in their own futures. Author Gertrude Stein called these writers "a lost generation." Writers who criticized American society in the 1920s thus became known as the **Lost Generation**.

Many members of the Lost Generation moved to Paris in the 1920s and formed a community of **expatriates**—people who leave their home country to live elsewhere. Hemingway wrote about the expatriate community in his best-selling novel *The Sun Also Rises*. Another Lost Generation writer was F. Scott Fitzgerald. His novel *The Great Gatsby* focused on what he saw as the loss of morality behind the seemingly fun and free-spirited times of the Jazz Age. Criticizing a glamorous couple, Fitzgerald wrote:

"They were careless people . . . they smashed up things and creatures and then retreated back into their money or their vast carelessness or whatever it was that kept them together, and let other people clean up the mess they had made."

—F. Scott Fitzgerald, *The Great Gatsby*

Another writer of the time, Sinclair Lewis, became the first American to receive the Nobel Prize in literature.

New Directions in Art

Painters were also experimenting with new artistic styles in the 1920s. Edward Hopper painted images of the loneliness of modern urban life. **Georgia O'Keeffe** was well known for her detailed paintings of flowers and of the Southwest.

Architects of the 1920s embraced a style they called art deco. Buildings constructed in this style had clean, sharp lines that resembled machines. Today art deco skyscrapers still stand out in American city skylines.

READING CHECK **Comparing and Contrasting** How were the artists of the Harlem Renaissance and the Lost Generation similar and different?

BIOGRAPHY

Georgia O'Keeffe

1887–1986

Georgia O'Keeffe grew up in Wisconsin and studied art in Chicago and New York. While teaching art at a college in Canyon, Texas, she would sometimes hike in Palo Duro Canyon, where she sketched scenes of amazing colors and rock formations. This was the start of a lifelong fascination with the beauty of the desert landscape. O'Keeffe lived much of her life in rural New Mexico, where many of her paintings were created. Animal bones, rocks, and desert flowers fill her works. She would often paint these objects in close-up view, showing tiny details. O'Keeffe said, "Most people in the city rush around so, they have no time to look at a flower. I want them to see it whether they want to or not."

Finding Main Ideas How did Georgia O'Keeffe's life influence her painting?

SUMMARY Americans became interested in new forms of entertainment and art in the 1920s.

Section 3 Assessment

hmhsocialstudies.com ONLINE QUIZ

Reviewing Ideas, Terms, and People

1. a. **Recall** What new forms of entertainment dominated American society during the 1920s?
   b. **Identify** What was the first **talkie**?
2. a. **Explain** Why were the 1920s called the **Jazz Age**?
   b. **Make Inferences** Why do you think jazz music became so popular?
3. a. **Recall** How did writers and artists express new ideas during the 1920s?
   b. **Describe** What did the **Lost Generation** writers express in their works?
   c. **Predict** How might the artists of the **Harlem Renaissance** influence African American artists of later generations?

Critical Thinking

4. **Categorizing** Review your notes on examples of popular culture in the 1920s. Then copy the graphic organizer below. Use it to categorize examples of popular culture in the 1920s.

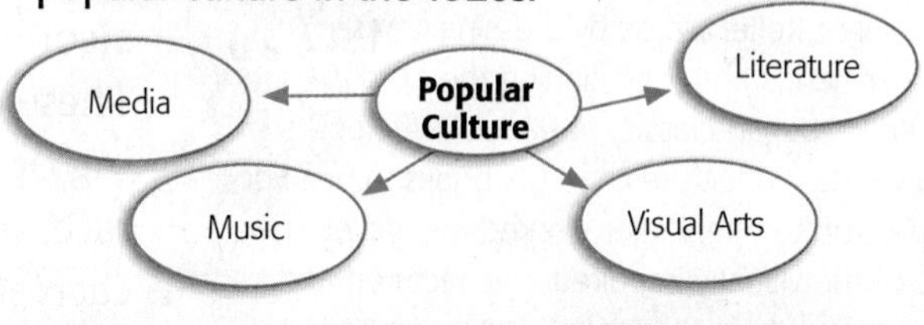
Popular Culture
Media
Literature
Music
Visual Arts

FOCUS ON WRITING

5. **Taking Notes on Entertainment** Make a list of popular forms of entertainment in the 1920s. How would you persuade people to attend a sports event, a talkie, or a jazz club? Begin to think about which product or form of entertainment you will choose for your radio advertisement.

© Houghton Mifflin Harcourt Publishing Company • Image Credits: (t), ©Georgia O'Keeffe Museum, Santa Fe/Art Resource

Case Study

Society During the 1920s

The Modern Woman

At the turn of the nineteenth century, the lives of American women were changing drastically. New inventions allowed housework such as dishwashing, laundry, and cooking to be done much more quickly. Because of this, middle-class women had more leisure time. In some cases, they were able to gain more economic freedom and opportunities for education.

The Club Movement

In addition, more women had greater access to education. In 1870, less than 1 percent of women attended college. By 1900, almost 3 percent did. Women formed societies and clubs that held informative lectures, speaking events, and classes. The clubs encouraged women to become more comfortable with their organizational and public-speaking abilities. Although the idea of women speaking before groups of both men and women shocked some people, the idea became more accepted over time.

Often, these clubs and societies were organized to help reform a particular problem in society such as race relations or alcohol abuse. Others focused on women's issues in general. These clubs held lectures on topics such as efficient homekeeping or childcare. The clubs were almost always segregated by race, however. Networks of women's clubs developed across each state and the nation. The General Federation of Women's Clubs was organized in 1890 and the National Association of Colored Women was formed in 1896. Through these umbrella organizations, women coordinated larger efforts.Although the women's clubs were dominated by educated women from cities in the Northeast, they helped spread the idea of the independent, educated, and intelligent woman to the rest of society.

BIOGRAPHY

Helen Keller

The women of the club movement faced many social limitations. Helen Keller, however, faced an even tougher struggle. She became deaf and blind before the age of two, after a severe fever. She was unable to communicate with most people, and she developed behavior problems. Her parents brought Anne Sullivan to live with them in their Tuscumbia, Alabama, home and be Keller's tutor. Sullivan began teaching her to sign words a letter at a time. She taught Keller words by pressing items into her hands and then signing the word. At age 20, Keller began classes at Radcliffe College. Sullivan signed lectures and textbooks to her. For the rest of her life, Keller worked to improve the lives of the visually impaired. She lectured and wrote about their challenges and worked to prevent blindness.

Identify How did Helen Keller overcome the challenges she faced?

© Houghton Mifflin Harcourt Publishing Company • Image Credits: (c) ©Library of Congress Prints & Photographs Division

New Roles for Women

Daredevils such as Gladys Roy walked and performed acrobatics on the wings of planes in flight.

During World War I, women's support of the war effort showed that they were capable of performing many of the jobs traditionally held by men. When the Nineteenth Amendment granted women the right to vote in 1920, they were ready to demand even more rights and freedom. During the 1920s, many women chose to ignore many of the traditional ideas of the older generations.

One such woman was Amelia Earhart. She became one of the most well-known women in the world for her accomplishments as a pilot. The airplane had been invented in 1903, and by 1920 they had captured the public's imagination. Airshows were held across the nation to demonstrate the new invention. It was at one of these shows that Earhart first decided she wanted to be a pilot. Her first flying lesson was in 1921, and six months later she purchased her first plane. She quickly began setting records for women pilots.

In 1928, Earhart became the first woman to fly across the Atlantic. She accomplished this feat with two men. Four years later she made the trip solo and non-stop. Only Charles Lindbergh had accomplished this before she did. When she returned, she was awarded the Distinguished Flying Cross, the first woman to win this honor. She said that her flight proved that women were equal to men in "jobs requiring intelligence, coordination, speed, coolness, and willpower." In her marriage, she demanded an equal voice in decisions.

Earhart continued to break flight records of both men and women. In 1937, she tried to become the first woman to fly around the world. She and a navigator completed three quarters of the trip. In July, however, after taking off from New Guinea, her plane lost radio contact and disappeared. A large search operation was launched, but her plane has never been found.

Amelia Earhart made history by becoming the first woman to accomplish many achievements in early flight.

Case Study Assessment

1. What kinds of issues did women's clubs focus on?
2. Why is Amelia Earhart remembered for changing women's roles?
3. **Activity** Alabama had numerous women's clubs. Find information about one historical women's club and present your findings to the class.

© Houghton Mifflin Harcourt Publishing Company • Image Credits: (b) ©Bettmann/Corbis; (t) ©Topical Press Agency/Hulton Archives/Getty Image

The Tuskegee Institute

At the end of the Civil War, African Americans gained their freedom. But they were still kept separate from white society. They formed their own communities, and had their own schools and businesses. Soon an educated and wealthy class of African Americans emerged. Leaders debated the best way to bring opportunities to more African Americans.

The Tuskegee Institute became a center of education and social reform for African Americans.

The Tuskegee Spirit

Many people believed the best way to increase the economic prosperity of African Americans was through education. They founded numerous schools and colleges. In 1881 Booker T. Washington, who had been born into slavery, founded the Tuskegee Institution in Tuskegee, Alabama. Its goal was to teach agriculture and manual trades to African Americans. Washington brought the best black educators in the country to the school. Washington hoped to teach the skills needed for African Americans to be self-reliant and economically independent. Another goal was interracial harmony in the South. He called this mission the Tuskegee Spirit.

George Washington Carver

In 1896 Washington brought George Washington Carver to the school to be the head of the agriculture department. Carver had also been born as a slave, in 1864. He was raised by the owners of his mother. Carver attended a high school in Kansas because few schools in the South would accept black students. He was accepted at Highland College, but was denied entry when the school discovered his race. After this, he began a farm, where he did botanical experiments. Eventually he went to study botany at Iowa State. He was the first black student there. He then became the first black teacher at the school. While studying and teaching at Iowa State, Carver earned a national reputation as a gifted botanist.

He arrived at Tuskegee in 1896. There he taught classes such as crop rotation. He also developed a program to bring teachers to farms so that black sharecroppers would have access to the most current knowledge about farming techniques. While teaching at Tuskegee, he began researching new uses for crops that grew well in the South. His research led to the invention of hundreds of new products including paints, shampoo, and colored paper. These products used peanuts, soybeans, sweet potatoes, and pecans. These crops became

© Houghton Mifflin Harcourt Publishing Company • Image Credits: (t) ©Library of Congress Prints & Photographs Division more valuable. Carver also encouraged farmers to grow these crops for food, which made their diets healthier.

Margaret Murray-Washington

Margaret Murray was born in Mississippi, and her father died when she was seven. Like many African American children who lost their parents, her education was provided by Quakers.

At the same time that men were taught farming techniques and manual trades, the Girl's Institute at Tuskegee taught classes to African American women. In 1892 Margaret Murray became a teacher there. She married Booker T. Washington the same year. Murray-Washington was born in 1865 to a sharecropping family. After her father died she was taken in by a family of Quakers, who educated her. She then attended Fisk University, one of the oldest black universities.

While dean of women at Tuskegee, Murray-Washington oversaw the teaching of classes in dressmaking, sewing, laundering, cooking, and childcare. Her programs were also designed to support the "Tuskegee Spirit" of self-reliance and interracial cooperation in the South. She wrote articles and lectured on ways women could create a healthy and happy home.

Murray-Washington was also a leader of the African American women's club movement. She helped found the National Federation of Afro-American Women in 1895. She was elected president of the organization the next year, and led its merger with the Colored Women's League (CWL) to form the National Association of Colored Women (NACW). She then became the president of the Alabama Association of Women's Clubs. In 1914 she began serving as the president of the NACW.

In the 1920s, Tuskegee grew from an agriculture and trade school into an accredited institution. Some of the most important African American writers and intellectuals of the Harlem Renaissance were students at Tuskegee. Both Ralph Ellison and Claude McKay attended classes at Tuskegee before moving to New York City. Langston Hughes visited the school with Zora Neale Hurston and wrote an anthem for the school. Tuskegee became a symbol of the abilities of African Americans to define their own voice.

Case Study Assessment

1. What was the Tuskegee Spirit?
2. Who was Margaret Murray?
3. **Activity** George Washington Carver invented hundreds of products. Research some of the products that he created. Then make a visual display of several products and the plants they came from.

© Houghton Mifflin Harcourt Publishing Company • Image Credits: (c) ©Buyenlarge/Contributor/Getty Images

Music of the 1920s

The artists of the 1920s produced works of music and literature that still are considered some of the greatest in American history. Many artists used their works to describe the social changes that were occurring during the decade. The decade became known as the Jazz Age, but jazz music was only one of the types of music that were popular in the 1920s.

Tin Pan Alley

Until 1887, there was not a way to record music. People had to attend concerts or play music at home. Instead of CDs or mp3s, people bought the sheet music of popular songs and learned to play them with their own instruments.

George Gershwin became famous for his musical compositions. He wrote songs to be performed in concert, as musical theater, and in movies.

Many of the most important publishers of sheet music were located on the same street in New York City. The street was full of songs being played in their offices. The block was nicknamed "Tin Pan Alley," and the term became linked with the music industry centered there.

Many songwriters who sold their music as sheet music also wrote songs for musical theater shows. The sheet music for those songs was also sold to people who wanted to hear them at home. Songwriters such as Irving Berlin and George M. Cohan were some of the most popular entertainers of their day.

Like many other popular songwriters, George Gershwin began his career writing songs for Tin Pan Alley publishers. In 1919, he scored his first big hit with "Swanee." It sold more than a million copies. That same year he wrote the music for his first Broadway musical. He wrote songs for several musicals, many of which had lyrics written by his brother Ira. In 1935 they wrote *Porgy and Bess*. This opera is considered one of the classics of American theater.

Gershwin wanted to do more than write popular songs, however. He also composed jazz and orchestral works. His jazz-influenced song "Rhapsody in Blue" has come to represent

© Houghton Mifflin Harcourt Publishing Company • Image Credits: (c) ©GAB Archive/Redferns/Getty Images the 1920s. It is still heard in movies and commercials today. George and Ira moved to Hollywood and wrote music for several movies. Their songs include "Let's Call the Whole Thing Off" and "They Can't Take That Away from Me."

The Blues and Jazz

Another style of music that was popular during the 1920s was the blues. It was inspired by the African American songs played throughout the South. In 1912, W.C. Handy wrote "Memphis Blues," which is considered the first true blues song. The style takes its name from the "blue notes" that define it. These notes are a slurring of two notes. Blues songs also have a particular order for lyrics and musical structure.

In addition to writing music, Handy also published the works of other songwriters. Artists such as Mamie Smith, Bessie Smith, and Louis Armstrong recorded songs written by Handy. Many of these became popular hits. Although Handy didn't like jazz music, many of his songs became popular after jazz musicians recorded versions of them. The structure of jazz music is similar to the blues, but uses different combinations of chords.

Jazz evolved from small bands with only a few instruments into several different styles. During the 1920s, bands became larger and added more brass instruments. "Big band" music was a type of jazz that used a string section. It was closely related to swing music, which had a heavy rhythm and a fast beat. People attended nightclubs and performed the latest dances to go along with the music. The Cotton Club in Harlem was the most famous of these. It was one of the few places where African Americans and whites could meet socially.

W.C. Handy became famous for writing classic blues songs including "Saint Louis Blues."

Case Study Assessment

1. Who wrote "Rhapsody in Blue"?
2. How did W.C. Handy contribute to music in the United States?
3. **Activity** George Gershwin wrote many of the most famous songs in American history. Find recordings of some of his songs and play them in class.

© Houghton Mifflin Harcourt Publishing Company • Image Credits: (t) ©Michael Ochs Archives/Getty Images

Social Studies Skills

Analysis | Critical Thinking | Civic Participation | **Study**

Comparing Graphs

Define the Skill

Graphs are often a very useful way to organize historical information. They can present a large amount of detailed information clearly. Graphs can be an especially good way of showing how something like population or average income changed over time.

When information is organized in a graph, it is often easy to see patterns. Looking at two related graphs, you can compare patterns and make conclusions. For example, you can ask yourself, "Do the numbers in the graphs go up or down for the same reasons? What are the causes behind the changes shown by these graphs?"

Learn the Skill

These guidelines will help you to compare information in two or more graphs.

1. Use your basic graph-interpreting skills. Identify each graph's subject, purpose, and type. Study its parts and categories.
2. Analyze the data in each graph. Then compare any increases, decreases, changes, or patterns you find.
3. Finally, draw conclusions about the relationship between the information in each graph. Think about what could cause such relationships. It will probably help you to review what you know about related events at the same time.

Practice the Skill

Compare the graphs below to answer the following questions.

1. What are the topics of these graphs?
2. What percentage of American households had electricity in 1922? What was the first year when more than half of American households had electricity?
3. Based on the information in the graphs, draw a conclusion about how electricity changed American households.

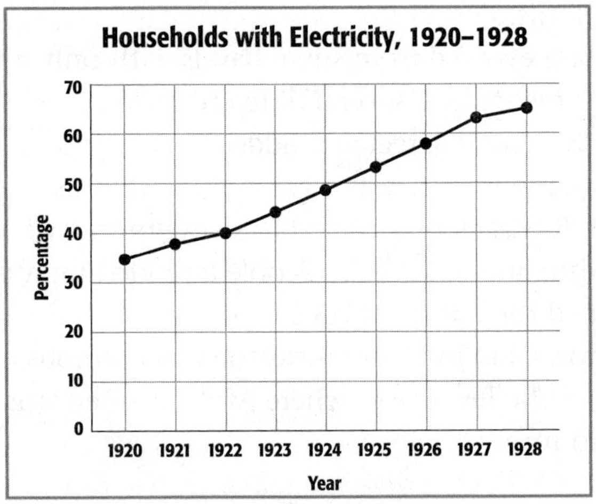

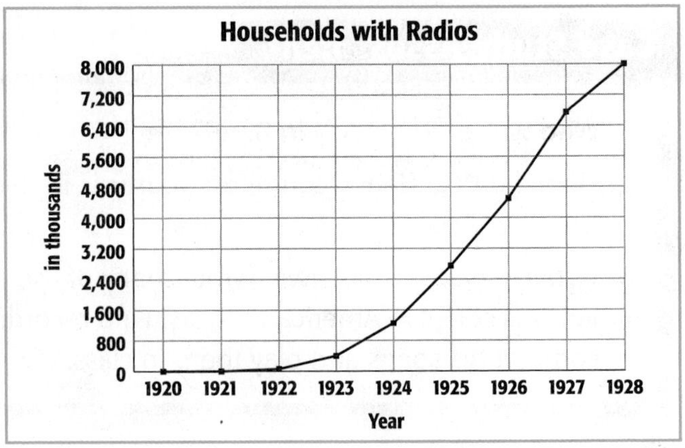

Source: *Historical Atlas of the United States*

© Houghton Mifflin Harcourt Publishing Company

CHAPTER 9 Chapter Review

History's Impact
▶ **video series**
Review the video to answer the closing question:
How did the post–World War I economy have an impact on film, literature, and music?

Visual Summary

QUICK FACTS

Use the visual summary below to help you review the main ideas of the chapter.

Political leaders tried to create economic prosperity during the 1920s.

Women found new freedom and opportunity in post–World War I America.

People enjoyed new forms of entertainment during the 1920s.

Reviewing Vocabulary, Terms, and People

Complete each sentence by filling in the blank with the correct term or person from the chapter.

1. Harlem Renaissance writer _________ wrote poems, plays, and novels about African American life.
2. The United States and other nations signed the _________, which outlawed war.
3. In the _________, Clarence Darrow defended a high school teacher tried for teaching evolution.
4. The _________ repealed prohibition.
5. Writers who criticized American culture during the 1920s were known as the _________.
6. African Americans moved north for jobs during the _________.

Comprehension and Critical Thinking

SECTION 1

7. a. **Describe** What was President Warren Harding's plan for strengthening the U.S. economy?

   b. **Explain** What methods did Henry Ford's competitors use to attract customers?

   c. **Elaborate** What do you think might have made the Kellogg-Briand Pact more effective?

SECTION 2

8. a. **Recall** What was the Red Scare?

   b. **Analyze** What are some reasons women had more opportunities in the 1920s?

   c. **Evaluate** Would you have become involved in the youth culture if you had lived during the 1920s? Why or why not?

© Houghton Mifflin Harcourt Publishing Company

SECTION 3

9. **a. Identify** What were talkies?

   b. Explain How did African Americans play an important role in Jazz Age culture?

   c. Predict How do you think new aspects of American culture affected life after the 1920s?

Reviewing Themes

10. **Society and Culture** How did the prosperity of the 1920s change American culture?
11. **Science and Technology** What new forms of technology emerged in the 1920s?

Social Studies Skills 21ST CENTURY

Comparing Graphs *Use the Social Studies Skills taught in this chapter to answer the question below.*

12. Look back at the line graphs on page 770. Do you think a graph showing the number of radio stations in the United States during the 1920s would look similar to these graphs? Explain your answer.

Using the Internet 21ST CENTURY

13. **Activity: Experiencing the Jazz Age** The arts flourished in America during the 1920s. There were amazing developments in the literary and visual arts, and new forms of performing arts, like blues and jazz, became popular. Use your online book to research some of the most influential writers, artists, and musicians of the 1920s. Choose one and conduct an imaginary interview with that person about his or her work and impact on American culture. Document your conversation by creating an audio recording or by writing a transcript.

hmhsocialstudies.com

Reading Skills 21ST CENTURY

Synthesizing Information *Use the Reading Skills taught in this chapter to answer the question below.*

> The number of women in the workforce continued to grow as well. Women with college degrees worked as nurses, teachers, librarians, and social workers . . . Women were still discouraged from pursuing fields such as medicine, law, and architecture, however. By the end of the 1920s, less than 5 percent of the country's doctors, lawyers, and architects were women. The percentage was small—but it was beginning to rise.

14. Which of the following sources might have been used to synthesize the information above?

    a. a history of architecture

    b. an instructional manual for nurses

    c. a history of working women in the 1920s

    d. the list of graduates from a women's college in 1910

Focus on Writing

15. **Writing Your Radio Advertisement** Look over your notes and choose one product that was popular in the 1920s. Think about these questions as you design your radio ad: Who is your audience? How will this product improve people's lives? What words or sounds will best describe your product? Write the dialogue for your ad, including directions for the actors. Also, include information about music or sound effects you want to use.

© Houghton Mifflin Harcourt Publishing Company

Standardized Test Practice

DIRECTIONS: Read each question and write the letter of the best response.

1 President Warren Harding's secretary of the interior was convicted and jailed for his participation in the

A Scopes trial.

B Teapot Dome scandal.

C Red Scare.

D Kellogg-Briand Pact.

2 Marcus Garvey was a leader in which of the following movements?

A black nationalism

B fundamentalism

C socialism

D communism

3 Which of the following is a reason why consumers bought more manufactured products in the 1920s?

A More Americans had electricity in their homes, so they could use new electric appliances.

B Radio and print advertising made it easier to buy products.

C Immigrants came to the United States in record numbers and bought new goods.

D The Lost Generation felt separated from American culture.

4 Which of the following was a famous jazz musician and composer?

A Zora Neale Hurston

B Mary Pickford

C Charles Lindbergh

D Edward "Duke" Ellington

5 One effect of the Red Scare was

A the election of Herbert Hoover in 1928.

B the trial and execution of Nicola Sacco and Bartolomeo Vanzetti.

C new opportunities for women, immigrants, and minorities.

D the Scopes trail.

6 Which of the following quotes is attributed to Calvin Coolidge?

A "The business of America is business."

B "I will build a motor car for the great multitude."

C "I want my girl to be a flapper, because flappers are brave."

D "America's present need is not heroics, but healing; not nostrums but normalcy."

7 Read the following excerpt from a 1928 campaign speech by Herbert Hoover and use it to answer the question below.

> "We in America today are nearer to the final triumph over poverty than ever before in the history of any land . . . We have not yet reached the goal, but given a chance to go forward with the policies of the last eight years, we shall soon with the help of God be in sight of the day when poverty will be banished from this nation."
>
> — Herbert Hoover, 1928 inaugural speech

Document-Based Question What did Hoover believe about poverty in the United States?

© Houghton Mifflin Harcourt Publishing Company

CHAPTER 10 1929–1939

The Great Depression

Essential Question What changes occurred because of the economic disaster of the Great Depression?

ALABAMA COURSE OF STUDY

4 Identify cultural and economic developments in the United States from 1900 through the 1930s.

- Identifying notable persons of the early 1900s.
- Comparing results of the economic policies of the Warren G. Harding, Calvin Coolidge, and Herbert Hoover Administrations.

5 Explain causes and effects of the Great Depression on the people of the United States.

- Identifying patterns of migration during the Great Depression.
- Locating on a map the area of the United States known as the Dust Bowl.
- Describing the importance of the election of Franklin D. Roosevelt as President of the United States, including the New Deal alphabet agencies.
- Locating on a map river systems utilized by the Tennessee Valley Authority (TVA).

Focus on Writing

Journal Entry We know a lot about life during the Great Depression because many Americans described their experiences in journals and letters. In this chapter you will read about how people struggled through hard times in the 1930s. Read the chapter and then write a one-page journal entry as if you were a person living during the Depression. You may choose to write from the point of view of a student, artist, farmer, or other individual. As you read, think about how the events in the 1930s may have affected this person.

STAGE BROADWAY SCREEN
VARIETY 25¢
WALL ST. LAYS AN EGG

UNITED STATES

1929 The U.S. stock market crashes on Black Tuesday.

1930

1930 Mahatma Gandhi and a group of followers begin the Salt March.

WORLD

Image Credits: (b), The Granger Collection, New York; (t), ©Bettmann/Corbis

© Houghton Mifflin Harcourt Publishing Company

$100. WILL
BUY THIS CAR.
MUST HAVE CASH,
LOST ALL ON THE
STOCK MARKET

The Great Depression forced many people to sell everything they owned just to survive.

HISTORY FDR's New Deal

hmhsocialstudies.com VIDEO

SWEEPING
THE DEPRESSION OUT

1932 Franklin D. Roosevelt wins his first presidential election, beating Herbert Hoover.

1932 At least 30 million people worldwide are unemployed.

1933 Adolf Hitler becomes chancellor of Germany.

1935 The CIO is organized.

1936 Jesse Owens wins four gold medals at the Berlin Olympics.

1937 The first Social Security payments are made.

1937 War officially begins between Japan and China.

1938 Violence against German Jews erupts into *Kristallnacht* ("night of broken glass").

1939 The film *The Wizard of Oz* is released.

1932 | 1934 | 1936 | 1938 | 1940

Image Credits: (t), ©Bettmann/Corbis; (bl), ©Bettmann/Corbis; (cr), Courtesy Everett Collection; (cl), Janice L. and David J. Frent Collection of Political Americana

© Houghton Mifflin Harcourt Publishing Company

Reading Social Studies

Economics | Geography | **Politics** | Society and Culture | Science and Technology

Focus on Themes In this chapter, you will learn about the Great Depression, one of the most serious **economic** crises in America's history. You will also learn about the **politics** that arose to try to deal with this crisis. Finally, you will read about how the Depression affected the global economy and how world leaders responded to it.

Recognizing Implied Main Ideas

Focus on Reading When you read, you will notice that not every paragraph has a main idea sentence. Sometimes the main idea is implied.

Implied Main Ideas While main ideas give a basic structure to a paragraph, supporting details help convince the reader of the author's point. Main ideas can be presented in a sentence, or simply implied. Usually, a paragraph without a main idea sentence will still have an implied main idea that ties the sentences together.

Notice how one reader found the main idea of the following paragraph.

> During the boom years of the 1920s, one General Motors executive boldly declared: "Anyone not only can be rich, but ought to be rich." For almost all of the Roaring Twenties, the stock market was a bull market, or one with rising stock values. It seemed easy to make money by investing in stocks. For example, you could have bought shares in the Radio Corporation of America for $85 each at the beginning of 1928. You could have sold them a year later for $549 each.

This quote is about making money and being rich. Maybe the main idea is about money or economics.

This sentence is about making money through the stock market. I guess the main idea has to do with investing.

Here is a great example of how easy it was to make money in the late 1920s. I think the main idea is something like "The stock market provided an easy way for many to become rich in the 1920s."

© Houghton Mifflin Harcourt Publishing Company

You Try It!

Read the following paragraph and then answer the questions below.

The action began when Roosevelt called Congress into a special session. Known as the Hundred Days, the session started just after the inauguration and lasted until the middle of June. During the Hundred Days, Roosevelt and Congress worked together to create new programs to battle the Depression and aid economic recovery. These programs became known as the New Deal.

1. List two ideas that this paragraph discusses.
2. How are these two ideas related to each other?
3. Write an example of the main idea of this paragraph.
4. Which details support your main idea?

As you read this chapter, think of a main idea for any paragraph that does not have a main idea sentence.

Key Terms and People

Chapter 10

Section 1

buying on margin
Black Tuesday
business cycle
Great Depression
Bonus Army
Franklin D. Roosevelt

Section 2

New Deal
fireside chats
Tennessee Valley Authority
Frances Perkins
Eleanor Roosevelt
Social Security Act
Congress of Industrial Organizations
sit-down strike

Section 3

Dust Bowl
Mary McLeod Bethune
John Steinbeck
Woody Guthrie

Academic Vocabulary

In this chapter you will learn the following academic words:

implement
authority

© Houghton Mifflin Harcourt Publishing Company

SECTION 1

The End of Prosperity

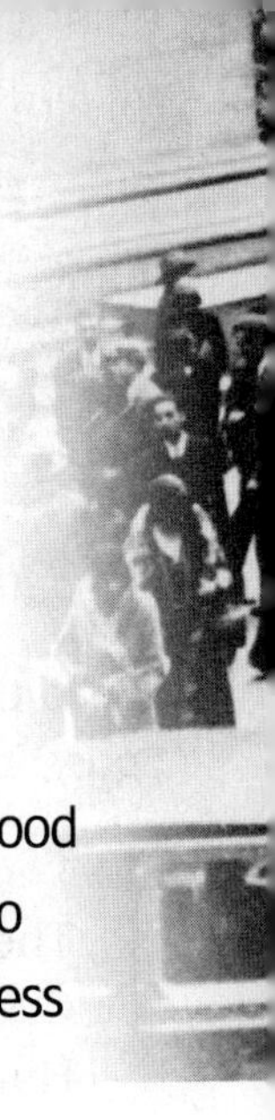

What You Will Learn...

Main Ideas

1. The U.S. stock market crashed in 1929.
2. The economy collapsed after the stock market crash.
3. Many Americans were dissatisfied with Hoover's reaction to economic conditions.
4. Roosevelt defeated Hoover in the election of 1932.

The Big Idea

The collapse of the stock market in 1929 helped lead to the start of the Great Depression.

Key Terms and People

buying on margin
Black Tuesday
business cycle
Great Depression
Bonus Army
Franklin D. Roosevelt

hmhsocialstudies.com
TAKING NOTES

Use the graphic organizer online to take notes about the American economy in the 1920s and 1930s.

If YOU were there...

For almost a year you've been working part-time at a neighborhood store. You earn money for your family and still have time to go to school. But when you arrive at work today, your boss says business has been so bad that he can't afford to pay you anymore. With your father out of work, your family had been counting on your income from this job.

How can you continue earning money to help your family?

BUILDING BACKGROUND By the late 1920s many Americans were used to year after year of economic expansion. It was easy to believe that the prosperity of the 1920s would last forever. But the U.S. economy historically has experienced periods of prosperity followed by periods of economic downturn. This cycle would continue in a way that shocked Americans in the 1930s.

The Stock Market Crashes

During the boom years of the 1920s, one General Motors executive boldly declared: "Anyone not only can be rich, but ought to be rich." For almost all of the Roaring Twenties, the stock market was a bull market, or one with rising stock values. It seemed easy to make money by investing in stocks. For example, you could have bought shares in the Radio Corporation of America for $85 each at the beginning of 1928. You could have sold them a year later for $549 each.

The chance to make huge profits from small investments encouraged many people to buy stocks. Some who could not afford the stocks' full price began **buying on margin**—purchasing stocks on credit, or with borrowed money. These stockholders planned to sell the stocks at a higher price, pay back the loan, and keep what remained as profit. But this plan only worked if stock values went up. Few considered what would happen if the bull market turned into a bear market, or one with declining stock prices.

© Houghton Mifflin Harcourt Publishing Company • Image Credits: (t) ©Bettmann/Corbis

Black Tuesday

More than 16 million shares were traded on Wall Street on Black Tuesday, a record that stood for 39 years. Just weeks later, roughly one-third of the value of the stock market had disappeared.

How are the events of Black Tuesday shown on the chart?

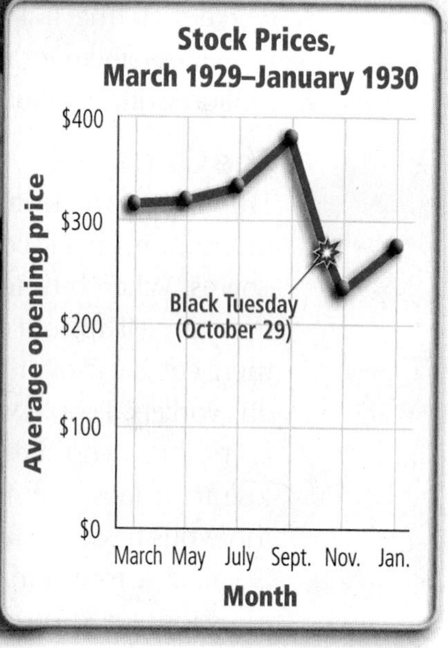
Stock Prices, March 1929–January 1930
$400
$300
$200
$100
$0
Average opening price
Black Tuesday (October 29)
March May July Sept. Nov. Jan.
Month

Stock prices peaked in the late summer of 1929. Then prices started to drop. Frightened investors who had bought stocks on margin rushed to sell their stocks in order to pay off their loans. On Thursday, October 24, panic hit the stock market. Within three hours the market had lost $11 billion in value. The following Monday, prices dropped again. On Tuesday, October 29—a day that became known as **Black Tuesday**—the stock market crashed. So many people wanted to sell their stocks, and so few wanted to buy, that stock prices collapsed. One journalist described the nightmare:

> "The wires to other cities were jammed with frantic orders to sell [stock]. So were the cables, radio, and telephones to Europe and the rest of the world. Buyers were few, sometimes wholly absent . . . This was real panic . . . When the closing bell rang, the great bull market was dead and buried."
>
> —Jonathan Norton Leonard, from *Three Years Down*

In September 1929 the total value of all stocks was $87 billion. Less than two months later, more than $30 billion in stock value had disappeared.

READING CHECK **Analyzing Information** Why was buying on margin risky?

The Economy Collapses

President Herbert Hoover tried to calm public fears by assuring Americans that the economy was still strong. "The fundamental business of the country . . . is on a sound and prosperous basis," he said. But this was just the beginning of more than 10 years of economic hard times.

The Banking Crisis

One immediate effect of the stock market crash was a banking crisis. Banks had invested heavily in the stock market, so they lost heavily when the market crashed. Banks had also lent their customers money to buy stocks on margin. Now those customers were unable to pay back their loans. Some banks went out of business. People who had deposited their life savings in those banks lost everything.

This created a panic all over the country, as customers rushed to their banks to withdraw their money. But since banks usually do not keep enough cash on hand to cover all deposits, the banks soon ran out of money. Many had to close their doors. In 1931 alone, more than 2,200 banks closed. The banking crisis contributed to a business crisis. Some businesses lost their savings in failed banks and had to close. Others were forced to cut back production, which meant they needed fewer workers. In the last three months of 1929, U.S. unemployment soared from under half a million workers to more than 4 million.

The Causes

Throughout the history of the United States, the economy has followed a pattern of ups and downs. When businesses produce more than they can sell, unsold goods pile up. Businesses then cut back on their production and lay off workers. People who have lost their jobs, and others who are afraid they might soon lose their jobs, buy fewer goods. This causes more businesses to fail. This economic event is called a recession. Deep and long-lasting recessions are known as depressions.

As time passes, an economy will tend to bounce back. Consumers buy surplus goods, and companies increase production to meet the demand. Soon, more workers are hired and unemployment drops. This up-and-down pattern is known as the **business cycle**.

The United States had experienced recessions and depressions before 1929. Each time, the economy followed the business cycle and recovered. But the economy did not recover quickly from the downturn that began in 1929. Because of its severity and length, it was called the **Great Depression**.

hmhsocialstudies.com
ANIMATED GEOGRAPHY AND HISTORY
Great Depression Unemployment 1934

Historians and economists still debate the exact causes of the Great Depression. Some believe that the government's monetary policy was a cause. Most agree that a major factor was the overproduction of goods at a time when the market for those goods was shrinking. Companies built millions of cars and appliances during the 1920s. By the late 1920s, however, most people who could afford these products already had them. That meant that American businesses were producing far more goods than people were consuming.

Uneven distribution of wealth made this problem worse. In 1929 the wealthiest 5 percent of Americans earned one-third of all income, while the bottom 40 percent earned only one-eighth of all income. Millions of Americans simply did not earn enough money to buy expensive new products.

Declining world trade also hurt American manufacturers. Europeans were still recovering from World War I and could not afford many American goods. At the same time, high tariffs made it difficult for European nations to sell products to the United States. As a result, Europeans had even less money to buy American goods.

READING CHECK **Making Predictions** Do you think the Great Depression could have been avoided? How?

Unemployment during the Depression

CONNECT TO ECONOMICS

People are considered unemployed if they are trying to find work but do not have a job. High rates of unemployment hurt the economy because unemployed people cannot buy many goods and services. This causes businesses to lose money.

During what year was unemployment the highest?

Unemployment, 1929–1941
Percentage of the Labor Force Unemployed
30
25
20
15
10
5
0
1929 1931 1933 1935 1937 1939 1941
Year

WORK-IS-WHAT-I
WANT-AND-NOT-CHAR
WHO-WILL-HELP-ME-
GET-A-JOB.-7 YEARS
IN-DETROIT. NO-MONE
SENT-AWAY- FURNISH-
BEST-OF-REFERENCE.
PHONE RANDOLPH

Primary Source

POLITICAL CARTOON

"Blame It on Hoover"

Presidents can affect the economy to some degree through their policies. During the Great Depression, President Hoover was blamed for the financial crisis. Political cartoons like this one gave voice to those Americans who thought Hoover could have prevented the crisis or could have brought it to an end quickly through government programs.

How does the cartoonist show Hoover reacting to the crisis?

What kind of people are blaming Hoover?

A Most Vicious Circle

—Costello in the Albany "News."

ANALYSIS SKILL **ANALYZING PRIMARY SOURCES**

Why is this cartoon useful for showing the feelings of the American public during the Great Depression?

Hoover's Reaction

As unemployment skyrocketed, more and more Americans struggled just to feed themselves and their families. Hungry people searched city dumps for scraps of food. One woman remembered taking off her glasses when she cooked so she could not see the maggots in the meat her family was about to eat. Private charities, as well as state and local governments, set up soup kitchens and breadlines. But the need far exceeded the available resources. Many people turned to President Herbert Hoover and the federal government to lead the relief effort.

Hoover knew that many Americans needed help. He did not believe, however, that it was the federal government's role to provide direct relief to Americans. Hoover felt it was up to private individuals and institutions, not the government, to offer relief. Despite this belief, Hoover did **implement** some new government programs. In 1932 he created the Reconstruction Finance Corporation (RFC). That year, the RFC loaned $1.2 billion to 5,000 different financial institutions, including banks and farm mortgage companies. Hoover continued to resist giving direct assistance to individuals.

This angered Americans who believed the president should do more to fix the economy. People bitterly referred to empty pockets turned inside out as Hoover flags. Groups of tin and cardboard shacks built by homeless families were nicknamed Hoovervilles.

In 1932 a new Hooverville was built in Washington, D.C. Its more than 17,000 residents were World War I veterans, some with their families. Called the **Bonus Army**, they had come to the capital to demand early payment of a military bonus. After the government denied the payment, most of the veterans returned home. About 2,000, however, stayed in their shantytown.

President Hoover authorized General Douglas MacArthur to use U.S. troops to evict the Bonus Army. MacArthur used force, including tear gas and tanks, to scatter the veterans. Several veterans were killed. The public reacted with outrage to the government's treatment of war veterans. Americans would have a chance to express this frustration in the upcoming election.

ACADEMIC VOCABULARY

implement put in place

READING CHECK **Making Generalizations**

How would you describe President Hoover's response to the Depression?

Election of 1932

The Republican Party nominated Herbert Hoover again for president in 1932, but few people believed he could win. Regarding his chances of re-election, even Hoover realized that "the prospects are dark." Still, he began campaigning hard for a second term.

THE IMPACT TODAY

Before 1932, candidates did not attend their party's nominating convention. Roosevelt broke with this tradition, setting a new precedent. Today presidential candidates give televised speeches at party conventions.

He called the election "a contest between two philosophies of government." He warned that the government aid programs Democrats were promising would weaken Americans' spirit of self-reliance.

By 1932, however, much of the public had lost confidence in Hoover. Many even blamed him for the Depression. In contrast, as governor of New York during the first years of the Depression, **Franklin D. Roosevelt** had taken active steps to provide aid. He directed the state government to provide relief for the state's citizens, especially farmers. He also helped establish the Temporary Emergency Relief Administration, which gave unemployment assistance to many out-of-work New Yorkers.

Roosevelt's confident and optimistic personality appealed to many voters. At the Democratic Party convention, Roosevelt declared to Americans: "I pledge you, I pledge myself, to a new deal for the American people." Voters responded overwhelmingly to this message of hope. Roosevelt won the 1932 election in a landslide. In addition, the Democrats won strong majorities in both houses of Congress.

READING CHECK **Analyzing Information** How did Franklin D. Roosevelt win the 1932 presidential election?

SUMMARY After the stock market crash and the start of the Great Depression, Franklin Roosevelt offered hope for the future.

Section 1 Assessment

hmhsocialstudies.com ONLINE QUIZ

Reviewing Ideas, Terms, and People

1. a. **Recall** Why did the stock market crash in 1929?
   b. **Compare** How is **buying on margin** similar to buying on an installment plan?
2. a. **Recall** What happened to the economy as a result of the stock market crash?
   b. **Explain** Why did many banks close in the late 1920s and early 1930s?
   c. **Draw Conclusions** What do you think was the goal of U.S. tariffs?
3. a. **Make Inferences** Why did many Americans blame President Hoover for the Depression?
   b. **Describe** What did the **Bonus Army** want?
   c. **Elaborate** Do you think Americans were justified in blaming Hoover for the hard times?
4. a. **Identify** Which party was more successful in the 1932 elections?
   b. **Make Inferences** Why do you think voters did not listen to Hoover's ideas about government?
   c. **Elaborate** How do you think **Franklin D. Roosevelt**'s experiences as governor of New York helped him appeal to voters?

Critical Thinking

5. **Identifying Cause and Effect** Review your notes on the American economy in the 1920s and 1930s. Then copy the graphic organizer below and use it to identify the economic causes of the Depression and their effects.

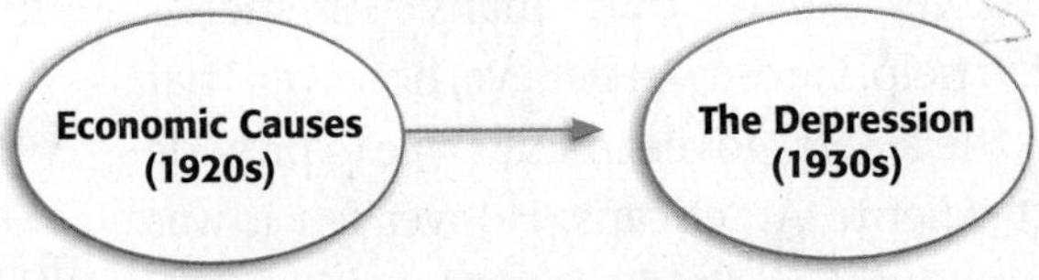
Economic Causes (1920s)
The Depression (1930s)

Focus on Writing

6. **Taking Notes on the End of Prosperity** To begin thinking about creating a character for your journal entry, answer the question at the end of the "If YOU were there" on page 778. Then make some notes on the stock market crash, the banking crisis, and rising unemployment. Decide how your character would feel about these developments.

BIOGRAPHY

Franklin Delano Roosevelt

How would you try to lead your country through times of national crisis?

When did he live? 1882–1945

Where did he live? Roosevelt lived much of his life in New York State, where he served in the state senate and as governor. He also lived in Washington, D.C., while he was serving as assistant secretary of the navy and later as president. He had a second home in Warm Springs, Georgia.

What did he do? He began the New Deal, a set of government programs designed to help the country survive and recover from the Great Depression. He gave many Americans hope for the future when he spoke to them in his fireside chats. Roosevelt also led the country through World War II. His support for strong ties between the Allied countries helped the Allies achieve victory.

Why is he so important? Roosevelt led the United States during two of the most serious crises that our country has ever faced: the Great Depression and World War II. He served as president for 12 years, longer than any other. Many of the programs he began in the 1930s expanded the role of government in American life.

Making Predictions How do you think Franklin Roosevelt's experience as president during the Depression might have helped him lead the country during World War II?

KEY EVENTS

- **1905** Marries Eleanor Roosevelt
- **1921** Stricken with polio; unable to walk without leg braces and canes for the rest of his life
- **1928** Elected governor of New York
- **1932** Elected president; re-elected in 1936, 1940, and 1944
- **1941** U.S. entry into World War II
- **1945** Dies at his home in Warm Springs, Georgia

"The only thing we have to fear is fear itself, nameless, unreasoning, unjustified terror."

Franklin Roosevelt, 1933 inaugural address

© Houghton Mifflin Harcourt Publishing Company

SECTION 2

Roosevelt's New Deal

What You Will Learn...

Main Ideas

1. Congress approved many new programs during the Hundred Days.
2. Critics expressed concerns about the New Deal.
3. New Deal programs continued through Roosevelt's first term in what became known as the Second New Deal.
4. Roosevelt clashed with the Supreme Court over the New Deal.

The Big Idea

Franklin Roosevelt's New Deal included government programs designed to relieve unemployment and help the economy recover.

Key Terms and People

New Deal
fireside chats
Tennessee Valley Authority
Frances Perkins
Eleanor Roosevelt
Social Security Act
Congress of Industrial Organizations
sit-down strike

hmhsocialstudies.com
TAKING NOTES

Use the graphic organizer online to take notes on the challenges that the nation and President Roosevelt faced during the Great Depression.

If YOU were there...

It has been five months since you lost your job. One of your friends has found work in a new government program that is hiring young people to work in national parks and forests. The pay is low, and you would have to leave home, but you would have enough food, a place to live, and a little money to send back to your family every month.

Would you take a job with the Civilian Conservation Corps? Why or why not?

BUILDING BACKGROUND When he ran for president in 1932, Franklin D. Roosevelt promised to provide relief to people suffering from the Depression. Even before he took office, Roosevelt began making plans with his Brain Trust, a group of expert advisers. People endured the harsh winter of 1932–1933, looking forward to Roosevelt's inauguration.

The Hundred Days

Immediately after taking the oath of office in March 1933, President Franklin Roosevelt spoke to the nation. In his first inaugural address, Roosevelt told nervous Americans that economic recovery was possible. "The only thing we have to fear is fear itself," he said, "nameless, unreasoning, unjustified terror." It was only fear of the future, he argued, that could keep America from moving forward. Roosevelt spoke openly of the severe problems facing the American people—unemployment, failing banks, and products with no markets. He promised that the government would help. "This nation asks for action," he said, "and action now."

The action began when Roosevelt called Congress into a special session. Known as the Hundred Days, the session started just after the inauguration and lasted until the middle of June. During the Hundred Days, Roosevelt and Congress worked together to create new programs to battle the Depression and aid economic recovery. These programs became known as the **New Deal**.

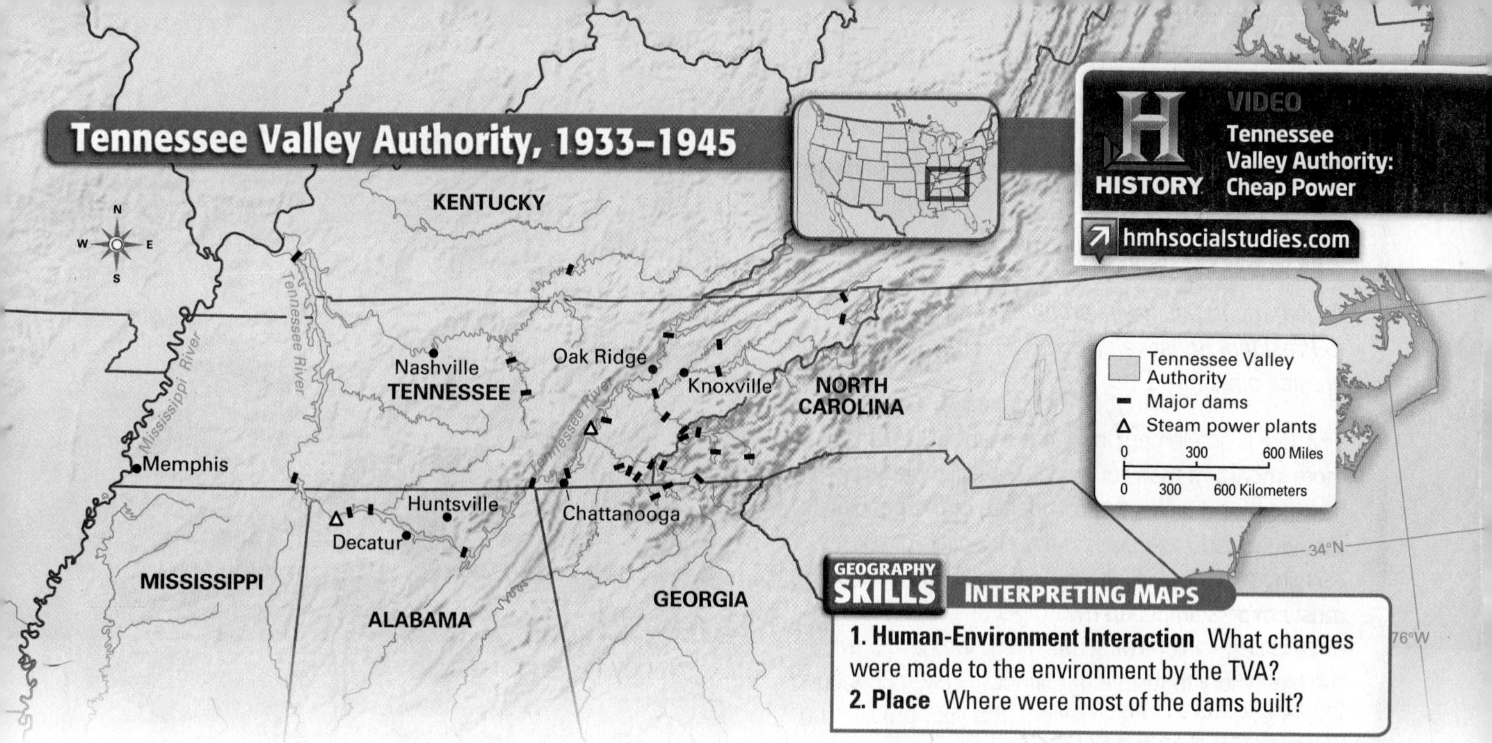

GEOGRAPHY SKILLS INTERPRETING MAPS

1. **Human-Environment Interaction** What changes were made to the environment by the TVA?
2. **Place** Where were most of the dams built?

Restoring Confidence

One of Roosevelt's first goals was to restore confidence in American banks. The day after his inauguration, Roosevelt announced a "bank holiday," ordering all banks to close temporarily. Three days later, Congress's special session began. Congress quickly passed the Emergency Banking Relief Act, and President Roosevelt signed it into law.

That Sunday, President Roosevelt gave the first of his **fireside chats**—radio addresses in which he spoke directly to the American people. In this first fireside chat, he explained the new bank relief law. The government would inspect the finances of every bank and allow only healthy banks to reopen. The new bank law and Roosevelt's fireside chat helped Americans trust banks with their money again. As banks reopened, there were no rushes to withdraw money. Over the next month, Americans deposited almost $1 billion in banks.

Relief and Recovery

Roosevelt next turned his attention to other serious problems. In 1933 some 13 million Americans—about 25 percent of the nation's workforce—were unemployed. New Deal programs helped to get Americans back to work. The Civil Works Administration (CWA) employed more than 4 million Americans, building roads and airports. One grateful CWA worker expressed the feelings of many when he said, "I was working, and I could again hold my head up when I met people." The Civilian Conservation Corps (CCC) provided jobs for hundreds of thousands of people through projects such as planting trees and improving national parks.

Another federal project, the **Tennessee Valley Authority** (TVA), hired people to build dams and generators, bringing electricity and jobs to communities in the Tennessee River valley. The New Deal also included programs to help farmers. The Farm Credit Administration (FCA) helped farmers refinance their mortgages so they could keep their farms. The Agricultural Adjustment Act (AAA) helped stabilize agricultural prices.

FOCUS ON READING

What is the main idea of this paragraph?

The National Industrial Recovery Act (NIRA) addressed business concerns by eliminating unfair competition among companies. This law was passed with support from Secretary of Labor **Frances Perkins**, the nation's first woman cabinet member.

READING CHECK **Categorizing** Which New Deal programs employed people to build public projects?

Primary Source

RADIO BROADCAST

Fireside Chats

An American family sits around the radio listening to President Roosevelt answer his critics in his first fireside chat.

"There is an element in . . . our financial system more important than currency [money], more important than gold, and that is the confidence of the people. Confidence and courage are the essentials of success in carrying out our plan. You people must have faith; you must not be stampeded by rumors or guesses. Let us unite in banishing [driving away] fear. We have provided the machinery to restore our financial system; it is up to you to support and make it work. It is your problem no less than it is mine. Together we cannot fail."

ANALYSIS SKILL ANALYZING PRIMARY SOURCES

According to Roosevelt, how should the American people help the government deal with the banking crisis?

New Deal Critics

While many Americans approved of the New Deal, others criticized President Roosevelt's programs. New Deal critics fell into two main groups—those who believed the New Deal went too far, and those who believed it did not go far enough.

Those who felt the New Deal went too far criticized the enormous expansion of the federal government. For example, members of the American Liberty League said that New Deal laws gave the president too much **authority**. Many business leaders were concerned that the high cost of new government programs would lead to new taxes. As one writer explained:

ACADEMIC VOCABULARY

authority power, right to rule

> "It's simple arithmetic to figure that taxpayers must pay the bills for current billions of emergency expenditures. The question is, Which taxpayers? Under this administration the answering finger points pretty much in the direction of business interests. Thus higher taxes of the future will eat into profits."
>
> —W. H. Kiplinger, quoted in *The New Deal and the American People,* edited by Frank Freidel

One critic who thought the New Deal did not go far enough was a U.S. senator from Louisiana, Huey Long. Long proposed a program called Share Our Wealth, which would tax rich Americans and use the money to help the poor. Every family would be guaranteed an annual income of $5,000. As Long prepared to challenge Roosevelt in the 1936 election, he announced his goal "to break up the swollen fortunes of America and to spread the wealth among all our people." Long's White House dreams ended when an assassin shot him in 1935.

Another fierce critic of Roosevelt's New Deal was Father Charles Edward Coughlin. Coughlin was a Roman Catholic priest in Detroit who developed a large following by broadcasting sermons over the radio. Although he initially supported Roosevelt and his programs, Coughlin eventually decided that the New Deal helped only business interests. Coughlin wanted the government to nationalize, or take over, all of the country's wealth and natural resources.

READING CHECK **Supporting a Point of View** Do you agree with any of the New Deal critics? Why or why not?

The New Deal Continues

Despite criticism of the New Deal, Democrats increased their majorities in both houses of Congress in the 1934 election. With this show of support from the American people, Roosevelt continued to introduce additional New Deal legislation. These later laws were known as the Second New Deal.

The Second New Deal

After the Civil Works Administration ended in 1934, Congress formed a new agency to provide jobs for unemployed Americans. Between 1935 and 1943, the Works Progress Administration (WPA) employed some 8.5 million people on tens of thousands of projects all over the country. WPA employees built more than 650,000 miles of roads; 75,000 bridges; 8,000 parks; and 800 airports. WPA workers also built the Grand Coulee Dam in Washington and New York City's Lincoln Tunnel, as well as prisons, swimming pools, hospitals, and courthouses nationwide.

First Lady **Eleanor Roosevelt** was an active supporter of New Deal programs. She was concerned, however, that the WPA was not solving the problem of unemployment among young Americans in their teens and early twenties. "I live in real terror when I think we may be losing this generation," she said. "We have got to bring these young people into the active life of the community and make them feel that they are necessary." The first lady helped convince the president to create the National Youth Administration (NYA). The NYA gave part-time jobs to many students. These jobs allowed young workers to stay in school and help their families. One NYA worker said, "I tell you, the first time I walked through the front door with my paycheck, I was somebody!"

President Roosevelt also wanted to help those who were "unable . . . to maintain themselves independently . . . through no fault of their own." The **Social Security Act**, passed in 1935, provided some financial security for the elderly, the disabled, children, and the unemployed. To help pay for these programs, the law placed a new tax on workers and employers. The passage of the Social Security Act marked the first time the federal government took direct responsibility

HISTORY

VIDEO
FDR's
New Deal

hmhsocialstudies.com

THE IMPACT TODAY

Social Security is still an important financial safety net for many Americans. Nine out of ten individuals over the age of 65 receive benefits from the program.

Selected New Deal Programs

QUICK FACTS

Program	Purpose
Emergency Banking Relief Act	Gave the executive branch the right to regulate banks
Farm Credit Act (FCA)	Refinanced loans to keep farmers from losing their land
Civilian Conservation Corps (CCC)	Created jobs for single, unemployed young men
Agricultural Adjustment Act (AAA)	Paid farmers to grow less (declared unconstitutional)
Tennessee Valley Authority (TVA)	Built dams and power plants in the Tennessee Valley
Federal Deposit Insurance Corporation (FDIC)	Guaranteed deposits in individual bank accounts
National Industrial Recovery Act (NIRA)	Established fair competition laws (declared unconstitutional)
Civil Works Administration (CWA)	Provided jobs for the unemployed
Works Progress Administration (WPA)	Created jobs in construction, research, and the arts
National Youth Administration (NYA)	Provided part-time jobs to students
National Labor Relations Act (Wagner Act)	Recognized unions' right to bargain collectively
Social Security Act	Provided government aid to the retired and unemployed

© Houghton Mifflin Harcourt Publishing Company

for many citizens' economic well-being. In a national radio address, Secretary of Labor Perkins told Americans she believed Social Security was "a most significant step in our national development, a milestone in our progress toward the better-ordered society."

New Deal Labor Programs

The National Industrial Recovery Act of 1933 helped regulate business by requiring minimum wage and allowing collective bargaining. In 1935, however, the Supreme Court declared the NIRA unconstitutional.

In response to this setback, Congress passed the National Labor Relations Act (NLRA). This law is sometimes called the Wagner Act after its sponsor, Senator Robert F. Wagner of New York. This law allowed workers to join labor unions and take part in collective bargaining. It also established the National Labor Relations Board to oversee union activities. Union membership grew after the passage of the Wagner Act. Organized labor became a powerful political force.

At the start of the Depression, many skilled workers belonged to craft unions. Such unions were often associated with the American Federation of Labor, which had existed since the 1880s. Unskilled workers, however, such as those who worked on assembly lines, did not qualify to belong to AFL unions. In 1935 a new union called the **Congress of Industrial Organizations** (CIO) organized workers into unions based on industry, not skill level. For example, all workers in the automobile industry would belong to the same union. The CIO also welcomed African American and Hispanic members, as well as women and immigrants.

Unions led a number of major strikes during the Depression. On New Year's Eve 1936, the CIO went on strike against General Motors for 44 days. Instead of leaving the buildings as strikers usually did, workers stayed in the factories so they could not be replaced by new workers. This strategy became known as the **sit-down strike**. The success of the General Motors strike attracted more workers to CIO unions.

READING CHECK **Comparing and Contrasting** How were the WPA and the Social Security Act similar, and how were they different?

National Youth Administration

A New Deal program called the National Youth Administration (NYA) helped thousands of young people continue their education while working to support their families. Eleanor Roosevelt was a strong supporter of the program, which aimed to teach young people the skills they would need to remain part of the workforce.

How did the NYA demonstrate the ideals of the New Deal?

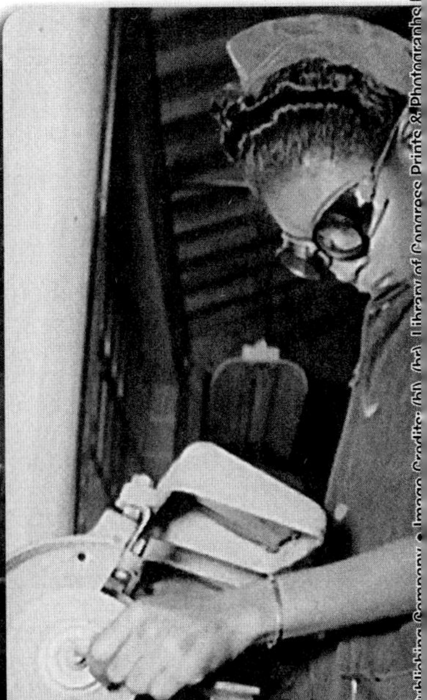

© Houghton Mifflin Harcourt Publishing Company • Image Credits: (b), (bg) Library of Congress Prints & Photographs Division, Washington, D.C.

Clashes with the Court

Roosevelt won re-election by a huge margin in 1936, carrying every state but Maine and Vermont. Democrats expanded their dominant control of Congress. But Roosevelt and the Democrats in Congress could not control the Supreme Court.

In 1935 the Supreme Court issued a series of rulings declaring several New Deal programs, including the AAA, unconstitutional. Roosevelt and his advisers felt that the entire New Deal was in danger. "Mr. President, they mean to destroy us," said Attorney General Homer Cummings.

Roosevelt decided to propose a plan for reorganizing the federal judiciary that was soon to be labeled the "court-packing" bill. This bill would allow the president to appoint a new Supreme Court justice for every justice who was 70 years old or older. Roosevelt would be able to appoint six new justices immediately.

Roosevelt's judiciary plan drew harsh criticism from Congress and the public. Critics charged that Roosevelt was trying to change the balance of power so carefully defined in the U.S. Constitution. After a heated debate, Congress rejected the bill. The Supreme Court, however, did not overturn any more New Deal legislation. Roosevelt eventually had the opportunity to nominate nine new Supreme Court justices to replace those who had retired or died.

READING CHECK **Analyzing Information** Why did Roosevelt try to alter the Supreme Court?

SUMMARY Roosevelt's New Deal programs brought economic relief to many Americans.

Section 2 Assessment

hmhsocialstudies.com
ONLINE QUIZ

Reviewing Ideas, Terms, and People

1. a. **Recall** What were the Hundred Days?
   b. **Make Inferences** What was the purpose of the bank holiday Roosevelt declared?
   c. **Evaluate** Which of the **New Deal** programs that passed during the Hundred Days was most effective? Why?
2. a. **Describe** Who were some of the critics of the New Deal?
   b. **Contrast** How were the ideas of Huey Long and the American Liberty League different?
   c. **Elaborate** Why do you think people supported New Deal critics such as Huey Long and Father Coughlin?
3. a. **Identify** What programs were part of the Second New Deal?
   b. **Make Inferences** Why did the Wagner Act encourage people to join unions?
4. a. **Recall** What happened to some of the New Deal programs when they were challenged in court?
   b. **Make Inferences** What was the purpose of Roosevelt's judiciary reorganization bill?

Critical Thinking

5. **Problem Solving** Review your notes on the challenges faced by the nation and the president during the Depression. Then copy the graphic organizer below and use it to identify Depression problems and New Deal solutions.

Problems	New Deal solutions

FOCUS ON WRITING

6. **Thinking about New Deal Programs** Take notes on the New Deal programs. Think about how your character might be affected by one or more of the programs. For example, how do you think he or she would feel about getting a construction job with the Works Progress Administration?

Case Study

The Great Depression

Wheeler Dam, in northern Alabama, has provided electric power to the region since the Great Depression.

Social Changes During the Great Depression

The Great Depression not only affected our economy and government policies, it changed society in many ways. On an individual level, many Americans faced personal hardships such as separated families and forced moves to find work. People migrated to new areas of the country to look for a job, or to be near family members who could help support them.

Many families left their farms that had been ruined by the Dust Bowl. Some went to cities, others moved to different farming areas and looked for new jobs there. The farms and orchards of California experienced a huge growth in the number of families arriving from the Great Plains. There were so many, in fact, that there were more workers than jobs. As a result, even people who could find work earned very little and their living conditions did not improve much.

Part of Franklin Roosevelt's plan for economic recovery was to create government projects for the unemployed to carry out. The jobs created by these projects were spread across the nation. Agencies such as the Works Projects Administration (WPA), Civilian Conservation Corps (CCC), and the Federal Works Agency (FWA) built public facilities and roads, installed telephone and electric lines, and maintained forests. Workers would crisscross the nation to work on projects organized by one of the many "alphabet agencies." Workers from Florida, for example, might be sent to Oregon to build a telephone line.

The Resettlement Administration was created to help struggling families relocate to federally supported communities. Most of these communities were located in the South or in California. Cahaba, Gee's Bend Farms, and Greenwood Homesteads were three of the towns located in

TVA River Systems

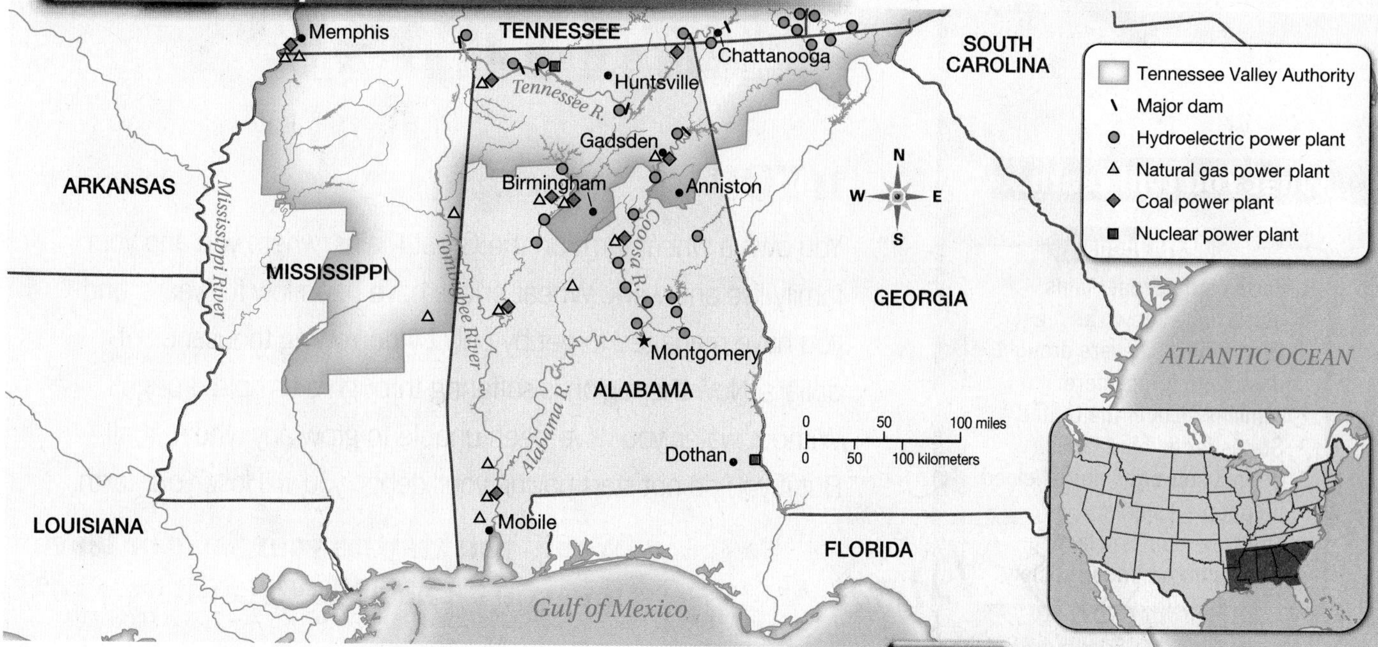

Memphis
TENNESSEE
Chattanooga
Huntsville
Tennessee R.
Gadsden
Birmingham
Anniston
ARKANSAS
Mississippi River
MISSISSIPPI
Tombigbee River
Coosa R.
Montgomery
ALABAMA
Alabama R.
Dothan
Mobile
LOUISIANA
FLORIDA
GEORGIA
SOUTH CAROLINA
ATLANTIC OCEAN
Gulf of Mexico
N
S
E
W
0 50 100 miles
0 50 100 kilometers
Tennessee Valley Authority
Major dam
Hydroelectric power plant
Natural gas power plant
Coal power plant
Nuclear power plant

GEOGRAPHY SKILLS **INTERPRETING MAPS**

Place Which type of power plant is most common in Alabama?

Alabama. Almost 1,000 homes were built by the government for use by Alabamians hit by the Great Depression.

By the end of the Great Depression, many people had better access to roads, electricity, and recreation areas. The Tennessee Valley Authority was a large government project to bring electricity to rural areas from Mississippi to Virginia. Hydroelectric dams built along the Tennessee River and its tributaries still provide electricity to millions of people. Large dams like Wheeler Dam in northern Alabama created huge reservoirs for water storage, flood control, and recreation. Other, smaller dams were built along tributaries of the Tennessee, such as those along the Bear Creek system in Alabama and Clinch River in Tennessee.

Both the TVA and the CCC increased the accessibility of Americans to basic services such as electricity. Along with an economic rebound, Roosevelt's polices drastically changed both society and the role of government in people's lives.

Case Study Assessment

1. Where did people move during the Great Depression?
2. What were the "alphabet agencies"?
3. **Activity** Popular music during the Great Depression often told the stories of people experiencing hardships. Write song lyrics that you think tell the story of someone forced to move during the Great Depression.

SECTION 3

Americans Face Hard Times

What You Will Learn...

Main Ideas

1. Parts of the Great Plains came to be known as the Dust Bowl as severe drought destroyed farms there.
2. Families all over the United States faced hard times.
3. Depression-era culture helped lift people's spirits.
4. The New Deal had lasting effects on American society.

The Big Idea

All over the country, Americans struggled to survive the Great Depression.

Key Terms and People

Dust Bowl
Mary McLeod Bethune
John Steinbeck
Woody Guthrie

hmhsocialstudies.com TAKING NOTES

Use the graphic organizer online to take notes on people's lives during the Depression.

If YOU were there...

You own a wheat farm on the Great Plains, where you and your family live and work. Wheat prices have been low for years, and you have managed to get by only by borrowing thousands of dollars. Now the region is suffering through a terrible drought. Without water, you have been unable to grow any wheat at all. But if you do not start paying your debts, you will lose your farm.

Would you stay on your farm or leave and start a new life somewhere else?

BUILDING BACKGROUND The New Deal provided jobs and relieved suffering for many Americans, but it did not end the Great Depression. Unemployment fell to about 14 percent in 1937 but then rose again to about 17 percent in 1939. All over the country, people still struggled to survive.

The Dust Bowl

For American farmers, hard times began well before the start of the Great Depression. Despite the widespread prosperity of the 1920s, prices for farm products remained low. The Depression worsened this already bad situation. Conditions worsened again when a severe drought hit the Great Plains in the early 1930s and lasted most of the decade. From North Dakota to Texas, crops withered away. With no roots to hold it in place, topsoil began to blow away.

Massive dust storms swept the region, turning parts of the Great Plains into the **Dust Bowl**. "These storms were like rolling black smoke," recalled one Texas schoolboy. "We had to keep the lights on all day. We went to school with the headlights on, and with dust masks on." A woman from Kansas remembered dust storms "covering everything—including ourselves—in a thick, brownish gray blanket . . . Our faces were as dirty as if we had rolled in the dirt; our hair was gray and stiff and we ground dirt between our teeth."

Unable to raise crops, farmers in the Dust Bowl region could not pay their mortgages. Many lost their farms. Several New Deal programs tried to assist farmers by offering loans and by working to stabilize prices for farm products. Scientists also began thinking of ways to prevent dust storms during future droughts. Soil conservation experts encouraged farmers to adopt new farming methods to protect the soil. Grass was planted to hold soil in place, and rows of trees were planted to help break the wind. These changes have helped prevent another Dust Bowl in the years since the Great Depression.

For many farmers in the 1930s, however, the new programs came too late. After losing their crops and livestock to dust storms, about 2.5 million people left the area. Many packed up whatever they could fit in the family car or truck and drove to California to look for any kind of work they could find. Once there, they often found that there were already more workers than available jobs.

READING CHECK **Identifying Cause and Effect** How did the Dust Bowl affect farmers?

Hard Times

The Great Depression took a heavy toll on families all over the United States. Many families were forced to split up, as individual members roamed the country in search of work. To help their families buy food, children often had to drop out of school and take very low-paying jobs. Others left home

Primary Source

PERSONAL ACCOUNT

The Dust Bowl

Lawrence Svobida was a Kansas wheat farmer who saw his life's work destroyed in the 1930s.

"When I knew that my crop was irrevocably [forever] gone I experienced a deathly feeling which, I hope, can affect a man only once in a lifetime. My dreams and ambitions . . . and my shattered ideals seemed gone forever. The very desire to make a success of my life was gone, the spirit and urge to strive were dead within me. Fate had dealt me a cruel blow above which I felt utterly unable to rise."

ANALYSIS SKILL **ANALYZING PRIMARY SOURCES**

How did Svobida feel after his crop was destroyed?

hmhsocialstudies.com INTERACTIVE MAP

The Dust Bowl

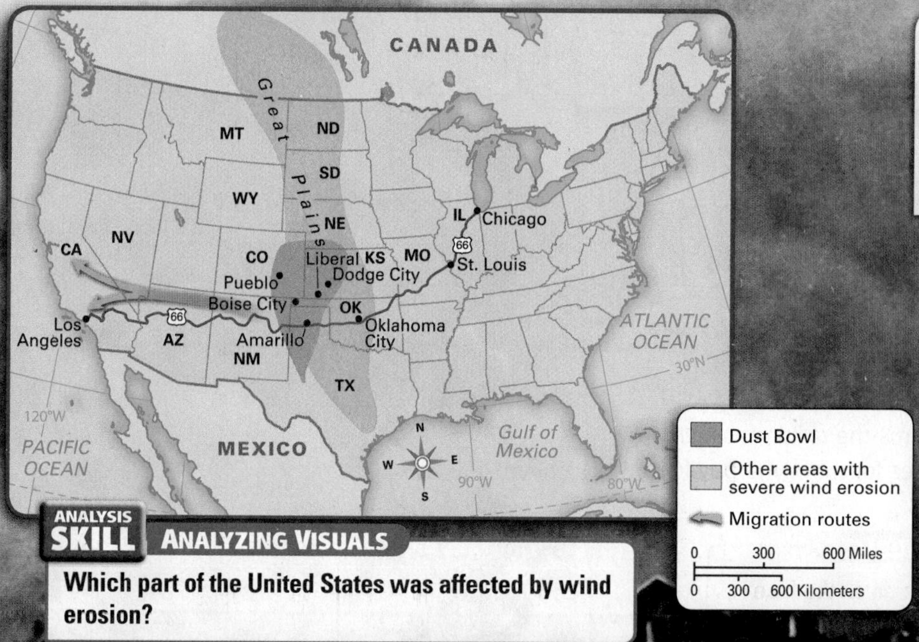

ANALYSIS SKILL **ANALYZING VISUALS**

Which part of the United States was affected by wind erosion?

Severe drought during the 1930s destroyed the livelihood of many Great Plains farmers. Here, a black cloud of dust rages toward the outbuildings of a farm.

to fend for themselves. One boy wrote this diary entry in 1932:

> "Slept in paper box. Bummed swell breakfast three eggs and four pieces meat . . . Rode freight [train] to Roessville. Small burg [town], but got dinner. Walked Bronson . . . Couple a houses. Rode to Sidell . . . Hit homes for meals and turned down. Had to buy supper 20 cents. Raining."
>
> —Anonymous, quoted in *The Great Depression,* by Thomas Minehan

The Great Depression was especially hard on minority groups. As white families moved west in search of jobs, Mexican Americans found it harder to get work. In California local leaders and unions convinced the government to deport many Mexican-born workers. Some of the workers' children were American-born, which made them U.S. citizens, but they were deported anyway.

African Americans also faced discrimination. Many lost jobs to unemployed white workers. One man recalled traveling around Michigan in search of work. He went into a factory that was hiring workers:

> "They didn't hire me because I didn't belong to the right kind of race. Another time I went into Saginaw, it was two white fellas and myself made three. The fella there hired the two men and didn't hire me. I was back out on the streets. That hurt me pretty bad, the race part."
>
> —Louis Banks, quoted in *Hard Times: An Oral History of the Great Depression,* by Studs Terkel

In spite of this type of discrimination, hundreds of thousands of African Americans were able to find work though relief programs such as the CCC and WPA. President Roosevelt also consulted with African American leaders, including educator **Mary McLeod Bethune**. Bethune was one of several African Americans who Roosevelt appointed to his administration. Other members included Walter White and William Henry Hastie. These advisers became known as the Black Cabinet. Their role was to advance the concerns of African Americans in the Roosevelt White House.

First Lady Eleanor Roosevelt was a strong supporter of equal rights. She encouraged the president to include African Americans in his recovery programs. In 1939 the Daughters of the American Revolution (DAR) refused to rent their auditorium to the African American singer Marian Anderson. In protest, Eleanor Roosevelt resigned her membership in the DAR. She then helped Anderson arrange a concert at the base of the Lincoln Memorial. Some 75,000 people attended.

READING CHECK **Drawing Inferences** What weakened families during the Depression?

Primary Source

PHOTOGRAPH

Migrant Mother

Photographer Dorothea Lange gained fame in the 1930s for documenting the conditions of the poor during the Depression. Lange took this famous photograph of a widowed migrant worker and two of her seven children. The woman worked in the pea fields of Nipomo, California. Her family survived by eating frozen peas and birds the children caught. The woman had just sold her car's tires for money to buy food.

ANALYSIS SKILL **ANALYZING PRIMARY SOURCES**

How would you describe the expression on the face of the woman in the photograph?

Depression-Era Culture

Starting in 1935, new Works Progress Administration projects began to put the country's painters, sculptors, writers, and actors to work. When he was criticized for hiring artists, WPA director Henry Hopkins said, "They've got to eat just like other people."

Some of the work done by WPA artists has become an important part of American culture. For example, WPA musicians went into the nation's rural areas to record cowboy ballads, folk songs, and African American spirituals. This music might have been lost without these recordings. Artists employed by the WPA made more than 2,500 murals and 17,000 pieces of sculpture for public spaces. WPA writers created a permanent record of American life by interviewing Americans of many different backgrounds about their lives and memories.

Like many people at the time, author **John Steinbeck** was deeply affected by the Great Depression. Depression life became a main theme of Steinbeck's most famous novel, *The Grapes of Wrath*. The novel tells the story of the Joads, a family of farmers who are forced to move to California for work.

Some of the music of the day expressed themes similar to Steinbeck's. Oklahoma-born folk singer **Woody Guthrie** crisscrossed the country singing his songs of loss and struggle. One contained the line, "All along your green valley I'll work till I die"—a grim reality for some Americans.

Swing music, meanwhile, became popular for a different reason. Instead of focusing on the sadness of the Depression, swing helped people forget their troubles. Big band leaders such as Duke Ellington, Benny Goodman, and Count Basie helped make swing wildly popular in the 1930s. People tuned into swing music shows on inexpensive radios and danced to the fast-paced rhythms. Radios provided people with other forms of entertainment as well. Every week millions of Americans put aside their worries to listen to radio shows such as *Little Orphan Annie* and *The Lone Ranger*.

Movies offered Americans another welcome escape from reality. One boy remembered how he and his friends would save their pennies for movie tickets. "[It] was two for a nickel," he said. "You'd come to the movie in the summer like 8:30 in the mornin' and you'd see about 200 kids." For 25 cents or less, adults, too, could forget their troubles as they watched historical dramas, gangster films, comedies, and musicals.

READING CHECK **Evaluating** How was the work of writers and musicians affected by the Great Depression?

Escape to the Movies

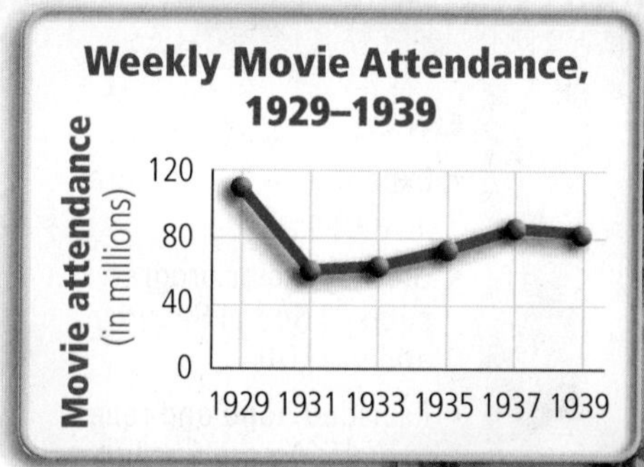

ANALYSIS SKILL **ANALYZING INFORMATION**

How many Americans attended movies in 1930?

THE IMPACT TODAY

Today many of the thousands of interviews conducted by WPA writers are available on the Internet. You can read the stories of former slaves, pioneers, Native American leaders, and others in their own words.

Causes and Effects of the New Deal

QUICK FACTS

Causes	Effects
• Stock market crash • Banking crisis • Soaring unemployment • Farmers' troubles • Widespread poverty	• Expanded role of federal government • Created major programs such as Social Security and the FDIC • Provided hope and relief to many Americans but did not end the Great Depression

Effects of the New Deal

People are still debating the effects of the New Deal today. New Deal critics point out that Roosevelt's programs did not end the Great Depression. Full recovery occurred in the early 1940s, after the United States entered World War II. Roosevelt's supporters, however, believe that the New Deal gave Americans help and hope in a time of severe economic crisis.

People today do agree that the New Deal greatly expanded the role of the federal government. Some of the programs and agencies created as part of the New Deal, such as Social Security and the Federal Deposit Insurance Corporation (FDIC), remain part of our lives. Social Security still provides economic relief to the elderly, children, and those with disabilities. The FDIC protects the savings of bank customers.

READING CHECK **Finding the Main Idea** What are some current government programs that began during the New Deal?

SUMMARY The New Deal helped Americans but did not end the Great Depression. The Depression finally ended after the United States entered World War II.

Section 3 Assessment

hmhsocialstudies.com
ONLINE QUIZ

Reviewing Ideas, Terms, and People

1. **a. Identify** What was the **Dust Bowl**?
   b. Explain What factors contributed to farmers' difficulties in the 1920s and 1930s?
2. **a. Recall** What were some of the problems people faced during the Depression?
   b. Compare How was the experience of African Americans and Mexican Americans in the Depression similar?
   c. Evaluate Do you think President Roosevelt did enough to help African Americans? Explain your answer.
3. **a. Draw Conclusions** Why do you think swing music, radio shows, and movies were popular during the Great Depression?
   b. Identify How did the WPA help the arts?
4. **a. Recall** What are the different viewpoints on the success of the New Deal?
   b. Elaborate How are Social Security and the FDIC still important today?

Critical Thinking

5. **Categorizing** Review your notes on life during the Great Depression. Then copy the graphic organizer below and use it to identify challenges people faced during the Depression and the ways they coped.

Challenges people faced	Ways people coped with challenges

FOCUS ON WRITING

6. **Taking Notes on the Hard Times** As you read this section, add notes about the Dust Bowl, family life, and Depression-era culture. What would it have been like to be a farmer at this time? How would you describe your experiences?

Depression-Era Literature

GUIDED READING

WORD HELP

migrant a person who moves regularly

Divide The Continental Divide separates rivers that flow east from those that flow west.

tributary stream that feeds into a larger river or lake (Steinbeck applies the word to the road system.)

❶ ***From what are people on Highway 66 fleeing?***

❷ ***How does Steinbeck describe what people are running from?***

from *The Grapes of Wrath*

by John Steinbeck (1902–1968)

About the Reading *Published in 1939,* The Grapes of Wrath *described the impact of the Great Depression on the nation. In this passage, Steinbeck describes a journey of Dust Bowl families to California.*

AS YOU READ **Look for details that appeal to the five senses.**

Highway 66 is the main migrant road. 66—the long, concrete path across the country, waving gently up and down the map, from the Mississippi [River] to Bakersfield [California]—over the red lands and the gray lands, twisting up into the mountains, crossing the Divide and down into the bright and terrible desert to the mountains again, and into the rich California valleys.

66 is the path of people in flight,❶ refugees from dust and shrinking land, from the thunder of tractors and shrinking ownership, from the desert's slow northward invasion, from the twisting winds that howl up out of Texas, from the floods that bring no richness to the land and steal what little richness is there.❷ From all of these the people are in flight, and they come into 66 from the tributary side roads, from the wagon tracks and the rutted country roads. 66 is the mother road, the road of flight.

CONNECTING LITERATURE TO HISTORY

1. **Steinbeck describes in vivid detail the fear that people on the road felt.** According to this passage, why might driving between towns be a terror? What does this tell you about the migrants?

2. ***The Grapes of Wrath* became a favorite among readers for its honest portrayal of the realities of the Depression.** Based on Steinbeck's description and on what you already know, how might people traveling on Route 66 have felt? Why?

Having a Debate

Define the Skill

The First Amendment to the U.S. Constitution guarantees freedom of speech, assembly, and the press. These freedoms have become a key part of American democracy. They guarantee that both government officials and citizens can express their opinions. People also have the right to express disagreement with leaders or the government.

The ability to discuss opposing points of view is key to a democratic society. In the United States, citizens vote for their leaders. Having access to different points of view helps people decide which candidates to support in elections.

One way to express opposing points of view is to have a debate. Debates are organized to present two sides of an issue. Debate rules make sure that both sides are treated fairly. By learning about the strengths and weaknesses of two positions on an issue, people can decide which position is more convincing.

Learn the Skill

Think about the opposition President Franklin D. Roosevelt faced when he tried to begin new programs during the Great Depression. He had to convince people to support his ideas. Roosevelt and members of his administration used radio programs and newspaper articles to promote their point of view and answer questions from their critics.

In a debate, it is important to make your point of view clear. Explain why you support a certain position or give specific reasons why you oppose it. The more detailed the argument, the more persuasive it will be. When you are in a debate, make sure to prepare plenty of evidence and examples to support your case.

Debaters have the chance not only to present a case but also to argue against the opposite point of view. One way to get ready for this is to think of possible arguments against your position. Prepare responses to each of these arguments in advance. Having good answers to criticism makes your position stronger.

In a debate, it is important to follow any rules that have been set up. Not all debates have the same rules. They do share some basic guidelines, however. Only one person is allowed to speak at once, and speaking time is limited. The two sides take turns presenting their arguments. Debates may have additional rules as well.

Practice the Skill

Suppose that your class is the Senate in 1933. President Roosevelt has already begun several new government programs. Now he is asking you to pass more new laws, which he believes will help the economy. Follow the guidelines above to have a debate about the New Deal. One group should support expanding the New Deal, and one group should oppose it. When the debate is over, answer the following questions.

1. Did your group make its point of view clear? Did it explain the reasons for taking that position? What do you think was your group's most persuasive supporting detail or example?
2. Did your group prepare arguments against the other side in advance? Were any of these arguments particularly effective?

CHAPTER 10

Chapter Review

History's Impact
▶ **video series**
Review the video to answer the closing question:
How did some of Roosevelt's programs lessen the damage caused by the recessions of 1987 and the early 2000s?

Visual Summary

QUICK FACTS

Use the visual summary below to help you review the main ideas of the chapter.

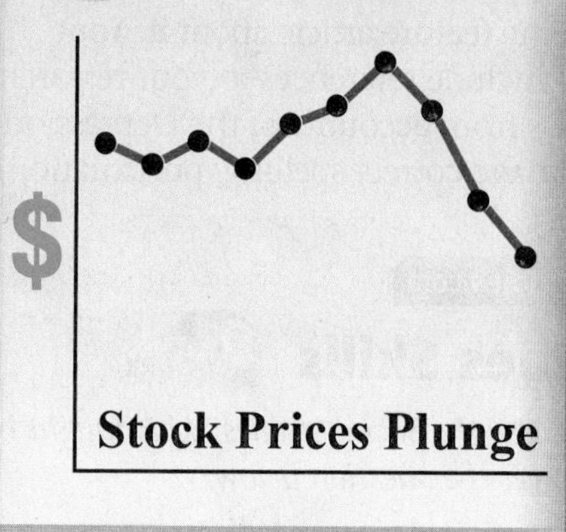

$
Stock Prices Plunge

The economy began to decline when the stock market crashed in 1929.

Many farmers from the Great Plains moved elsewhere to escape the devastation of the Dust Bowl.

President Roosevelt and Congress tried to end the financial crisis.

Reviewing Vocabulary, Terms, and People

Read each question and write the letter of the best response.

1. Which of the following refers to a severe economic downturn that lasted for more than 10 years?

a. the Bonus Army **c.** the bull market
b. the Great Depression **d.** the business cycle

2. Who was Franklin Roosevelt's secretary of labor and the first woman cabinet member?

a. Frances Perkins **c.** Eleanor Roosevelt
b. Mary McLeod Bethune **d.** Dorothea Lange

3. Parts of the Great Plains where a severe drought struck were known as the

a. Tennessee Valley. **c.** Dust Bowl.
b. New Deal. **d.** Hoovervilles.

4. Which of the following means purchasing stocks on credit with a loan?

a. the installment plan **c.** the banking crisis
b. buying on margin **d.** bear market

Comprehension and Critical Thinking

SECTION 1

5. a. Describe What happened on Black Tuesday—October 29, 1929?

b. Summarize How did President Hoover respond to the Depression?

c. Elaborate Why do you think Americans were so unprepared for difficult times?

SECTION 2

6. a. Recall What New Deal programs did lawmakers create during the Hundred Days?

b. Explain How did the Works Progress Administration help Americans?

c. Evaluate Do you think the New Deal was successful? Explain your answer.

SECTION 3

7. a. **Recall** How did the Great Depression affect Mexican Americans?

   b. **Contrast** How did Depression-era culture show both hope and the difficulties of everyday life?

   c. **Draw Conclusions** Why do you think many African Americans supported President Roosevelt, even though they continued to face discrimination and segregation?

Reviewing Themes

8. **Economics** How did the economy of the country change during the Great Depression?
9. **Politics** What role did politics play in easing the Great Depression?

Reading Skills 21st Century

Recognizing Implied Main Ideas *Use the Reading Skills taught in this chapter to answer the question about the reading selection below.*

> Banks had invested heavily in the stock market, so they lost heavily when the market crashed. Banks had also lent their customers money to buy stocks on margin. Now those customers were unable to pay back their loans. Some banks went out of business. People who had deposited their life savings in those banks lost everything.

10. Write a main idea for the paragraph above.

Using the Internet 21st Century

11. **Activity: Writing an Article** During the 1930s, part of the Great Plains region of the United States became known as the Dust Bowl. The troubled region earned its nickname from the dust storms that swept through the dry, drought-stricken area. Through your online textbook, research accounts of the Dust Bowl and write a magazine feature article about it. Your article should include references to your research and quotations from accounts of the Depression, and it should have correct spelling, punctuation, and grammar.

hmhsocialstudies.com

Social Studies Skills 21st Century

Having a Debate *Use the Social Studies Skills taught in this chapter to answer the question below.*

12. Suppose you have been invited to participate in a debate on Franklin Roosevelt's plan to "pack" the Supreme Court by adding extra justices. First decide on your position. Then prepare several supporting arguments. Summarize the main points of your argument in a paragraph.

Focus on Writing

13. **Writing Your Journal Entry** Review your notes. Then decide on a fictional character and a set of circumstances for your character. Choose one or more events from the Great Depression for your character to talk about. Write a one-page journal entry about the life of this person. Begin by placing a date from the 1930s at the top of the page. Think about what life would have been like for this person. Remember to describe how the character feels about his or her experiences. What are your character's hopes and fears for the future?

CHAPTER 10 Standardized Test Practice

DIRECTIONS: Read each question and write the letter of the best response.

1 President Roosevelt successfully used his fireside chats to

- **A** promote the American movie industry.
- **B** hold negotiations between labor unions and business owners.
- **C** persuade many Americans to vote for him in the election of 1932.
- **D** convince people that it was safe to keep their money in reopened banks.

2 Dorothea Lange contributed to our understanding of Depression life by

- **A** writing novels about Dust Bowl farmers.
- **B** singing songs about loss and hardship.
- **C** photographing migrant workers.
- **D** making movies that helped people forget their troubles.

3 How did the National Labor Relations Act affect organized labor?

- **A** It increased the power of labor unions and helped them grow.
- **B** It banned all strikes and increased the power of big business.
- **C** It created new government jobs but did not affect labor unions.
- **D** It gave relief money directly to labor unions to help unemployed workers.

4 What part of the business cycle contributes to a depression?

- **A** Consumers begin buying more, and companies increase production.
- **B** Businesses produce more than they can sell, and manufacturing slows.
- **C** The stock market is a bull market, and investors make large profits.
- **D** People are buying products with cash.

5 Which of the following was a part of the New Deal?

- **A** nationalizing businesses
- **B** relieving unemployment
- **C** guaranteeing every family an income of at least $5,000
- **D** discouraging negotiations between labor unions and business owners

6 Which of the following was a way many families coped with the Depression?

- **A** They bought stocks on margin.
- **B** They sent their children to boarding schools in California.
- **C** They moved to the Dust Bowl looking for farm jobs.
- **D** They separated to look for work.

7 Read the excerpt from John Steinbeck's *The Grapes of Wrath* and use it to answer the question below.

> "66 is the path of people in flight, refugees from dust and shrinking land, from the thunder of tractors and shrinking ownership, from the desert's slow northward invasion, from the twisting winds that howl up out of Texas, from the floods that bring no richness to the land and steal what little richness is there."
>
> —John Steinbeck, *The Grapes of Wrath*

Document-Based Question Why did people travel on Highway 66, according to Steinbeck?

© Houghton Mifflin Harcourt Publishing Company

The Great Depression

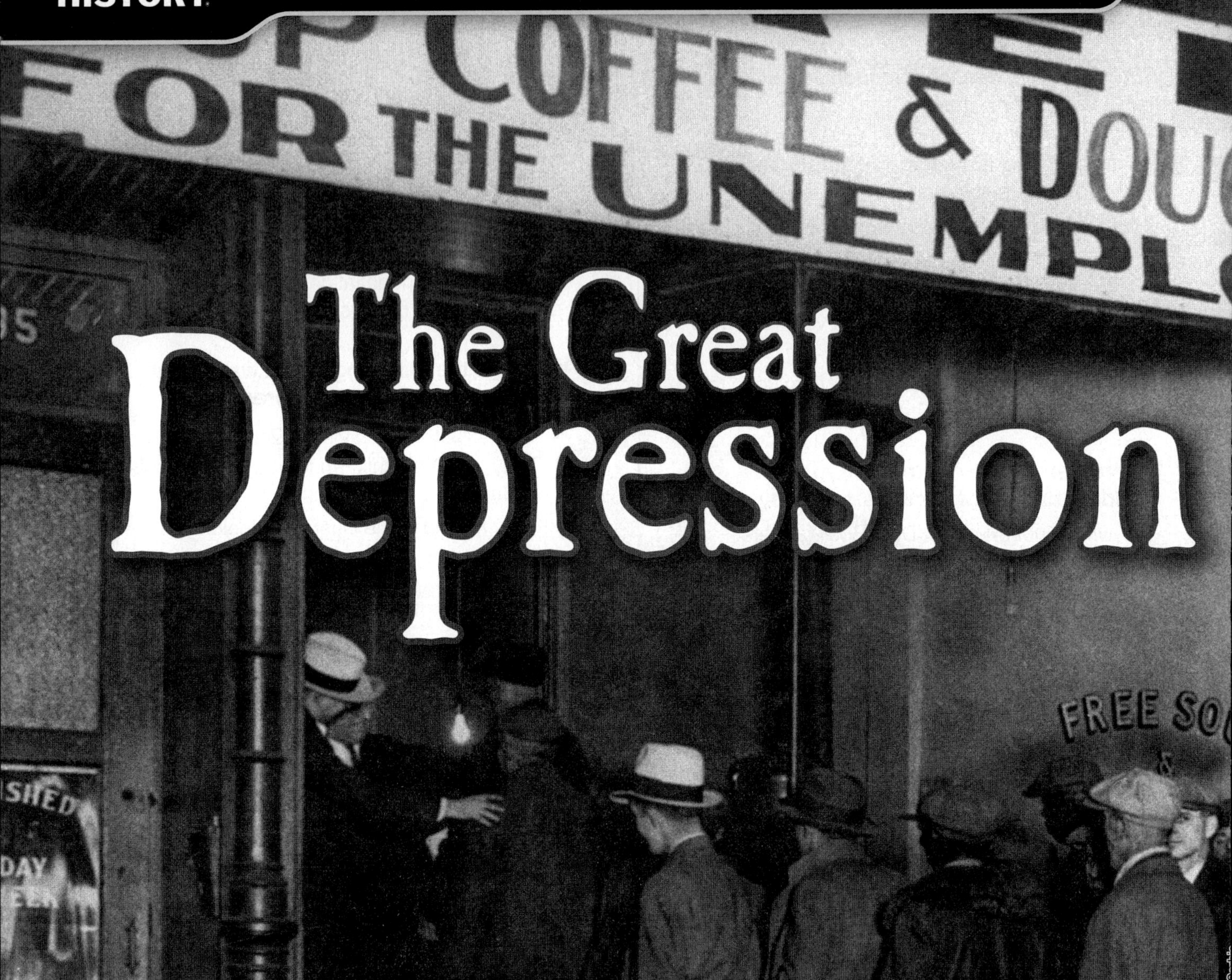

The Great Depression, which lasted from 1929 to 1939, was the most severe economic downturn in the history of the United States. The boom times of the 1920s concealed severe weaknesses in the American economy. The stock market crash of 1929 exposed the economy's shaky foundations and plunged the country into a deep economic depression. To stimulate the economy, President Franklin Delano Roosevelt introduced a host of government programs. This New Deal alleviated the worst aspects of the Great Depression. However, it would take a world war to bring the country to full economic recovery.

Explore the impact of the Great Depression online. You can find a wealth of information, video clips, primary sources, activities, and more at hmhsocialstudies.com.

A Picture Worth 1,000 Words

Watch the video to learn about the work of photographer Dorothea Lange, who chronicled the Great Depression.

CLICK THROUGH INTER/ACTIVITIES

hmhsocialstudies.com

A New Deal

Watch the video to see how President Roosevelt intended to fight the Great Depression.

Public Works

Watch the video to see examples of the New Deal programs introduced by President Roosevelt.

From Depression to War

Watch the video to see how the American economy finally recovered from the Great Depression.

© Houghton Mifflin Harcourt Publishing Company • Image Credits: (c), ©Bettmann/Corbis; (t), Library of Congress, Prints and Photographs Division, Farm Security Administration, Office of War Information Photograph Collection.

CHAPTER 11 1938–1945

World War II

Essential Question How did events and battles during World War II change American society and the nation's role in the world?

ALABAMA COURSE OF STUDY

6 Identify causes and consequences of World War II and reasons for entry of the United States into the war.

- Locating on a map Allied countries and Axis Powers.
- Locating on a map key engagements of World War II, including Pearl Harbor; the battles of Normandy, Stalingrad, and Midway; and the Battle of the Bulge.
- Identifying key figures of World War II, including Franklin D. Roosevelt, Sir Winston Churchill, Harry S. Truman, Joseph Stalin, Adolf Hitler, Benito Mussolini, Michinomiya Hirohito, and Hideki Tojo.
- Describing the development of and the decision to use the atomic bomb.
- Describing human costs associated with World War II.
- Explaining the importance of the surrender of the Axis Powers ending World War II.

7 Identify changes on the American home front during World War II.

- Recognizing the retooling of factories from consumer to military production.
- Identifying new roles of women and African Americans in the workforce.
- Describing increased demand on Birmingham steel industry and Port of Mobile facilities
- Describing the experience of African Americans and Japanese Americans in the United States during World War II, including the Tuskegee Airmen and occupants of internment camps.

8 Describe how the United States' role in the Cold War influenced domestic and international events.

- Recognizing Alabama's role in the Cold War.

10 Analyze changing economic priorities and cycles of economic expansion and contraction for their impact on society since World War II.

- Identifying policies and programs that had an economic impact on society since World War II.

Focus on Writing

A Radio News Broadcast During World War II, millions of Americans had relatives fighting overseas. They relied on radio broadcasts for up-to-date news from the battlefronts around the world. In this chapter, you will read about American involvement in World War II. Then you will write a radio news broadcast about an event from the war.

UNITED STATES

1938 Orson Welles broadcasts "War of the Worlds."

1938

WORLD

Image Credits: (t), ©Corbis

© Houghton Mifflin Harcourt Publishing Company

HISTORY

Japanese Attack Pearl Harbor

hmhsocialstudies.com VIDEO

The D-Day invasion at Normandy, France, was one of the most successful Allied invasions of the war.

1941 On December 7, the Japanese attack the U.S. fleet at Pearl Harbor, Hawaii.

1942 German submarines begin attacking the United States.

1944 U.S. forces participate in the D-Day invasion.

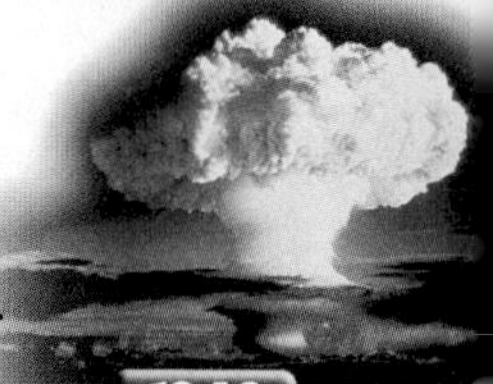

1945 The United States drops atomic bombs on Hiroshima and Nagasaki, Japan.

1940 — 1942 — 1944 — 1946

1940 Alan Turing devises a way to break the code of the German Enigma machine.

1943 Mussolini is overthrown and executed in Italy.

1944 The Allies enter Paris.

1945 Hideki Tojo, prime minister of Japan, attempts suicide after atomic bombs are dropped on Japan.

© Houghton Mifflin Harcourt Publishing Company

Image Credits: (t), ©Corbis; (bc), ©MPI/Getty Images; (bl), AKG-Images, London; (cr), Reuters/HO/Hulton Archive/Getty Images

Reading Social Studies

Economics | Geography | Politics | Society and Culture | Science and Technology

Focus on Themes In this chapter, you will read about the causes and consequences of World War II. You will learn about how **geography** played an important role in the fighting of the war. You will also read about how **society and culture** reacted to the Second World War.

Categorizing

Focus on Reading Have you ever read a schoolbook and been overwhelmed by the amount of information it contained? Categorizing events, people, and ideas can help you make sense of the facts you learn in this book.

Understanding Categorizing Ideas, people, events, and things can all be categorized in many different ways. For the study of history, some of the most useful ways are by time period and by similarity between events. Categorizing events by the people involved can also be helpful. Within a category, you can make subcategories to further organize the information.

People involved in WWII	Events of WWII
• Winston Churchill • Franklin D. Roosevelt • Adolf Hitler • Benito Mussolini • Hideki Tojo • Soldiers • Civilians	• Key battles • Treaties • Invasions ↓ **Invasions** • China • Rhineland • Czechoslovakia • Poland • Dunkirk • French Indochina • D-Day

© Houghton Mifflin Harcourt Publishing Company

You Try It!

As you read the passage, look for ways to organize the information.

Japan Advances

American and Filipino forces under the command of American general Douglas MacArthur could not stop Japan's advance in the Philippines. MacArthur left the islands in March 1942, vowing to return. More than 70,000 American and Filipino soldiers surrendered to the Japanese. The exhausted soldiers were forced to march 63 miles up the Bataan Peninsula to prison camps. Many prisoners were starved and beaten by Japanese soldiers. More than 600 Americans and about 10,000 Filipinos died in the Bataan Death March.

After you read the passage, answer the following questions.

1. What are two categories you could use to organize the information in this passage?

2. How many different kinds of people are mentioned in this passage?

3. What different places are mentioned in this passage?

4. Complete the chart below using the information from the passage above.

People involved	Countries involved	Places mentioned

As you read this chapter, remember to look for categories that can help you organize the information you read.

Key Terms and People

Chapter 11

Section 1

totalitarianism
Benito Mussolini
fascism
Adolf Hitler
Nazis
Joseph Stalin
Axis Powers
appeasement
Winston Churchill
Allied Powers
Lend-Lease Act
Pearl Harbor

Section 2

War Production Board
A. Philip Randolph
Tuskegee Airmen
Benjamin O. Davis Jr.
zoot-suit riots
internment

Section 3

Battle of El Alamein
Dwight D. Eisenhower
Battle of Stalingrad
D-Day

Section 4

Douglas MacArthur
Bataan Death March
Chester Nimitz
Battle of the Coral Sea
Battle of Midway
island hopping
Battle of Leyte Gulf
kamikaze

Section 5

Battle of the Bulge
Harry S. Truman
Holocaust
genocide
Manhattan Project
atomic bomb

Academic Vocabulary

In this chapter, you will learn the following academic word:

execute

© Houghton Mifflin Harcourt Publishing Company

SECTION 1

The War Begins

What You Will Learn...

Main Ideas

1. During the 1930s, totalitarian governments rose to power in Europe and Japan.
2. German expansion led to the start of World War II in Europe in 1939.
3. The United States joined the war after Japan attacked Pearl Harbor in 1941.

The Big Idea

The rise of aggressive totalitarian governments led to the start of World War II.

Key Terms and People

totalitarianism
Benito Mussolini
fascism
Adolf Hitler
Nazis
Joseph Stalin
Axis Powers
appeasement
Winston Churchill
Allied Powers
Lend-Lease Act
Pearl Harbor

hmhsocialstudies.com
TAKING NOTES

Use the graphic organizer online to take notes on the countries in which totalitarian governments gained power before World War II.

If YOU were there...

The year is 1933, and your family is struggling through the Great Depression along with millions of others. Sometimes your parents wonder if they should have left Italy to come to the United States. But conditions in Italy are far from ideal. A dictator rules the country, and the people have little personal freedom.

What would you say to your parents?

BUILDING BACKGROUND The devastating effects of the Great Depression reached well beyond the United States. In Europe, war debt and the huge costs of rebuilding after World War I made economic recovery even more difficult.

The Rise of Totalitarianism

Desperate to end the hard times, many people were willing to give up their individual rights to leaders who promised to deliver prosperity and national glory. As a result, in the 1920s and 1930s, several European countries moved toward **totalitarianism**, a political system in which the government controls every aspect of citizens' lives.

Italy

In the years after World War I, the people of Italy suffered through economic depression, unemployment, strikes, and riots. Many Italians looked for a strong leader who could bring stability to the country. They found such a leader in **Benito Mussolini**, who gained complete control of Italy in 1922. Mussolini's rule was based on **fascism**, a political system in which the "state"—or government—is seen as more important than individuals. Fascist systems are typically militaristic and headed by a strong leader.

Mussolini restored order to Italy and improved the economy through public works projects. But the fascist government violently crushed all opposition, destroying basic individual rights such as freedom of speech. In 1935 Mussolini tried to expand Italy's territory by attacking the nation of Ethiopia, making it a colony. Haile Selassie, Ethiopia's overthrown emperor, warned the world, "It is us today. It will be you tomorrow."

© Houghton Mifflin Harcourt Publishing Company

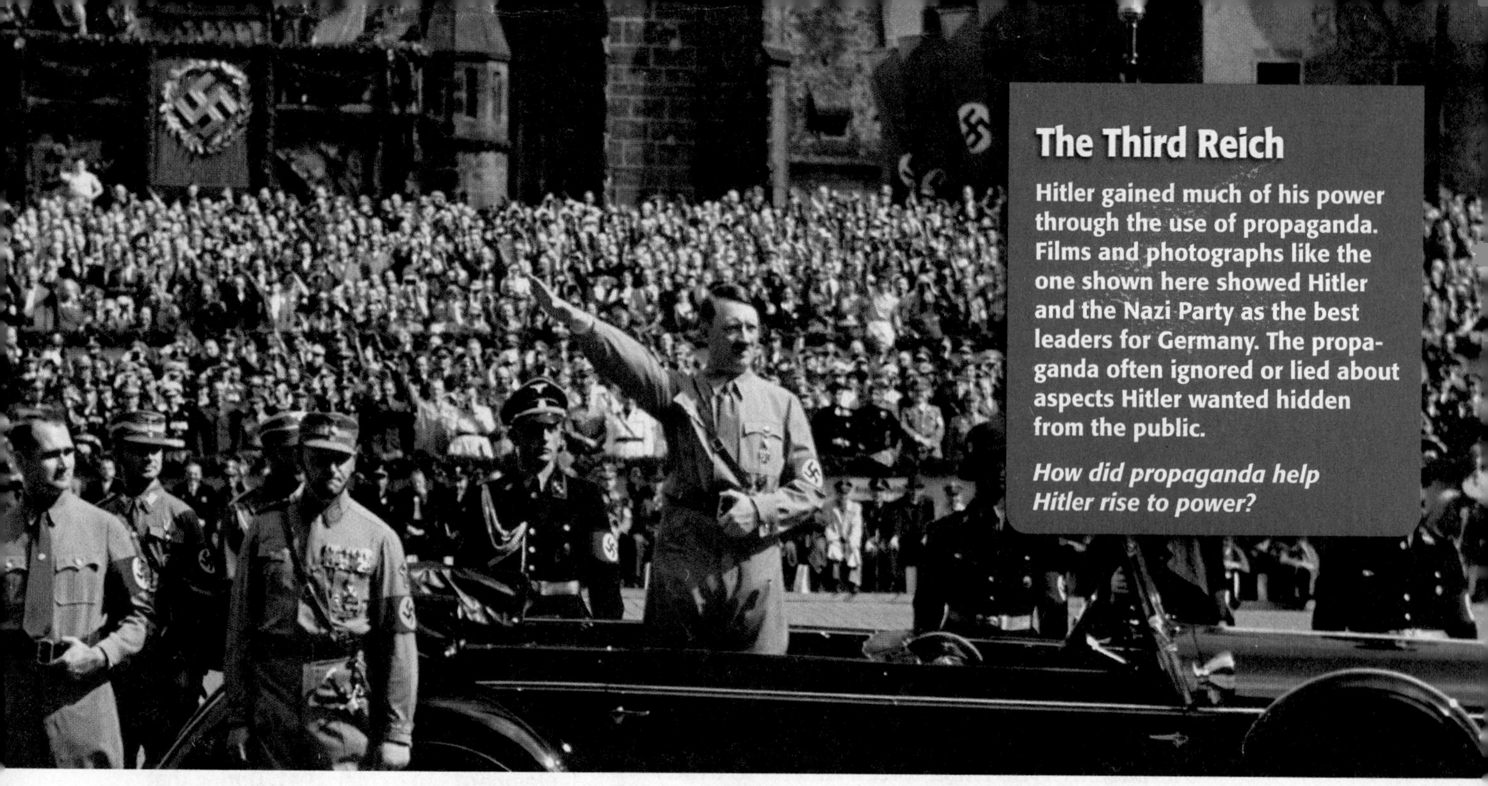

The Third Reich

Hitler gained much of his power through the use of propaganda. Films and photographs like the one shown here showed Hitler and the Nazi Party as the best leaders for Germany. The propaganda often ignored or lied about aspects Hitler wanted hidden from the public.

How did propaganda help Hitler rise to power?

Germany

Germany was also suffering the effects of the global depression. In addition, many Germans were furious about the Treaty of Versailles, which forced Germany to make crippling re-paration payments for its role in World War I. Politician and World War I veteran **Adolf Hitler** took advantage of public anger to gain power. A fiery speaker, he inspired huge audiences by vowing to restore Germany to prosperity and a position of international power.

Hitler also offered Germans a scapegoat, or someone to blame for their problems. He accused intellectuals, Communists, and especially Jews of causing Germany's defeat in World War I and its economic problems after the war. Only by ridding itself of Jews, Hitler declared, would Germany again rise to greatness. Hitler's National Socialist Party, or **Nazis**, gained a large following. Hitler became chancellor in 1933 and quickly seized all government power.

The Soviet Union

Hitler spoke with fury of his hatred of communism. But he had something in common with the Communist ruler of the Soviet Union—both ruled as ruthless dictators. By 1928 **Joseph Stalin** had become dictator of the Soviet Union. In the 1930s Stalin terrorized those he saw as political enemies, killing or imprisoning millions of Soviet citizens. As one Soviet artist put it, "There isn't a single thinking adult in this country who hasn't thought that he might get shot."

Japan

Though Japan never had one single dictator, a group of military leaders slowly gained complete control over the government during the early 1900s. By the early 1930s this group had more influence than the Japanese emperor. The military leaders wanted to build a large Japanese empire in East Asia. In 1931 Japan invaded and conquered a region in northern China and called it Manchukuo. From 1937 to 1938, at least 360,000 Chinese were killed by the invading Japanese in the fall of Nanjing. The United States protested the invasion. Fearful of another world war, however, most Americans opposed using force to help China.

hmhsocialstudies.com

ANIMATED GEOGRAPHY AND HISTORY

Axis Powers' Aggression to 1941

READING CHECK **Comparing and Contrasting** What did the leaders of totalitarian governments have in common?

© Houghton Mifflin Harcourt Publishing Company • Image Credits: (t) ©Hugo Jaeger/Timepix/Time Life Pictures/Getty Images

Germany Expands

Hitler dreamed of avenging Germany's defeat in World War I. "The lost land will never be won back by solemn appeals to God," he told Germans, "nor by hopes in any League of Nations, but only by force of arms." Hitler wanted to build an empire, uniting all German-speaking people in Europe. He also wanted "living space" for the growing German population.

In violation of the Treaty of Versailles, Hitler began to rebuild the German military. In 1936 Nazi troops invaded the Rhineland, a former German territory lost during World War I. That year he also signed an alliance with Mussolini, forming the **Axis Powers**. Japan later joined this pact. In 1938 Hitler forced Austria to unite with Germany. Then he demanded control of the Sudetenland, a region in Czechoslovakia where many Germans lived. When the Czechs refused, Hitler threatened war.

Appeasement Fails

Czech leaders looked to their allies in France and Great Britain for help. But neither country wanted to be pulled into an armed conflict. British prime minister Neville Chamberlain organized a meeting with Hitler to work out a peaceful solution. At the 1938 Munich Conference, Germany was given control over the Sudetenland in return for a promise not to demand more land. This approach was known as **appeasement**—a policy of avoiding war with an aggressive nation by giving in to its demands. British admiral **Winston Churchill** was convinced that this strategy would not stop Hitler. "The government had to choose between shame and war," Churchill warned. "They have chosen shame. They will get war."

Churchill was right. In March 1939, German troops seized the rest of Czechoslovakia and began demanding territory from Poland. Great Britain and France pledged to defend Poland if Hitler attacked. To keep the Soviets out of the conflict, Hitler signed a nonaggression pact with Joseph Stalin in August 1939. In

Nazi planes bombed London from September 1940 to May 1941. During that time, residents of London sought shelter wherever they could, including subway stations. Here, a relief effort passes out food to Londoners who have lost their homes.

addition to promising not to attack each other, the two countries secretly agreed to divide Poland between them.

On September 1, 1939, Hitler's troops and tanks rushed into Poland. This was the start of World War II. Two days later, Britain and France, known as the **Allied Powers**, declared war on Germany. Neville Chamberlain spoke bitterly of the failure of appeasement, saying, "Everything that I believed in during my public life has crashed into ruins."

Hitler Moves West

The Allied Powers had little time to organize their forces to protect Poland. Using a strategy called *blitzkrieg*, or "lightning war," German tanks and airplanes broke through Polish defenses. As German forces drove into Poland from the west, the Soviets attacked from the east. Within a month, the two powers had taken control of Poland.

With Poland secure, Hitler turned toward western Europe. In the spring of 1940, Germany quickly conquered Denmark, Norway,

© Houghton Mifflin Harcourt Publishing Company • Image Credits: (t) ©Corbis

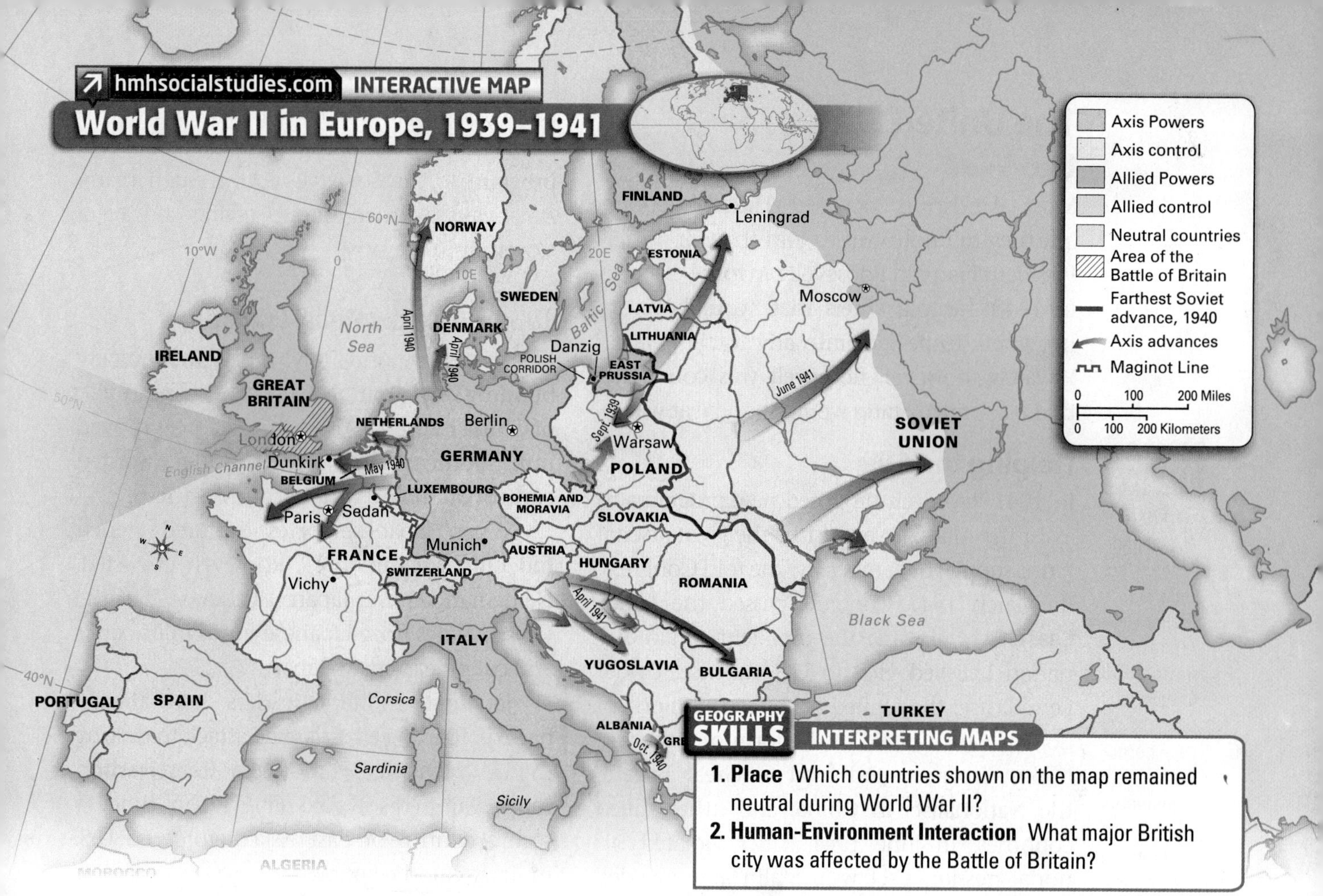

GEOGRAPHY SKILLS INTERPRETING MAPS

1. **Place** Which countries shown on the map remained neutral during World War II?
2. **Human-Environment Interaction** What major British city was affected by the Battle of Britain?

Belgium, Luxembourg, and the Netherlands. German troops then invaded France, trapping hundreds of thousands of Belgian, British, and French soldiers in the French port city of Dunkirk. British ships raced to Dunkirk and carried the soldiers across the English Channel to safety in Britain.

German forces, meanwhile, continued their march through France. As the Germans approached the French capital of Paris, Italy declared war on the Allied powers. France surrendered to Germany on June 22, 1940. Many of the French soldiers who had escaped at Dunkirk, however, continued to resist Germany's occupation of France. In London, French general Charles de Gaulle organized a "Free French" army to fight alongside the Allies. "France has lost a battle," de Gaulle declared. "But France has not lost the war!"

The Battle of Britain

Great Britain now stood alone against Hitler's war machine. "The final German victory over England is now only a question of time," said German general Alfred Jodl. Hitler prepared to invade Britain. To safely move troops and equipment across the English Channel, Germany first had to defeat the British Royal Air Force (RAF). In July 1940 the Luftwaffe, or German air force, began attacking British planes and airfields in what became known as the Battle of Britain.

In August Hitler ordered the Luftwaffe to begin bombing British cities in the hope of crushing British morale. But Winston Churchill, the new prime minister, refused to give in. "We shall fight on the beaches," he vowed. "We shall fight in the fields and in the streets, we shall never surrender." Using the new technology of radar, the RAF was able to detect and destroy some 2,300 of the Luftwaffe's aircraft. Hitler canceled the invasion of Britain.

READING CHECK **Sequencing** What event sparked World War II?

© Houghton Mifflin Harcourt Publishing Company

The United States Joins the War

Most Americans opposed Hitler's actions, but they did not want to join the war. When President Franklin Roosevelt ran for re-election in 1940, he told voters that "your boys are not going to be sent into any foreign wars." Privately, however, Roosevelt was convinced that the United States would soon be at war.

THE IMPACT TODAY

Pearl Harbor is still the headquarters of the U.S. Pacific Fleet today. The sunken USS *Arizona*, still visible beneath the harbor waters, is a national memorial to the victims of the Pearl Harbor attack.

Helping the Allies

In 1941 Roosevelt proposed new programs to assist the Allies. "We must be the great arsenal [arms supply] of democracy," he told Congress. In March 1941 Congress passed the **Lend-Lease Act**, allowing the president to aid any nation believed vital to U.S. defense. Under Lend-Lease, the United States sent billions of dollars' worth of aid in the form of weapons, tanks, airplanes, and food to Great Britain, the Nationalists in China, and other Allied countries. In June 1941 Hitler violated his nonaggression pact with Stalin and invaded the Soviet Union. The Soviets then joined the Allies in the fight against Germany. In November the United States extended the Lend-Lease program to the Soviet Union, though many Americans worried about giving aid to a Communist country.

Japan Attacks Pearl Harbor

Like Germany and Italy, Japan was quickly building an empire. After conquering much of China in the 1930s, Japanese forces moved into Southeast Asia. Japan's leaders wanted control of oil and other resources there.

When Japanese forces captured French Indochina in July 1941, Roosevelt protested. He demanded that Japan withdraw. Then the United States froze Japanese funds in its banks and cut off exports to Japan.

Japanese military leaders had already begun planning a large-scale attack to destroy the U.S. naval fleet stationed at **Pearl Harbor**, in Hawaii. This would give Japan time to secure control of East Asia before the U.S. military could respond.

hmhsocialstudies.com INTERACTIVE MAP

Pearl Harbor, 1941

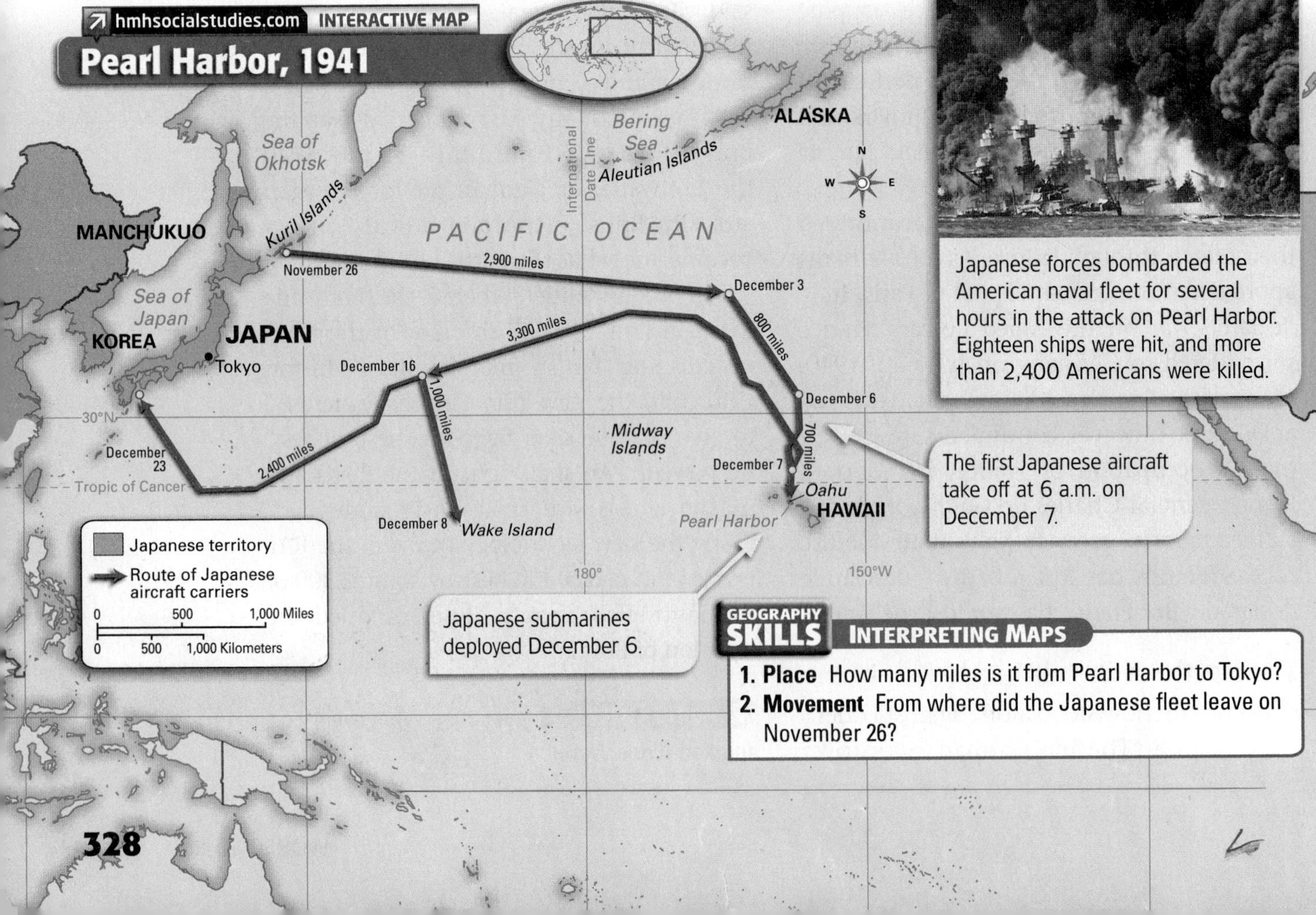

Japanese forces bombarded the American naval fleet for several hours in the attack on Pearl Harbor. Eighteen ships were hit, and more than 2,400 Americans were killed.

GEOGRAPHY SKILLS INTERPRETING MAPS

1. **Place** How many miles is it from Pearl Harbor to Tokyo?
2. **Movement** From where did the Japanese fleet leave on November 26?

© Houghton Mifflin Harcourt Publishing Company • Image Credits: (cr), ©Corbis

At 7:55 a.m. on Sunday, December 7, 1941, Japanese airplanes dove from the sky and attacked Pearl Harbor. An American sailor aboard the USS *Arizona* remembered how quickly his battleship was hit and destroyed:

> "I began to realize there were dead men all around me . . . it was obvious the ship was doomed. I made my way to the side of the ship, which by this time was sinking fast, and jumped off."
>
> —George D. Phraner, quoted in *World War II*, by H. P. Willmott

In just a few hours, the Japanese sank or damaged all of the battleships anchored at Pearl Harbor. More than 2,400 Americans were killed. Almost 200 airplanes were destroyed.

Speaking to Congress the next day, President Roosevelt called December 7, 1941, "a date which will live in infamy [disgrace]." Congress voted to declare war on Japan. Germany then declared war on the United States. Less than 25 years after entering World War I, the United States joined the Allies in another global war. This one would be even more devastating.

BIOGRAPHY

Daniel Inouye

1924–2012

Daniel Inouye was born in Honolulu, Hawaii, to Japanese parents. When the Japanese attacked Pearl Harbor, the 17-year-old Inouye used his medical aid training to help treat victims. He joined the army the next year, winning several medals for bravery in combat. In an attack in Italy, Inouye was shot three times, and his right arm had to be amputated. After the war, Inouye studied law and entered politics. In 1959 he became Hawaii's first representative in Congress, as well as the first Japanese American to serve in Congress. He was elected to the U.S. Senate in 1962 and became an important figure in U.S. politics.

Drawing Conclusions Why do you think Inouye went into politics?

READING CHECK **Identifying Cause and Effect** What did Japan hope to gain by attacking Pearl Harbor?

SUMMARY Military aggression in Europe and Asia drew the United States into war.

Section 1 Assessment

hmhsocialstudies.com
ONLINE QUIZ

Reviewing Ideas, Terms, and People

1. **a. Identify** What types of leaders came to power in Italy, Germany, and the Soviet Union before World War II?
   b. Explain Why did some Europeans have faith in these leaders?
2. **a. Summarize** What did **Adolf Hitler** promise the German people, and how did he act on this promise?
   b. Recall Which countries formed the **Axis Powers** and the **Allied Powers**?
   c. Elaborate Do you think **Winston Churchill** was a good choice for Britain's prime minister? Explain your answer.
3. **a. Explain** What event brought the United States into World War II?
   b. Describe How did the **Lend-Lease Act** help the Allies?

Critical Thinking

4. **Identifying Cause and Effect** Review your notes on totalitarian countries and their leaders prior to World War II. Then copy the graphic organizer below and use it to give details on the causes of World War II.

Focus on Writing

5. **Taking Notes on Pearl Harbor** Look back at what you have read about the attack on Pearl Harbor. Take notes on who attacked Pearl Harbor, where the attack took place, and when. What were the results of the attack?

© Houghton Mifflin Harcourt Publishing Company • Image Credits: (t) ©Brooks Kraft/Corbis

The Alabama Home Front

A statue of Vulcan, the Roman god of the forge, stands over the city of Birmingham. The city is well-known for its steel production.

Steel and Ship Production

Even before the United States entered World War II, the demand for war materials had increased dramatically. The Allied Powers already at war relied on weapons, ammunition, ships, and airplanes made in the United States. Almost everything that was needed by the troops required steel, aluminum, or other metals. Alabama became a major supplier of these metals before and during World War II.

Birmingham Steel

Alabama had become a center of the steel industry by the end of the nineteenth century. The state had plentiful deposits of iron ore, coal, and limestone. In the area surrounding Birmingham, these deposits were located especially near to one another. This made the production of steel and pig iron easier and more profitable than many other areas of the state and the nation. During the Great Depression, however, the demand for steel plummeted. Birmingham was one of the hardest-hit cities in the country.

The rapid increase in the need for steel for troops in World War II brought the industry back to life. At one of the major steel producers in the city, Tennessee Coal and Iron (TCI), the number of employees more than tripled between 1939 and 1941. By the end of the war, the TCI plant was producing more than 1.5 million tons of steel a day. Today the city is still known for its steel production.

Industries in Mobile

The state's economy also saw a boost from the enormous increase in shipbuilding in Mobile. Two shipyards there, Gulf Shipbuilding and Alabama Dry Dock and Shipbuilding, provided about 60,000 jobs. More than 90,000 people moved into the

© Houghton Mifflin Harcourt Publishing Company • Image Credits: (l) ©Hulton Archive/Getty Images city and surrounding areas in search of jobs. The Alcoa plant in Mobile also provided about a third of the entire amount of aluminum output of the United States. Aluminum was one of the major components of the aircraft used in the war.

Many training sites used by each of the U.S. armed forces were located in Alabama. The most famous of these is the Tuskegee Army Air Field, where the first African American pilots were trained. Other important airfields included Brookley Field and Maxwell Field.

Postwar Industries and the Cold War

The Cold War between the United States and the USSR involved developing new and more powerful weapons, but the countries also competed in space travel. After the war, the companies and government installations that produced war equipment continued to be leaders in technological research. Redstone Arsenal, for example, had produced explosives during the war. It became a center for rocket research. A group of German scientists were brought to the facility, where they developed rockets during the Space Race with the USSR. The scientists moved to the George C. Marshall Space Flight Center in 1960, and there developed several of the components needed to carry humans into space.

In 1955, the Army Aviation Center was created at Fort Rucker. Again Alabama became a center for training military pilots. Other Army offices were opened at or near Fort Rucker, including sites for medical personnel training and for safety matters. Pilots trained at the site have taken part in military actions since the Korean War. In the early 1970s, the air force sent the first classes of helicopter trainees to the site. These early pilots were important in the Vietnam War.

Wernher Von Braun, a German weapons scientist during World War II, moved to the United States at the end of the war. He led a group of scientists in developing rockets at the Marshall Space Flight Center.

Case Study Assessment

1. How did World War II affect Alabama's industry?
2. What role did Alabama have during the Cold War?
3. **Activity** Soldiers often have uniform patches that identify which unit they belong to. Research one of the units that trained in Alabama during World War II. Create a patch that illustrates something that made it unique.

© Houghton Mifflin Harcourt Publishing Company • Image Credits: (cr) ©Hulton Archive/Stringer/Archive Photos/Getty Images

SECTION 2

The Home Front

What You Will Learn...

Main Ideas

1. Businesses, soldiers, and citizens worked to prepare the United States for war.
2. The war brought new opportunities for many women and minorities.
3. Japanese Americans faced internment during the war.

The Big Idea

American involvement in World War II helped the U.S. economy and changed the lives of many Americans.

Key Terms and People

War Production Board
A. Philip Randolph
Tuskegee Airmen
Benjamin O. Davis Jr.
zoot-suit riots
internment

hmhsocialstudies.com
TAKING NOTES

Use the graphic organizer online to take notes on how World War II brought both opportunities and challenges to minorities.

If YOU were there...

Shopping for food has become a whole new experience since the United States entered World War II. When your mother sends you to the grocery store these days, she gives you government-issued ration stamps. These stamps limit the amount of sugar, butter, and meat each family can buy. The sacrifice is difficult, but you know it will help the soldiers fighting overseas.

In what other ways can you help the war effort?

BUILDING BACKGROUND As World War II raged in 1940 and 1941, the Allies relied on war supplies and food from the United States. President Roosevelt and Congress also increased defense spending at home, believing that the United States would soon join the fighting. The increased spending boosted the U.S. economy.

Preparing for War

The United States was still experiencing the effects of the Great Depression when the Japanese attacked Pearl Harbor in December 1941. The enormous effort of mobilizing for war finally brought the Depression to an end. Factories ran 24 hours a day, producing ships, tanks, jeeps, guns, and ammunition. Americans turned their knowledge of mass production toward the production of war supplies. One remarkable example was the building of Liberty ships—transport vessels for troops and supplies. Workers could build an entire 441-foot-long Liberty ship in as little as four days.

American workers were soon doubling the war production of Germany, Japan, and all other Axis Power countries combined. Unemployment fell to 1 percent in 1944. Agricultural production increased as well, as farmers sent food overseas to feed Allied soldiers. To organize the war effort, the government created the **War Production Board** (WPB) to oversee the conversion of factories to war production. In 1942, for example, the WPB banned the production of cars so that auto plants could produce military equipment.

The United States also needed millions of soldiers. Congress had begun to prepare for war by passing the Selective Training and Service Act in 1940. This was the first peacetime draft in the country's history.

© Houghton Mifflin Harcourt Publishing Company

Men from the ages of 21 to 35 (later 18 to 38) were required to register for the draft. More than 16 million Americans served during the war.

To finance the war effort, the government increased taxes and sold war bonds. War bonds were essentially loans that people made to the government. People who bought war bonds in 1942, for example, would get their money back 10 years later, with interest.

Americans also contributed to the war effort by collecting scrap metal that could be used in weapons factories. People learned to adjust to government rations limiting the supply of gasoline, rubber, shoes, and some foods. Posters urged Americans to "Use it up, wear it out, make it do, or do without."

READING CHECK **Identifying Cause and Effect** How did the war affect the U.S. economy?

Wartime Opportunities

You read that wartime production during World War I created new opportunities for many women and minorities. The same thing happened on an even larger scale during World War II.

New Roles for Women

With so many men leaving home to fight in World War II, factories badly needed new workers. The government urged women to fill these positions. Women found themselves doing work that had traditionally been considered "unladylike." One female riveter (a person who fastens parts on a machine) recalled her experiences building airplanes:

> "[I] learned to use an electric drill . . . and I soon became an outstanding riveter . . . The war really created opportunities for women. It was the first time we got a chance to show that we could do a lot of things that only men had done before."
>
> —Winona Espinosa, quoted in *Ordinary Americans*, edited by Linda Monk

Women also filled new roles in military service. About 300,000 women served in the armed forces through special divisions such as the Women's Auxiliary Army Corps (WAAC) and Women's Airforce Service Pilots (WASP). WASP pilots flew test flights and ferried planes between factories and air bases. Army and navy nurses served in combat areas.

Primary Source

POSTERS

Supporting the War

Posters like these encouraged Americans to support their troops in a variety of ways. Building weaponry, growing food, saving scrap metal, and rationing all helped the war effort and allowed soldiers to have necessary supplies.

We Can Do It!
WAR PRODUCTION CO-ORDINATING COMMITTEE

"Rosie the Riveter" became a symbol of women's work to support the war.

WAR GARDENS
FOR
VICTORY
GROW VITAMINS AT YOUR KITCHEN DOOR

Victory gardens planted at home allowed more commercially produced food to be sent from farms to troops overseas.

ANALYSIS SKILL **ANALYZING PRIMARY SOURCES**

How did posters like these aim to help troops overseas?

© Houghton Mifflin Harcourt Publishing Company • Image Credits: (br), Library of Congress Prints & Photographs Division, Washington, D.C.; (bc), Picture Research Consultants, Inc.

African Americans

The Great Migration that began during World War I continued as African Americans moved to northern cities to find factory jobs. In most cases, however, black workers received lower pay than did white workers. They also were restricted in what kinds of jobs they were hired to perform.

To protest this unfair treatment, African American labor leader **A. Philip Randolph** began to organize a march to Washington, D.C., in 1941. "If freedom and equality are not [granted for] the peoples of color, the war for democracy will not be won," he argued. Randolph canceled the march, however, after President Roosevelt issued an order prohibiting racial discrimination in the government and in companies producing war goods.

About 1 million African Americans served in the armed forces during the war, mostly in segregated units. In the Navy, African Americans were assigned only to support positions and denied the right to participate in combat. Despite this, many black soldiers became national heroes during the war, including Dorie Miller. Leaving his post as ship's cook, Miller manned a machine gun on the deck of the USS *West Virginia* until he was ordered to abandon the ship because it was sinking.

The **Tuskegee Airmen** were African American pilots who trained at the Tuskegee Army Air Field in Alabama. **Benjamin O. Davis Jr.**, who later became the first African American general in the U.S. Air Force, led the group. Davis and his pilots had to overcome prejudice in the military as well as the hazards of war. He later described the pilots as "outstanding Americans who served their country unselfishly. Despite treatment that would have demoralized men of lesser strength and character, they persisted through humiliations and dangers to earn the respect of their fellows." The Tuskegee Airmen flew thousands of successful combat missions in North Africa and Italy.

Struggles at Home

Although members of every race participated in the war as American soldiers, life for minorities at home changed very little. African Americans were still subject to segregation, and Mexican Americans continued to have very little economic opportunity. After the attack on Pearl Harbor, Japanese Americans were removed from their communities and ordered into internment camps far away from the West Coast.

FOR
COLORED
ONLY

Primary Source

AUTOBIOGRAPHY

Tuskegee Airmen

Benjamin O. Davis was a graduate of West Point who became the first African American Air Force officer to achieve the rank of general. During World War II he led the first African American flying unit, the 99th Fighter Squadron. These men had been trained at the Tuskegee Institute in Alabama.

"While no AAF [American Air Force] unit had gone into combat better trained or better equipped than the 99th Fighter Squadron, we lacked actual combat experience. So as we approached our first missions, my own inexperience and that of my flight commanders was a major source of concern. On the other hand, we had averaged about 250 hours per man in a P-40 (quite a lot for pilots who had not yet flown their first missions), and we possessed an unusually strong sense of purpose and solidarity."

—Benjamin O. Davis,
Benjamin O. Davis, American: An Autobiography

ANALYSIS SKILL ANALYZING PRIMARY SOURCES

What advantages did the Tuskegee Airmen bring to battle?

© Houghton Mifflin Harcourt Publishing Company • Image Credits: (t), Corbis/Bettman; (bl), ©U.S. Air Force/Collection of David Ethell

Japanese American Internment
Not interned
6%
Japanese citizens living in America interned
37%
57%
American citizens of Japanese descent interned

Mexican Americans

About 300,000 Mexican Americans served in the military during the war. Many Mexican Americans also found wartime jobs on the West Coast and in the Midwest. Because of a shortage of farm workers, the federal government asked Mexico to provide agricultural workers. The workers, called *braceros*, were guaranteed a minimum wage, food, shelter, and clean living conditions. About 200,000 Mexicans worked in the *bracero* program.

Young Mexican Americans of the time created their own culture by blending different music styles and clothing styles. Some men wore zoot suits—fancy, loose-fitting outfits with oversized hats. Despite their aiding of the war effort, many faced discrimination. In Los Angeles in June 1943, groups of sailors attacked Mexican Americans wearing zoot suits, beginning the **zoot-suit riots**. During the 10-day period, white mobs attacked many Mexican Americans.

READING CHECK **Evaluating** How did the war create both opportunities and challenges for minorities?

Japanese American Internment

Japanese Americans faced a different form of prejudice during World War II. After the Japanese attack on Pearl Harbor, some Americans began to look at Americans of Japanese descent with fear and suspicion. Most Japanese Americans lived on the West Coast at this time. It was feared that they would serve as secret agents for Japan and help Japan prepare an invasion of the West Coast or try to sabotage U.S. war efforts.

The U.S. government had no evidence to support these fears. In spite of this fact, President Roosevelt issued Executive Order 9066. This order allowed the government to begin the process of **internment**, or forced relocation and imprisonment, of Japanese Americans. About 115,000 Japanese Americans were evacuated from their homes and held in isolated internment camps. Half of those held in the camps were children. A smaller number of Americans of German and Italian ancestry were also held in internment camps during the war.

THE IMPACT TODAY

Congress passed the Civil Liberties Act of 1988 to compensate victims of internment. Each living Japanese American who had been interned—60,000 in all—received $20,000 and a formal apology signed by President Ronald Reagan.

© Houghton Mifflin Harcourt Publishing Company • Image Credits: (tl), ©Hulton-Deutsch Collection/Corbis; (tr), ©Seattle Post-Intelligencer Collection/Museum of History and Industry/Corbis

At this time, some Japanese Americans were *Issei*, or immigrants born in Japan. But most were *Nisei*, American citizens born in the United States to Japanese immigrant parents. Whether they were U.S. citizens or not, Japanese Americans lost their jobs, homes, and belongings when they were forced to move to internment camps. A farm owner named Yuri Tateishi spoke of feeling betrayed by his government. "You hurt," he said. "You give up everything that you worked for that far, and I think everybody was at the point of just having gotten out of the Depression and was just getting on his feet. And then all that happens! You have to throw everything away."

After the Pearl Harbor attack, the government banned young Japanese American men from serving in the military. But Roosevelt reversed this policy in 1943. Daniel Inouye remembered the excitement he and his fellow Japanese Americans in Hawaii felt when they heard that the government was going to form an all-*Nisei* combat team. An army recruiter had prepared a pep talk for the young Japanese Americans, but this proved to be unnecessary:

"As soon as he said that we were now eligible to volunteer, that room exploded into a fury of yells and motion. We went bursting out of there and ran—ran!—the three miles to the draft board . . . jostling for position, like a bunch of marathoners gone berserk."

—Daniel Inouye, quoted in *Only What We Could Carry*, edited by Lawson Fusao Inada

Inouye was one of about 33,000 *Nisei* who served in World War II. The Japanese American 100th/442nd Regimental Combat Team received more than 18,000 decorations for bravery—more than any other unit of its size in U.S. military history. Many of the soldiers of the 100th/442nd served while their families were held in internment camps back home.

READING CHECK **Evaluating** Why were Japanese Americans interned?

SUMMARY The war effort changed life on the home front.

Section 2 Assessment

hmhsocialstudies.com ONLINE QUIZ

Reviewing Ideas, Terms, and People

1. a. **Describe** How did people on the home front support the war effort?
   b. **Identify** What government agency oversaw factory production during the war?
2. a. **Recall** What were the WAAC and the WASP?
   b. **Explain** Why did **A. Philip Randolph** organize a march on Washington and then cancel it?
   c. **Elaborate** How did the *bracero* program benefit both Mexicans and Americans?
3. a. **Define** What was the **internment** program?
   b. **Contrast** How did the U.S. government change its policy toward Japanese Americans serving in the military? How did many respond?

Critical Thinking

4. **Categorizing** Review your notes on challenges and opportunities for different groups of people in America during World War II. Then copy the graphic organizer below and use it to list opportunities that women, African Americans, and Mexican Americans found during the war.

Wartime Opportunities

Women	African Americans	Mexican Americans

Focus on Writing

5. **Taking Notes on the Home Front** Radio broadcasts often reminded Americans to "do your part" in winning World War II. Take notes on the ways ordinary citizens helped the troops by supporting the war effort on the home front. How might you convince someone to support the effort?

© Houghton Mifflin Harcourt Publishing Company • Image Credits: (b) Everett Collection

War in Europe and North Africa

SECTION 3

If YOU were there...

The year is 1943, and you are a senior in high school. You know that you will be drafted into the armed forces as soon as you graduate. Every day after school you listen to radio reports about the battles being fought around the world. Your future, and the future of the whole world, seems so uncertain.

How do you feel about fighting in this war?

BUILDING BACKGROUND By the time the United States entered the war, the Allies were in trouble. The Axis Powers controlled much of western Europe and were advancing in North Africa and the Soviet Union. German submarine attacks on Allied ships were making it difficult to get American supplies to the British.

What You Will Learn...

Main Ideas

1. The Allies fought back against the Axis Powers in North Africa and Europe.
2. Key Allied victories halted the German advance.
3. In the D-Day invasion, Allied forces attacked German-controlled France.

The Big Idea

After fierce fighting in North Africa and Europe, the Allies stopped the German advance and slowly began driving back German forces.

Key Terms and People

Battle of El Alamein
Dwight D. Eisenhower
Battle of Stalingrad
D-Day

hmhsocialstudies.com
TAKING NOTES

Use the graphic organizer online to make a list of the major battles and campaigns in different areas of the world.

The Allies Fight Back

In December 1941, soon after the United States entered the war, President Roosevelt met with British prime minister Winston Churchill to work out a plan to defeat the Axis Powers. Roosevelt agreed that the United States would place "Europe first" in its plans to defeat the Axis, while still aiding China in the fight against Japan in the Pacific. In addition, Roosevelt and Churchill agreed on two initial strategies: a buildup of troops in Great Britain to be used to invade France, and an assault on German forces in North Africa.

Meanwhile, the Soviets had been demanding Allied help on the eastern front, where they had borne the brunt of the European war for months after Hitler's invasion. Stalin wanted the Allies to attack

The Allies began using sonar to destroy German U-boats, shown here in a German harbor.

© Houghton Mifflin Harcourt Publishing Company • Image Credits: (b), Everett Collection in Europe immediately, to take some of the pressure off of the Soviet forces in the east. In July 1942, however, the Allies decided to put a European invasion on hold and launch an initial offensive in North Africa. Stalin was angry. The Soviets would have to continue to fight the war on the eastern front without a western European assault to distract the Germans.

As they prepared their battle plans, the Allies faced many obstacles. One major threat the Allies had to combat was U-boat attacks. In 1942 alone German U-boats sank more than 6,000,000 tons of Allied materials. To prevent further damage, the Allies used the convoy system of multiple ships traveling at once, along with new sonar technology. Sonar, which uses sound waves to detect objects underwater, helped Allied ships find and destroy German U-boats. In addition, new long-range Allied planes protected the convoys from the air. Long-range planes could also fly into German territory to drop bombs on factories, railroads, and cities, inflicting tremendous damage on German targets.

FOCUS ON READING

What categories could you use to organize the information in this paragraph?

hmhsocialstudies.com

ANIMATED GEOGRAPHY

WWII in Europe and Africa 1939–1945

READING CHECK **Explaining** What battle plan did the Allies agree to pursue after American entry into the war?

BIOGRAPHY

Dwight D. Eisenhower

1890–1969

Dwight D. Eisenhower was born in Denison, Texas. "Ike," as his friends called him, attended the U.S. Military Academy at West Point and trained soldiers for tank warfare during World War I. With a strong ability to organize and plan strategies, as well as a persuasive and optimistic personality, Eisenhower rose to the rank of general during World War II. He was named supreme commander of Allied forces in western Europe in 1943. His standing as a war hero helped him win the presidential elections of 1952 and 1956.

Drawing Inferences What were some of Eisenhower's strengths?

Halting the German Advance

Churchill predicted that the road to victory would be long and difficult. By winning several key battles, however, Allied forces finally stopped the German advance.

North Africa and Italy

As you have read, a main focus for the Allies when the United States entered the war was North Africa. The Germans and British were battling for control there because Axis leaders wanted to grab control of the Suez Canal, a crucial supply route in Egypt. Germany's Afrika Korps was led by General Erwin Rommel, nicknamed the Desert Fox for his bold, surprise attacks.

In the summer of 1942, Rommel began an offensive to take Egypt. General Bernard Montgomery led the British forces to stop the Germans. The British stopped the Afrika Korps in July at the **Battle of El Alamein**. At the same time, U.S. and British troops, led by American general **Dwight D. Eisenhower**, came ashore in Morocco and Algeria, west of Egypt. Caught between two Allied forces, the Afrika Korps surrendered in May 1943.

With North Africa under their control, the Allies prepared to attack the Axis Powers in Europe. Churchill identified Italy as the "soft underbelly" of the Axis. Allied forces invaded the island of Sicily in July 1943 and moved from there to the Italian mainland. Italian leaders overthrew Mussolini and surrendered to the Allies. But Hitler refused to recognize the Axis defeat. He sent German troops to Italy to block the Allied advance.

In January 1944, Allied forces tried to get behind the Germans with a surprise attack at Anzio, on the western coast of Italy. American and British troops landed at Anzio but were pinned down on the beach for several months. The "soft underbelly" proved to be much tougher than expected. Finally, the Allied forces in southern Italy battled north to Anzio. The combined forces captured Rome, the capital of Italy, in June

© Houghton Mifflin Harcourt Publishing Company • Image Credits: (b) ©Bettmann/Corbis

Major Leaders of the War in Europe

QUICK FACTS

Winston Churchill
Prime Minister of Great Britain

Franklin Roosevelt
President of the United States

Joseph Stalin
Premier of the Soviet Union

Adolf Hitler
Chancellor of Germany

Benito Mussolini
Prime Minister of Italy

1944. Early in 1945, German forces were driven out of Italy. Italian freedom fighters executed Mussolini.

The Battle of Stalingrad

Meanwhile, massive German and Soviet armies were battling on the eastern front. By the middle of 1942, Axis armies had driven deep into Soviet territory. Millions of Soviet soldiers had been killed or captured.

German forces then advanced to the key industrial city of Stalingrad. German firebombs set much of the city on fire. But Soviet leader Joseph Stalin was determined to hold on to Stalingrad at all costs. Savage street fighting dragged on for months. Soviet snipers used the ruined buildings to their advantage, firing at German soldiers from behind piles of stone and brick.

German supplies began to run desperately low as the harsh Russian winter began. Hitler remained obsessed with capturing Stalingrad, however. He ordered his troops to keep fighting, though he did not send enough new supplies or soldiers. Thousands of Germans froze or starved to death. In late January 1943 the German commander at Stalingrad defied Hitler and surrendered to save his remaining troops. The **Battle of Stalingrad** thus became a key turning point of the war.

The Soviet victory came at an enormous cost—more than 1 million Soviet soldiers died at Stalingrad. About 800,000 Axis soldiers were killed. After Stalingrad, the Soviets won another victory in the city of Kursk, in the biggest tank battle ever fought. The Axis Powers now began to retreat from the Soviet Union. The tide of the war in the east had turned.

READING CHECK **Sequencing** What events led to the Allied victories in Italy and Russia?

The D-Day Invasion

After hard-fought victories in North Africa and Italy, the Allies were ready for an even tougher task—the invasion of German-occupied France. This was the first step toward the goal of liberating Europe and forcing Hitler to surrender.

© Houghton Mifflin Harcourt Publishing Company • Image Credits: (all), Bettmann/Corbis

hmhsocialstudies.com INTERACTIVE MAP

World War II in Europe, 1942–1945

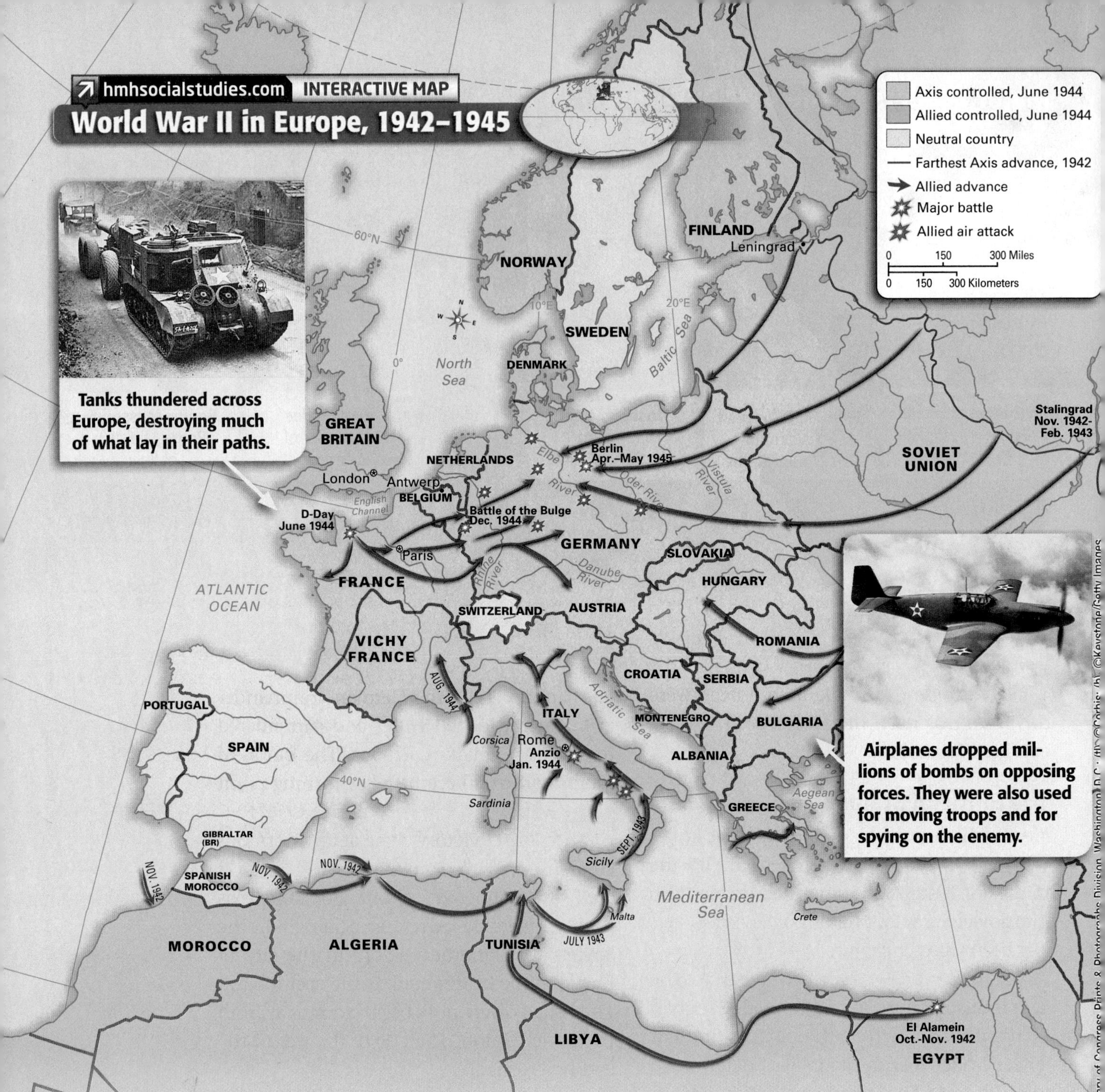

Axis controlled, June 1944
Allied controlled, June 1944
Neutral country
Farthest Axis advance, 1942
Allied advance
Major battle
Allied air attack
0 150 300 Miles
0 150 300 Kilometers
FINLAND
Leningrad
NORWAY
SWEDEN
Baltic Sea
DENMARK
North Sea
60°N
10°E
20°E
0°
GREAT BRITAIN
NETHERLANDS
London
Antwerp
BELGIUM
English Channel
D-Day June 1944
Paris
Battle of the Bulge Dec. 1944
Berlin Apr.–May 1945
Elbe River
Oder River
Vistula River
GERMANY
Rhine River
Danube River
FRANCE
ATLANTIC OCEAN
SWITZERLAND
AUSTRIA
SLOVAKIA
HUNGARY
ROMANIA
VICHY FRANCE
AUG. 1944
CROATIA
SERBIA
Adriatic Sea
ITALY
MONTENEGRO
BULGARIA
PORTUGAL
SPAIN
Corsica
Rome
Anzio Jan. 1944
ALBANIA
40°N
Sardinia
GREECE
Aegean Sea
GIBRALTAR (BR)
SEPT. 1943
Sicily
NOV. 1942
SPANISH MOROCCO
NOV. 1942
NOV. 1942
Mediterranean Sea
Malta
Crete
MOROCCO
ALGERIA
TUNISIA
JULY 1943
LIBYA
El Alamein Oct.-Nov. 1942
EGYPT
Stalingrad Nov. 1942- Feb. 1943
SOVIET UNION

Tanks thundered across Europe, destroying much of what lay in their paths.

Airplanes dropped millions of bombs on opposing forces. They were also used for moving troops and for spying on the enemy.

1942

November 1942
Allies win the Battle of El Alamein.

February 1943
Final German troops surrender at Stalingrad.

May 1943
Axis forces in North Africa surrender.

July 1943
Allies begin an invasion of Sicily.

© Houghton Mifflin Harcourt Publishing Company • Image Credits: (cr) Library of Congress Prints & Photographs Division, Washington D.C.; (b) ©Corbis; (tl) ©Keystone/Getty Images

Dwight Eisenhower was in charge of planning what would be the largest sea-to-land invasion ever attempted. Eisenhower knew that German forces were expecting an invasion of France. The Germans had planted mines and stretched barbed wire along the French coastline. Heavily armed German soldiers waited on the beaches in bombproof bunkers. Eisenhower warned his troops of the danger but expressed confidence in their ability to succeed. "The hopes and prayers of liberty-loving people everywhere march with you," he told them.

American, British, and Canadian troops invaded France on June 6, 1944—known as **D-Day**, or "designated day." They crossed the choppy waters of the English Channel and landed on five beaches in Normandy. More than 6,000 ships, 11,000 planes, and 156,000 men were part of the invasion. Soldiers jumped from boats and waded ashore, often under heavy fire.

The Americans landed on two beaches, codenamed Utah and Omaha. Fighting was especially fierce on Omaha Beach, where almost 3,000 men were killed or wounded. "The entire beach was strewn with mines," wrote one U.S. soldier to his wife. "With a stream of lead coming towards us, we were at the mercy of the Germans."

June 5, 1944
Allies capture Rome.
June 6, 1944
Allied forces invade France on D-Day.
1945

American soldiers landed on the beaches of Normandy during the D-Day invasion.

© Houghton Mifflin Harcourt Publishing Company • Image Credits: (b), ©Keystone/Getty Images

By the end of D-Day, all five beaches were secured. The Allies then began driving east through French villages and countryside toward Germany.

READING CHECK **Summarizing** What was the goal of the D-Day invasion?

SUMMARY Allied victories led to the D-Day invasion.

Section 3 Assessment

hmhsocialstudies.com
ONLINE QUIZ

Reviewing Ideas, Terms, and People

1. **a. Describe** What new strategies did the Allies use in the fight in Europe and North Africa?
   b. Draw Conclusions Why was it important for no individual Allied Power to make peace with the Axis countries?
2. **a. Recall** What role did **Dwight D. Eisenhower** play in the North Africa campaign?
   b. Analyze Why did the Allies decide to invade North Africa and Italy?
   c. Evaluate Why do you think people call the **Battle of Stalingrad** a turning point in the war?
3. **a. Define** What was **D-Day**?
   b. Elaborate What did Eisenhower mean when he said, "The hopes and prayers of liberty-loving people everywhere march with you"?

Critical Thinking

4. **Categorizing** Review your list of the major battles and campaigns in different areas of the world. Then copy the graphic organizer below and use it to explain the significance of each event shown.

Event	Significance
Battle of El Alamein	
Capture of Rome	
Battle of Stalingrad	
D-Day invasion	

Focus on Writing

5. **Taking Notes on the Progress of the War** Take notes on the major battles involving American soldiers. How did American leaders, strategies, and individual soldiers contribute to victories in Europe and North Africa?

SECTION 4

War in the Pacific

What You Will Learn...

Main Ideas

1. The Japanese continued advancing across the Pacific in 1942.
2. The Allies stopped Japan's advance with key victories over the Japanese navy.
3. The Allies began battling toward Japan.

The Big Idea

Allied forces reversed Japan's expansion in the Pacific and battled toward the main Japanese islands.

Key Terms and People

Douglas MacArthur
Bataan Death March
Chester Nimitz
Battle of the Coral Sea
Battle of Midway
island hopping
Battle of Leyte Gulf
kamikaze

hmhsocialstudies.com
TAKING NOTES

Use the graphic organizer online to take notes on the main events of the war in the Pacific.

If YOU were there...

It is spring 1945, and your older brother is fighting the Japanese in the Pacific. You've been following the news reports closely, and you know that fighting in the Pacific is terribly fierce. You hear that the Japanese soldiers often refuse to surrender, fighting to the death instead. Your brother reveals in his letters that he is lonely and suffering many hardships. Now you are writing to him.

What would you say to encourage him?

BUILDING BACKGROUND Japan attacked China in the early 1930s, leading to all-out war between Japan and China in 1937. Japanese forces captured key Chinese cities, including Nanjing, where they killed up to 300,000 civilians. Under the command of General Hideki Tojo, Japanese forces continued to expand the Japanese empire in Asia.

Japan Advances

Japan's attack on Pearl Harbor left the U.S. Pacific Fleet so weakened that it could not immediately respond to the Japanese advance. While the United States recovered from Pearl Harbor, Japan conquered Thailand, Burma, the British colonies of Hong Kong and Singapore, and the U.S. territories of Guam and Wake Island. The same day as the attack on Pearl Harbor, Japan invaded Hong Kong. British, Canadian, and Indian forces attempting to stop the invasion were outnumbered. Japan attacked the American-controlled Philippines the same day.

American and Filipino forces under the command of American general **Douglas MacArthur** could not stop Japan's advance in the Philippines. MacArthur left the islands in March 1942, vowing to return. More than 70,000 American and Filipino soldiers surrendered to the Japanese. The exhausted soldiers were forced to march 63 miles up the Bataan Peninsula to prison camps. Many prisoners were starved and beaten by Japanese soldiers. More than 600 Americans and about 10,000 Filipinos died in the **Bataan Death March**.

READING CHECK **Identifying Cause and Effect** Why could the U.S. Pacific Fleet not immediately stop the Japanese advance?

© Houghton Mifflin Harcourt Publishing Company

Code Talkers

More than 40,000 Native Americans served in the U.S. armed forces during the war. About 400 Navajo Native Americans served as "Code Talkers," relaying coded messages based on the complex Navajo language. Japan's expert code breakers were never able to crack the Navajo code.

Why might the Japanese have been unable to break the Navajo code?

Key Allied Victories

The Allies feared the Japanese might next attack India, Australia, or even the United States mainland. Admiral **Chester Nimitz** led the U.S. Pacific Fleet. Nimitz was determined to stop the Japanese advance, and he had an important advantage—the ability to crack secret Japanese codes.

American code breakers helped the Allies in two key naval battles in the Pacific. Nimitz learned that the Japanese were planning an attack on Port Moresby, New Guinea, an island just north of Australia. If the Japanese took New Guinea, they would have a base from which to invade Australia. In May 1942 Nimitz sent Allied forces to stop the Japanese fleet. American and Japanese aircraft carriers and fighter planes clashed in the **Battle of the Coral Sea**. Neither side won a clear victory, but the Japanese assault on Port Moresby was stopped.

Allied leaders then learned that the Japanese planned a surprise attack on the Midway Islands. Nimitz was prepared. The **Battle of Midway** began on June 4, 1942, when Japan started bombing the islands. American aircraft carriers launched their planes, catching the Japanese aircraft carriers while many of their planes were refueling on deck. American dive bombers destroyed four of Japan's aircraft carriers, severely weakening Japanese naval power. "Pearl Harbor has now been partially avenged," said Nimitz.

The Allies then began the enormous and difficult task of recapturing territory from Japan. In August 1942 American marines invaded Guadalcanal, one of the Solomon Islands northeast of Australia. Intense fighting raged for nearly six months. Marine Louis Ortega remembered that enemy bombs and bullets were only part of the danger in the hot, rainy jungles of Guadalcanal. Soldiers also suffered from diseases, such as malaria, and from hunger due to lack of supplies. "I had gone to Guadalcanal weighing about 150," Ortega said. "I left weighing about 110." American forces finally took control of the island in February 1943.

READING CHECK **Drawing Conclusions** How did the Allied victory at Midway change the course of the war in the Pacific?

Battling toward Japan

Allied victories at Midway and Guadalcanal helped change the course of the war in the Pacific. The Allies now saw their chance to go on the offensive, with the goal of reaching Japan itself.

Island Hopping

To fight their way toward Japan, Allied war planners developed a strategy called **island hopping**, where Allied forces took only the most strategically important islands, instead of each Japanese-held island. They could use each captured island as a base for the next attack, while isolating the Japanese forces on the bypassed islands.

ACADEMIC VOCABULARY
execute perform, carry out

Island hopping proved to be a successful strategy, though very costly to execute. Japanese forces fortified key islands and fought fiercely to hold on to them. In November 1943, U.S. Marines leapt off their boats and waded toward Tarawa, one of the Gilbert Islands. They advanced into ferocious fire from Japanese machine guns. "The water seemed never clear of . . . men," one marine said. "They kept falling, falling, falling." Both sides sustained heavy casualties at Tarawa, but the marines captured the island. The Allies won similar victories in the Marshall, Mariana, Volcano, and Bonin islands.

hmhsocialstudies.com
ANIMATED GEOGRAPHY
WWII in the Pacific 1941–1945

In October 1944 General MacArthur led a mission to retake the Philippines. The Japanese navy confronted the Allies at the **Battle of Leyte Gulf**, the largest naval battle in history. The Allies crushed the Japanese fleet, crippling Japan's naval power for the remainder of the war. It also gave the Allies a base from which to attack the main shipping routes that supplied Japan. After splashing ashore on Leyte, MacArthur proudly declared: "People of the Philippines: I have returned." Securing the Philippines took many more months of fighting. Allied forces and Filipino guerrillas finally drove out or captured all of the Japanese defenders by the summer of 1945.

Final Battles

With key islands close to Japan secured, Allied planes began bombing targets in Japan in November 1944. American B-29 bombers, able to carry 20,000 pounds of explosives each, led bombing raids on more than 60 major Japanese cities. A March 1945 raid set Japan's capital city of Tokyo on fire, leaving 1 million people homeless. Japanese factories were destroyed, and food became so scarce that many people neared starvation. Still, Japan refused to surrender.

Two of the war's fiercest battles occurred on Japan's outer islands early in 1945. In February U.S. Marines stormed the beaches of Iwo Jima, now known as Iwo To. Japanese defenders were dug into caves, with orders to fight to the death. "On Iwo, we hardly ever saw the enemy," recalled one marine. After the marines raised the American flag on Iwo Jima, a month of bloody fighting followed. Of more than 20,000 Japanese defenders on Iwo Jima, about a thousand were taken prisoner—the rest were killed or wounded in battle. About 6,800 Americans had died.

Beginning in April an even deadlier battle was fought for the island of Okinawa. There were an estimated 100,000 Japanese soldiers on the island when U.S. forces began their attack. One U.S. Marine officer described the hard fighting at the Battle of Okinawa:

> "We poured a tremendous amount of metal in on those positions . . . It seemed nothing could possibly be living in that churning mass where the shells were falling and roaring but when we next advanced, [Japanese troops] would still be there and madder than ever."
>
> —Colonel Wilburt S. Brown, quoted in *The Final Campaign: Marines in the Victory on Okinawa* by Colonel Joseph H. Alexander

In the waters near the island, Japanese planes struck U.S. ships with the tactic of **kamikaze**—purposely crashing piloted planes into enemy ships. In wave after wave, kamikaze pilots flew planes loaded with explosives straight down onto the decks of Allied ships. An American sailor who was on the deck of an aircraft carrier when a kami-

hmhsocialstudies.com INTERACTIVE MAP

War in the Pacific, 1941–1945

SOVIET UNION
ALASKA
60°N
Bering Sea
Aleutian Islands
1943
1945
MONGOLIA
MANCHUKUO
45°N
Beijing
KOREA
Hiroshima
Aug. 6,
1945
JAPAN
Tokyo
PACIFIC
OCEAN
CHINA
1944
Chengdu
Nagasaki
Aug. 9,
1945
1944–1945
Volcano
Islands
Okinawa
April-
June,
1945
Iwo Jima (Iwo To)
Feb.–Mar. 1945
Midway
June 1942
Midway
Islands
30°N
Hawaiian Islands
Japanese attack
Pearl Harbor
Dec. 7, 1941
BURMA
Hong
Kong
Taiwan
Mariana
Islands
BATAAN
PENINSULA
Tinian
FRENCH
INDOCHINA
PHILIPPINE
ISLANDS
Philippine Sea
June 1944
Guam
NIMITZ
1944
Marshall
Islands
15°N
THAILAND
Leyte Gulf
Oct. 1944
MALAYA
MACARTHUR
Gilbert
Islands
0° Equator
Bismarck Sea
March 1943
Guadalcanal
Aug. 1942-
Feb. 1943
Solomon
Islands
DUTCH EAST INDIES
1942–1943
Port Moresby
Coral Sea
May 1942
150°E
135°E
AUSTRALIA
Japan (Axis Power)
Controlled by Japan, July 1942
Allied
Allied control
Major battle
Allied advance
Allied air attack
Atomic bombing
0 500 1,000 Miles
0 500 1,000 Kilometers
N
S
E
W

Kamikaze pilots as young as 17 flew their airplanes directly into enemy targets, committing suicide to fulfill their duty.

GEOGRAPHY SKILLS INTERPRETING MAPS

1. **Location** Did the area controlled by Japan by July 1942 include the Hawaiian Islands? How can you tell?
2. **Human-Environment Interaction** Which major battles occurred south of the equator?

© Houghton Mifflin Harcourt Publishing Company • Image Credits: (bl), ©Hulton-Deutsch Collection/Corbis

Six marines are shown raising the American flag atop Mount Suribachi on the island of Iwo Jima after an important battle there. They were instructed to raise the flag on the highest point of the island so that all the men still fighting could see it.

kaze attacked the ship described the scene. The plane "cartwheeled the length of the carrier and plowed into the planes we had on the [flight deck]. We were burning bow to stern . . . All the guys manning the guns were dead. Standing up. Pointing their guns. They never left their posts."

More than 2,500 kamikaze missions were flown, killing more than 4,000 Allied sailors. The fighting on Okinawa lasted nearly three months and led to terrible casualties. By the time the island was secure, some 12,000 Allied troops were dead and 36,000 wounded. The Japanese losses were staggering—some 110,000 troops and 80,000 civilians had been killed.

After their victories at Iwo Jima and Okinawa, the Allies were one step closer to final victory. Allied leaders began to plan for an all-out assault on the main Japanese islands.

READING CHECK **Analyzing** How did the Allied strategy in the Pacific change starting in 1943?

SUMMARY The Allies made major gains in the Pacific war, moving closer to Japan.

Section 4 Assessment

hmhsocialstudies.com
ONLINE QUIZ

Reviewing Ideas, Terms, and People

1. a. **Identify** Why were the Japanese able to advance in the Pacific in 1942?
   b. **Explain** Why did so many prisoners die on the **Bataan Death March**?
2. a. **Recall** What Allied victories halted Japan's advance?
   b. **Analyze** Why was the **Battle of the Coral Sea** important?
   c. **Elaborate** How do you think the war might have been different if the Allies had lost at Midway?
3. a. **Define** What was **island hopping**?
   b. **Sequence** What event led to the retaking of the Philippines?
   c. **Evaluate** Why do you think someone would serve as a **kamikaze** pilot?

Critical Thinking

4. **Sequencing** Review your notes on the main events of the Pacific war. Then copy the graphic organizer below and use it to put the events in the correct sequence.

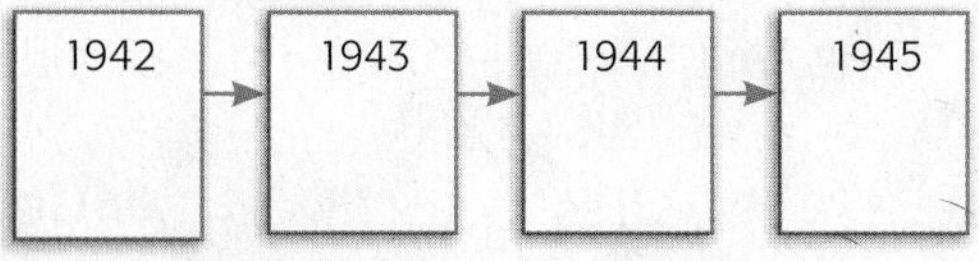

1942
1943
1944
1945

Focus on Writing

5. **Taking Notes on Military Achievements** Take notes on the challenges U.S. soldiers faced in the Pacific. How was fighting in the Pacific different from and similar to fighting in Africa and Europe? How might you describe a Pacific battle to someone?

© Houghton Mifflin Harcourt Publishing Company • Image Credits: (t) ©Underwood Photo Archives/SuperStock

Victory and Consequences

SECTION 5

If YOU were there...

It is August 1944. You are an American soldier in France. You have seen the horrors of battle up close, but today is a day to rejoice. You and other Allied soldiers are marching through the streets of Paris, celebrating its liberation from Nazi control. It seems as if the whole city has come out to greet the Americans. People rush up to shake your hand. Children cheer and hand you flowers.

How does it feel to be part of this moment in history?

BUILDING BACKGROUND By late 1944 Allied forces were advancing in Europe and Asia. But Germany and Japan were both resisting, showing no signs of being willing to surrender. Allied leaders knew there was much more fighting still to be done.

What You Will Learn...

Main Ideas

1. The Allies gained victory in Europe with Germany's surrender.
2. Nazis murdered millions of Jews and other people in the Holocaust.
3. Victory in the Pacific came after the United States dropped atomic bombs on Japan.

The Big Idea

The Allies won World War II, the most devastating war in world history.

Key Terms and People

Battle of the Bulge
Harry S. Truman
Holocaust
genocide
Manhattan Project
atomic bomb

hmhsocialstudies.com
TAKING NOTES

Use the graphic organizer online to take notes on the final days of the war in both Europe and the Pacific.

Germany Surrenders

In the weeks after the successful D-Day invasion, hundreds of thousands of Allied troops landed in France. Led by American general Omar Bradley, Allied forces began fighting their way across France toward Germany. At the same time, the Soviets were closing in on Germany from the east. Although Germany's defeat seemed certain to the Allies, Hitler refused to surrender.

In July 1944 Allied tank forces led by American general George Patton broke through German lines on the western front. While Patton drove forward, more Allied forces invaded southern France. Both groups of Allied forces fought their way toward Paris. Encouraged by the Allies' success, the citizens of Paris rebelled against the German occupying force. By the end of August, General Bradley was leading Allied troops through the streets of the freed city. "All Paris surged out to meet the Allied columns and welcome their liberators," remembered one witness. After securing Paris, the Allies continued driving through Belgium and Luxembourg, making their way toward Germany. Hitler drafted every able-bodied German man from the age of 16 to 60 and planned one last desperate attack.

Hitler's goal was for German forces to drive through a weak spot in the Allied lines and capture the city of Antwerp, Belgium. On December 16 the Germans seized a moment when Allied planes were grounded due to bad weather. In heavy snow some 25 German divisions attacked the Ardennes (ahr-DEN), a densely forested region defended by just a few American divisions. The Germans quickly pushed the Allied forces back about 65 miles, creating a huge bulge in the Allied lines. This gave the battle its name—the **Battle of the Bulge**.

Allied forces recovered rapidly and stopped the German advance. When the skies cleared in late December, Allied planes began pounding German troops. In early January 1945 the Germans began to retreat. American losses were heavy—between 70,000 and 81,000 casualties. Germany's losses were even greater, and Hitler's ability to wage offensive war was now completely crushed.

In the final months of the war, Allied bombing raids devastated major German cities such as Berlin and Hamburg. Both sides in World War II had used these kinds of bombing raids against the enemy's cities. German raids, for example, killed about 30,000 civilians in the British capital of London. In February 1945 Allied bombers attacked the German city of Dresden, igniting a firestorm that destroyed the city and killed more than 35,000 civilians. "Dresden was an inferno," recalled one U.S. soldier. "I have nightmares, even today."

As Allied forces surrounded Berlin, Hitler retreated to an underground bunker in the heart of the ruined city. On April 30, as Soviet troops entered Berlin, Hitler committed suicide. A week later, the Germans surrendered. The war in Europe had finally come to an end. The Allies celebrated May 8, 1945, as V-E (Victory in Europe) Day.

President Franklin Roosevelt, who had led the United States throughout World War II, did not live to see V-E Day. He died of a stroke on April 12. **Harry S. Truman** became president and immediately faced the challenge of winning the war in the Pacific.

READING CHECK **Sequencing** What events led to Germany's surrender?

Primary Source

INTERVIEW TRANSCRIPT

Battle of the Bulge

In the Battle of the Bulge, American soldiers faced a strong German attack in snowy forests during the coldest winter northern Europe had seen in 40 years. Private Dave Nutt described the long, tense nights on the front lines:

> "The cold, the snow, and the darkness were enough to set young nerves on edge. The thud of something as innocuous [harmless] as snow plopping to the ground from a tree branch could be terrifying. Was it snow? Was it maybe a German patrol? Should you fire at the sound and risk giving away your position, or worse, hitting one of your own men? But did the Germans have us surrounded?"

—Dave Nutt, quoted in *Citizen Soldiers*, by Stephen Ambrose

ANALYSIS SKILL ANALYZING PRIMARY SOURCES

What factors made the Battle of the Bulge especially hard on soldiers?

Buchenwald

Jews, Gypsies, and other victims of Hitler and the Nazis were sent to concentration camps. Many were killed immediately upon arrival at the camps, while others were executed later. Families were forced apart, and prisoners were poorly fed and clothed. Some were used as subjects for medical experiments. This photo shows survivors of the Buchenwald concentration camp after their liberation.

How did Hitler use the concentration camps to fulfill part of his goals for Germany?

Horrors of the Holocaust

When Allied forces liberated Europe, they uncovered evidence of horrifying Nazi crimes against humanity. In a program of mass murder that became known as the **Holocaust**, Hitler and the Nazis had attempted to exterminate the entire Jewish population of Europe in the name of Aryan supremacy.

The Final Solution

Soon after gaining power in Germany, Hitler began his campaign of terror against the Jews. The Nazis stripped German Jews of their citizenship and seized their property. On the "night of broken glass," or *Kristallnacht*, many Jewish homes and businesses were destroyed. Many Jews who did not escape the country were imprisoned in concentration camps such as Dachau (DAH-kow), near Munich.

When Germany conquered huge sections of Europe and the Soviet Union early in World War II, nearly 10 million Jews came under Hitler's control. The Nazis forced many Jews into urban centers called ghettos. Others were sent to concentration camps and used as slave labor. Many died from hunger or disease. The Nazis also formed special killing squads that rounded up groups of Jews, shot them, and buried them in mass graves. When the Germans invaded the Soviet Union, these squads murdered more than 33,000 Soviet Jews near Kiev in three days. By the end of 1941, the death squads had executed nearly 1 million people.

The Death Camps

In January 1942 senior Nazi officials met to plan what they called "a final solution to the Jewish question." Hitler's "final solution" was **genocide**, or the extermination of an entire group of people. The Nazi plan was to kill the Jews in specially built death camps, mainly in German-occupied Poland. The camps were equipped with gas chambers designed to kill large numbers of people, and furnaces were used to cremate the bodies of victims.

By mid-1942 the Nazis had begun to ship Jews from throughout German-occupied Europe to the camps. Several hundred thousand Jews, for example, were transported by train from the ghetto in the Polish capital of Warsaw to a death camp called Treblinka. In April 1943 Jews in the Warsaw ghetto staged a violent uprising, attacking the Germans with guns and homemade bombs. It took German troops nearly a month to crush the revolt. Survivors were sent to Treblinka.

THE IMPACT TODAY

There are more than 50 museums in the world that honor victims of the Holocaust. The United States Holocaust Memorial Museum in Washington, D.C., displays historical film footage and artifacts from the Holocaust.

HISTORY

VIDEO
The Holocaust

hmhsocialstudies.com

At the death camps most children, the elderly, and the sick were immediately executed. Those strong enough to work were used as laborers. When they became too weak to work, they too were sent to the gas chambers. Moritz Vegh was 13 when his family was sent from Czechoslovakia to Auschwitz, one of the most notorious of the death camps. He later described what happened to his mother and sister:

> "When we got off the cattle truck, they ordered, 'Men, right; women, left.' . . . I went with my father. My little sister, Esther, she went with my mother. Esther was only eleven. She was holding my mother's hand. When they made a selection of the women, Esther clung to my mother. My mother wouldn't give her up . . . They went straight to the gas chamber."
>
> —Moritz Vegh, quoted in *The Boys: Triumph over Adversity*

Moritz survived the war, working as a laborer at Auschwitz.

The Allied soldiers who liberated the death camps were horrified by what they found. About 6 million Jews—some two-thirds of Europe's prewar Jewish population—had been killed in the Holocaust. The Nazis had also murdered millions of others, including Gypsies, Slavs, political opponents, and people with physical or mental disabilities.

READING CHECK **Summarizing** What was the purpose of the Nazis' "final solution"?

HISTORY

VIDEO
Bombing of Hiroshima and Nagasaki

hmhsocialstudies.com

Victory in the Pacific

In the Pacific Allied war planners prepared for an invasion of Japan. They estimated that the invasion could result in more than 1 million Allied casualties.

The Allies had another option. Since 1942 Allied scientists had been working on a secret program known as the **Manhattan Project**. The goal was to develop an **atomic bomb**, a weapon that produces tremendous power by splitting atoms. On July 16, 1945, the Allies successfully tested the first atomic bomb in the New Mexico desert. The massive explosion melted the desert sand into glass for 800 yards in all directions.

When Japanese leaders refused the Allies' demand for an unconditional surrender, President Truman gave the order to use the atomic bomb. On August 6, 1945, the B-29 bomber *Enola Gay* dropped an atomic bomb above the city of Hiroshima. "When I saw a very strong light, a flash, I put my arms over my face unconsciously," said one Japanese survivor. "Almost instantly I felt my face was inflating . . . I saw people looking for water and they died soon after they drank it . . . The whole city was destroyed and burning. There was no place to go." The explosion killed almost 80,000 people instantly. Thousands more died later from burns and radiation poisoning.

The atomic blast over Hiroshima destroyed the city. Over 80,000 people were killed instantly, and thousands more died later from the effects of radiation.

Japanese leaders still refused to surrender. On August 9 U.S. forces dropped a second atomic bomb on the city of Nagasaki. About one-third of the city was destroyed, and approximately 22,000 people died immediately. The Japanese announced their surrender on August 15, 1945. VJ day

After six years, World War II was finally over. More than 50 million people had been killed—more than half of them civilians. National economies in Europe and Asia were devastated, and millions of people were left without food, water, or shelter. Since the war had been fought far from American soil, the United States escaped this level of destruction. As the strongest power left in the world, much of the responsibility for postwar rebuilding fell to the United States.

READING CHECK **Drawing Conclusions** Why did Japan surrender?

SUMMARY In this section you learned how World War II ended.

Causes and Effects of World War II

QUICK FACTS

Causes

- Global and local economic problems
- Totalitarian governments
- Germany's aggression in Europe
- Japanese aggression in Asia and the Pacific

Effects

- Millions of deaths worldwide
- Widespread destruction of cities and industries
- The Holocaust
- Rise of the United States as the leading world power

Section 5 Assessment

hmhsocialstudies.com
ONLINE QUIZ

Reviewing Ideas, Terms, and People

1. a. **Identify** What was the last major battle of the war in Europe?
   b. **Evaluate** What was the biggest task facing **Harry S. Truman** when he became president?
2. a. **Define** What was the **Holocaust**?
   b. **Elaborate** How did the oppression of Jews increase during the war?
3. a. **Recall** What was the purpose of the **Manhattan Project**, and how did it result in the end of the war against Japan?
   b. **Explain** What was the status of the United States after the war?
   c. **Predict** How do you think the invention of the **atomic bomb** changed people's views of war?

Critical Thinking

4. **Identifying Causes** Review your notes on the final days of the war in both Europe and the Pacific. Then copy the graphic organizer below and use it to show the short-term causes of Germany's and Japan's surrenders.

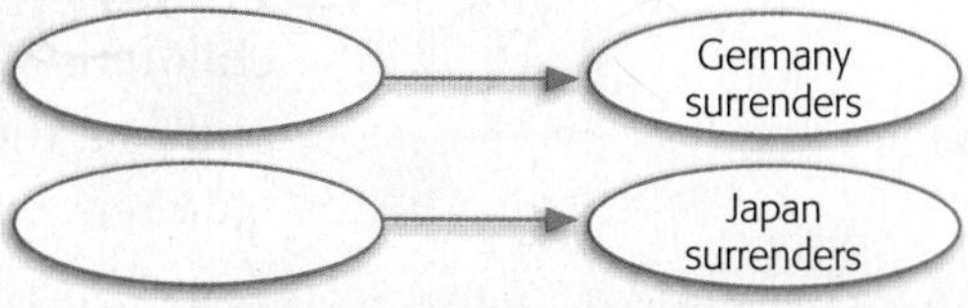
Germany surrenders
Japan surrenders

Focus on Writing

5. **Taking Notes on the Impact of the War** Take notes on the last days of World War II. How did the Allies finally win the war? What impact did the war have on people and countries around the world?

Literature of the Holocaust

GUIDED READING

WORD HELP

Mr. Dussel a friend of Anne's father

droves large numbers

Gestapo German military police

Westerbork a concentration camp on the Dutch-German border

Drenthe a province of the Netherlands

❶ ***Jews suffered harsh treatment before and after arrest.***

❷ ***Jews in hiding knew that they would be sent to concentration camps if discovered.***

❸ ***Anne cannot hide her feelings at seeing innocent victims of the Germans being treated poorly.***

from *Diary of Anne Frank*

by Anne Frank (1929–1945)

About the Reading *Anne Frank was a Jewish teenager in Amsterdam who experienced the Nazi occupation of the Netherlands firsthand. Frank and her family hid for more than two years in the sealed-off back room of an office. The family was betrayed to the Gestapo in 1944. Frank and her family members were sent to concentration camps in Germany. Frank died in 1945 at the Bergen-Belsen concentration camp.*

AS YOU READ **Notice how Frank describes the oppression of Jews.**

9th October, 1942

Our many Jewish friends and acquaintances are being taken away in droves. The Gestapo is treating them very roughly and transporting them in cattle-trucks to Westerbork, the big camp in Drenthe to which they're sending all the Jews. ❶

19th November, 1942

Mr. Dussel has told us much about the outside world we've missed for so long. He had sad news. Countless friends and acquaintances have been taken off to a dreadful fate. ❷ Night after night, green and grey military vehicles cruise the streets. They knock on every door, asking whether any Jews live there. If so, the whole family is immediately taken away. If not, they proceed to the next house. It's impossible to escape their clutches unless you go into hiding. They often go around with lists, knocking only on those doors where they know there's a big haul to be made... In the evenings when it's dark, I often see long lines of good, innocent people, accompanied by crying children, walking on and on, ordered about by a handful of men who bully and beat them until they nearly drop. No one is spared. The sick, the elderly, children, babies and pregnant women—all are marched to their death. ❸

© Houghton Mifflin Harcourt Publishing Company

from *Night*

by Elie Wiesel (1928–), translated by Marion Wiesel

About the Reading *Elie Wiesel, a Hungarian Jew, was taken to Auschwitz when he was age 15. Though he survived the camp, not all of his family did. Years after the war, Wiesel wrote about his time spent imprisoned at Auschwitz.*

AS YOU READ **Look for ways that Wiesel describes the trauma of being taken away.**

By eight o'clock in the morning, weariness had settled into our veins, our limbs, our brains, like molten lead. I was in the midst of prayer when suddenly there was shouting in the streets. I quickly unwound my phylacteries and ran to the window. Hungarian police had entered the ghetto and were yelling in the street nearby.

"All Jews, outside! Hurry!"

They were followed by Jewish police, who, their voices breaking, told us:

"The time has come . . . you must leave all this . . ."

The Hungarian police used their rifle butts, their clubs to indiscriminately strike old men and women, children and cripples. ❶

One by one, the houses emptied and the streets filled with people carrying bundles. By ten o'clock, everyone was outside. The police were taking roll calls, once, twice, twenty times. The heat was oppressive. Sweat streamed from people's faces and bodies.

Children were crying for water.

Water! There was water close by inside the houses, the backyards, but it was forbidden to break rank.

"Water, Mother, I am thirsty!"

Some of the Jewish police surreptitiously went to fill a few jugs. My sisters and I were still allowed to move about, as we were destined for the last convoy, and so we helped as best we could.

GUIDED READING

WORD HELP

molten melted

phylacteries wooden prayer boxes strapped to the forehead and arm

ghetto neighborhood set aside for Jews

indiscriminately without care

surreptitiously secretly

convoy military escort

❶ ***The Hungarian police used physical force to gather people together.***

CONNECTING LITERATURE TO HISTORY

1. **The Nazi oppression of Jews eventually led to the Gestapo taking Jews from their homes.** How does Frank describe the job that the Gestapo did?
2. **The oppression soon changed to removal.** How does Wiesel describe the removal of the Jews from his hometown?
3. **Jews were treated with physical violence by Nazi supporters.** Give two examples of violence against Jews found in these passages.

© Houghton Mifflin Harcourt Publishing Company • Image Credits: (t), ©A H Productions/Getty Images

Analysis | Critical Thinking | Civic Participation | Study

Constructing Time Lines

Define the Skill

Time lines are a good way to organize historical information. Time lines clearly show a sequence of historical events over a certain period of time. Many time lines focus on a specific theme within a time period.

When you construct a time line, it often makes the sequence of events easier to follow. Time lines show events in the order they happened and the amount of time between events. Constructing a time line can therefore help you better understand events' context. For example, organizing events on a time line can help you determine their causes and effects.

Learn the Skill

When you construct a time line, you need to make some basic decisions. First, the time line needs a topic. This topic can be general or specific. One example of a general topic is the 1940s. A more specific topic might be major battles of World War II. The time line should cover a time period that includes the main events related to the topic. For example, it would make sense for a time line on American battles in World War II to cover the period 1941 to 1945.

The next step in constructing a time line is gathering information. This includes taking notes on events from the chosen time period related to the topic. It is important to write down the date when each event happened. Putting the events in order before making the time line is often helpful. If there are too many events, it is a good idea to include only the most important ones.

The first step in actually constructing the time line is to draw a straight line using a ruler. The next step is to mark even intervals on the line. Intervals are dates that divide the time line into smaller, equal time periods. For example, a time line of the 1940s might include two-year intervals: 1940, 1942, 1944, and so on. Then add events in the correct places on the time line. The beginning and end of the time line, each interval, and each event should be labeled with dates. The finished time line should include at least six events. As a final touch, the time line needs a title. The title tells what the entries in the time line are about and may include the dates the time line covers.

Practice the Skill

Follow these instructions to construct a time line.

1. Using your textbook, choose a topic related to World War II for your time line. Decide on the dates your time line will need to cover.
2. Use your textbook to take notes on events to include in your time line and their dates. Put the events in order.
3. Following the steps described above, construct your time line. The finished time line should include clearly labeled dates, at least six events, and a title.

© Houghton Mifflin Harcourt Publishing Company

CHAPTER 11 Chapter Review

History's Impact
▶ **video series**
Review the video to answer the closing question:
Why do you think the United States made the GI Bill of Rights a permanent policy?

Visual Summary

QUICK FACTS

Use the visual summary below to help you review the main ideas of the chapter.

The bombing of Pearl Harbor drew the United States into World War II.

To help supply the troops, women worked in jobs usually held by men.

American soldiers helped defeat the Axis Powers in Europe and the Pacific.

Reviewing Vocabulary, Terms, and People

Identify the term or person from the chapter that best fits each of the following descriptions.

1. The first African American flying unit in the U.S. military

2. American general who retreated from and then retook the Philippines

3. The dictator of the Soviet Union

4. A weapon that produces a massive explosion by splitting atoms

5. Battle at which British troops stopped the German Afrika Korps

6. Policy of avoiding war with an aggressive nation by giving in to its demands

7. Extermination of an entire group of people

Comprehension and Critical Thinking

SECTION 1

8. a. Define What is fascism?

b. Make Inferences Before Pearl Harbor, what U.S. policies suggested that the United States would join the Allies?

c. Evaluate How well did the policy of appeasement work? Explain your answer.

SECTION 2

9. a. Recall What happened during the zoot-suit riots?

b. Analyze Why was the War Production Board important to the war effort?

c. Elaborate How do you think Japanese Americans felt about internment?

© Houghton Mifflin Harcourt Publishing Company

SECTION 3

10. **a. Identify** What led the Axis powers to retreat from the Soviet Union?

    b. Summarize In which regions and countries did the Allies win major victories against Germany?

    c. Draw Conclusions Why do you think D-Day succeeded?

SECTION 4

11. **a. Describe** What did kamikaze pilots do?

    b. Explain How did cracking Japanese codes help the Allies in the Pacific?

    c. Draw Conclusions Why do you think Japan was determined to continue fighting?

SECTION 5

12. **a. Recall** What were the effects of the atomic bombs on Hiroshima and Nagasaki?

    b. Contrast How was the Holocaust different from other wartime tragedies?

    c. Evaluate Do you think the strategy of bombing civilian centers was fair? Why or why not?

Reviewing Themes

13. **Geography** How did geography affect the course of World War II?

14. **Society and Culture** What changes in society did World War II bring about?

Using the Internet 21ST CENTURY

15. **Activity: Understanding Code Talkers** Guns and bombs were not the only weapons of World War II. Cryptography, or the use of secret codes, was also an important tool for the Allied forces. Some Native Americans in the U.S. military used their own language as a form of cryptography. They spoke Navajo, a complex language, and adapted it for battlefield communications and to transmit secret information by radio and telephone. Soldiers who could speak it became known as code talkers. Using the online textbook, research the Navajo code talkers of World War II and then create a poster to present your findings.

hmhsocialstudies.com

Reading Skills 21ST CENTURY

Categorizing *Use the Reading Skills taught in this chapter to answer the question from the reading selection below.*

> American, British, and Canadian troops invaded France on June 6, 1944—known as D-Day or "designated day." They crossed the choppy waters of the English Channel and landed on five beaches in Normandy. More than 6,000 ships, 11,000 planes, and 156,000 men were part of the invasion. Soldiers jumped from boats and waded ashore, often under heavy fire.

16. Which of the following general categories could help you organize this information?

    a. generals of the American forces

    b. types of ammunition used

    c. resources of invading forces

    d. leaders of Allied nations

Social Studies Skills

Constructing Time Lines *Use the Social Studies Skills taught in this chapter to answer the question below.*

17. Make a time line about the end of World War II, covering the events of 1945.

Focus on Writing

18. **Writing Your Radio News Broadcast** Review your notes. Choose one event or story from World War II as the focus of your radio broadcast. You can include quotes from soldiers or national leaders. Remember that people cannot see your broadcast, so use descriptive language. Be sure to answer the following questions: Who? What? Where? When? Why? and How?

© Houghton Mifflin Harcourt Publishing Company

CHAPTER 11

Standardized Test Practice

DIRECTIONS: Read each question and write the letter of the best response. Use the map below to answer question 1.

1

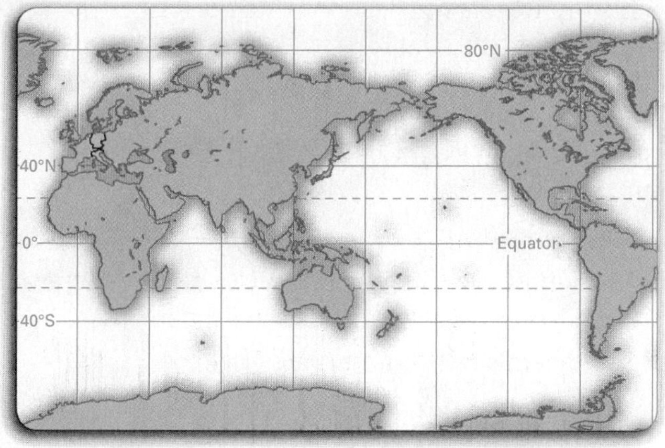

The yellow countries above represent the

A Central Powers.

B Allied Powers.

C Axis Powers.

D Big Three.

2 Which one of the following battles took place in the Pacific?

A Battle of Omaha Beach

B Battle of El Alamein

C Battle of Stalingrad

D Battle of Midway

3 During the war, many American women

A did work that traditionally had been done by men.

B served in battlefront combat positions in the military.

C worked as *braceros.*

D participated in labor strikes.

4 The Allies' successful 1944 invasion of France is known as

A D-Day.

B the Desert Fox.

C sonar.

D the Battle of Britain.

5 Who became president when Franklin D. Roosevelt died in 1945?

A Eleanor Roosevelt

B Harry S. Truman

C Winston Churchill

D Douglas MacArthur

6 The majority of Nazi victims were

A Slavs.

B Japanese.

C disabled people.

D Jews.

7 Read the following excerpt from the diary of Anne Frank, a Dutch Jew who died in the Holocaust, and use it to answer the question below.

> July 15, 1944
>
> "It's a wonder I haven't abandoned all my ideals, they seem so absurd and impractical. Yet I cling to them because I still believe, in spite of everything, that people are truly good at heart."
>
> —Anne Frank, *The Diary of Anne Frank*

Document-Based Question Why does Frank call her ideals "absurd and impractical"?

© Houghton Mifflin Harcourt Publishing Company

Memories of WORLD WAR II

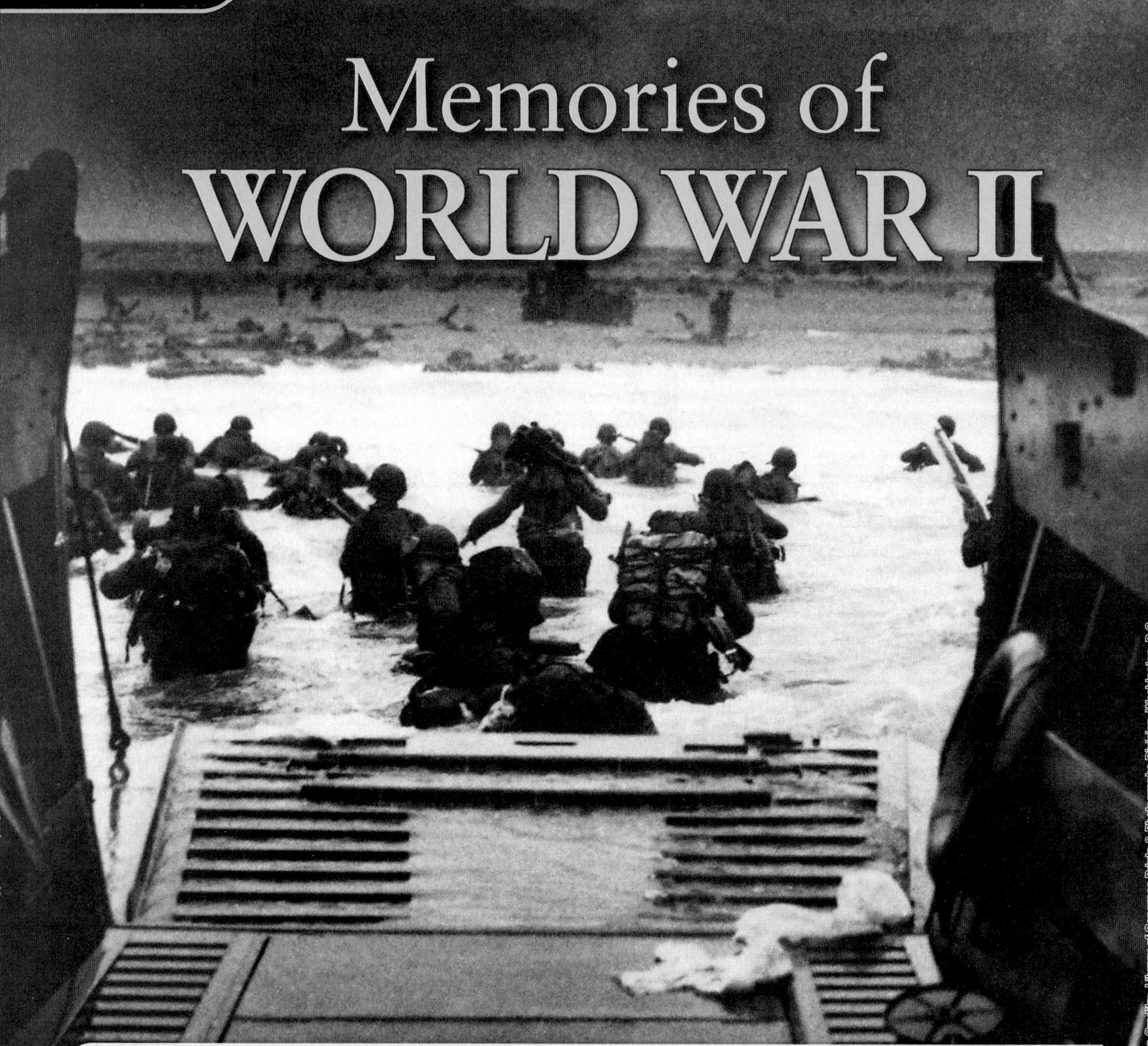

A global conflict, World War II shaped the history of both the United States and the world. Americans contributed to the war effort in numerous ways. Many enlisted in the military and served in Africa, Europe, and the Pacific. Others contributed by working in factories to produce the massive amounts of ships, planes, guns, and other supplies necessary to win the war. In the process, these Americans left behind firsthand accounts of their experiences during the war, both at home and abroad.

Explore some of the personal stories and recollections of World War II online. You can find a wealth of information, video clips, primary sources, activities, and more at hmhsocialstudies.com.

© Houghton Mifflin Harcourt Publishing Company • Image Credits: Library of Congress Prints & Photographs Division, Washington, D.C.

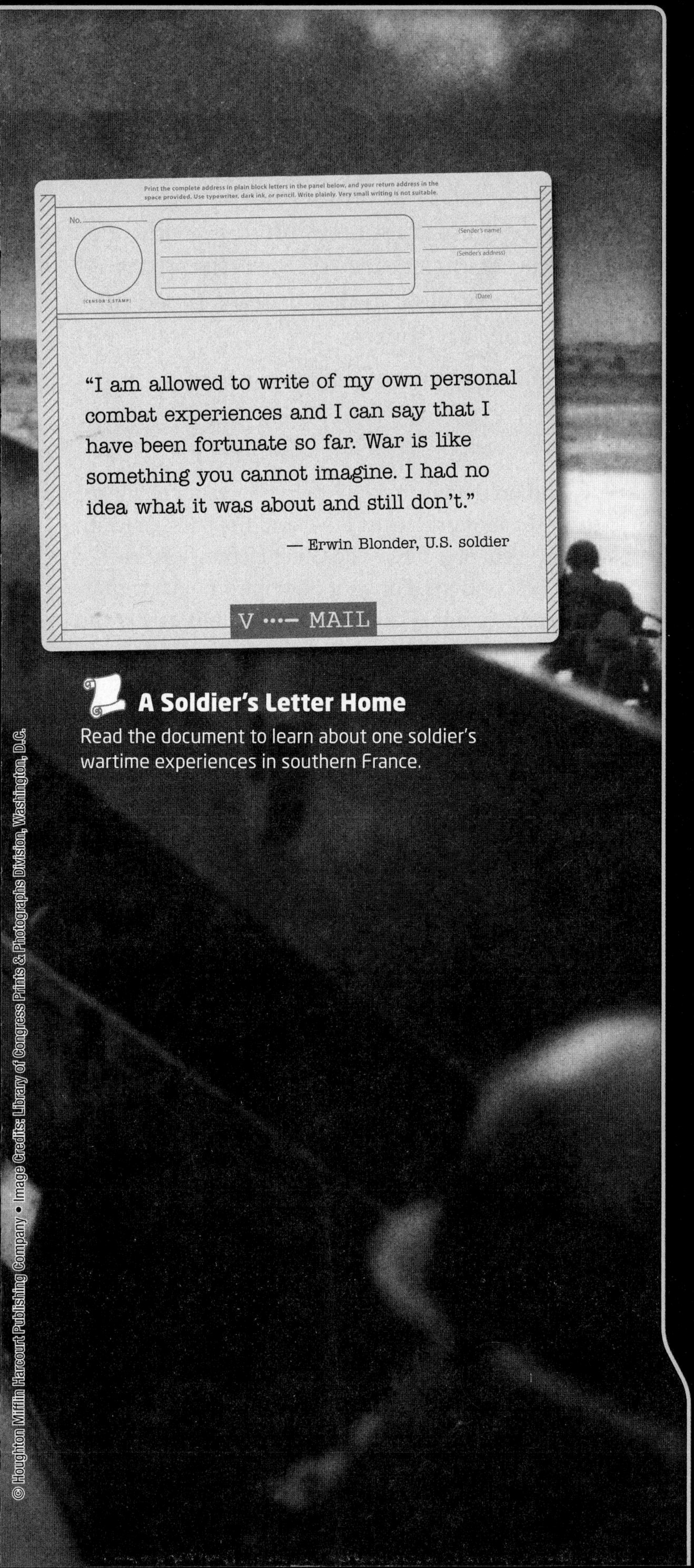

Print the complete address in plain block letters in the panel below, and your return address in the space provided. Use typewriter, dark ink, or pencil. Write plainly. Very small writing is not suitable.

No.

(Sender's name)

(Sender's address)

(CENSOR'S STAMP)

(Date)

"I am allowed to write of my own personal combat experiences and I can say that I have been fortunate so far. War is like something you cannot imagine. I had no idea what it was about and still don't."

— Erwin Blonder, U.S. soldier

V ···– MAIL

A Soldier's Letter Home

Read the document to learn about one soldier's wartime experiences in southern France.

America Mobilizes for War

Watch the video to see how the United States mobilized its citizens for war and how society changed as a result.

Air War Over Germany

Watch the video to see how the P-51 Mustang helped the Allies win the air war over Germany.

The Pacific Islands

Watch the video to hear veterans describe their experiences fighting in the Pacific theater.

© Houghton Mifflin Harcourt Publishing Company • Image Credits: Library of Congress Prints & Photographs Division, Washington, D.C.

Assignment

Write an essay describing either Hoovervilles or the Dust Bowl during the Great Depression.

A Descriptive Essay

Vivid descriptions of a place and time can help us understand history. Primary sources often provide such descriptions from one person's point of view. Historians provide a different point of view in descriptions based on many primary and secondary sources.

1. Prewrite

Getting Started

Descriptive essays depend on details that will help the reader create a mental picture. The quotes about the Dust Bowl and the passage from *The Grapes of Wrath* in the chapter titled The Great Depression are good examples of vivid descriptions. For your description, review that chapter and look in various sources. Collect as many details as you can about Hoovervilles or the Dust Bowl. Try to find details that involve all of the five senses (sight, sound, smell, touch, and taste). Good description depends on strong details.

TIP **Using Visual Images** Look at visual images such as photographs from the 1930s. What do they show about Hoovervilles or the Dust Bowl and the people who lived there? Use this information in your description.

go to 426

Organizing Information

Make one generalization that sums up all your details. This will be your main idea. Then organize the details and examples you have found into two, three, or four categories. These will become the body paragraphs of the essay. All of these categories should support the main idea.

For example, the main idea of an essay could be that the name *Dust Bowl* was an accurate description of the area. One detail might be that the gritty dirt often became caught in people's skin, hair, and clothing. This detail could fit into the category of people in the Dust Bowl.

2. Write

You can use this framework to help you write your first draft.

A Writer's Framework

Introduction

- Make a generalization about your topic.
- List the categories that will be included in the body paragraphs.

Body

- Separate details into paragraphs by category.
- Use vivid details that involve the five senses.
- Use details from different sources.

Conclusion

- Summarize your information.
- Explain how your topic is related to larger issues.

© Houghton Mifflin Harcourt Publishing Company

3. Evaluate and Revise

Evaluating

Use these questions to discover ways to improve your essay.

Evaluation Questions for a Descriptive Essay

- Do you begin with a generalization about your topic?
- Do you separate details into separate paragraphs by category?
- Do you use vivid details that involve the five senses?
- Do you use details from different sources?
- Do you explain how your topic is related to larger issues?

TIP **Show, Don't Tell** Writers are often advised, "Show, don't tell." This phrase means that writers should use strong words, details, and examples to make a point. Choose vivid, clear examples for your description. They should not need much explanation.

Revising

When you revise your essay, make examples and details as specific as possible. This will make your description more vivid.

General: *People built flimsy houses in Hoovervilles.*

Specific: *In Hoovervilles, people built shelters out of scraps of lumber, tin, and cardboard.*

4. Proofread and Publish

Proofreading

Check your sentences for fragments and run-ons. A fragment is an incomplete sentence. Adding a subject or a verb can often make a fragment into a complete sentence. A run-on has too many subjects and verbs for one sentence. It usually needs to be broken into two or more separate sentences.

Publishing

Share your essay with one or more classmates. Make illustrations based on the descriptions in each other's essays.

5. Practice and Apply

Use the steps and strategies in this workshop to write your descriptive essay.

© Houghton Mifflin Harcourt Publishing Company

UNIT 5 1945–1975

Postwar America

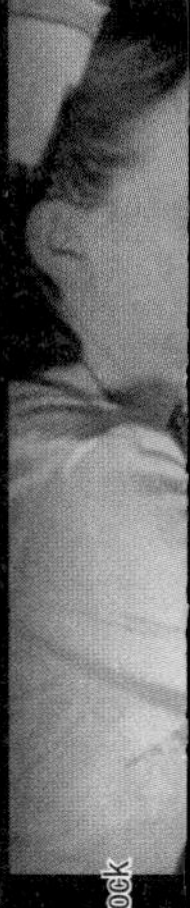

© Houghton Mifflin Harcourt Publishing Company • Image Credits: ©New York Times Co./Hulton Archive/Getty Images; (inset) ©Lazlo Willinger/SuperStock

What You Will Learn…

After the end of World War II, Americans became concerned with the global spread of communism. The government began taking steps to defend the nation against possible aggression from Communist nations. At home, many Americans enjoyed the economic prosperity of 1950s society. Not everyone benefited, however. Some Americans spoke out against American society and a government that did not guarantee equality to all citizens.

During the civil rights movement many Americans demanded equal rights for minority groups. Despite sometimes violent opposition, many successes were achieved. Differing viewpoints within society were further exposed, however, by reactions to the Vietnam War, a war fought in Southeast Asia over Communist expansion.

Explore the Art

The movies of the 1950s often portrayed American life as prosperous and content, although this was not true for everyone. What does this image suggest about the prosperity of postwar America?

© Houghton Mifflin Harcourt Publishing Company • Image Credits: ©New York Times Co./Hulton Archive/Getty Images; (inset) ©Lazlo Willinger/SuperStock

CHAPTER 12 1945–1959

Early Years of the Cold War

Essential Question How did the Cold War and domestic changes in the postwar years affect the nation?

ALABAMA COURSE OF STUDY

6 Identify causes and consequences of World War II and reasons for entry of the United States into the war.
- Explaining the importance of the surrender of the Axis Powers ending World War II.

8 Describe how the United States' role in the Cold War influenced domestic and international events.
- Describing the origin and meaning of the Iron Curtain and communism.
- Identifying strategic diplomatic initiatives that intensified the Cold War, including the policies of Harry S. Truman, Dwight D. Eisenhower, and John F. Kennedy.
- Identifying how Cold War tensions resulted in armed conflict.
- Describing the impact of the Cold War on technological innovations.

9 Critique major social and cultural changes in the United States since World War II.
- Recognizing the impact of music genres and artists on United States' culture since World War II.
- Identifying the impact of media, including newspapers, AM and FM radio, television, twenty-four hour sports and news programming, talk radio, and Internet social networking, on United States' culture since World War II.

10 Analyze changing economic priorities and cycles of economic expansion and contraction for their impact on society since World War II.
- Identifying policies and programs that had an economic impact on society since World War II.

12 Evaluate significant political issues and policies of presidential administrations since World War II.
- Identifying domestic policies that shaped the United States since World War II.
- Recognizing domestic issues that shaped the United States since World War II.
- Identifying issues of foreign affairs that shaped the United States since World War II.

Focus on Writing

Song Lyrics The end of World War II brought economic prosperity to the United States, along with new fears and challenges. Americans adjusted to changes in their everyday lives and the new threat of nuclear war. In this chapter you will read about life at the beginning of the Cold War. Then you will write the words to a song that reflects some aspect of American life in the 1950s.

UNITED STATES

1945 After Roosevelt's death, Harry S. Truman becomes president.

1945

1946 Winston Churchill declares an "iron curtain" between Western powers and the Soviet Union.

WORLD

Image Credits: (tc), ©Bettmann/Corbis

© Houghton Mifflin Harcourt Publishing Company

October 4, 1957
Sputnik

HISTORY Sputnik

hmhsocialstudies.com VIDEO

you can protect
yourself from...
RADIOACTIVE
FALLOUT
CD
GET THE FACTS!
FROM YOUR CIVIL DEFENSE DIRECTOR
FREE
COURSE ON FALLOUT

After World War II, the United States and the Soviet Union engaged in a nuclear arms race. Here, American students practice a "duck-and-cover" drill, designed to protect them from a nuclear bomb blast, shown in the government poster above.

1952 Grace Hopper creates the first compiler, which translates English into computer language.

1953 Julius and Ethel Rosenberg are executed for Communist activities.

1956 Fats Domino's "Blueberry Hill" tops the charts.

1958 The National Aeronautics and Space Administration (NASA) is formed.

1950

1955

1960

1948 The State of Israel is established.

1955 The Warsaw Pact is formed between Eastern European powers.

1957 The Soviet Union launches the first satellite, *Sputnik*, into orbit.

1959 Fidel Castro takes over Cuba.

© Houghton Mifflin Harcourt Publishing Company

Image Credits: (tc), ©Bettmann/Corbis; (tr), Civil Defense Museum; (cl), ©Bettmann/Corbis; (c), ©Hulton Archive/Getty Images; (bl), ©Carl & Ann Purcell/Corbis; (cr), ©AP/Wide World Photos; (br), ©Bettman/Corbis

Reading Social Studies

Economics | Geography | **Politics** | Society and Culture | Science and Technology

Focus on Themes In this chapter, you will learn about the Cold War between the United States and the Soviet Union. This war was unlike other wars in that it was often fought between **politicians** instead of soldiers. Each country used developments in **science and technology** to declare itself superior. You will also read about U.S. society and its reaction to the Cold War.

Visualizing

Focus on Reading Visualizing how your life might have been different if you had been alive during a period in history can help you understand life at that time.

Understanding Visualizing Using clues about everyday life that you find in a history book like this one can help you imagine what life was like in the past. You can imagine yourself and your life, and how life would have been different if you had lived in the past. Or, you can try to imagine what life was like for the people alive then.

Notice the clues in this passage that give you an idea of the feelings of people living during the Cold War.

> All the time, in the homely [plain], cluttered rooms of our private lives the television displayed the continuing spectacle of public life—all of it still going on in the windless places on the other side of the screen. Presidents and First Secretaries trod [climbed] down the metal staircases from the bellies of great aircraft to shake hands on the tarmac [runway] and climb into big black cars. Tanks wheeled down blind streets and across muddy fields. Rolls of heavy wire netting were unwound and veered [turned] upwards against a dawn sky.
>
> — From *The Cruel Peace*, by Fred Inglis

The author is using description to inform the reader about the feeling of watching the Cold War unfold on television.

Here the author uses frightening images to help the reader understand the fear of the Cold War.

© Houghton Mifflin Harcourt Publishing Company

You Try It!

As you read the following passage, look for details that help you visualize the past.

In 1946 Winston Churchill described how Soviet control cut these countries off from the Western world. "An iron curtain has descended [fallen] across the [European] Continent," he said. The term *iron curtain* thus came to be used to describe this division. Presidential adviser Bernard Baruch warned of the seriousness of the Soviet threat, saying, "Let us not be deceived—we are today in the midst of a cold war." The phrase *Cold War* came to be used to describe the struggle for global power between the United States and the Soviet Union.

After you read the passage, answer the following questions.

1. Which details help you understand the attitude existing between the United States and the Soviet Union?

2. How does the quote by Winston Churchill help you visualize the political atmosphere of the time?

3. How does the phrase *Cold War* help you visualize the political atmosphere of the time?

As you read this chapter, look for details that help you visualize the past.

Key Terms and People

Chapter 12

Section 1

Yalta Conference
Nuremberg trials
United Nations
Cold War
containment
Truman Doctrine
Marshall Plan
North Atlantic Treaty Organization
GI Bill of Rights
Fair Deal

Section 2

Mao Zedong
38th parallel
Joseph McCarthy
hydrogen bomb
arms race
Sputnik
brinkmanship

Section 3

baby boom
Sun Belt
urban renewal
beats

Academic Vocabulary

In this chapter, you will learn the following academic words:

concrete

© Houghton Mifflin Harcourt Publishing Company

SECTION 1

Adjusting to Peace

What You Will Learn...

Main Ideas

1. As World War II ended, leaders began planning the future of the postwar world.
2. The United States and the Soviet Union went from being allies to enemies after World War II.
3. Americans adjusted to postwar life.

The Big Idea

After World War II, Americans adjusted to new challenges both at home and around the world.

Key Terms

Yalta Conference
Nuremberg trials
United Nations
Cold War
containment
Truman Doctrine
Marshall Plan
North Atlantic Treaty Organization
GI Bill of Rights
Fair Deal

hmhsocialstudies.com
TAKING NOTES

Use the graphic organizer online to take notes on the results of the end of World War II.

If YOU were there...

You are an adviser to President Harry S. Truman in July 1945. You have traveled with him to Potsdam, outside the ruined city of Berlin, where Allied leaders are discussing postwar plans. Everyone agrees that steps must be taken to prevent another world war. But you are worried that Soviet leader Joseph Stalin cannot be trusted.

What advice would you give to President Truman?

BUILDING BACKGROUND U.S. leaders had mistrusted the Soviet government before World War II. The goals of the totalitarian, Communist Soviet state conflicted with American democratic, capitalistic ideals. In addition, Soviet dictator Joseph Stalin used brutal tactics, including murder, to maintain power and control political opposition. During the war, the rivals put aside their differences to defeat Germany. After the war, however, old tensions resurfaced.

The Future of the Postwar World

As 1945 began, it was becoming clear that the Allies were going to win World War II. In February Allied leaders known as the Big Three—Franklin D. Roosevelt of the United States, Winston Churchill of Great Britain, and Joseph Stalin of the Soviet Union—met in the Soviet city of Yalta to discuss plans for peace.

At the **Yalta Conference**, the three leaders made important decisions about the future of European governments. They expressed support for the creation of an international peacekeeping organization. They also agreed that nations freed from Germany should have the right "to create democratic institutions of their own choice." Stalin promised to allow free elections in the Soviet-occupied countries in Eastern Europe. However, after driving German troops out of Poland, Soviet forces set up a pro-Soviet Communist government.

In July 1945 President Truman met with British and Soviet leaders near Berlin, Germany, at the Potsdam Conference. The Allied leaders divided conquered Germany into four zones. Britain, France, the United States, and the Soviet Union would each occupy one zone. The capital city of Berlin—located deep inside the Soviet zone—was also divided into four zones.

© Houghton Mifflin Harcourt Publishing Company

War Crimes Trials

After World War II, Allied leaders formed a special court, called the International Military Tribunal, to try Axis leaders accused of war crimes. In November 1945 the tribunal put high-ranking Nazis on trial in the German city of Nuremberg in what became known as the **Nuremberg trials**. U.S. Supreme Court justice Robert H. Jackson served as the chief American attorney. In his opening statement, Jackson explained the importance of the trials:

> "The wrongs which we seek to condemn and punish have been so calculated [well planned], so malignant [evil] and devastating, that civilization cannot tolerate their being ignored because it cannot survive their being repeated."
>
> —Robert H. Jackson, quoted in *The Nuremberg Trial*, edited by Mitchell Bard

The court charged Nazi officials with "crimes against humanity." One defendant was Hermann Goering, a key planner of Hitler's "final solution." Another was Hans Frank, Poland's wartime governor, who had organized the killing of hundreds of thousands of Poles and Polish Jews. The tribunal found 19 Nazi leaders guilty. Of these, 12, including Goering and Frank, were sentenced to death.

The International Military Tribunal for the Far East held trials in Japan. Japan's wartime leader Hideki Tojo was convicted and executed. Seven other Japanese leaders were also sentenced to death. The trials in Germany and Japan helped establish the principle that individuals must be held responsible for committing war crimes, even when acting on behalf of a government.

Focus on Reading

How does the quote from Robert H. Jackson help you visualize the atmosphere of the Nuremberg trials?

The United Nations

During the war, President Roosevelt had spoken of the need for a new international organization to promote world peace. Roosevelt did not believe the United States alone could bring peace to the whole world. "The structure of world peace," he said, "must be a peace which rests on the cooperative effort of the whole world."

Quick Facts

Yalta Conference, February 1945

Who attended?

- Franklin Roosevelt, United States
- Winston Churchill, Great Britain
- Joseph Stalin, Soviet Union

What was the outcome?

- Free elections for countries liberated from German control
- Strong support for creation of an international peacekeeping organization

Winston Churchill, Franklin Roosevelt, and Joseph Stalin (seated left to right) met at Yalta in 1945.

Quick Facts

Potsdam Conference, July 1945

Who attended?

- Harry S. Truman, United States
- Winston Churchill and Clement Attlee, Great Britain
- Joseph Stalin, Soviet Union

What was the outcome?

- Germany and the city of Berlin would be divided into four zones. Britain, France, the United States, and the Soviet Union would each control one zone.

Clement Attlee, Harry Truman, and Joseph Stalin (seated left to right) met at Potsdam in 1945.

© Houghton Mifflin Harcourt Publishing Company • Image Credits: (br), UPI/Corbis-Bettmann; (bl), ©Hulton-Deutsch Collection/Corbis

LINKING TO TODAY

The United Nations

Written in 1945, the United Nations Charter declared the organization's commitment "to unite our strength to maintain international peace and security." Since 1945 the UN has grown from 51 member nations to more than 190. In addition to working to prevent war, the United Nations today works to provide disaster relief, prevent hunger and disease, and combat international terrorism.

ANALYSIS SKILL **ANALYZING INFORMATION**

How have the goals of the United Nations expanded since 1945?

In 1944 American, British, Soviet, and Chinese representatives met to draft a plan for the **United Nations** (UN)—an organization dedicated to resolving international conflicts. In 1945, representatives from 50 countries met to write the UN Charter. President Truman appointed Eleanor Roosevelt as one of the first U.S. delegates to the UN.

One of the UN's first actions concerned the Palestine Mandate, occupied by the British after World War I. The UN General Assembly voted to divide the area into separate Arab and Jewish states. Jews had begun moving to Palestine, an area important to the Jewish, Christian, and Muslim religions, in the late 1800s. Many more moved there before and during World War II. On May 14, 1948, Jewish leaders announced the creation of the nation of Israel.

The United States quickly recognized the new Jewish state. Arab leaders refused to do so and claimed the land as their own. Armies from five Arab states attacked Israel. Israeli forces drove them back, and the two sides reached a truce in 1949. Israel then joined the UN. But tensions remained high.

READING CHECK **Finding Main Ideas** What steps did world leaders take to establish peace?

From Allies to Enemies

During World War II, the United States and the Soviet Union cooperated to win the war. Afterward, the differences between the two nations led to new hostility. The Soviet Union hoped to spread communism around the world. Americans remained committed to capitalism and democracy.

The Iron Curtain

After Stalin created a Communist government in Poland, the Soviet Union expanded its control over Eastern Europe by creating "satellite states"—countries under complete Soviet control. In 1946 Winston Churchill described how Soviet control cut these countries off from the Western world. "An iron curtain has descended [fallen] across the [European] Continent," he said. The term *iron curtain* thus came to be used to describe this division. Presidential adviser Bernard Baruch warned of the seriousness of the Soviet threat, saying, "Let us not be deceived—we are today in the midst of a cold war." The phrase **Cold War** came to be used to describe the struggle for global power between the United States and the Soviet Union.

© Houghton Mifflin Harcourt Publishing Company • Image Credits: (tc) ©Corbis; (tr) ©AP Photo/United Nations

Cold War Policies

The United States quickly developed a new foreign policy to deal with the Cold War. It was based on the goal of **containment**, or preventing the Soviet Union from expanding its influence around the world.

In 1945 the Soviet Union began demanding control over areas in the Mediterranean Sea that were under Turkish authority. In 1946 Communist rebels in Greece threatened to topple the Greek monarchy. At Truman's request, Congress passed an aid package worth millions of dollars for Greece and Turkey. The money, the president said, would "support free peoples who are resisting attempted subjugation [conquest] by armed minorities or outside pressures." U.S. aid helped the Greek army defeat the Communist rebels and protected Turkey from Soviet expansion. This policy of providing aid to help foreign countries fight communism became known as the **Truman Doctrine**.

The nations of Europe, meanwhile, were still devastated from World War II. American secretary of state George C. Marshall saw this as a threat both to stability in Europe and to the U.S. economy, which depended on trade with Europe. Marshall called on European leaders to develop plans for economic recovery, which the United States would help fund. Under the **Marshall Plan**, Western Europe received more than $13 billion in U.S. loans and grants for European economic recovery between 1948 and 1952. Soviet leaders rejected Marshall Plan aid. They also kept Eastern European nations from participating.

Cold War tensions rose further in 1948 when France, Britain, and the United States

CZECHO-SLOVAKIA

This cartoon shows Czechoslovakia's freedom being crushed by the Soviet Union.

Cold War Europe, 1955

Cold War Europe, 1955
60°N
50°N
40N
20E
10E
0
10°W
N
S
E
W
NORWAY
SWEDEN
FINLAND
North Sea
Baltic Sea
DENMARK
IRELAND
GREAT BRITAIN
NETHERLANDS
BELGIUM
LUXEMBOURG
ATLANTIC OCEAN
Berlin
EAST GERMANY
WEST GERMANY
POLAND
CZECHOSLOVAKIA
Iron Curtain
SOVIET UNION
SWITZERLAND
AUSTRIA
HUNGARY
ROMANIA
FRANCE
Yalta
PORTUGAL
ANDORRA
SPAIN
ITALY
YUGOSLAVIA
Adriatic Sea
BULGARIA
ALBANIA
Iron Curtain
Dardanelles
GREECE
Aegean Sea
TURKEY
Mediterranean Sea
NATO member, 1955
Warsaw Pact member, 1955
Nonaligned Communist nation
Nonaligned nation
The United States, Canada, and Iceland were also NATO members.
0 200 400 Miles
0 200 400 Kilometers

GEOGRAPHY SKILLS **INTERPRETING MAPS**

1. **Place** Which countries remained nonaligned during the Cold War?
2. **Location** What is the northernmost NATO member country shown on the map?

© Houghton Mifflin Harcourt Publishing Company • Image Credits: (t) Editorial cartoon by Tom Little, 1948, courtesy of the Nashville Tennessean decided to join their occupation zones of Germany into one unit. The Soviet Union had good reason to fear the creation of a strong West German state. On June 24, the Soviet Union suddenly blocked all rail, highway, and water traffic between western Germany and the city of Berlin. West Berlin's 2 million residents were trapped behind the iron curtain.

To respond to this crisis without using military force, U.S. and British planes began airlifting supplies into West Berlin. For more than a year, planes delivered lifesaving food, fuel, and machinery to West Berliners. The Soviet Union made no determined effort to stop the airlift, fearing a war. It then lifted the blockade in May 1949.

THE IMPACT TODAY

When the Cold War ended, many former Warsaw Pact nations joined NATO. Today NATO has 28 member nations.

That same year, the United States joined nine Western European countries, along with Iceland and Canada, to form the **North Atlantic Treaty Organization** (NATO). NATO members promised to defend each other if attacked. In 1955 the Soviet Union created the Warsaw Pact, which provided a unified system of military command between the Soviet Union and its Eastern European satellite countries for their mutual defense.

READING CHECK **Comparing** How were NATO and the Warsaw Pact similar?

BIOGRAPHY

Harry S. Truman

1884–1972

Harry S. Truman grew up in Independence, Missouri. He was an artillery officer in France during World War I; then he returned to Missouri and later became active in politics. He was elected to the U.S. Senate in 1934, where he served until becoming vice president in 1945. When President Roosevelt died, Truman was sworn in as president of the United States. "I felt like the moon, the stars, and all the planets had fallen on me," he said. Truman later called his first year in office a "year of decisions," as he led the country through the end of World War II and the start of the Cold War.

Analyzing Information What made Truman's first year as president especially challenging?

Postwar America

You have read about the economic depression that followed the end of World War I. As World War II ended, President Truman was worried about a similar downturn. More than 16 million Americans had served in the armed forces during the war. Now they were coming home, and most would be looking for work.

The Postwar Economy

To provide jobs for returning veterans, the government urged the millions of women who had gone to work during the war to give up their jobs. New laws also eased the transition for returning soldiers. The Servicemen's Readjustment Act, or **GI Bill of Rights**, offered veterans money for school as well as loans for houses, farms, and businesses. The GI Bill's home loans enabled veterans to buy about 20 percent of the new houses built right after the war. Some 8 million veterans used the GI Bill's educational benefits to attend colleges and technical schools. Bob Dole, former U.S. senator from Kansas, described how the GI Bill changed his life:

> "In my case, I went from a couple of nondescript [ordinary] years in college before the war, and came back and made excellent grades. I went on to law school and got involved in politics. None of that would have happened without the GI Bill."
>
> —Bob Dole, quoted in *GI Bill: The Law That Changed America*, by Milton Greenberg

Another major postwar change was Truman's decision to end the rationing of scarce products. Prices skyrocketed as people rushed to buy gasoline and other products that had been limited during the war. The inflation rate in 1946 rose above 18 percent. The U.S. economy remained strong, however.

Labor Unrest

More than 35 percent of all nonfarm workers were members of unions in 1946, more than ever before. With prices rising quickly,

Jackie Robinson

On April 15, 1947, Jackie Robinson played his first game for the Brooklyn Dodgers. Robinson became a hero to millions by ending segregation in major league baseball. He went on to be a Hall of Fame player—and an outspoken supporter of equal rights. "The right of every American to first-class citizenship is the most important issue of our time," Robinson said.

How did Robinson show his support for equal rights for all Americans?

workers went on strike to demand higher wages. In 1946 alone, 4.5 million workers participated in nearly 5,000 strikes.

The strikes became a major political problem for President Truman. Many people began to wonder if he could handle the presidency. In April 1946 the 400,000-member United Mine Workers Union went on strike. When Truman was unable to negotiate a settlement, he placed the mines under government control. In May Truman ended a railroad strike by threatening to draft all the striking workers into the army.

To reduce the power of labor unions, Congress passed the Taft-Hartley Act in 1947. This act outlawed closed shops—businesses that could hire only union members. It also allowed the president to order an 80-day "cooling-off" period before a strike began. In addition, union leaders had to swear they were not Communists. In spite of his clashes with unions, Truman thought this bill went too far to weaken unions. He vetoed the bill, but Congress overrode his veto.

Civil Rights

After serving their country in World War II, many African Americans faced prejudice and segregation at home. "Black servicemen were overseas dying for this country," said civil rights lawyer Constance Baker Motley. "And . . . they would be coming home to a situation that said, in effect, You're a second-class citizen." African American veterans helped lead a major effort to gain equal rights.

Truman responded in 1946 by appointing the Committee on Civil Rights to investigate discrimination and suggest solutions. As a result of the committee's report, Truman recommended that Congress pass anti-lynching laws, outlaw segregation, and protect civil rights. Congress failed to act on Truman's ideas. But in 1948, under pressure from African American groups, Truman issued an executive order ending segregation in the armed forces. He also banned discrimination in the hiring of federal employees.

The Election of 1948

As the election of 1948 drew near, President Truman's chances of re-election looked bleak. The Republicans had gained control of Congress in 1946. They felt confident that their presidential candidate, New York governor Thomas Dewey, could beat Truman.

Truman faced challenges from within the Democratic Party as well. Some southern Democrats protested Truman's support for

© Houghton Mifflin Harcourt Publishing Company • Image Credits: (t) The Granger Collection, New York civil rights laws by walking out of the 1948 Democratic National Convention. Many joined the States' Rights Party, or Dixiecrats, which favored racial segregation. The Dixiecrats nominated their own presidential candidate—South Carolina governor Strom Thurmond.

Truman took his case for re-election directly to the American people. He traveled more than 30,000 miles by train and delivered hundreds of speeches. He attacked what he called the "do-nothing, good-for-nothing" Congress for refusing to pass his legislation. "I spoke I believe altogether to between fifteen and twenty million people," he later said. "I met them face to face, and I convinced them, and they voted for me." Truman won a surprise victory. The Democratic Party also regained control of both houses of Congress.

In his 1949 State of the Union Address, Truman urged Congress to support his plans for the nation. Truman's domestic program, called the **Fair Deal**, included a higher minimum wage, the creation of a national health insurance plan for all Americans, and expanded Social Security benefits for the elderly. It also asked for federal protection of civil rights and an end to racial discrimination in hiring.

Congress approved some parts of the Fair Deal, such as a higher minimum wage and expanded Social Security benefits. Congress rejected other Fair Deal proposals. These included civil rights legislation that would have created a permanent Fair Employment Practices Committee.

QUICK FACTS

The Fair Deal

The Fair Deal included
- National health insurance
- Expanded social security
- Higher minimum wage
- Public housing
- Civil rights legislation
- Federal aid to education

READING CHECK **Analyzing** How did the GI Bill help returning soldiers?

SUMMARY The United States faced a series of new challenges after World War II.

Section 1 Assessment

hmhsocialstudies.com ONLINE QUIZ

Reviewing Ideas, Terms, and People

1. **a. Describe** How did the Allies divide Germany at the Potsdam Conference?
   b. Explain Why were the **Nuremberg trials** important?
   c. Predict Based on its founding and early years, do you think the **United Nations** would be an effective organization?
2. **a. Define** What was the **Truman Doctrine**?
   b. Analyze How did the **Marshall Plan** help stabilize Western Europe?
   c. Elaborate Why do you think the United States and Western European countries were concerned about Soviet expansion?
3. **a. Recall** What kinds of programs were included in President Truman's **Fair Deal**?
   b. Explain What was the purpose of the Taft-Hartley Act?
   c. Evaluate Do you think President Truman did enough to promote civil rights? Why or why not?

Critical Thinking

4. **Categorizing** Review your notes on the results of World War II. Then copy the graphic organizer below and use it to identify the effects of the war's end on the United States and the world.

Results of World War II	
In the United States	In the World

Focus on Writing

5. **The Postwar World** Take notes on postwar developments in the United States and the world. Which events might have given Americans hope? Which might have made them concerned? If you had lived during the 1950s, which issue would have been of the most interest to you?

Eleanor Roosevelt

How would you work for human rights for all?

When did she live? 1884–1962

Where did she live? She lived much of her life in New York, where she married Franklin D. Roosevelt in 1905. She also lived in Washington, D.C., when her husband was assistant secretary of the navy and, later, president.

What did she do? During the Great Depression, Eleanor Roosevelt acted as President Roosevelt's "eyes and ears" by traveling around the United States to study conditions among the people. She investigated New Deal programs and reported on their effectiveness. She also worked for equal rights for African Americans. Serving on the UN Commission on Human Rights from 1946 to 1951, she helped write the Universal Declaration of Human Rights, which the UN adopted in 1948. In 1961 President John F. Kennedy chose her to chair his Commission on the Status of Women.

Why is she so important? She changed the role of First Lady by acting as a public figure. She held her own press conferences, made speeches, and wrote newspaper columns. She was a leading figure in the movements to promote human rights, children's welfare, and equal rights for women and minorities.

Making Inferences How did Eleanor Roosevelt's different jobs and activities reflect her values and beliefs?

KEY EVENTS

1905
Marries Franklin D. Roosevelt

1921
Becomes active in politics

1936
Begins writing daily newspaper columns; holds press conferences for women correspondents

1945
Appointed delegate to the UN

1946
Becomes chair of the UN Commission on Human Rights

1961
Appointed chair of the Commission on the Status of Women

1962
Dies in New York City

Image Credits: (br), The Granger Collection, New York

© Houghton Mifflin Harcourt Publishing Company

SECTION 2

War in Korea and a New Red Scare

What You Will Learn...

Main Ideas

1. The United States fought Communist North Korea in the Korean War.
2. Fear of Communists led to a new Red Scare at home.
3. President Eisenhower faced Cold War crises around the world.

The Big Idea

During the Cold War, the U.S. government confronted communism globally and within the United States.

Key Terms and People

Mao Zedong
38th parallel
Joseph McCarthy
hydrogen bomb
arms race
Sputnik
brinkmanship

hmhsocialstudies.com
TAKING NOTES

Use the graphic organizer online to take notes on the conflicts and crises of the Cold War.

If YOU were there...

A radio broadcast on June 26, 1950, delivers a shocking announcement. Communist forces from North Korea have just invaded South Korea. President Truman has demanded that the North Koreans halt their invasion, but they seem to be ignoring this demand. Now Truman has to decide whether to use American military force to stop the North Koreans.

Do you think the United States should send troops to Korea? Why or why not?

BUILDING BACKGROUND The earliest Cold War conflicts were in Central and Eastern Europe, where countries were divided by the Iron Curtain. But the Truman Doctrine committed the United States to containing communism on a wider scale. The Communist takeover of China in 1949 soon focused Cold War fears on Asia.

The Korean War

The Cold War began in Europe but quickly spread to the Asian nations of China and Korea. In China, the Communist Party and the Nationalist Party had been struggling for control of the country since the early 1900s. The two rivals joined forces against Japan during World War II but then resumed their civil war after Japan's defeat. The United States, as part of its commitment to stop the spread of communism, backed the Nationalists. The Nationalists were defeated, however, and were forced to flee to the island of Taiwan. Led by **Mao Zedong**, the Communists officially established the People's Republic of China on October 1, 1949. Many Americans saw this as a disastrous failure of U.S. foreign policy. They feared that all of Asia might soon fall to communism.

These fears were heightened by a crisis in Korea. Japan had controlled Korea from 1910 to the end of World War II. After the war, the Allies divided Korea at the **38th parallel**. The Soviet Union

The Korean War

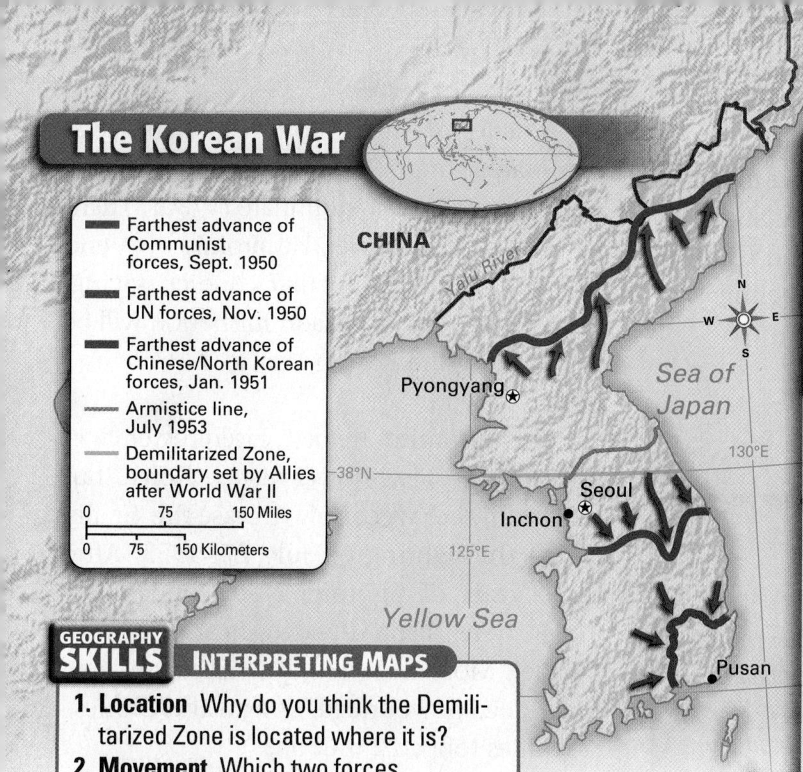

Farthest advance of Communist forces, Sept. 1950
Farthest advance of UN forces, Nov. 1950
Farthest advance of Chinese/North Korean forces, Jan. 1951
Armistice line, July 1953
Demilitarized Zone, boundary set by Allies after World War II
0 75 150 Miles
0 75 150 Kilometers
CHINA
Yalu River
Pyongyang
Sea of Japan
38°N
130°E
Seoul
Inchon
125°E
Yellow Sea
Pusan
N
S
E
W

GEOGRAPHY SKILLS INTERPRETING MAPS

1. **Location** Why do you think the Demilitarized Zone is located where it is?
2. **Movement** Which two forces advanced into South Korea?

BIOGRAPHY

Douglas MacArthur

1880–1964

Douglas MacArthur grew up on a series of military bases, where his father served in the U.S. Army. "It was here I learned to ride and shoot even before I could read or write," he later said. After graduating first in his class at West Point, MacArthur began an army career that would last more than 50 years. He reached the rank of general in 1918 and commanded troops in World War I, World War II, and the Korean War. "When I joined the Army," he told Congress in 1951, "it was the fulfillment of all my boyhood hopes and dreams."

Drawing Inferences How can you tell how MacArthur felt about the U.S. Army?

controlled the northern part of Korea, and the United States occupied the south. Both sides set up governments, neither of which recognized the other as legitimate.

Fighting in Korea

On June 25, 1950, North Korea's Soviet-trained and equipped army stormed across the 38th parallel and invaded South Korea. The United Nations called for a cease-fire. But the North Koreans continued their attack.

President Truman had to make an immediate decision: Should the United States use force to try to stop the North Korean invasion? On June 27 Truman announced: "I have ordered United States air and sea forces to give the [South] Korean government troops cover and support." That same day, the UN decided to help South Korea "to repel the armed attack." American general Douglas MacArthur was put in command of the UN forces, which included troops from the United States and 15 other countries. The majority of the troops were from the United States and South Korea.

In the early battles, MacArthur's forces were driven back to the southeastern tip of the Korean Peninsula, near the city of Pusan. Fierce fighting raged for six weeks before the UN troops turned the tide of the war with a surprise attack. Landing at the port city of Inchon on September 15, UN forces attacked the North Koreans from behind. About a month later, MacArthur's troops captured Pyongyang, North Korea's capital. They then advanced north to the Yalu River, the border between North Korea and China. MacArthur told Truman he would "have the boys home by Christmas."

Then China suddenly sent hundreds of thousands of soldiers across the border to join the North Koreans. They drove UN forces south again, back below the 38th parallel. MacArthur suggested air strikes on Chinese cities and an attack on mainland China. Truman refused permission. He was determined to contain the war in Korea.

When MacArthur publicly criticized the president's strategy, Truman relieved the general of command. "I fired General MacArthur because he wouldn't respect the authority of the president," Truman said. This was a very unpopular decision with the American public. MacArthur came home to a hero's welcome.

HISTORY

VIDEO
Korean War Begins

hmhsocialstudies.com

The War Ends

By the spring of 1951 the fighting in Korea settled into a violent stalemate. The UN forces had driven the North Koreans and Chinese back across the 38th parallel. But neither side seemed able to win the war.

Primary Source

POLITICAL CARTOON

Fear of Communism

In the 1950s the fear of communism caused some government leaders to ignore the civil liberties of suspected Communists. Some critics, like this cartoonist, believed these tactics threatened the freedom of all Americans. Here, a frightened man climbs the arm of the Statue of Liberty to put out her torch.

"FIRE!"
The Statue of Liberty's burning torch symbolizes freedom.
HYSTERIA
Hysteria means "senseless excitement."
The frightened man carries water to put out the fire.
HERBLOCK

ANALYSIS SKILL **ANALYZING PRIMARY SOURCES**

Why is the man shown to be putting out Liberty's torch?

Americans' frustration with the war dominated the 1952 presidential election. The Republicans nominated war hero Dwight D. Eisenhower. He promised to end the increasingly unpopular conflict, saying, "The first task of a new administration will be to . . . bring the Korean War to an early and honorable end."

This promise helped Eisenhower win the election. Eisenhower visited Korea, but the conflict dragged on. A cease-fire finally ended the fighting on July 27, 1953. After three years of fighting, North and South Korea were again divided near the 38th parallel. More than 130,000 Americans had been killed or wounded. Korean and Chinese casualties topped 2 million.

READING CHECK **Summarizing** What were the effects of the Korean War?

A New Red Scare

The first Red Scare swept America after the Russian Revolution in 1917. Cold War fears led to another Red Scare in the late 1940s and 1950s. Attorney General J. Howard McGrath summed up these fears when he said, "There are today many Communists in America. They are everywhere—in factories, offices, butcher shops, on street corners."

Fear of Communists

A congressional committee called the House Un-American Activities Committee (HUAC) investigated Communist influence in America. In 1947 HUAC launched a series of hearings to expose what it believed was Communist influence in the Hollywood movie industry. The committee branded as "red," or Communist, actors and writers who would not answer questions or who refused to reveal the names of suspected Communists. People suspected of Communist sympathies were often blacklisted, or denied work. Some of these people never worked in movies again.

© Houghton Mifflin Harcourt Publishing Company • Image Credits: (l), 'FIRE!' from Herblock: A Cartoonist's Life (Times Books 1998)/Library of Congress Prints & Photographs Division, Washington, D.C.

Primary Source

POINTS OF VIEW

McCarthyism

Journalist Edward R. Murrow frequently criticized Senator McCarthy's tactics. This drew a furious response from McCarthy.

"If none of us ever read a book that was 'dangerous,' nor had a friend who was 'different,' or never joined an organization that advocated 'change,' we would all be just the kind of people Joe McCarthy wants. Whose fault is that? Not really [McCarthy's]. He didn't create this situation of fear. He merely exploited [took advantage of] it, and rather successfully."

—Edward R. Murrow

"Murrow is a symbol—the leader and the cleverest of the jackal [wild dog] pack which is always found at the throat of anyone who dares to expose individual Communists and traitors. I am compelled by the facts to say to you that Mr. Edward R. Murrow, as far back as twenty years ago, was engaged in propaganda for Communist causes."

—Joseph McCarthy

ANALYSIS SKILL **ANALYZING POINTS OF VIEW**

How would you describe Murrow's criticism of McCarthy's ideas?

Explosive spy cases also fed the fears that Communists were at work in the United States. In 1950 a German-born physicist was convicted of providing the Soviets information about the atomic bomb project at Los Alamos, New Mexico, that allowed them to develop an atomic bomb at least one year earlier than they would have. In 1951 Julius and Ethel Rosenberg also were tried for providing Soviet spies with secret details about atomic bomb design. The Rosenbergs denied the charges but were found guilty and executed in 1953.

The Rise of McCarthy

Wisconsin senator **Joseph McCarthy** contributed to fears in the early 1950s by charging that Communists were working inside the State Department. He claimed to have the names of 57 people who were "either card-carrying members or certainly loyal to the Communist Party."

McCarthy produced no <u>concrete</u> proof of crimes. When challenged, he made up new charges, labeling those who questioned him as "soft on communism." This method of making aggressive accusations without proof became known as McCarthyism.

ACADEMIC VOCABULARY

concrete specific, real

McCarthy finally went too far in 1954. In televised Senate hearings, he charged that there were Communists in the U.S. Army. For five weeks, Americans watched McCarthy's bullying tactics. At one point, McCarthy tried to discredit Joseph Welch, the army's attorney, by attacking a young assistant in Welch's law firm. This shocked Welch—and the nation. "Let us not assassinate this lad further, Senator," Welsh said. "Have you left no sense of decency?" A later Senate vote condemned McCarthy's actions, but it came too late for those whose careers had been ruined by his attacks.

READING CHECK **Comparing** How were HUAC's and McCarthy's actions similar?

Eisenhower and the Cold War

Cold War tensions increased around the world during the presidency of Dwight Eisenhower. In this hostile atmosphere, Americans adjusted to the reality of living with the constant threat of nuclear war.

The Arms Race

THE IMPACT TODAY

Today Americans, Russians, and astronauts from other countries work side by side on the International Space Station, which has been in orbit since 1998.

In 1950 President Truman approved work on the **hydrogen bomb**, a weapon far more powerful than the atomic bombs used in World War II. American scientists tested the first hydrogen bomb in the South Pacific in 1952. "The fireball expanded to three miles in diameter," said a test observer. He soon saw that the entire island on which the bomb exploded "had vanished, vaporized."

The Soviet Union tested its first atomic bomb in 1949 and its first hydrogen bomb in 1953. In what became a nuclear **arms race**, both the United States and the Soviet Union rushed to build more and more weapons. American school children practiced "duck-and-cover" drills, in which they were taught to crouch under their desks in case of nuclear attack. Some families built underground bomb shelters in their backyards.

In October 1957 the Soviets launched ***Sputnik,*** the world's first artificial satellite. Americans feared that if the Soviet Union could launch a satellite, it could launch missiles to attack the United States. In January 1958 the United States responded by launching its own satellite. Later that year, the U.S. government established the National Aeronautics and Space Administration (NASA) to conduct space research.

Cold War Crises

President Eisenhower modified Truman's policy of containment. He and Secretary of State John Foster Dulles supported **brinkmanship**—a willingness to go to the brink of war to oppose communism. "The ability to get to the verge [edge] without getting into war is the necessary art," Dulles explained. The president and Dulles also

History Close-up

Inside a Bomb Shelter

Many families built personal bomb shelters for use in a nuclear emergency. The shelters were stocked with essentials like food and water and were often located in the family's backyard.

underground shelter
entrance
beds
food
water

threatened the Soviet Union with "massive retaliation" against Soviet advances.

As part of his effort, Eisenhower used covert, or secret, operations around the world. In 1953, for example, the Central Intelligence Agency (CIA) helped overthrow the premier of Iran. American officials had feared he was a Communist. In 1954 the CIA helped organize the removal of the Guatemalan president for similar reasons.

In 1956 a crisis in Egypt seemed to push the world to the brink of a third world war. Egyptian leader Gamal Abdel Nasser nationalized the Suez Canal, a vital waterway connecting the Mediterranean and Red seas, in an attempt to collect tolls from the canal to finance a major dam project. Britain and France, which relied on the canal for trade, allied with Israel, a longtime enemy of Egypt, and invaded the area around the canal. The Soviet Union, an ally of Egypt, threatened to crush the invaders. This would force the United States to defend its allies. Finally, the Americans and the Soviet Union agreed to condemn the invasion, and the Suez crisis ended. After the brief moment of cooperation, the Cold War continued.

READING CHECK **Analyzing** How was the arms race a display of brinkmanship?

Families practiced getting into their shelters as quickly as possible. Some families spent free time in the shelters to adjust to spending weeks or months there.

ANALYSIS SKILL **ANALYZING INFORMATION**

Which essentials did families keep in their bomb shelters?

SUMMARY After World War II, Americans responded to Communist threats at home and abroad.

Section 2 Assessment

hmhsocialstudies.com ONLINE QUIZ

Reviewing Ideas, Terms, and People

1. a. **Identify** What is the **38th parallel**, and why was it important in the Korean War?
   b. **Analyze** How did the outcome of China's civil war affect the U.S. response to North Korea's attack?
   c. **Evaluate** Do you think President Truman should have fired MacArthur? Explain your answer.
2. a. **Describe** Why did a second Red Scare occur in the late 1940s and 1950s?
   b. **Explain** How did television affect **Joseph McCarthy**'s power?
   c. **Elaborate** Why do you think the Red Scare lasted so long?
3. a. **Recall** How did Eisenhower deal with Cold War crises during his administration?
   b. **Make Inferences** How can you tell that the U.S. government took the launch of ***Sputnik*** seriously?
   c. **Elaborate** Why do you think the United States and the Soviet Union were able to cooperate during the Suez crisis?

Critical Thinking

4. **Categorizing** Review your notes on Cold War conflicts and crises. Then copy the graphic organizer below and use it to list each event under its appropriate location.

Asia	Soviet Union	United States	Other

Focus on Writing

5. **Taking Notes on Challenges at Home and Abroad** Take notes on the challenges and fears Americans faced during the Korean War, McCarthy era, and Eisenhower presidency. How did the government and individuals respond to these challenges and fears?

The Cold War

Flags of the United States and the USSR

Threats During the Cold War

The Cold War began shortly after World War II ended, as the world's countries adjusted to new postwar relationships. Cold War tension between the United States and the Soviet Union affected diplomatic relationships around the globe. Many countries based their foreign policy on their alliance with one of the two main superpowers.

The Soviet Union had an economy and political system based on communism, a system first described by the German writer Karl Marx. In Marx's version of communism, a country

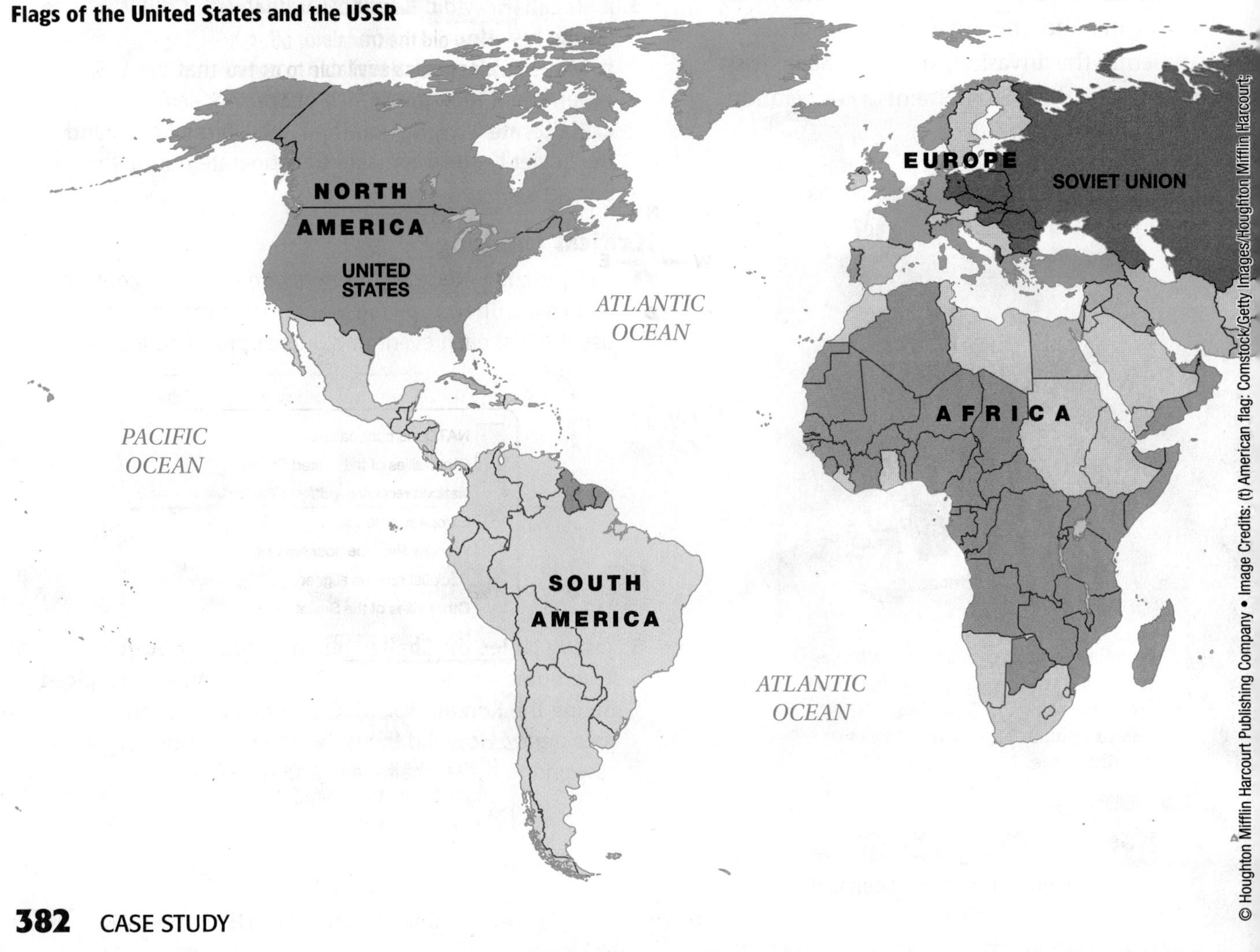

© Houghton Mifflin Harcourt Publishing Company • Image Credits: (t) American flag: Comstock/Getty Images/Houghton Mifflin Harcourt;

would ultimately be ruled by a collective government. But before true communism took hold, the country would go through a transition based on socialism. In a socialist society, there would still be a government. However, the government would decide what workers produced, not business owners.

After World War II, both the Soviet Union and China worked to build communist societies. They encouraged other countries to embrace communism and reject capitalism. The United States and its allies saw the spread of communism as a threat to their capitalist societies. In places around the world, the two sides opposed each other and supported different countries.

LINKING TO TODAY

Modern Technology

Scientists and engineers developed many new technologies during the Cold War. The first computers were created during this time, including ENIAC. This room-sized computer was invented to process information for the military. In 1947 the transistor was invented. The transistor allowed items such as radios, computers, and televisions to become much smaller. It also enabled new devices such as calculators and digital watches to be produced.

Many technologies were discovered through research on unrelated projects. The microwave oven, for example, was invented after a scientist working to improve radar technology discovered accidently that his project cooked food placed nearby. Almost every electronic gadget commonly used by people today was invented or improved upon using technology developed during the Cold War.

ANALYSIS SKILL **ANALYZING INFORMATION**

How did the transistor affect the range of electronics available to consumers?

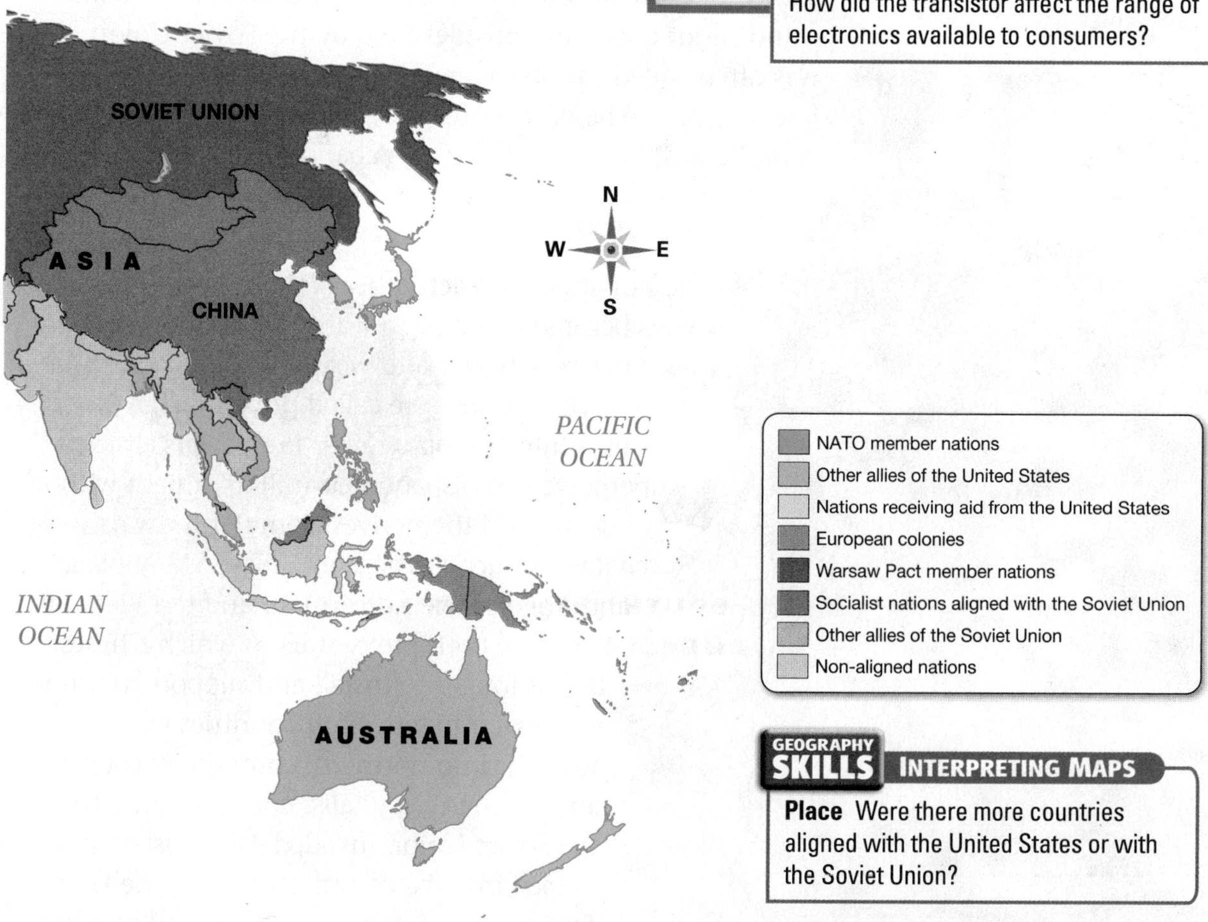

SOVIET UNION
ASIA
CHINA
N
W
E
S
PACIFIC OCEAN
INDIAN OCEAN
AUSTRALIA
NATO member nations
Other allies of the United States
Nations receiving aid from the United States
European colonies
Warsaw Pact member nations
Socialist nations aligned with the Soviet Union
Other allies of the Soviet Union
Non-aligned nations

GEOGRAPHY SKILLS **INTERPRETING MAPS**

Place Were there more countries aligned with the United States or with the Soviet Union?

The Arms Race

Both the United States and the Soviet Union built more and more nuclear weapons in an arms race. The nuclear bombs were much more powerful than even the atom bombs that destroyed Hiroshima and Nagasaki. New missile technologies also made it possible to launch warheads over longer distances. Soon, each side had so many nuclear weapons that both knew that if they attacked first, the nuclear counterattack would cause massive destruction within their own countries. No matter who attacked first, both sides would be completely destroyed. This situation, known as mutually assured destruction (MAD), kept each side from attacking the other.

In addition to nuclear weapons, the United States and the Soviet Union developed chemical and biological weapons that could kill hundreds or thousands of people at once or destroy whole towns. Along with nuclear weapons, these are called weapons of mass destruction and have become an important issue in today's world.

In the 1980s, President Ronald Reagan proposed the Strategic Defense Initiative (SDI). The plan involved building a system of missiles, satellites, and high-powered lasers that could shoot down any missiles fired by the Soviet Union. It was often called the Star Wars program because some of the lasers would be based in space. The plan was so expensive and complicated, however, that it was abandoned.

During Greece's civil war, the United States sent support to the opponents of the Greek communist army forces.

Proxy Wars

While not attacking each other directly, both superpowers became involved in wars fought in other countries. They sent troops and weapons to opposite sides of the war. These wars were called proxy wars. A "*proxy*" is a substitute or replacement. Proxy wars allowed the superpowers to display their military might without being attacked themselves. Some proxy wars were civil wars, such as those in Greece, Cambodia, and Angola. The Korean War and the Vietnam War were both proxy wars in which Chinese troops fought to install and support communist governments. Both countries were eventually split into northern, communist countries and southern, capitalist countries. In 1979 the Soviet Union invaded Afghanistan and helped install a communist ruler. The United States sent military equipment and supplies to

© Houghton Mifflin Harcourt Publishing Company • Image Credits: (bl) ©Bert Hardy/Stringer/Getty Images support a rebellion against the new communist government. The struggle continued until 1989, just before the Soviet Union broke apart.

Economic Policies

Another way that the United States opposed the Soviet Union and its allies was through economic policies. The United States passed laws called trade embargoes that prevented companies from exporting certain goods to communist countries. For example, anything that could be used to build weapons could not be sold. Food products and goods such as clothing or electronics were also restricted. In some cases, however, the Soviet Union was able to import American goods. During the 1970s, for example, severe droughts caused wheat crops in the Soviet Union to die, and the country was forced to import large amounts of grain from the United States.

Trade embargoes were a common part of U.S. foreign policy throughout the Cold War. Trade with China, North Korea, and Vietnam was heavily restricted until the period of improved relations under President Richard Nixon. When the Soviets invaded Afghanistan, however, President Jimmy Carter returned to stronger embargoes. Ronald Reagan then put even stronger laws in place in a more confrontational stance toward the Soviets. Embargoes against the Dominican Republic, Brazil, Chile, Nicaragua, and Panama helped force out leaders that did not support the United States.

The Soviet Union sent soldiers into Afghanistan to support an unpopular communist government.

The United States also tried to require its allies to impose their own sanctions on communist countries. Most of these countries arranged for exceptions, however, and freely traded with communist nations. Few trade embargoes were very effective in limiting the economies of communist nations. In Cuba, a strict embargo by the United States and countries in North and South America actually gave the Soviets a chance to strengthen its ties with Cuban dictator Fidel Castro.

Sports and International Relations

During the Cold War, tensions and competition between communist and capitalist countries affected many areas of international relations. The superpowers competed intensely at international sporting events to try to show the superiority of their way of life. The Olympics were especially important in political contests between Cold War rivals.

© Houghton Mifflin Harcourt Publishing Company • Image Credits: (c) ©Romano Cagnoni/Getty Images

The Olympics

The Soviet Union joined the Olympic organization for the first time at the 1952 Helsinki games. Instead of staying in the Olympic Village with the other athletes, however, athletes from the Soviet Union and their allies lived in a separate camp.

The number of medals won by each country became very important, especially for communist countries. It was so important that some countries began cheating. The Soviet Union, for example, created programs to train its athletes as if they were professionals, in violation of the rules. Because of this, the Soviets dominated the games until the 1980s. East Germany became famous for the success of its female athletes, but many used performance-enhancing drugs.

Sometimes, countries would boycott the games for political reasons. In 1956, several countries boycotted the games to protest the Soviet invasion of Hungary, while Egypt boycotted because it was at war with Israel. African nations boycotted the games for many years to protest South Africa's policy of apartheid. In 1980 the United States boycotted the Moscow games in response to the Soviet invasion of Afghanistan. At the next games held in Los Angeles in 1984, the Soviets boycotted, and several other communist countries joined them.

The IOC's decisions about which countries to invite to the Olympics sometimes reflected political developments. The decision to include East Germany as its own team did not occur until 1968. By that time the hope that East and West

The 1980 Olympic hockey match between the U.S. and the USSR ended with the United States winning 4–3. It became known as "the Miracle on Ice" because the Soviets were expected to win easily.

© Houghton Mifflin Harcourt Publishing Company • Image Credits: (b) ©Staff/AFP/Getty Images

Germany would be reunited had faded. When the Nationalist Chinese government fled from the communist takeover of the country, the IOC was forced to choose which government to recognize for the 1952 Games. By 1984, there were two Chinese teams, Chinese Taipei and the People's Republic of China. Disagreement continues, however.

In 2009 members of the U.S. ping-pong team that visited China in 1971 returned to China for a special tournament.

Symbolic Competitions

In 1971, the U.S. national table tennis team was surprised by an invitation to visit communist China for a competition. Americans had not been allowed in the country since 1949. Although the team lost the games, the event reflected a new relationship between the United States and China. This success in "ping-pong diplomacy" encouraged Americans to support Nixon's policy of détente. In 1972 Nixon visited communist China, the first U.S. president to do so.

Because science and technology were so important in winning the Cold War, both superpowers attempted to highlight the intelligence of their people. The United States, for example, increased funding for science and math education. The game of chess was viewed as a highly intellectual one. Tournaments were held every three years to determine the world chess champion. The Soviets dominated these competitions for decades. In 1972, however, American champion Bobby Fischer reached the world championship. He faced the reigning Soviet champion, Boris Spassky. The match became a symbol of the struggle between the United States and the Soviet Union. Fischer won the match and became famous around the world.

Case Study Assessment

1. How effective were trade embargoes during the Cold War?
2. What was the most common way that the Olympics were affected by the Cold War?
3. **Activity** The technological innovations of the Cold War produced many consumer products that have affected modern society. Research some of the new products available because of technological advances. Then create an illustrated poster showing the products and how they have changed life in the United States.

© Houghton Mifflin Harcourt Publishing Company • Image Credits: (tr) ©Hao Aimin/Xinhua Press/Corbis

SECTION 3

The Nation Prospers

What You Will Learn...

Main Ideas

1. America's economy boomed in the 1950s.
2. Americans enjoyed new forms of popular culture.
3. Social critics found fault with 1950s society.

The Big Idea

An expanding economy led to new ways of life for many Americans in the 1950s.

Key Terms and People

baby boom
Sun Belt
urban renewal
beats

hmhsocialstudies.com
TAKING NOTES

Use the graphic organizer online to take notes on the suburban lifestyle and culture of the 1950s.

If YOU were there...

You live with your parents in an apartment building in 1954. You have grown up in the city, and you are used to walking or taking the subway everywhere you need to go. But your parents are talking about moving out to the suburbs. They like the idea of having a house of their own, with a driveway and a backyard. They ask what you think about moving to the suburbs.

How would you respond?

BUILDING BACKGROUND A long economic boom after World War II led to a rapid rise in the income of many Americans. By the mid-1950s nearly 60 percent of the U.S. population qualified as middle class, with annual incomes between $3,000 and $10,000. The prosperity of the 1950s brought many changes to American life.

America's Economy in the 1950s

The American economy boomed during the 1950s. Millions of Americans earned more money than ever before and, therefore, had more money to spend on homes, cars, vacations, and large appliances. Feeling better off than they had during the Depression and World War II, many young Americans were getting married and starting families. This led to a **baby boom**, or a significant increase in the number of babies born.

A Nation on the Move

Americans were also on the move in the 1950s, as people relocated to new parts of the country to take jobs and improve the quality of their lives. Many businesses and workers moved to the **Sun Belt**—southern and western states that offered a warm climate year-round and low tax rates. As a result, the region's population doubled in the 30 years after World War II.

The 1956 Highway Act also encouraged travel. This new law provided billions of dollars for the construction of a 41,000-mile

© Houghton Mifflin Harcourt Publishing Company

Postwar Boom, 1945–1960 QUICK FACTS

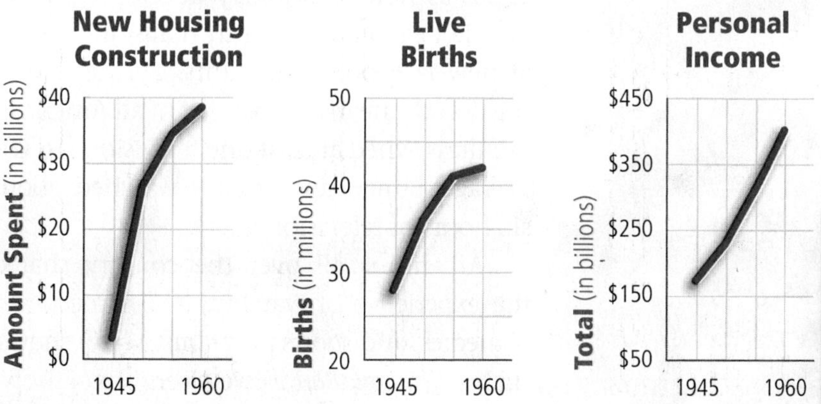
New Housing Construction
Amount Spent (in billions)
$40
$30
$20
$10
$0
1945
1960
Live Births
Births (in millions)
50
40
30
20
1945
1960
Personal Income
Total (in billions)
$450
$350
$250
$150
$50
1945
1960

Many American families used their newfound wealth to buy consumer products like houses, automobiles, and appliances. Advertisements like this one used an idealized version of an American family to sell products.

ANALYSIS SKILL ANALYZING VISUALS

How did rising wealth affect families in the 1950s?

interstate highway system. New highways helped to greatly increase both business and personal travel between cities throughout the country. The roads also made it easier for people to move to suburbs and commute to jobs in cities.

Suburbs and Cities

The rising demand for homes in the suburbs encouraged developers to build new suburban neighborhoods. On Long Island, New York, William Levitt created Levittown, one of the nation's first preplanned suburbs. Between 1946 and 1951, Levitt built more than 17,000 low-priced, mass-produced houses. Like Henry Ford's Model T, Levitt's homes were designed to be simple and affordable. By the mid-1950s, builders were constructing similar suburban homes all over the country. By 1970 more Americans lived in suburbs than in cities.

Many families welcomed the comfort and convenience of suburban living. Suburban homes usually had driveways, large lawns, and labor-saving appliances. Suburban children could participate in a wide variety of sports and other activities. Many mothers spent so much time driving their children from one activity to another that one commentator referred to the task as "motherhood on wheels."

Some critics of suburbs complained that suburban life was too heavily based on consumer culture. They also criticized the suburbs for encouraging conformity, or sameness. Most of the people living in the suburbs were white and middle class. In fact, some communities—including Levittown—refused to sell homes to black families.

As middle-class families moved to the suburbs, cities collected fewer tax dollars. This led to a decline in city services. Those who were unable to afford a move to the suburbs lived in increasingly decaying urban areas. As conditions worsened, the federal government began an **urban renewal** program—a plan to improve life in cities. Urban renewal projects focused on improving city services and urban housing. In reality, however, the programs sometimes led to more problems for urban residents.

READING CHECK **Contrasting** How was life different in suburbs and cities?

© Houghton Mifflin Harcourt Publishing Company • Image Credits: (tr), Image courtesy of The Advertising Archives

Life in the 1950s

Life for the average citizen in the United States changed dramatically in the prosperous years after World War II. More money was available to buy a wider variety of products, and technological advances made life safer and easier for many.

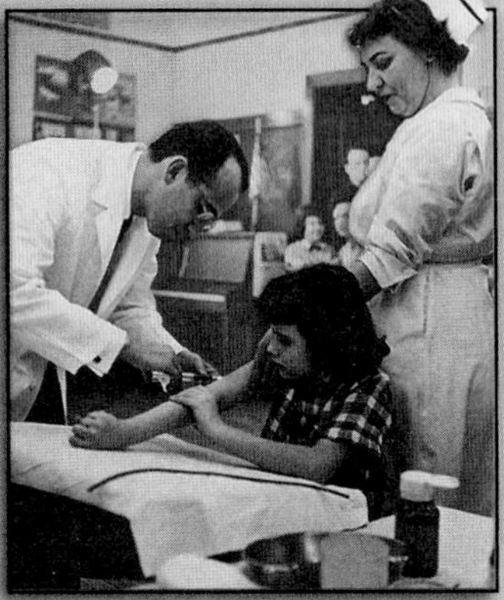

In 1952 Dr. Jonas Salk developed a vaccine for the paralyzing disease of polio.

Teenagers enjoyed the music of Elvis Presley and other rock 'n' roll stars.

Ralph Ellison began his writing career with the Federal Writers' Project during the Great Depression. He eventually became famous for writing about discrimination against African Americans.

DRIVE-IN
GREGORY PECK & ANNE BAXTER
YELLOW SKY
MY LITTLE CHICKADEE
MAE WEST & W C FIELDS
EXIT

Drive-in movie theaters became increasingly popular during the 1950s. Movies were shown on large outdoor screens as patrons watched from their cars. The largest drive-ins could accommodate 3,000 cars.

American Pop Culture

American life was changing quickly in the 1950s as new technology developed. Many people began shopping in malls and eating at new fast-food restaurants. By the end of the decade, nearly 90 percent of all American families owned at least one television set. On average, American families watched about six hours of television a day.

Americans all over the country shared the experience of watching the same news, comedies, and sports programs. Many shows, such as *The Lone Ranger*, were versions of shows that began on the radio. Early hits included Milton Berle's variety show *Texaco Star Theater* and the Western drama *Gunsmoke*. But the most popular show was *I Love Lucy*, a situation comedy (or sitcom) starring Lucille Ball and her real-life husband, Cuban American bandleader Desi Arnaz. About 44 million Americans tuned in to one episode of *I Love Lucy* in 1953 to see the birth of their son—twice the number that watched President Eisenhower's inauguration the next day.

New styles of music also helped reshape American culture in the 1950s. African American jazz greats Charlie Parker and Dizzy Gillespie became known as the Fathers of Bebop, a complex jazz style often played at a rapid pace. Meanwhile, musicians like Elvis Presley, Buddy Holly, Chuck Berry, and Little Richard helped rock 'n' roll sweep the nation. Teenage music fans powered the rock 'n' roll revolution, buying more than 70 percent of all records sold in the late 1950s. Just like jazz in the 1920s, rock music drew criticism from some adults. One journalist even labeled rock 'n' roll "a menace to morals." An Arizona teenager responded to this type of criticism by saying, "Man, I believe the older generation just doesn't want the younger generation to have any fun."

READING CHECK **Finding Main Ideas** What changes took place in American pop culture during the 1950s?

© Houghton Mifflin Harcourt Publishing Company • Image Credits: (bl), ©Bettmann/Corbis; (c), Courtesy Elvis Presley Enterprises; (cl), ©Ben Martin//Time Life Pictures/Getty Image; (tl), ©Bettmann/Corbis

Social Critics

Though the postwar years were happy and productive for many Americans, not everyone was happy with American society in the 1950s. Some women, for instance, were frustrated that they could only find work in a limited number of fields such as teaching, nursing, or office work. Others were discouraged by the expectation that they would give up their jobs when they got married. One woman recalled,

> "There was always the assumption, even when I was getting my graduate degree in education, that any work I did was temporary, something to do until I assumed [began] my principal role in life which was to be the perfect wife and mother, supported by my husband."
>
> —Sally Ann Carter, quoted in *The Fifties: A Women's Oral History*, by Brett Harvey

Many writers commented on 1950s society in their work. In 1951 J. D. Salinger published *The Catcher in the Rye*. The novel's teenage narrator, Holden Caulfield, criticizes the "phoniness" of the adults around him, who he believed loved only money and wanted everyone to be the same. In his 1952 novel *Invisible Man*, Ralph Ellison wrote about how African Americans felt left out by American society. "I am an invisible man," Ellison wrote. "I am invisible, understand, simply because people refuse to see me."

Young people known as beatniks, or **beats**, criticized society with unusual writing styles and rebellious behavior. The works of beat poet Allen Ginsberg and novelist Jack Kerouac inspired many young people to question the rules of mainstream American society. Many young people also identified with rebellious characters in popular movies of the 1950s. In the 1953 film *The Wild One,* actor Marlon Brando plays Johnny, a wild biker who challenges the rules of society. When asked, "Hey Johnny, what are you rebelling against?" Johnny replies, "Whadda ya got?"

READING CHECK **Finding Main Ideas** Why did people criticize 1950s society?

SUMMARY In the 1950s, suburban life, television, and pop culture changed American society.

Section 3 Assessment

hmhsocialstudies.com
ONLINE QUIZ

Reviewing Ideas, Terms, and People

1. a. **Recall** How did a booming economy affect life in the United States in the 1950s?
   b. **Explain** How did the growth of suburbs affect cities?
   c. **Elaborate** How do you think the **baby boom** affected 1950s society?
2. a. **Identify** How did American pop culture change in the 1950s?
   b. **Make Inferences** Based on what you have read, how was teenage culture in the 1950s different from adult culture?
3. a. **Describe** What was *Invisible Man* about?
   b. **Compare** What did J. D. Salinger and Jack Kerouac have in common?
   c. **Predict** How do you think some women in the 1950s might have wanted to change their lives?

Critical Thinking

4. **Analyzing Information** Review your notes on 1950s suburban life and culture. Then copy the graphic organizer below and use it to list the benefits and challenges of suburban life and culture.

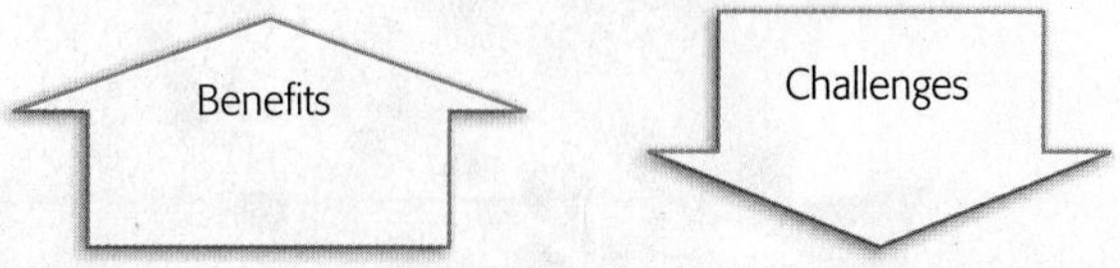

Focus on Writing

5. **Taking Notes on Daily Life and Culture** Take notes on daily life and pop culture during the 1950s. What did Americans want, and what was important to them? What kind of music would be appropriate for a song about the 1950s?

© Houghton Mifflin Harcourt Publishing Company

Case Study

Postwar Music

Music's Influence on Postwar Culture

During World War II, the most popular songs were upbeat dance songs played by "big bands." These bands featured horns, woodwinds, and drums and combined elements of jazz and swing. "Western" music described life on the ranches of the West using fiddles, guitars, and drawling lyrics. Songs based on the traditional songs played in the Appalachians and southeastern United States were called "country." The musical act the Carter Family typified this kind of music.

Country music became popular through local radio shows, which featured names like *The Louisiana Hayride and The Midnight Jamboree*. The most famous of these shows was *The Grand Ole Opry*. Stars such as Bill Monroe, Patsy Cline, Charley Pride, Dolly Parton, Garth Brooks, Taylor Swift, and Brad Paisley have all played on the show. The show is still broadcast today, and performing on the Opry stage is considered one of the highest honors for country musicians.

Rock and Roll Is Born

During the early 1950s, artists who played traditional African American blues songs and artists who played country music began to influence each other more. Rock and roll was the result. Early artists such as Chuck Berry and Buddy Holly revolutionized the sound of music. The young generation that listened to it broke with the traditions of the past. Older generations worried that rock and roll threatened the moral stability of the nation.

Taylor Swift is one of hundreds of stars that have appeared on the stage of the Grand Ole Opry.

© Houghton Mifflin Harcourt Publishing Company • Image Credits: (bl) ©Debby Wong/Shutterstock

The Beatles took the United States and the rest of the world by storm during the 1960s.

Perhaps the first true international rock star was Elvis Presley. He grew up in Memphis and listened to both blues and country music from a young age. His song "Heartbreak Hotel" became the number one song on both the pop and country charts, and number five on the rhythm and blues chart. Known as the "King of Rock and Roll," Elvis had 45 records that earned more than a million dollars and starred in 33 popular movies.

Rock and roll took hold of youth culture across the world. In the mid-1960s, the British band the Beatles brought a new, modern, blues-inspired type of rock and roll to America. Teenagers caught up in "Beatlemania" arrived in huge numbers screaming, crying, and even fainting when they saw their idols. The Beatles are still seen as the most influential rock band in history.

© Houghton Mifflin Harcourt Publishing Company • Image Credits: (t) ©Bettmann/Corbis

Soul, Rap, and Hip-Hop

During the late 1950s and 1960s another style of music developed that was most often performed by African Americans. Most of the record labels that produced soul music were owned by African Americans as well. The music business was one of the few areas in which black entrepreneurs could thrive. Many of the records made it into the hands of white audiences, and they helped with the gradual integration of entertainment venues. Soul music was influenced by gospel and blues and featured quick beats, horns, and strong backup vocals.

The center of soul music was Detroit (nicknamed Motor City), and Berry Gordy's Motown Records was the biggest label. Stars included Smokey Robinson and the Miracles, the Temptations, and the Jackson 5. Aretha Franklin, called the "Queen of Soul," viewed soul as a voice of the 1960s black power movement. The music lost much of its political and social significance by the late 1970s.

In the late 1970s and early 1980s, on the streets of New York City, a new kind of music was born. It incorporated elements of rock and soul, but the lyrics were spoken instead of sung. The slang term "rap" meant "to talk," and the new music style took rap as its name. Rap music had a strong beat and featured spoken lyrics that were heavy with rhymes influenced by spoken word poetry. Soon musicians called MCs were using new techniques to make vinyl records scratch in time with the beat. They often played short pieces of other songs to build their own music. This style became known as hip-hop. Today rap and hip-hop artists are some of the most popular in the world.

Queen Latifah was an early rap artist. She was one of the few women who found success in the early years of the genre.

© Houghton Mifflin Harcourt Publishing Company • Image Credits: (bl) ©Featureflash/Shutterstock

Folk and Social Critics

During World War II the social commentary of folk musicians such as Woody Guthrie and Josh White moved away from the topic of the Great Depression. They began singing songs protesting involvement in the war. Traditionally, folk music was defined as older songs that had no known composer and were not usually performed for profit. During the twentieth century, however, the term "folk music" became associated with a type of music that carried a social message. Today, traditional music is often called "roots music."

During the 1950s acts such as the Weavers, which included Pete Singer, became associated with communism. Many were accused of being communists and had to testify before Joseph McCarthy in Congress. The man who accused the Weavers later said that he lied. Folk music became less popular with mainstream listeners, but it was still spread among smaller groups. Antiwar, anti-racism, and anti-government songs became popular among protest movements. "We Shall Overcome" was a rallying song during the civil rights movement. Artists such as Bob Dylan and Joan Baez wrote popular songs protesting the Vietnam War.

Bob Dylan became known as the voice of the young generation of baby boomers that protested segregation, Vietnam, and traditional institutions. His songs include "The Times They Are a-Changin'" and "Blowin' in the Wind." Both songs are poetic expressions of the drastic social changes that were occurring during the 1960s and 1970s.

BIOGRAPHY

Hank Williams

1923–1953

Hiram King Williams, better known as Hank Williams, was born in Mount Olive, Alabama. In his short life, he created an iconic sound that became a standard for country music. The style he played was called honky tonk, and it still heavily influences musicians today. His hits included "Your Cheatin' Heart," "I'm So Lonesome I Could Cry," and "Lovesick Blues." He sang about heartbreak, loneliness, and nights spent having fun. His songs are still played by bands with very different styles, including jazz, R&B, and punk bands.

Make Inferences Why do you think Hank Williams' music is still popular today?

Case Study Assessment

1. How did popular music reflect the influence of the baby boomers on U.S. culture?
2. What role did music play in the civil rights movement?
3. **Activity** Popular music today is still influenced by bands and songs from the past. Choose one of the artists discussed in the text and find modern artists who use elements of his or her songs in their work. Create a list of three to five songs and present your work to the class.

© Houghton Mifflin Harcourt Publishing Company • Image Credits: (t) ©Michael Ochs Archives/Corbis

Social Studies Skills

Analysis | Critical Thinking | Civic Participation | **Study**

Interpreting Battle Maps

Define the Skill

Battle maps show events during a battle or war. They may show army movements or locations of battles. A single battle map often shows events that occurred at different times. Reading the map key is very important when you interpret battle maps. Battle maps usually include many different symbols. The map key explains the symbols used on the map.

Learn the Skill

Follow these steps to interpret battle maps.

1. Read the title to determine what the map is about.
2. Study the map key to understand what the symbols on the map mean. Locate the symbols from the key on the map.
3. Look for labels and other information on the map. Use what you already know about the time period to determine the importance of these features.
4. Use the map to make a generalization about a battle or war, such as which side won.

Practice the Skill

1. What is this map about?
2. What does the solid blue line on this map represent? What does the solid red line represent?
3. What does the green line on the 38th parallel show? Why is this important?

Based on this map, make a generalization about the Korean War.

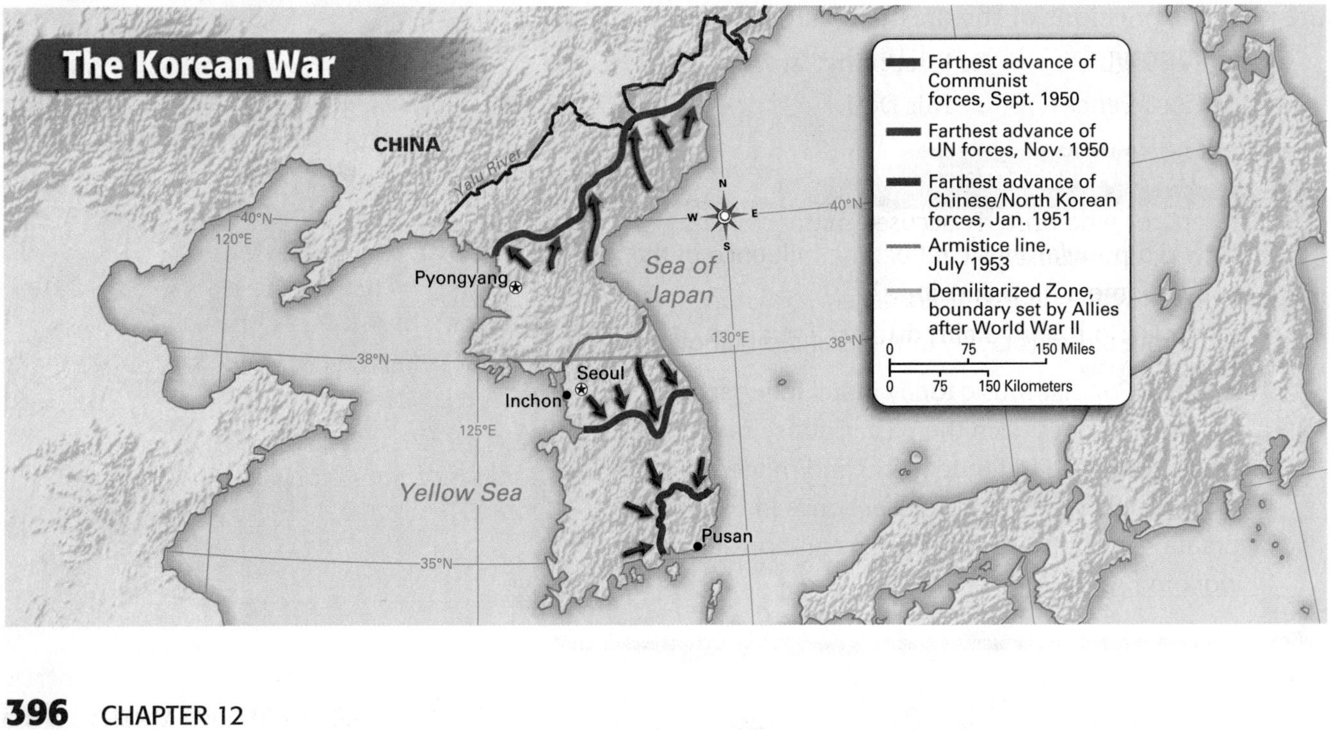
The Korean War
CHINA
Yalu River
Pyongyang
Seoul
Inchon
Pusan
Sea of Japan
Yellow Sea
40°N
120°E
38°N
125°E
35°N
130°E
N
S
E
W
Farthest advance of Communist forces, Sept. 1950
Farthest advance of UN forces, Nov. 1950
Farthest advance of Chinese/North Korean forces, Jan. 1951
Armistice line, July 1953
Demilitarized Zone, boundary set by Allies after World War II
0 75 150 Miles
0 75 150 Kilometers

© Houghton Mifflin Harcourt Publishing Company

CHAPTER 12

Chapter Review

History's Impact
▶ **video series**
Review the video to answer the closing question:
How might Americans' awareness of world events have changed once television became popular?

Visual Summary

QUICK FACTS

Use the visual summary below to help you review the main ideas of the chapter.

American prosperity during the 1950s was sometimes overshadowed by a fear of communism.

Reviewing Vocabulary, Terms, and People

Match the numbered person or term with the correct lettered definition.

1. GI Bill of Rights
2. Yalta Conference
3. Truman Doctrine
4. Joseph McCarthy
5. Fair Deal

a. U.S. senator who unfairly accused many citizens of being Communists
b. meeting at which Franklin Roosevelt, Winston Churchill, and Joseph Stalin discussed strategy for postwar peace
c. package of domestic reforms proposed by President Truman
d. U.S. policy of containing communism through economic aid
e. program that offered veterans money for school after World War II

Comprehension and Critical Thinking

SECTION 1

6. a. Recall What is the United Nations?
b. Explain Why did Franklin Roosevelt support the formation of the UN?
c. Elaborate Would you have supported the policy of containment? Why or why not?

SECTION 2

7. a. Identify How did the United States battle communism in Asia in the 1950s?
b. Explain What effect did the launch of *Sputnik* have on the United States?
c. Evaluate What were some risks and advantages of the strategy of brinkmanship?

© Houghton Mifflin Harcourt Publishing Company

SECTION 3

8. a. **Describe** How did life in the United States change in the 1950s?

   b. **Summarize** Why were some women frustrated with 1950s society?

   c. **Elaborate** How has American popular culture changed since the 1950s? How has it stayed the same?

Reviewing Themes

9. **Politics** How did the Cold War affect political relations between the United States and the Soviet Union?

10. **Science and Technology** How did science and technology advance during the 1950s?

Reading Skills

Visualizing *Use the Reading Skills taught in this chapter to answer the question below.*

> Wisconsin senator Joseph McCarthy contributed to fears in the early 1950s by charging that Communists were working inside the State Department. He claimed to have the names of 57 people who were "either card-carrying members or certainly loyal to the Communist Party."

11. What elements of the selection above help you visualize the feelings created by the Red Scare?

Social Studies Skills

Interpreting Battle Maps *Use the Social Studies Skills taught in this chapter to answer the question below.*

12. Look back at the battle map. In what year did North Korean forces make their farthest advance?

Using the Internet

13. **Activity: Researching the Second Red Scare** Fear of communism and spies grew during the late 1940s and 1950s. What were Americans' fears? How did Senator Joseph McCarthy and congressional hearings affect the lives of those accused of Communist activities? What did the hearings accomplish? Through your online textbook, learn more about the second Red Scare. Then write a journal entry from the point of view of Senator McCarthy, a blacklisted writer, or Joseph Welch, attorney for the U.S. Army. Your journal entry should include direct references to your research.

hmhsocialstudies.com

Focus on Writing

14. **Writing Your Song Lyrics** Review your notes. Decide on a theme for your song about the 1950s. It can focus either on one event or idea or on several. Remember that the lyrics should address something specific about what it was like to live in the United States in the 1950s. You may even want to write from the point of view of a young person living in the 1950s. What would that person think about? What would be his or her hopes and fears?

© Houghton Mifflin Harcourt Publishing Company • Image Credits: (b), HMH Photo

CHAPTER 12

Standardized Test Practice

DIRECTIONS: Read each question and write the letter of the best response.

1 At the Yalta Conference, Joseph Stalin promised

A to allow free elections in the Soviet Union.

B to allow free elections in Eastern Europe.

C to prosecute Soviet war criminals.

D that the Soviet Union would join the United Nations.

2 The United Nations was formed to

A promote world peace.

B deal with problems in Palestine.

C bring Nazi leaders responsible for the Holocaust to justice.

D plan how to divide Germany among the Allies.

3 What is McCarthyism?

A denying people work

B a type of communism

C going to the brink of nuclear war

D making accusations of Communist activity without proof

4 Which president decided to use U.S. troops to help defend South Korea in 1950?

A Franklin Roosevelt

B Dwight Eisenhower

C Harry Truman

D Herbert Hoover

5 What new kind of music was popular with teenagers in the 1950s?

A suburban swing

B big band jazz

C rock 'n' roll

D beatnik

6 Which country sent hundreds of thousands of troops to fight alongside North Korean forces in the Korean War?

A Japan

B China

C the United States

D the Soviet Union

7 Social critics in the 1950s spoke out against which of the following?

A containment

B the United Nations

C Douglas MacArthur

D consumer culture

8 Read the following excerpt from a 1953 speech by President Eisenhower and use it to answer the question below.

> "Every gun that is made, every warship launched, every rocket fired signifies, in the final sense, a theft from those who hunger and are not fed, those who are cold and not clothed. This world in arms is not spending money alone. It is spending the sweat of its laborers, the genius of its scientists, the hopes of its children."
>
> —Dwight D. Eisenhower, April 16, 1953

Document-Based Question What desire do you think Eisenhower was expressing in this passage?

© Houghton Mifflin Harcourt Publishing Company

CHAPTER 13 1945–1975

The Civil Rights Movement

Essential Question How did Americans respond to discrimination during the civil rights movement?

ALABAMA COURSE OF STUDY

9 Critique major social and cultural changes in the United States since World War II.

- Identifying key persons and events of the modern Civil Rights Movement.
- Describing the changing role of women in United States' society and how it affected the family unit.
- Identifying the impact of media, including newspapers, AM and FM radio, television, twenty-four hour sports and news programming, talk radio, and Internet social networking, on United States' culture since World War II.

10 Analyze changing economic priorities and cycles of economic expansion and contraction for their impact on society since World War II.

- Identifying policies and programs that had an economic impact on society since World War II.

12 Evaluate significant political issues and policies of presidential administrations since World War II.

- Identifying domestic policies that shaped the United States since World War II.
- Recognizing domestic issues that shaped the United States since World War II.

Focus on Writing

A Civil Rights Bill In the 1950s and 1960s, African Americans began successfully to challenge the discrimination they had faced for so many years. In this chapter, you will read about the civil rights movement and about the passage of new civil rights laws. Imagine that you are a member of Congress at this time. You will write a new civil rights bill to help people gain fair treatment under the law.

UNITED STATES

1954 Thurgood Marshall argues against segregation in the Supreme Court case *Brown* v. *Board of Education.*

1945

1953 Soviet leader Joseph Stalin dies.

WORLD

© Houghton Mifflin Harcourt Publishing Company

Image Credits: (t), ©Flip Schulke/Corbis; (br), ©Hank Walker/Time Life Pictures/Getty Images

HISTORY Civil Rights Act of 1964

hmhsocialstudies.com VIDEO

African Americans launched a major civil rights movement in the years following World War II. Members of the movement organized demonstrations to protest unfair treatment, like the March on Washington shown here.

1957 The Soviets launch *Sputnik*, the first human-made satellite.

1960

1961 The Berlin Wall divides East and West Berlin.

1963 Lee Harvey Oswald assassinates President John F. Kennedy.

1966 The National Organization for Women is formed.

1966 Indira Gandhi becomes prime minister of India.

1969 La Raza Unida is organized to support the rights of Mexican Americans.

1970

1973 The American Indian Movement protests at Wounded Knee.

© Houghton Mifflin Harcourt Publishing Company

Image Credits: (t), ©Flip Schulke/Corbis; (bc), ©Bettmann/Corbis (cr), ©Bettmann/Corbis

Reading Social Studies

Economics | Geography | **Politics** | **Society and Culture** | Science and Technology

Focus on Themes In this chapter, you will read about the important changes in American **society** during the period called the civil rights era. You will learn about how many people came to see **politics** as a way to correct social inequalities that existed for minority groups in the United States, such as African Americans, women, Mexican Americans, Native Americans, and people with disabilities. You will also read about life in the 1960s.

Using Context Clues: Synonyms

Focus on Reading Some words mean almost the same thing. Understanding the similarities can help you understand words whose meaning you may not know.

Understanding Synonyms Words that have similar meanings are called synonyms. Often, a synonym is given as a definition. The synonym will probably be a word you already understand. This will help you learn the new word through context clues.

Notice how one reader uses synonyms to understand words she does not understand.

> An AIM leader described the group's goals, saying, "We don't want civil rights in the white man's society—we want our own *sovereign [self-governing]* rights."

This is a word I don't know the meaning of.

These brackets mean that the word inside is a synonym of the word or phrase that comes before. The word inside is a synonym of sovereign.

↓

The word *sovereign* must mean to govern on one's own.

© Houghton Mifflin Harcourt Publishing Company

You Try It!

As you read the following passage, look for synonyms in the definitions of unfamiliar words.

On February 1, 1960, the students went into Woolworth and staged a sit-in—a demonstration in which protesters sit down and refuse to leave. They sat in the "whites-only" section of the lunch counter and ordered coffee. They were not served, but they stayed until the store closed. The next day, they returned with dozens more students to continue the sit-in. Soon, another sit-in began at the lunch counter of a nearby store.

After you read the passage, answer the following questions.

1. What word is a synonym of sit-in that is given in that word's definition?
2. What clue is given that helps you find the synonym in the above passage?
3. Can you think of another synonym for sit-in that might have been used?

As you read this chapter, look for synonyms that can help you define words you don't know.

Key Terms and People

Chapter 13

Section 1
Thurgood Marshall
Brown v. *Board of Education*
Little Rock Nine
Rosa Parks
Montgomery bus boycott
Martin Luther King Jr.
sit-in
Student Nonviolent Coordinating Committee

Section 2
John F. Kennedy
Freedom Rides
March on Washington
Lyndon B. Johnson
Civil Rights Act of 1964
Voting Rights Act of 1965
Great Society
Black Power
Malcolm X

Section 3
Cesar Chavez
United Farm Workers
Betty Friedan
National Organization for Women
Shirley Chisholm
Equal Rights Amendment
Phyllis Schlafly
American Indian Movement
Disabled in Action

Academic Vocabulary
In this chapter, you will learn the following academic words:
implement
consequences

SECTION 1

The Civil Rights Movement Takes Shape

What You Will Learn...

Main Ideas

1. Civil rights leaders battled school segregation in court.
2. The Montgomery bus boycott helped end segregation on buses.
3. Students organized sit-ins to protest segregation.

The Big Idea

Civil rights activists used legal challenges and public protests to confront segregation.

Key Terms and People

Thurgood Marshall
Brown v. *Board of Education*
Little Rock Nine
Rosa Parks
Montgomery bus boycott
Martin Luther King Jr.
sit-in
Student Nonviolent Coordinating Committee

hmhsocialstudies.com
TAKING NOTES

Use the graphic organizer online to take notes on key events in the fight against segregation.

If YOU were there...

You are an African American student in the 1950s. You get up early every day and take a long bus ride across the city to an African American public school. There is another school just three blocks from your home, but only white students are welcome there. You have heard, however, that this school will soon be opening its doors to black students as well.

Would you want to be one of the first African Americans to attend this school? Why or why not?

BUILDING BACKGROUND African Americans continued to face segregation and discrimination after World War II. Early victories in the civil rights movement included the end of segregation in baseball in 1947 and President Truman's ban on segregation in the military in 1948. These successes were the beginning of a national movement for civil rights.

Battling School Segregation

The 1896 Supreme Court case *Plessy* v. *Ferguson* established the "separate-but-equal" doctrine. This doctrine stated that federal, state, and local governments could allow segregation as long as separate facilities were equal. One result of this ruling was that states in both the North and South maintained separate schools for white and black students. Government officials often insisted that though these schools were separate, they were equal in quality.

In fact, however, schools for black children typically received far less funding. Early civil rights leaders, led by members of the National Association for the Advancement of Colored People (NAACP), focused on ending segregation in America's public schools.

Brown v. *Board of Education*

The NAACP's strategy was to show that separate schools were unequal. The NAACP attorneys **Thurgood Marshall**, who went on to become Supreme Court justice, and Jack Greenberg led the courtroom battles against segregation. In the early 1950s, five school segregation cases from Delaware, Kansas, South Carolina, Virginia, and Washington, D.C., came together under the title of ***Brown* v. *Board of Education***. The "Brown" in the case title was a seven-year-old African American girl from Topeka, Kansas, named Linda Brown. Though she lived near a school for white children, Linda Brown had to travel across town to a school for black children. Linda's father and the NAACP sued to allow Linda to attend the school closer to her home.

On May 17, 1954, the Supreme Court issued a unanimous ruling on *Brown* v. *Board of Education*. Segregation in schools and other public facilities was illegal.

The next year, the Court ordered public schools to desegregate, or integrate, "with all deliberate speed." These rulings would prove difficult to enforce.

Little Rock Nine

In the entire South, only three school districts began desegregating in 1954. Most others implemented gradual integration plans. In Little Rock, Arkansas, the school board started by integrating one high school. It allowed nine outstanding black students to attend Central High School. These students became known as the **Little Rock Nine**. Arkansas governor Orval Faubus worked to prevent desegregation at Central High School, however. He used National Guard troops to block the Little Rock Nine from entering the school.

On the morning of September 4, 1957, eight of the nine students arrived at the school together and were turned away by the National Guard. Then the ninth student, 15-year-old Elizabeth Eckford, arrived at the school by herself. She found the entrance blocked by the National Guard. Turning around, she faced a screaming mob. Someone began yelling, "*Lynch her! Lynch her!*" Finally, a white man and woman guided Eckford to safety.

Elizabeth Eckford and the rest of the Little Rock Nine went home. For weeks, Governor

ACADEMIC VOCABULARY

implement put in place

FOCUS ON READING

What is a synonym for *desegregrate*?

hmhsocialstudies.com

ANIMATED GEOGRAPHY AND HISTORY

School Segregation 1952

SUPREME COURT DECISIONS

Brown v. *Board of Education* (1954)

Background of the Case In 1896 the Supreme Court had ruled in *Plessy* v. *Ferguson* that "separate-but-equal" facilities were constitutional. In 1951 the NAACP sued the Board of Education of Topeka, Kansas. It argued that segregated schools did not give equal opportunities to black and white children. After hearing many arguments, the Court made its ruling in 1954.

The Court's Ruling

The Supreme Court overturned the *Plessy* doctrine of "separate-but-equal." It ruled that racially segregated schools were not equal and were therefore unconstitutional. All of the justices agreed to the ruling, making it unanimous.

The Court's Reasoning

The Supreme Court decided that segregation violated the Fourteenth Amendment's guarantee of "equal protection of the laws." Its opinion stated, "We conclude that, in the field of public education, the doctrine of 'separate-but-equal' has no place. Separate educational facilities are inherently [naturally] unequal."

Why It Matters

The ruling in *Brown* v. *Board of Education* led to integrated public schools. It also opened the door to other successful challenges to segregation in public places.

Linda Brown, age 9

ANALYSIS SKILL **ANALYZING INFORMATION**

1. How did the ruling in *Brown* v. *Board of Education* overturn the 1896 Supreme Court ruling in *Plessy* v. *Ferguson*?
2. How might parents of both black and white children at the time have reacted to the ruling in *Brown* v. *Board of Education*?

LINKING TO TODAY

An Apology

The famous photograph to the right shows Elizabeth Eckford walking to Little Rock's Central High School on September 4, 1957. The young woman shouting at Eckford is Hazel Massery. In 1963 Massery apologized to Eckford. Massery had decided she did not want to be, she said, the "poster child of the hate generation." The two women have since become friends. In 1999 President Bill Clinton presented Eckford and the other Little Rock Nine with Congressional Gold Medals for their contributions to the civil rights movement.

Faubus refused to allow them to attend the school. The tense situation lasted until President Eisenhower sent federal troops to escort the students into the school.

The Little Rock Nine began attending classes, but resistance to integration continued. Some white students insulted, harassed, and attacked the black students. In spite of these obstacles, eight of the nine remained at the school. In May 1958 Ernest Green became the first African American student to graduate from Central High. When Green's name was called at the graduation ceremony, no one clapped. "But I figured they didn't have to," he later said. "After I got that diploma, that was it. I had accomplished what I had come there for."

READING CHECK **Summarizing** What obstacles faced supporters of desegregation?

Montgomery Bus Boycott

The victory in *Brown* v. *Board of Education* was part of a larger struggle against segregation. Most facilities in the South, including public transportation, remained segregated.

The NAACP decided to continue the battle against segregation in Montgomery, Alabama. Black passengers there were required to sit in the back of city buses. If the whites-only front section filled up, black passengers had to give up their seats.

On December 1, 1955, a seamstress and NAACP worker named **Rosa Parks** boarded a bus and sat in the front row of the section reserved for black passengers. When the bus became full, the driver told Parks and three others to give their seats to white passengers. Parks refused. The bus driver called the police, and Parks was taken to jail.

ANALYSIS SKILL FINDING THE MAIN IDEA

Why did Hazel Massery apologize to Elizabeth Eckford?

To protest Parks's arrest, African American professor Jo Ann Robinson organized a boycott of Montgomery buses. Local leaders formed the Montgomery Improvement Association (MIA) to help strengthen the boycott. In the **Montgomery bus boycott**, thousands of African Americans stopped riding the buses. Some white residents supported the boycott as well. Bus ridership fell by 70 percent.

To lead the MIA, African American leaders turned to **Martin Luther King Jr.**, a young Baptist minister. The 26-year-old King already had a reputation as a powerful speaker whose words could motivate and inspire listeners.

As the boycott continued, bus drivers guided nearly empty buses down the city streets. Leaders planned a carpool system that helped people find rides at more than 40 locations throughout Montgomery. For 381 days, boycotters carpooled, took taxis, rode bicycles, and walked. Still, Montgomery's leaders refused to integrate the bus system.

As in Little Rock during the school segregation fight, many white residents were angry about the attempt to end segregation. Some people resorted to violence. King's home was bombed, and he received hate mail and phone calls threatening him and his family. The police also harassed and arrested carpool drivers. In spite of this intimidation, the boycott gained national attention, sparking similar protests in other cities.

Finally, in November 1956 the Supreme Court ruled that segregation on public transportation was illegal. The next month, King joined other black and white ministers to ride the first integrated bus in Montgomery. "It . . . makes you feel that America is a great country and we're going to do more to make it greater," remembered Jo Ann Robinson.

The Montgomery bus boycott helped make Martin Luther King Jr. a nationally known civil rights leader. He formed the Southern Christian Leadership Conference (SCLC), which led campaigns for civil rights throughout the South.

READING CHECK **Identifying Cause and Effect** What event sparked the Montgomery bus boycott?

BIOGRAPHY

Rosa Parks

1913–2005

Rosa Parks was born in Tuskegee, Alabama, and spent most of her childhood in Montgomery. While working as a seamstress, Parks became an active member of the NAACP.

She was fired from her seamstress job for her leading role in the Montgomery bus boycott. After the boycott succeeded, she and her husband moved to Detroit, Michigan. She continued working for fair treatment for all Americans and started a program to teach children about the Underground Railroad and the civil rights movement.

Finding the Main Idea How did Rosa Parks work for equal rights?

Sit-ins and the SNCC

Like public schools and buses, many private businesses in the South were segregated. In Greensboro, North Carolina, four students decided to challenge this form of segregation. They targeted a lunch counter at Woolworth, a popular department store. Black customers were supposed to eat standing up at one end of the counter. White customers sat down to eat at the other end.

On February 1, 1960, the students went into Woolworth and staged a **sit-in**—a demonstration in which protesters sit down and refuse to leave. They sat in the whites-only section of the lunch counter and ordered coffee. They were not served, but they stayed until the store closed. The next day, they returned with dozens more students to continue the sit-in. Soon, another sit-in began at the lunch counter of a nearby store.

THE IMPACT TODAY

Today Bob Moses runs the Algebra Project. Its goals include helping students in poor communities become skilled in math, get into college, and compete for jobs.

People across the country read newspaper stories about the Greensboro sit-ins. Other black students in the South began to hold similar protests. The student protesters practiced the strategy of nonviolent resistance. No matter how much they were insulted or threatened, they refused to respond with violence. They were inspired by Martin Luther King Jr., who was a strong supporter of nonviolent action.

Over time, some restaurants and businesses, including Woolworth, began the process of integration. To continue the struggle for civil rights, the leaders of the student protests formed the **Student Nonviolent Coordinating Committee** (SNCC) in the spring of 1960. The SNCC activists trained protesters and organized civil rights demonstrations. Bob Moses, a leader of the SNCC, helped organize sit-ins and voter registration drives.

READING CHECK **Comparing** How were sit-ins similar to other civil rights protests?

SUMMARY In the 1950s court rulings and protests challenged segregation.

Section 1 Assessment

hmhsocialstudies.com ONLINE QUIZ

Reviewing Ideas, Terms, and People

1. a. **Summarize** How did the Supreme Court impact the desegregation of public schools?
   b. **Identify** Who were the **Little Rock Nine**?
2. a. **Recall** What was the purpose of the **Montgomery bus boycott**?
   b. **Analyze** Why was the arrest of **Rosa Parks** a turning point in the civil rights movement?
   c. **Elaborate** Why do you think the bus boycott lasted so long?
3. a. **Identify** What means did the **Student Nonviolent Coordinating Committee** use to protest segregation?
   b. **Make Inferences** What might have inspired the Greensboro students to stage a **sit-in**?
   c. **Evaluate** Do you think nonviolent resistance is an effective form of protest? Why or why not?

Critical Thinking

4. **Sequencing** Review your notes on events that challenged segregation. Then copy the graphic organizer below and use it to show the sequence of major events in the civil rights movement described in this section.

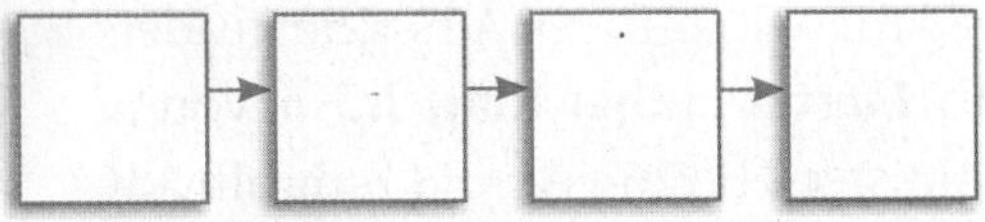

Focus on Writing

5. **Explaining Major Issues** Take notes on the major issues behind the civil rights movement. What were these issues? Why were they important to African Americans? What changes did the movement try to make?

Martin Luther King Jr.

How would you help lead a national movement?

When did he live? 1929–1968

Where did he live? King grew up in Atlanta, Georgia, where his father was a pastor. He studied to become a minister in Pennsylvania. He received his doctorate in Massachusetts, then became pastor of a church in Alabama. He traveled throughout the country as a civil rights leader.

What did he do? As a powerful and moving speaker, King became one of the leading voices of the civil rights movement. He was committed to achieving equality through nonviolent protest. He led a series of successful marches and protests, including the 1955 Montgomery bus boycott and the 1963 March on Washington.

Why is he so important? His leadership helped make the civil rights movement a success. His belief in and passion for nonviolence led to the boycotts, sit-ins, and marches that helped African Americans gain equal treatment. King's work helped bring an end to legal segregation and led to new laws guaranteeing equal rights for all Americans.

Evaluating Which of Martin Luther King Jr.'s contributions to the civil rights movement was most important? Why?

KEY EVENTS

- **1953** Marries Coretta Scott
- **1955** Becomes leader of the Montgomery Improvement Association
- **1957** Founds Southern Christian Leadership Conference
- **1963** Writes "Letter from Birmingham Jail"; gives the "I Have a Dream" speech at the March on Washington
- **1964** Wins the Nobel Peace Prize; Civil Rights Act of 1964 is passed
- **1968** Shot and killed in Memphis, Tennessee
- **1986** Martin Luther King Jr. Day becomes a national holiday.

"I have a dream that my four children will one day live in a nation where they will not be judged by the color of their skin but by the content of their character."

—Martin Luther King Jr., speech at March on Washington

© Houghton Mifflin Harcourt Publishing Company

SECTION 2

Kennedy, Johnson, and Civil Rights

What You Will Learn...

Main Ideas

1. John F. Kennedy was elected president in 1960.
2. Civil rights leaders continued to fight for equality.
3. Lyndon B. Johnson became president when Kennedy was assassinated.
4. Changes occurred in the civil rights movement in the late 1960s.

The Big Idea

The civil rights movement made major advances during the presidencies of John F. Kennedy and Lyndon B. Johnson.

Key Terms and People

John F. Kennedy
Freedom Rides
March on Washington
Lyndon B. Johnson
Civil Rights Act of 1964
Voting Rights Act of 1965
Great Society
Black Power
Malcolm X

hmhsocialstudies.com
TAKING NOTES

Use the graphic organizer online to take notes on the leaders of the civil rights movement and their goals.

If YOU were there...

You are a civil rights activist living and working in the South. It is 1960, a presidential election year. The battle for fair treatment has been difficult, and you hope that the next president will support civil rights. Both major presidential candidates will be visiting your area soon, and you might have a chance to meet them and ask some questions.

What questions would you ask the candidates?

BUILDING BACKGROUND In the 1960 presidential election Republican Richard M. Nixon, who had served as Eisenhower's vice president, ran against Democrat John F. Kennedy, a senator from Massachusetts. For the first time, presidential candidates debated each other on television. Kennedy's performance in the televised debates helped him win a very close election.

Kennedy Elected

When **John F. Kennedy** won the election of 1960, he became the youngest person ever elected president of the United States. For many Americans, Kennedy and his wife, Jacqueline, brought a sense of style and excitement to the White House. Kennedy was also the first Roman Catholic to become president.

In his inaugural address, Kennedy spoke of the opportunities and dangers facing Americans. "Man holds in his mortal hands the power to abolish all forms of human poverty and all forms of human life," he said. He encouraged all Americans to support freedom throughout the world, saying, "And so, my fellow Americans, ask not what your country can do for you—ask what you can do for your country."

As president, Kennedy pursued a set of proposals he called the New Frontier. His plan included a higher minimum wage and tax cuts to help stimulate economic growth. It called for new spending on the military and on the space program, and new programs to help

hmhsocialstudies.com INTERACTIVE MAP

Freedom Rides, 1961

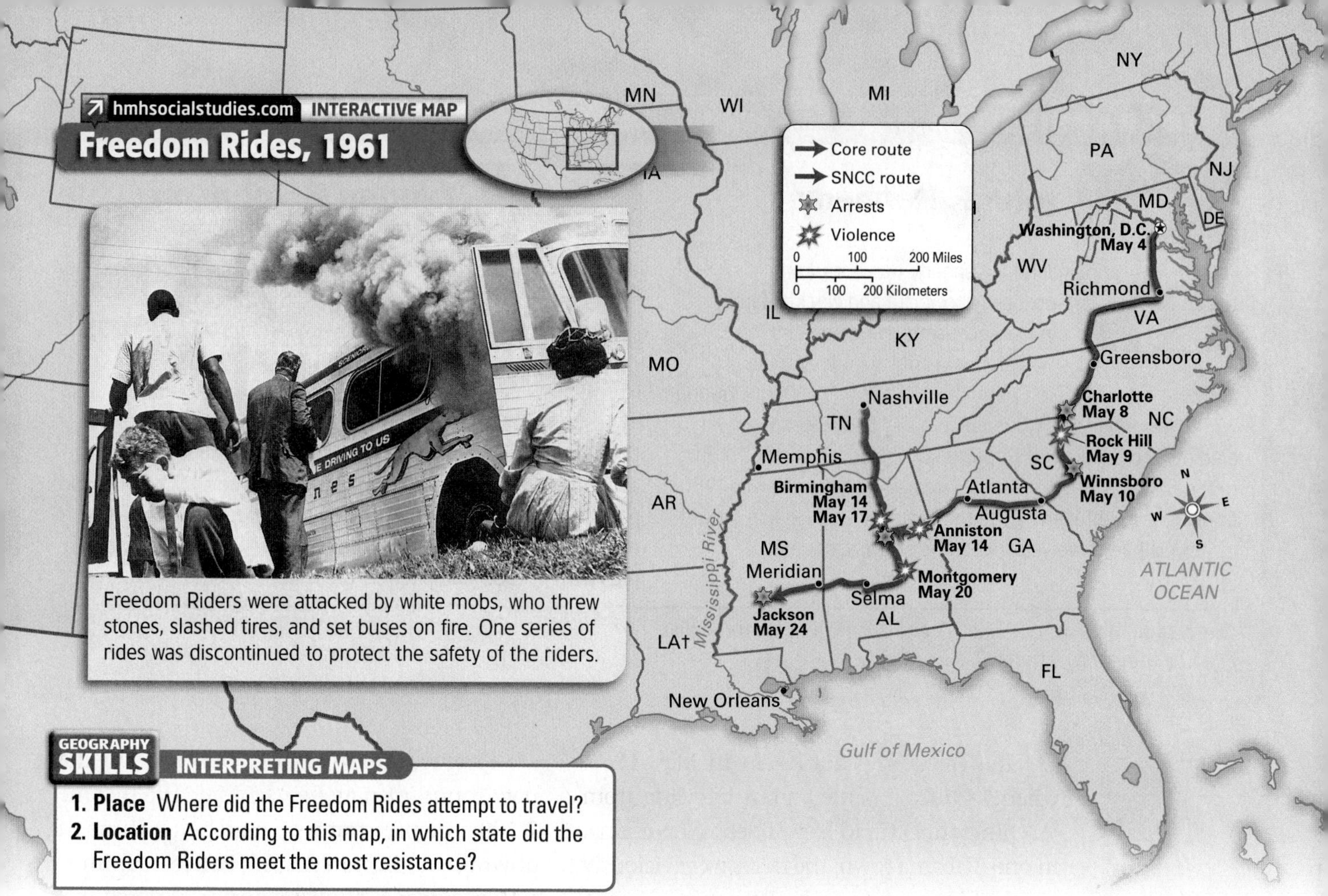

Core route
SNCC route
Arrests
Violence
0 100 200 Miles
0 100 200 Kilometers
MN
WI
MI
NY
PA
NJ
MD
DE
IA
IL
MO
KY
WV
VA
Washington, D.C. May 4
Richmond
Greensboro
Charlotte May 8
NC
Rock Hill May 9
Winnsboro May 10
SC
TN
Nashville
Memphis
AR
Birmingham May 14 May 17
Atlanta
Augusta
Anniston May 14
GA
MS
Meridian
Montgomery May 20
Selma
AL
Jackson May 24
LA
Mississippi River
New Orleans
FL
Gulf of Mexico
ATLANTIC OCEAN
N
E
S
W

Freedom Riders were attacked by white mobs, who threw stones, slashed tires, and set buses on fire. One series of rides was discontinued to protect the safety of the riders.

GEOGRAPHY SKILLS **INTERPRETING MAPS**

1. **Place** Where did the Freedom Rides attempt to travel?
2. **Location** According to this map, in which state did the Freedom Riders meet the most resistance?

poor and unemployed Americans. Kennedy also proposed providing greater financial help to public schools. Fearing a budget imbalance, Republicans and conservative southern Democrats blocked much of the legislation Kennedy introduced.

Kennedy also spoke of his support for the goals of the civil rights movement. This had helped convince many African Americans to vote for him in the election of 1960. As president, however, Kennedy moved slowly on civil rights legislation. He was reluctant to anger Republicans and conservative southern Democrats in Congress, whose support he needed to pass other items on his agenda. Kennedy was also busy dealing with foreign policy crises, as you will read in the next chapter.

READING CHECK **Drawing Inferences** What do you think African American voters hoped for from the new president?

The Fight for Rights Continues

Public schools and some businesses had begun to desegregate. But other facilities remained strictly segregated.

Freedom Rides

In 1947 a civil rights group called the Congress of Racial Equality (CORE) began protests in which African Americans rode in the whites-only section of interstate buses. In 1960 the Court ruled that segregation of bus stations was illegal. CORE decided to put pressure on President Kennedy to enforce this ruling.

To accomplish this, CORE organized a series of protests called the **Freedom Rides,** in which black and white bus riders traveled together to segregated bus stations in the South. White riders planned to use facilities set aside for African Americans in bus stations. Black riders would use whites-only facilities.

BIOGRAPHIES

John F. Kennedy

1917–1963

John F. Kennedy was born to a politically powerful and wealthy family in Massachusetts. He graduated from Harvard University, then joined the U.S. Navy. He commanded a patrol boat in the South Pacific during World War II and was wounded in a sea battle. Kennedy was elected to the House of Representatives at the age of 29 and to the Senate six years later. He was elected president in 1960, bringing a youthful energy to the White House. He had served for fewer than three years when he was assassinated.

Lyndon B. Johnson

1908–1973

Lyndon B. Johnson grew up in rural Texas. After working his way through college, Johnson taught school for a year. In 1937, at the age of 29, he was elected to the House of Representatives. He was elected to the Senate in 1948. Johnson was known for his ability to guide bills through Congress by convincing members from both political parties to support them. As one fellow member of Congress said, "Lyndon got me by the lapels [jacket collar] and put his face on top of mine and he talked and talked." Johnson was elected vice president in 1960 and became president in 1963.

Contrasting How were Kennedy's and Johnson's careers similar, and how were they different?

The Freedom Rides began in May 1961, when 13 riders boarded a bus traveling from Washington, D.C., to New Orleans, Louisiana. In one Alabama town, the riders were viciously attacked by a white mob. After more attacks, CORE leaders decided to stop the protest to protect the riders' lives.

The leaders of the SNCC decided to continue the Freedom Rides. The SNCC activists faced the same violence as the CORE riders. Arriving in Montgomery, Alabama, in late May, they were attacked by a furious mob. Many freedom riders were jailed in Jackson, Mississippi. That same month, President Kennedy ordered the Interstate Commerce Commission to enforce strict bans on segregation in interstate bus terminals.

King in Birmingham

In 1963 Martin Luther King Jr. organized marches in Birmingham, Alabama. King was arrested and jailed for marching without a permit. While jailed, he wrote a "Letter from Birmingham Jail," explaining his commitment to nonviolence. "We will reach the goal of freedom in Birmingham and all over the nation, because the goal of America is freedom."

King was released from prison and led a new round of marches. In May 1963, some 2,500 demonstrators marched through downtown Birmingham. Police commissioner Eugene "Bull" Connor ordered his officers to unleash their attack dogs and blast the marchers with high-pressure water hoses. Televised images of their tactics shocked Americans.

The March on Washington

Pressure for civil rights legislation continued to grow. President Kennedy called racial discrimination "a moral crisis." In June 1963 he announced support for a sweeping civil rights bill to end racial discrimination completely.

To demonstrate support for the civil rights bill, African American leaders held the **March on Washington**—a massive demonstration for civil rights. On August 28, 1963, Martin Luther King Jr. stood at the Lincoln Memorial before a diverse crowd of more than 200,000 people. In his famous "I Have a Dream" speech, King expressed his hope for a future in which all Americans would enjoy equal rights and opportunities.

READING CHECK **Summarizing** How did the Birmingham marches affect public opinion?

Johnson and Civil Rights

After he became president, Lyndon Johnson promised to continue Kennedy's plans for civil rights legislation. Johnson worked with Congress and African American leaders to create and pass laws that would help ensure equality for all Americans. Here, Johnson is shown signing the Civil Rights Act of 1964 as Martin Luther King Jr. and other leaders look on.

How did Johnson work to continue Kennedy's campaign promises?

Johnson Becomes President

In the months following the March on Washington, Congress debated Kennedy's civil rights legislation. In November 1963 Kennedy began a quick tour of Texas cities.

Kennedy Assassinated

On November 22, 1963, Kennedy rode through Dallas in a convertible, waving to supporters in the streets. Suddenly, gunshots rang out. Kennedy had been shot twice, and he died soon afterward in a Dallas hospital. Vice President **Lyndon B. Johnson** was quickly sworn in as president. Dallas police arrested an alleged assassin, Lee Harvey Oswald.

The assassination stunned Americans, who grieved the young president's death. Many of Kennedy's goals were left unfinished. Vowing to continue Kennedy's work, President Johnson urged Congress to pass a civil rights bill.

Civil Rights Laws

On July 2, 1964, President Johnson signed the **Civil Rights Act of 1964**. The act banned segregation in public places. It also outlawed discrimination in the workplace on the basis of color, gender, religion, or national origin.

That summer, activists began to push for equal voting rights for African Americans in the South. Legally, of course, African Americans had the right to vote. But in much of the South, threats and unfair election rules often kept them from the polls. During the "Freedom Summer" of 1964, hundreds of volunteers, including many white college students, came to Mississippi. Their goal was to help African Americans register to vote.

Volunteers were threatened and attacked. On June 21 three civil rights workers—James Chaney, a young black Mississippian plasterer's apprentice; Andrew Goodman, a Jewish Queens College student; and Michael Schwerner, a Jewish social worker from New York City—were murdered by members of the Ku Klux Klan. Martin Luther King Jr. organized a voting rights march from Selma, Alabama, to Montgomery, during which many marchers were beaten and jailed. Violence against civil rights workers convinced many people to support voter registration efforts.

Congress approved the **Voting Rights Act of 1965**, which Johnson signed into law in August. This law gave the federal government new powers to protect African Americans' voting rights. Within three years, more than half of all qualified African Americans in the South registered to vote.

HISTORY

VIDEO
Assassination of JFK

hmhsocialstudies.com

THE IMPACT TODAY

In June 2005 a judge in Mississippi sentenced Edgar Ray Killen to 60 years in prison for his role in the murder of the three civil rights workers. The 1967 case had ended in a deadlocked jury.

QUICK FACTS

The Great Society

Great Society Legislation:

- Civil Rights Act of 1964
- Voting Rights Act of 1965
- Elementary and Secondary Education Act of 1965
- Medicare and Medicaid Bill, 1965
- Department of Housing and Urban Development Act of 1965

The Great Society

President Johnson won the election of 1964 by a huge margin. He saw this as a vote of approval for his program of domestic reforms that he called the **Great Society**. "The Great Society rests on abundance and liberty for all," Johnson said.

Congress quickly passed most of Johnson's Great Society legislation. Great Society programs included Medicare and Medicaid, which help senior citizens and low-income citizens afford health care. Another act gave local schools more than $1 billion to help students with special needs. The Department of Housing and Urban Development (HUD) was created to help low-income families get better housing. Robert Weaver served as HUD's secretary, becoming the first African American appointed to a presidential cabinet.

READING CHECK **Summarizing** How did President Johnson support civil rights?

hmhsocialstudies.com
ANIMATED HISTORY
Technology of the Time: The Power of Images

Changes in the Civil Rights Movement

Many young civil rights reformers found the pace of change too slow. Others entirely rejected the goal of racial integration.

New Directions

One such activist was Stokely Carmichael, who had participated in the Freedom Rides and many marches. But in the mid-1960s, he broke with the goal of nonviolence. Carmichael was a founder of the **Black Power** movement, which called for African American independence. Black Power activists believed that blacks should reject integration, focusing instead on controlling their own communities.

Malcolm X helped inspire the Black Power movement. He was a leader of the Nation of Islam, an organization that combined ideas about African American independence with the teachings of Islam. Malcolm X argued that African Americans should work for social and political independence. He believed that African Americans had the right to defend themselves, using violence if necessary.

Time Line

Civil Rights Movement, Key Events

1955 An African American tailor's assistant named Rosa Parks refused to give up her seat on a Montgomery, Alabama, bus, sparking a citywide bus boycott that would last more than a year.

1950

1960 The first sit-in at a lunch counter occurs in Greensboro, North Carolina. During these sit-ins, young African Americans sat at segregated lunch counters along with their white counterparts and asked to be served.

In 1964 Malcolm X traveled to the Muslim holy city of Mecca, where he met Muslims of many races. He began to hope that different races could coexist in peace, although he still supported freedom "by any means necessary." But in 1965 Malcolm X broke with the Nation of Islam and was killed by three of its members.

Violence in the Streets

Slow progress in the civil rights movement frustrated many members of the black community. In some U.S. cities, tensions exploded into violent, sometimes deadly, riots. One such riot occurred in August 1965 in the Watts section of Los Angeles. Twenty-four people were killed, and much of Watts was destroyed.

In April 1968 Martin Luther King Jr. was shot and killed in Memphis, Tennessee. As televised reports spread the news of King's assassination, furious rioters took to the streets in more than 100 American cities. The movement had lost its most visible leader.

1963 Four young girls die in the racially motivated bombing of a Birmingham, Alabama, church. The deaths lead to riots and civil unrest during which police attack African Americans. Televised images of the events shocked many people.

1965

1964 Civil rights leader Martin Luther King Jr. receives the Nobel Peace Prize for his work in nonviolent demonstrations against segregation.

READING CHECK **Contrasting** How did Malcolm X's goals differ from Martin Luther King Jr.'s?

SUMMARY Under Kennedy and Johnson, major civil rights legislation was passed.

Section 2 Assessment

hmhsocialstudies.com ONLINE QUIZ

Reviewing Ideas, Terms, and People

1. a. **Describe** How was **John F. Kennedy** different from previous presidents?
   b. **Analyze** Why did many African Americans vote for Kennedy?
2. a. **Identify** What were the **Freedom Rides**?
   b. **Explain** How did television influence public opinion about the civil rights movement?
3. a. **Recall** What happened in Dallas, Texas, on November 22, 1963?
   b. **Draw Conclusions** Based on Johnson's plans for the **Great Society**, what do you think he believed was the purpose of government?
4. a. **Recall** What challenges did the civil rights movement face in the late 1960s?
   b. **Elaborate** Why did **Malcolm X** reject the goal of racial integration?

Critical Thinking

5. **Evaluating** Review your notes on the goals and achievements of leaders who supported civil rights. Then copy the graphic organizer below and use it to evaluate the leaders discussed in the section. Tell whether or not you think the leaders' actions were effective.

Leader	Evaluation

Focus on Writing

6. **Listing Laws** List new civil rights laws passed in the 1960s. What were the goals of these laws? What problems or events did they respond to? As a member of Congress, would you have approved of these laws? Why or why not?

Case Study

Alabama and Civil Rights

Fred Shuttlesworth

A Center of Struggle

Many of the most important and dramatic events of the civil rights movement occurred in Alabama. Several prominent leaders of the movement, as well as some of its most well-known opponents, lived in Alabama and focused their efforts in the state.

Despite attempts by the federal government to end segregation, state governments continued to make laws enforcing the system known as Jim Crow. In 1954 the unanimous Supreme Court decision in *Brown* v. *Board of Education* demanded that states desegregate public schools. One of the most important justices on this court, Hugo Black, was from Alabama. Although he had briefly been a member of the Ku Klux Klan, his time spent in public office was dedicated to ensuring African Americans had equal protection under the Constitution.

A year after the *Brown* decision, Rosa Parks made her historic bus ride in Montgomery. Her refusal to give her seat to a white passenger sparked the year-long boycott of city buses. It ended only after the U.S. Supreme Court decided in Parks' favor. The boycott inspired leaders in other southern cities to challenge similar segregation laws. Birmingham leader Fred Shuttlesworth organized a boycott of buses in 1956 that proceeded even after his home was bombed.

Organizations Across the South

Soon, several organizations were coordinating larger protests across several states. The NAACP had been banned in Alabama, and in response leaders founded new groups. Fred Shuttlesworth was one of seven founding members, along

© Houghton Mifflin Harcourt Publishing Company • Image Credits: (bl) ©Everett Collection Inc/Alamy Limited

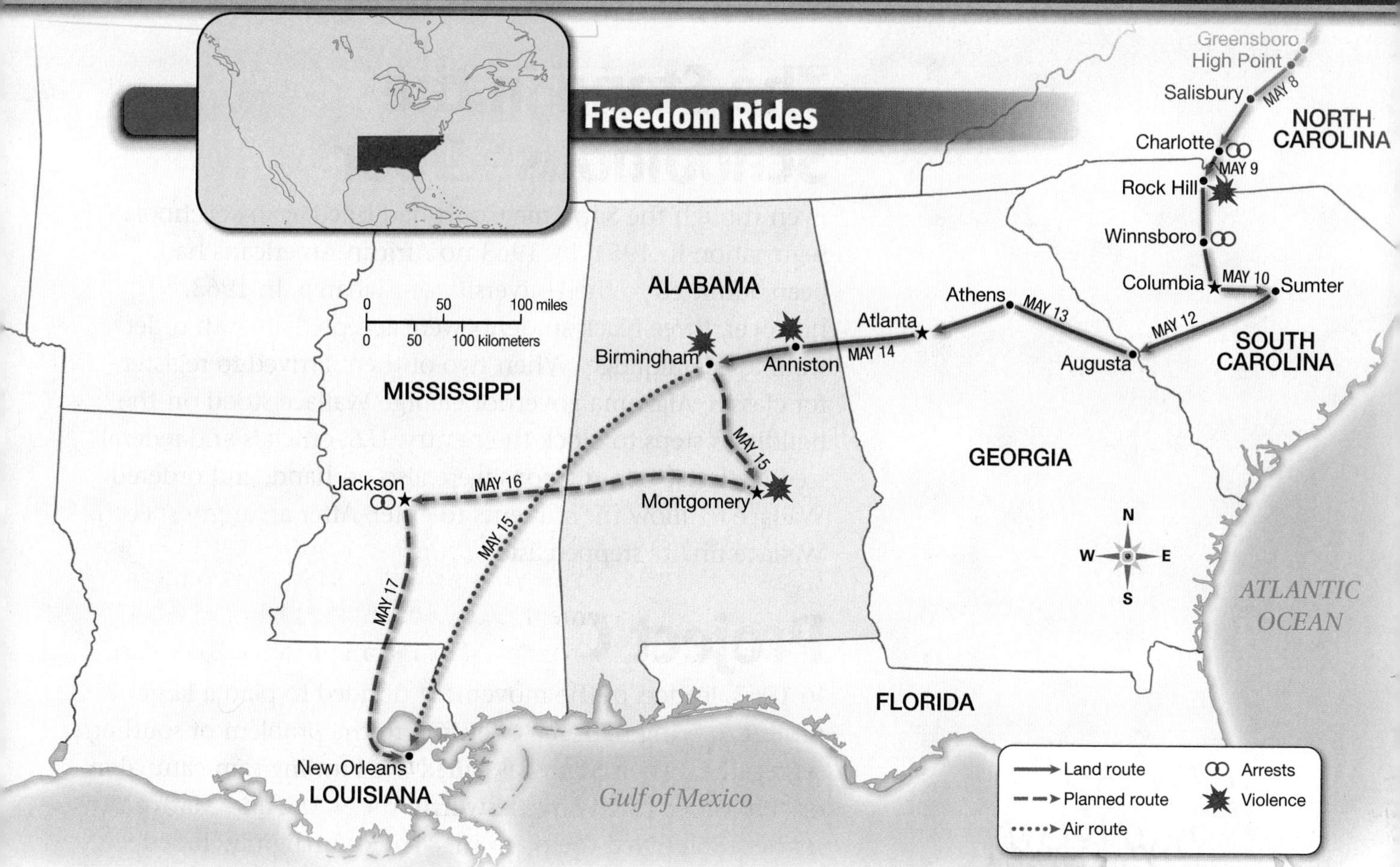
Freedom Rides
Greensboro
High Point
Salisbury
MAY 8
NORTH CAROLINA
Charlotte
MAY 9
Rock Hill
Winnsboro
Columbia
MAY 10
Sumter
SOUTH CAROLINA
MAY 12
Augusta
Athens
MAY 13
Atlanta
MAY 14
Anniston
Birmingham
ALABAMA
MAY 15
Montgomery
MAY 16
Jackson
MISSISSIPPI
MAY 15
MAY 17
New Orleans
LOUISIANA
GEORGIA
FLORIDA
Gulf of Mexico
ATLANTIC OCEAN
0 50 100 miles
0 50 100 kilometers
N
W
E
S
Land route
Planned route
Air route
Arrests
Violence

with Dr. Martin Luther King Jr., of the Southern Christian Leadership Conference (SCLC). This group recruited community organizations to support the movement and was dedicated to the practice of nonviolent resistance.

The Supreme Court delivered more decisions that declared states' segregation laws unconstitutional. Lunch counter sit-ins were happening in cities and towns across Alabama and the rest of the South. In 1961 the Freedom Rides were organized to challenge segregation on interstate bus travel. Still, however, state lawmakers resisted the push toward integration. White authorities and citizens used tactics of intimidation and violence to squash protests. The Freedom Riders were badly beaten at several stops along their route, including Birmingham. They continued on.

One Alabamian Freedom Rider, John Lewis, would soon become one of the most recognized leaders in the civil rights movement. As chairman of the Student Nonviolent Coordinating Committee (SNCC), he helped King organize the 1963 March on Washington. He and the other "Big Six" leaders of the movement all spoke at the event. The next year he took a leading role in organizing the Mississippi voter registration drive known as "Freedom Summer."

GEOGRAPHY SKILLS INTERPRETING MAPS

Location Where in Alabama did Freedom Riders meet with violence?

The Stand in the Schoolhouse Door

Even though the Supreme Court had ruled against school segregation in 1954, by 1963 no African Americans had been admitted to the University of Alabama. In 1963, however, three black students were accepted after an order from a federal judge. When two of them arrived to register for classes, Alabama governor George Wallace stood on the building's steps to block their entry. U.S. officials and federalized National Guard troops were also on hand, and ordered Wallace to allow the students to enter. After an angry speech, Wallace finally stepped aside.

Project C

In 1963, leaders of the movement decided to plan a large protest to bring national attention to the problem of southern segregation. Their plan was called the Birmingham campaign or "Project C." Fred Shuttlesworth, the SCLC, and Martin Luther King Jr. led the planning. The campaign included marches, sit-ins, and voter registration drives. It was during this campaign that King was arrested and wrote his "Letter from Birmingham Jail."

Governor George Wallace blocked the entrance of a University of Alabama school office to prevent the registration of African American students. He was confronted by a federal Deputy Attorney General and National Guard troops. Eventually Wallace allowed the students to enter.

© Houghton Mifflin Harcourt Publishing Company • Image Credits: (b) ©MPI/Getty Images

Alabama's Jim Crow System

One of the most powerful novels to come out of the civil rights movement was *To Kill a Mockingbird.* Harper Lee, a native of Monroeville, Alabama, wrote the novel. It was first published in 1960. Lee describes the racism faced by African Americans through the story of a court case that unjustly targets a black man. Lee's narrator is a young girl named Scout. During the court case she learns about the violence and unfairness that African Americans endured under the Jim Crow system.

The novel is set in the 1930s, and some of the story is very similar to the event of the Scottsboro Trials. These trials began in 1931 with a criminal case against a group of African American teenagers accused of attacking a white girl on a train in Alabama. Despite the flimsy case against them, they were found guilty. The case went to the Supreme Court, which ruled that the conviction be overturned because there were no African Americans on the jury. A retrial again found five of the men guilty, but they were eventually pardoned and released. The series of trials lasted almost 20 years, and became a symbol of the unequal treatment of African Americans by southern laws.

Harper Lee, author of *To Kill a Mockingbird*, won a Pulitzer Prize for the book and a Medal of Freedom from President George W. Bush.

ANALYSIS **SKILL** **ANALYZING INFORMATION**

Predict How might *To Kill a Mockingbird* have affected the civil rights movement?

The *C* in the name of the plan stood for "confrontation." Shuttlesworth and other leaders hoped to show the rest of the nation that their nonviolent tactics would be met with assaults by white authorities. The Commissioner of Public Safety in Birmingham, Eugene "Bull" Connor, was known to be especially forceful in his response to protestors.

In early May, with the city jail full, Connor ordered police to use fire hoses and attack dogs against the marchers, including children. Televised images of these attacks angered many Americans and helped win support for the Civil Rights Act of 1964. Many of the same leaders, including Shuttlesworth, then organized a march from Selma to Montgomery. Marchers were beaten and jailed, but national support for the marchers encouraged support for the Voting Rights Act of 1965.

John Lewis, one of the Big Six civil rights leaders, spoke at the 2012 Democratic National Convention.

Case Study Assessment

1. Who were some key leaders of the civil rights movement from Alabama?
2. Who planned Project C?
3. **Activity** Many groups were organized to protest segregation. Research the activities of one of these groups in Alabama. Then construct a time line of important events that the group took part in.

SECTION 3

Rights for Other Americans

What You Will Learn...

Main Ideas

1. Hispanic Americans organized for civil rights and economic opportunities.
2. The women's movement worked for equal rights.
3. Other Americans also fought for change.

The Big Idea

Encouraged by the success of the civil rights movement, many groups worked for equal rights in the 1960s.

Key Terms and People

Cesar Chavez
United Farm Workers
Betty Friedan
National Organization for Women
Shirley Chisholm
Equal Rights Amendment
Phyllis Schlafly
American Indian Movement
Disabled in Action

hmhsocialstudies.com
TAKING NOTES

Use the graphic organizer online to take notes on the major events that occurred as various groups worked for equal rights.

If YOU were there...

Your parents came to the United States from Mexico, and you were born in California in the 1950s. You and your family work year-round picking crops—the work is hard, and the pay is low. You're trying to put aside some money for school, but your family barely makes enough to get by. Some farmworkers are talking about going on strike for better wages.

Would you join the strike? Why or why not?

BUILDING BACKGROUND Many Americans faced unfair treatment in the 1960s. Women were paid lower wages and had fewer job opportunities than men. Hispanic Americans had long faced discrimination as well. The victories of the civil rights movement inspired many groups to struggle for equal rights.

Hispanic Americans Organize for Change

The Hispanic population of the United States grew to 4 million by 1960, and to more than 10 million by 1970. Though people of Mexican descent made up the majority of this population, Hispanic Americans were a diverse group. Many people from Puerto Rico, Cuba, and other Latin American countries also lived in the United States.

The success of African Americans encouraged Hispanic Americans to fight for their own rights. **Cesar Chavez** was one of many Hispanic Americans who worked to improve conditions. In 1962 Chavez formed a union that would later become the **United Farm Workers** (UFW). This union was committed to the goal of better pay and working conditions for migrant farmworkers—those who move seasonally from farm to farm for work. Chavez led the UFW in a five-year strike and boycott against California grape growers. The workers finally won better wages and benefits in 1970. The UFW became a national organization in 1976.

Chavez shared the commitment to nonviolent protest. To those who complained about the slow pace of change, he replied:

© Houghton Mifflin Harcourt Publishing Company

> "Nonviolence takes time . . . I despise exploitation [unfair gain] and I want change, but I'm willing to pay the price in terms of time. There's a Mexican saying, 'Hay más tiempo que vida'—there's more time than life. We've got all the time in the world."
>
> —Cesar Chavez, quoted in *Chávez, César: Autobiography of La Causa*

Chavez helped inspire young leaders in what became known as the Chicano movement. To fight discrimination and gain greater political influence, Chicano activists formed a political party called *La Raza Unida*, or the United Race. The Hispanic civil rights movement had important consequences. A 1968 amendment to the Elementary and Secondary Education Act required schools to teach students whose first language was not English in both languages until they learned English. The Voting Rights Act of 1975 required communities with large immigrant populations to print ballots in the voters' preferred language.

READING CHECK **Sequencing** What group helped inspire the Chicano movement?

BIOGRAPHY

Cesar Chavez

1927–1993

Cesar Chavez was born on a small family ranch in Arizona. After losing their land during the Great Depression, Chavez and his family began working as migrant farmworkers. Moving from town to town in search of work, Chavez went to more than 30 different schools. He served in the U.S. Navy during World War II, then returned to the fields to help migrant workers fight for better pay and working conditions. The soft-spoken Chavez seemed to many an unlikely leader of a protest movement. But Chavez quickly became an influential leader, continuing to lead the struggle for farmworkers' rights into the 1990s. Before his death, Chavez insisted, "It's not me who counts, it's the Movement."

Making Inferences Why do you think Chavez began the farmworkers' movement?

The Women's Movement

Activists also brought public attention to women's position in society. In 1963 a government commission reported that women had fewer job opportunities than men and were often paid less for the same work. President Kennedy responded by ordering an end to discrimination based on gender in civil service jobs. That same year Congress passed the Equal Pay Act, which required many employers to pay men and women equal salaries for the same work. The Civil Rights Act of 1964 banned discrimination based on both gender and race.

Some women also began to question their traditional roles in society. In her 1963 book *The Feminine Mystique*, Jewish author **Betty Friedan** described the dissatisfaction some women felt with their traditional roles of wife, mother, and homemaker.

Friedan became a leader of the modern women's rights movement. In 1966 she helped found the **National Organization for Women** (NOW) to fight for equal educational and career opportunities for women. Other women worked for change by running for public office. In 1968 **Shirley Chisholm** was elected to represent a New York City district in the House of Representatives. She was the first African American woman elected to the U.S. Congress.

ACADEMIC VOCABULARY
consequences the effects of a particular event or events

In the early 1970s, NOW and other women's rights activists supported an amendment to the Constitution. The **Equal Rights Amendment** (ERA) would outlaw all discrimination based on sex. The ERA was approved by Congress in 1972.

THE IMPACT TODAY
Ninety-six women served in the 111th Congress, the highest total in history. In 2007, Nancy Pelosi was elected the first female Speaker of the House. She was elected to serve a second term as Speaker in 2009.

For an amendment to go into effect, it must be ratified by three-fourths of the states—or 38 out of 50 states. The ERA was ratified by 30 state legislatures by the end of 1973. But many opponents came forward to block the ERA. **Phyllis Schlafly**, a conservative activist, founded the group STOP ERA to prevent its ratification. Schlafly and her supporters argued that the ERA would hurt

© Houghton Mifflin Harcourt Publishing Company • Image Credits: (t) ©Arthur Schatz/Time Life Pictures/Getty Images

Debate over Women's Rights

In the 1960s, women began to organize to demand equal rights. The movement became known as women's liberation. Many activists supported a woman's right to equal pay and equal protection under the law. Some opposing activists worked to maintain what they saw as women's protected status under the law.

Shirley Chisholm became the first African American woman elected to Congress in 1968.

Betty Friedan authored *The Feminine Mystique*, a book declaring that many women wanted achievements beyond those of becoming a wife and mother.

Phyllis Schlafly argued against the Equal Rights Amendment, saying it would reduce the legal rights of wives and mothers.

families by encouraging women to focus on careers rather than on motherhood. Such opposition weakened support for the ERA. In June 1982 the amendment fell three states short of ratification.

Despite this failure, the women's movement achieved many of its goals. Women found new opportunities in education and the workplace. For example, women began attending many formerly all-male universities. Increasing numbers of women pursued careers in traditionally all-male fields such as law and medicine. Many women also won political office at all levels of government.

READING CHECK **Finding Main Ideas**
What were some achievements of the women's movement of the 1960s?

Other Voices for Change

Other Americans also began to demand change in laws and other discriminating practices during the 1960s and 1970s. In 1974 the Asian American Legal Defense and Education Fund was founded with the purpose of building an "informed and active Asian America." The National Italian American Foundation (1975) advocates for Italian Americans. League of United Latin American Citizens, which was founded much earlier, played an important activist role for Hispanic Americans during this period as well and continues to do so today. Native Americans and people with disabilities were also inspired by the civil rights movement.

Native Americans

One major issue for Native Americans was their lack of control over tribal lands. Many worked through the National Congress of American Indians (NCAI) to gain more control over reservation lands from the federal government. They helped win passage of the Indian Civil Rights Act of 1968.

Other activists thought that groups like the NCAI worked too slowly. In November 1969 a group of young Native Americans occupied Alcatraz Island in San Francisco Bay to protest the government's takeover of Native American lands.

© Houghton Mifflin Harcourt Publishing Company • Image Credits: (all) ©Bettmann/Corbis

One of the groups that participated in the Alcatraz protest was the **American Indian Movement** (AIM), founded in 1968 to fight for Native Americans' rights. In February 1973 AIM activists seized a trading post and church at Wounded Knee, South Dakota—the site of the U.S. Army's massacre of Sioux Indians in 1890. Federal marshals surrounded Wounded Knee, and the standoff ended with a gun battle killing two protesters and wounding one federal agent.

Such protests brought attention to issues facing Native Americans. In the early 1970s Congress began passing laws granting Native Americans greater self-government on tribal lands.

Disabled in Action

Judy Heumann and other activists formed Disabled in Action in 1970. The group promotes legislation and access to independent living for people with disabilities.

What kind of rights might people with disabilities seek?

The Disability Rights Movement

In 1970 Judy Heumann and other activists created **Disabled in Action** (DIA) to make people aware of challenges facing people with disabilities. People with disabilities often lacked access to both job opportunities and to public places. The DIA's work led to the passage of new laws. The Rehabilitation Act of 1973 banned federal agencies from discriminating against people with disabilities. The Education of Handicapped Children Act of 1975 required public schools to provide a quality education to children with disabilities. In 1990 the Americans with Disabilities Act (ADA) outlawed all discrimination against people with disabilities.

READING CHECK **Contrasting** How were the tactics of AIM and DIA different?

SUMMARY The fight for equal rights had far-reaching effects on American society.

Section 3 Assessment

hmhsocialstudies.com
ONLINE QUIZ

Reviewing Ideas, Terms, and People

1. **a. Evaluate** How did Hispanic Americans fight for civil rights?
   b. Describe Who benefited from laws like the Elementary and Secondary Education Act of 1968 and the Voting Rights Act of 1975?
2. **a. Recall** What were the goals of the women's movement?
   b. Explain What happened during the ratification process of the **Equal Rights Amendment**?
   c. Elaborate Do you think we need the ERA today? Explain your answer.
3. **a. Compare** In what way was the **American Indian Movement** similar to the Black Power movement?
   b. Identify What laws banned discrimination against people with disabilities?

Critical Thinking

4. **Categorizing** Review your notes on the achievements of groups that worked for equal rights. Then copy the graphic organizer below and use it to identify the achievements of each group.

Hispanic Americans	Women	Native Americans	People with Disabilities

Focus on Writing

5. **Describing New Movements** Describe new rights movements inspired by the success of the African American civil rights movement. What groups did these movements represent? What were their goals? What did they accomplish?

© Houghton Mifflin Harcourt Publishing Company • Image Credits: (t), William Philpott/Reuters/NewsCom

Case Study

Changing Postwar Culture

Men were once expected to dress in formal suits and hats to go to work. Women usually had to wear skirts or dresses. Today most office workers wear more casual clothing.

Cultural Shifts Since World War II

The culture of the United States has changed dramatically since the end of World War II. Some of these changes are the result of women and minorities gaining wider access to the economic, social, and political life of the nation. In addition, social interactions, speech patterns, and clothing are much less strict than in the past. During the 1940s and 1950s, for example, most men were expected to wear suits and hats to their offices. Women wore dresses and skirts much more often.

People in modern society also have more access to information and are much more mobile than in the past. The interstate highway system, increased car ownership, and air travel have all contributed to the modern American's sense of mobility. Technological advances such as smart phones, laptops, and wireless Internet have allowed people to take advantage of this mobility in ways few imagined in the 1940s.

Women in the Workforce

Since the 1970s, when women began gaining more rights, their voice in society has grown. For example, there are more women politicians and business owners than in the past, and they have more influence on important public decisions. Women are also more likely to receive higher education today. However, on average women's wages are still only about 80 percent of what men receive for the same job.

As more women joined the workforce, traditional roles within the family also changed. Men used to provide all or a majority of the money a family needed. Once women began earning part of a family's income, they could have more influence over family purchases and other decisions.

© Houghton Mifflin Harcourt Publishing Company • Image Credits: (l) ©Ocean/Corbis

Working women could also leave a marriage more easily. Increasing divorce rates have led to a higher number of remarriages, blended families, and single-parent households.

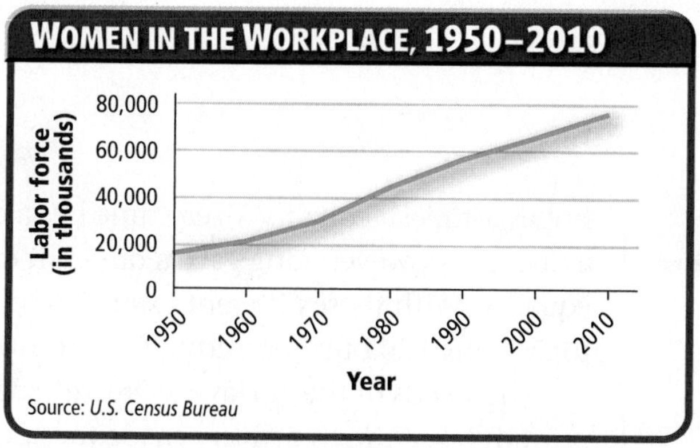

ANALYSIS SKILL **INTERPRETING CHARTS**

Location How many women joined the workforce between 1970 and 2010?

Effects on Children

Because more single women can support themselves financially, many are choosing to focus first on their career and delay marriage. They are also choosing to have fewer children, or none at all. As more mothers have begun working outside the home, children's lives have changed. More children attend afterschool programs or childcare centers while their parents are at work, or they stay at home alone or with siblings until their parents return from work. These children are known as "latchkey children" from the door key that some would carry to let themselves into their house. Some studies suggest that latchkey children might develop more social problems than others, but these findings are disputed. Other studies suggest that girls with working mothers have higher self-esteem and are high achievers.

Today many children take care of themselves after school.

Case Study Assessment

1. How have families changed since more women have entered the workforce?
2. What are "latchkey children"?
3. **Activity** While American culture has changed a lot since World War II, some things remain the same. Choose a part of modern culture such as clothing, eating habits, or entertainment choices to research. Create an illustrated time line that compares and contrasts developments in the decades since 1945.

© Houghton Mifflin Harcourt Publishing Company • Image Credits: (r) ©Ocean/Corbis

Social Studies Skills

Analysis | Critical Thinking | Civic Participation | Study

21ST CENTURY

Making Speeches

Define the Skill

In a democracy, activists, government leaders, and candidates for public office often need to address people directly. Speeches allow public figures to deliver a message to many people at once. People can use speeches to make their views known. They can use speeches to try to persuade people to support their ideas or programs.

Learn the Skill

Think about the role of speeches in the civil rights movement. Speakers increased awareness of and support for the movement's goals. Civil rights leader Martin Luther King Jr. is remembered as a powerful and effective speaker. His words moved and inspired many listeners—and continue to do so today. Here is a brief excerpt from King's famous "I Have a Dream" speech, delivered during the March on Washington on August 28, 1963:

"I have a dream that one day on the red hills of Georgia the sons of former slaves and the sons of former slaveowners will be able to sit down together at the table of brotherhood."

"I have a dream that my four little children will one day live in a nation where they will not be judged by the color of their skin but by the content of their character."

"I have a dream today."

In his speech, King followed one basic idea. He used the same words over and over to emphasize his hopes for racial equality. Every time he said "I have a dream," however, King gave a different example of equality. With these different examples on the same topic, King laid out a powerful vision for the future.

The words of the "I Have a Dream" speech are powerful, but King's delivery made the speech even stronger. King spoke with confidence in a loud, clear voice. He also looked at his audience and connected with them.

Following these steps can help you make a persuasive speech.

1. **Write the speech.** Make sure it includes a clear main idea, good examples, and convincing language.
2. **Practice.** Practice reading your speech out loud to a friend. You can also practice at home in front of a mirror.
3. **Give the speech.** Remember to speak loudly and clearly and to look at your audience.

Practice the Skill

Suppose that you are a civil rights leader in the 1960s. Following the steps above, write a short speech in favor of equal rights for African Americans, Hispanic Americans, women, Native Americans, or Americans with disabilities. After you have written and practiced your speech, give the speech to the class.

© Houghton Mifflin Harcourt Publishing Company

CHAPTER 13

Chapter Review

History's Impact
▶ **video series**
Review the video to answer the closing question:
How did the Civil Rights Act of 1964 inspire a push for equality among other minority groups?

Visual Summary

QUICK FACTS

Use the visual summary below to help you review the main ideas of the chapter.

Many groups of Americans organized to demand their civil rights during the 1960s and 1970s.

Reviewing Vocabulary, Terms, and People

Complete each sentence by filling in the blank with the correct term or person from the chapter.

1. _________ was an African American civil rights leader and minister who believed in nonviolent, direct action.
2. In 1960, black students staged a _________ at a Woolworth lunch counter in Greensboro, North Carolina.
3. The Congress of Racial Equality organized the _________ to protest segregation in bus stations throughout the South.
4. The _________ protected the voting rights of African Americans.
5. The _________ worked to get better pay and working conditions for migrant farmworkers.
6. _________ was the first African American woman elected to the U.S. Congress.

Comprehension and Critical Thinking

SECTION 1

7. a. **Describe** What was the Court's ruling in the *Brown* v. *Board of Education* case?
   b. **Explain** What did the Student Nonviolent Coordinating Committee do to fight segregation?
   c. **Draw Conclusions** Why do you think Martin Luther King Jr. was chosen to lead the MIA?

SECTION 2

8. a. **Recall** What was the New Frontier?
   b. **Contrast** What roles did leaders from CORE and SNCC play in the Freedom Rides?
   c. **Contrast** How did Malcolm X's ideas about integration differ from those of Martin Luther King Jr.?

© Houghton Mifflin Harcourt Publishing Company

SECTION 3

9. a. **Identify** What is the National Organization for Women?

   b. **Summarize** How did Cesar Chavez help migrant farmworkers?

   c. **Elaborate** How did the Americans with Disabilities Act help disabled Americans?

Reviewing Themes

10. **Politics** How did political changes help minorities achieve their goals?
11. **Society and Culture** How did society change during the civil rights era?

Reading Skills

Using Context Clues: Synonyms *Use the Reading Skills taught in this chapter to answer the question below.*

> The Little Rock Nine began attending classes, but resistance to integration continued. Some white students insulted, harassed, and attacked the black students. In spite of these obstacles, eight of the nine remained at the school.

12. Which of the following would be a good synonym for the word *harassed*?

    a. comforted

    b. assisted

    c. helped

    d. insulted

Social Studies Skills

Making Speeches *Use the Social Studies Skills taught in this chapter to answer the question below.*

13. What steps should you follow to make a persuasive speech?

Using the Internet

14. **Activity: Creating a Newspaper** Even after the ruling in *Brown* v. *Board of Education*, integration was slow to take effect. Many districts began gradual integration plans, as in Little Rock, Arkansas, where local leaders chose the Little Rock Nine to start the process. Through your online textbook, research the Little Rock Nine. Then create two pages of a newspaper about them. Make sure your newspaper articles include direct references to your research. Include quotations from the historical figures that were involved in the integration of Central High School.

hmhsocialstudies.com

Focus on Writing

15. **Writing Your Bill** Review your notes. Then start writing your civil rights bill. What is its goal? Explain how it will expand civil rights. Is it designed to help a certain group of people? Discuss the reasons you believe it is important to expand civil rights in this way. You may refer to problems or events the bill responds to as well as to earlier civil rights laws and legal decisions.

© Houghton Mifflin Harcourt Publishing Company • Image Credits: (b), HMH Photo

CHAPTER 13

Standardized Test Practice

DIRECTIONS: Read each question and write the letter of the best response.

1 Use the following graph to answer the question below.

By about how much did the percentage of women in the workforce increase between 1960 and 1980?

A 5 percent

B 25 percent

C 15 percent

D 50 percent

2 The Supreme Court case that led to the integration of public schools was called

A *Plessy* v. *Ferguson.*

B *Brown* v. *Board of Education.*

C *Chisholm* v. *Marshall.*

D *King* v. *Alabama.*

3 Leaders of the MIA organized the Montgomery Bus Boycott after

A black students staged a sit-in at a Woolworth lunch counter.

B Martin Luther King Jr. founded the Southern Christian Leadership Conference.

C Rosa Parks was arrested for sitting in the whites-only section of a public bus.

D the Little Rock Nine began attending Central High School.

4 In the 1960s Cesar Chavez became

A the first Hispanic American to serve in the U.S. Congress.

B a nationally recognized Hispanic rights leader.

C a member of President Johnson's cabinet.

D a leader of the Native American rights movement.

5 In 1969 a group of activists seized Alcatraz Island to

A demand better wages and conditions for migrant farmworkers.

B protest the government's takeover of Native American lands.

C demonstrate in favor of the Equal Rights Amendment.

D call attention to the needs of Americans with disabilities.

6 Read the following excerpt from Martin Luther King Jr.'s "I Have a Dream" speech and use it to answer the question below.

> "When we allow freedom to ring, when we let it ring from every village and every hamlet [community], from every state and every city, we will be able to speed up that day when all of God's children, black men and white men, Jews and Gentiles [non-Jews], Protestants and Catholics, will be able to join hands and sing in the words of the old Negro spiritual, 'Free at last! Free at last! Thank God Almighty, we are free at last!'"
>
> —Martin Luther King Jr.,
> speech at the March on Washington

Document-Based Question What is the main idea King is expressing in this passage?

© Houghton Mifflin Harcourt Publishing Company

CHAPTER 14 1960–1975

The Vietnam War Years

Essential Question What were the causes and effects of the Vietnam War?

ALABAMA COURSE OF STUDY

8 Describe how the United States' role in the Cold War influenced domestic and international events.

- Identifying strategic diplomatic initiatives that intensified the Cold War, including the policies of Harry S. Truman, Dwight D. Eisenhower, and John F. Kennedy.
- Identifying how Cold War tensions resulted in armed conflict.
- Describing the impact of the Cold War on technological innovations.

9 Critique major social and cultural changes in the United States since World War II.

- Identifying key persons and events of the modern Civil Rights Movement.
- Identifying the impact of media, including newspapers, AM and FM radio, television, twenty-four hour sports and news programming, talk radio, and Internet social networking, on United States' culture since World War II.

10 Analyze changing economic priorities and cycles of economic expansion and contraction for their impact on society since World War II.

- Identifying policies and programs that had an economic impact on society since World War II.

12 Evaluate significant political issues and policies of presidential administrations since World War II.

- Recognizing domestic issues that shaped the United States since World War II.
- Identifying issues of foreign affairs that shaped the United States since World War II.

Focus on Writing

Newscast Writing in the 1960s, Michael Arlen called the Vietnam War the first American "living room war." For the first time, Americans could sit in their homes and watch scenes from the war on TV newscasts. In this chapter, you will read about American involvement in Cold War conflicts, such as the Cuban missile crisis and the Vietnam War. Then you will present a newscast on major events of the Cold War.

UNITED STATES

1961 Kennedy sends military advisers to Vietnam.

1960

WORLD

1960 Cuba and the Soviet Union sign a trade agreement and establish diplomatic relations.

Image Credits: (t), ©AP/Wide World Photos

© Houghton Mifflin Harcourt Publishing Company

Soldiers from the U.S. 173rd Airborne Brigade take part in the Iron Triangle assault.

HISTORY Causes of the Vietnam War

hmhsocialstudies.com VIDEO

1968 Martin Luther King Jr. and Robert Kennedy are assassinated.

1969 Joan Baez, The Who, and Jimi Hendrix headline the Woodstock Music Festival.

1973 Last U.S. ground troops leave Vietnam.

1965 — 1970 — 1975

1965 North Vietnamese leader Ho Chi Minh refuses peace talks with President Lyndon Johnson.

1969 Ho Chi Minh dies in Hanoi.

1975 North Vietnamese troops capture Saigon.

Image Credits: (t), ©AP/Wide World Photos; (cr), ©Blank Archives/Getty Images; (br), ©Dirck Halstead/Getty Images; (bl), ©Hulton Archive/Getty Images; (cl), ©Flip Schulke/Corbis

© Houghton Mifflin Harcourt Publishing Company

Reading Social Studies

Economics | Geography | Politics | Society and Culture | Science and Technology

Focus on Themes In this chapter, you will learn about the Vietnam War years. American soldiers faced many obstacles in Vietnam, including the country's **geography**. Jungles and mountains prevented Americans from gaining an easy victory. You will read about how the long, drawn-out conflict caused divisions between the nation's leaders and many Americans.

Setting a Purpose

Focus on Reading Setting a purpose for your reading can help you to understand the things that you read. Understanding the author's goal is often an important part of this task.

Setting a Purpose When you open this book to a page you have been assigned to read, there will be clues about what you will be learning. The information in this book is organized under headings that help explain the text. When you read a section like the one below, try to determine how the text explains the heading.

Notice how one reader used the headings to determine his purpose for reading the passage below.

Society in the 1960s

As the Vietnam War continued, growing numbers of Americans began to criticize the war . . .

This large heading lets me know that the text below will be about everyday life during the 1960s.

Antiwar Protests

College students often took the lead in organizing antiwar protests . . .

The text below this heading might answer questions about what antiwar protests are and who took part in them.

I guess protests were frequent during the 1960s. I should read to find out what they were and why they took place.

© Houghton Mifflin Harcourt Publishing Company

Key Terms and People

Chapter 14

Section 1
Peace Corps
Fidel Castro
Berlin Wall
Cuban missile crisis
Neil Armstrong
Edwin "Buzz" Aldrin
Ho Chi Minh
domino theory
Vietcong

Section 2
Tonkin Gulf Resolution
Ho Chi Minh Trail
escalation
William Westmoreland
search-and-destroy missions
Tet Offensive
doves
hawks

Section 3
Students for a Democratic Society
hippies
Richard M. Nixon
Henry Kissinger
Vietnamization
Twenty-sixth Amendment
War Powers Act
Vietnam Veterans Memorial

Academic Vocabulary
In this chapter, you will learn the following academic words:
aspect
values

You Try It!

As you read the following passage, look for information in the headings that tells you what to look for.

The Vietnam War Ends

While Nixon was running for re-election in 1972, Henry Kissinger started peace negotiations with the North Vietnamese . . .

The Impact in Southeast Asia

The war ended when North Vietnamese forces captured Saigon in April 1975 . . .

The Impact at Home

The Vietnam War carried heavy costs for the United States as well . . .

After you read the passage, answer the following questions.

1. After reading the headings, what do you think this section is going to be about?
2. What are some questions you might ask before reading this section?
3. What information do you think you will learn from the section?

As you read this chapter, set a purpose before you read each section.

© Houghton Mifflin Harcourt Publishing Company

SECTION 1

Kennedy and Foreign Policy

MEXI
PACIFIC

What You Will Learn...

Main Ideas

1. President Kennedy confronted Communist threats around the world.
2. The United States and the Soviet Union raced to send a person to the moon.
3. The Cold War conflict in Vietnam led the United States into war.

The Big Idea

The United States confronted Communist nations in Cold War conflicts around the world.

Key Terms and People

Peace Corps
Fidel Castro
Berlin Wall
Cuban missile crisis
Neil Armstrong
Edwin "Buzz" Aldrin
Ho Chi Minh
domino theory
Vietcong

hmhsocialstudies.com
TAKING NOTES

Use the graphic organizer online to take notes on the Cold War crises that took place during the Kennedy administration.

If YOU were there...

You are a student in 1960. Whenever you discuss current events in class, students talk nervously about the ongoing nuclear arms race between the United States and the Soviet Union. If Cold War tensions ever spark an all-out nuclear war, entire cities and populations could be destroyed in just a matter of minutes.

Do you think Cold War tensions will lead to a nuclear war?

BUILDING BACKGROUND In the 1950s some Americans feared that the United States was falling behind the Soviet Union in missile production. The United States began using U-2 spy planes to gather information about Soviet military technology. On May 1, 1960, a U-2 plane was shot down over Soviet territory. Soviet leaders reacted angrily. Cold War tensions were running high as the Kennedy presidency began in 1961.

Kennedy Confronts Communism

As president, John F. Kennedy was committed to the Cold War policy of stopping the spread of communism worldwide. He maintained strong military forces and expanded the nation's supply of nuclear weapons. He also sought nonmilitary ways to defeat communism. For example, in a program called the Alliance for Progress, the United States pledged $20 billion in aid to countries in Latin America. This assistance did little to improve conditions in Latin America or U.S.–Latin American relations, however. Another nonmilitary program was more successful. Beginning in 1961, the **Peace Corps** sent volunteers to developing countries to help with projects such as digging wells and building schools.

Bay of Pigs

Much of Kennedy's attention, in his early days as president, involved confronting communism with U.S. military forces. The first Cold

© Houghton Mifflin Harcourt Publishing Company

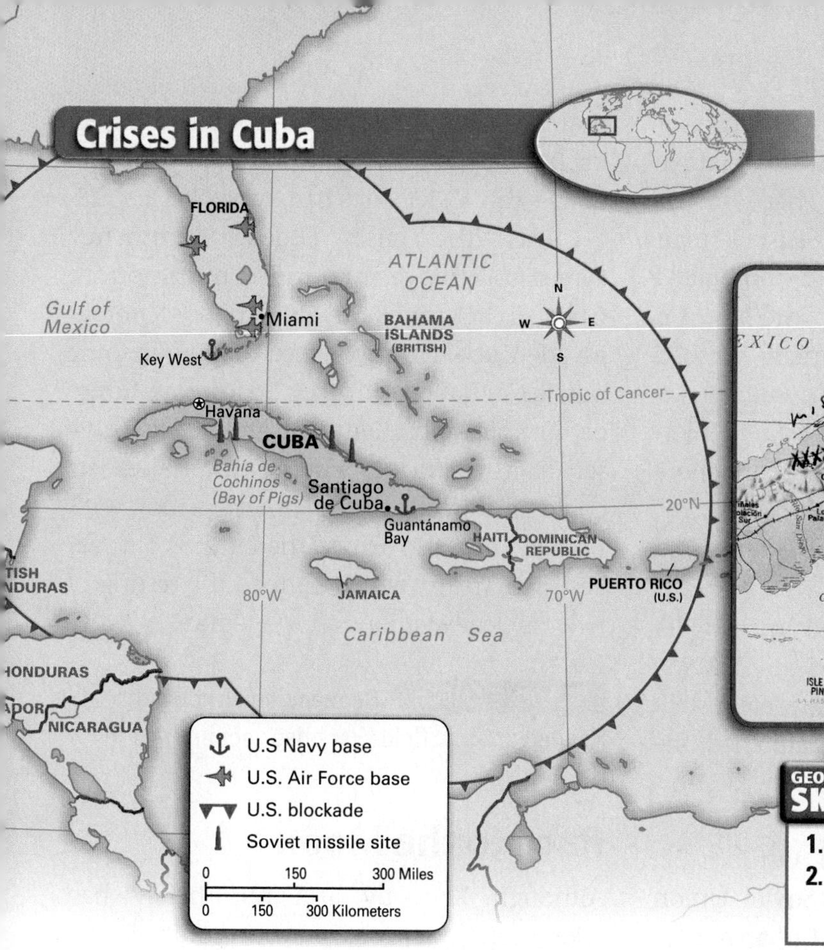

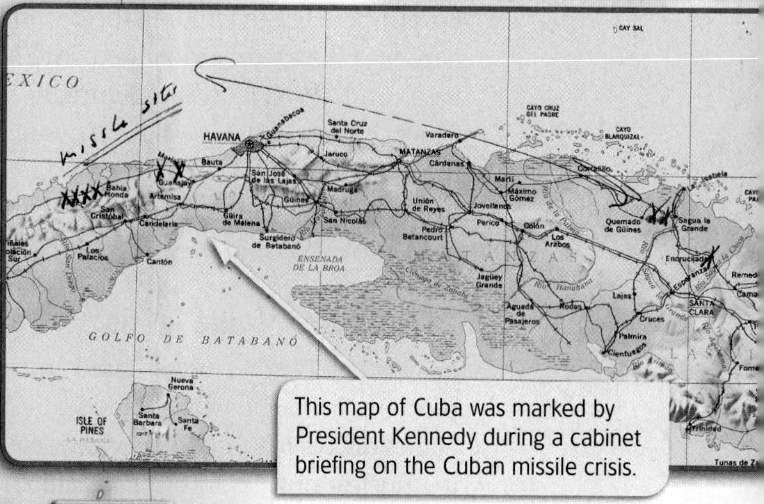

This map of Cuba was marked by President Kennedy during a cabinet briefing on the Cuban missile crisis.

HISTORY VIDEO Cuban Missile Crisis

hmhsocialstudies.com

GEOGRAPHY SKILLS INTERPRETING MAPS

1. **Location** How far is Havana from Miami?
2. **Human-Environment Interaction** Why was the Cuban military presence so dangerous for the United States?

War crisis during his administration took place in Cuba. In the late 1950s Cuban rebel **Fidel Castro** had led a revolution against an unpopular dictator. In 1959 he overthrew the dictator and soon established a Communist government allied to the Soviet Union. Many Cubans who had opposed Castro fled to the United States.

Castro's close ties with the Soviet Union worried Kennedy, especially since Cuba is only about 90 miles from Florida. Soviet leaders could use Cuba as a base from which to attack the United States.

While president, Dwight Eisenhower had developed a plan to remove Castro from power. The Central Intelligence Agency began training Cuban exiles to invade the island and overthrow Castro. Kennedy learned of the plan when he became president. He approved the operation.

On April 17, 1961, about 1,500 Cuban exiles landed by boat at Cuba's Bay of Pigs. Castro's forces quickly responded, killing about 300 of the invaders and capturing the rest. Many Americans criticized Kennedy for the disastrous invasion attempt. His administration was off to a shaky start.

The Berlin Wall

Located behind the Iron Curtain in East Germany, the city of Berlin was the site of Kennedy's second crisis. East Berlin was part of Communist East Germany. West Berlin remained a part of democratic West Germany and stood as a model of prosperity and freedom. Desperate for freedom and better economic opportunities, about 2.5 million East Germans fled to West Berlin between 1949 and 1961. The steady loss of skilled workers alarmed Communist officials. Calling the open border between East and West Berlin a "handy escape route," Soviet premier Nikita Khrushchev demanded that the border be closed.

Khrushchev threatened to take over West Berlin. President Kennedy responded

© Houghton Mifflin Harcourt Publishing Company

by vowing to defend the free city. "We cannot and will not permit the Communists to drive us out of Berlin," he warned. Then, on the night of August 12–13, 1961, the East German government began building the **Berlin Wall**, a barrier of concrete and barbed wire between East and West Berlin. Kennedy rushed American troops to West Berlin. But he was unwilling to go to war with the Soviet Union over the Berlin Wall. The wall stood as a symbol of the Cold War for nearly three decades.

The Cuban Missile Crisis

In October 1962 Kennedy faced yet another problem in Cuba when American U-2 spy planes discovered that the Soviets were installing nuclear missiles in Cuba. If launched, the missiles could reach, and possibly destroy, American cities within minutes.

At a press conference on October 22, Kennedy demanded that the Soviet Union remove the missiles. During the **Cuban missile crisis**, the U.S. Navy formed a blockade around Cuba to prevent Soviet ships from bringing in more weapons. As Soviet ships approached the blockade, terrified Americans waited tensely for news updates. Then came some welcome news—the Soviet ships had turned back.

ACADEMIC VOCABULARY
aspect
part

After the crisis ended, Khrushchev agreed to remove the nuclear missiles from Cuba. In return, Kennedy promised not to invade Cuba. He also agreed to remove some missiles in Italy and Turkey. To improve future communication, Kennedy and Khrushchev set up a telephone "hotline" so the leaders could talk directly to each other at a moment's notice. They also signed the Limited Nuclear Test Ban Treaty, which banned the testing of new nuclear weapons aboveground.

READING CHECK **Sequencing** When did Kennedy's three Cold War crises occur?

Race to the Moon

Although Kennedy and Khrushchev had taken some steps to prevent conflicts, the Cold War continued. One aspect of the Cold War that heated up in the 1960s was the space race—the competition between the United

Primary Source

BOOK

Thirteen Days

During the Cuban missile crisis, President Kennedy considered several options: blockade Cuba, invade the island, or bomb missile sites by air. After choosing the blockade, Kennedy and his advisers could only wait to see how Khrushchev would respond. The president's brother, Attorney General Robert F. Kennedy, later described these tense moments in the White House.

I think these few minutes were the time of gravest concern for the President. Was the world on the brink of a holocaust? Was it our error? A mistake? Was there something further that should have been done? Or not done?. . . The minutes in the Cabinet Room ticked slowly by. What could we say now—what could we do?

Robert Kennedy describes the doubts he and others in the room felt.

Then it was 10:25—a messenger brought in a note . . . 'Mr. President . . . some of the Russian ships have stopped dead in the water . . . Six ships . . . have stopped or have turned back toward the Soviet Union' . . .

Then we were back to the details. The meeting droned on. But everyone looked like a different person. For a moment the world had stood still, and now it was going around again.

—Robert F. Kennedy, from *Thirteen Days: A Memoir of the Cuban Missile Crisis*

ANALYSIS SKILL **ANALYZING PRIMARY SOURCES**

What details from the passage show that the moment was tense?

States and the Soviet Union to explore space. The Soviet Union pulled ahead in April 1961 when Soviet cosmonaut Yuri Gagarin became the first person to travel into space, orbiting Earth once.

The United States was determined to catch up to and surpass the Soviet Union in the space race. Kennedy outlined a bold plan in a 1961 speech to Congress:

> "I believe that this nation should commit itself to achieving the goal, before this decade is out, of landing a man on the moon and returning him safely to the earth."
>
> —John F. Kennedy, speech to Congress, May 25, 1961

It is difficult for us to imagine what it was like for Kennedy's audience to hear these words. Space travel seems normal to us today. But to people in the early 1960s, the idea of humans landing on the moon seemed like something out of a science fiction novel. Still, Americans supported the project. Congress provided NASA with billions of dollars to fund the development of new technology.

In May 1961 astronaut Alan Shepard Jr. became the first U.S. astronaut in space. The next year, John Glenn became the first American to orbit Earth. Then NASA pushed ahead with Project Apollo, with the goal of landing an astronaut on the moon. Even with careful planning, Apollo astronauts faced great danger. Three astronauts died in a fire during a prelaunch test in 1967.

Mission to the Moon

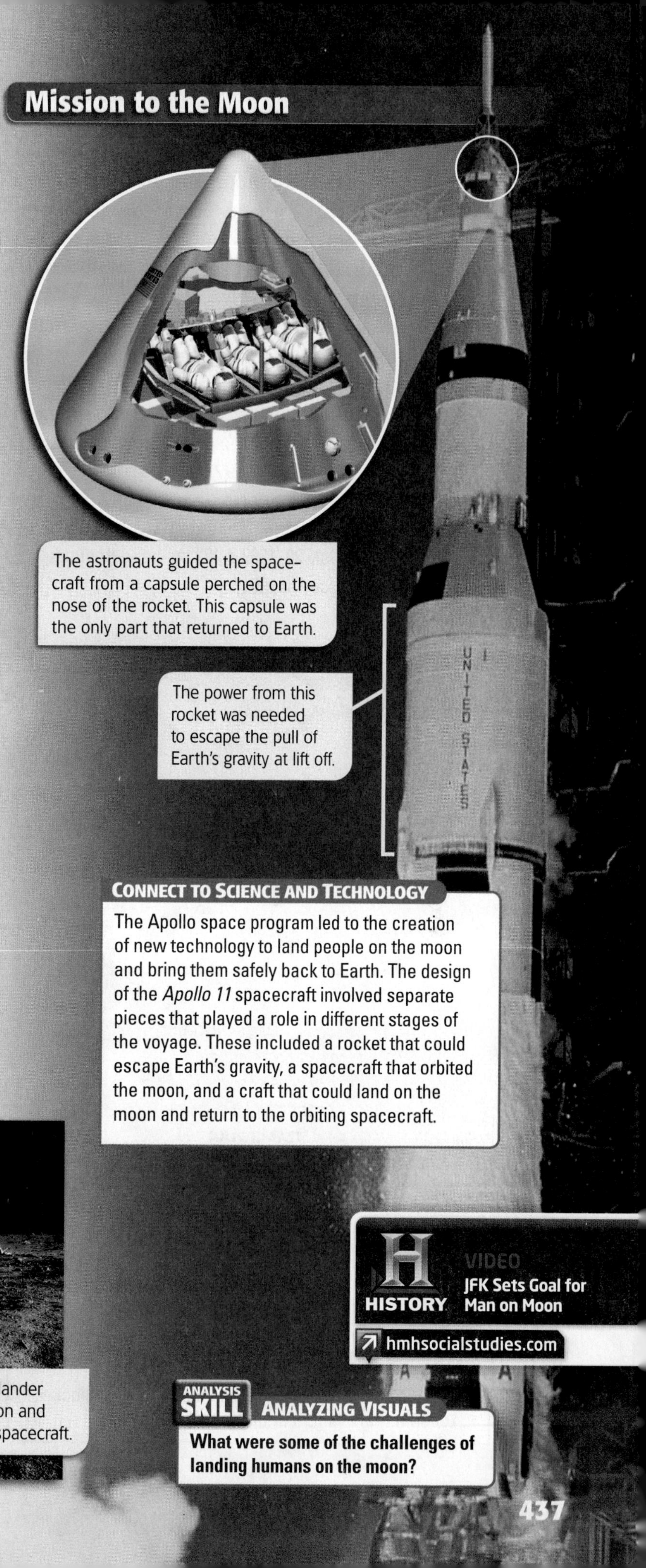

The astronauts guided the spacecraft from a capsule perched on the nose of the rocket. This capsule was the only part that returned to Earth.

The power from this rocket was needed to escape the pull of Earth's gravity at lift off.

CONNECT TO SCIENCE AND TECHNOLOGY

The Apollo space program led to the creation of new technology to land people on the moon and bring them safely back to Earth. The design of the *Apollo 11* spacecraft involved separate pieces that played a role in different stages of the voyage. These included a rocket that could escape Earth's gravity, a spacecraft that orbited the moon, and a craft that could land on the moon and return to the orbiting spacecraft.

A vehicle known as the moon lander took two astronauts to the moon and returned them to the orbiting spacecraft.

HISTORY VIDEO
JFK Sets Goal for Man on Moon
hmhsocialstudies.com

ANALYSIS SKILL ANALYZING VISUALS

What were some of the challenges of landing humans on the moon?

© Houghton Mifflin Harcourt Publishing Company • Image Credits: (bl), ©1996 Corbis; Original image courtesy of NASA/Corbis; (r), NASA

On July 20, 1969, while millions of people around the world watched on television, the lunar module *Eagle* landed on the surface of the moon. American astronauts **Neil Armstrong** and **Edwin "Buzz" Aldrin** climbed out and became the first people to walk on the moon. "That's one small step for [a] man, one giant leap for mankind," said Armstrong as he touched the lunar surface. Armstrong and Aldrin planted the American flag on the moon's surface and collected samples of moon rocks. The Apollo program continued, achieving five more successful moon landings by 1972.

hmhsocialstudies.com
ANIMATED GEOGRAPHY AND HISTORY
Southeast Asia 1954

READING CHECK **Analyzing** How did the events of July 20, 1969, fulfill the hope Kennedy had expressed in 1961?

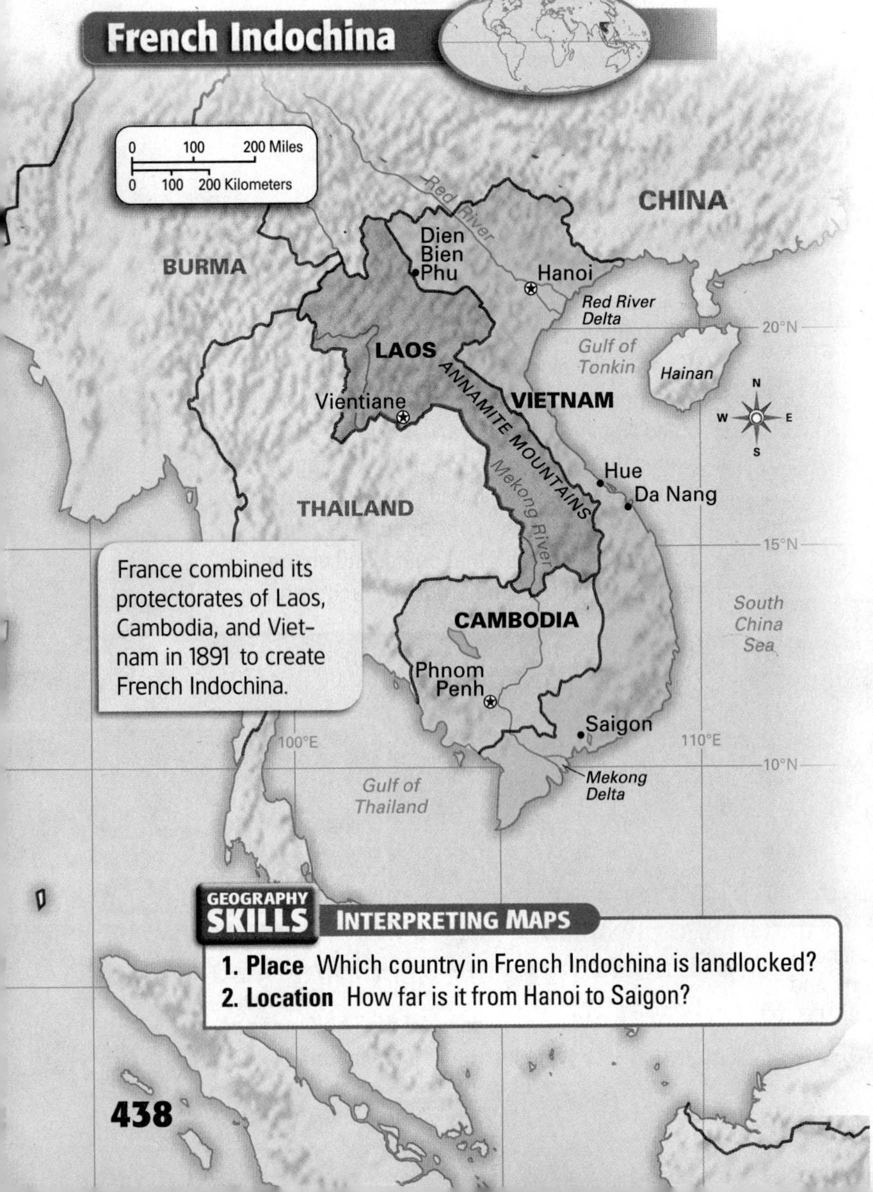

France combined its protectorates of Laos, Cambodia, and Vietnam in 1891 to create French Indochina.

GEOGRAPHY SKILLS **INTERPRETING MAPS**

1. **Place** Which country in French Indochina is landlocked?
2. **Location** How far is it from Hanoi to Saigon?

Conflict in Vietnam

The most serious and deadly event of the Cold War took place in Vietnam, a country in Southeast Asia. The Vietnamese struggled against the domination of China for centuries. By the early 1880s all of Vietnam was conquered by France. The French combined Vietnam with neighboring Laos and Cambodia to create a colony called French Indochina. French leaders imposed harsh taxes and put limits on political freedoms. Vietnamese nationalists began a struggle for independence in the early 1900s.

France and Vietnam

One of the leading Vietnamese nationalists was **Ho Chi Minh**. Ho believed that only a Communist revolution could free the Vietnamese people.

During World War II, Japan drove the French out of Indochina. Ho Chi Minh did not want Vietnam to be controlled by yet another foreign power. He organized a group called the Vietminh to resist Japanese occupation. When Japan was defeated by the Allies in 1945, Ho declared Vietnamese independence. Using words echoing those of the American Declaration of Independence, he said, "All men are born equal: the Creator has given us inviolable rights, life, liberty, and happiness." In reality, Ho did not believe in the democratic principles outlined in the American document.

Vietnam was still not free of foreign rule. France insisted that Vietnam was a French colony. French forces moved to regain control of Vietnam, leading to new fighting between the two sides.

Presidents Truman and Eisenhower both supported France with military aid. They were concerned that a Vietminh victory would lead to the spread of communism in Asia. American leaders feared that if one country became Communist, nearby countries would also fall to communism. This was called the **domino theory**. Americans had already watched Communist victories in China and North Korea. They did not want Vietnam to be next.

The Vietminh had fewer weapons and supplies than the French, but they used hit-and-run guerrilla tactics to gradually weaken French forces. In May 1954 the Vietminh trapped a French army at Dien Bien Phu, where the French surrendered. In July French and Vietnamese leaders worked out an agreement called the Geneva Accords. This compromise temporarily divided Vietnam into North and South. It also called for democratic elections in July 1956 that would unite the two countries under one government.

North and South Vietnam

North Vietnam became a Communist dictatorship led by Ho Chi Minh. South Vietnam had a Western-style government led by Ngo Dinh Diem (en-GOH DIN de-EM) and supported by the United States. U.S. officials hoped Diem would win control of the country in the 1956 elections.

Diem, however, quickly proved to be a disappointing leader. He put his own family members in top government positions and used his security forces to imprison and torture his political enemies. President Eisenhower was concerned, but he and his advisers saw Diem as the only realistic alternative to a Communist Vietnam.

In North Vietnam, meanwhile, Ho Chi Minh introduced land redistribution plans. Like Diem, Ho and the Vietminh violently persecuted their opponents. During the land redistribution process, they imprisoned and killed thousands of landowners.

As the 1956 reunification elections approached, however, a growing number of South Vietnamese supported Ho and the Vietminh. Diem refused to allow South Vietnam to participate in the elections. The United States backed this decision. Diem also arrested thousands of people who supported Ho.

In 1960 members of the North Vietnamese government formed the National Liberation Front (NLF). The NLF recruited South Vietnamese who were opposed to Diem to fight against the South Vietnamese

South Vietnamese soldiers plot a firing pattern under the guidance of American military personnel.

government. The NLF relied on Communist guerrilla forces called the **Vietcong** as its army, which was supplied and funded by the North Vietnamese.

American Involvement

President Eisenhower sent aid, weapons, and military advisers to South Vietnam to aid Diem. Soon after taking office in 1961, President Kennedy sent more advisers and special forces. Although they were not official combat troops, the U.S. military advisers often accompanied the South Vietnamese army on combat missions. Some were killed in action. By late 1963 about 16,000 U.S. military personnel were serving in Vietnam.

The increased U.S. support did not help Diem, who was becoming less and less popular in South Vietnam. Several attempts were made to overthrow his government, all of which failed. Diem would not hold elections, and his opponents began to consider violence as their only option. He lost more support when he ordered his troops to fire on Buddhist demonstrators.

© Houghton Mifflin Harcourt Publishing Company • Image Credits: (tr), ©AP/Wide World Photos

Some Buddhist monks protested by setting themselves on fire. Horrifying images of these protests helped turn U.S. public opinion against Diem.

In November 1963 a group of South Vietnamese army officers seized power and killed Diem and his brother. Only weeks later, Kennedy was assassinated, and Vice President Lyndon Johnson became president. Johnson immediately faced tough decisions about how to handle an increasingly unstable South Vietnam.

READING CHECK **Evaluating** Why did the United States see the Vietnam conflict as a Cold War struggle?

SUMMARY In the 1950s and early 1960s, Cold War tensions caused conflicts around the world.

The Beginning of the Vietnam War

QUICK FACTS

Causes

- French lose control of Vietnam
- Cold War tensions
- Civil war in Vietnam
- Assassination of President Diem

Effects

- Eisenhower and Kennedy send military advisers
- Gulf of Tonkin Resolution

Section 1 Assessment

hmhsocialstudies.com ONLINE QUIZ

Reviewing Ideas, Terms, and People

1. a. **Describe** What nonmilitary tactics did President Kennedy use to confront communism?
   b. **Explain** How was the **Cuban missile crisis** resolved?
   c. **Evaluate** In which Cold War crisis do you think President Kennedy showed the strongest leadership? Explain your answer.
2. a. **Recall** How did the Soviet Union take the lead in the space race in 1961?
   b. **Predict** How do you think the Soviet Union responded to the successful U.S. landing of a man on the moon?
3. a. **Identify** Who was **Ho Chi Minh?**
   b. **Describe** According to the **domino theory,** what did U.S. leaders think might happen if Vietnam became a Communist country?
   c. **Analyze** Do you think the United States was justified in supporting Ngo Dinh Diem? Why or why not?

Critical Thinking

4. **Identifying Cause and Effect** Review your notes on Cold War crises during the Kennedy administration. Then copy the graphic organizer below and use it to list the causes and effects of each crisis.

Cause →	Bay of Pigs	→ Effect
Cause →	Berlin Wall	→ Effect
Cause →	Cuban Missile Crisis	→ Effect

Focus on Writing

5. **Listing Cold War Conflicts** List Cold War conflicts the United States faced during the 1960s. Who was involved in each conflict? How could you explain each conflict to a television audience? What could you show in your newscast to illustrate the conflicts?

Escalation in Vietnam

SECTION 2

If YOU were there...

It is 1965, and you have just been elected to Congress. You know voters are concerned about events in Vietnam, and you are carefully following the progress of the war. No one knows what will happen if the United States gets more deeply involved in the conflict. It might turn back the tide of communism. On the other hand, thousands of young soldiers might die.

Would you support sending U.S. troops to Vietnam? Why or why not?

BUILDING BACKGROUND Lyndon Johnson had spent most of his political career focused on domestic issues. After becoming president, he dedicated himself to civil rights legislation and his Great Society programs. But Johnson also had the same goal as presidents before him—to stop the spread of communism around the world.

Johnson Commits to Victory

Lyndon Johnson was determined to prevent Communists from taking over in South Vietnam. "We have the resources and the will to follow this course as long as it may take," Johnson said. He waited for a spark that might allow him to take action.

The Tonkin Gulf Resolution

In the summer of 1964, a naval skirmish led to a rapid expansion of U.S. involvement in Vietnam. On August 2, 1964, the USS *Maddox* reportedly exchanged gunfire with North Vietnamese torpedo boats in the Gulf of Tonkin, off the North Vietnamese coast. Two days later, during a night of thunderstorms, U.S. ships reported a second attack. The captain of the *Maddox* was not sure his ship had actually been attacked, but the USS *Turner Joy* claimed to have picked up high-speed vessels on its radar. Despite the conflicting stories, President Johnson declared the incident an act of war.

What You Will Learn...

Main Ideas

1. President Johnson committed the United States to victory in Vietnam by expanding U.S. involvement.
2. American soldiers faced new challenges fighting the Vietnam War.
3. The Tet Offensive was an important turning point in the war.

The Big Idea

Johnson quickly expanded U.S. involvement in Vietnam, but American soldiers faced a determined enemy.

Key Terms and People

Tonkin Gulf Resolution
Ho Chi Minh Trail
escalation
Willliam Westmoreland
search-and-destroy missions
Tet Offensive
doves
hawks

hmhsocialstudies.com
TAKING NOTES

Use the graphic organizer online to take notes on the events that led to the escalation of U.S. involvement in the Vietnam War.

© Houghton Mifflin Harcourt Publishing Company

Johnson asked Congress to give him the authority to take military action. Congress passed the **Tonkin Gulf Resolution**, giving the president the authority "to take all necessary measures to repel any armed attack against the forces of the United States." Johnson used the Tonkin Gulf Resolution to greatly expand the U.S. role in Vietnam.

Air Strikes Begin

Johnson sent the first U.S. combat troops to South Vietnam in March 1965. At the same time, he ordered Operation Rolling Thunder, a series of air strikes on war industries in North Vietnam. The air strikes were also designed to disrupt the **Ho Chi Minh Trail**, a supply route used by the North Vietnamese. The trail was a network of paths and tunnels that led from North Vietnam, through Laos and Cambodia, and into South Vietnam.

Because some of the Ho Chi Minh Trail was located in neutral countries, U.S. soldiers could not surround it on the ground. Instead, U.S. airplanes bombed the route, sometimes with napalm, or jellied gasoline, to kill troops and destroy supplies. Planes also released chemicals such as Agent Orange to kill the dense forests on the trail and to increase visibility from the air. American veterans and Vietnamese civilians later suffered serious health problems from exposure to these chemicals.

By late 1968 more than a million tons of explosives had been dropped on North and South Vietnam. Many Vietnamese soldiers and civilians were killed. The Communists' ability to wage war, however, was not destroyed.

READING CHECK **Summarizing** What authority did the Tonkin Gulf Resolution give to President Johnson?

U.S. Soldiers in Vietnam

From 1965 to 1968, President Johnson pursued a policy of **escalation**, or increased involvement, in the war. By 1968 more than 500,000 U.S. troops were serving in Vietnam. Backed by superior military technology, U.S. generals expected to win a quick victory. But the Vietnam War proved to be different from previous wars.

Strategies and Tactics

In Vietnam, there was rarely a front line where armies met face to face. Much of the war was

BIOGRAPHY

John McCain

1936–

John McCain's father and grandfather were both U.S. Navy admirals. The younger McCain also attended the Naval Academy and served in Vietnam as a combat pilot. On a bombing mission over Hanoi in 1967, his plane was shot down. McCain was held as a prisoner of war (POW) for more than five years and was often tortured and kept in solitary confinement. McCain entered politics after the war. In 2004 he was elected to his fourth term as U.S. senator from Arizona. One of his priorities as a senator was to help repair and strengthen U.S. relations with Vietnam. McCain was the Republican nominee for president in 2008.

Drawing Inferences If you were John McCain, would you want to establish good relations with Vietnam? Why or why not?

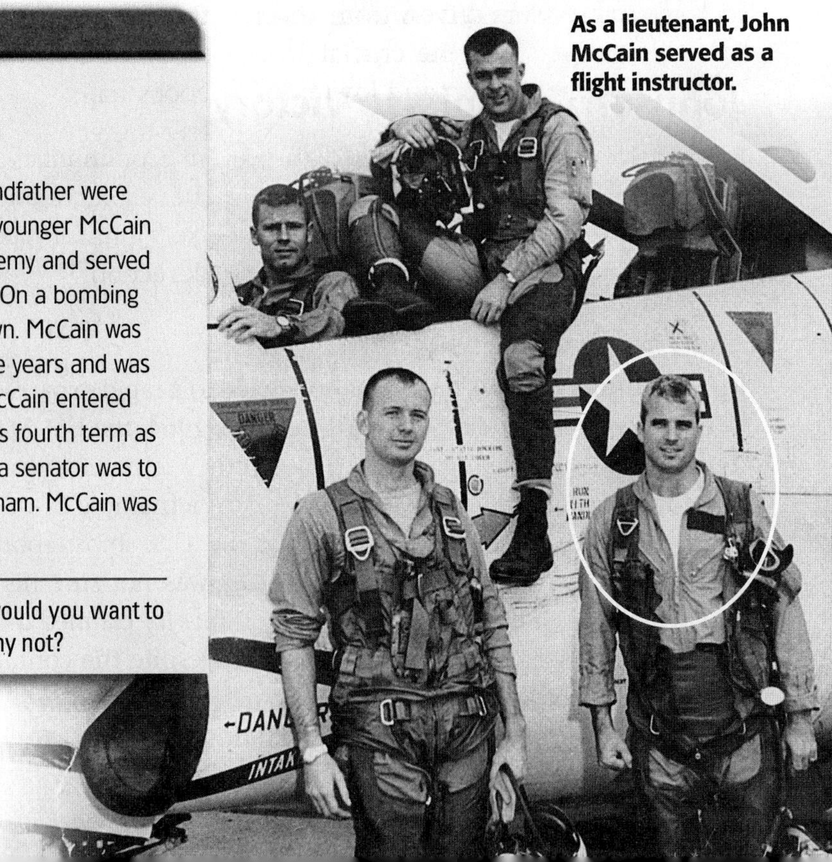

As a lieutenant, John McCain served as a flight instructor.

© Houghton Mifflin Harcourt Publishing Company • Image Credits: (bl) ©Larry Downing/Reuters/Corbis; (br) ©Sygma/Corbis fought in the jungles and villages of South Vietnam. General **William Westmoreland** commanded the U.S. ground forces involved in Vietnam. He developed a strategy based on **search-and-destroy missions**, where U.S. patrols searched for hidden enemy camps, then destroyed them with massive firepower and air raids.

To make up for their disadvantage in firepower, Vietcong and North Vietnamese Army (NVA) troops used guerrilla warfare tactics. Moving quickly, they set deadly traps and land mines. They also knew the local geography, which allowed them to make quick surprise assaults on small groups of U.S. soldiers. Though the Vietcong and NVA suffered high casualty rates, they were able to match U.S. escalation by continuing to send new troops into combat. They also received supplies and weapons from Communist China and the Soviet Union.

The civilians of South Vietnam were often caught in the middle of the fighting. Vietcong forces entered villages at night and killed people they believed were cooperating with the South Vietnamese government. South Vietnamese and American troops attacked villages they suspected of assisting the Vietcong. About 4 million South Vietnamese were driven from their homes. This undermined the crucial U.S. goal of winning the support and loyalty of South Vietnamese civilians.

Primary Source

ORAL HISTORY

Vietnam War

Charley Trujillo was a soldier in the Vietnam War. He later became a writer and filmmaker, focusing on the experiences of Latinos and Chicanos in the Vietnam War. Below he describes a day in Vietnam.

"Throughout the day we received mortar and sniper fire. By that evening we had suffered more casualties. The one I remember most was a guy we called the yippie. He was totally against the war and usually tried to avoid any violence. He was even thinking, for a while, of not carrying a rifle. It didn't help him much because the dude lost his leg that afternoon."

—Charley Trujillo, quoted in *Soldados: Chicanos In Việt Nam*

ANALYSIS SKILL **ANALYZING PRIMARY SOURCES**

Why might Trujillo have remembered this casualty the most?

Soldiers' Stories

More than 2 million American soldiers served in the Vietnam War. Their average age was 18–21, several years younger than in previous American wars. About one-quarter of the soldiers were drafted, many from minority groups and poor families. College students—most of whom were white and from wealthier families—were able to get draft releases called deferments.

American troops patrolled jungles and rice paddies, carrying 75–90 pounds of equipment through 100-degree heat and rainstorms that could last for days. They never knew when they might run into enemy fire. Soldiers also faced the constant danger of land mines and booby traps. "We required this kind of instant hair-trigger alertness," said marine Philip Caputo. "You simply trusted absolutely no one. I mean, from a 5-year-old kid to a 75-year-old woman."

While American troops were often able to win individual battles, they were rarely able to control the territory they had won for long. "You were just constantly walking out over the same ground," Caputo explained. "The enemy you were supposed to be defeating statistically kept coming back for more."

READING CHECK **Comparing and Contrasting**
How was Vietnam different from previous wars for U.S. soldiers?

Turning Points in Vietnam

By the end of 1967, U.S. military leaders argued that they were nearing victory in Vietnam. General Westmoreland said that he saw "a light at the end of the tunnel." But events in 1968 weakened the American public's confidence in this claim.

The Tet Offensive

On January 30, 1968, the Vietnamese celebrated their New Year, called Tet. In previous years, a cease-fire had halted fighting on this holiday. In 1968, however, Vietcong and North Vietnamese forces launched the **Tet Offensive**—surprise attacks all over South Vietnam, including an attack on the U.S. Embassy in Saigon, South Vietnam's capital.

South Vietnamese and U.S. forces successfully fought off the enemy strikes. Still, the massive size of the Tet Offensive shocked Americans. They had been told that the war would soon be over. Now they saw that the enemy was still strong and determined. Many began to wonder if government officials were being honest about the war. One poll taken after the Tet Offensive showed that only 33 percent of Americans believed that the United States was winning the war in Vietnam. About 49 percent said that the United States should never have become involved in the war.

In February 1968 Westmoreland asked for some 200,000 more troops. Many Americans questioned the wisdom of further escalation in Vietnam. President Johnson denied the general's request.

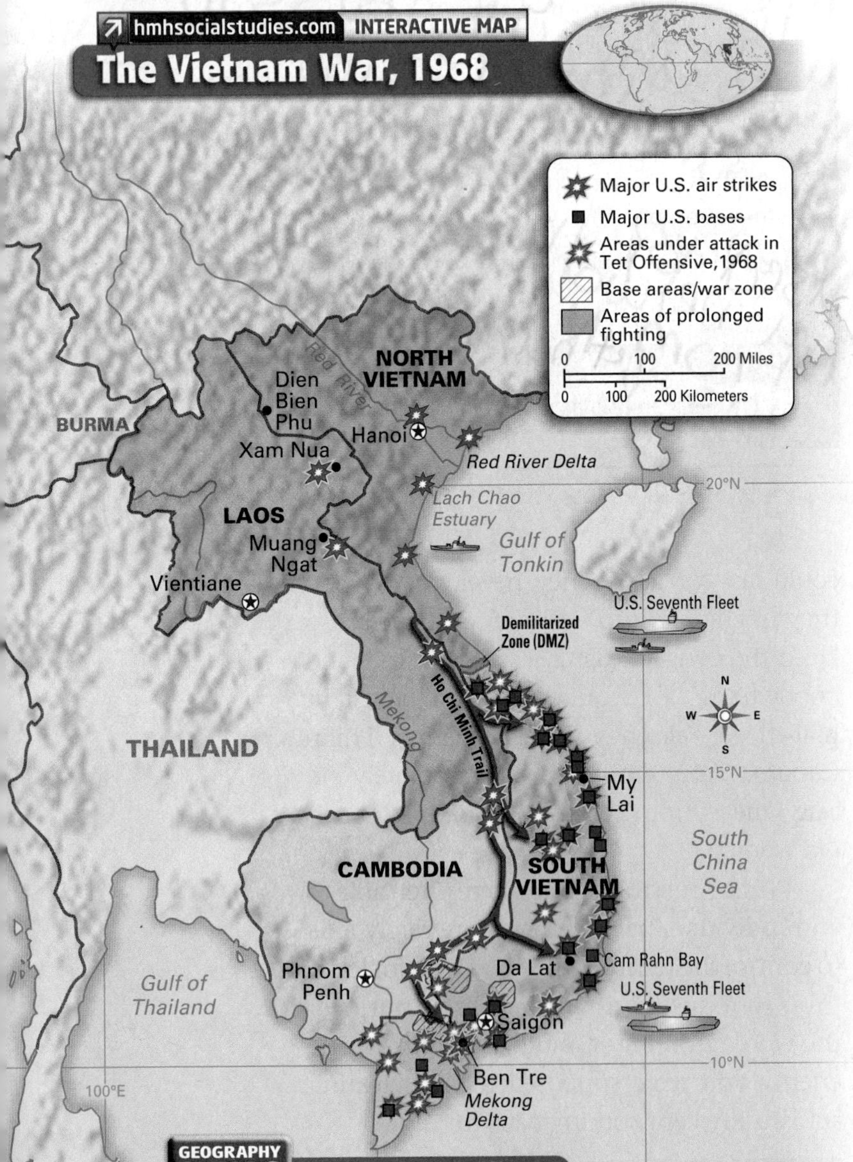

hmhsocialstudies.com INTERACTIVE MAP
The Vietnam War, 1968
Major U.S. air strikes
Major U.S. bases
Areas under attack in Tet Offensive, 1968
Base areas/war zone
Areas of prolonged fighting
0 100 200 Miles
0 100 200 Kilometers
NORTH VIETNAM
Red River
Dien Bien Phu
Hanoi
BURMA
Xam Nua
Red River Delta
20°N
Lach Chao Estuary
LAOS
Muang Ngat
Gulf of Tonkin
Vientiane
U.S. Seventh Fleet
Demilitarized Zone (DMZ)
Ho Chi Minh Trail
Mekong
N
W
E
S
THAILAND
15°N
My Lai
South China Sea
CAMBODIA
SOUTH VIETNAM
Cam Rahn Bay
Da Lat
Phnom Penh
Gulf of Thailand
U.S. Seventh Fleet
Saigon
Ben Tre
10°N
100°E
Mekong Delta

GEOGRAPHY SKILLS INTERPRETING MAPS

1. **Place** In which countries did major U.S. air strikes occur?
2. **Human-Environment Interaction** Which country experienced most of the fighting in the Vietnam War?

105°E 110°E

Hawks and Doves

Television reports had an important impact on public opinion about the war. Americans could watch action from the battlefield and see real images of the war's brutality on nightly news broadcasts. Many were dismayed by what they saw.

Gradually, some Americans who had been supporters of the Vietnam War began to call for an end to U.S. involvement. Opponents of the war were called **doves**—named after the birds that symbolize peace. Many doves believed that the war was draining money that should be spent on social programs at home. Supporters of the war were called **hawks**. Hawks called for increased military spending, based on the belief that winning the Cold War took priority over domestic programs.

The bitter divisions between hawks and doves deepened as the Vietnam War continued. On March 16, 1968, a company of U.S. soldiers under the command of

© Houghton Mifflin Harcourt Publishing Company

Lieutenant William Calley entered the South Vietnamese village of My Lai. Calley and his men expected to find Vietcong forces in My Lai. Their search-and-destroy mission turned into a massacre when American soldiers opened fire, killing about 500 unarmed villagers, including women and children.

At first, U.S. military officials tried to cover up news of the massacre. But former soldiers eventually made details of the events public. Lieutenant Calley was tried by the military and convicted of murder. As with the Tet Offensive, the My Lai massacre caused many Americans to question U.S. involvement in Vietnam.

READING CHECK **Summarizing** What events made some Americans oppose the war?

SUMMARY The Vietnam War escalated steadily under President Johnson.

A Reporter in the Field

Millions of Americans watched correspondent Walter Cronkite report the Vietnam War from the field. When Cronkite called the war a stalemate, or tie, President Johnson said "I've lost middle America."

How did Cronkite affect American's view of the war?

Section 2 Assessment

hmhsocialstudies.com
ONLINE QUIZ

Reviewing Ideas, Terms, and People

1. a. **Recall** What events led Johnson to ask Congress for authority to take military action in Vietnam?
   b. **Explain** Why was the **Ho Chi Minh Trail** the target of U.S. air strikes?
   c. **Predict** What problems might arise from giving a president powers such as those defined in the **Tonkin Gulf Resolution**?
2. a. **Define** What was **escalation**?
   b. **Contrast** How did strategies and tactics of U.S. troops differ from those of the NVA and Vietcong?
3. a. **Describe** What were the goals of the **doves** and the **hawks** during the Vietnam War?
   b. **Analyze** How did television influence public opinion during the Vietnam War?
   c. **Elaborate** Why was the Tet Offensive such a surprise to U.S. forces?

Critical Thinking

4. **Sequencing** Review your notes on events that led to increased U.S. involvement in the Vietnam War. Then copy the graphic organizer below and use it to put these events in the correct order.

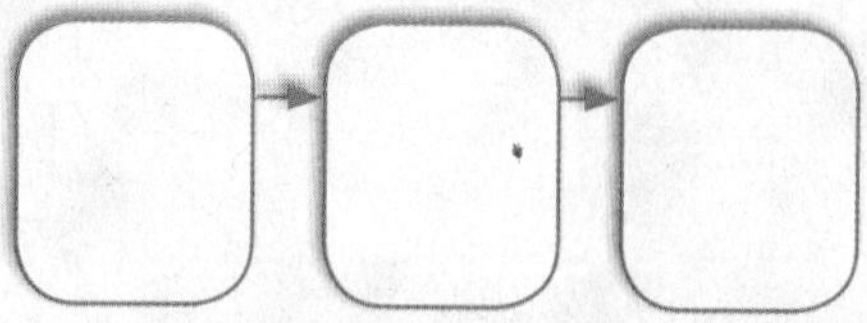

Focus on Writing

5. **Comparing Points of View** Take notes on different people's points of view on the war. What different points of view should you present in your newscast to give a complete picture of the war in Vietnam? What kinds of people might you want to interview?

The Vietcong Tunnels

Besides knowing the geography and terrain much better than U.S. forces, the Vietcong had the advantage of an underground system of tunnels. One large system of tunnels was installed some 47 miles north of Saigon in the Cu Chi district of South Vietnam. The picture on these pages is a re-created representation of these tunnels. The tunnels provided a place from which to fight that the Americans could not attack. A tunnel complex included special rooms in which to sleep, eat, plan, store weapons and supplies, and tend wounded soldiers.

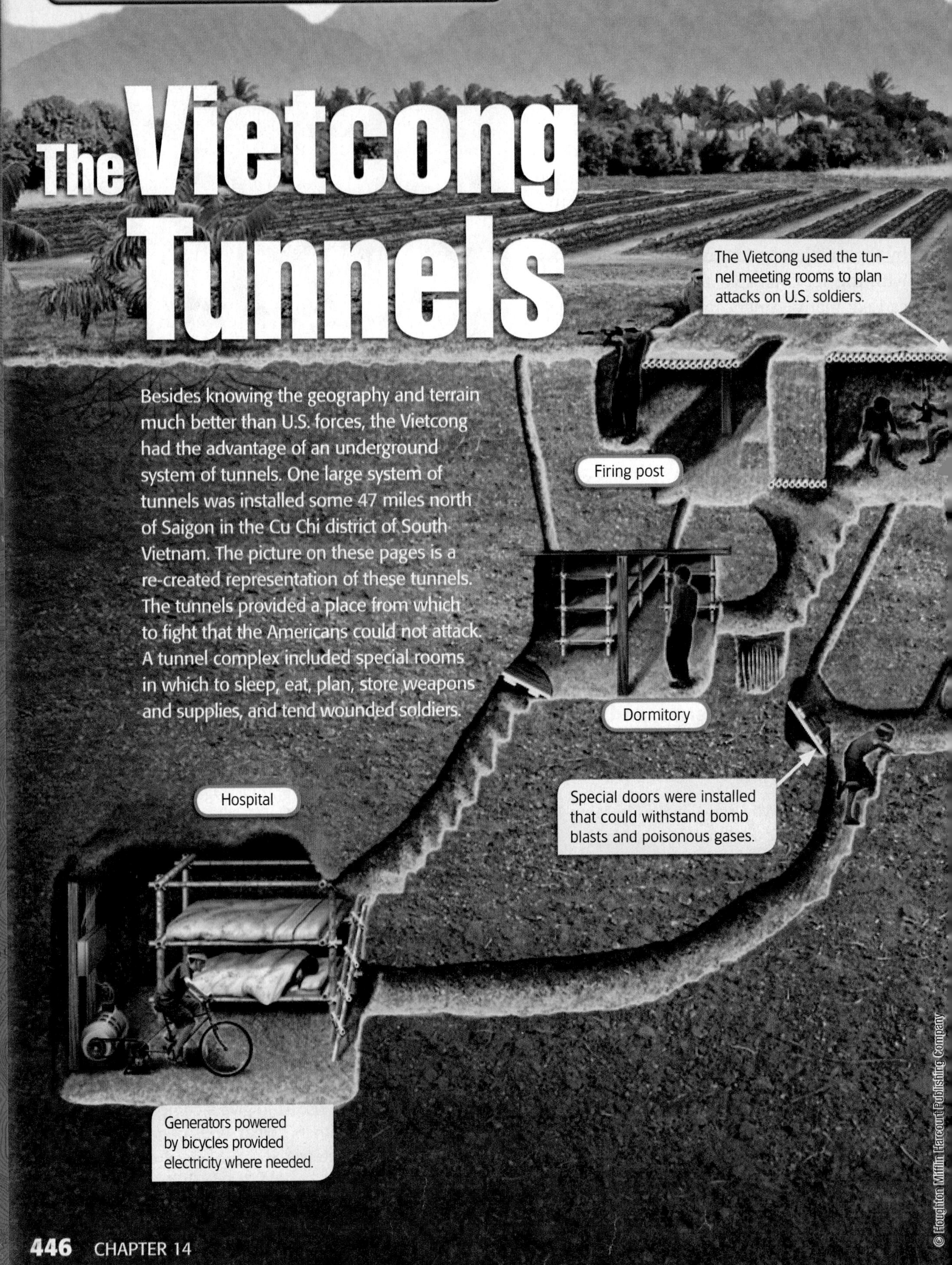
The Vietcong used the tunnel meeting rooms to plan attacks on U.S. soldiers.
Firing post
Dormitory
Hospital
Special doors were installed that could withstand bomb blasts and poisonous gases.
Generators powered by bicycles provided electricity where needed.

© Houghton Mifflin Harcourt Publishing Company

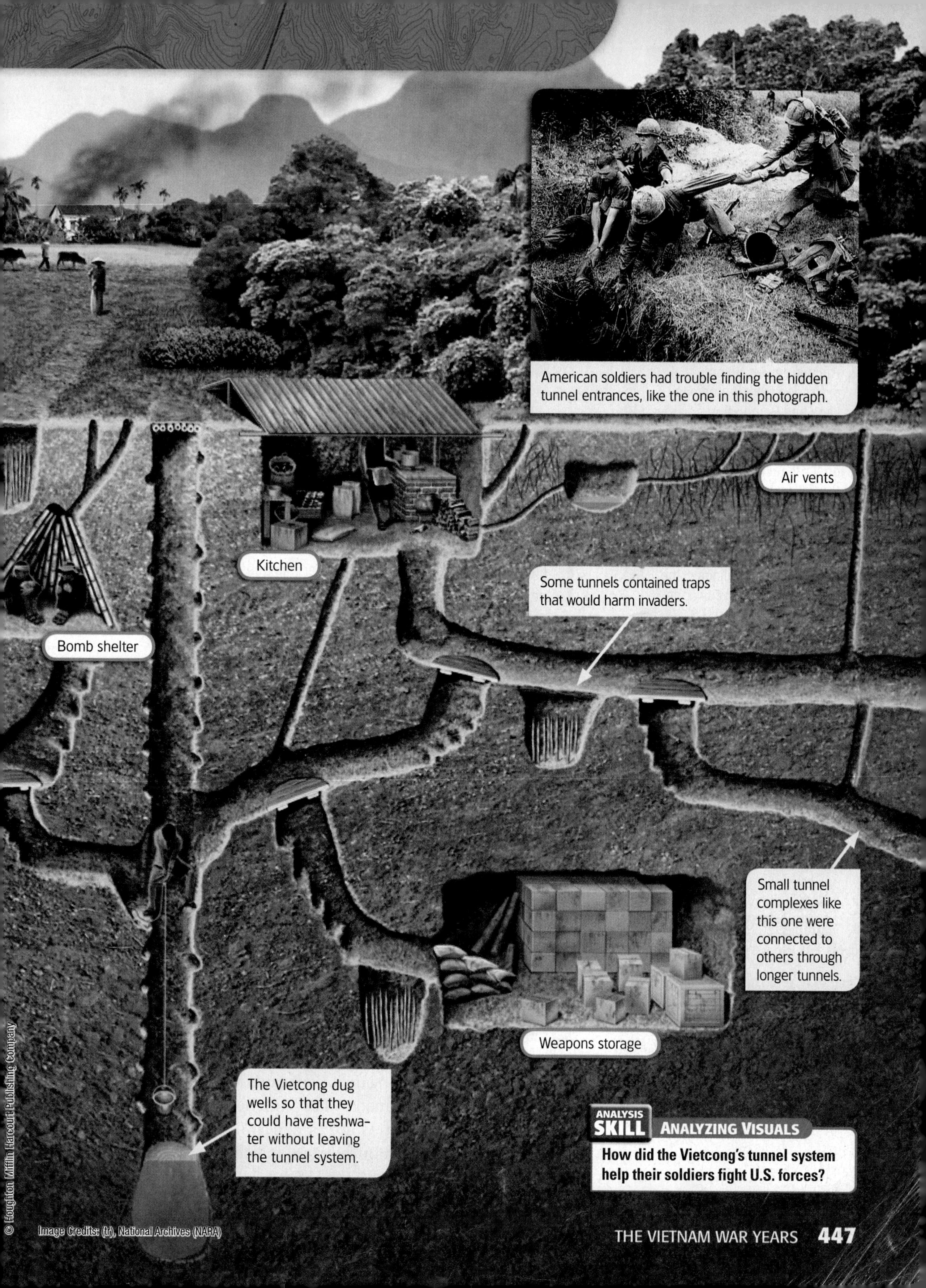
Air vents
Kitchen
Some tunnels contained traps that would harm invaders.
Bomb shelter
Small tunnel complexes like this one were connected to others through longer tunnels.
Weapons storage
The Vietcong dug wells so that they could have freshwater without leaving the tunnel system.

American soldiers had trouble finding the hidden tunnel entrances, like the one in this photograph.

ANALYSIS SKILL **ANALYZING VISUALS**

How did the Vietcong's tunnel system help their soldiers fight U.S. forces?

Image Credits: (tr), National Archives (NARA)

© Houghton Mifflin Harcourt Publishing Company

SECTION 3

The End of the War

What You Will Learn...

Main Ideas

1. Opinions about the Vietnam War divided American society in the 1960s.
2. The war under Nixon expanded from Vietnam to Laos and Cambodia.
3. The Vietnam War ended in 1973, but it had lasting effects on Vietnam and the United States.

The Big Idea

Growing antiwar feelings in the United States helped convince the government to end U.S. involvement in the Vietnam War.

Key Terms and People

Students for a Democratic Society
hippies
Richard M. Nixon
Henry Kissinger
Vietnamization
Twenty-sixth Amendment
War Powers Act
Vietnam Veterans Memorial

hmhsocialstudies.com
TAKING NOTES

Use the graphic organizer online to take notes on the causes of the end of the Vietnam War.

If YOU were there...

You are a high school student in 1969. You follow events in Vietnam very closely and often talk about the war with your friends. Some of your friends are active in the antiwar movement, but you also have friends who support the war. You think each group makes good points, but you are having a hard time deciding which position you support.

Would you join the antiwar protests? Why or why not?

BUILDING BACKGROUND Should the United States continue fighting in Vietnam? The debate over this question caused deep divisions in American society in the late 1960s. Antiwar demonstrators marched in cities and on college campuses. Others demonstrated in support of the war.

Society in the 1960s

As the Vietnam War continued, growing numbers of Americans began to criticize the war. "The peaceniks [war protesters] these days are legion [many]," said Charlotte Keyes, who helped organize a group called Women Strike for Peace. "They are ninety-years-old and fifteen, heads of families and housewives with babies, students, [and] young people."

Antiwar Protests

College students often took the lead in organizing antiwar protests. One of the most active protest groups was **Students for a Democratic Society** (SDS). Members of SDS protested the draft, as well as companies that made weapons used in Vietnam.

By the end of 1968, students had held antiwar demonstrations on nearly 75 percent of college campuses. Some young men protested by publicly burning their draft cards. Others avoided military service by moving to Canada. Many Americans, however, criticized the antiwar movement as anti-American. In 1970, for example, thousands of construction workers marched in New York City, shouting, "All the way with the U.S.A."

© Houghton Mifflin Harcourt Publishing Company

A Society Divided

Some young Americans supported the war in Vietnam. Many saw it as the only way to stop the spread of communism.

Other young Americans protested the war. They believed the United States should not be involved in a violent conflict far from home.

ANALYSIS SKILL **ANALYZING INFORMATION**

What differing views did young Americans have about the Vietnam War?

For some Americans, the antiwar movement was part of a rejection of traditional <u>values</u> and government authority. Some young people chose to "drop out" of mainstream society and built a counterculture—a culture with its own values and ways of behaving. Members of this counterculture, called **hippies**, emphasized individual freedom, nonviolence, and communal sharing. Hippies expressed their rejection of traditional society by growing their hair long and wearing unusual clothes. The views of hippies and war protesters upset many Americans. Commentators described a "generation gap," or division between older and younger Americans. "I know of no time in our history when the gap between the generations has been wider," said one university professor.

The Election of 1968

News of the Tet Offensive led to a sharp drop in the popularity of President Johnson. In early 1968 the percentage of Americans who approved of Johnson's performance as president fell from 48 to 36. The number of Americans who approved of the way Johnson was handling the war was even lower. As the 1968 presidential election approached, Johnson was even losing support within his own Democratic Party. On March 31 he went on live television and told Americans: "I shall not seek, and I will not accept, the nomination of my party for another term as president."

Several other candidates campaigned for the Democratic nomination. Johnson backed his vice president, Hubert Humphrey. Eugene McCarthy, a senator from Minnesota, ran as an outspoken antiwar candidate. Senator Robert F. Kennedy of New York argued that the United States should do everything possible to negotiate a quick and peaceful end to the war.

Kennedy won the California primary on June 5, 1968—an important step before the upcoming Democratic National Convention in Chicago. After giving his victory speech that night, he was assassinated by a man named Sirhan Sirhan.

The Democrats were badly divided going into their party's convention in Chicago.

ACADEMIC VOCABULARY

values ideas that people hold dear and try to live by

©Houghton Mifflin Harcourt Publishing Company • Image Credits: (bkgd), ©The Image Bank/Getty Images; (tl), (tr), ©David J. & Janice L. Frent Collection/Corbis; (tcr), ©Dick Swanson/Time Life Pictures/Getty Images; (tcl), ©Leif Skoogfors/Corbis

Vice President Humphrey seemed certain to win the nomination. But many delegates disliked his close ties with President Johnson and the Vietnam War. Angry debates inside the convention hall were matched by antiwar protests on the streets. When police officers moved in to stop the demonstrations, a riot broke out. Television cameras broadcast live images of the violent chaos in Chicago. More than 100 police and 100 demonstrators were injured.

Humphrey won the Democratic nomination for president, but the events in Chicago damaged his chances of victory. Republican nominee **Richard M. Nixon** promised to restore order to American society and bring "peace with honor" to Vietnam. Nixon won the election, receiving 301 electoral votes to Humphrey's 191. Southern voters gave 46 electoral votes to George Wallace, a segregationist candidate of the American Independent Party.

READING CHECK **Summarizing** Who were the candidates in the 1968 election? What was the outcome of the election?

The War under Nixon

President Nixon wanted to get U.S. troops out of Vietnam without creating the appearance of an American defeat. "I will not be the first president of the United States to lose a war," he told his fellow Republicans. With his national security adviser, **Henry Kissinger**, Nixon created a plan to pull U.S. troops from Vietnam and have the South Vietnamese Army take over all the fighting. This strategy was called **Vietnamization**.

Nixon began slowly withdrawing American troops from Vietnam. Without the knowledge of Congress or the American public, however, he approved bombing raids on Cambodia and Laos. The goal of these raids was to disrupt Vietcong supply lines. On April 30, 1970, Nixon announced that he had sent U.S. troops into Cambodia to attack Communist bases. "If, when the chips are down," he said, "the United States of America acts like a pitiful helpless giant, the forces of totalitarian anarchy will threaten free nations." Many Americans were furious. Rather than seeking peace, Nixon seemed to be expanding the war.

LINKING TO TODAY

The United States and Vietnam Today

Since the end of the Vietnam War, relations between the United States and Vietnam have slowly improved. In 1994 the United States lifted its long-standing trade embargo against Vietnam. In 1995 the former enemies officially established diplomatic relations. It became more common for American veterans and tourists to visit Vietnam.

According to a 2007 U.S. Census survey, more than a million Vietnamese immigrants now live in the United States. Vietnamese, Laotian, and Cambodian immigrants to the United States have made significant contributions to the communities they join, many of which are along the West and Gulf coasts.

GEOGRAPHY SKILLS **ANALYZING INFORMATION**

How did the relationship between Vietnam and the United States change from the end of the war to today?

© Houghton Mifflin Harcourt Publishing Company • Image Credits: (b), ©Paula Bronstein/Getty Images

The Election of 1972

Richard M. Nixon

George McGovern

Candidate (Political Party)	Electoral Vote	Popular Vote
Nixon (Republican)	520	47,165,234
McGovern (Democrat)	17	29,170,774

*One elector from Virginia cast his vote for John Hospers of California.

ANALYSIS SKILL **INTERPRETING CHARTS**

Location Why was the 1972 election considered a landslide victory for Nixon?

Student protests erupted on hundreds of college campuses. On May 4, at Kent State University in Ohio, the National Guard was called in to break up a demonstration. When the students refused to leave, guard troops used tear gas. Some students began throwing rocks at the National Guard. Several guard troops then opened fire into the crowd. Four students were killed. Horrified by the killings, antiwar activists expanded their protests all over the nation.

Antiwar feelings grew in June 1971 when the *New York Times* published secret government documents known as the Pentagon Papers. These documents revealed that U.S. officials had been lying to the American public about the progress of the war for years.

Public opinion was hardening against the war as the 1972 presidential race began. Democratic candidate George McGovern was an outspoken opponent of the war who promised voters an immediate U.S. troop withdrawal from Vietnam. "The doors of government will be opened, and that brutal war will be closed," he said.

McGovern hoped to appeal to young voters, many of whom would be voting for the first time. The **Twenty-sixth Amendment**, which was ratified in 1971, lowered the federal voting age from 21 to 18. McGovern did win a majority of these younger voters in 1972, but a majority of voters over 21 from both parties supported Nixon. Many of these voters feared that a McGovern victory would lead to greater disorder and protests. Nixon won by a landslide, receiving 520 electoral votes to McGovern's 17.

READING CHECK **Drawing Conclusions** Why did McGovern lose in a landslide?

The Vietnam War Ends

FOCUS ON READING
What is a purpose you can set for reading this section?

While Nixon was running for re-election in 1972, Henry Kissinger continued peace negotiations with the North Vietnamese. On January 27, 1973, the United States signed a cease-fire called the Paris Peace Accords with representatives of North Vietnam, South Vietnam, and the Vietcong. The United States agreed to withdraw all its troops from Vietnam. North Vietnam agreed to return all American prisoners of war. Despite the peace agreement, fighting broke out between North and South Vietnam

© Houghton Mifflin Harcourt Publishing Company • Image Credits: (tr), ©Bettmann/Corbis; (tl), ©Corbis in 1974. The United States refused to send troops back to South Vietnam.

In 1975 North Vietnam invaded the South. Thousands of panic-stricken American Embassy workers and South Vietnamese scrambled to evacuate Saigon. "The city was in flames," remembered one American worker. "And the Communists had the city surrounded with missiles . . . We realized that we were down to hours if not minutes." Helicopters lifted many people to ships waiting off the coast.

THE IMPACT TODAY

Today the U.S. government is more prepared to meet the needs of veterans with post-traumatic stress disorder. It offers counseling and information to vets and their families on how to deal with symptoms of trauma.

The Impact in Southeast Asia

The war ended when North Vietnamese forces captured Saigon in April 1975. Communist leaders created the Socialist Republic of Vietnam, uniting the former countries of North and South Vietnam. Hanoi became the capital, and Saigon was renamed Ho Chi Minh City.

Life remained extremely difficult in Vietnam. Cities, villages, forests, and farms had been destroyed. Some 250,000 South Vietnamese soldiers died in the war. About 1 million North Vietnamese and Vietcong soldiers were killed. The number of civilians killed is estimated at 2 million. Hundreds of thousands of former soldiers, officials, and other professionals were forced to live in "re-education camps." Another 1.5 million Vietnamese fled the country—about half of them settling in the United States.

Communist dictators took over Laos and Cambodia in 1975. The Cambodian Communist army, the Khmer Rouge, killed about 1.5 million people in a massive campaign to destroy supposed enemies of communism.

The Impact at Home

The Vietnam War carried heavy costs for the United States as well. Some 58,000 Americans were killed, and more than 300,000 were wounded.

Returning American soldiers were not always welcomed home as heroes as other war veterans had been. Some were insulted by antiwar protesters. As veterans struggled

BIOGRAPHY

Maya Ying Lin

1959–

Ohio-born Maya Lin was a 21-year-old architecture student when she designed the Vietnam Veterans Memorial. Her design was chosen from more than 1,400 proposed memorial designs. The memorial is a V-shaped black granite wall that lists the names of more than 58,000 dead and missing Americans. Explaining the design, Lin said, "It was important to me to be extremely honest; not be concerned with the politics of war, but the results. I wanted to bring the visitor a concrete realization of the great loss." The memorial is now one of the most-visited spots in Washington, D.C. Many visitors leave letters, flowers, or other objects at the memorial to honor loved ones.

Drawing Conclusions How does Lin's design achieve the goal she describes?

© Houghton Mifflin Harcourt Publishing Company • Image Credits: (b) ©James P. Blair/Corbis; (c) ©Richard Howard/Time Life Pictures/Getty Images to readjust to civilian life, many suffered from post-traumatic stress disorder. This condition includes symptoms such as nightmares and flashbacks to traumatic experiences.

Another effect of the war was that Americans had less trust in government officials, including the president. This led to passage in 1973 of the **War Powers Act**, which requires the president to get congressional approval before committing U.S. troops to an armed struggle.

Americans took a step toward healing the wounds of the war with the 1982 dedication of the **Vietnam Veterans Memorial**. Designed by Maya Ying Lin, the black granite memorial lists the names of dead or missing American soldiers.

READING CHECK **Summarizing** What were the long-term effects of the Vietnam War?

SUMMARY American society was deeply divided by the Vietnam War.

Causes and Effects of the Vietnam War

QUICK FACTS

Long-Term Causes
- Fear of Communist expansion
- U.S. support of South Vietnam's government

Immediate Causes
- Gulf of Tonkin incident
- Communist attacks against South Vietnam

Vietnam War

Effects
- Many thousands of Americans and millions of Vietnamese killed and injured
- Vietnam united as a Communist nation
- Political divisions created in the United States
- Increased Vietnamese immigration to the United States

Section 3 Assessment

hmhsocialstudies.com
ONLINE QUIZ

Reviewing Ideas, Terms, and People

1. a. **Identify** What was **Students for a Democratic Society**?
   b. **Elaborate** How did **hippies** express their disapproval of traditional culture?
   c. **Evaluate** How did the Republicans win the presidential election of 1968?
2. a. **Explain** What was **Vietnamization**?
   b. **Summarize** Why did the Pentagon Papers fuel antiwar feelings?
   c. **Elaborate** How did the **Twenty-sixth Amendment** affect the 1972 presidential election?
3. a. **Recall** How did the Vietnam War end?
   b. **Describe** What was the experience of veterans returning home from Vietnam?
   c. **Analyze** Do you think U.S. leaders made the right decision in signing the Paris Peace Accords? Why or why not?

Critical Thinking

4. **Identifying Effects** Review your notes on the causes of the end of the Vietnam War. Then copy the graphic organizer below and use it to list the effects of the end of the war.

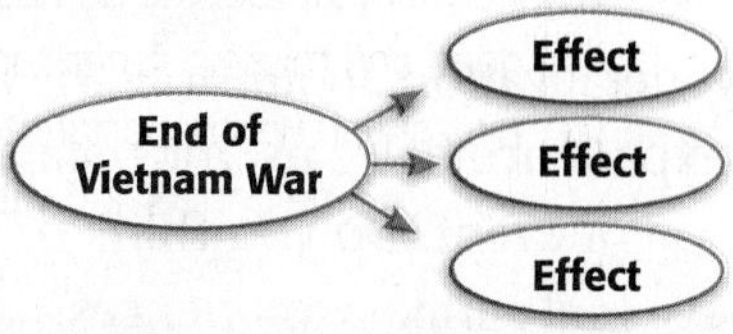

FOCUS ON WRITING

5. **Taking Notes on the Effects of the War** Take notes on the effects of the Vietnam War. How did it affect American politics? How did it affect American culture? How did it affect the American and Vietnamese people? How will you explain these effects to television viewers?

Using Primary Sources: Oral Histories

Define the Skill

An important part of history is understanding the lives and experiences of people in the past. Oral histories and personal memoirs are primary sources that help historians understand how people in the past acted and felt.

Oral histories are interviews in which people talk about events they participated in or witnessed. In personal memoirs, people write about their memories of such events. Both oral histories and personal memoirs are different from other kinds of primary sources because they can be written long after an event takes place. However, they both include descriptions of firsthand experiences.

Learn the Skill

Follow these guidelines to analyze oral histories and personal memoirs.

1. Identify the situation that the oral history or memoir describes.
2. Find the emotions or events that stand out in the description.
3. Make a generalization about how the individual's experience helps us understand the time period or event. Do you think other people might have had similar experiences?

In the following quotation, Diana Dwan Poole describes her experience serving in the Army Nurse Corps in Vietnam.

> "One of my rules was that nurses were not allowed to cry. The wounded and dying men in our care need our strength, I told them. We couldn't indulge in the luxury of our own feelings ... I was always straight with the soldiers. I would never say, 'Oh, you're going to be just fine,' if they were on their way out. I didn't lie."

Poole was a nurse in Vietnam. In this quotation, she describes working with other nurses and with wounded and dying patients. Her strength in the face of sadness and her honesty stand out.

Other nurses might have had experiences similar to Poole's. The nurses' situation—treating the wounded and the dying—also suggests the dangers soldiers faced.

Practice the Skill

Harold Bryant was a combat engineer in Vietnam. Read the primary source quotation from Bryant below.

> "Today I'm constantly thinking about the war. I walk down streets different. I look at places where individuals could hide. Maybe assault me or rob me or just harass me. I hear things that other people can't hear. My wife, she had a habit at one time of buying cheap watches and leaving them on top of the dresser. I could hear it ticking, so she would put it in a drawer. I could still hear it ticking."

1. What situation does Bryant describe?
2. Based on this description, how do you think Bryant felt at the time?
3. How can Bryant's experience help us better understand soldiers serving in Vietnam?

© Houghton Mifflin Harcourt Publishing Company

CHAPTER 14

Chapter Review

History's Impact
▶ **video series**
Review the video to answer the closing question:
How was the passing of the War Powers Act a reaction to the Vietnam War?

Visual Summary

QUICK FACTS

Use the visual summary below to help you review the main ideas of the chapter.

The spread of communism encouraged the United States to escalate the Vietnam War.

The Vietcong's superior knowledge of the geography helped them win the war.

Richard Nixon won the 1968 presidential election and pulled troops out of Vietnam.

Reviewing Vocabulary, Terms, and People

Identify the descriptions below with the correct term or person from the chapter.

1. The Cuban rebel who overthrew an unpopular dictator and established a Communist government
2. A barrier made of concrete and barbed wire that separated East Berlin and West Berlin
3. The commander of U.S. ground forces in Vietnam who developed the strategy of search-and-destroy missions
4. Supporters of the Vietnam War who believed winning the Cold War took priority over domestic reform
5. The Republican nominee who won the 1968 election for president of the United States
6. The amendment that lowered the voting age from 21 to 18

Comprehension and Critical Thinking

SECTION 1

7. **a. Recall** What is the Peace Corps?

   b. Sequence Describe the sequence of events that led to American astronauts landing on the moon in 1969.

   c. Evaluate How do you think the Cuban missile crisis would have ended had the United States pursued air strikes or an invasion of Cuba?

SECTION 2

8. **a. Define** What is guerrilla warfare?

   b. Describe How did the American military try to disrupt the Ho Chi Minh Trail?

   c. Predict Do you think Americans' opinions about the war would have been different had there been no television reporting? Explain your answer.

© Houghton Mifflin Harcourt Publishing Company

SECTION 3

9. a. **Identify** What was the War Powers Act?

   b. **Explain** What was Henry Kissinger's role in the Vietnam War?

   c. **Summarize** What long-term effects did the Vietnam War have on the United States?

Reviewing Themes

10. **Geography** How did the geography of Vietnam help the Vietcong?
11. **Geography** How did the geography of Vietnam affect American forces?

Reading Skills

Setting a Purpose *Use the Reading Skills taught in this chapter to answer the question about the reading selection below.*

Johnson Commits to Victory

Lyndon B. Johnson was determined to prevent Communists from taking over in South Vietnam. "We have the resources and the will to follow this course as long as it may take," Johnson said . . .

The Tonkin Gulf Resolution

In the summer of 1964, a naval skirmish led to a rapid expansion of U.S. involvement in Vietnam. On August 2, 1964, the USS *Maddox* reportedly exchanged gunfire with North Vietnamese torpedo boats in the Gulf of Tonkin, off the North Vietnamese coast . . .

12. Which of the following is an example of a purpose you could set for the passage above?
    a. Find out why the Vietnam War was fought.
    b. Find out Johnson's view of the Vietnam War.
    c. Find out when the Vietnam War ended.
    d. Find out what the Vietnam Veterans Memorial is.

Social Studies Skills 21st CENTURY

Using Primary Sources: Oral Histories *Read this passage from marine officer Philip Caputo. Then use the Social Studies Skills taught in this chapter to answer the question below.*

> "You simply trusted absolutely no one. I mean, from a 5-year-old kid to a 75-year-old woman."

13. How do you think Caputo felt about not being able to trust anyone? Do you think he felt safe? Why or why not?

Using the Internet 21st CENTURY

14. **Activity: Mapping the Terrain** Geography played a very important role in the Vietnam War. American soldiers struggled to fight against enemy soldiers who knew the land and were able to use that knowledge to their advantage. Through your online textbook, find information about the geography of Southeast Asia. Then create a map showing the area's various geographic features. Include notes on the map that describe some of the geographical challenges American soldiers faced.

hmhsocialstudies.com

Focus on Writing

15. **Presenting Your Newscast** Review your notes and prepare your newscast. You will have about five minutes for your newscast. Include several segments on different topics from the chapter. One could be an interview with a friend in the role of a soldier back from Vietnam, a government official, or an antiwar protester. You can also use pictures to illustrate the events you are reporting. Write your script and practice reading it before your presentation.

© Houghton Mifflin Harcourt Publishing Company

CHAPTER 14

Standardized Test Practice

DIRECTIONS: Read each question and write the letter of the best response.

1 The Berlin Wall separated

A Eastern Europe and Western Europe.
B East Berlin and West Berlin.
C West Germany and the Soviet Union.
D East Germany and the Soviet Union.

2 Ho Chi Minh was the leader of

A Laos.
B Cambodia.
C North Vietnam.
D South Vietnam.

3 President Johnson's policy of escalation called for

A a gradual withdrawal of U.S. troops from Vietnam.
B an immediate withdrawal of U.S. troops from Vietnam.
C a rapid buildup of U.S. forces in Vietnam.
D expanding the war into Laos and Cambodia.

4 During the war, the Vietcong and NVA fought using what tactics?

A quick, surprise assaults
B air strikes
C search-and-destroy missions
D blockades

5 Who were the Democratic and Republican candidates in the 1972 election?

A Lyndon Johnson and Richard Nixon
B Eugene McCarthy and John McCain
C Robert F. Kennedy and Henry Kissinger
D George McGovern and Richard M. Nixon

6 The Pentagon Papers revealed that

A the Bay of Pigs invasion was a disaster.
B U.S. officials had been lying about the progress of the war.
C the USS *Maddox* was attacked by North Vietnamese torpedo boats.
D the 1968 election was won by Richard Nixon.

7 What was the main purpose of the War Powers Act?

A It allowed President Kennedy to blockade Cuba.
B It allowed President Johnson to expand the U.S. role in Vietnam.
C It repealed the Tonkin Gulf Resolution.
D It limited the right of any president to commit troops to an armed struggle.

8 Read the following quote from Attorney General Robert F. Kennedy and use it to answer the question below.

> "On Tuesday morning, October 16, 1962, shortly after 9:00, President Kennedy called and asked me to come to the White House. He said only that we were facing great trouble. Shortly afterward, in his office, he told me that a U-2 had just finished a photographic mission and that the Intelligence Community had become convinced that Russia was placing missiles and atomic weapons in Cuba."
>
> —Robert F. Kennedy, *Thirteen Days: A Memoir of the Cuban Missile Crisis*

Document-Based Question What clues can you read that tell you how frightening the Cuban missile crisis was for Americans?

© Houghton Mifflin Harcourt Publishing Company

OCTOBER FURY:
THE CUBAN MISSILE CRISIS

The Cuban missile crisis was perhaps the most dangerous event of the Cold War period. For several days in October 1962, the United States and the Soviet Union stood on the brink of nuclear war. The crisis began when the Soviet Union sent weapons, including nuclear missiles, to Cuba. It deepened when the United States blockaded Cuba to prevent the Soviets from delivering more missiles. With Soviet ships sailing toward the blockade, a confrontation seemed inevitable. However, at the last moment, the Soviet ships turned back and war was averted.

Explore the development and resolution of the Cuban missile crisis online. You can find a wealth of information, video clips, primary sources, activities, and more at hmhsocialstudies.com.

© Houghton Mifflin Harcourt Publishing Company • Image Credits: (c) ©Bettmann/Corbis

CLICK THROUGH INTERACTIVITIES

hmhsocialstudies.com

Prelude to Crisis

Watch the video to learn about the buildup to the Cuban missile crisis.

Getting Ready for War

Watch the video to see how the missiles in Cuba created tension between the United States and the Soviet Union.

Crisis Averted?

Watch the video to see how the Cuban missile crisis brought the United States and the Soviet Union to the brink of nuclear war.

Lessons Learned

Watch the video to learn about the impact of the Cuban missile crisis.

© Houghton Mifflin Harcourt Publishing Company • Image Credits: (c), ©Bettmann/Corbis; (cr), Cold War Civil Defense Museum

21ST CENTURY

Assignment

Write a news article about the anniversary of either (1) the Nuremberg trials, (2) the Supreme Court's *Brown* v. *Board of Education* decision, or (3) the opening of the Vietnam Veterans Memorial.

A News Article

You have probably read many news articles in newspapers and magazines. News articles keep people informed about events in their communities, the nation, and the world. Sometimes they also remind people about important events from the past.

1. Prewrite

Considering Purpose and Audience

Remember that you are writing for people who have a choice about what to read. Your story must keep readers interested. How will you relate the topic of your story to their lives or emotions? At the same time, your story should give people information they need. In order to share information effectively, you must choose the most important details to include in your article.

TIP Brainstorming Brainstorm ways to interest people in the topic of your article. Take a few minutes to review what you know about the topic. Then write down as many questions, interesting points, and examples as you can.

Writing a Compelling Article

Make your article vivid and compelling by including

- **A short headline** showing what the article is about.
- **A "hook"**—an interesting fact or detail—to get the reader's attention at the beginning of the article.
- **Clear descriptions** of people and events.
- **Specific examples and quotations.**
- **Reasons** why the event is important.

2. Write

You can use this framework to help you write the first draft of your article.

A Writer's Framework

Introduction
- Grab your reader's attention with a strong headline.
- Begin with a striking detail or quotation for a hook.
- Introduce the event and its importance to people today.

Body
- Describe what happened, who was involved, and where, when, and why the event took place.
- Explain the significance of the event.
- Use details to connect the event to readers' lives or emotions.

Conclusion
- Finish any incomplete thoughts.
- End with a quotation or example that sums up the main point of the article.

© Houghton Mifflin Harcourt Publishing Company

3. Evaluate and Revise

Evaluating

Use these questions to discover ways to improve your news article.

Evaluation Questions for a News Article

- Do you begin with a strong headline and hook?
- Do you introduce the event and its importance to people today?
- Do you describe what happened, who was involved, and where, when, and why the event took place?
- Do you explain the significance of the event?
- Do you use details to connect the event to readers' lives or emotions?
- Do you end with a quotation or example that sums up the main point of the article?

TIP **Vivid Writing** Make sentences more interesting by using vivid words and images. Use strong words that help readers create a mental picture.

Revising

Newspapers and magazines often have limited space. News articles must express a sharply focused idea briefly. To make sure that your article does this, read each sentence carefully. Each sentence should

- Be clear and to-the-point.
- Contain no unnecessary words or phrases.
- Use only precise words. Eliminate words such as *very* unless they add meaning to the sentence.

4. Proofread and Publish

Proofreading

Read your essay aloud to catch any mistakes in your spelling or grammar. If something looks or sounds wrong, mark it. Come back to it later to correct the mistake. This is also a good strategy for identifying and fixing awkward sentences.

Publishing

Exchange articles with a classmate who wrote about a different topic. Did you learn from your classmate's article? Did you find it interesting? Put together a class newspaper that includes all the articles and headlines. Add pictures and display the newspaper on a bulletin board.

5. Practice and Apply

Use the steps and strategies in this workshop to write your news article.

© Houghton Mifflin Harcourt Publishing Company

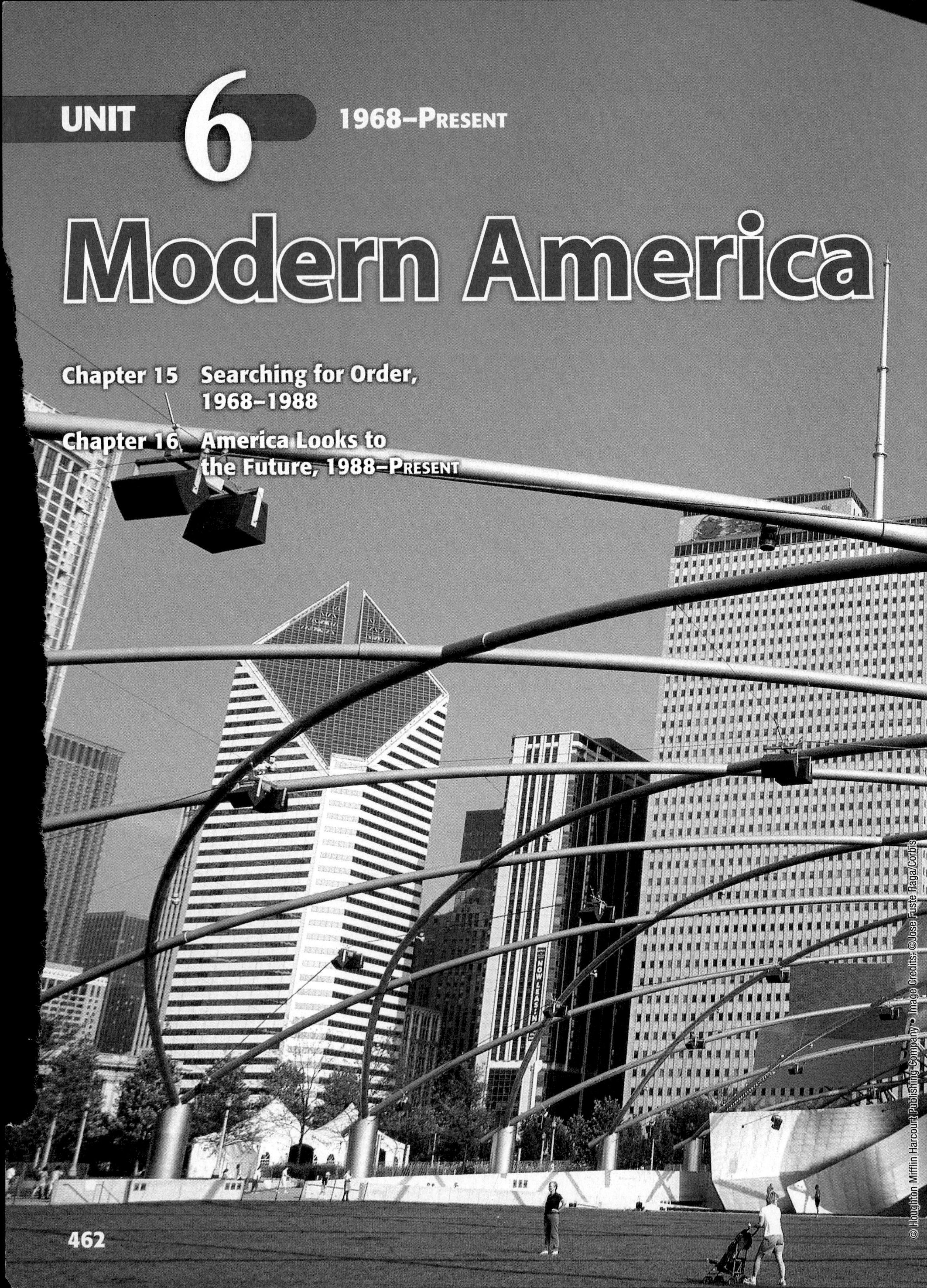

UNIT 6 1968–PRESENT

Modern America

© Houghton Mifflin Harcourt Publishing Company • Image Credits: ©Jose Fuste Raga/Corbis

What You Will Learn...

By the end of the Vietnam War, Americans were living in a society very different from previous eras. Economic and political changes continue today. People are choosing new kinds of jobs in new industries, and the role of the United States in international affairs is increasing. Rapid advances in technology will also affect the future of American society. As the population becomes larger and more diverse, new solutions are needed to provide all Americans with equality and opportunity.

Explore the Art

Millennium Park in Chicago was designed to be an exciting public place for the people of the large city to enjoy. How might the people of Chicago use the park?

© Houghton Mifflin Harcourt Publishing Company • Image Credits: ©Jose Fuste Raga/Corbis

CHAPTER 15 1968–1988

Searching for Order

Essential Question How did the presidencies of the 1970s and 1980s deal with the Cold War?

ALABAMA COURSE OF STUDY

8 Describe how the United States' role in the Cold War influenced domestic and international events.
- Recognizing how the Cold War conflict manifested itself through sports.
- Identifying how Cold War tensions resulted in armed conflict.
- Assessing effects of the end of the Cold War Era.

9 Critique major social and cultural changes in the United States since World War II.
- Describing the changing role of women in United States' society and how it affected the family unit.

10 Analyze changing economic priorities and cycles of economic expansion and contraction for their impact on society since World War II.
- Identifying policies and programs that had an economic impact on society since World War II.

12 Evaluate significant political issues and policies of presidential administrations since World War II.
- Identifying domestic policies that shaped the United States since World War II.
- Recognizing domestic issues that shaped the United States since World War II.
- Identifying issues of foreign affairs that shaped the United States since World War II.
- Explaining how conflict in the Middle East impacted life in the United States since World War II.

Focus on Writing

Historical Novel Suppose you have decided to write a historical novel set during the 1970s or 1980s. You want your story to bring one or more of the major events of this time period to life for readers. As you read this chapter, you will take notes on the important people and conflicts of this time. You will choose which historical figures and events to include in your story. Then you will write the first page of your novel.

United States

1968 Richard Nixon is elected president.

1969

World

1969 Golda Meir becomes prime minister of Israel.

Image Credits: (t), ©Wally McNamee/Corbis; (b), ©Bettmann/Corbis

© Houghton Mifflin Harcourt Publishing Company

The nation's 200th birthday was celebrated on July 4, 1976.

HISTORY

Watergate Ends Nixon's Presidency

hmhsocialstudies.com VIDEO

1970 America celebrates its first Earth Day.

1973 Egypt and Syria attack Israel.

1974 Nixon resigns the presidency. Gerald Ford is sworn in.

1975 South Vietnam surrenders to North Vietnam.

1976 Jimmy Carter is elected president.

1979 The Three Mile Island accident creates doubts about nuclear energy.

1979 The Soviet Union invades Afghanistan.

1985 Ronald Reagan is sworn in to his second term as president.

1970 — 1975 — 1980 — 1985

Image Credits: (t), ©Wally McNamee/Corbis; (cr), ©Tim Shaffer/AP/Wide World Photos (cl), ©Bill Pierce/Getty Images; (br), AP Photo/Herve Merliac

© Houghton Mifflin Harcourt Publishing Company

Reading Social Studies

Economics | Geography | Politics | Society and Culture | Science and Technology

Focus on Themes In this chapter, you will learn about issues faced by several modern presidents. You will also read about crises in the **economy** and in **politics** that changed the way Americans viewed their role as a nation. Finally, you will learn about American society in the 1970s.

Summarizing

Focus on Reading After reading a large amount of information, you can summarize it into a shorter amount that is easier for you to understand.

Understanding Summarizing Using the ideas and information presented in a book can be easier if you summarize what the author is saying. When you summarize, you can use some of the key ideas and words to write your own sentences that explain the information. When you write a summary, some details can be left out.

Read the following passage and its summary. Notice which details the author chose to include and which to leave out.

The American population was changing in the 1970s. Throughout American history, most immigrants to the United States had come from Europe. Beginning in the 1970s, however, a majority of new immigrants came from the Americas and Asia. This pattern continues today.

Summary:

The population immigrating to the United States began changing during the 1970s. Now the majority of immigrants come from Latin America and Asia.

This passage contains most of the same information but is shorter. Not all of the information is included.

© Houghton Mifflin Harcourt Publishing Company

You Try It!

As you read the following passage, look for information that is important enough to go in a summary.

> "Are you better off than you were four years ago?" That was the question Republican candidate Ronald Reagan asked voters during the 1980 presidential campaign. Millions of voters answered "No," giving Reagan an easy victory over President Carter. Reagan won 489 electoral votes to Carter's 49. On January 20, 1981—the day of Reagan's inauguration—Iran finally released the American hostages after 444 days in captivity.

After you read the passage, answer the following questions.

1. Do you think the campaign slogan from the passage above is essential information for a summary of the election?

2. Do you think the number of electoral votes should be included in your summary?

3. Write a two-sentence summary of the passage above.

As you read this chapter, practice summarizing the information from several paragraphs.

Key Terms and People

Chapter 15

Section 1
stagflation
Organization of Petroleum Exporting Countries
realpolitik
Strategic Arms Limitation Talks
détente
Watergate
Gerald Ford
pardon

Section 2
affirmative action
Rachel Carson
Jimmy Carter
human rights
apartheid
sanctions
Camp David Accords
Iran hostage crisis

Section 3
Ronald Reagan
supply-side economics
deficit
Iran-Contra affair
Mikhail Gorbachev

Academic Vocabulary

In this chapter, you will learn the following academic words:
consequences
implications

© Houghton Mifflin Harcourt Publishing Company

SECTION 1

Nixon's Presidency and Watergate

What You Will Learn...

Main Ideas

1. Americans faced domestic challenges, including an energy and economic crisis.
2. Nixon's foreign policy led to improved relations with Communist powers.
3. The Watergate scandal forced Nixon to resign.
4. Gerald Ford became president upon Nixon's resignation and faced many challenges.

The Big Idea

Richard Nixon's policies helped ease Cold War tensions before the Watergate scandal brought down his presidency.

Key Terms and People

stagflation
Organization of Petroleum Exporting Countries
realpolitik
Strategic Arms Limitation Talks
détente
Watergate
Gerald Ford
pardon

hmhsocialstudies.com
TAKING NOTES

Use the graphic organizer online to take notes on facts about Nixon's domestic policy, foreign policy, and the Watergate scandal.

If YOU were there...

You experienced a decade of conflict and change in the 1960s. You were a witness to major events in the civil rights movement, and you lived through frightening Cold War crises. You saw leaders assassinated and astronauts walk on the moon. You have some friends who fought in Vietnam and others who led antiwar protests.

Do you think the United States is now headed in the right direction? Why or why not?

BUILDING BACKGROUND Protests over the Vietnam War led to bitter divisions among Americans in the 1960s. When Republican Richard Nixon ran for president in 1968, he said he would work to restore law and order to American society. Nixon won a close election over Democratic candidate Hubert Humphrey.

Domestic Challenges

As president, Richard Nixon promised to work on behalf of Americans who opposed protests and supported his plan for ending the war. Nixon called these Americans the Silent Majority. He criticized student protesters and called on them to stop their activities. He did not believe Americans should leave Vietnam quickly.

New Federalism

Nixon also had a new plan for government. Nixon knew that his supporters blamed the federal government for setting high taxes and interfering in citizens' lives. He proposed a plan called the New Federalism, which would limit the power of the federal government. His policies represented a major shift in direction from Lyndon Johnson's Great Society ideas. Under Nixon's plan, grants of money from the federal government went directly to state and local governments, who decided how to spend the money. This plan reflected Nixon's conservatism, or a belief in limiting the involvement of government in citizens' lives.

The Energy Crisis

GAS SHORTAGE!
Sales Limited to
10 GALS. OF GAS.
PER CUSTOMER

CONNECT TO ECONOMICS

Rising oil prices in the early 1970s had a major impact on the U.S. economy. Because oil was more expensive, the cost of everything made from oil—gasoline, heating oil, electricity, and other key products—also shot up. These higher prices led to rising inflation.

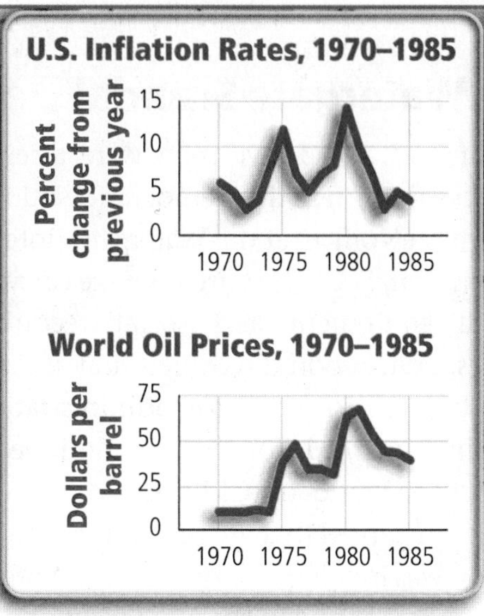
U.S. Inflation Rates, 1970–1985
Percent change from previous year
15
10
5
0
1970 1975 1980 1985
World Oil Prices, 1970–1985
Dollars per barrel
75
50
25
0
1970 1975 1980 1985

ANALYSIS SKILL **ANALYZING GRAPHS**

Comparing How were trends in oil prices and inflation similar during the 1970s?

President Nixon promised to reduce welfare spending and to restore law and order. He supported policies that gave more power to police and to the courts.

His political philosophy affected the Supreme Court as well. As president, he appointed four new justices. Many Court decisions soon began to reflect a more conservative point of view.

Nixon did not push for new civil rights legislation. He believed that the government had done enough in the 1960s, saying, "The laws have caught up with our consciences."

Economic Troubles

Nixon faced the difficult economic challenge of so-called **stagflation**—the economic condition of combined stagnant economic growth and high inflation. From 1967 to 1974, rising prices reduced the purchasing power of the U.S. dollar by more than 30 percent.

One cause of inflation was the rising cost of oil. By the early 1970s, the United States was importing about one-third of its oil. Much of this oil was purchased from Middle Eastern nations that were members of the **Organization of Petroleum Exporting Countries**, or OPEC. This group worked to control the production and sale of oil to keep prices high.

THE IMPACT TODAY

Today about half of U.S. oil imports comes from OPEC countries.

Most OPEC countries were Arab countries that had been opposed to the creation of the Jewish state of Israel. On October 6, 1973, the Jewish holy day of Yom Kippur, Egypt and Syria attacked Israel in what would become known as the Yom Kippur War. The United States sent military supplies to help Israel.

Arab members of OPEC responded angrily to support for Israel by declaring an embargo, or ban, on oil sales to the United States. The oil embargo and soaring oil prices caused an energy crisis. This worsened an already weak U.S. economy.

READING CHECK **Identifying Cause and Effect** What was one cause of inflation?

© Houghton Mifflin Harcourt Publishing Company • Image Credits: (t) ©Owen Franken/Corbis

Nixon's Foreign Policy

As the energy crisis demonstrated, international events could have a serious impact on life in the United States. Henry Kissinger, a German American professor who became Nixon's senior foreign policy adviser, helped Nixon develop a new approach to foreign policy. Nixon's foreign policy decisions would be based on practical American interests, not on moral or political ideals. This approach was known as **realpolitik**, the German term meaning "actual politics." Nixon credited his realpolitik strategies with bringing an end to the Vietnam War by using political pressure from the Soviet Union and China to convince the North Vietnamese to negotiate.

Realpolitik was controversial. In several Latin American countries, for example, the United States backed harsh military governments because they were friendly to U.S. interests.

In the ongoing Cold War rivalries with China and the Soviet Union, the realpolitik approach led to important changes. American officials had long feared China and the Soviet Union would work together to spread communism. But by 1970, it was clear that these two Communist powers had become bitter rivals. Nixon believed it was in America's interest to widen this split and to improve U.S. relations with both Communist powers.

Nixon first turned his attention to China. He lifted restrictions on trade and travel and opened negotiations with its leaders. In 1972 Nixon became the first U.S. president to make an official visit to China. Newscasts showed Nixon and Chinese leader Mao Zedong shaking hands and trading jokes.

Nixon's trip led to improved U.S.–China relations. It also caught the attention of Soviet leaders, who became more open to talks with the United States. In May 1972 Nixon flew to Moscow, where he and Soviet leader Leonid Brezhnev participated in the **Strategic Arms Limitation Talks** (SALT). These talks led to a treaty limiting each country's nuclear weapons. The SALT agreement opened a period of **détente** (day-TAHNT), or less hostile relations, between the United States and the Soviet Union. Détente brought economic benefits, as the Soviets began buying millions of tons of grain from American farmers.

READING CHECK **Supporting a Point of View** Do you think realpolitik was a good strategy? Why or why not?

The Watergate Scandal

On June 17, 1972, five men were arrested while breaking in to the Democratic National Committee's offices at the Watergate Hotel in Washington, D.C. The burglars were carrying camera equipment and secret recording devices. Police soon discovered that some of them had ties to the Nixon administration. One had worked for the Committee to Re-elect the President (CRP).

Nixon denied that anyone in his administration was involved in the Watergate break-in. He went on to win the 1972 election in a landslide. But early in Nixon's second term,

Watergate Scandal

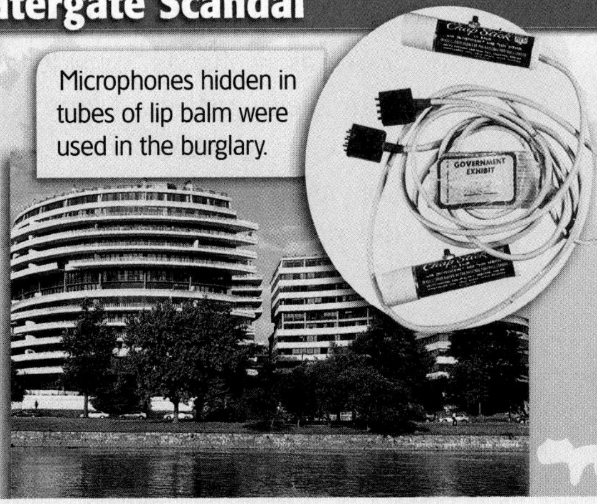

Microphones hidden in tubes of lip balm were used in the burglary.

On May 28, 1972, five men burglarized the Democratic National Committee headquarters in the Watergate Hotel, shown here. They took pictures of files and bugged telephones. The burglars returned for more information on June 17 and were arrested.

the seemingly minor break-in exploded into a massive political scandal that became known as **Watergate**.

Investigating the Break-in

Did Nixon administration officials have anything to do with the Watergate break-in? Reporters Bob Woodward and Carl Bernstein investigated that question in a series of articles in the *Washington Post*. Key figures in the Nixon administration refused to talk to the reporters. Then Woodward was contacted by a government official who had inside information on the Watergate investigation. To protect the identity of their source, Woodward called him by a secret codename. With the informant's information, Woodward and Bernstein began publishing stories about illegal activities by Nixon administration officials. The stories revealed that the CRP had hidden illegal campaign contributions and spread false rumors about Democratic candidates. They also presented evidence that officials in the Nixon White House were trying to cover-up the facts of the Watergate break-in.

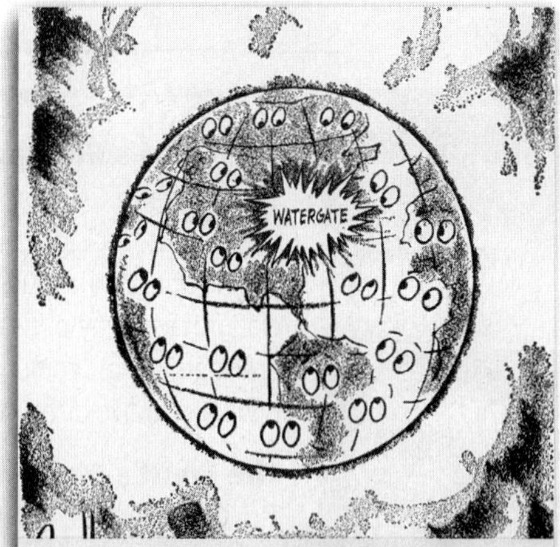

Americans and the rest of the world watched the Watergate drama unfold through the intense media coverage of the scandal.

A Senate committee led by Senator Sam Ervin launched its own investigation of Watergate. When the committee began televised hearings in May 1973, millions of Americans tuned in. The most damaging witness was former White House attorney John Dean, who testified that Nixon was personally involved in the Watergate cover-up. Dean could not prove this, however. Then another witness revealed that Nixon had tape-recorded almost all of his Oval Office conversations.

THE IMPACT TODAY

The identity of the *Post's* informant remained confidential for more than 30 years. In 2005 W. Mark Felt, second-in-command at the FBI during Watergate, revealed that he was the inside source for information.

Washington Post reporters soon linked the break-in to the presidential re-election campaign. A White House cover-up began.

The Senate formed a committee to investigate the break-in and possible cover-up. Its hearings (shown above) were televised.

Faced with impeachment for an illegal cover-up of the break-in, Nixon resigned. He was later pardoned by President Gerald Ford.

ANALYSIS SKILL **ANALYZING INFORMATION**

Why was Nixon threatened with impeachment by the House?

© Houghton Mifflin Harcourt Publishing Company • Image Credits: (inset) ©Bettmann/Corbis; (bl) ©Alex Webb/Magnum Photos; (t) The Granger Collection, New York

Supreme Court Decisions

United States v. Nixon (1974)

Background of the Case During the Watergate investigation, a special prosecutor asked for the tapes of President Nixon's Oval Office conversations. Nixon claimed that he did not have to obey court orders to turn over the tapes because of executive privilege. On July 8, 1974, the case went before the Supreme Court.

The Court's Ruling

The Supreme Court announced its unanimous decision on July 24. It stated, "the legitimate [lawful] needs of the judicial process may outweigh presidential privilege." Nixon could not use executive privilege to avoid the subpoenas.

The Court's Reasoning

The Court decided to hear the case more quickly than most cases because of its importance to the functioning of government and the interest of the American public. The Supreme Court ruled that to claim executive privilege a president would have to show a compelling national security reason. Nixon had no such reason for refusing to hand over the tapes.

Why It Matters

The Supreme Court ruling showed that, despite their unique and important position, presidents do have to obey the law. It also showed that the government could use the powers defined in the Constitution to prevent one branch from becoming too powerful. Less than a week later, the House Judiciary Committee voted to impeach Nixon.

ANALYSIS SKILL **ANALYZING INFORMATION**

1. How is this case an example of the checks and balances system?
2. What do you think was the most important impact of this Supreme Court decision?

Committee members asked Nixon to allow them to listen to the tapes. Nixon refused to hand the tapes over to a special prosecutor, claiming executive privilege—a president's right to keep information secret for reasons of national security. In July 1974 the Supreme Court ordered Nixon to turn over the tapes. The recordings proved that Nixon had directed the Watergate cover-up and lied about it to Congress and the public.

While this investigation was unfolding, Vice President Spiro Agnew resigned amid charges that he had taken bribes and failed to pay taxes. Nixon appointed Michigan congressman **Gerald Ford** as vice president.

ACADEMIC VOCABULARY
consequences the effects of a particular event or events

Nixon Resigns

After studying the case, the House Judiciary Committee recommended impeachment. Judiciary Committee member Barbara Jordan of Texas explained why she thought Nixon should be impeached:

> "My faith in the Constitution is whole, it is complete, it is total. And I am not going to sit here and be an idle spectator to the . . . destruction of the Constitution."
>
> —Barbara Jordan, in a speech before Congress, 1974

On July 27, 1974, the committee approved its first article of impeachment, charging Nixon with obstruction of justice. Within the next week, two more articles were approved by the committee, one for the abuse of power and one for contempt of Congress.

On August 8, 1974, Nixon appeared on national television and announced, "I shall resign the presidency effective at noon tomorrow." He became the first president in American history to resign from office. Gerald Ford was sworn in as president on August 9.

One of the consequences of Watergate was that many Americans lost faith in government officials. In a poll taken in 1974, just 36 percent of Americans said they trusted the government. Others, however, saw a more positive side of Watergate. Senator Sam Ervin viewed the hearings and Nixon's resignation as evidence that the government was able to rid itself of corruption. "Watergate . . . proved our Constitution works," he said.

READING CHECK **Sequencing** What events led to Nixon's resignation?

Ford as President

Vice President Gerald Ford became the first modern president to hold the office without being elected to it. Ford lost some public support when he granted Richard Nixon a **pardon**, or freedom from punishment. He declared it was best for the nation that Nixon not be tried for his crime because he would be "cruelly and excessively penalized" and "ugly passions would again be aroused [stirred]."

Adding to Ford's difficulties, oil prices and unemployment remained high, and stagflation continued. The United States also had an increasing trade deficit, an imbalance in which a country imports more than it exports.

Arguing that inflation was the main cause of the economic troubles, Ford began a campaign called Whip Inflation Now (WIN). WIN encouraged people to save money and businesses to hold down wages and prices. Ford's plan met with resistance from many members of Congress, who wanted to increase spending to help the poor and unemployed. In 1975 Ford and Congress began to compromise. Still, inflation and unemployment remained high.

A U.S. Marine changes the official presidential photograph from one of Nixon to one of Ford.

READING CHECK **Evaluating** Do you think President Ford was right to pardon Nixon?

SUMMARY Gerald Ford became president after the Watergate scandal ended Nixon's presidency.

Section 1 Assessment

hmhsocialstudies.com ONLINE QUIZ

Reviewing Ideas, Terms, and People

1. a. **Describe** What challenges did the United States face during President Nixon's terms of office?
   b. **Make Inferences** Why do you think the **Organization of Petroleum Exporting Countries** objected to U.S. support for Israel?
2. a. **Identify** Who was Henry Kissinger?
   b. **Contrast** How was **realpolitik** different from other foreign policy approaches?
   c. **Draw Conclusions** Why do you think improved U.S.–China relations made the Soviets more open to talks with the United States?
3. a. **Recall** What was the **Watergate** scandal?
   b. **Explain** Why were President Nixon's tapes important?
   c. **Elaborate** Why do you think President Nixon decided to resign?
4. a. **Describe** How did **Gerald Ford** become president of the United States?
   b. **Predict** Do you think WIN was effective in helping the economy?

Critical Thinking

5. **Sequencing** Review your notes on Richard Nixon's presidency. Then copy the graphic organizer below and use it to list, in order, events in his presidency.

Event	Date

Focus on Writing

6. **Describing Major Events** Take notes on Nixon's domestic policy, Cold War strategy, and the Watergate scandal. What were the major events of this time period? Who were the major public figures involved, and what roles did they play? Which of these events and people do you find the most interesting?

© Houghton Mifflin Harcourt Publishing Company • Image Credits: (t), ©AP/Wide World Photos

SECTION 2

America in the 1970s

What You Will Learn...

Main Ideas

1. American society debated key social issues during the 1970s.
2. Jimmy Carter was elected president in 1976.
3. Carter had successes as well as failures in foreign policy during his administration.

The Big Idea

Americans faced major challenges both at home and around the world in the 1970s.

Key Terms and People

affirmative action
Rachel Carson
Jimmy Carter
human rights
apartheid
sanctions
Camp David Accords
Iran hostage crisis

hmhsocialstudies.com
TAKING NOTES

Use the graphic organizer online to take notes on new government policies in the 1970s.

If YOU were there...

It is July 4, 1976. Today the entire nation is celebrating the 200th anniversary of the signing of the Declaration of Independence. As you sit with your family watching a spectacular fireworks show, you think about the challenges this country has faced throughout its history. You think about the economic and foreign policy challenges facing Americans right now.

What are your hopes for the nation's future?

BUILDING BACKGROUND The celebration of the country's bicentennial, or 200th birthday, was a much-needed break from worries about political scandals, economic troubles, and Cold War dangers. This was a moment of renewal and hope—though many Americans still disagreed about how the country should move forward.

Social Issues of the 1970s

The American population was changing in the 1970s. Throughout American history, most immigrants to the United States had come from Europe. Beginning in the 1970s, however, a majority of new immigrants came from the Americas and Asia. This pattern continues today. Another change was that the birthrate, or number of births per 1,000 people, was declining. By 1970 Americans 65 and older became one of the fastest-growing population groups.

As the population grew and changed, American society faced the challenges of how to balance the views of all Americans. You read earlier that the Equal Rights Amendment caused nationwide debate in the 1970s. Although the ERA was not ratified, the women's movement did make important gains. A 1972 federal law known as Title IX banned discrimination on the basis of sex in educational programs that receive federal funds. The number of women admitted to medical and law schools climbed quickly. Title IX also opened the door for many more women to participate in

© Houghton Mifflin Harcourt Publishing Company

college sports and earn athletic scholarships. In 1973 the Supreme Court legalized abortion in the case *Roe* v. *Wade*.

In the 1970s Americans also debated **affirmative action**, the practice of giving special consideration to nonwhites or women to make up for past discrimination. Supporters of affirmative action argued that it was needed to improve educational and job opportunities for minorities and women. Opponents insisted that any race- or gender-based preferences were unfair.

Many African Americans benefited from new opportunities in the 1970s. For example, the number of African Americans attending college in 1976 was four times higher than it had been a decade earlier. Many people credited affirmative action programs with this increase.

The environment also became a major issue in the 1970s. In her book *Silent Spring*, biologist **Rachel Carson** brought attention to the dangers of pollution. She explained how chemicals used to kill insects travel through the food chain and affect people's health.

> "Man, however much he may like to pretend the contrary, is part of nature. Can he escape a pollution that is now so thoroughly distributed throughout our world?"
>
> —Rachel Carson, *Silent Spring*

First published in 1962, *Silent Spring* helped inspire a nationwide movement to improve the environment. Environmentalists in the United States celebrated the first Earth Day on April 22, 1970. "Earth Day is to remind each person of his [or her] . . . equal responsibility . . . to preserve and improve the Earth," explained activists.

Congress passed new laws to limit the release of pollutants. The Environmental Protection Agency (EPA) was established in 1970 to enforce these laws. As protections increased, debates sprung up about how to balance business interests with environmental concerns.

READING CHECK **Comparing and Contrasting** How are Title IX and affirmative action similar and different?

Issues of the 1970s

Environmental protection, women's rights, and affirmative action were among the major issues of the 1970s.

Activists brought the environment to the forefront of national debate, urging legislation and individual action to help protect the Earth.

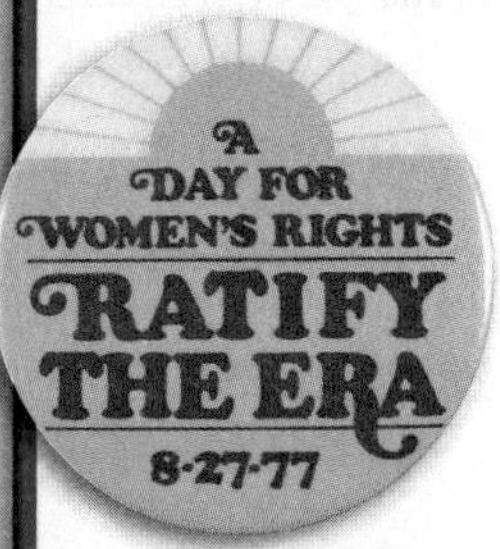

Supporters of the Equal Rights Amendment urged states to ratify the amendment they believed would ensure equal protection to women under the Constitution.

African Americans over 25 with a 4-Year College Degree, 1960–2000

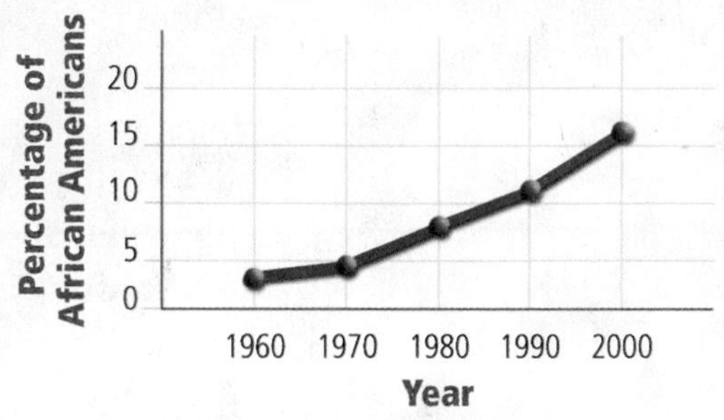

Affirmative action helped African Americans and other minorities gain access to universities and certain jobs but also created much debate.

FOCUS ON READING

Summarize the information in this paragraph.

Carter Elected

To oppose Republican Gerald Ford in the 1976 presidential election Democrats nominated **Jimmy Carter**, a little-known former governor of Georgia. The Democrats purposely chose a candidate who was untouched by the recent scandals. Carter knew that the Vietnam War and Watergate had badly shaken American voters' trust in government. "I will never lie to you," he told voters.

Carter defeated Ford in a close election. As president, Carter wanted to show a new spirit of informality and openness at the White House. On inauguration day, he and his family broke with tradition by walking to the inauguration rather than riding in a limousine.

While Americans seemed to respond positively to his straightforward style, Carter faced serious challenges. High unemployment and inflation continued. The ongoing energy crisis also kept oil prices high. Many Americans became frustrated with the president's inability to solve these problems.

Although Democrats controlled Congress, Carter had a hard time convincing members to support his proposals. For example, Carter proposed a national energy plan that called for conservation and the use of alternative fuels such as solar energy. Congress demanded changes to the complex plan. The plan was never fully enacted.

One way Carter hoped to decrease the country's dependence on imported oil was by expanding the use of nuclear power. But an accident at the Three Mile Island nuclear power plant in Pennsylvania caused new worries about the safety of nuclear energy. On March 28, 1979, a reactor core at Three Mile Island overheated, and the plant released a small amount of radioactive gas into the air. This frightening incident damaged the nuclear power industry, and the federal government put in place a ban on building new reactors.

READING CHECK **Drawing Conclusions** How did the Three Mile Island incident affect Carter's energy plan?

Carter and Foreign Policy

President Carter rejected Nixon's realpolitik approach to foreign policy. He argued that "fairness, not force, should lie at the heart of our dealings with the nations of the world."

The Election of 1976

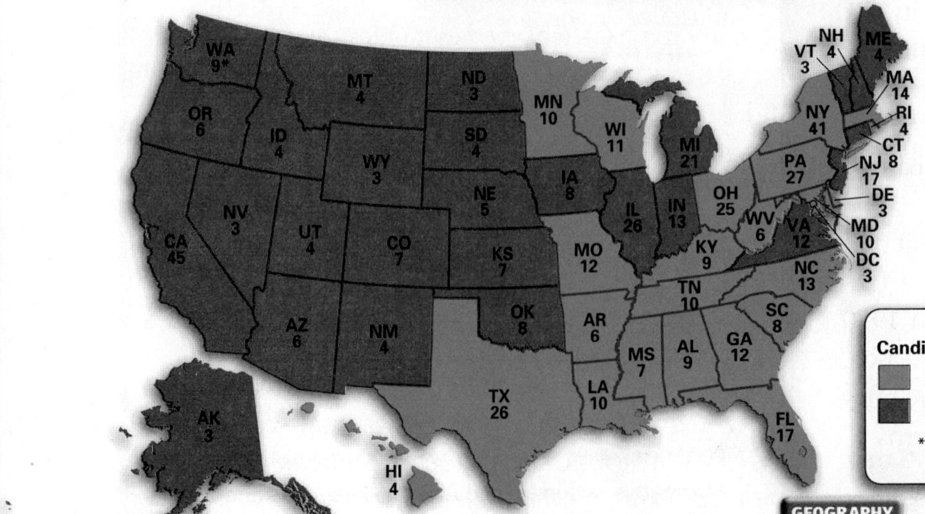

Jimmy Carter

Gerald Ford

Candidate	Party	Electoral Vote	Popular Vote	% Popular Vote
Carter	Democrat	297	40,828,929	50.1
Ford	Republican	240	39,148,940	48.0

*One electoral vote was cast for Ronald Reagan.

Source: *World Almanac and Book of Facts, 2004*

GEOGRAPHY SKILLS **INTERPRETING MAPS**

Place Which areas of the country did Carter win in 1976?

© Houghton Mifflin Harcourt Publishing Company • Image Credits: (all) White House Collection, copyright White House Historical Association

Primary Source

HISTORIC DOCUMENT

The Camp David Accords

During the long and often bitter Camp David negotiations, Carter worked hard to keep Israel's Menachem Begin and Egypt's Anwar el-Sadat from walking out. He later wrote about one moment when the talks nearly broke down.

"Within a few minutes Sadat announced angrily that a stalemate [standstill] had been reached. He saw no reason for the discussions to continue. As far as he was concerned, they were over . . . They [Sadat and Begin] were moving toward the door, but I got in front of them to partially block the way. I urged them not to break off their talks, to give me another chance to use my influence and analysis, to have confidence in me. Begin agreed readily. I looked straight at Sadat; finally, he nodded his head. They left without speaking to each other."

Leaders Anwar el-Sadat (left), Jimmy Carter, and Menachem Begin reached a peace agreement for the Middle East in the Camp David Accords.

ANALYSIS SKILL **ANALYZING PRIMARY SOURCES**

Why do you think Begin and el-Sadat agreed to continue their negotiations?

Changing Policies

Carter favored policies that promoted **human rights**—the basic rights and freedoms of all people. He reduced U.S. aid to several former allies that committed human rights violations. In South Africa, Carter hoped to pressure the government into ending **apartheid**, a system of laws requiring racial segregation. He called for **sanctions**, or economic penalties, to encourage reform.

Carter's approach to foreign policy had effects in Latin America as well. Many Latin Americans resented previous U.S. interference in their countries. American control of the Panama Canal stood as a symbol of power in the region. In 1977 Carter signed treaties that would transfer control of the canal to Panama by the year 2000.

Carter had less success improving relations with the Soviet Union. Détente broke down when he criticized the Soviet Union for committing human rights abuses. Then in 1979 the Soviet Union invaded Afghanistan. Carter responded by breaking off arms-control talks and refusing to allow U.S. athletes to participate in the 1980 Summer Olympics in Moscow.

The Middle East

While Cold War tensions increased, Carter worked to ease tensions in the Middle East. Egypt and Israel had been in conflict for 30 years. In 1978 Carter invited Egyptian president Anwar el-Sadat and Israeli prime minister Menachem Begin (men-AHK-uhm BAY-guhn) to the presidential retreat at Camp David, Maryland. After 13 days of meetings, the two leaders reached a peace agreement called the **Camp David Accords**, considered by many to be Carter's greatest achievement.

Carter also experienced disaster in the Middle East. Since the 1950s, the United States had supported the pro–American shah, or king, of Iran. Many Iranians resented the shah's reform efforts and the country's shift from a traditional and agricultural society to a more urban and industrial one. The government severely punished its opponents and controlled all political participation. Many members of the opposition supported the views of Islamic spiritual leader Ruhollah Khomeini, who had been forced to leave the country because of his criticisms of the shah's policies. In 1979 Khomeini's supporters drove the shah out of Iran, and a month later, Khomeini took control of the government. On November 4, a group of Iranian students attacked the U.S. embassy in Tehran, the capital of Iran, seizing about 90 American hostages. The **Iran hostage crisis** lasted for more than a year.

In the early days of the crisis, some hostages were released. These remaining hostages were often blindfolded and beaten by their Iranian captors. Carter ended Iranian oil imports and froze Iranian assets in American banks. After a failed rescue attempt in April 1980, many Americans lost confidence in Carter's leadership.

READING CHECK **Making Generalizations** Overall, do you think President Carter's foreign policy was effective? Why or why not?

SUMMARY President Carter's policies included both successes and failures.

Hostages Released

Approximately 52 Americans were held hostage by Iranian militants during the Iran hostage crisis. The men and women were kept blindfolded by their captors. After 444 days in captivity, the Americans were released.

How do these photographs show the experiences of the hostages?

Section 2 Assessment

hmhsocialstudies.com
ONLINE QUIZ

Reviewing Ideas, Terms, and People

1. a. **Define** What social issues did Americans debate during the 1970s?
   b. **Contrast** How had immigration patterns changed by the 1970s?
   c. **Draw Conclusions** Why do you think *Silent Spring* remained important in the 1970s?
2. a. **Describe** How did **Jimmy Carter** break with tradition at his inauguration?
   b. **Analyze** Why did Carter's promise of honesty appeal to voters?
   c. **Elaborate** How did the Three Mile Island accident affect the energy crisis?
3. a. **Recall** Describe the successes and failures of President Carter's foreign policy.
   b. **Explain** What did the treaties Carter signed about the Panama Canal promise?
   c. **Draw Conclusions** Why do you think many people consider the **Camp David Accords** Carter's greatest achievement?

Critical Thinking

4. **Evaluating** Review your notes on new policies in the 1970s. Then copy the graphic organizer below and use it to show President Carter's successes and failures.

Focus on Writing

5. **Identifying Important Issues** Identify important issues and challenges facing Americans during the 1970s. Which of these issues or challenges do you think you will write about? What do you know about this subject? What more would you have to learn before writing about it?

© Houghton Mifflin Harcourt Publishing Company • Image Credits: (inset) ©Bettmann/Corbis; (t) ©AP/Wide World Photos

The Reagan Presidency

SECTION 3

If YOU were there...

It is 1980, and you are a top adviser to the newly elected president, Ronald Reagan. You think about the challenges Reagan will face. High inflation and unemployment are plaguing the economy. Relations with the Soviet Union are falling apart. Also 52 Americans are still being held hostage in Iran.

What would be your first recommendation to the president?

BUILDING BACKGROUND Many Americans blamed President Carter for the nation's economic problems and the continuing hostage crisis in Iran. These became major issues in the presidential election of 1980. Republican candidate Ronald Reagan promised to take the country in a new direction.

Reagan and Conservative Ideas

"Are you better off than you were four years ago?" That was the question Republican candidate **Ronald Reagan** asked voters during the 1980 presidential campaign. Millions of voters answered "No," giving Reagan an easy victory over President Carter. Reagan won 489 electoral votes to Carter's 49. On January 20, 1981—the day of Reagan's inauguration—Iran finally released the American hostages after 444 days in captivity.

Reagan's approach to government was based on conservative ideas. He wanted to cut taxes and reduce regulations on businesses. He promised to scale back the size of government, arguing that government involvement in business and society harmed individual ambition. "Government is not the solution to our problem; government is the problem," Reagan declared in his inaugural address.

Just two months into his presidency, Reagan was shot and severely wounded in an assassination attempt by John Hinckley Jr. Reagan was released from the hospital within two weeks and returned to work.

What You Will Learn...

Main Ideas

1. President Reagan based his policies on conservative ideas.
2. Reagan took a tough stand against communism in his foreign policy.

The Big Idea

President Reagan enacted conservative policies at home and took a strong anti-Communist stance in the Cold War.

Key Terms and People

Ronald Reagan
supply-side economics
deficit
Iran-Contra affair
Mikhail Gorbachev

hmhsocialstudies.com
TAKING NOTES

Use the graphic organizer online to take notes on President Reagan's domestic and foreign policies.

© Houghton Mifflin Harcourt Publishing Company

BIOGRAPHY

Sandra Day O'Connor

1930–

Sandra Day O'Connor grew up on a ranch in Arizona and entered Stanford University at age 16. She graduated third in her class from Stanford Law School in 1952. When she applied for jobs as a lawyer, however, she found that law firms were not willing to hire women. She turned instead to public service in Arizona, holding jobs including assistant attorney general, state senator, and judge. She was serving on the Arizona Court of Appeals when she was nominated to the Supreme Court by Ronald Reagan. The Senate confirmed O'Connor's appointment by a vote of 99–0. O'Connor retired from the bench in 2005.

Analyzing Information Why did Sandra Day O'Connor begin working in public service?

Reaganomics

Reagan's economic policies, which some called Reaganomics, were based on a theory called **supply-side economics**. This theory calls for sharp tax cuts with the goal of increasing the amount of money people and businesses have to invest. This investment would lead to economic growth and the creation of new jobs. Over time, the expanding economic activity would produce increased tax revenues for the government.

ACADEMIC VOCABULARY
implications effects of a decision

Though many Democrats opposed this theory, Congress approved most of Reagan's plan for large cuts in business and personal taxes. To help balance the budget, Reagan called for spending cuts as well. Congress agreed to cut the rate of the growth of spending on social programs such as school lunches, low-income housing, and food stamps.

The economy experienced a brief recession early in Reagan's presidency. Then in 1983 the economy rebounded and began a long period of expansion. Business profits and tax revenues increased.

At the same time, spending on defense was increased dramatically, from $180 billion in 1981 to nearly $280 billion in 1985. The new spending outpaced the new tax revenues. The result was a rapidly rising **deficit**—the amount by which a government's spending exceeds its revenues.

Conservative Goals

One of Reagan's conservative goals was to reduce government regulation of key industries. Reagan hoped fewer rules would encourage expansion in those industries, thereby improving the U.S. economy. Congress responded by reducing regulations on industries such as television, airlines, and banking.

Reagan was also able to move the Supreme Court in a more conservative direction by appointing politically conservative judges. In 1981 he appointed Sandra Day O'Connor to the Court. She became the first woman to serve as a Supreme Court justice. Reagan later appointed two more conservative justices: Antonin Scalia and Anthony M. Kennedy.

Election of 1984

President Reagan ran for re-election in 1984 against Democratic candidate Walter Mondale, who had served as Jimmy Carter's vice president. Mondale chose Geraldine Ferraro as his running mate. Ferraro was the first woman to run for vice president on a major-party ticket. She spoke of the **implications** of her nomination:

> "By choosing an American woman to run for our nation's second-highest office, you send a powerful signal to all Americans . . . We will place no limits on achievement. If we can do this, we can do anything."
>
> —Geraldine Ferraro, *Ferraro: My Story*

The economy was booming as the election approached. Mondale argued that Reagan's economic policies unfairly favored the wealthy. Voters, however, gave Reagan a landslide victory. Reagan received 59 percent of the popular vote and captured 525 of the 538 electoral votes.

READING CHECK **Summarizing** What theories did Reaganomics include?

© Houghton Mifflin Harcourt Publishing Company • Image Credits: (t) Pam Price/CNP/Getty Images

Reagan and Foreign Policy

President Reagan was an outspoken critic of communism and the Soviet Union, which he called an "evil empire." He saw the Cold War as a fight of "good versus evil, right versus wrong."

Conflicts in Central America

Civil wars raged in several Central American countries in the 1980s as communism spread in the area. Reagan supported anti-Communist governments in El Salvador and Guatemala with financial aid. Critics of this policy charged that the aid went to military governments that committed major human rights violations.

In Nicaragua, a revolutionary group called the Sandinistas overthrew the country's pro-American dictator in 1979. U.S. leaders became concerned when the Sandinistas formed closer ties with Communist Cuba. Reagan cut all U.S. aid to Nicaragua and began supporting anti-Sandinista rebels known as the Contras. This led to fears that the United States could be drawn into war. In 1984 Congress passed a ban on further U.S. military aid to the Contras.

A group of Reagan administration officials secretly found a way to continue funding the Contras. One member of the group was Oliver North, a marine officer serving as a national security aide. North helped arrange the sale of U.S. missiles to Iran. In exchange, Iran released U.S. hostages that had been taken by Iranian terrorists. Profits from this secret deal were sent to the Contras, in violation of the congressional ban. The so-called **Iran-Contra affair** became a national controversy when it was exposed in 1986. Congressional hearings concluded that President Reagan was not guilty of illegal activity. Several White House officials, however, were convicted of crimes related to the affair.

HISTORY

VIDEO
Soviet War Scare
hmhsocialstudies.com

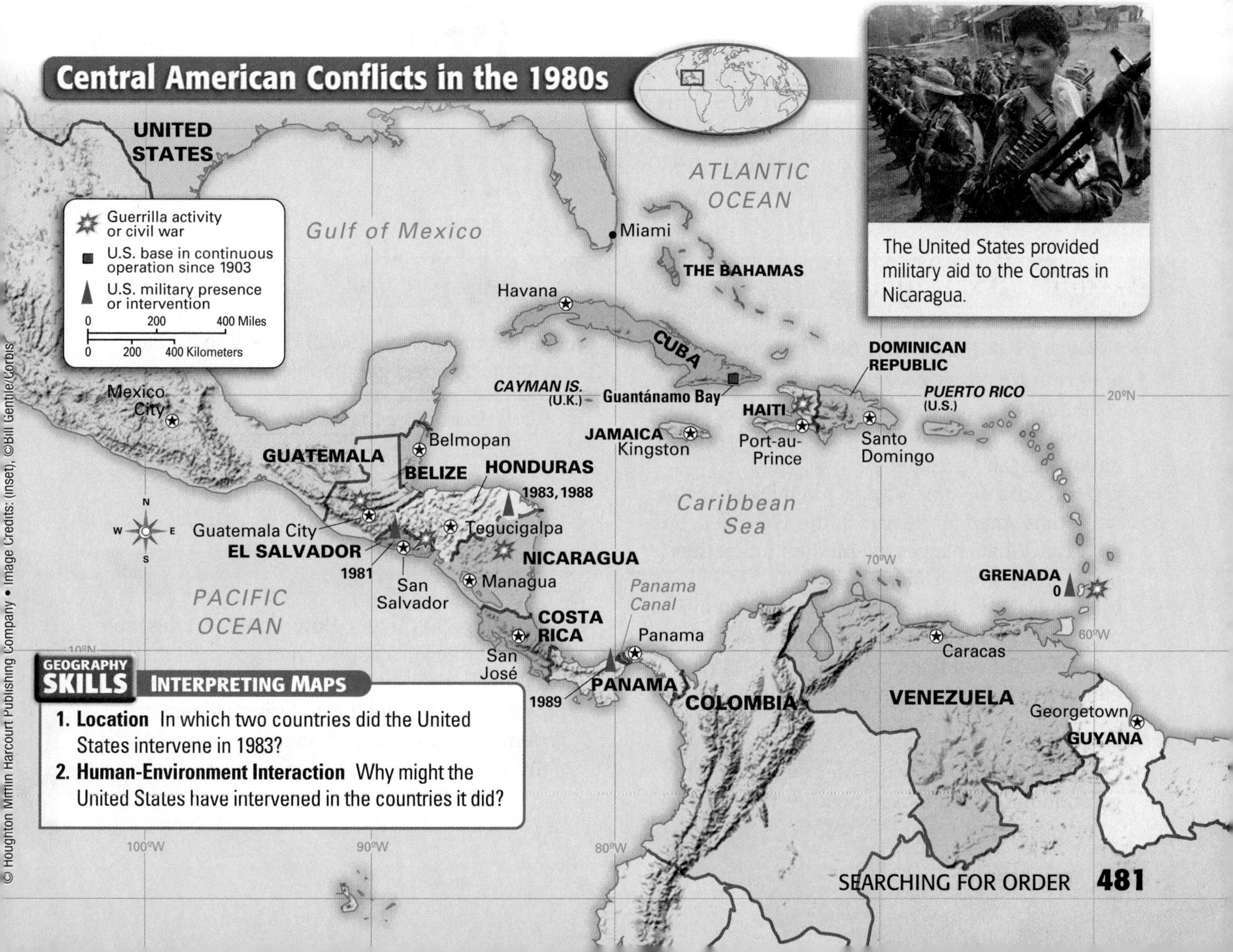

Central American Conflicts in the 1980s
UNITED STATES
Gulf of Mexico
ATLANTIC OCEAN
Miami
THE BAHAMAS
Havana
CUBA
Guerrilla activity or civil war
U.S. base in continuous operation since 1903
U.S. military presence or intervention
0 200 400 Miles
0 200 400 Kilometers
Mexico City
CAYMAN IS. (U.K.)
Guantánamo Bay
DOMINICAN REPUBLIC
HAITI
PUERTO RICO (U.S.)
20°N
JAMAICA
Kingston
Port-au-Prince
Santo Domingo
Belmopan
GUATEMALA
BELIZE
HONDURAS
1983, 1988
Caribbean Sea
Guatemala City
Tegucigalpa
EL SALVADOR
NICARAGUA
1981
San Salvador
Managua
70°W
GRENADA
1983
Panama Canal
PACIFIC OCEAN
COSTA RICA
Panama
60°W
San José
Caracas
PANAMA
1989
COLOMBIA
VENEZUELA
Georgetown
GUYANA
100°W
90°W
80°W

The United States provided military aid to the Contras in Nicaragua.

GEOGRAPHY SKILLS **INTERPRETING MAPS**

1. **Location** In which two countries did the United States intervene in 1983?
2. **Human-Environment Interaction** Why might the United States have intervened in the countries it did?

© Houghton Mifflin Harcourt Publishing Company • Image Credits: (inset), ©Bill Gentile/Corbis

An Easing of Tensions

President Reagan and his wife Nancy developed a friendship with Mikhail Gorbachev and his wife Raisa that symbolized the easing of Cold War tensions between their countries. Gorbachev's policies helped greatly to bring about this change in foreign affairs.

How did the friendship between the Reagans and the Gorbachevs help unite the two countries?

Reagan and Gorbachev

During his first term, President Reagan took a tough stand against the Soviet Union. He halted arms negotiations and quickly expanded the U.S. military.

The Soviet Union tried to keep up with American spending in the arms race. This contributed to desperate economic times in the Soviet Union during the 1980s. In 1985 **Mikhail Gorbachev** became the new Soviet leader. To deal with his country's economic problems, he began a process of political and economic reforms called *perestroika.* He also adopted a new policy of political openness called *glasnost.* The newfound freedoms introduced by Gorbachev's policies threatened other leaders of the Soviet Union but were mostly supported by its citizens and by leaders in the West.

Reagan became convinced of Gorbachev's desire for change. In 1987 the two leaders signed the Intermediate-Range Nuclear Forces Treaty, eliminating all medium-range nuclear weapons in Europe. Cold War tensions were decreasing for the first time since the early 1970s.

READING CHECK **Identifying Cause and Effect** Why did President Reagan change his tough stand toward the Soviet Union?

SUMMARY Conservative ideas influenced many of Ronald Reagan's policies.

Section 3 Assessment

hmhsocialstudies.com
ONLINE QUIZ

Reviewing Ideas, Terms, and People

1. a. **Recall** What was **Ronald Reagan**'s view of government?
   b. **Analyze** Why did the federal budget deficit rise during Reagan's presidency?
   c. **Draw Conclusions** Why do you think so many Americans voted for Reagan in the 1984 election?
2. a. **Recall** What changes did **Mikhail Gorbachev** make in the Soviet Union?
   b. **Explain** How did Reagan administration officials violate the law in the **Iran-Contra affair**?
   c. **Predict** Do you think Reagan's policies were effective in fighting communism?

Critical Thinking

3. **Categorizing** Review your notes on Ronald Reagan's domestic and foreign policies. Then copy the graphic organizer below and use it to list each policy with its correct geographic focus.

United States	Central America	Soviet Union

Focus on Writing

4. **Describing Characters** How would you describe President Reagan's approach to government? What major decisions did he make during his presidency? How did these decisions influence government, politics, and foreign relations? Make notes on what you will use in your historical novel.

© Houghton Mifflin Harcourt Publishing Company • Image Credits: (t), Mike Sargent/AFP/Getty Images

BIOGRAPHY

Ronald Reagan

How would you lead your country during the Cold War?

When did he live? 1911–2004

Where did he live? Ronald Reagan grew up in Illinois. In 1937 he moved to California, where he became a well-known movie actor. He later entered politics and was elected governor of California. After serving eight years as president, he retired to his California ranch.

What did he do? Reagan worked to reshape the American government and economy based on conservative principles. In foreign policy, he took an aggressive stand toward communism and the Soviet Union. In a famous speech at the Berlin Wall, he challenged the Soviet leader to allow freedom in Eastern Europe, saying, "Mr. Gorbachev, open this gate! Mr. Gorbachev, tear down this wall!" Reagan and Gorbachev later signed the Intermediate-Range Nuclear Forces (INF) Treaty, the first treaty reducing the number of nuclear weapons held by both countries.

Why is he so important? Nicknamed the Great Communicator, Reagan inspired many Americans with his sense of humor and his optimistic view of America's future. Many voters credited him with restoring their confidence after the difficulties of the 1970s. Reagan's buildup of the U.S. military is believed by many to have contributed to major changes in the Cold War and the eventual fall of Communist governments in the Soviet Union and Eastern Europe.

Finding Main Ideas What was Reagan's biggest foreign policy achievement? Use evidence from the reading to support your answer.

KEY EVENTS

1937
Becomes a movie actor

1952
Marries his second wife, Nancy Davis

1966
Elected governor of California

1980
Elected president

1981
Shot by John Hinckley Jr.

1984
Elected to second term

1987
Signs INF Treaty

2004
Dies in California

HISTORY

VIDEO
President Reagan Shot

hmhsocialstudies.com

Ronald Reagan used his California ranch as a retreat during his years in the White House.

© Houghton Mifflin Harcourt Publishing Company

Image Credits: (br), Courtesy Ronald Reagan Library

Case Study

America's Economy

The New York Stock Exchange is one of the most important indicators of the economic health of the United States.

Business Cycles

The economy of the United States changes over time. Many factors influence the expansion or contraction of the economy. As the economy changes, it impacts the business cycle. A boom happens when the economy has a period of high growth for a long time. The demand for goods and services may be greater and people are willing to pay higher prices. The taxes collected on these goods and services helps the economy. A bust happens when the economic activity slows down and there is less demand for the goods and services. During this period, prices and value of goods and services go down and the government collects less in taxes.

Domestic Policies

Boom and bust business cycles are affected by policies set by the U.S. government. A domestic policy is a rule or regulation that guides how American businesses and citizens make decisions. Our country has many economic policies that set rules for businesses, such as worker and product safety regulations. The government decides how strongly to enforce these regulations and may fine a business if they do not follow them. But such regulations cost a business money. Businesses may raise prices to help pay for new safety equipment or other taxes.

The government also has policies for tax rates. Many people pay taxes on the money they earn. People also pay sales taxes on purchases they make. If the tax rate is raised, the government collects more money. If it is too low, the government may not have enough money to pay for federal goods and services.

Often presidents create policies in response to what people want or need. In the 1950s, there was public pressure to improve the road system. President Dwight Eisenhower established a committee that created the Interstate Highway System. Better transportation routes connected major cities and helped business ship goods more quickly and easily, thereby helping the economy.

© Houghton Mifflin Harcourt Publishing Company • Image Credits: (l) ©Image Source/Getty Images

Foreign Policies

Unlike domestic policies and programs, foreign policies relate to how our government interacts with other nations, both in business and politics. Good relationships make it easier for countries to trade goods and make decisions together.

Presidents can play an important role in foreign policy. In 1972, President Richard Nixon became the first U.S. president to visit China. This historic meeting helped to establish more trade between the United States and China, impacting the economy in both countries. Since this time, China's economy has grown tremendously and it has become an economic power. India has become an economic power as well. Relations with both countries are affected by the U.S. need for trade with companies within each country.

Globalization

One reason India and China have risen as economic powers is globalization. In today's global economy, nations depend on one another for resources, goods, and services. Many goods and services made in the United States may have certain parts made or tasks done in another country. This means workers in India may be writing a software code for a product made by an American business. Some businesses insource to change where money is spent. Rather than sending a particular job out to be done an outside company, many businesses are training employees to do that same job at locations within the United States.

Although countries are interdependent, they still have different policies and regulations. Some differences relate to environmental protection. Recently, some countries have begun to charge businesses carbon taxes. Companies are charged a tax based on the amount of fossil fuels that they use. By paying taxes, government leaders hope to have businesses rethink how much fuel they use and to look for greener energy sources.

ECONOMIC GROWTH, 2000–2012

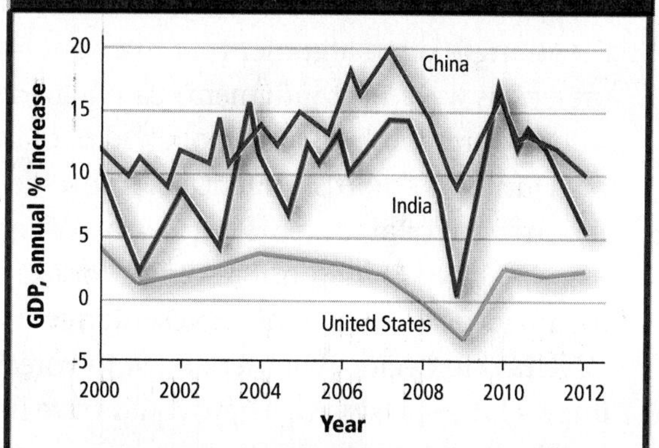

Source: *U.S. Bureau of Economic Analysis, Reserve Bank of Australia*

ANALYSIS SKILL — ANALYZING VISUALS

In what year did India see the greatest percent of increase in GDP? What about China?

Case Study Assessment

1. What is the boom and bust cycle?
2. How is globalization affecting U.S. foreign policy?
3. **Activity** Carbon taxes are designed to reduce pollution. Research carbon pollution in Alabama. Then create a poster that shows the dangers of carbon pollution and how local businesses are dealing with the issue.

© Houghton Mifflin Harcourt Publishing Company

Determining the Strength of an Argument

Define the Skill

Studying history often involves learning about different opinions. In order to understand these opinions, it is important to recognize strong arguments. Strong arguments are based on convincing supporting evidence. Examples and points should be true and should make sense in the context of the argument. For example, supporting points should relate to the main idea of the argument. It is also important to consider any evidence against the argument.

Many people in the past have made decisions based on the strength of an argument. Determining the strength of an argument is important for the present as well. Your judgments can help you decide whether or not to support a policy, idea, or candidate.

During the 1970s, Americans had to determine the strength of arguments during the Watergate scandal. If Nixon had not resigned, for example, members of the House of Representatives would have had to decide whether or not to vote to impeach the president. They would have had to weigh the evidence and determine the strength of arguments for and against him.

Learn the Skill

In *Silent Spring,* Rachel Carson argued that environmental pollution was harmful and had to be stopped. Here is part of her argument:

> "Man, however much he may like to pretend the contrary, is part of nature. Can he escape a pollution that is now so thoroughly distributed throughout our world?"

How strong is Carson's argument? In *Silent Spring,* she gives many examples of the harmful effects of pollutants and insect poisons. This makes her argument stronger. In the quotation above, Carson points out that humans rely upon nature. As nature becomes polluted, she argues, humans will not be able to avoid the harmful health effects of that pollution.

Carson's argument was strong enough to convince the American people and Congress to take action. The environmental movement grew, and new laws were passed to protect the nation's air and water.

Practice the Skill

Suppose that you are a member of Congress during the Watergate scandal. You have to decide whether or not to impeach President Nixon. Your decision will depend on the strength of the arguments in favor of impeachment. Review the chapter and answer the following questions to help determine the strength of those arguments.

1. What is the evidence against President Nixon? How does this evidence strengthen or weaken the case against him?
2. Is there any evidence that President Nixon is innocent? How strong is this evidence?
3. Would you vote to impeach the president? Explain your answer.

© Houghton Mifflin Harcourt Publishing Company

CHAPTER 15

Chapter Review

History's Impact
▶ **video series**
Review the video to answer the closing question:
How did the Supreme Court contribute to the series of checks and balances that eventually led to President Nixon's resignation?

Visual Summary

QUICK FACTS

Use the visual summary below to help you review the main ideas of the chapter.

Positives and Negatives of the Presidencies

Richard Nixon
Positive: Nixon brought China and the United States together diplomatically.
Negative: His administration ended because of the Watergate scandal.

Jimmy Carter
Positive: Carter helped create the Camp David Accords.
Negative: He also faced the Iran hostage crisis.

Ronald Reagan
Positive: Reagan signed a major arms treaty with several countries.
Negative: His administration was linked to the Iran-Contra affair.

Reviewing Vocabulary, Terms, and People

Read each question and write the letter of the best response.

1. Which of the following refers to a period of less hostile U.S.–Soviet relations in the 1970s?
a. détente **c.** realpolitik
b. stagflation **d.** *perestroika*

2. The South African government's system of official racial segregation was known as
a. Title IX. **c.** sanctions.
b. the ERA. **d.** apartheid.

3. Which of the following was a theory that influenced President Reagan's policies?
a. Whip Inflation Now **c.** SALT
b. supply-side economics **d.** *glasnost*

Comprehension and Critical Thinking

SECTION 1

4. a. Identify Who were the reporters who uncovered the Watergate scandal?
b. Analyze What were some results of Nixon's visit to China?
c. Elaborate Why do you think Nixon called his supporters the Silent Majority?

SECTION 2

5. a. Recall What happened at Three Mile Island?
b. Contrast How were the foreign policies of Nixon and Carter different?
c. Draw Conclusions Why do you think many Americans responded to *Silent Spring*?

© Houghton Mifflin Harcourt Publishing Company

SECTION 3

6. a. **Describe** What happened in the election of 1980?

   b. **Summarize** What were some results of Reagan's conservative policies?

   c. **Evaluate** Do you think Congress was right to ban aid to the Contras in Nicaragua?

Reviewing Themes

7. **Economics** How did the energy crisis affect the economy of the United States?
8. **Politics** How did the politics of the presidents discussed in this chapter affect the foreign policy of the United States?

Reading Skills

Summarizing *Use the Reading Skills taught in this chapter to answer the question below.*

Carter also experienced disaster in the Middle East. Since the 1950s, the United States had supported the pro–American shah, or king, of Iran. Many Iranians resented the shah's reform efforts and the country's shift from a traditional and agricultural society to a more urban and industrial one. The government severely punished its opponents and controlled all political participation. Many members of the opposition supported the views of Islamic spiritual leader Ruhollah Khomeini, who had been forced to leave the country because of his criticisms of the shah's policies. In 1979 Khomeini's supporters drove the shah out of Iran, and a month later, Khomeini took control of the government. On November 4, a group of Iranian students attacked the U.S. embassy in Tehran, the capital of Iran, seizing about 90 American hostages. The Iran hostage crisis lasted for more than a year.

9. Summarize the beginning of the Iran hostage crisis in three sentences.

Using the Internet

10. **Activity: Making Connections** The cost of oil rose steadily in the early 1970s, and it reached a new high after Arab nations placed an embargo on oil exports to the United States. Americans felt the impact as costs increased for all products that were made from oil, further weakening the already struggling U.S. economy. Through your online textbook, research the causes, effects, results, and connections between the Yom Kippur War and the Arab oil embargo. Create a model or diagram to illustrate your research. You should label your model or diagram and be prepared to explain it to the class.

hmhsocialstudies.com

Social Studies Skills

Determining the Strength of an Argument *Use the Social Studies Skills taught in this chapter to answer the question about the selection below.*

In this chapter, you have read about the Supreme Court case *United States v. Nixon.* Nixon argued that executive privilege, a president's right to keep information secret for reasons of national security, protected him from having to give up tapes of his official conversations.

11. In your opinion, how strong was Nixon's argument?

Focus on Writing

12. **Writing Your Historical Novel** Review your notes about important events and people from the 1970s and 1980s. Choose a subject that you would like to focus on in your novel. Think about the main events you will describe and main characters your story will include. Then write the first page of your novel. Be sure to describe where and when your story is taking place. Since this is a novel, you should feel free to write dialogue for historical figures who appear in your story.

© Houghton Mifflin Harcourt Publishing Company

CHAPTER 15

Standardized Test Practice

DIRECTIONS: Read each question and write the letter of the best response.

1 The Camp David Accords were

- **A** secret deals supplying Iran with weapons and the Nicaraguan Contras with money.
- **B** the negotiations that ended the Iran hostage crisis.
- **C** U.S.–Soviet nuclear arms reduction treaties.
- **D** a set of peace agreements between Israel and Egypt.

2 Which of the following was a result of Reagan's economic plan?

- **A** The deficit decreased.
- **B** Tax rates were lowered.
- **C** Military spending was cut.
- **D** Unemployment and inflation rose.

3 Which president participated in the 1972 Strategic Arms Limitation Talks?

- **A** Gerald Ford
- **B** Richard Nixon
- **C** Ronald Reagan
- **D** Jimmy Carter

4 The *main* job of the Environmental Protection Agency is to

- **A** enforce the laws that help protect air and water quality.
- **B** raise environmental awareness through Earth Day celebrations.
- **C** negotiate arms-control agreements.
- **D** prevent inflation and unemployment.

5 What was one aspect of Reagan's tough stance against communism?

- **A** He dramatically increased military spending.
- **B** He made peace agreements in the Middle East.
- **C** He visited and established diplomatic relations with China.
- **D** He focused on human rights.

6 How did the Watergate scandal begin?

- **A** Government officials were caught giving information to newspaper reporters.
- **B** Five men were caught breaking in to the Democrats' headquarters.
- **C** Richard Nixon refused to share his tapes with Congress.
- **D** Gerald Ford pardoned Richard Nixon.

7 How were Nixon's and Reagan's influences on the Supreme Court similar?

- **A** Both tried to give the Supreme Court more power.
- **B** Both denied the authority of the Supreme Court to issue subpoenas.
- **C** Both appointed women as Supreme Court justices.
- **D** Both appointed conservative Supreme Court justices.

8 *Stagflation* refers to the unusual economic condition of

- **A** high oil prices but low inflation.
- **B** stagnant economic growth and high inflation.
- **C** low unemployment and low inflation.
- **D** stagnant deficits and falling exports.

9 Read the following quote from a U.S. senator urging Nixon's impeachment and use it to answer the question below.

> "What the president has done threatens to destroy our system of law. It smacks of dictatorship. Unless Congress responds in the only way provided in the Constitution for resisting such a usurpation [stealing] of authority, we endanger our country's future."
>
> —Senator Edmund S. Muskie, quoted in the *Washington Post*, October 21, 1973

Document-Based Question Why did Muskie feel Nixon should be impeached?

© Houghton Mifflin Harcourt Publishing Company

CHAPTER 16 1988–PRESENT

America Looks to the Future

Essential Question What events have shaped the United States today?

ALABAMA COURSE OF STUDY

8 Describe how the United States' role in the Cold War influenced domestic and international events.
- Assessing effects of the end of the Cold War Era.

9 Critique major social and cultural changes in the United States since World War II.
- Identifying the impact of media, including newspapers, AM and FM radio, television, twenty-four hour sports and news programming, talk radio, and Internet social networking, on United States' culture since World War II.

10 Analyze changing economic priorities and cycles of economic expansion and contraction for their impact on society since World War II.
- Identifying policies and programs that had an economic impact on society since World War II.
- Analyzing consequences of immigration for their impact on national and Alabama economies since World War II.

11 Identify technological advancements on society in the United States since World War II.

12 Evaluate significant political issues and policies of presidential administrations since World War II.
- Identifying domestic policies that shaped the United States since World War II.
- Recognizing domestic issues that shaped the United States since World War II.
- Identifying issues of foreign affairs that shaped the United States since World War II.
- Explaining how conflict in the Middle East impacted life in the United States since World War II.
- Recognizing the election of Barack Obama as the culmination of a movement in the United States to realize equal opportunity for all Americans.
- Identifying the 2008 presidential election as a watershed in the use of new technology and mass participation in the electoral process.

Focus on Writing

Web Site The popularity of the Internet dramatically increased in the 1990s, changing the way we communicate and share information. The attacks of September 11, 2001, made terrorism a major concern for Americans. In this chapter you will learn about these and other important events that have taken place in your lifetime. Then you will write the text for a Web site about America in the late twentieth century and early twenty-first century.

UNITED STATES

1988 George H. W. Bush is elected president.

1980

WORLD

1989 Most of the Berlin Wall is dismantled.

Image Credits: (t), ©Jeff Greenberg/PhotoEdit; (b), HMH Photo

© Houghton Mifflin Harcourt Publishing Company

HISTORY Election 2008
hmhsocialstudies.com VIDEO

Young people like these are helping to shape the future of the United States.

1990 U.S. and UN forces liberate Kuwait from Iraqi control in the Persian Gulf War.

1990

1994 Nelson Mandela is elected president of South Africa.

1995 Extremists bomb a federal building in Oklahoma.

1997 Hong Kong returns to Chinese control.

2000

2001 Terrorists attack the World Trade Center and the Pentagon on September 11.

2005 Pope John Paul II dies.

2008 Barack Obama is elected the first African American president of the United States.

PRESENT

2008 For the first time in the world's history, more people live in cities than in rural areas.

© Houghton Mifflin Harcourt Publishing Company

Image Credits: (t), ©Jeff Greenberg/PhotoEdit; (cl), ©Peter Turnley/Corbis (bl), Per-Anders Pettersson/Getty Images

Reading Social Studies

Economics | Geography | Politics | Society and Culture | Science and Technology

Focus on Themes In this chapter, you will read about the most recent presidents and their administrations. You will learn about the changing role the United States has gained in global **politics** and the global **economy.** You will also read about the terrorist attacks against the United States on September 11, 2001, and learn how that event helped shape the world you live in today.

Predicting

Focus on Reading Often when you are reading, predicting what might come next can help you understand what is happening in the story of history.

Understanding Predicting Predicting what may come next in the logical progression of a story relies on understanding what has happened in the past. You have learned many different responses to crises that have occurred throughout U.S. history. You can use this knowledge to predict what may come in the future.

Notice how one reader uses information from the past to predict what may happen in the future.

> ...On March 20, 2003, the United States and a coalition of allies launched a ground attack on Iraq. Saddam [Hussein]'s government collapsed, and Saddam was eventually captured.... Violence continued, however, with attacks on U.S. soldiers and Iraqis who were working to rebuild the country.... The war in Iraq caused fierce debate at home. After months of searching, no weapons of mass destruction were uncovered, and no concrete ties between Saddam and al Qaeda could be proven.

After reading this section, one reader thought:

I have read about other wars in which the American public was divided over the action the country should take. In the War of 1812, there was a convention of delegates opposed to the war. During the Civil War, President Lincoln silenced antiwar Democrats by imprisoning them. In the 1960s and 1970s, many citizens publicly protested the Vietnam War, while others supported the war. What happened in these past wars might also happen in the war against terrorism.

© Houghton Mifflin Harcourt Publishing Company

You Try It!

As you read the following passage, look for the facts that can help you predict what might happen in the future.

> The Internet was first developed in 1969 by scientists at the U.S. Department of Defense. Early computer networks were used mainly by government and university researchers. Then in the 1990s, computer programmers developed the World Wide Web, enabling people to access information from computers around the world. Internet use exploded in the 1990s. Computers and the Internet made it easier and faster for people at home, work, and school to access and share information. This important development was known as the Information Revolution.

After you read the passage, answer the following questions.

1. What other revolutions have you read about in the study of American history, and how have they affected American society?
2. Is the Information Revolution similar to any other revolution you have read about?
3. How might the Information Revolution affect American society in the future?

As you read this chapter, use the information given to predict what may happen in American society in the next 10 years.

Key Terms and People

Chapter 16

Section 1

George H. W. Bush
Saddam Hussein
Operation Desert Storm
Colin Powell
Bill Clinton
North American Free Trade Agreement
Madeleine Albright
terrorism

Section 2

Al Gore
George W. Bush
World Trade Center
Pentagon
al Qaeda
Osama bin Laden
weapons of mass destruction

Section 3

service economy
globalization
Internet
Information Revolution
AIDS
ozone layer
global warming

Academic Vocabulary

In this chapter, you will learn the following academic words:

facilitate
ideals

© Houghton Mifflin Harcourt Publishing Company

SECTION 1

The End of the Twentieth Century

What You Will Learn...

Main Ideas

1. Major global changes took place during the presidency of George H. W. Bush.
2. During Bill Clinton's presidency, the nation experienced scandal, economic growth, and the rise of terrorist threats.

The Big Idea

The United States and the world faced many new challenges at the end of the twentieth century.

Key Terms and People

George H. W. Bush
Saddam Hussein
Operation Desert Storm
Colin Powell
Bill Clinton
North American Free Trade Agreement
Madeleine Albright
terrorism

hmhsocialstudies.com
TAKING NOTES

Use the graphic organizer online to take notes on the key events that happened during the presidencies of George H. W. Bush and Bill Clinton.

If YOU were there...

You are visiting the city of West Berlin in 1989. Just after midnight on November 9, you see huge crowds of people pouring into the streets to celebrate. You rush outside to find out what's going on. "The wall is falling!" people shout. You run toward the Berlin Wall, and there you see East and West Germans working together to rip down the hated wall.

What might the fall of the Berlin Wall mean for the future?

BUILDING BACKGROUND Mikhail Gorbachev began a process of political and economic reforms in the Soviet Union in the late 1980s. Encouraged by these changes, people from many Eastern European countries continued to demand change as well. They were eager to break free from Soviet domination and establish their own democratic governments.

George H. W. Bush

Ronald Reagan was popular with a majority of voters as his second term as president came to an end. Republicans hoped this would help Reagan's vice president, **George H. W. Bush**, win the election of 1988. Bush's Democratic opponent was Massachusetts governor Michael Dukakis. After a hard-fought campaign, Bush won the election with 426 electoral votes to Dukakis's 111.

The Cold War Ends

As Bush began his presidency, Mikhail Gorbachev continued his reform programs in the Soviet Union. In the Soviet-controlled states of Eastern Europe, people demanded even faster change and more freedom. Prodemocracy movements in Hungary, Poland, and other nations put increasing pressure on Communist governments. This pressure produced world-changing results in 1989, as pro-Soviet governments across Eastern Europe began to fall.

© Houghton Mifflin Harcourt Publishing Company

In October 1989 massive protests in East Germany lead to the resignation of Communist leader Erich Honecker. The new government agreed to open the borders of East Germany—including the border guarded by the Berlin Wall. At midnight on November 9, a wild celebration broke out as East and West Berliners jumped onto the Berlin Wall, shouting and dancing. Some smashed through parts of the wall with hammers and chisels. The wall, which had stood as a symbol of the Cold War since 1961, began crumbling to the ground. Within a year, the two Germanys reunited as one democratic country.

Several Soviet republics soon declared independence from the Soviet regime. In a desperate attempt to hold on to power, hard-line Communists took Gorbachev hostage and tried to seize the government. Thousands of Soviets took to the streets in protest. Ignoring orders to stop the protesters, many soldiers joined the crowds. Prodemocracy leader Boris Yeltsin encouraged the protesters to stand strong. The Soviet Union soon broke apart, confirming the end of the Cold War.

The Persian Gulf War

President Bush called for all countries to work together, especially during times of crisis. A major crisis soon developed in the Middle East. In August 1990 Iraq's dictator, **Saddam Hussein**, invaded neighboring oil-rich Kuwait.

Members of the United Nations called for the immediate withdrawal of Iraqi troops. President Bush, with strong public support, began assembling a coalition of nations to drive Iraq from Kuwait by force.

When Saddam refused to withdraw from Kuwait, a U.S.-led multinational coalition launched **Operation Desert Storm**. This air offensive was led by U.S. generals Norman Schwarzkopf and **Colin Powell**—chair of the joint chiefs of staff and the highest-ranking African American ever to serve in the U.S. military. After a six-week bombing campaign, ground forces entered Kuwait. Within days, Iraq agreed to a cease-fire.

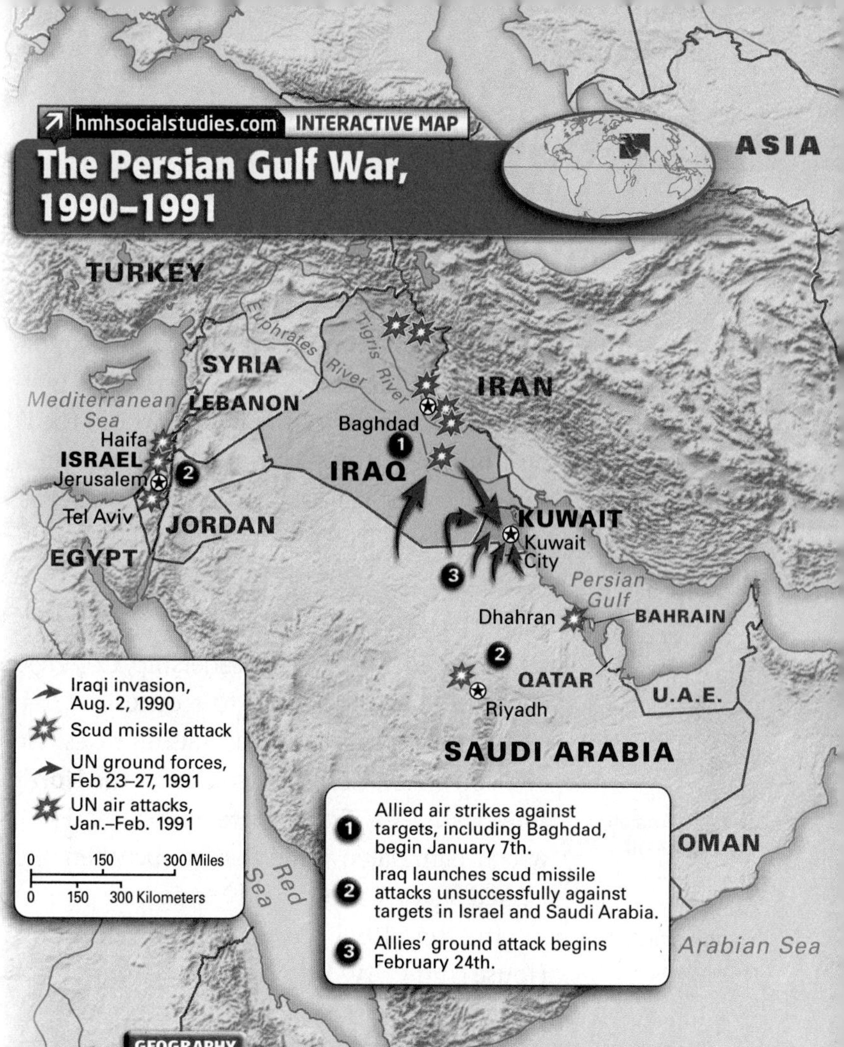

hmhsocialstudies.com INTERACTIVE MAP
The Persian Gulf War, 1990–1991
ASIA
TURKEY
SYRIA
LEBANON
IRAN
IRAQ
Baghdad
Euphrates River
Tigris River
Mediterranean Sea
Haifa
ISRAEL
Jerusalem
Tel Aviv
JORDAN
EGYPT
KUWAIT
Kuwait City
Persian Gulf
Dhahran
BAHRAIN
QATAR
Riyadh
U.A.E.
SAUDI ARABIA
OMAN
Red Sea
Arabian Sea
Iraqi invasion, Aug. 2, 1990
Scud missile attack
UN ground forces, Feb 23–27, 1991
UN air attacks, Jan.–Feb. 1991
0 150 300 Miles
0 150 300 Kilometers
1 Allied air strikes against targets, including Baghdad, begin January 7th.
2 Iraq launches scud missile attacks unsuccessfully against targets in Israel and Saudi Arabia.
3 Allies' ground attack begins February 24th.

GEOGRAPHY SKILLS **INTERPRETING MAPS**

1. **Place** Where did Iraqi forces invade?
2. **Location** From which country did UN ground forces attack Iraq?

About 22,300 Iraqi soldiers and civilians were killed in the Persian Gulf War. The coalition forces lost around 223 soldiers, 148 of whom were American. More than 35,000 American women served in the war, though federal laws prevented them from serving in combat.

President Bush explained the importance of the war, telling Congress:

> "Now, we can see a new world coming into view. A world in which there is the very real prospect of a new world order . . . A world in which freedom and respect for human rights find a home among all nations."
>
> —George H. W. Bush, March 6, 1991

READING CHECK **Summarizing** How did the world change between 1989 and 1991?

HISTORY
VIDEO
Eastern Block Uprisings
hmhsocialstudies.com

© Houghton Mifflin Harcourt Publishing Company

Clinton's Presidency

An overwhelming majority of Americans supported President Bush's handling of the Gulf War. By the time of the 1992 election, however, the struggling U.S. economy had become a more important issue for most voters. The Democratic nominee, Arkansas governor **Bill Clinton**, told voters he would focus on improving the economy. Clinton won a three-way race against Bush and H. Ross Perot, who ran as an independent candidate.

THE IMPACT TODAY

In 2005 Congress approved a similar accord with the Dominican Republic and the Central American countries of Costa Rica, El Salvador, Guatemala, Honduras, and Nicaragua. The treaty is known as CAFTA-DR. Costa Rica did not implement the terms of the treaty until 2009.

Clinton and Congress

Under President Clinton's leadership, Congress passed a budget designed to reduce the deficit by cutting spending and raising taxes. He also convinced Congress to support the **North American Free Trade Agreement** (NAFTA), which eliminated trade barriers between the United States, Canada, and Mexico.

In the 1994 congressional elections, House minority leader Newt Gingrich of Georgia helped lead Republicans to an important victory. Gingrich and other Republicans promoted a set of policies called the Contract with America, promising lower taxes and smaller government. Republicans gained control of both houses of Congress for the first time since 1952.

A growing economy helped Clinton win a second term in 1996 over Senator Bob Dole of Kansas. By 1998 the U.S. government was taking in more money than it was spending. Clinton's second term, however, was dominated by questions about his personal and official conduct. Government investigators charged that the president had conducted an improper relationship with a White House intern and then lied about it under oath. In 1998 the House of Representatives voted to impeach Clinton for obstruction of justice. The Senate acquitted him of the charges in 1999. The scandal damaged Clinton's public image, though his approval ratings remained high, due in part to the booming economy.

Primary Source

POINTS OF VIEW

NAFTA

Just before Congress voted on NAFTA in 1993, Vice President Al Gore and former presidential candidate H. Ross Perot debated the controversial issue on national television.

"If we keep shifting our manufacturing jobs across the border [to Mexico] and around the world and deindustrializing our country, we will not be able to defend this great country, and that is a risk we will never take."

—H. Ross Perot

"Everything that he [Perot] is worried about will get worse if NAFTA is defeated. We want jobs for America's working men and women. We want to get rid of the barriers that have prevented us from selling what we make in other countries. This is an historic opportunity to do that."

—Al Gore

ANALYSIS SKILL **ANALYZING POINTS OF VIEW**

According to Perot, how would NAFTA affect the United States? Why does Gore disagree?

© Houghton Mifflin Harcourt Publishing Company • Image Credits: (bl), ©Shelly Katz/Time Life/Getty Images; (br), ©AFP/Getty Images

A Dangerous World

The collapse of the Soviet Union left the United States as the world's only superpower. In 1997 President Clinton appointed **Madeleine Albright** as the first woman to be secretary of state. Albright had been born in Prague before her family moved to the United States, fleeing the Holocaust. She helped adapt U.S. foreign policy to this complex new world.

The United States worked to protect global peace and democracy. In the Balkan region of Europe, for example, the former nation of Yugoslavia broke apart. Different ethnic and religious groups fought for control of territory. U.S. diplomats helped negotiate an end to the bloody war. President Clinton then sent 20,000 U.S. troops to the region to help maintain peace.

In the 1990s **terrorism**—the use of violence by individuals or small groups to advance political goals—became a major issue. In April 1995 American terrorists bombed the Alfred P. Murrah Federal Building in Oklahoma City, killing 168 people. The United States also faced increasingly deadly attacks by extremist Islamic groups. Hundreds were killed in bomb attacks on U.S. embassies in Africa in 1998.

BIOGRAPHY

Bill Clinton
1946–

Bill Clinton was born in Hope, Arkansas. As a teenager he met and shook hands with President John Kennedy—an experience that heightened his interest in becoming a politician. He became a Rhodes scholar at Oxford after graduating from college. After graduating from Yale Law School, Clinton returned to Arkansas and was elected governor in 1978. He lost his bid for re-election in 1980 but ran again in 1982 and won, serving 10 more years as governor. Clinton was elected president in 1992 and re-elected in 1996. The country experienced the longest period of continued economic growth during his presidency. In 1998, however, Clinton became only the second president in U.S. history to be impeached.

Drawing Conclusions Why might meeting President Kennedy have influenced Clinton?

READING CHECK **Identifying Cause and Effect** How did the end of the Cold War change the U.S. role in the world?

SUMMARY The Cold War ended in 1990.

Section 1 Assessment

hmhsocialstudies.com
ONLINE QUIZ

Reviewing Ideas, Terms, and People

1. a. **Summarize** What were some of the major world events during **George H. W. Bush**'s presidency?
   b. **Identify** What was the purpose of **Operation Desert Storm**?
   c. **Evaluate** How did the Persian Gulf War test President Bush's vision of a new world order?
2. a. **Recall** What were some of the high points and low points of **Bill Clinton**'s presidency?
   b. **Contrast** How is **terrorism** different from standard warfare?
   c. **Elaborate** Do you think Congress was right to pass the **North American Free Trade Agreement**? Explain your answer.

Critical Thinking

3. **Sequencing** Review your notes on the presidencies of George H. W. Bush and Bill Clinton. Then copy the graphic organizer below and use it to identify major events and the year they occurred.

Year	Event

FOCUS ON WRITING

4. **Identifying Important Figures** Take notes on the main people in the chapter. Identify why each of these people was important. In what major events was each person involved? How did he or she affect the United States?

© Houghton Mifflin Harcourt Publishing Company • Image Credits: (t), Courtesy The White House

SECTION 2

George W. Bush in Office

What You Will Learn...

Main Ideas

1. George W. Bush won the disputed 2000 presidential election.
2. Americans debated the future of the War on Terror that began after terrorists attacked the United States.
3. The nation faced difficult challenges during President Bush's second term.

The Big Idea

George W. Bush led the country in response to terrorist attacks and through domestic challenges.

Key Terms and People

Al Gore
George W. Bush
World Trade Center
Pentagon
al Qaeda
Osama bin Laden
weapons of mass destruction

hmhsocialstudies.com
TAKING NOTES

Use the graphic organizer online to take notes on the major policies of George W. Bush.

If YOU were there...

It is the December after the presidential election between George W. Bush and Al Gore. For weeks, people have been talking about whether the votes can be recounted by hand. The race was too close to call on election night, and now the candidates are involved in a court case that will decide who the next president will be.

How would you solve the problem of recounting votes?

BUILDING BACKGROUND In the 1990s extremist Islamic groups in the Middle East vowed to attack the United States. They carried out deadly attacks on U.S. embassies in Africa and against the ship the USS *Cole*. Terrorism was not a major issue in the 2000 presidential election, but it would soon begin to dominate American politics.

The 2000 Presidential Election

The United States was at peace and enjoying economic prosperity as the 2000 presidential election neared. The Democrats chose **Al Gore**, who had served as Bill Clinton's vice president, as their nominee. The Republican candidate was Texas governor **George W. Bush**, the son of former president George H. W. Bush.

Campaign Issues

One major campaign issue was how to use the federal budget surplus, which totaled nearly $100 billion in 1999. Gore said he would use the money for education and health care and to pay off a part of the national debt. Bush promised to return the money to taxpayers in the form of tax cuts. Bush and Gore also debated the role that the United States—now the world's only superpower—should play in global affairs. Campaign polls showed that the race was very close.

On election night, the voting in some states was so close that no winner could be declared. It soon became clear that Florida's 25 electoral votes would determine the outcome of the election. The popular vote

© Houghton Mifflin Harcourt Publishing Company

The Election of 2000

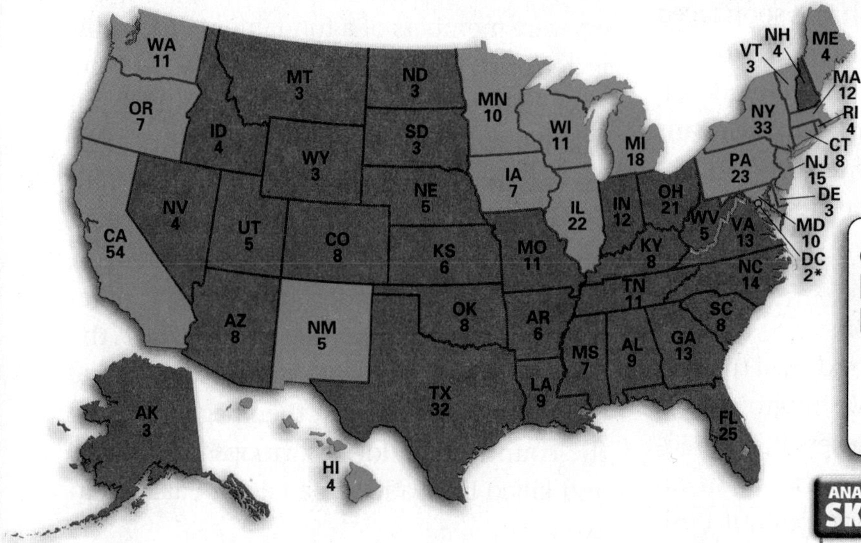

George W. Bush

Al Gore

Candidate	Party	Electoral Vote	Popular Vote	% Popular Vote
Bush	Republican	271	50,459,211	47.89
Gore	Democrat	266	51,003,894	48.41
Nader	Green		2,834,410	2.69
Other			1,062,745	1.01

*One elector from the District of Columbia abstained.

Source: *The World Almanac and Book of Facts,* 2002

ANALYSIS SKILL INTERPRETING CHARTS

Interpreting Charts By how many electoral votes did Bush win? How many more popular votes did Gore have than Bush?

in Florida was so close that state law required the votes to be recounted. A machine recount found that Bush had received a few hundred more votes than Gore. But Gore supporters wanted the votes in four counties to be counted by hand, arguing that this would ensure all votes were counted. The Bush campaign challenged this manual recount in court.

After several weeks of suspense, the Supreme Court ruled that the manual recounts could not ensure that all votes would be counted the same way. They ordered the recount to stop. Florida's electoral votes went to Bush, making him the winner of the election. He was the first president in more than 100 years to win the electoral vote while receiving fewer popular votes than his opponent.

At his inauguration, President Bush urged Americans to come together.

> "This is my solemn pledge: I will work to build a single nation of justice and opportunity... Today, we affirm a new commitment to live out our nation's promise through civility, courage, compassion, and character."
>
> —George W. Bush, January 20, 2001

Bush's Early Days in Office

The disputed election, however, caused lingering bitterness between Democrats and Republicans. Republicans held a small majority in the House of Representatives, while the Senate was split 50–50. When votes in the Senate are tied, the vice president casts the tie-breaking vote. This gave Vice President Dick Cheney an important role in helping to pass Republican legislation.

Bush put together his cabinet, appointing Colin Powell to the key position of secretary of state. Powell became the first African American to hold this office. Bush carried through with his campaign promise to cut taxes. Six months after taking office, he signed into law a $1.35 trillion tax-cut plan. He also signed into law an education reform plan called No Child Left Behind. This act created a national set of standards for every student and every school to meet. It also raised funding for schools.

READING CHECK **Analyzing** What was unusual about the outcome of the 2000 presidential election?

© Houghton Mifflin Harcourt Publishing Company • Image Credits: (tc), (tr), ©Brooks Kraft/Corbis

Fighting Terrorism

Despite many plans for educational and economic reform, President Bush was soon faced with the challenge of confronting terrorism. His administration became focused on developing a foreign policy to protect Americans from the growing threat of terrorist attacks after the events of September 11, 2001.

September 11, 2001

HISTORY
VIDEO
9/11: Watershed Event
hmhsocialstudies.com

On September 11, 2001, terrorists took control of four commercial airliners and used them as weapons to attack sites in Washington, D.C., and New York City. The hijackers flew an airplane into each of two towers that made up the **World Trade Center**, an important business center in New York City. The resulting fires caused the buildings, which had been the tallest in the nation, to crumble to the ground. About 2,500 people were killed in the collapsing buildings. Another airplane was flown into the **Pentagon**—the headquarters of the Department of Defense located outside of Washington, D.C. A fourth hijacked airplane crashed in a Pennsylvania field. The tragedy brought Americans together, and the nation received support from foreign leaders and citizens. One French newspaper's headline read, "WE ARE ALL AMERICANS." President Bush promised to find and punish those responsible for the attacks.

U.S. officials determined that the hijackers were members of a fundamentalist Islamic terrorist group called **al Qaeda**, or "the Base." The group was led by a wealthy Saudi Arabian exile, **Osama bin Laden**. Bin Laden and his followers were based in Afghanistan. The Taliban, an extreme Islamic group, ruled the country. After Taliban leaders refused to turn over bin Laden, the United States took military action. In October 2001 the United States attacked Afghanistan, drove the Taliban from power, then began helping the country rebuild. U.S. troops later found and killed bin Laden in a raid in Pakistan in 2011.

War in Iraq

After the attack on Afghanistan, President Bush argued that Saddam Hussein, the dictator of Iraq, posed an immediate threat to U.S. security. When the Persian Gulf War ended in 1991, Saddam had agreed to give up Iraq's **weapons of mass destruction**—chemical, biological, or nuclear weapons that can kill thousands. However, Saddam failed to fully cooperate with UN weapons inspectors.

Leaders from France, Germany, and Russia argued that the UN inspectors should be

Time Line

9/11 and Beyond

2001

September 11, 2001 About 3,000 Americans are killed in terrorist attacks on the United States. Al Qaeda claims responsibility three years later.

October 7, 2001 The war in Afghanistan begins.

November/December 2001 The Taliban regime is driven from power in Afghanistan.

January 2003 The Department of Homeland Security is created to oversee domestic security.

March 20, 2003 The air war in Iraq begins.

© Houghton Mifflin Harcourt Publishing Company • Image Credits: (bc), ©Oleg Nikishin/Getty Images; (bl), ©Ricky Flores/Corbis

given more time to search for weapons. President Bush and British prime minister Tony Blair said force should be used to ensure Iraq was complying with the weapons ban. On March 20, 2003, the United States and a coalition of allies launched a ground attack on Iraq. Saddam's government collapsed, and Saddam was eventually captured.

As in Afghanistan, U.S. officials began working with Iraqis to establish a democratic government. Violence continued, however, with attacks on U.S. soldiers and Iraqis who were working to rebuild the country. Iraqi voters elected new government leaders and approved a new constitution in 2005. In 2006 an Iraqi court sentenced Saddam to death, and he was executed a short time later. Deep divisions among Iraqis remained an issue, however, threatening the stability of the new government.

Debates at Home

The war in Iraq caused fierce debate at home. After months of searching, no weapons of mass destruction were uncovered, and no concrete ties between Saddam and al Qaeda could be proven. Critics began to accuse the Bush administration of exaggerating the danger Saddam posed to the United States. The continuing violence between Iraqi insurgents and U.S. soldiers led many Americans to call for an end to the war. Meanwhile, growing concerns that Iraq's neighbor, Iran, was working to develop nuclear weapons caused additional tensions in the region. President Bush lost much of his support among voters, and during the elections of 2006 Democrats gained a majority in both houses of Congress. The new Congress elected Nancy Pelosi the first female Speaker of the House of Representatives. In response to the outcome of the election, Secretary of Defense Donald Rumsfeld resigned and a new secretary, Robert Gates, was appointed. The newly elected Congress began calling for a plan to withdraw from Iraq.

READING CHECK **Summarizing** What led to the war in Iraq?

HISTORY

VIDEO
Fighting the War on Terrorism

hmhsocialstudies.com

Domestic Issues

After the 2004 election, Secretary of State Colin Powell resigned. Bush appointed Condoleezza Rice as his replacement. She became the first African American woman to hold the office. Bush's other new cabinet appointees included Alberto Gonzales, the first Hispanic attorney general.

December 13, 2003 Saddam Hussein is captured.

October 9, 2004 Afghanistan holds elections for a new government.

2005

January 30, 2005 Iraqis choose new leaders in a democratic election. Violence continues.

2006 Four men attack the U.S. Embassy in Damascus, Syria, highlighting tensions between Middle-Eastern nations and the United States.

May 2, 2011 U.S. troops kill Osama bin Laden in Pakistan.

ANALYSIS SKILL **READING TIME LINES**

How long did it take American forces to capture Saddam Hussein after the war in Iraq began?

© Houghton Mifflin Harcourt Publishing Company • Image Credits: (cr) ©Hasan Sarbakhshian/AP/WideWorld; (bl) ©Mirrorpix/Getty Images

BIOGRAPHY

George W. Bush

1946–

George W. Bush was born in Connecticut and grew up mainly in Texas. His family has a long history of political success—his grandfather was a U.S. senator and his father served as president from 1989 to 1993. Bush was a member of the National Guard during the Vietnam War, then attended Harvard Business School. After running unsuccessfully for Congress in 1978, he started several oil businesses in Texas and became part owner of the Texas Rangers baseball team. He was elected governor of Texas in 1994 and re-elected in 1998. In 2000 he defeated Al Gore in one of the closest presidential races in American history.

Sequencing What did George W. Bush do before he was elected president?

In late 2005 Bush nominated two new Supreme Court justices, John Roberts and Samuel Alito. The Senate investigated each thoroughly before approving them. With the confirmation of Bush's nominees, the court began making more conservative rulings.

Bush's administration faced much criticism for its response to the natural disaster of Hurricanes Katrina and Rita. Rain associated with Hurricane Katrina flooded many parts of the Gulf Coast and the city of New Orleans. The director of the Federal Emergency Management Agency (FEMA) stepped down amid criticism that the local, state, and federal governments responded inadequately to the crisis. As victims tried to rebuild their towns and cities, Hurricane Rita struck a second blow to the region. Although alone not as serious as Hurricane Katrina, the combined effects of the two storms caused many residents to move permanently from their homes along the Gulf Coast.

READING CHECK **Analyzing** What issues did Bush face in his second term?

SUMMARY Terrorism became a major concern after September 11, 2001.

Section 2 Assessment

hmhsocialstudies.com
ONLINE QUIZ

Reviewing Ideas, Terms, and People

1. a. **Describe** What was the outcome of the 2000 presidential election?
   b. **Explain** How did **George W. Bush** promise to use the government surplus?
   c. **Elaborate** How do you think the election of 2000 shows the importance of voting?
2. a. **Identify** What is al Qaeda?
   b. **Explain** Why did the United States enter into the war with Iraq?
   c. **Predict** What do you think the future holds for the war on terror?
3. a. **Recall** Who is Condoleezza Rice?
   b. **Interpret** How might Hurricane Katrina have affected people's view of government?

Critical Thinking

4. **Categorizing** Review your notes on the major policies of George W. Bush. Then copy the graphic organizer below and use it to describe George W. Bush's approach to dealing with terrorism.

Fighting Terrorism
→ Afghanistan
→ Iraq

FOCUS ON WRITING

5. **Describing the Effects of September 11** Take notes on the effects of the September 11, 2001, terrorist attacks. How did Americans respond to the attacks? How did the attacks change the focus of the American people? How did they affect the presidency of George W. Bush?

© Houghton Mifflin Harcourt Publishing Company • Image Credits: (tl), Courtesy the White House/Photo by Eric Draper

The Road Ahead

SECTION 3

If YOU were there...

You are a student studying American history. You have read about the dramatic impact that inventions, new industries, political changes, and wars have had on daily life over the years. In your own life, you have seen how much things can change in just a few years. Now picture yourself living in the United States 50 years from now.

What will be different about life in America?

BUILDING BACKGROUND Think of the challenges Americans have faced throughout our history. Consider how much the country has changed since it was founded and how much progress has been made. Today the United States continues to face challenges and to search for solutions.

What You Will Learn...

Main Ideas

1. The American economy and job market are changing.
2. Technological advances continue to solve everyday problems.
3. Americans are a diverse people united by shared ideals.

The Big Idea

The United States continues to grow and change as we move ahead in the twenty-first century.

Key Terms

service economy
globalization
Internet
Information Revolution
AIDS
ozone layer
global warming

hmhsocialstudies.com
TAKING NOTES

Use the graphic organizer online to take notes on changes taking place in the United States.

America's Changing Economy

In public opinion polls taken in 2010, Americans listed economic recovery and unemployment among the most important challenges facing the United States. Other major concerns included health insurance reform, terrorism, and immigration. The growing national debt was another key concern. After several years of surpluses, the government began running a deficit again in 2002. Slow economic growth, the cost of the war in Iraq, and tax cuts all contributed to the rising budget imbalance. Beginning with the 2010 budget, the deficit was expected to fall from previous years, but remain high as a percentage of Gross Domestic Product (GDP).

The American economy has experienced important ups and downs in recent years. During the 1990s the stock market boomed, and unemployment fell to its lowest level in 30 years. Much of this economic growth was powered by Internet companies and other high-tech firms. When some high-tech firms failed to earn profits, however, their stocks lost value, and many went out of business. Unemployment began rising again. A similar financial crisis began in 2007 when risky mortgages led to huge losses by some of the largest investment firms in the nation. Amid controversy, the federal government provided money to help these firms recover.

In recent years, many traditional industries have declined in importance to the U.S. economy. Many textile companies, for example, have closed mills and shifted their operations to countries where labor is less expensive. This is part of a larger trend in which the percentage of Americans working in manufacturing has steadily fallen. The U.S. economy has moved toward becoming a **service economy**. This means that most people have jobs providing services, such as medical care or entertainment, rather than producing goods.

By the end of the 1990s, about 75 percent of American workers were employed in service jobs. By 2010, this number had risen to above 80 percent, and is expected to keep rising. Health care, computer engineering, and education are expected to be among the fastest-growing fields. Such predictions are based partly on population trends. As the number of older Americans increases, for example, so will the need for nurses and other health-care professionals.

Another ongoing change in our economy is the process of **globalization**—growing connections among economies and cultures all over the world. Multinational corporations—companies that do business in more than one country—play a large part in globalization. For example, you can find American fast-food restaurants in Russia and Japanese car factories in the United States. Increasing international trade has also contributed to globalization. In 1995 more than 120 nations joined to form the World Trade Organization (WTO). The WTO's goal is to promote international trade by removing political and economic trade barriers between nations.

Americans have different opinions about how globalization will affect the United States. Supporters believe globalization will lead to increased U.S. exports and new jobs at home. Opponents worry that Americans will lose jobs as U.S. companies move their operations to countries where wages are lower. Still others insist that globalization can help our economy if it is well managed. Senator Joseph Lieberman of Connecticut said, "Only education, innovation, investment, trade, training, and hard work will give us the growth and jobs we want and need."

READING CHECK **Identifying Cause and Effect** What economic trend led to the creation of the World Trade Organization?

Life in the Twenty-first Century

QUICK FACTS

Financial Crisis

Slowing home sales and failed investments led to an economic downturn that resulted in federal payments to several banks and manufacturing firms.

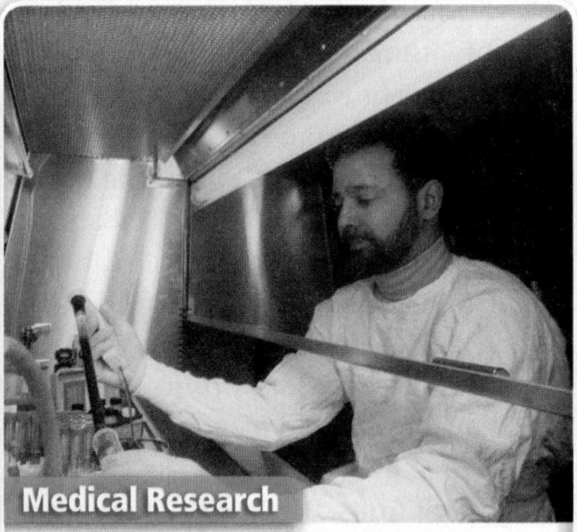

Medical Research

Medical research has improved the lives of millions, as new medicines combat old and new diseases. In 2009, a new vaccine was created to curb the spread of a strain of swine flu that many feared would lead to a world-wide pandemic.

© Houghton Mifflin Harcourt Publishing Company • Image Credits: (bkgd) ©Digital Art/Corbis; (br) Custom Medical Stock Photo; (bl) ©Ariel Skelley/Corbis

Technology Moves Forward

As you have seen throughout this book, technological changes and new inventions have dramatic effects on life in the United States and around the world. This continues to be true of our lives today. Just think about all the ways you use technology every day.

One of the new technologies that has changed everyday life is the **Internet**—a global system of computer networks through which people anywhere in the world can communicate and share information. The Internet was first developed in 1969 by scientists at the U.S. Department of Defense. Early computer networks were used mainly by government and university researchers. Then in the 1990s, computer programmers developed the World Wide Web, enabling people to access information from computers around the world.

Internet use exploded in the 1990s. Computers and the Internet made it easier and faster for people at home, work, and school to access and share information. This important development was known as the **Information Revolution**. Bill Gates, a leader in the computer industry, described the exciting changes this revolution promised:

> "We are watching something historic happening, and it will affect the world . . . the same way the scientific method, the invention of printing, and the arrival of the Industrial Age did."
>
> —Bill Gates, quoted in *Newsweek*

Excitement about the Internet and the Information Revolution helped fuel the economic boom of the 1990s. Although not all Internet companies succeeded, the Internet has changed the way we find information and communicate with each other. Internet use continues to grow rapidly around the world today.

Technology is also helping to **facilitate** new medical research. For example, researchers have made important breakthroughs in understanding connections between genetics and illness. In 2003 scientists completed the Human Genome Project, a project to identify more than 30,000 genes in human DNA. Medical researchers hope to use this information to find treatments for a wide range of diseases.

Another ongoing challenge for medical reasearchers is fighting **AIDS** — acquired immune deficiency syndrome. Caused by the human immunodeficiency virus (HIV), AIDS shuts down the body's immune system.

FOCUS ON READING

Predict how the use of the Internet might change American society.

HISTORY

VIDEO

Computers

hmhsocialstudies.com

ACADEMIC VOCABULARY

facilitate
bring about

New Technology

Advances in computing power and wireless devices have changed the way people across the world communicate. Social networking has become an important part of everyday life for many Americans.

Environmental Issues

The nation and the world face the issues of environmental damage and an increase in population. A 2009 international summit on global warming acknowledged the need for curbs on emissions, but no binding resolutions were agreed upon.

Terrorism

Increases in the number and severity of terrorist attacks directed at the United States and its interests overseas have led to stricter controls on people and goods coming into the nation.

ANALYSIS SKILL ANALYZING VISUALS

What are some ways people are responding to the challenges of the twenty-first century?

© Houghton Mifflin Harcourt Publishing Company • Image Credits: (bkgd), ©Digital Art/Corbis; (br), ©Robert Nickelsberg/Getty Images; (bc), ©Digital Vision/Getty Images; (bl), ©Comstock/Jupiterimages Corporation

BIOGRAPHY

Barack Obama

1961–

In 2008 Barack Obama became the first African American to be elected president of the United States. Obama worked as a lawyer and community organizer in Chicago before entering politics. He won his first race, for the Illinois State Senate, but then lost a bid for a seat in the U.S. House of Representatives. He also served Illinois in the U.S. Senate. Obama came to national attention with his keynote address at the 2004 Democratic National Convention, and became the Democratic Party nominee for president four years later. Foreign policy and the economy were the primary focus of Obama's first years in office, as the nation faced two wars and a financial crisis when he took office. In 2009 Obama won the Nobel Peace Prize, becoming the fourth American president to win this honor.

Summarizing What political offices has Barack Obama held?

HISTORY

VIDEO
Election 2008

hmhsocialstudies.com

hmhsocialstudies.com

ANIMATED GEOGRAPHY AND HISTORY
Satellite View of Earth

This makes it more likely that people with AIDS will contract other illnesses and die. As of 2005, more than 23 million people worldwide had died from AIDS. Scientists have developed drugs that help control the HIV virus but have not yet found a cure. In 2002 leaders from around the world founded the Global Fund to Fight AIDS, Tuberculosis, and Malaria. The Global Fund provides money to treat these deadly diseases and search for cures.

Scientists are also searching for ways to help protect the environment. Because environmental quality affects every nation, international solutions are required. In the 1980s, for example, many people became concerned about the condition of the **ozone layer**—a thin layer of gas in the upper atmosphere that blocks harmful solar rays. The United States joined with more than 100 other nations to ban the use of chemicals that were harming the ozone layer. By 2004 some scientists reported that damage to the ozone layer was slowly being repaired.

Another environmental issue facing the world is climate change, or **global warming**. The burning of fossil fuels such as gasoline and coal releases carbon dioxide into Earth's atmosphere. Many scientists warn that rising levels of carbon dioxide are causing a greenhouse effect that traps heat from the sun in Earth's atmosphere. This could cause temperatures to rise, which could cause rising sea levels and more severe weather patterns. A 2001 United Nations scientific report predicted that Earth's average temperature could rise between 2 and 10 degrees by 2100. World leaders continue to meet to discuss methods for reducing the effects of global warming.

Concerns about global warming and high oil prices have encouraged development of new transportation technologies. In 2007 Americans bought record numbers of hybrid cars, which run partially on electricity. Scientists are also developing vehicles that will run entirely on hydrogen and release almost no pollution.

Even as some scientists take on issues facing our planet, others look to the challenge of exploring space. In 2004 NASA landed two robotic vehicles on Mars. The rovers began exploring the Martian surface, sending back images that people could see on NASA's Web site. In 2009 a probe discovered a significant amount of water on the moon's surface, and more unmanned missions are planned. Human exploration of space continues on the International Space Station and with successful shuttle flights, although shuttle accidents in 1986 and 2003 killed 14 astronauts. In 2010, President Obama proposed a cut to NASA's budget for Constellation, a program that planned to send humans to the moon for the first time since 1972.

READING CHECK **Summarizing** In what key areas is technology changing modern life?

© Houghton Mifflin Harcourt Publishing Company • Image Credits: (tl) Official White House photo by Pete Souza

The American People

The American population will continue to grow and change in the twenty-first century. The U.S. Census Bureau reports that our population is more ethnically diverse than ever before. In 2005 the bureau reported that Hispanics made up 14 percent of the country's total population, making them the country's largest minority group. African Americans made up just over 13 percent of the American population, and Asian Americans about 5 percent.

These changes are greatly influenced by immigration patterns. Of the more than 37.5 million foreign-born residents, 53 percent were born in Latin America and 26 percent were born in Asia. Based on these trends, the Census Bureau predicts that the country's white and nonwhite populations will be about equal by the year 2050.

Increased diversity is reflected not only in American society but also in individual Americans. In the year 2000 the Census Bureau began allowing people to indicate in official surveys that they were of more than one race, and more than 6.8 million Americans did so. In 2008, American voters chose a man of mixed race, Barack Obama, as president for the first time.

While the diversity of our population grows, Americans of all backgrounds share a belief in many basic **ideals**. Our shared commitment to the ideals of freedom, equality, and justice helps keep our nation strong. So does our shared dedication to the responsibilities of citizenship. Americans also share many of the same hopes and dreams for the future.

ACADEMIC VOCABULARY
ideals ideas or goals that people try to live up to

READING CHECK **Predicting** How might the U.S. population change over the next 100 years?

SUMMARY The United States continues to create opportunities and face challenges. How would you like to contribute to your country's future?

Section 3 Assessment

hmhsocialstudies.com ONLINE QUIZ

Reviewing Ideas, Terms, and People

1. a. **Recall** How has the American economy changed in the past several decades?
   b. **Explain** What caused government deficits to rise in the early 2000s?
   c. **Draw Conclusions** How do you think **globalization** has changed the U.S. economy?
2. a. **Identify** What are some of the world's most recent technological advances?
   b. **Explain** How did the **Internet** spark an **Information Revolution**?
   c. **Predict** Do you think **global warming** will affect your life in the future? Why or why not?
3. a. **Describe** Describe the U.S. population today.
   b. **Make Inferences** Why do you think the Census Bureau started allowing people to mark more than one race?
   c. **Elaborate** How do you think diversity and shared ideals affect America?

Critical Thinking

4. **Categorizing** Review your notes on changes taking place in the United States. Then copy the graphic organizer below and use it to describe major technological challenges for the future.

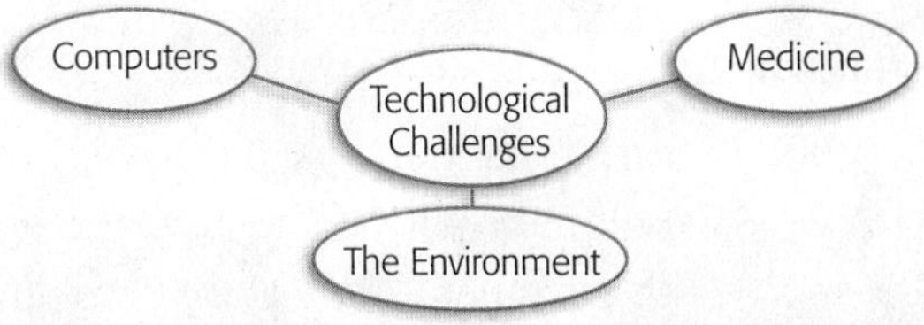

FOCUS ON WRITING

5. **Elaborating on Key Themes** Identify key elements of American life today. In your opinion, what are some great things about life in America? What do you think are the major challenges facing Americans today? What are some possible solutions? Which subjects would you like to read more about? Think about links you could include on your Web site that would provide readers with more information about these topics.

© Houghton Mifflin Harcourt Publishing Company

Case Study

Modern Society

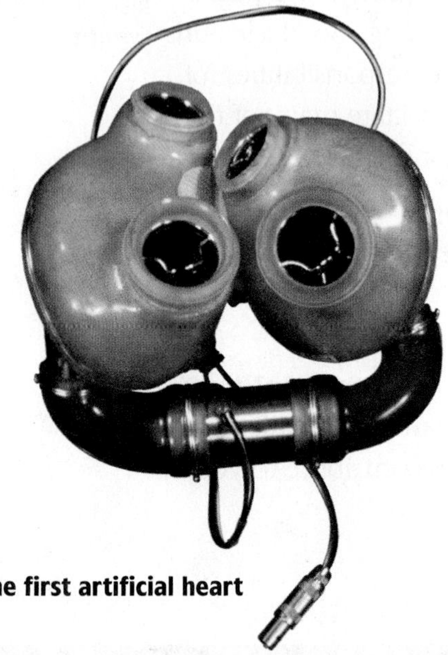

The first artificial heart

Advances in Technology

The rapid advances in technology after World War II helped to create modern society in the United States. Because of rationing, Americans had done without many goods during the war. After the war, they wanted to buy cars, televisions, new clothes, and many other products. Innovation and the economy boomed as companies and entrepreneurs raced to meet these demands.

Plastics Everywhere

During the war, the raw materials used in manufacturing were in short supply. Advances in plastics technology helped to fill these shortages. After the war, plastics began to be used in making many different products. Plastics were used to make some basic parts for appliances and automobiles, in packaging for foods and other products, and even to make children's toys, such as dolls and action figures. As toys became less expensive to produce, more children were able to have similar ones. Plastics technology even allowed doctors to build a successful artificial heart. Today, plastics can be found in almost every product sold in the United States.

Consumer Goods

Many of the technological advancements after World War II were driven by the demand for consumer goods. Companies strived to make improvements to existing technologies like televisions, radios, and appliances. They also worked to develop new technologies and products. First audiocassettes in the 1950s and later videotapes and then compact discs (CD) and digital video diskettes (DVD) in the 1990s

Early computers took up entire rooms, yet they could not do many of the tasks the smallest computers of today can.

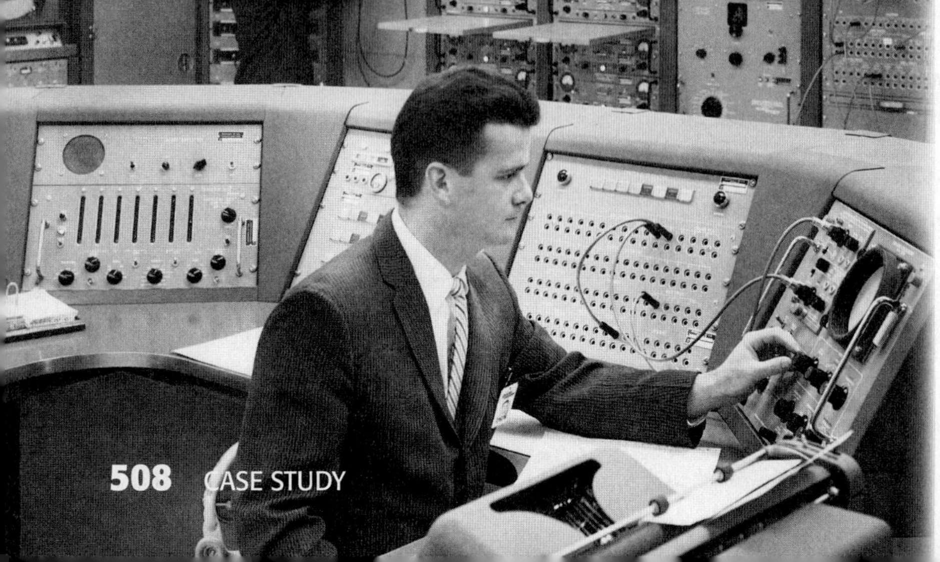

© Houghton Mifflin Harcourt Publishing Company • Image Credits: (b) ©Superstock/Getty Images; (t) ©Hank Morgan/Photo Researchers/Getty Images

provided people with new ways to access entertainment. Later, people could purchase electronic devices that could play songs and movies from digital files.

Other electronic devices improved the way people worked. Calculators made it easier for people to add, subtract, divide, multiply and even solve complex mathematical equations. Word processors made typing and producing documents much quicker and easier. People also began playing video games at coin-operated consoles. Then, the personal computer combined aspects of many devices. Computer technology also changed the way people played, spawning the home video game industry.

Cell phones and later smart phones allowed people to communicate more effectively from almost anywhere around the world. Through the end of the twentieth century and into the 2000s, advances in consumer goods have helped shaped the way Americans live, work, and play.

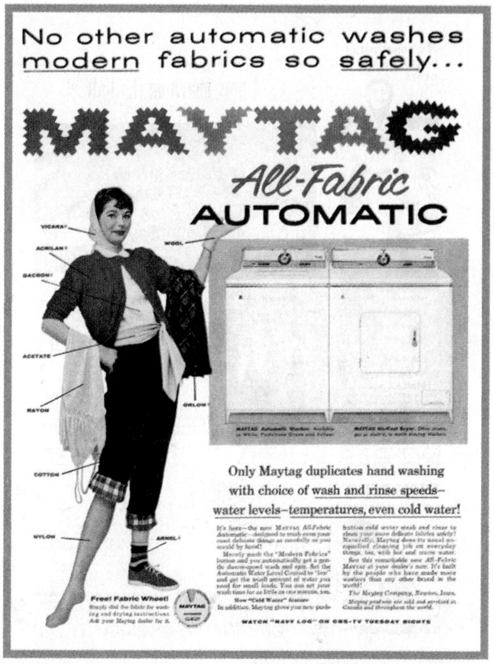

Electrical appliances like washers and dryers became cheaper to produce and buy, making them available to larger numbers of people.

The Government Helps

The United States government has played a large role in developing many of the new technologies that have shaped modern society. NASA launched the first United States satellite in 1958. Today, satellites provide the infrastructure for many other technologies, including television, mobile telephones, and the Internet. Using satellite technology, the United States military developed the Global Positioning System (GPS). Today, an individual can buy an inexpensive GPS receiver that will tell them their location anywhere on Earth.

The Internet itself was first developed by a United States government program. In the late 1960s, American researchers connected several computers in different cities through the phone lines. Through this network, they were able to get the computers to communicate with one another. This early computer network, called ARPANET, was the predecessor of the World Wide Web (WWW), which connects millions of computers today.

Case Study Assessment

1. Why were plastics first used?
2. What helped drive technological advancements after World War II?
3. **Activity** Identify one technological advancement that you could not live without. Make a poster that describes the benefits of this technology.

Impact of Technology

Since World War II, advances in technology have had enormous influence in shaping our modern society. New technologies have changed the foods we eat, the clothes we wear, and the places we live. They have had an impact in almost every part of our lives—from school to work to leisure.

In many cases, technology has had a positive impact in people's lives. For example, the Internet has opened up new ways for people to work, sell and buy products, and communicate. Improvements in refrigeration and food preservatives have made food safer. In addition, improved irrigation, chemical fertilizers, and insect controls have improved soil and crop management, increasing the amount of food that farmers can produce. Technology has even enhanced some leisure activities, like fishing. Sonar technology, or sound waves, has allowed anglers to locate fish under the water.

Sometimes, though, technology can have an unintended negative impact. Some of the same pesticides used by farmers to control insects were found to have harmful effects on animals and potentially people. In the 1960s, widespread use of the pesticide DDT was believed to be causing reductions in the bald eagle population. Because of this, the chemical was banned for agricultural use in 1972. Nuclear power, although clean and sustainable, has been at the center of several catastrophic accidents; most recently, the Fukushima Daiichi disaster in Japan in 2011.

Nuclear power plants have become an increasingly important source of electricity in every region of the nation. Many people are concerned about the environmental effects of the plants, however. Nuclear plants produce about one-fourth of the electricity in Alabama.

Linking to Today

In the past, the most reliable weather forecasting might be found in a farmer's almanac or by consulting a thermometer and barometer. Today, meteorologists can track weather patterns using satellites and Doppler radar. They can then use the data they collect to predict conditions for hurricanes, tornadoes, and lightning. Radar was widely used during World War II to track enemy aircraft. *Sputnik*, the first satellite, was launched by the Soviet Union in 1957. The first satellite used for weather prediction was launched two years later. Today the United States uses four satellites to monitor the nation's weather.

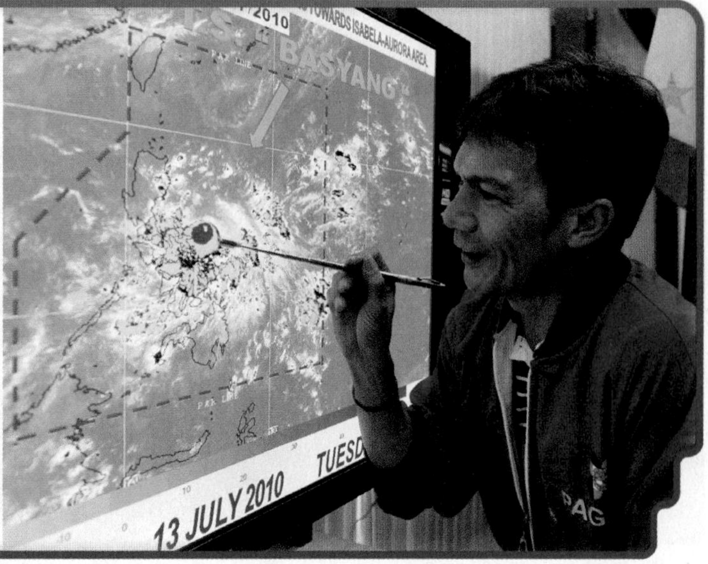

ANALYSIS SKILL **ANALYZING INFORMATION**

How has technology improved people's ability to predict the weather?

Mass Media and Society

By 1850, there were more than 3,000 newspapers in the United States. In the 1930s, 60 percent of American households had radios. By 1955, more than half of all American households had a television set. From these devices, people got both news and entertainment.

At the end of the twentieth century, newspaper readership began to decline. Twenty-four-hour news and sports channels on television have allowed people to get information much more quickly than from a traditional newspaper.

Post World War II, the popularity of television also caused a decline in radio listenership. However, in the last few decades, radio has seen a resurgence of popularity with talk radio, which blends the current events elements of news with opinion and audience participation.

Today, people have access to more information than at any time in human history. The Internet is pushing the boundaries of mass media. Smart phones allow people to have 24-hour access to information right at their fingertips from almost anywhere on Earth.

Cultures today are connected like never before in the history of the world. Through social media, people can share what interests them, and not just with their friends, but also with strangers in different countries. Cultural trends that might once have been contained to a specific geographic region can now influence people around the world.

Access to Mass Media

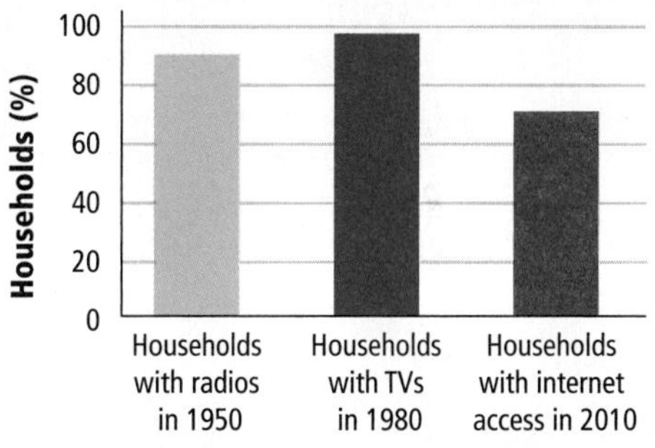

Source: *U.S. Census Bureau*

ANALYSIS SKILL **INTERPRETING CHARTS**

What conclusion can you draw about the number of televisions in 2010?

© Houghton Mifflin Harcourt Publishing Company • Image Credits: (t) ©Jay Directo/AFP/Getty Images

In the 1930s and 1940s, radio was the primary form of mass communication. President Franklin Roosevelt used national radio addresses to share his views with Americans. Today, politicians use hand-held internet devices to send emails and tweets to the nation.

Mass Media and Politics

Mass media has been a part of politics in the United States since before the Revolutionary War. Thomas Paine famously published *Common Sense*, a pamphlet he used to argue that the Thirteen Colonies should claim their independence. The yellow journalism of the late 1800s led the U.S. military into the Spanish-American War. Graphic news stories of Spanish brutality in Cuba caused many Americans to support the Cuban rebels. In the 1930s, President Franklin D. Roosevelt used the radio to give his fireside chats. He used these talks to ease the fears of Americans and to try to gain support for his New Deal policies.

Mass media became an even more influential political tool with television. The first televised presidential debate between John F. Kennedy and Richard Nixon took place in 1960. Those who watched the debate on TV felt that Kennedy clearly won. Those who listened on radio felt the debate was much closer.

Today, televised presidential debates are much more commonplace, and both candidates are usually well prepared. However, the Internet has offered new powerful tools for mass communication. In 2008, a little-known one-term senator named Barack Obama utilized the Internet and social media in his campaign for president. Obama's campaign surprised many of his opponents by taking advantage of social media's ability to organize and motivate people on a mass scale.

© Houghton Mifflin Harcourt Publishing Company • Image Credits: (b) ©Ron Sachs/Pool/Corbis; (t) ©MPI/Archive Photos/Getty Images

Politics and Reform

Modern American society has also been changed by reforms to governmental policies. In the 1930s, President Franklin Roosevelt helped create a welfare program to help people who are in need. Since that time, other presidents have worked to reform, or improve, the welfare system. In 1996, President Bill Clinton signed the Personal Responsibility and Work Opportunity Act, which set new limits to help move people off welfare and into jobs.

President Lyndon Johnson helped develop a preschool program called Head Start for children in need. This full-day, full-year preschool program has expanded to serve almost 30 million children since it first began. The Elementary and Secondary Education Act (ESEA) also set high standards and protected equal education for all students. In 2001, President George W. Bush signed the No Child Left Behind Act (NCLB) to reauthorize ESEA and to expand the federal role in education.

Children across the nation benefit from afterschool programs provided by federal funds.

Lawmakers have begun other programs to help make health insurance affordable. Medicare provides health insurance for Americans who are 65 years and older or those who have disabilities. Medicaid provides affordable health insurance for low-income children, families, elderly, and people with disabilities. The Children's Health Insurance Program (CHIP) provides low-cost health insurance for children in low-income families who cannot afford private insurance and do not qualify for Medicaid. In 2010, the Patient Protection and Affordable Care Act signed by President Obama was designed to increase access to health care for all Americans.

Case Study Assessment

1. Give an example of a positive impact of technology. Give an example of a negative impact of technology.
2. How did technology influence the presidential election of 1960?
3. **Activity** Write a speech that will be delivered on television to help President Lyndon Johnson convince people to support one of the programs of the Great Society.

© Houghton Mifflin Harcourt Publishing Company • Image Credits: (t) ©Monkey Business/Fotolia

Immigration Today

Immigrants from Asia make up about 26 percent of all foreign-born U.S. residents. Although Chinese and Japanese immigrants have been coming to the United States for generations, Southeast Asians such as the Hmong, Laotians, Vietnamese, and Cambodians are groups that have only recently begun to arrive.

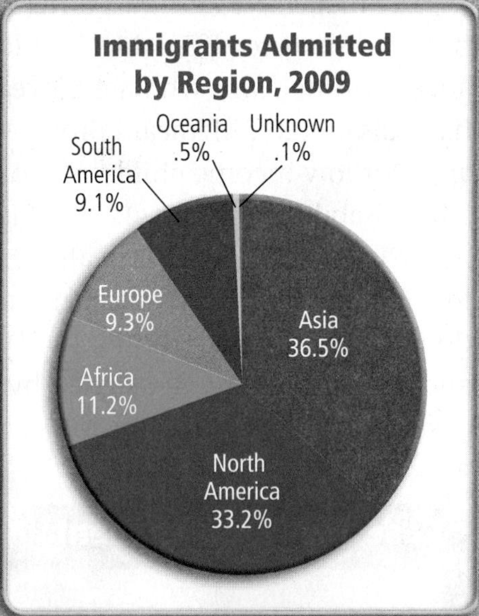
Immigrants Admitted by Region, 2009
Oceania .5%
Unknown .1%
South America 9.1%
Europe 9.3%
Asia 36.5%
Africa 11.2%
North America 33.2%

America has always been a nation of immigrants. Today people from every country move to the United States. In 2008 approximately 14 percent of the U.S. population was foreign born. Many of these people will eventually choose to become naturalized citizens. With the threat of global terrorism, however, U.S. immigration policy is becoming more strict. People from certain countries are now required to register with the Department of Homeland Security.

Image Credits: (c), ©Elise Amendola/AP/Wide World Photos

© Houghton Mifflin Harcourt Publishing Company

Many immigrants from Eastern and Western Europe come to the United States seeking a better life. They accounted for about 9 percent of the immigrants admitted in 2009.

Immigrants from around the world often choose to become naturalized U.S. citizens. The day they take the oath of American citizenship is often a day of celebration, as it was for this mother and daughter from Uganda.

Immigrants arrive in the United States searching for economic, educational, and political opportunities. Immigrants from Mexico and Central America made up about 19 percent of new permanent residents of the United States in 2009.

GEOGRAPHY SKILLS INTERPRETING MAPS

1. **Human-Environment Interaction** From which continent does the largest number of immigrants come?
2. **Movement** How do you think immigration affects U.S. society today?

© Houghton Mifflin Harcourt Publishing Company

Image Credits: (t), ©Rob Schoenbaum/AP/Wide World Photos; (br), ©Bizuayehu Tesfaye/AP/Wide World Photos; (bl), ©Chabruken/Getty Images

Case Study

Immigration in Alabama

Immigration and the Economy

Since World War II, the economic prosperity of the United States has drawn large numbers of foreign immigrants to the nation. Migration among the states has also increased as technological changes have allowed people to become more mobile. Alabama's population and economy have changed as a result.

FOREIGN-BORN POPULATION OF ALABAMA

Total Foreign-Born Population 168,596 (2010)

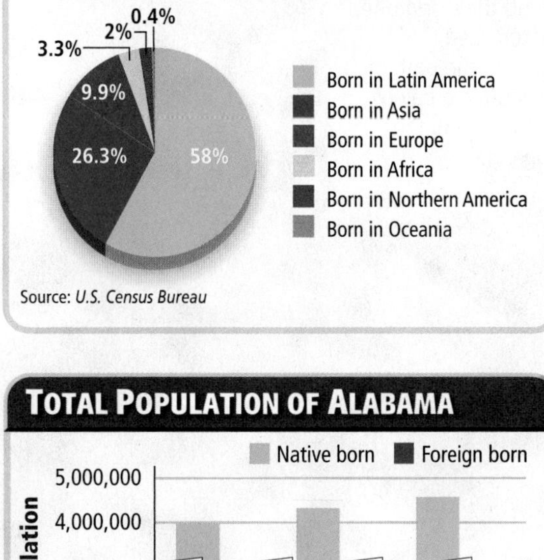

0.4%
2%
3.3%
9.9%
26.3%
58%
Born in Latin America
Born in Asia
Born in Europe
Born in Africa
Born in Northern America
Born in Oceania

Source: *U.S. Census Bureau*

TOTAL POPULATION OF ALABAMA

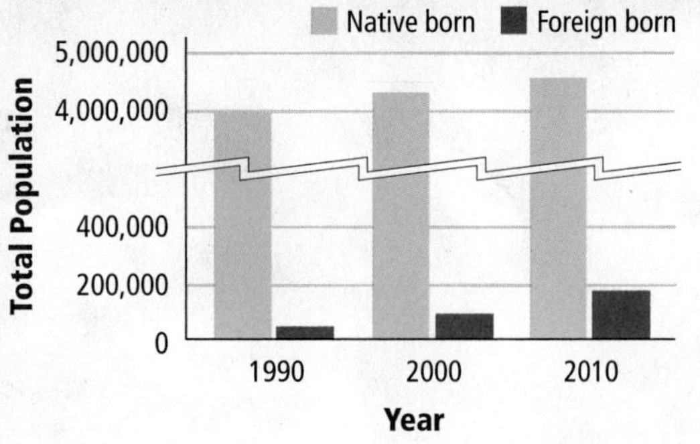

Native born
Foreign born
5,000,000
4,000,000
400,000
200,000
0
Total Population
1990
2000
2010
Year

Source: *U.S. Census Bureau*

ANALYSIS SKILL ANALYZING VISUALS

About how many Alabamians were born in Asia?

International Immigration

According to the 2010 census, about 13 percent of the U.S. population is foreign-born. More than a third of these immigrants have entered the nation since 2000. People move to the United States from every region of the world. A little more than half arrive from Latin America and the Caribbean, and another 28 percent from Asia. California has the largest number of immigrants, about twice the national average. In Alabama, the number of immigrants is much lower. About 3.4 percent of Alabama residents are foreign-born.

How does immigration affect the economy of the United States and Alabama? In general immigration encourages growth and leads to higher wages for both native-born and immigrant populations. Immigrants make up nearly 16 percent of the American workforce. Highly skilled immigrants contribute to the many technological innovations that have benefited the U.S. economy since World War II. In fact, of the scientists working in the United States today who have a Ph.D., about 40 percent are immigrants. In addition, less skilled immigrants work in many different sectors of the economy, such as service

© Houghton Mifflin Harcourt Publishing Company

industries, manufacturing, and farming. Immigrants also start new businesses at a much higher rate than the native-born population.

While most immigrants enter the country legally, others are undocumented. The number of undocumented residents is very difficult to determine, but studies estimate between one fourth and one third of immigrants since 1980 may be undocumented. Some Americans believe that undocumented residents take jobs and services away from legal residents. In 2011, Alabama joined many other states in passing a law designed to deny government services to undocumented residents. Many undocumented workers left their jobs after the law was passed, and several industries faced labor shortages. About 2.5 percent of the Alabama population is estimated to be undocumented.

ALABAMA AND UNITED STATES POPULATIONS, 2011

	Alabama	United States
Total Population	4,802,740	311,591,917
Whites	70.1%	78.1%
Blacks	26.5%	13.1%
Hispanics	4.0%	16.7%
Foreign-born	3.4%	12.7%
Language other than English spoken at home	4.9%	20.1%

Source: *U.S. Census Bureau*

ANALYSIS SKILL ANALYZING VISUALS

What is the second-largest population group in Alabama?

Interstate Migration

Immigrants are not the only ones who move to find a better life. In the years since World War II, many Americans have moved internally within the country. People have moved from farms and small towns to cities and from city centers to surrounding suburbs. There has also been a population shift away from the colder, industrial regions of the Northeast "Rust Belt" and toward the warmer, southern areas of the "Sun Belt." This has spurred economic growth in Alabama and the region.

Case Study Assessment

1. From what parts of the world do immigrants arrive to Alabama today?
2. How has immigration affected the economies of Alabama and the United States since World War II?
3. **Activity** People move to Alabama for a variety of economic reasons. Research what jobs might draw someone to Alabama. Prepare a short report on the information you find.

© Houghton Mifflin Harcourt Publishing Company

Confronting Controversial Issues

Define the Skill

The United States and the world face many challenges in the twenty-first century. People often have different opinions on how to deal with these challenges, which can lead to controversy. Some of the issues discussed in this book remain controversial.

As citizens of a democracy, Americans have a responsibility to confront controversial issues. This includes learning about different issues and why they are controversial. It also involves discussing the issues and forming opinions about them. Part of the democratic system is listening to other people's ideas about how to solve controversial issues and presenting your own ideas in a helpful way. In this way, everyone's ideas can be heard and discussed, so that the best course of action can be followed.

Learn the Skill

To confront controversial issues, it is important to understand them. You can start by identifying them. For example, one controversial issue in the 21st century is globalization—the process of economies and cultures becoming more closely connected. Some people think that globalization is a good way to improve the lives of all the world's citizens. Others think that globalization destroys what is unique about individual cultures.

Once the issue has been identified, you can learn more about it. Books, news reports, and articles are good sources of information on controversial issues. They can provide different points of view on an issue. Gathering different opinions about globalization, for example, can help you see why it is controversial. It can also help you determine your own point of view on the issue.

Follow these guidelines to confront other controversial issues.

1. Identify the issue.
2. Learn about the issue. Gather information on the subject from different sources. Determine why the issue is controversial.
3. Figure out your own point of view on the issue.
4. Discuss the issue with others. Because the issue is controversial and may lead to disagreements, it is important to be respectful of differences of opinion.

Practice the Skill

Follow these instructions to confront the controversial issue of how to deal with terrorism.

1. Find at least three articles showing different points of view about dealing with terrorism.
2. Read and take notes on the articles you have found. Based on what you have learned, determine your own point of view.
3. Have a class discussion about dealing with terrorism. Listen to opposing points of view. Share your own ideas and explain how you arrived at your point of view.

© Houghton Mifflin Harcourt Publishing Company

CHAPTER 16

Chapter Review

History's Impact
▶ **video series**
Review the video to answer the closing question:
The National Park Service is constantly challenged to find a balance between wildlife and visitors. Why is this?

Visual Summary

QUICK FACTS

Use the visual summary below to help you review the main ideas of the chapter.

The United States today acts as a member of the global community as it faces the future.

Challenges
- Environmental issues
- Diseases
- Terrorism

Benefits
- Technology
- Political alliances

Reviewing Vocabulary, Terms, and People

Match the numbered person or term with the correct lettered definition.

1. World Trade Center
2. Colin Powell
3. Al Gore
4. global warming
5. Saddam Hussein
6. Madeleine Albright
7. AIDS
8. terrorism

a. 2000 Democratic presidential candidate
b. the rise in average temperatures around the world
c. dictator of Iraq overthrown in 2003
d. buildings attacked on September 11, 2001
e. deadly disease that shuts down the body's immune system
f. the use of violence by individuals or small groups to achieve political goals
g. the first woman secretary of state
h. the first African American secretary of state

Comprehension and Critical Thinking

SECTION 1

9. a. Recall What important Cold War symbol was destroyed in Germany in 1989?

b. Explain How did U.S. foreign policy change in the Clinton administration?

c. Evaluate Do you think NAFTA helped the U.S. economy? Why?

SECTION 2

10. a. Identify Who was responsible for the September 11, 2001, terrorist attacks on the United States?

b. Explain Why was the 2000 U.S. presidential election controversial?

c. Evaluate Do you think the United States was right to go to war with Iraq in 2003? Why?

© Houghton Mifflin Harcourt Publishing Company

SECTION 3

11. a. **Identify** What trend is responsible for increasing diversity in the United States?
   b. **Analyze** Why are some people concerned about globalization?
   c. **Predict** What aspects of life do you think will be most affected by new technology in the future?

Reviewing Themes

12. **Economics** How have changes in the economy affected American society since the 1990s?
13. **Politics** How did international politics change over the course of George W. Bush's presidency?

Reading Skills 21st CENTURY

Predicting *Use the Reading Skills taught in this chapter to answer the question below.*

14. What might you predict for the future of society in the United States? What about the U.S. economy? How might American politics stay the same or change? What ideas in the chapter lead you to these conclusions?

Using the Internet 21st CENTURY

15. **Activity: Ending the Cold War** By the 1980s, the Cold War had been going on for decades. But times were changing—communism was falling apart, and the Soviet Union would never be the same again. Use the online book to research the factors that led to the decline of the Soviet Union's political and economic power. Then create a brochure on the fall of communism in the Soviet Union, the factors that led to this decline, and the impact on Russian society.

hmhsocialstudies.com

Social Studies Skills 21st CENTURY

Confronting Controversial Issues *Use the Social Studies Skills taught in this chapter to answer the question below.*

16. Name one controversial issue today. What are two different points of view on the issue?

FOCUS ON WRITING

17. **Designing Your Web Site** Review your notes and plan your Web site. Decide whether it will be just one page or multiple linked pages. Remember to include information on significant people, events, and ideas. Include ideas for photos, audio, or video you would like to place on your site. You might also want to provide links to other Web sites where viewers can find more information. Make sure your links connect to reliable Web sites, such as government sites or those for newspapers or museums. Finally, choose the Web site address you would like to use.

© Houghton Mifflin Harcourt Publishing Company • Image Credits: (br), HMH/Sam Dudgeon

CHAPTER 16

Standardized Test Practice

DIRECTIONS: Read each question and write the letter of the best response.

1 Madeleine Albright and Colin Powell both

A conducted breakthrough medical research.
B lost close presidential elections.
C served as secretary of state.
D commanded troops in Iraq.

2 One way the U.S. economy is changing is that

A more people are working in service industries.
B more people are working in manufacturing.
C the health care and computer industries are shrinking.
D textile mills are hiring thousands of new workers.

3 Saddam Hussein was

A removed from power in Operation Desert Storm.
B elected to the new Iraqi government in 2005.
C killed in the September 11, 2001, attacks.
D captured as a result of the 2003 U.S. invasion of Iraq.

4 The Cold War came to an end after

A Communists lost power in East Germany.
B prodemocracy movements began in Eastern Europe.
C the Soviet Union dissolved in 1991.
D Iraq invaded Kuwait in 1990.

5 What trend did the Internet help bring about?

A terrorism
B the Information Revolution
C a service economy
D global warming

6 Which of the following was one of Bill Clinton's achievements as president?

A gaining the passage of the North American Free Trade Agreement
B creating the Department of Homeland Security
C allowing women in the military to serve in combat
D setting new education standards in the No Child Left Behind act

7 Which state's electoral votes were contested in the election of 2000?

A California
B Florida
C New York
D Arkansas

8 Read the following speech by New York City mayor Rudolph Giuliani following the 9/11 attacks and use it to answer the question below.

> "We're a city of immigrants unlike any other city, within a nation of immigrants. Like the victims of the World Trade Center attack, we're of every race, we're of every religion, we're of every ethnicity . . . It's the thing that renews us and revives us in every generation, our openness to new people from all over the world."
>
> —Rudolph Giuliani, quoted in *The Washington Post*

Document-Based Question What did Mayor Giuliani say was a unique strength of New York City? Why was this an important message to deliver after the attacks of September 11?

© Houghton Mifflin Harcourt Publishing Company

Assignment

Write an oral history, based on an interview with an adult you know, about one of the events in this chapter.

An Oral History

Oral histories can provide excellent sources of information about events in the recent past. An oral history is a report based on an interview with a person who experienced or remembers a historical event. Oral histories preserve personal experiences and memories for future generations.

TIP Use question words like *Who? What? When? Where? Why?* and *How?* in your interview questions.

1. Prewrite

Getting Started

Think about all the events you read about in this unit. Which ones interested you the most? Which ones do you think made the strongest impression on people at the time? Choose one as your subject.

Writing Questions

- Focus on finding out how the person you are interviewing experienced the event you chose.
- Write at least 10 questions.

Conducting an Interview

- Find an adult family member or friend to interview who remembers participating in or reacting to the event.
- Come prepared with your questions, paper, and something to write with.
- Take notes on the answers. Indicate direct quotations with quotation marks.
- Ask follow-up questions, even if you did not prepare them in advance.

2. Write

You can use this framework, along with your interview notes, to help you write your first draft.

A Writer's Framework

Introduction	Body	Conclusion
■ Grab your reader's attention with an interesting quote from your interview. ■ Introduce the event you chose and why it was important. ■ Explain how the event affected the person you interviewed.	■ Describe the memories and experiences of the person you interviewed about the event. ■ Summarize what you learned from the interview. ■ Use quotes from the interview.	■ Make a generalization about how people reacted to the event. ■ Draw conclusions about how people's reactions to the event affected history.

© Houghton Mifflin Harcourt Publishing Company

3. Evaluate and Revise

Evaluating

Use these questions to discover ways to improve your oral history.

Evaluation Questions for an Oral History

- Do you introduce the event and the person you interviewed in the first paragraph?
- Do you focus on the event from a personal point of view?
- Do you describe the memories and experiences of the person you interviewed about the event?
- Do you summarize what you learned and use quotes from the interview?
- Do you make generalizations and draw conclusions about people's reactions to the event?

Revising

When you revise your oral history, you may need to add background information. Check the material you have included from your interview. If anything is unclear, add more details about the event or time period. Make sure to explain clearly the connections between the personal experience and the event.

4. Proofread and Publish

Proofreading

In your oral history, you have been using quotations from the person you interviewed. Check the punctuation marks around these direct quotations. Also, check the spelling and capitalization of all proper names, such as the name of the person you interviewed.

Publishing

Share your oral history with classmates who wrote about the same event. How were the experiences of the people you interviewed similar and different? Share your oral history with the class. The person you interviewed would probably also like to see the finished project.

5. Practice and Apply

Use the steps and strategies in this workshop to write your oral history.

TIP Using Quotations Effectively Quotations from your interview will make your oral history more interesting. Introduce quotations with a phrase or a sentence that makes it clear what they are about. Always identify the person who is quoted.

EXAMPLE

Simon remembered taking part in a demonstration in Washington, D.C., the night before President Nixon resigned. "There were thousands of people in Lafayette Park across from the White House," Simon recalled.

TIP Using Ellipses To make a quotation shorter, you can delete some words and replace them with an ellipsis—the symbol "...". Make sure the quotation still makes sense after you do this.

EXAMPLE

Original quotation: "On the morning of September 11, I woke up, brushed my teeth, ate breakfast, and did everything like any other day."

Quotation with an ellipsis: "On the morning of September 11, I ... did everything like any other day."

© Houghton Mifflin Harcourt Publishing Company

© Houghton Mifflin Harcourt Publishing Company • Image Credits: ©Royalty-free/Corbis

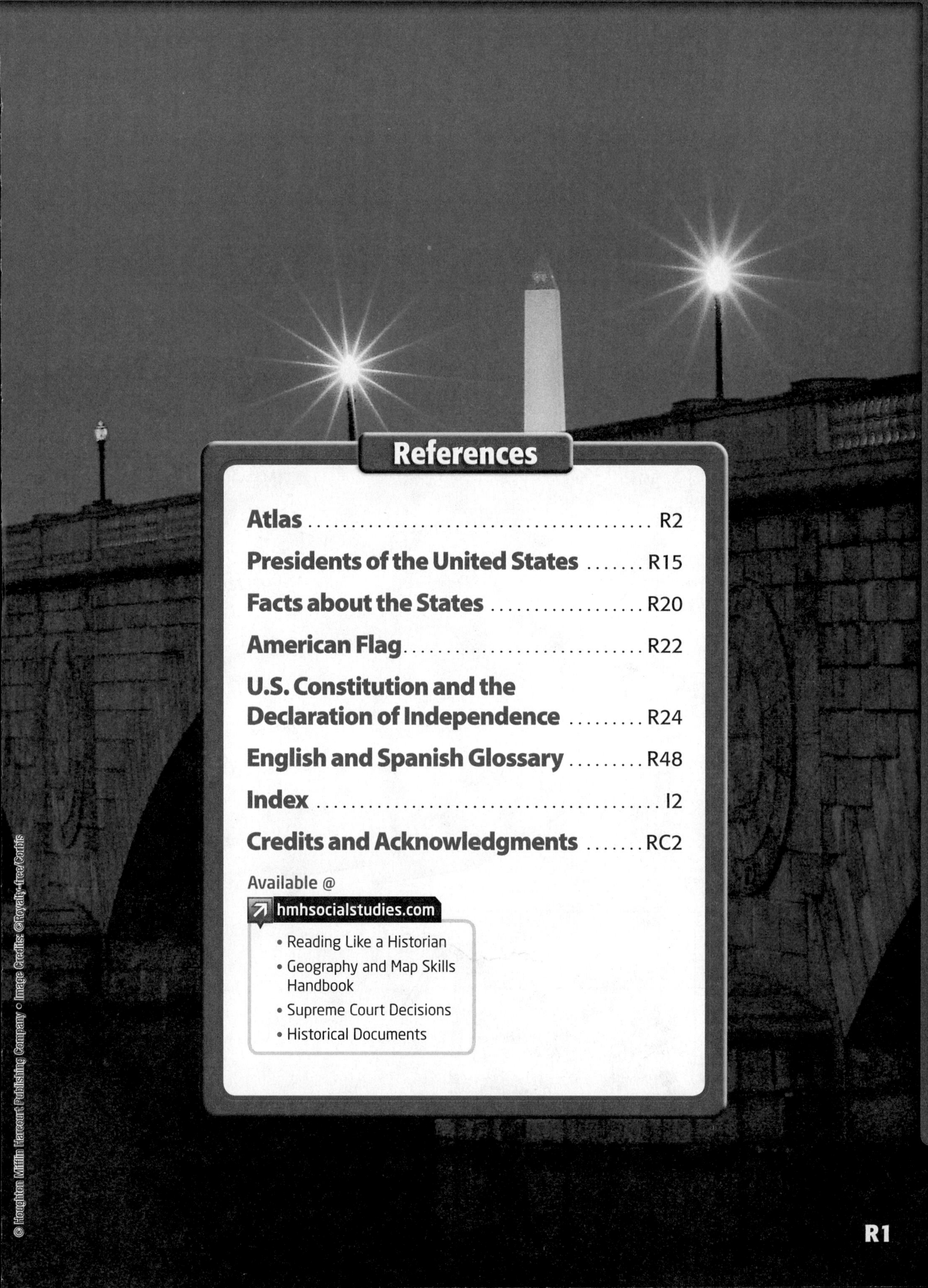

References

Available @

hmhsocialstudies.com

- Reading Like a Historian
- Geography and Map Skills Handbook
- Supreme Court Decisions
- Historical Documents

© Houghton Mifflin Harcourt Publishing Company • Image Credits: ©Royalty-free/Corbis

The United States of America: Political

Strait of Juan de Fuca
Puget Sound
Seattle
Tacoma
Olympia
Franklin D. Roosevelt Lake
Spokane
WASHINGTON
Pend Oreille
Flathead Lake
Portland
Columbia River
Salem
Eugene
OREGON
45°N
Missouri River
Great Falls
Helena
MONTANA
Fort Peck Lake
Yellowstone River
Billings
NORTH DAKOTA
Lake Sakakawea
Bismarck
Lake Oahe
SOUTH DAKOTA
Pierre
Rapid City
IDAHO
Boise
Sun Valley
Snake River
Pocatello
Yellowstone Lake
WYOMING
Cheyenne
NEBRASKA
Platte River
Goose Lake
Cape Mendocino
40°N
Shasta Lake
Sacramento River
Pyramid Lake
Reno
Carson City
Lake Tahoe
NEVADA
Berkeley
Oakland
San Francisco
San Francisco Bay
Sacramento
San Joaquin River
San Jose
Monterey Bay
Fresno
CALIFORNIA
125°W
35°N
Great Salt Lake
Ogden
Salt Lake City
Provo
Utah Lake
UTAH
Green River
Lake Powell
COLORADO
Boulder
Vail
Denver
Aspen
Colorado Springs
Pueblo
Arkansas River
KANSA
Las Vegas
Colorado River
Lake Mead
Santa Barbara
Ventura
Channel Islands
Los Angeles
Long Beach
Riverside
Palm Springs
Anaheim
Santa Ana
Salton Sea
San Diego
PACIFIC OCEAN
Flagstaff
ARIZONA
Phoenix
Gila River
Casa Grande
Tucson
Taos
Santa Fe
Albuquerque
NEW MEXICO
Las Cruces
El Paso
OKLAHOM
Canadian River
Oklahoma C
Amarillo
Lawt
Lubbock
Brazos River
Fort Wo
Abilene
Midland
Odessa
TEXAS
Colorado River
Pecos River
Amistad Reservoir
Austin
San Antonio
Rio Grande
Corpus Chris
Laredo
MEXICO
120°W
30°N
Gulf of California
To understand the relative locations of Alaska and Hawaii, as well as the vast distances separating them from the rest of the United States, see the world map.
Kauai
Niihau
Oahu
HAWAII
Honolulu
Molokai
Maui
Lanai
PACIFIC OCEAN
Kahoolawe
Hilo
Hawaii
22°N
155°W
160°W
19°N
0 75 150 Miles
0 75 150 Kilometers
Projection: Mercator
N S E W
ARCTIC OCEAN
RUSSIA
Arctic Circle
Bering Strait
Nome
Yukon River
St. Lawrence Island
St. Matthew Island
Fairbanks
ALASKA
CANADA
Nunivak Island
Bering Sea
Anchorage
Valdez
Skagway
Juneau
Gulf of Alaska
Kodiak Island
Alexander Archipelago
Attu Island
ALEUTIAN ISLANDS
PACIFIC OCEAN
0 250 500 Miles
0 250 500 Kilometers
Projection: Albers Equal Area
170°E
55°N
50°N
180°
170°W
160°W
150°W
140°W
55°N

© Houghton Mifflin Harcourt Publishing Company

CANADA
MINNESOTA
WISCONSIN
MICHIGAN
IOWA
ILLINOIS
INDIANA
OHIO
MISSOURI
KENTUCKY
TENNESSEE
ARKANSAS
MISSISSIPPI
ALABAMA
GEORGIA
FLORIDA
LOUISIANA
SOUTH CAROLINA
NORTH CAROLINA
VIRGINIA
WEST VIRGINIA
PENNSYLVANIA
NEW YORK
MAINE
VT
NH
MA
CT
RI
NJ
DE
MD
ATLANTIC OCEAN
BAHAMAS
Gulf of Mexico
Lake Superior
Lake Michigan
Lake Huron
Lake Erie
Lake Ontario
Lake Champlain
St. Lawrence River
Hudson R.
Connecticut R.
Susquehanna River
Mississippi River
Missouri River
Illinois River
Ohio River
Minnesota River
Red River
Savannah River
Chattahoochee R.
Lake of the Ozarks
Lake Barkley
Kentucky Lake
Keystone Lake
Lake Texoma
Toledo Bend Reservoir
Lake Okeechobee
Chesapeake Bay
Delaware Bay
Long Island Sound
Long Island
Cape Cod
Cape Hatteras
Cape Canaveral
Cape Sable
Sea Islands
Chandeleur Islands
Florida Keys
Straits of Florida
Grand Forks
Fargo
Duluth
Superior
Minneapolis
St. Paul
Sioux Falls
Sioux City
Marquette
Sault Ste. Marie
Green Bay
Madison
Milwaukee
Grand Rapids
Lansing
Saginaw
Detroit
Ann Arbor
Rockford
Chicago
Cedar Rapids
Davenport
Des Moines
Gary
South Bend
Fort Wayne
Toledo
Cleveland
Youngstown
Akron
Erie
Buffalo
Rochester
Syracuse
Albany
Burlington
Montpelier
Augusta
Portland
Concord
Manchester
Boston
Worcester
Springfield
Providence
Hartford
New Haven
Bridgeport
Yonkers
Jersey City
Newark
New York City
Trenton
Camden
Allentown
Harrisburg
Philadelphia
Pittsburgh
Atlantic City
Baltimore
Dover
Annapolis
Washington, D.C.
Peoria
Springfield
Columbus
Indianapolis
Dayton
Cincinnati
Kansas City
Kansas City
St. Louis
East St. Louis
Jefferson City
Springfield
Louisville
Evansville
Frankfort
Lexington
Charleston
Richmond
Newport News
Norfolk
Virginia Beach
Greensboro
Durham
Raleigh
Winston-Salem
Knoxville
Asheville
Charlotte
Nashville
Chattanooga
Memphis
Tulsa
Fayetteville
Little Rock
Pine Bluff
Huntsville
Birmingham
Atlanta
Greenville
Columbia
Charleston
Macon
Columbus
Savannah
Meridian
Montgomery
Vicksburg
Jackson
Shreveport
Mobile
Pensacola
Tallahassee
Jacksonville
Gainesville
Baton Rouge
Biloxi
New Orleans
Beaumont
Houston
Galveston
Orlando
Tampa
St. Petersburg
Fort Myers
Fort Lauderdale
Miami
N
S
E
W
40°N
35°N
30°N
25°N
70°W
75°W
80°W
85°W
90°W
95°W
National capital
State capitals
Other cities
0
100
200 Miles
0
100
200 Kilometers
Projection: Albers Equal Area

© Houghton Mifflin Harcourt Publishing Company

The United States of America: Physical

Strait of Juan de Fuca
Puget Sound
Mount Rainier 14,410 ft (4,392 m)
CASCADE RANGE
COAST RANGES
Franklin D. Roosevelt Lake
Pend Oreille Lake
Clark Fork
Flathead River
Lewis Range
Flathead Lake
ROCKY MOUNTAINS
Milk River
Missouri River
Fort Peck Lake
Lake Sakakawea
Columbia River
Willamette River
Bitterroot Range
Salmon River
Salmon River Mts.
Sawtooth Mts.
Columbia Plateau
CONTINENTAL DIVIDE
Yellowstone River
Yellowstone Lake
Bighorn Mts.
Bighorn River
Powder River
Lake Oahe
GREAT PLAINS
Grand Tetons
Snake River
Wind River
Wind River Range
Gannett Peak 13,804 ft (4,207 m)
Black Hills
Cheyenne River
White River
Klamath River
Goose Lake
Cape Mendocino
Shasta Lake
Niobrara River
North Platte River
Platte River
Wasatch Range
Front Range
Pyramid Lake
Great Salt Lake
Utah Lake
Uinta Mts.
SIERRA NEVADA
Sacramento River
Central Valley
GREAT BASIN
Lake Tahoe
San Francisco Bay
South Platte River
Green River
Republican River
San Joaquin River
Monterey Bay
Colorado River
Mount Elbert 14,433 ft (4,400 m)
Pikes Peak 14,110 ft (4,301 m)
Smoky Hill River
COLORADO PLATEAU
Lake Powell
Coast Ranges
Mount Whitney 14,494 ft (4,419 m)
Death Valley
San Juan River
Grand Canyon
Lake Mead
Mojave Desert
San Luis Valley
Sangre De Cristo Mts.
Painted Desert
Channel Islands
PACIFIC OCEAN
Salton Sea
Imperial Valley
Canadian River
Rio Grande
Gila River
Sonoran Desert
Gulf of California
Pecos River
Amistad Reservoir
Nueces
MEXICO
45°N
40°N
35°N
30°N
125°W
120°W
To understand the relative locations of Alaska and Hawaii, as well as the vast distances separating them from the rest of the United States, see the world map.
HAWAII
Kauai
Niihau
Oahu
Molokai
Maui
Lanai
Kahoolawe
Mauna Kea 13,796 ft (4,206 m)
Hawaii
PACIFIC OCEAN
22°N
19°N
160°W
155°W
0 75 150 Miles
0 75 150 Kilometers
Projection: Mercator
ARCTIC OCEAN
RUSSIA
Bering Strait
Arctic Circle
BROOKS RANGE
Yukon River
Tanana River
St. Lawrence Island
St. Matthew Island
CANADA
Kuskokwim River
ALASKA RANGE
Mount McKinley 20,320 ft (6,194 m)
Nunivak Island
Bering Sea
Attu Island
Gulf of Alaska
Kodiak Island
Alexander Archipelago
ALEUTIAN ISLANDS
PACIFIC OCEAN
0 250 500 Miles
0 250 500 Kilometers
Projection: Albers Equal Area
55°N
50°N
170°E
180°
170°W
160°W
150°W
140°W

© Houghton Mifflin Harcourt Publishing Company

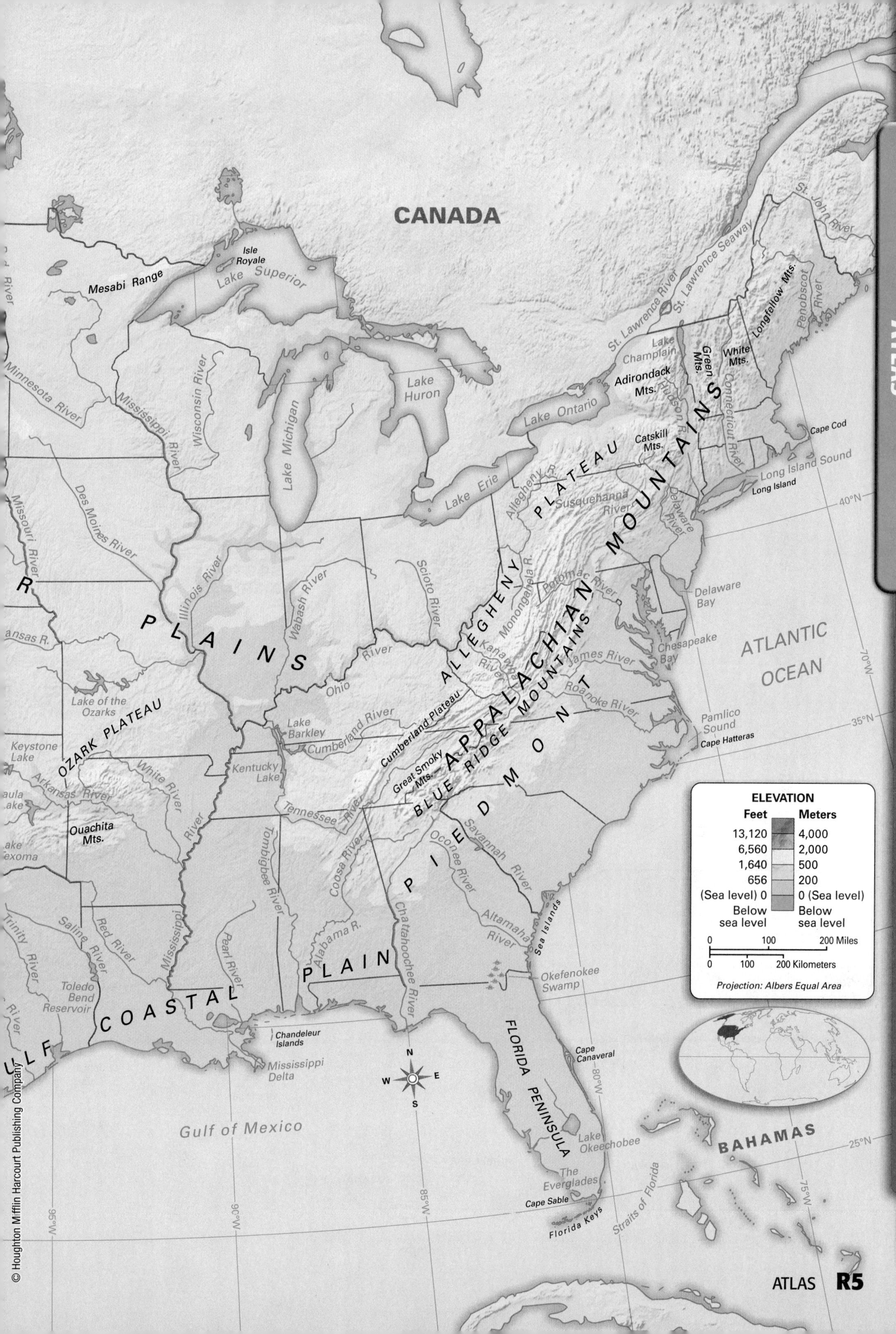
CANADA
Isle Royale
Mesabi Range
Lake Superior
Lake Michigan
Lake Huron
Lake Ontario
Lake Erie
Lake Champlain
Adirondack Mts.
Green Mts.
White Mts.
Longfellow Mts.
Catskill Mts.
St. Lawrence River
St. Lawrence Seaway
St. John River
Penobscot River
Connecticut River
Hudson R.
Cape Cod
Long Island Sound
Long Island
Delaware River
Delaware Bay
Susquehanna River
Allegheny R.
Monongahela R.
Potomac River
Chesapeake Bay
James River
Roanoke River
Pamlico Sound
Cape Hatteras
ATLANTIC OCEAN
APPALACHIAN MOUNTAINS
ALLEGHENY PLATEAU
BLUE RIDGE MOUNTAINS
PIEDMONT
Cumberland Plateau
Great Smoky Mts.
Kanawha River
Ohio River
Scioto River
Wabash River
Illinois River
Wisconsin River
Mississippi River
Minnesota River
Des Moines River
Missouri River
PLAINS
Lake of the Ozarks
OZARK PLATEAU
Keystone Lake
Arkansas River
White River
Ouachita Mts.
Kentucky Lake
Lake Barkley
Cumberland River
Tennessee River
Tombigbee River
Coosa River
Alabama R.
Chattahoochee River
Oconee River
Savannah River
Altamaha River
Sea Islands
Okefenokee Swamp
Red River
Saline River
Trinity River
Pearl River
Toledo Bend Reservoir
GULF COASTAL PLAIN
Chandeleur Islands
Mississippi Delta
Gulf of Mexico
FLORIDA PENINSULA
Cape Canaveral
Lake Okeechobee
The Everglades
Cape Sable
Florida Keys
Straits of Florida
BAHAMAS
40°N
35°N
25°N
70°W
75°W
80°W
85°W
90°W
95°W
N
S
E
W
ELEVATION
Feet
Meters
13,120
4,000
6,560
2,000
1,640
500
656
200
(Sea level) 0
0 (Sea level)
Below sea level
Below sea level
0
100
200 Miles
0
100
200 Kilometers
Projection: Albers Equal Area

© Houghton Mifflin Harcourt Publishing Company

World: Political

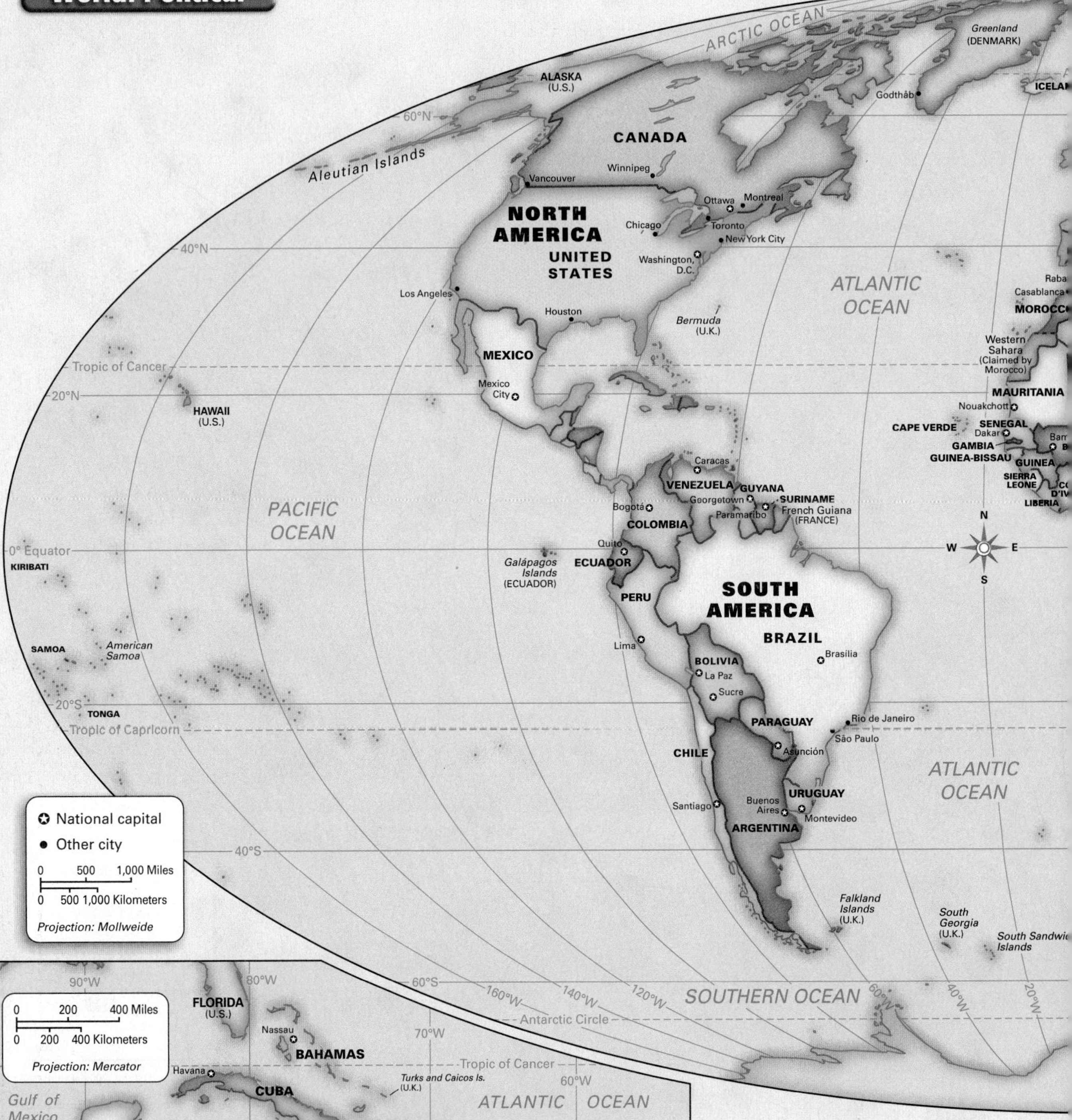
ARCTIC OCEAN
Greenland (DENMARK)
Godthåb
ICELA
ALASKA (U.S.)
60°N
Aleutian Islands
CANADA
Winnipeg
Vancouver
Ottawa
Montreal
NORTH AMERICA
Chicago
Toronto
New York City
UNITED STATES
Washington, D.C.
40°N
Los Angeles
Houston
ATLANTIC OCEAN
Raba
Casablanca
MOROCC
Bermuda (U.K.)
Western Sahara (Claimed by Morocco)
MEXICO
Tropic of Cancer
Mexico City
20°N
HAWAII (U.S.)
MAURITANIA
Nouakchott
CAPE VERDE
SENEGAL
Dakar
GAMBIA
GUINEA-BISSAU
GUINEA
SIERRA LEONE
LIBERIA
Caracas
VENEZUELA
GUYANA
Georgetown
SURINAME
Paramaribo
French Guiana (FRANCE)
PACIFIC OCEAN
Bogotá
COLOMBIA
0° Equator
KIRIBATI
Quito
Galápagos Islands (ECUADOR)
ECUADOR
SOUTH AMERICA
PERU
BRAZIL
SAMOA
American Samoa
Lima
Brasília
BOLIVIA
La Paz
Sucre
20°S
TONGA
Tropic of Capricorn
PARAGUAY
Rio de Janeiro
São Paulo
Asunción
CHILE
ATLANTIC OCEAN
URUGUAY
Santiago
Buenos Aires
Montevideo
ARGENTINA
National capital
Other city
0 500 1,000 Miles
0 500 1,000 Kilometers
Projection: Mollweide
40°S
Falkland Islands (U.K.)
South Georgia (U.K.)
South Sandwic Islands
60°S
160°W
140°W
120°W
SOUTHERN OCEAN
60°W
40°W
20°W
Antarctic Circle

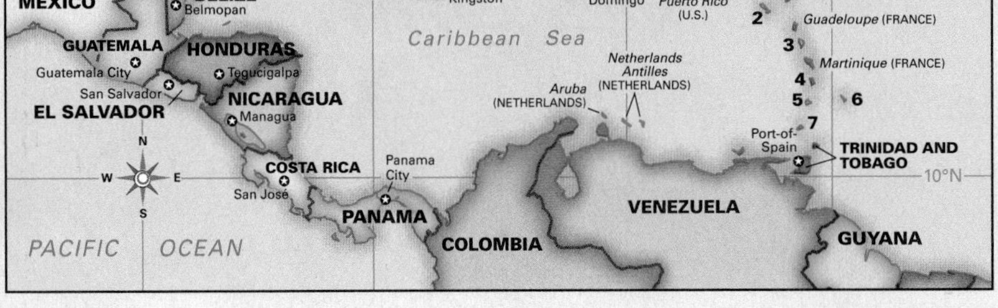
90°W
80°W
0 200 400 Miles
0 200 400 Kilometers
Projection: Mercator
FLORIDA (U.S.)
Nassau
BAHAMAS
70°W
Tropic of Cancer
Havana
CUBA
Turks and Caicos Is. (U.K.)
60°W
Gulf of Mexico
ATLANTIC OCEAN
20°N
Cayman Is. (U.K.)
HAITI
DOMINICAN REPUBLIC
Port-au-Prince
Virgin Islands (U.S. and U.K.)
BELIZE
Belmopan
JAMAICA
Kingston
Santo Domingo
Puerto Rico (U.S.)
MEXICO
1
2
Guadeloupe (FRANCE)
GUATEMALA
HONDURAS
Caribbean Sea
3
Guatemala City
Tegucigalpa
Netherlands Antilles (NETHERLANDS)
Martinique (FRANCE)
4
San Salvador
NICARAGUA
Aruba (NETHERLANDS)
5
6
EL SALVADOR
Managua
7
Port-of-Spain
TRINIDAD AND TOBAGO
COSTA RICA
Panama City
10°N
San José
PANAMA
VENEZUELA
PACIFIC OCEAN
COLOMBIA
GUYANA

	COUNTRY	CAPITAL
1	Antigua and Barbuda	St. Johns
2	St. Kitts and Nevis	Basseterre
3	Dominica	Roseau
4	St. Lucia	Castries
5	St. Vincent and the Grenadines	Kingstown
6	Barbados	Bridgetown
7	Grenada	St. George's

© Houghton Mifflin Harcourt Publishing Company

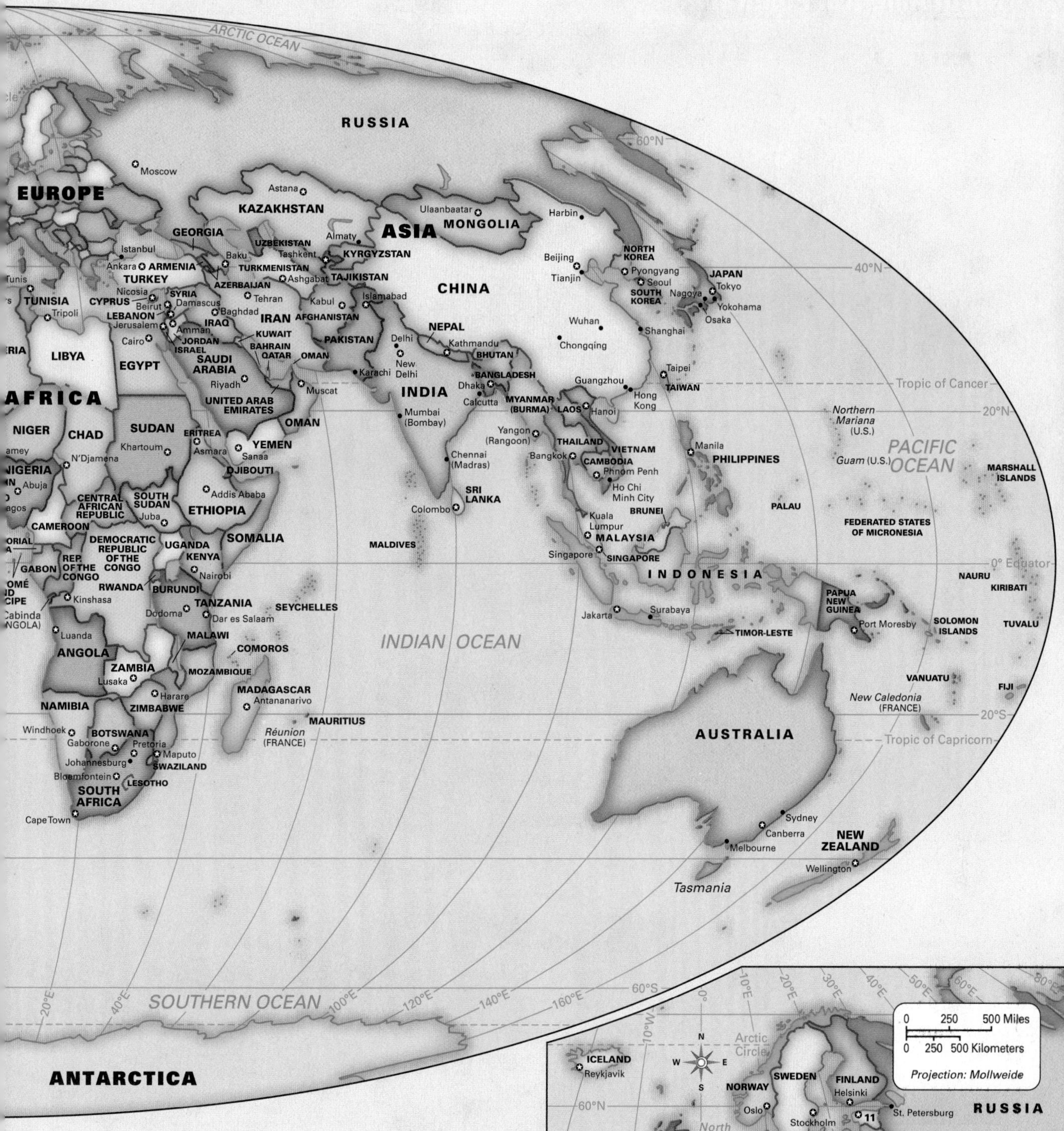

COUNTRY		CAPITAL
1	Czech Republic	Prague
2	Slovakia	Bratislava
3	Slovenia	Ljubljana
4	Croatia	Zagreb
5	Bosnia and Herzegovina	Sarajevo
6	Macedonia	Skopje
7	Serbia	Belgrade
8	Montenegro	Podgorica
9	Lithuania	Vilnius
10	Latvia	Riga
11	Estonia	Tallinn
12	Kosovo	Pristina

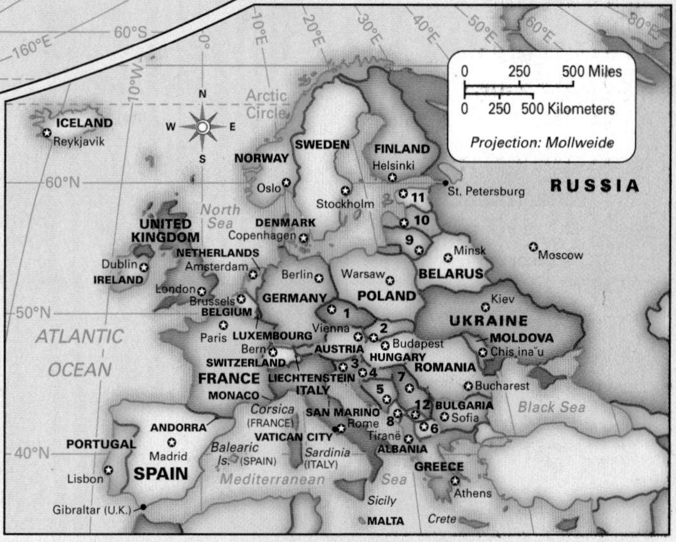

© Houghton Mifflin Harcourt Publishing Company

ATLAS

North America: Political

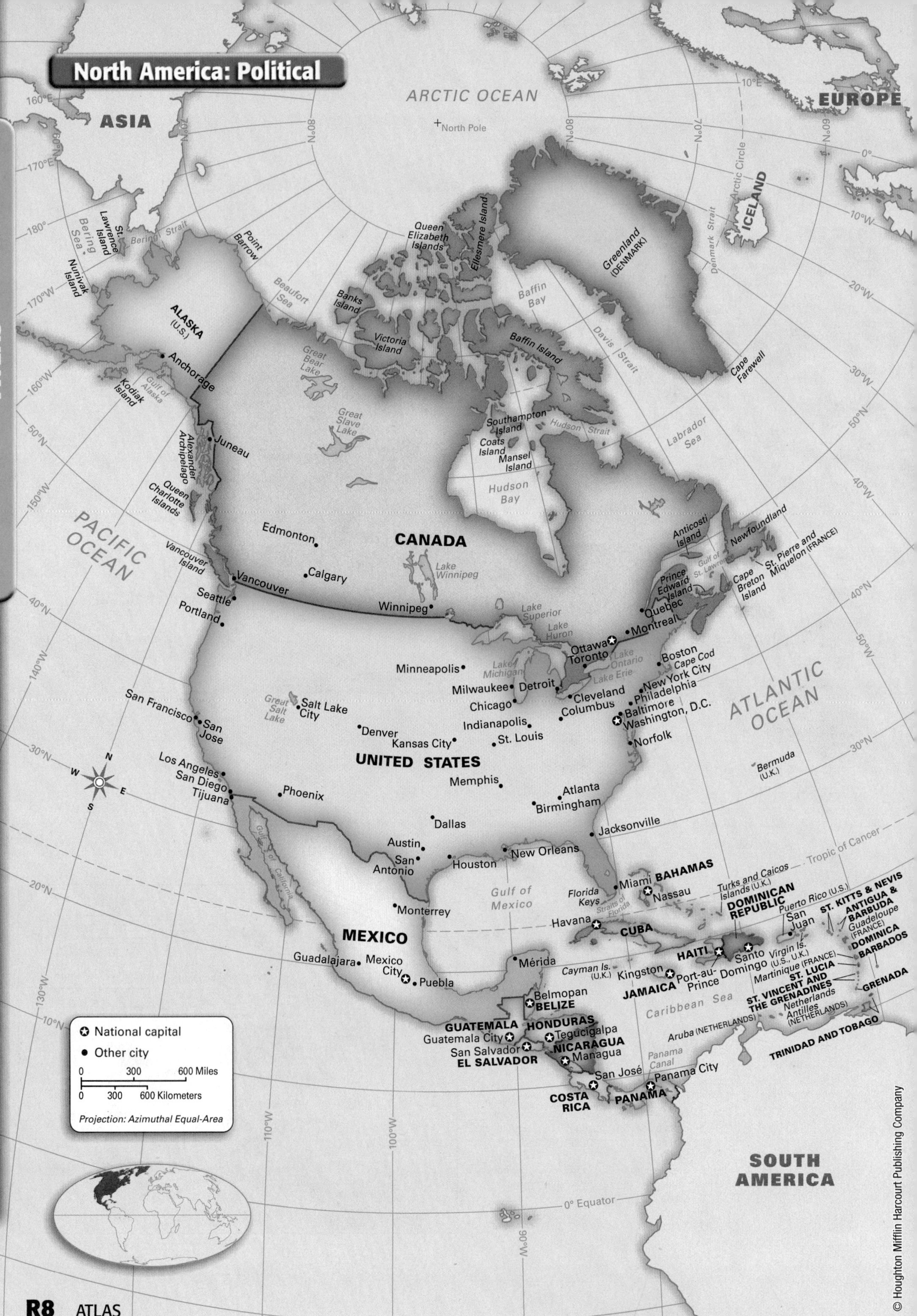
ARCTIC OCEAN
North Pole
ASIA
EUROPE
ICELAND
Greenland (DENMARK)
Queen Elizabeth Islands
Ellesmere Island
Baffin Bay
Baffin Island
Davis Strait
Denmark Strait
Arctic Circle
Cape Farewell
Labrador Sea
Hudson Strait
Southampton Island
Coats Island
Mansel Island
Hudson Bay
Banks Island
Victoria Island
Beaufort Sea
Point Barrow
Bering Strait
Bering Sea
St. Lawrence Island
Nunivak Island
ALASKA (U.S.)
Anchorage
Gulf of Alaska
Kodiak Island
Great Bear Lake
Great Slave Lake
Juneau
Alexander Archipelago
Queen Charlotte Islands
PACIFIC OCEAN
Vancouver Island
Vancouver
Edmonton
Calgary
CANADA
Lake Winnipeg
Winnipeg
Anticosti Island
Gulf of St. Lawrence
Newfoundland
St. Pierre and Miquelon (FRANCE)
Prince Edward Island
Cape Breton Island
Quebec
Montreal
Lake Superior
Lake Huron
Lake Michigan
Lake Ontario
Lake Erie
Ottawa
Toronto
Boston
Cape Cod
New York City
Philadelphia
Baltimore
Washington, D.C.
Norfolk
ATLANTIC OCEAN
Bermuda (U.K.)
Seattle
Portland
Minneapolis
Milwaukee
Detroit
Chicago
Cleveland
Columbus
Indianapolis
St. Louis
Great Salt Lake
Salt Lake City
Denver
Kansas City
San Francisco
San Jose
UNITED STATES
Los Angeles
San Diego
Tijuana
Phoenix
Memphis
Atlanta
Birmingham
Dallas
Jacksonville
Austin
San Antonio
Houston
New Orleans
Gulf of California
Tropic of Cancer
Miami
BAHAMAS
Nassau
Florida Keys
Straits of Florida
Gulf of Mexico
Monterrey
Havana
CUBA
Turks and Caicos Islands (U.K.)
DOMINICAN REPUBLIC
Puerto Rico (U.S.)
San Juan
ST. KITTS & NEVIS
ANTIGUA & BARBUDA
Guadeloupe (FRANCE)
DOMINICA
BARBADOS
MEXICO
Guadalajara
Mexico City
Puebla
Mérida
Cayman Is. (U.K.)
Kingston
JAMAICA
HAITI
Port-au-Prince
Santo Domingo
Virgin Is. (U.S., U.K.)
Martinique (FRANCE)
ST. LUCIA
ST. VINCENT AND THE GRENADINES
GRENADA
Netherlands Antilles (NETHERLANDS)
Caribbean Sea
Aruba (NETHERLANDS)
TRINIDAD AND TOBAGO
Belmopan
BELIZE
GUATEMALA
Guatemala City
HONDURAS
Tegucigalpa
NICARAGUA
Managua
San Salvador
EL SALVADOR
San José
COSTA RICA
Panama Canal
Panama City
PANAMA
SOUTH AMERICA
0° Equator
National capital
Other city
0 300 600 Miles
0 300 600 Kilometers
Projection: Azimuthal Equal-Area
160°E
170°E
180°
170°W
160°W
150°W
140°W
130°W
110°W
100°W
90°W
80°N
70°N
60°N
50°N
40°N
30°N
20°N
10°N
10°E
0°
10°W
20°W
30°W
40°W
50°W

© Houghton Mifflin Harcourt Publishing Company

South America: Political

Caribbean Sea
CENTRAL AMERICA
Barranquilla
Cartagena
Caracas
Lake Maracaibo
VENEZUELA
Medellín
Bogotá
COLOMBIA
Cali
Malpelo Island (COLOMBIA)
Georgetown
GUYANA
Paramaribo
SURINAME
Cayenne
French Guiana (FRANCE)
ATLANTIC OCEAN
Quito
ECUADOR
Guayaquil
Galápagos Islands (ECUADOR)
0° Equator
Belém
PERU
BRAZIL
Recife
Trujillo
Callao
Lima
Salvador
Brasília
PACIFIC OCEAN
Lake Titicaca
Arequipa
La Paz
Lake Poopó
BOLIVIA
Sucre
Belo Horizonte
PARAGUAY
Campinas
São Paulo
Rio de Janeiro
Asunción
Curitiba
Tropic of Capricorn
San Ambrosio Island (CHILE)
San Félix Island (CHILE)
CHILE
Pôrto Alegre
Córdoba
Rosario
URUGUAY
Juan Fernández Islands (CHILE)
Valparaíso
Santiago
Buenos Aires
Montevideo
ATLANTIC OCEAN
ARGENTINA
National capital
Other city
0 250 500 Miles
0 250 500 Kilometers
Projection: Azimuthal Equal-Area
Strait of Magellan
Falkland Islands (U.K.)
Tierra del Fuego
South Georgia Island (U.K.)
20°N
10°N
10°S
20°S
30°S
40°S
50°S
90°W
80°W
70°W
60°W
50°W
40°W
30°W
20°W
100°W
N
S
E
W

© Houghton Mifflin Harcourt Publishing Company

ATLAS

Europe: Political

National capital
Other city
0 150 300 Miles
0 150 300 Kilometers
Projection: Azimuthal Equal-Area
ARCTIC OCEAN
ATLANTIC OCEAN
North Cape
Barents Sea
White Sea
Arctic Circle
ICELAND
Reykjavik
Faeroe Islands (DENMARK)
Shetland Islands
North Sea
NORWAY
Bergen
Oslo
SWEDEN
Stockholm
Göteborg
Gulf of Bothnia
Gulf of Finland
FINLAND
Helsinki
ESTONIA
Tallinn
LATVIA
Riga
LITHUANIA
Vilnius
RUSSIA
Baltic Sea
St. Petersburg
Moscow
Nizhny Novgorod
URAL MOUNTAINS
ASIA
BELARUS
Minsk
UKRAINE
Kiev
MOLDOVA
Chișinau
Caspian Sea
Black Sea
DENMARK
Copenhagen
NORTHERN IRELAND
SCOTLAND
Edinburgh
UNITED KINGDOM
Belfast
Dublin
IRELAND
Liverpool
WALES
ENGLAND
London
British Isles
THE NETHERLANDS
Amsterdam
Channel Islands (U.K.)
English Channel
Brussels
BELGIUM
LUXEMBOURG
Luxembourg
Hamburg
Berlin
GERMANY
Cologne
Bonn
Dresden
POLAND
Warsaw
Krakow
Prague
CZECH REPUBLIC
SLOVAKIA
Bratislava
Paris
FRANCE
SWITZERLAND
Lake Geneva
Bern
Vaduz
LIECHTENSTEIN
Munich
Vienna
AUSTRIA
Budapest
HUNGARY
ROMANIA
Bucharest
Bay of Biscay
Lyon
ALPS
Milan
Ljubljana
SLOVENIA
Zagreb
CROATIA
PYRENEES
Marseille
MONACO
Monaco
SAN MARINO
San Marino
BOSNIA AND HERZEGOVINA
Sarajevo
Belgrade
SERBIA
Adriatic Sea
PORTUGAL
Lisbon
Madrid
SPAIN
Andorra la Vella
ANDORRA
Barcelona
Valencia
Seville
Corsica (FRANCE)
ITALY
VATICAN CITY
Rome
MONTENEGRO
KOSOVO
Podgorica
Pristina
Tirana
Sofia
BULGARIA
Skopje
MACEDONIA
ALBANIA
Balearic Islands (SPAIN)
Sardinia (ITALY)
Naples
Strait of Gibraltar
Gibraltar (U.K.)
Mediterranean Sea
GREECE
Aegean Sea
Athens
Sicily
AFRICA
MALTA
Valletta
Rhodes
Crete
SOUTHWEST ASIA
70°N
60°N
50°N
40°N
30°W
20°W
10°W
0°
10°E
20°E
30°E
40°E
50°E

© Houghton Mifflin Harcourt Publishing Company

© Houghton Mifflin Harcourt Publishing Company

Asia: Political

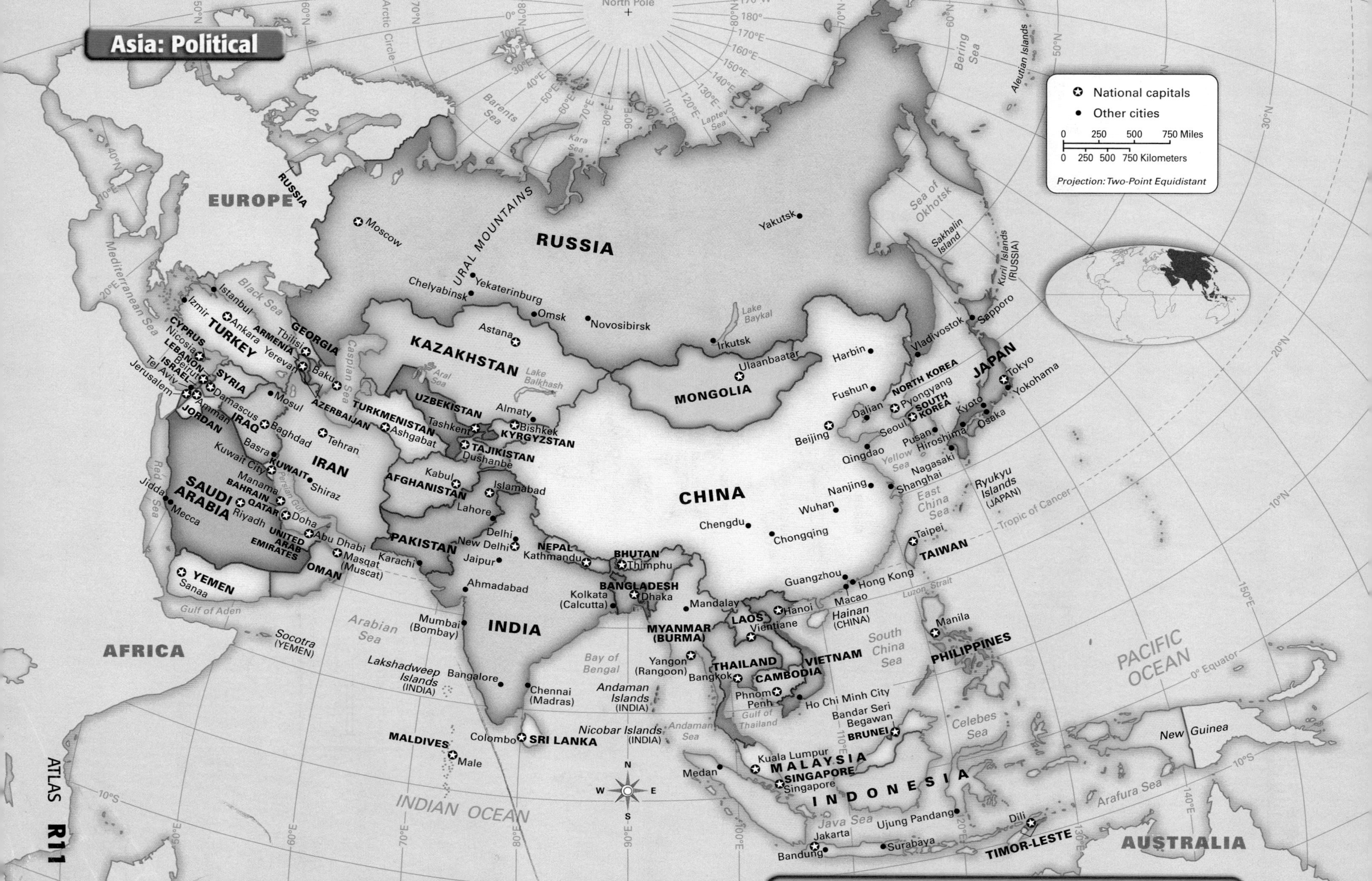
National capitals
Other cities
0 250 500 750 Miles
0 250 500 750 Kilometers
Projection: Two-Point Equidistant
North Pole
Arctic Circle
Tropic of Cancer
0° Equator
EUROPE
RUSSIA
URAL MOUNTAINS
Moscow
Yekaterinburg
Chelyabinsk
Omsk
Novosibirsk
Irkutsk
Yakutsk
Vladivostok
Barents Sea
Kara Sea
Laptev Sea
Bering Sea
Sea of Okhotsk
Sakhalin Island
Kuril Islands (RUSSIA)
Aleutian Islands
Lake Baykal
KAZAKHSTAN
Astana
Almaty
Lake Balkhash
Aral Sea
Caspian Sea
Black Sea
Mediterranean Sea
Red Sea
Persian Gulf
Gulf of Aden
TURKEY
Istanbul
Izmir
Ankara
GEORGIA
Tbilisi
ARMENIA
Yerevan
AZERBAIJAN
Baku
CYPRUS
Nicosia
LEBANON
Beirut
ISRAEL
Tel Aviv
Jerusalem
SYRIA
Damascus
JORDAN
Amman
IRAQ
Mosul
Baghdad
Basra
KUWAIT
Kuwait City
BAHRAIN
Manama
QATAR
Doha
UNITED ARAB EMIRATES
Abu Dhabi
SAUDI ARABIA
Riyadh
Mecca
Jidda
YEMEN
Sanaa
Socotra (YEMEN)
OMAN
Masqat (Muscat)
IRAN
Tehran
Shiraz
TURKMENISTAN
Ashgabat
UZBEKISTAN
Tashkent
TAJIKISTAN
Dushanbe
KYRGYZSTAN
Bishkek
AFGHANISTAN
Kabul
PAKISTAN
Islamabad
Lahore
Karachi
INDIA
Delhi
New Delhi
Jaipur
Ahmadabad
Mumbai (Bombay)
Bangalore
Chennai (Madras)
Kolkata (Calcutta)
NEPAL
Kathmandu
BHUTAN
Thimphu
BANGLADESH
Dhaka
SRI LANKA
Colombo
MALDIVES
Male
Lakshadweep Islands (INDIA)
Andaman Islands (INDIA)
Nicobar Islands (INDIA)
Arabian Sea
Bay of Bengal
Andaman Sea
INDIAN OCEAN
AFRICA
MONGOLIA
Ulaanbaatar
CHINA
Harbin
Fushun
Beijing
Dalian
Qingdao
Nanjing
Shanghai
Wuhan
Chengdu
Chongqing
Guangzhou
Hong Kong
Macao
Hainan (CHINA)
NORTH KOREA
Pyongyang
SOUTH KOREA
Seoul
Pusan
JAPAN
Tokyo
Yokohama
Sapporo
Kyoto
Osaka
Hiroshima
Nagasaki
Ryukyu Islands (JAPAN)
Yellow Sea
East China Sea
South China Sea
TAIWAN
Taipei
Luzon Strait
PHILIPPINES
Manila
MYANMAR (BURMA)
Mandalay
Yangon (Rangoon)
LAOS
Vientiane
THAILAND
Bangkok
Gulf of Thailand
VIETNAM
Hanoi
Ho Chi Minh City
CAMBODIA
Phnom Penh
MALAYSIA
Kuala Lumpur
SINGAPORE
Singapore
BRUNEI
Bandar Seri Begawan
INDONESIA
Medan
Jakarta
Bandung
Surabaya
Ujung Pandang
Java Sea
Celebes Sea
TIMOR-LESTE
Dili
New Guinea
Arafura Sea
AUSTRALIA
PACIFIC OCEAN
N
S
E
W

Africa: Political

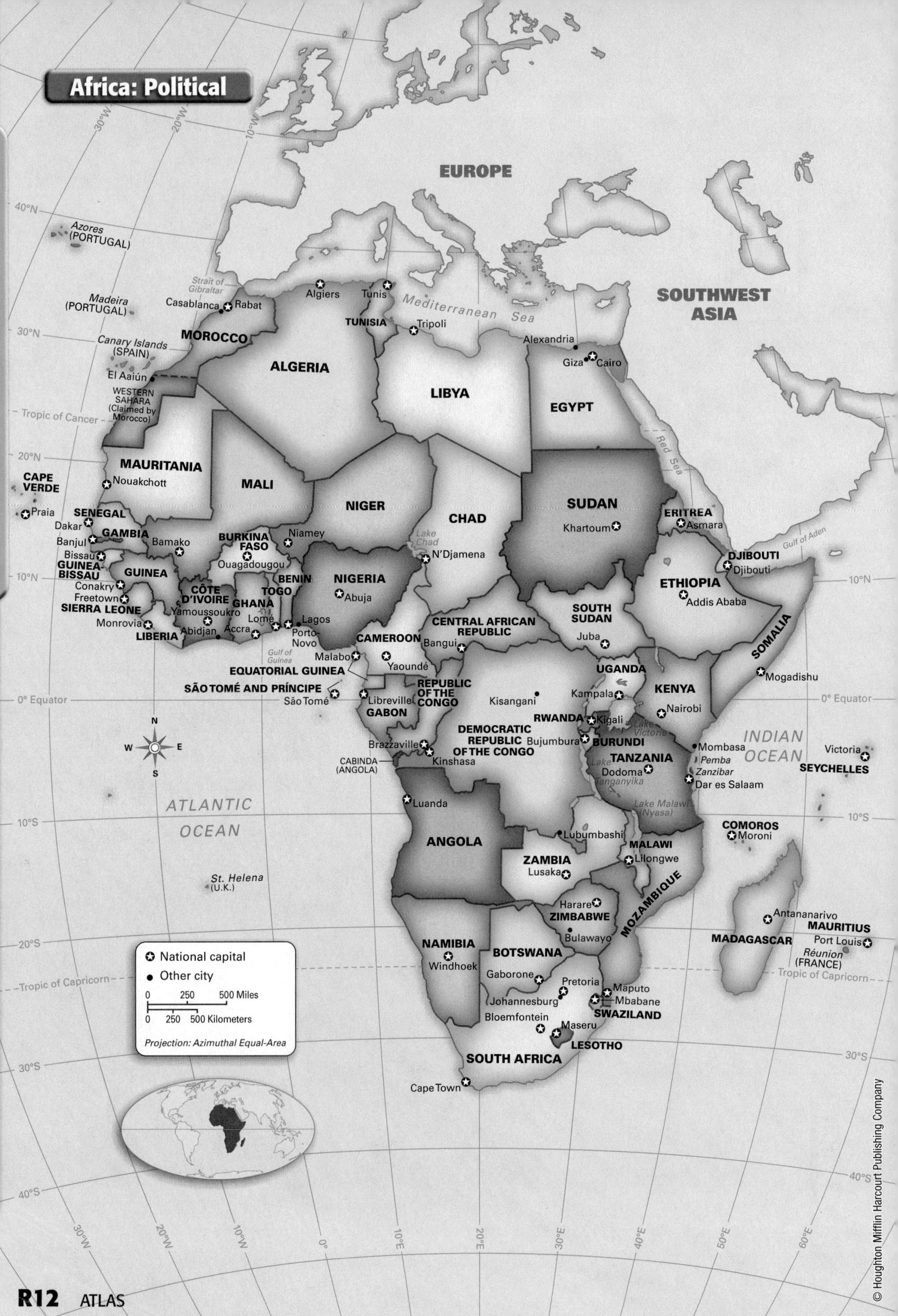
EUROPE
SOUTHWEST ASIA
Azores (PORTUGAL)
Madeira (PORTUGAL)
Canary Islands (SPAIN)
Strait of Gibraltar
Mediterranean Sea
Red Sea
Gulf of Aden
Casablanca
Rabat
Algiers
Tunis
TUNISIA
Tripoli
MOROCCO
ALGERIA
LIBYA
EGYPT
Alexandria
Giza
Cairo
El Aaiún
WESTERN SAHARA (Claimed by Morocco)
Tropic of Cancer
MAURITANIA
Nouakchott
MALI
NIGER
CHAD
SUDAN
Khartoum
ERITREA
Asmara
DJIBOUTI
Djibouti
ETHIOPIA
Addis Ababa
SOMALIA
Mogadishu
CAPE VERDE
Praia
SENEGAL
Dakar
GAMBIA
Banjul
Bissau
GUINEA-BISSAU
GUINEA
Conakry
Freetown
SIERRA LEONE
Monrovia
LIBERIA
Bamako
BURKINA FASO
Ouagadougou
Niamey
Lake Chad
N'Djamena
CÔTE D'IVOIRE
Yamoussoukro
Abidjan
GHANA
Accra
TOGO
Lomé
BENIN
Porto-Novo
Lagos
NIGERIA
Abuja
Gulf of Guinea
CAMEROON
Yaoundé
Malabo
EQUATORIAL GUINEA
SÃO TOMÉ AND PRÍNCIPE
São Tomé
Libreville
GABON
REPUBLIC OF THE CONGO
Brazzaville
Kinshasa
CABINDA (ANGOLA)
CENTRAL AFRICAN REPUBLIC
Bangui
SOUTH SUDAN
Juba
UGANDA
Kampala
KENYA
Nairobi
Mombasa
Kisangani
RWANDA
Kigali
Lake Victoria
DEMOCRATIC REPUBLIC OF THE CONGO
Bujumbura
BURUNDI
TANZANIA
Dodoma
Lake Tanganyika
Pemba
Zanzibar
Dar es Salaam
INDIAN OCEAN
Victoria
SEYCHELLES
Luanda
ANGOLA
Lake Malawi (Nyasa)
Lubumbashi
MALAWI
Lilongwe
ZAMBIA
Lusaka
COMOROS
Moroni
MOZAMBIQUE
Harare
ZIMBABWE
Bulawayo
Antananarivo
MADAGASCAR
MAURITIUS
Port Louis
Réunion (FRANCE)
NAMIBIA
Windhoek
BOTSWANA
Gaborone
Pretoria
Johannesburg
Maputo
Mbabane
SWAZILAND
Bloemfontein
Maseru
LESOTHO
SOUTH AFRICA
Cape Town
ATLANTIC OCEAN
St. Helena (U.K.)
N
E
S
W
National capital
Other city
0 250 500 Miles
0 250 500 Kilometers
Projection: Azimuthal Equal-Area
40°N
30°N
20°N
10°N
0° Equator
10°S
20°S
Tropic of Capricorn
30°S
40°S
30°W
20°W
10°W
0°
10°E
20°E
30°E
40°E
50°E
60°E

© Houghton Mifflin Harcourt Publishing Company

© Houghton Mifflin Harcourt Publishing Company

Australia and New Zealand: Political

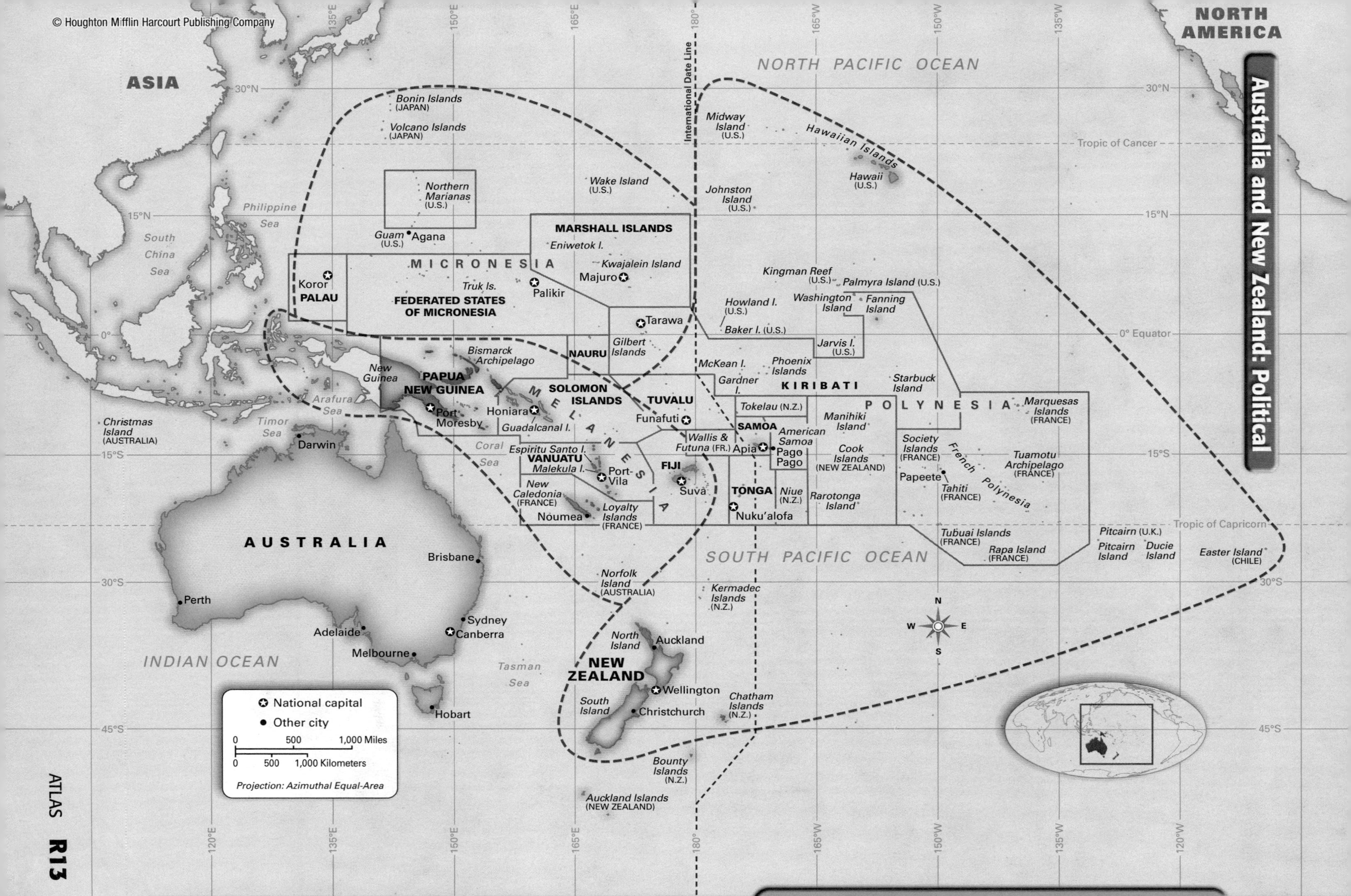
ASIA
NORTH AMERICA
NORTH PACIFIC OCEAN
SOUTH PACIFIC OCEAN
INDIAN OCEAN
AUSTRALIA
NEW ZEALAND
MICRONESIA
MELANESIA
POLYNESIA
PALAU
Koror
FEDERATED STATES OF MICRONESIA
Palikir
Truk Is.
MARSHALL ISLANDS
Majuro
Eniwetok I.
Kwajalein Island
Northern Marianas (U.S.)
Guam (U.S.)
Agana
Bonin Islands (JAPAN)
Volcano Islands (JAPAN)
Wake Island (U.S.)
Midway Island (U.S.)
Johnston Island (U.S.)
Hawaiian Islands
Hawaii (U.S.)
Kingman Reef (U.S.)
Palmyra Island (U.S.)
Washington Island
Fanning Island
Howland I. (U.S.)
Baker I. (U.S.)
Jarvis I. (U.S.)
NAURU
Gilbert Islands
Tarawa
KIRIBATI
McKean I.
Phoenix Islands
Gardner I.
Starbuck Island
Marquesas Islands (FRANCE)
PAPUA NEW GUINEA
Port Moresby
New Guinea
Bismarck Archipelago
SOLOMON ISLANDS
Honiara
Guadalcanal I.
TUVALU
Funafuti
Tokelau (N.Z.)
SAMOA
Apia
American Samoa
Pago Pago
Manihiki Island
Cook Islands (NEW ZEALAND)
Rarotonga Island
Niue (N.Z.)
TONGA
Nuku'alofa
Wallis & Futuna (FR.)
FIJI
Suva
VANUATU
Espiritu Santo I.
Malekula I.
Port-Vila
New Caledonia (FRANCE)
Noumea
Loyalty Islands (FRANCE)
Society Islands (FRANCE)
Papeete
Tahiti (FRANCE)
French Polynesia
Tuamotu Archipelago (FRANCE)
Tubuai Islands (FRANCE)
Rapa Island (FRANCE)
Pitcairn (U.K.)
Pitcairn Island
Ducie Island
Easter Island (CHILE)
Philippine Sea
South China Sea
Arafura Sea
Timor Sea
Coral Sea
Tasman Sea
Christmas Island (AUSTRALIA)
Darwin
Brisbane
Perth
Sydney
Canberra
Adelaide
Melbourne
Hobart
Norfolk Island (AUSTRALIA)
Kermadec Islands (N.Z.)
North Island
Auckland
Wellington
South Island
Christchurch
Chatham Islands (N.Z.)
Bounty Islands (N.Z.)
Auckland Islands (NEW ZEALAND)
International Date Line
Tropic of Cancer
0° Equator
Tropic of Capricorn
30°N
15°N
0°
15°S
30°S
45°S
120°E
135°E
150°E
165°E
180°
165°W
150°W
135°W
120°W
N
E
S
W
National capital
Other city
0 500 1,000 Miles
0 500 1,000 Kilometers
Projection: Azimuthal Equal-Area

ATLAS

© Houghton Mifflin Harcourt Publishing Company • Image Credits: (c), ©S. Wanke/Photodisc/Getty Images

Presidents

1 George Washington
Born: 1732 **Died:** 1799
Years in Office: 1789–97
Political Party: None
Home State: Virginia
Vice President: John Adams

2 John Adams
Born: 1735 **Died:** 1826
Years in Office: 1797–1801
Political Party: Federalist
Home State: Massachusetts
Vice President: Thomas Jefferson

3 Thomas Jefferson
Born: 1743 **Died:** 1826
Years in Office: 1801–09
Political Party: Republican*
Home State: Virginia
Vice Presidents: Aaron Burr, George Clinton

4 James Madison
Born: 1751 **Died:** 1836
Years in Office: 1809–17
Political Party: Republican
Home State: Virginia
Vice Presidents: George Clinton, Elbridge Gerry

5 James Monroe
Born: 1758 **Died:** 1831
Years in Office: 1817–25
Political Party: Republican
Home State: Virginia
Vice President: Daniel D. Tompkins

6 John Quincy Adams
Born: 1767 **Died:** 1848
Years in Office: 1825–29
Political Party: Republican
Home State: Massachusetts
Vice President: John C. Calhoun

7 Andrew Jackson
Born: 1767 **Died:** 1845
Years in Office: 1829–37
Political Party: Democratic
Home State: Tennessee
Vice Presidents: John C. Calhoun, Martin Van Buren

8 Martin Van Buren
Born: 1782 **Died:** 1862
Years in Office: 1837–41
Political Party: Democratic
Home State: New York
Vice President: Richard M. Johnson

* The Republican Party of the third through sixth presidents is not the party of Abraham Lincoln, which was founded in 1854.

© Houghton Mifflin Harcourt Publishing Company • Image Credits: (all), White House Historical Association (White House Collection)

9 William Henry Harrison
Born: 1773 **Died:** 1841
Years in Office: 1841
Political Party: Whig
Home State: Ohio
Vice President: John Tyler

10 John Tyler
Born: 1790 **Died:** 1862
Years in Office: 1841–45
Political Party: Whig
Home State: Virginia
Vice President: None

11 James K. Polk
Born: 1795 **Died:** 1849
Years in Office: 1845–49
Political Party: Democratic
Home State: Tennessee
Vice President: George M. Dallas

12 Zachary Taylor
Born: 1784 **Died:** 1850
Years in Office: 1849–50
Political Party: Whig
Home State: Louisiana
Vice President: Millard Fillmore

13 Millard Fillmore
Born: 1800 **Died:** 1874
Years in Office: 1850–53
Political Party: Whig
Home State: New York
Vice President: None

14 Franklin Pierce
Born: 1804 **Died:** 1869
Years in Office: 1853–57
Political Party: Democratic
Home State: New Hampshire
Vice President: William R. King

15 James Buchanan
Born: 1791 **Died:** 1868
Years in Office: 1857–61
Political Party: Democratic
Home State: Pennsylvania
Vice President: John C. Breckinridge

16 Abraham Lincoln
Born: 1809 **Died:** 1865
Years in Office: 1861–65
Political Party: Republican
Home State: Illinois
Vice Presidents: Hannibal Hamlin, Andrew Johnson

17 Andrew Johnson
Born: 1808 **Died:** 1875
Years in Office: 1865–69
Political Party: Democratic
Home State: Tennessee
Vice President: None

© Houghton Mifflin Harcourt Publishing Company • Image Credits: (all), White House Historical Association (White House Collection)

18 ULYSSES S. GRANT
Born: 1822 **Died:** 1885
Years in Office: 1869–77
Political Party: Republican
Home State: Illinois
Vice Presidents: Schuyler Colfax, Henry Wilson

19 RUTHERFORD B. HAYES
Born: 1822 **Died:** 1893
Years in Office: 1877–81
Political Party: Republican
Home State: Ohio
Vice President: William A. Wheeler

20 JAMES A. GARFIELD
Born: 1831 **Died:** 1881
Years in Office: 1881
Political Party: Republican
Home State: Ohio
Vice President: Chester A. Arthur

21 CHESTER A. ARTHUR
Born: 1829 **Died:** 1886
Years in Office: 1881–85
Political Party: Republican
Home State: New York
Vice President: None

22 GROVER CLEVELAND
Born: 1837 **Died:** 1908
Years in Office: 1885–89
Political Party: Democratic
Home State: New York
Vice President: Thomas A. Hendricks

23 BENJAMIN HARRISON
Born: 1833 **Died:** 1901
Years in Office: 1889–93
Political Party: Republican
Home State: Indiana
Vice President: Levi P. Morton

24 GROVER CLEVELAND
Born: 1837 **Died:** 1908
Years in Office: 1893–97
Political Party: Democratic
Home State: New York
Vice President: Adlai E. Stevenson

25 WILLIAM MCKINLEY
Born: 1843 **Died:** 1901
Years in Office: 1897–1901
Political Party: Republican
Home State: Ohio
Vice Presidents: Garret A. Hobart, Theodore Roosevelt

26 THEODORE ROOSEVELT
Born: 1858 **Died:** 1919
Years in Office: 1901–09
Political Party: Republican
Home State: New York
Vice President: Charles W. Fairbanks

© Houghton Mifflin Harcourt Publishing Company • Image Credits: (all), White House Historical Association (White House Collection)

27 William Howard Taft
Born: 1857 **Died:** 1930
Years in Office: 1909–13
Political Party: Republican
Home State: Ohio
Vice President: James S. Sherman

28 Woodrow Wilson
Born: 1856 **Died:** 1924
Years in Office: 1913–21
Political Party: Democratic
Home State: New Jersey
Vice President: Thomas R. Marshall

29 Warren G. Harding
Born: 1865 **Died:** 1923
Years in Office: 1921–23
Political Party: Republican
Home State: Ohio
Vice President: Calvin Coolidge

30 Calvin Coolidge
Born: 1872 **Died:** 1933
Years in Office: 1923–29
Political Party: Republican
Home State: Massachusetts
Vice President: Charles G. Dawes

31 Herbert Hoover
Born: 1874 **Died:** 1964
Years in Office: 1929–33
Political Party: Republican
Home State: California
Vice President: Charles Curtis

32 Franklin D. Roosevelt
Born: 1882 **Died:** 1945
Years in Office: 1933–45
Political Party: Democratic
Home State: New York
Vice Presidents: John Nance Garner, Henry Wallace, Harry S Truman

33 Harry S Truman
Born: 1884 **Died:** 1972
Years in Office: 1945–53
Political Party: Democratic
Home State: Missouri
Vice President: Alben W. Barkley

34 Dwight D. Eisenhower
Born: 1890 **Died:** 1969
Years in Office: 1953–61
Political Party: Republican
Home State: Kansas
Vice President: Richard M. Nixon

35 John F. Kennedy
Born: 1917 **Died:** 1963
Years in Office: 1961–63
Political Party: Democratic
Home State: Massachusetts
Vice President: Lyndon B. Johnson

© Houghton Mifflin Harcourt Publishing Company • Image Credits: (all), White House Historical Association (White House Collection)

36 LYNDON B. JOHNSON
Born: 1908 **Died:** 1973
Years in Office: 1963–69
Political Party: Democratic
Home State: Texas
Vice President: Hubert H. Humphrey

37 RICHARD M. NIXON
Born: 1913 **Died:** 1994
Years in Office: 1969–74
Political Party: Republican
Home State: California
Vice Presidents: Spiro T. Agnew, Gerald R. Ford

38 GERALD R. FORD
Born: 1913 **Died:** 2006
Years in Office: 1974–77
Political Party: Republican
Home State: Michigan
Vice President: Nelson A. Rockefeller

39 JIMMY CARTER
Born: 1924
Years in Office: 1977–81
Political Party: Democratic
Home State: Georgia
Vice President: Walter F. Mondale

40 RONALD REAGAN
Born: 1911 **Died:** 2004
Years in Office: 1981–89
Political Party: Republican
Home State: California
Vice President: George Bush

41 GEORGE BUSH
Born: 1924
Years in Office: 1989–93
Political Party: Republican
Home State: Texas
Vice President: J. Danforth Quayle

42 BILL CLINTON
Born: 1946
Years in Office: 1993–2001
Political Party: Democratic
Home State: Arkansas
Vice President: Albert Gore Jr.

43 GEORGE W. BUSH
Born: 1946
Years in Office: 2001–2009
Political Party: Republican
Home State: Texas
Vice President: Richard B. Cheney

44 BARACK OBAMA
Born: 1961
Years in Office: 2009–2016
Political Party: Democratic
Home State: Illinois
Vice President: Joe Biden

PRESIDENTS

© Houghton Mifflin Harcourt Publishing Company • Image Credits: (bc), The White House, photo by Eric Draper; (br), Official White House photo by Pete Souza; (all others), White House Historical Association (White House Collection)

Facts About the States

State	Year of Statehood	2009 Population	Area (Sq. Mi.)	Population Density (per Sq. Mi.)	Capital
Alabama	1819	4,708,708	50,744	88.7	Montgomery
Alaska	1959	698,473	571,951	1.1	Juneau
Arizona	1912	6,595,778	113,635	49.1	Phoenix
Arkansas	1836	2,889,450	52,068	52.3	Little Rock
California	1850	36,961,664	155,959	227.5	Sacramento
Colorado	1876	5,024,748	103,718	43.9	Denver
Connecticut	1788	3,518,288	4,845	719.0	Hartford
Delaware	1787	885,122	1,954	418.4	Dover
District of Columbia	—	599,657	61	9,235.8	—
Florida	1845	18,537,969	53,927	315.6	Tallahassee
Georgia	1788	9,829,211	57,906	150.0	Atlanta
Hawaii	1959	1,295,178	6,423	195.8	Honolulu
Idaho	1890	1,545,801	82,747	16.5	Boise
Illinois	1818	12,910,409	55,584	227.6	Springfield
Indiana	1816	6,423,113	35,867	172.7	Indianapolis
Iowa	1846	3,007,856	55,869	52.7	Des Moines
Kansas	1861	2,818,747	81,815	33.3	Topeka
Kentucky	1792	4,314,113	39,728	103.7	Frankfort
Louisiana	1812	4,492,076	43,562	103.2	Baton Rouge
Maine	1820	1,318,301	30,862	42.3	Augusta
Maryland	1788	5,699,478	9,774	563.6	Annapolis
Massachusetts	1788	6,593,587	7,840	820.6	Boston
Michigan	1837	9,969,727	56,804	177.5	Lansing
Minnesota	1858	5,266,214	79,610	63.6	St. Paul

© Houghton Mifflin Harcourt Publishing Company

State	Year of Statehood	2009 Population	Area (Sq. Mi.)	Population Density (per Sq. Mi.)	Capital
Mississippi	1817	2,951,996	46,907	61.4	Jackson
Missouri	1821	5,987,580	68,886	82.8	Jefferson City
Montana	1889	974,989	145,552	6.3	Helena
Nebraska	1867	1,796,619	76,872	22.6	Lincoln
Nevada	1864	2,643,085	109,826	20.4	Carson City
New Hampshire	1788	1,324,575	8,968	143.6	Concord
New Jersey	1787	8,707,739	7,417	1,164.7	Trenton
New Mexico	1912	2,009,671	121,356	15.4	Santa Fe
New York	1788	19,541,453	47,214	406.4	Albany
North Carolina	1789	9,380,884	48,711	172.6	Raleigh
North Dakota	1889	646,844	68,976	9.2	Bismarck
Ohio	1803	11,542,645	40,948	279.3	Columbus
Oklahoma	1907	3,687,050	68,667	51.1	Oklahoma City
Oregon	1859	3,825,657	95,997	37.1	Salem
Pennsylvania	1787	12,604,767	44,817	275.9	Harrisburg
Rhode Island	1790	1,053,209	1,045	1,029.8	Providence
South Carolina	1788	4,561,242	30,109	137.7	Columbia
South Dakota	1889	812,383	75,885	10.1	Pierre
Tennessee	1796	6,296,254	41,217	141.7	Nashville
Texas	1845	24,782,302	261,797	84.5	Austin
Utah	1896	2,784,572	82,144	28.6	Salt Lake City
Vermont	1791	621,760	9,250	66.9	Montpelier
Virginia	1788	7,882,590	39,594	186.6	Richmond
Washington	1889	6,664,195	66,544	92.1	Olympia
West Virginia	1863	1,819,777	24,078	75.2	Charleston
Wisconsin	1848	5,654,774	54,310	100.8	Madison
Wyoming	1890	544,270	97,100	5.2	Cheyenne

© Houghton Mifflin Harcourt Publishing Company

American Flag

The American flag is a symbol of the nation. It is recognized instantly, whether as a big banner waving in the wind or a tiny emblem worn on a lapel. The flag is so important that it is a major theme of the national anthem, "The Star-Spangled Banner." One of the most popular names for the flag is the Stars and Stripes. It is also known as Old Glory.

THE MEANING OF THE FLAG

The American flag has 13 stripes—7 red and 6 white. In the upper-left corner of the flag is the union—50 white five-pointed stars against a blue background.

The 13 stripes stand for the original 13 American states, and the 50 stars represent the states of the nation today. According to the U.S. Department of State, the colors of the flag also are symbolic:

Red stands for courage.

White symbolizes purity.

Blue is the color of vigilance, perseverance, and justice.

DISPLAYING THE FLAG

It is customary not to display the American flag in bad weather. It is also customary for the flag to be displayed outdoors only from sunrise to sunset, except on certain occasions. In a few special places, however, the flag is always flown day and night. When flown at night, the flag should be illuminated.

Near a speaker's platform, the flag should occupy the place of honor at the speaker's right. When carried in a parade with other flags, the American flag should be on the marching right or in front at the center. When flying with the flags of the 50 states, the national flag must be at the center and the highest point. In a group of national flags, all should be of equal size and all should be flown from staffs, or flagpoles, of equal height.

The flag should never touch the ground or the floor. It should not be marked with any insignia, pictures, or words. Nor should it be used in any disrespectful way—as an advertising decoration, for instance. The flag should never be dipped to honor any person or thing.

SALUTING THE FLAG

The United States, like other countries, has a flag code, or rules for displaying and honoring the flag. For example, all those present should stand at attention facing the flag and salute it when it is being raised or lowered or when it is carried past them in a parade or procession. A man wearing a hat should take it off and hold it with his right hand over his heart. All women and hatless men should stand with their right hands over their hearts to show their respect for the flag. The flag should also receive these honors during the playing of the national anthem and the reciting of the Pledge of Allegiance.

THE PLEDGE OF ALLEGIANCE

The Pledge of Allegiance was written in 1892 by Massachusetts magazine (*Youth's Companion*) editor Francis Bellamy. (Congress added the words "under God" in 1954.)

I pledge allegiance to the flag of the United States of America and to the republic for which it stands, one nation under God, indivisible, with liberty and justice for all.

Civilians should say the Pledge of Allegiance with their right hands placed over their hearts. People in the armed forces give the military salute. By saying the Pledge of Allegiance, we promise loyalty ("pledge allegiance") to the United States and its ideals.

© Houghton Mifflin Harcourt Publishing Company • Image Credits: (t), ©Photodisc/gettyimages

"THE STAR-SPANGLED BANNER"

"The Star-Spangled Banner" is the national anthem of the United States. It was written by Francis Scott Key during the War of 1812. While being detained by the British aboard a ship on September 13–14, 1814, Key watched the British bombardment of Fort McHenry at Baltimore. The attack lasted 25 hours. The smoke was so thick that Key could not tell who had won. When the air cleared, Key saw the American flag that was still flying over the fort. "The Star-Spangled Banner" is sung to music written by British composer John Stafford Smith. In 1931 Congress designated "The Star-Spangled Banner" as the national anthem.

I

Oh, say, can you see, by the dawn's early light,
What so proudly we hailed at the twilight's last gleaming,
Whose broad stripes and bright stars through the perilous fight,
O'er the ramparts we watched were so gallantly streaming?
And the rockets' red glare, the bombs bursting in air,
Gave proof through the night that our flag was still there.
Oh, say, does that star-spangled banner yet wave
O'er the land of the free, and the home of the brave?

II

On the shore, dimly seen through the mists of the deep,
Where the foe's haughty host in dread silence reposes,
What is that which the breeze, o'er the towering steep,
As it fitfully blows, half conceals, half discloses?
Now it catches the gleam of the morning's first beam,
In full glory reflected, now shines on the stream.
'Tis the star-spangled banner; oh, long may it wave
O'er the land of the free, and the home of the brave!

III

And where is that band who so vauntingly swore
That the havoc of war and the battle's confusion
A home and a country should leave us no more?
Their blood has washed out their foul footsteps' pollution.
No refuge could save the hireling and slave
From the terror of flight, or the gloom of the grave:
And the star-spangled banner in triumph doth wave
O'er the land of the free, and the home of the brave!

IV

Oh! thus be it ever when freemen shall stand
Between their loved homes and the war's desolation!
Blest with victory and peace, may the heaven-rescued land
Praise the Power that hath made and preserved us a nation!
Then conquer we must, for our cause it is just,
And this be our motto: "In God is our trust!"
And the star-spangled banner in triumph shall wave,
O'er the land of the free, and the home of the brave!

Sheet music to the national anthem

"AMERICA, THE BEAUTIFUL"

One of the most beloved songs celebrating our nation is "America, the Beautiful." Katharine Lee Bates first wrote the lyrics to the song in 1893 after visiting Colorado. The version of the song we know today is set to music by Samuel A. Ward. The first and last stanzas of "America, the Beautiful" are shown below.

O beautiful for spacious skies,
For amber waves of grain,
For purple mountain majesties
Above the fruited plain!
America! America!
God shed his grace on thee
And crown thy good with brotherhood
From sea to shining sea!

O beautiful for patriot dream
That sees beyond the years
Thine alabaster cities gleam
Undimmed by human tears!
America! America!
God shed his grace on thee
And crown thy good with brotherhood
From sea to shining sea!

© Houghton Mifflin Harcourt Publishing Company • Image Credits: (t), The Granger Collection, New York

The Declaration of Independence

In Congress, July 4, 1776
The unanimous Declaration of the thirteen united States of America,

When in the Course of human events, it becomes necessary for one people to dissolve the political bands which have connected them with another, and to assume among the Powers of the earth, the separate and equal station to which the Laws of Nature and of Nature's God entitle them, a decent respect to the opinions of mankind requires that they should declare the causes which **impel** them to the separation.

We hold these truths to be self-evident, that all men are created equal, that they are **endowed** by their Creator with certain unalienable Rights, that among these are Life, Liberty, and the pursuit of Happiness. That to secure these rights, Governments are instituted among Men, deriving their just powers from the consent of the governed, That whenever any Form of Government becomes destructive of these ends, it is the Right of the People to alter or to abolish it, and to institute new Government, laying its foundation on such principles and organizing its powers in such form, as to them shall seem most likely to effect their Safety and Happiness. Prudence, indeed, will dictate that Governments long established should not be changed for light and transient causes; and accordingly all experience hath shown, that mankind are more disposed to suffer, while evils are sufferable, than to right themselves by abolishing the forms to which they are accustomed. But when a long train of abuses and **usurpations**, pursuing invariably the same Object **evinces** a design to reduce them under absolute **Despotism**, it is their right, it is their duty, to throw off such Government, and to provide new Guards for their future security.—Such has been the patient sufferance of these Colonies; and such is now the necessity which constrains them to alter their former Systems of Government. The history of the present King of Great Britain is a history of repeated injuries and usurpations, all having in direct object the establishment of an absolute **Tyranny** over these States. To prove this, let Facts be submitted to a **candid** world.

Vocabulary

impel force

endowed provided

usurpations wrongful seizures of power

evinces clearly displays

despotism unlimited power

tyranny oppressive power exerted by a government or ruler

candid fair

He has refused his Assent to Laws, the most wholesome and necessary for the public good.

He has forbidden his Governors to pass Laws of immediate and pressing importance, unless suspended in their operation till his Assent should be obtained; and when so suspended, he has utterly neglected to attend to them.

He has refused to pass other Laws for the accommodation of large districts of people, unless those people would **relinquish** the right of Representation in the Legislature, a right **inestimable** to them and **formidable** to tyrants only.

He has called together legislative bodies at places unusual, uncomfortable, and distant from the depository of their Public Records, for the sole purpose of fatiguing them into compliance with his measures.

He has dissolved Representative Houses repeatedly, for opposing with manly firmness his invasions on the rights of the people.

He has refused for a long time, after such dissolutions, to cause others to be elected; whereby the Legislative Powers, incapable of **Annihilation**, have returned to the People at large for their exercise; the State remaining in the mean time exposed to all the dangers of invasion from without, and **convulsions** within.

He has endeavored to prevent the population of these States; for that purpose obstructing the Laws of **Naturalization of Foreigners**; refusing to pass others to encourage their migration hither, and raising the conditions of new **Appropriations of Lands**.

He has obstructed the Administration of Justice, by refusing his Assent to Laws for establishing Judiciary Powers.

He has made Judges dependent on his Will alone, for the **tenure** of their offices, and the amount and payment of their salaries.

He has erected **a multitude of** New Offices, and sent hither swarms of Officers to harass our people, and eat out their substance.

He has kept among us, in times of peace, Standing Armies without the Consent of our legislature.

He has affected to render the Military independent of and superior to the Civil Power.

He has combined with others to subject us to a jurisdiction foreign to our constitution, and unacknowledged by our laws; giving his Assent to their Acts of pretended legislation:

For **quartering** large bodies of armed troops among us:

For protecting them, by a mock Trial, from Punishment for any Murders which they should commit on the Inhabitants of these States:

For cutting off our Trade with all parts of the world:

For imposing taxes on us without our Consent:

For depriving us in many cases, of the benefits of Trial by Jury:

Vocabulary

relinquish release, yield

inestimable priceless

formidable causing dread

annihilation destruction

convulsions violent disturbances

naturalization of foreigners the process by which foreign-born persons become citizens

appropriations of lands setting aside land for settlement

tenure term

a multitude of many

quartering lodging, housing

DECLARATION OF INDEPENDENCE

Vocabulary

arbitrary not based on law

render make

abdicated given up

foreign mercenaries soldiers hired to fight for a country not their own

perfidy violation of trust

insurrections rebellions

petitioned for redress asked formally for a correction of wrongs

unwarrantable jurisdiction unjustified authority

magnanimity generous spirit

conjured urgently called upon

consanguinity common ancestry

acquiesce consent to

For transporting us beyond Seas to be tried for pretended offences:

For abolishing the free System of English Laws in a neighboring Province, establishing therein an **Arbitrary** government, and enlarging its Boundaries so as to **render** it at once an example and fit instrument for introducing the same absolute rule into these Colonies:

For taking away our Charters, abolishing our most valuable Laws, and altering fundamentally the Forms of our Governments:

For suspending our own Legislature, and declaring themselves invested with Power to legislate for us in all cases whatsoever.

He has **abdicated** Government here, by declaring us out of his Protection and waging War against us.

He has plundered our seas, ravaged our Coasts, burnt our towns, and destroyed the lives of our people.

He is at this time transporting large armies of **foreign mercenaries** to complete the works of death, desolation and tyranny, already begun with circumstances of Cruelty & **perfidy** scarcely paralleled in the most barbarous ages, and totally unworthy the Head of a civilized nation.

He has constrained our fellow Citizens taken Captive on the high Seas to bear Arms against their Country, to become the executioners of their friends and Brethren, or to fall themselves by their Hands.

He has excited domestic **insurrections** amongst us, and has endeavored to bring on the inhabitants of our frontiers, the merciless Indian Savages, whose known rule of warfare, is an undistinguished destruction of all ages, sexes and conditions.

In every stage of these Oppressions We have **Petitioned for Redress** in the most humble terms: Our repeated Petitions have been answered only by repeated injury. A Prince, whose character is thus marked by every act which may define a Tyrant, is unfit to be the ruler of a free People.

Nor have We been wanting in attention to our British brethren. We have warned them from time to time of attempts by their legislature to extend an **unwarrantable jurisdiction** over us. We have reminded them of the circumstances of our emigration and settlement here. We have appealed to their native justice and **magnanimity**, and we have **conjured** them by the ties of our common kindred to disavow these usurpations, which, would inevitably interrupt our connections and correspondence. They too have been deaf to the voice of justice and of **consanguinity**. We must, therefore, **acquiesce** in the necessity, which denounces our Separation, and hold them, as we hold the rest of mankind, Enemies in War, in Peace Friends.

We, therefore, the Representatives of the united States of America, in General Congress, Assembled, appealing to the Supreme Judge of the world for the **rectitude** of our intentions, do, in the Name, and by Authority of the good People of these Colonies, solemnly publish and declare, That these United Colonies are, and of Right ought to be Free and Independent States; that they are Absolved from all Allegiance to the British Crown, and that all political connection between them and the State of Great Britain, is and ought to be totally dissolved; and that as Free and Independent States, they have full Power to levy War, conclude Peace, contract Alliances, establish Commerce, and to do all other Acts and Things which Independent States may of right do. And for the support of this Declaration, with a firm reliance on the Protection of Divine Providence, we mutually pledge to each other our Lives, our Fortunes and our sacred Honor.

John Hancock
Button Gwinnett
Lyman Hall
George Walton
William Hooper
Joseph Hewes
John Penn
Edward Rutledge
Thomas Heyward, Jr.
Thomas Lynch, Jr.
Arthur Middleton
Samuel Chase
William Paca
Thomas Stone
Charles Carroll of Carrollton
George Wythe
Richard Henry Lee
Thomas Jefferson

Benjamin Harrison
Thomas Nelson, Jr.
Francis Lightfoot Lee
Carter Braxton
Robert Morris
Benjamin Rush
Benjamin Franklin
John Morton
George Clymer
James Smith
George Taylor
James Wilson
George Ross
Caesar Rodney
George Read
Thomas McKean
William Floyd
Philip Livingston
Francis Lewis

Lewis Morris
Richard Stockton
John Witherspoon
Francis Hopkinson
John Hart
Abraham Clark
Josiah Bartlett
William Whipple
Samuel Adams
John Adams
Robert Treat Paine
Elbridge Gerry
Stephen Hopkins
William Ellery
Roger Sherman
Samuel Huntington
William Williams
Oliver Wolcott
Matthew Thornton

Vocabulary

rectitude rightness

The Constitution of the United States

Preamble

We the People of the United States, in Order to form a more perfect Union, establish Justice, insure domestic Tranquility, provide for the common defense, promote the general Welfare, and secure the Blessings of Liberty to ourselves and our Posterity, do ordain and establish this Constitution for the United States of America.

Legislative Branch

Article I explains how the legislative branch, called Congress, is organized. The chief purpose of the legislative branch is to make laws. Congress is made up of the Senate and the House of Representatives.

Article I The Legislature

Section 1. Congress

All legislative Powers herein granted shall be vested in a Congress of the United States, which shall consist of a Senate and House of Representatives.

Section 2. The House of Representatives

1. Elections The House of Representatives shall be composed of Members chosen every second Year by the People of the several States, and the Electors in each State shall have the Qualifications requisite for Electors of the most numerous Branch of the State Legislature.

The House of Representatives

The number of members each state has in the House is based on the population of the individual state. In 1929 Congress permanently fixed the size of the House at 435 members.

2. Qualifications No Person shall be a Representative who shall not have attained to the Age of twenty five Years, and been seven Years a Citizen of the United States, and who shall not, when elected, be an Inhabitant of that State in which he shall be chosen.

3. Number of Representatives Representatives and direct Taxes shall be apportioned among the several States which may be included within this Union, according to their respective Numbers~~, which shall be determined by adding to the whole Number of free Persons, including~~ ~~**those bound to Service**~~[1] ~~for a Term of Years, and excluding Indians not taxed, three fifths of~~ ~~**all other Persons**~~.[2] The actual **Enumeration**[3] shall be made within three Years after the first Meeting of the Congress of the United States, and within every subsequent Term of ten Years, in such Manner as they shall by Law direct. The Number of Representatives shall not exceed one for every

Vocabulary

[1] **those bound to Service** indentured servants

[2] **all other Persons** slaves

[3] **Enumeration** census or official population count

Note: The parts of the Constitution that have been lined through are no longer in force or no longer apply because of later amendments. The titles of the sections and articles are added for easier reference.

thirty Thousand, but each State shall have at Least one Representative~~; and until such enumeration shall be made, the State of New Hampshire shall be entitled to choose three, Massachoosetts eight, Rhode-Island and Providence Plantations one, Connecticut five, New-York six, New Jersey four, Pennsylvania eight, Delaware one, Maryland six, Virginia ten, North Carolina five, South Carolina five, and Georgia three.~~

4. Vacancies When vacancies happen in the Representation from any State, the Executive Authority thereof shall issue Writs of Election to fill such Vacancies.

5. Officers and Impeachment The House of Representatives shall choose their Speaker and other Officers; and shall have the sole Power of impeachment.

Section 3. The Senate

1. Number of Senators The Senate of the United States shall be composed of two Senators from each State, ~~chosen by the Legislature thereof,~~ for six Years; and each Senator shall have one Vote.

2. Classifying Terms Immediately after they shall be assembled in Consequence of the first Election, they shall be divided as equally as may be into three Classes. The Seats of the Senators of the first Class shall be vacated at the Expiration of the second Year, of the second Class at the Expiration of the fourth Year, and of the third Class at the Expiration of the sixth Year, so that one third may be chosen every second Year; ~~and if Vacancies happen by Resignation, or otherwise, during the Recess of the Legislature of any State, the Executive thereof may make temporary Appointments until the next Meeting of the Legislature, which shall then fill such Vacancies.~~

3. Qualifications No Person shall be a Senator who shall not have attained to the Age of thirty Years, and been nine Years a Citizen of the United States, and who shall not, when elected, be an Inhabitant of that State for which he shall be chosen.

4. Role of Vice-President The Vice President of the United States shall be President of the Senate, but shall have no Vote, unless they be equally divided.

5. Officers The Senate shall choose their other Officers, and also a President **pro tempore**,[4] in the Absence of the Vice President, or when he shall exercise the Office of President of the United States.

6. Impeachment Trials The Senate shall have the sole Power to try all **Impeachments**.[5] When sitting for that Purpose, they shall be on Oath or Affirmation. When the President of the United States is tried, the Chief Justice shall preside: And no Person shall be convicted without the Concurrence of two thirds of the Members present.

7. Punishment for Impeachment Judgment in Cases of Impeachment shall not extend further than to removal from Office, and disqualification to hold

The Vice President

The only duty that the Constitution assigns to the vice president is to preside over meetings of the Senate. Modern presidents have usually given their vice presidents more responsibilities.

Vocabulary

[4] **pro tempore** temporarily

[5] **Impeachments** official accusations of federal wrongdoing

and enjoy any Office of honor, Trust or Profit under the United States: but the Party convicted shall nevertheless be liable and subject to Indictment, Trial, Judgment and Punishment, according to Law.

Section 4. Congressional Elections

1. Regulations The Times, Places and Manner of holding Elections for Senators and Representatives, shall be prescribed in each State by the Legislature thereof; but the Congress may at any time by Law make or alter such Regulations, except as to the Places of choosing Senators.

2. Sessions ~~The Congress shall assemble at least once in every Year, and such Meeting shall be on the first Monday in December, unless they shall by Law appoint a different Day.~~

Section 5. Rules/Procedures

1. Quorum Each House shall be the Judge of the Elections, Returns and Qualifications of its own Members, and a Majority of each shall constitute a **Quorum**[6] to do Business; but a smaller Number may **adjourn**[7] from day to day, and may be authorized to compel the Attendance of absent Members, in such Manner, and under such Penalties as each House may provide.

2. Rules and Conduct Each House may determine the Rules of its Proceedings, punish its Members for disorderly Behaviour, and, with the Concurrence of two thirds, expel a Member.

3. Records Each House shall keep a Journal of its Proceedings, and from time to time publish the same, excepting such Parts as may in their Judgment require Secrecy; and the Yeas and Nays of the Members of either House on any question shall, at the Desire of one fifth of those Present, be entered on the Journal.

4. Adjournment Neither House, during the Session of Congress, shall, without the Consent of the other, adjourn for more than three days, nor to any other Place than that in which the two Houses shall be sitting.

Section 6. Payment

1. Salary The Senators and Representatives shall receive a Compensation for their Services, to be ascertained by Law, and paid out of the Treasury of the United States. They shall in all Cases, except Treason, Felony and Breach of the Peace, be privileged from Arrest during their Attendance at the Session of their respective Houses, and in going to and returning from the same; and for any Speech or Debate in either House, they shall not be questioned in any other Place.

2. Restrictions No Senator or Representative shall, during the Time for which he was elected, be appointed to any civil Office under the Authority of the United States, which shall have been created, or the **Emoluments**[8]

Vocabulary

[6] **Quorum** the minimum number of people needed to conduct business

[7] **adjourn** to stop indefinitely

[8] **Emoluments** salary

whereof shall have been increased during such time; and no Person holding any Office under the United States, shall be a Member of either House during his **Continuance**[9] in Office.

Section 7. How a Bill Becomes a Law

1. Tax Bills All **Bills**[10] for raising Revenue shall originate in the House of Representatives; but the Senate may propose or concur with Amendments as on other Bills.

2. Lawmaking Every Bill which shall have passed the House of Representatives and the Senate, shall, before it become a Law, be presented to the President of the United States: If he approve he shall sign it, but if not he shall return it, with his Objections to that House in which it shall have originated, who shall enter the Objections at large on their Journal, and proceed to reconsider it. If after such Reconsideration two thirds of that House shall agree to pass the Bill, it shall be sent, together with the Objections, to the other House, by which it shall likewise be reconsidered, and if approved by two thirds of that House, it shall become a Law. But in all such Cases the Votes of both Houses shall be determined by yeas and Nays, and the Names of the Persons voting for and against the Bill shall be entered on the Journal of each House respectively. If any Bill shall not be returned by the President within ten Days (Sundays excepted) after it shall have been presented to him, the Same shall be a Law, in like Manner as if he had signed it, unless the Congress by their Adjournment prevent its Return, in which Case it shall not be a Law.

3. Role of the President Every Order, Resolution, or Vote to which the Concurrence of the Senate and House of Representatives may be necessary (except on a question of Adjournment) shall be presented to the President of the United States; and before the Same shall take Effect, shall be approved by him, or being disapproved by him, shall be repassed by two thirds of the Senate and House of Representatives, according to the Rules and Limitations prescribed in the Case of a Bill.

Section 8. Powers Granted to Congress

1. Taxation The Congress shall have Power To lay and collect Taxes, **Duties,**[11] **Imposts**[12] and **Excises,**[13] to pay the Debts and provide for the common Defense and general Welfare of the United States; but all Duties, Imposts and Excises shall be uniform throughout the United States;

2. Credit To borrow Money on the credit of the United States;

3. Commerce To regulate Commerce with foreign Nations, and among the several States, and with the Indian Tribes;

4. Naturalization and Bankruptcy To establish an uniform **Rule of Naturalization,**[14] and uniform Laws on the subject of Bankruptcies throughout the United States;

Vocabulary

[9] **Continuance** term

[10] **Bills** proposed laws

[11] **Duties** tariffs

[12] **Imposts** taxes

[13] **Excises** internal taxes on the manufacture, sale, or consumption of a commodity

[14] **Rule of Naturalization** a law by which a foreign-born person becomes a citizen

Vocabulary

[15] **Securities** bonds

[16] **Letters of Marque and Reprisal** documents issued by governments allowing merchant ships to arm themselves and attack ships of an enemy nation

5. Money To coin Money, regulate the Value thereof, and of foreign Coin, and fix the Standard of Weights and Measures;

6. Counterfeiting To provide for the Punishment of counterfeiting the **Securities**[15] and current Coin of the United States;

7. Post Office To establish Post Offices and post Roads;

8. Patents and Copyrights To promote the Progress of Science and useful Arts, by securing for limited Times to Authors and Inventors the exclusive Right to their respective Writings and Discoveries;

9. Courts To constitute Tribunals inferior to the supreme Court;

10. International Law To define and punish Piracies and Felonies committed on the high Seas, and Offences against the Law of Nations;

11. War To declare War, grant **Letters of Marque and Reprisal**,[16] and make Rules concerning Captures on Land and Water;

12. Army To raise and support Armies, but no Appropriation of Money to that Use shall be for a longer Term than two Years;

13. Navy To provide and maintain a Navy;

14. Regulation of the Military To make Rules for the Government and Regulation of the land and naval Forces;

15. Militia To provide for calling forth the Militia to execute the Laws of the Union, suppress Insurrections and repel Invasions;

16. Regulation of the Militia To provide for organizing, arming, and disciplining, the Militia, and for governing such Part of them as may be employed in the Service of the United States, reserving to the States respectively, the Appointment of the Officers, and the Authority of training the Militia according to the discipline prescribed by Congress;

17. District of Columbia To exercise exclusive Legislation in all Cases whatsoever, over such District (not exceeding ten Miles square) as may, by Cession of particular States, and the Acceptance of Congress, become the Seat of the Government of the United States, and to exercise like Authority over all Places purchased by the Consent of the Legislature of the State in which the Same shall be, for the Erection of Forts, Magazines, Arsenals, dock-Yards, and other needful Buildings;—And

The Elastic Clause

The framers of the Constitution wanted a national government that was strong enough to be effective. This section lists the powers given to Congress. The last portion of Section 8 contains the so-called elastic clause.

18. Necessary and Proper Clause To make all Laws which shall be necessary and proper for carrying into Execution the foregoing Powers, and all other Powers vested by this Constitution in the Government of the United States, or in any Department or Officer thereof.

Section 9. Powers Denied Congress

1. Slave Trade ~~The Migration or Importation of such Persons as any of the States now existing shall think proper to admit, shall not be prohibited~~

~~by the Congress prior to the Year one thousand eight hundred and eight, but a Tax or duty may be imposed on such Importation, not exceeding ten dollars for each Person.~~

2. Habeas Corpus The Privilege of the **Writ of Habeas Corpus**[17] shall not be suspended, unless when in Cases of Rebellion or Invasion the public Safety may require it.

3. Illegal Punishment No **Bill of Attainder**[18] or **ex post facto Law**[19] shall be passed.

4. Direct Taxes No **Capitation**,[20] or other direct, Tax shall be laid, unless in Proportion to the Census or enumeration herein before directed to be taken.

5. Export Taxes No Tax or Duty shall be laid on Articles exported from any State.

6. No Favorites No Preference shall be given by any Regulation of Commerce or Revenue to the Ports of one State over those of another; nor shall Vessels bound to, or from, one State, be obliged to enter, clear, or pay Duties in another.

7. Public Money No Money shall be drawn from the Treasury, but in Consequence of Appropriations made by Law; and a regular Statement and Account of the Receipts and Expenditures of all public Money shall be published from time to time.

8. Titles of Nobility No Title of Nobility shall be granted by the United States: And no Person holding any Office of Profit or Trust under them, shall, without the Consent of the Congress, accept of any present, Emolument, Office, or Title, of any kind whatever, from any King, Prince, or foreign State.

Section 10. Powers Denied the States

1. Restrictions No State shall enter into any Treaty, Alliance, or Confederation; grant Letters of Marque and Reprisal; coin Money; emit Bills of Credit; make any Thing but gold and silver Coin a Tender in Payment of Debts; pass any Bill of Attainder, ex post facto Law, or Law impairing the Obligation of Contracts, or grant any Title of Nobility.

2. Import and Export Taxes No State shall, without the Consent of the Congress, lay any Imposts or Duties on Imports or Exports, except what may be absolutely necessary for executing it's inspection Laws: and the net Produce of all Duties and Imposts, laid by any State on Imports or Exports, shall be for the Use of the Treasury of the United States; and all such Laws shall be subject to the Revision and Control of the Congress.

3. Peacetime and War Restraints No State shall, without the Consent of Congress, lay any Duty of Tonnage, keep Troops, or Ships of War in time of Peace, enter into any Agreement or Compact with another State, or with a foreign Power, or engage in War, unless actually invaded, or in such imminent Danger as will not admit of delay.

Vocabulary

[17] **Writ of Habeas Corpus** a court order that requires the government to bring a prisoner to court and explain why he or she is being held

[18] **Bill of Attainder** a law declaring that a person is guilty of a particular crime

[19] **ex post facto Law** a law that is made effective prior to the date that it was passed and therefore punishes people for acts that were not illegal at the time

[20] **Capitation** a direct uniform tax imposed on each head, or person

Article II The Executive

Section 1. The Presidency

1. Terms of Office The executive Power shall be vested in a President of the United States of America. He shall hold his Office during the Term of four Years, and, together with the Vice President, chosen for the same Term, be elected, as follows:

2. Electoral College Each State shall appoint, in such Manner as the Legislature thereof may direct, a Number of Electors, equal to the whole Number of Senators and Representatives to which the State may be entitled in the Congress: but no Senator or Representative, or Person holding an Office of Trust or Profit under the United States, shall be appointed an Elector.

3. Former Method of Electing President ~~The Electors shall meet in their respective States, and vote by Ballot for two Persons, of whom one at least shall not be an Inhabitant of the same State with themselves. And they shall make a List of all the Persons voted for, and of the Number of Votes for each; which List they shall sign and certify, and transmit sealed to the Seat of the Government of the United States, directed to the President of the Senate. The President of the Senate shall, in the Presence of the Senate and House of Representatives, open all the Certificates, and the Votes shall then be counted. The Person having the greatest Number of Votes shall be the President, if such Number be a Majority of the whole Number of Electors appointed; and if there be more than one who have such Majority, and have an equal Number of Votes, then the House of Representatives shall immediately choose by Ballot one of them for President; and if no Person have a Majority, then from the five highest on the List the said House shall in like Manner choose the President. But in choosing the President, the Votes shall be taken by States, the Representation from each State having one Vote; A quorum for this purpose shall consist of a Member or Members from two thirds of the States, and a Majority of all the States shall be necessary to a Choice. In every Case, after the Choice of the President, the Person having the greatest Number of Votes of the Electors shall be the Vice President. But if there should remain two or more who have equal Votes, the Senate shall choose from them by Ballot the Vice President.~~

4. Election Day The Congress may determine the Time of choosing the Electors, and the Day on which they shall give their Votes; which Day shall be the same throughout the United States.

5. Qualifications No Person except a natural born Citizen~~, or a Citizen of the United States, at the time of the Adoption of this Constitution~~, shall be eligible to the Office of President; neither shall any Person be eligible to

THE CONSTITUTION

Executive Branch

The president is the chief of the executive branch. It is the job of the president to enforce the laws. The framers wanted the president's and vice president's terms of office and manner of selection to be different from those of members of Congress. They decided on four-year terms, but they had a difficult time agreeing on how to select the president and vice president. The framers finally set up an electoral system, which varies greatly from our electoral process today.

Presidential Elections

In 1845 Congress set the Tuesday following the first Monday in November of every fourth year as the general election date for selecting presidential electors.

that Office who shall not have attained to the Age of thirty five Years, and been fourteen Years a Resident within the United States.

6. Succession In Case of the Removal of the President from Office, or of his Death, Resignation, or Inability to discharge the Powers and Duties of the said Office, the Same shall devolve on the Vice President, and the Congress may by Law provide for the Case of Removal, Death, Resignation or Inability, both of the President and Vice President, declaring what Officer shall then act as President, and such Officer shall act accordingly, until the Disability be removed, or a President shall be elected.

7. Salary The President shall, at stated Times, receive for his Services, a Compensation, which shall neither be increased nor diminished during the Period for which he shall have been elected, and he shall not receive within that Period any other Emolument from the United States, or any of them.

8. Oath of Office Before he enter on the Execution of his Office, he shall take the following Oath or Affirmation:—"I do solemnly swear (or affirm) that I will faithfully execute the Office of President of the United States, and will to the best of my Ability, preserve, protect and defend the Constitution of the United States."

Section 2. Powers of Presidency

1. Military Powers The President shall be Commander in Chief of the Army and Navy of the United States, and of the Militia of the several States, when called into the actual Service of the United States; he may require the Opinion, in writing, of the principal Officer in each of the executive Departments, upon any Subject relating to the Duties of their respective Offices, and he shall have Power to grant **Reprieves**[21] and **Pardons**[22] for Offences against the United States, except in Cases of Impeachment.

2. Treaties and Appointments He shall have Power, by and with the Advice and Consent of the Senate, to make Treaties, provided two thirds of the Senators present concur; and he shall nominate, and by and with the Advice and Consent of the Senate, shall appoint Ambassadors, other public Ministers and Consuls, Judges of the supreme Court, and all other Officers of the United States, whose Appointments are not herein otherwise provided for, and which shall be established by Law: but the Congress may by Law vest the Appointment of such inferior Officers, as they think proper, in the President alone, in the Courts of Law, or in the Heads of Departments.

3. Vacancies The President shall have Power to fill up all Vacancies that may happen during the Recess of the Senate, by granting Commissions which shall expire at the End of their next Session.

Presidential Salary

In 1999 Congress voted to set future presidents' salaries at $400,000 per year. The president also receives an annual expense account. The president must pay taxes only on the salary.

Commander in Chief

Today the president is in charge of the army, navy, air force, marines, and coast guard. Only Congress, however, can decide if the United States will declare war.

Appointments

Most of the president's appointments to office must be approved by the Senate.

Vocabulary

[21] **Reprieves** delays of punishment

[22] **Pardons** releases from the legal penalties associated with a crime

THE CONSTITUTION

The State of the Union

Every year the president presents to Congress a State of the Union message. In this message, the president introduces and explains a legislative plan for the coming year.

Section 3. Presidential Duties

He shall from time to time give to the Congress Information of the State of the Union, and recommend to their Consideration such Measures as he shall judge necessary and expedient; he may, on extraordinary Occasions, convene both Houses, or either of them, and in Case of Disagreement between them, with Respect to the Time of Adjournment, he may adjourn them to such Time as he shall think proper; he shall receive Ambassadors and other public Ministers; he shall take Care that the Laws be faithfully executed, and shall Commission all the Officers of the United States.

Section 4. Impeachment

The President, Vice President and all civil Officers of the United States, shall be removed from Office on Impeachment for, and Conviction of, Treason, Bribery, or other high Crimes and Misdemeanors.

Judicial Branch

The Articles of Confederation did not set up a federal court system. One of the first points that the framers of the Constitution agreed upon was to set up a national judiciary. In the Judiciary Act of 1789, Congress provided for the establishment of lower courts, such as district courts, circuit courts of appeals, and various other federal courts. The judicial system provides a check on the legislative branch: It can declare a law unconstitutional.

Article III The Judiciary

Section 1. Federal Courts and Judges

The judicial Power of the United States shall be vested in one supreme Court, and in such inferior Courts as the Congress may from time to time ordain and establish. The Judges, both of the supreme and inferior Courts, shall hold their Offices during good Behavior, and shall, at stated Times, receive for their Services a Compensation, which shall not be diminished during their Continuance in Office.

Section 2. Authority of the Courts

1. General Authority The judicial Power shall extend to all Cases, in Law and Equity, arising under this Constitution, the Laws of the United States, and Treaties made, or which shall be made, under their Authority;—to all Cases affecting Ambassadors, other public Ministers and Consuls;—to all Cases of admiralty and maritime Jurisdiction;—to Controversies to which the United States shall be a Party;—to Controversies between two or more States ~~—between a State and Citizens of another State;~~ —between Citizens of different States;—between Citizens of the same State claiming Lands under Grants of different States~~, and between a State, or the Citizens thereof, and foreign States, Citizens or Subjects.~~

2. Supreme Authority In all Cases affecting Ambassadors, other public Ministers and Consuls, and those in which a State shall be Party, the supreme Court shall have original Jurisdiction. In all the other Cases before mentioned, the supreme Court shall have appellate Jurisdiction, both as to Law and Fact, with such Exceptions, and under such Regulations as the Congress shall make.

3. Trial by Jury The Trial of all Crimes, except in Cases of Impeachment, shall be by Jury; and such Trial shall be held in the State where the said Crimes shall have been committed; but when not committed within any State, the Trial shall be at such Place or Places as the Congress may by Law have directed.

Section 3. Treason

1. Definition Treason against the United States, shall consist only in levying War against them, or in adhering to their Enemies, giving them Aid and Comfort. No Person shall be convicted of Treason unless on the Testimony of two Witnesses to the same overt Act, or on Confession in open Court.

2. Punishment The Congress shall have Power to declare the Punishment of Treason, but no Attainder of Treason shall work **Corruption of Blood**,[23] or Forfeiture except during the Life of the Person attainted.

Vocabulary

[23] **Corruption of Blood** punishing the family of a person convicted of treason

Article IV Relations among States

Section 1. State Acts and Records

Full Faith and Credit shall be given in each State to the public Acts, Records, and judicial Proceedings of every other State. And the Congress may by general Laws prescribe the Manner in which such Acts, Records and Proceedings shall be proved, and the Effect thereof.

Section 2. Rights of Citizens

1. Citizenship The Citizens of each State shall be entitled to all Privileges and Immunities of Citizens in the several States.

2. Extradition A Person charged in any State with Treason, Felony, or other Crime, who shall flee from Justice, and be found in another State, shall on Demand of the executive Authority of the State from which he fled, be delivered up, to be removed to the State having Jurisdiction of the Crime.

3. Fugitive Slaves ~~No Person held to Service or Labour in one State, under the Laws thereof, escaping into another, shall, in Consequence of any Law or Regulation therein, be discharged from such Service or Labour, but shall be delivered up on Claim of the Party to whom such Service or Labour may be due.~~

Section 3. New States

1. Admission New States may be admitted by the Congress into this Union; but no new State shall be formed or erected within the Jurisdiction of any other State; nor any State be formed by the Junction of two or more States, or Parts of States, without the Consent of the Legislatures of the States concerned as well as of the Congress.

The States

States must honor the laws, records, and court decisions of other states. A person cannot escape a legal obligation by moving from one state to another.

2. Congressional Authority The Congress shall have Power to dispose of and make all needful Rules and Regulations respecting the Territory or other Property belonging to the United States; and nothing in this Constitution shall be so construed as to Prejudice any Claims of the United States, or of any particular State.

Section 4. Guarantees to the States

The United States shall guarantee to every State in this Union a Republican Form of Government, and shall protect each of them against Invasion; and on Application of the Legislature, or of the Executive (when the Legislature cannot be convened), against domestic Violence.

Article V Amending the Constitution

The Congress, whenever two thirds of both Houses shall deem it necessary, shall propose Amendments to this Constitution, or, on the Application of the Legislatures of two thirds of the several States, shall call a Convention for proposing Amendments, which, in either Case, shall be valid to all Intents and Purposes, as Part of this Constitution, when ratified by the Legislatures of three fourths of the several States, or by Conventions in three fourths thereof, as the one or the other Mode of Ratification may be proposed by the Congress; Provided that ~~no Amendment which may be made prior to the Year One thousand eight hundred and eight shall in any Manner affect the first and fourth Clauses in the Ninth Section of the first Article; and that no State, without its Consent, shall be deprived of its equal Suffrage in the Senate.~~

National Supremacy

One of the biggest problems facing the delegates to the Constitutional Convention was the question of what would happen if a state law and a federal law conflicted. Which law would be followed? Who would decide? The second clause of Article VI answers those questions. When a federal law and a state law disagree, the federal law overrides the state law. The Constitution and other federal laws are the "supreme Law of the Land." This clause is often called the supremacy clause.

Article VI Supremacy of National Government

All Debts contracted and Engagements entered into, before the Adoption of this Constitution, shall be as valid against the United States under this Constitution, as under the Confederation.

This Constitution, and the Laws of the United States which shall be made in Pursuance thereof; and all Treaties made, or which shall be made, under the Authority of the United States, shall be the supreme Law of the Land; and the Judges in every State shall be bound thereby, any Thing in the Constitution or Laws of any State to the Contrary notwithstanding.

The Senators and Representatives before mentioned, and the Members of the several State Legislatures, and all executive and judicial Officers, both of the United States and of the several States, shall be bound by Oath or Affirmation, to support this Constitution; but no religious Test shall ever be required as a Qualification to any Office or public Trust under the United States.

Article VII **Ratification**

The Ratification of the Conventions of nine States, shall be sufficient for the Establishment of this Constitution between the States so ratifying the Same.

Done in Convention by the Unanimous Consent of the States present the Seventeenth Day of September in the Year of our Lord one thousand seven hundred and Eighty seven and of the Independence of the United States of America the Twelfth In witness whereof We have hereunto subscribed our Names,

George Washington—

President and deputy from Virginia

Delaware

George Read
Gunning Bedford Jr.
John Dickinson
Richard Bassett
Jacob Broom

Maryland

James McHenry
Daniel of St. Thomas Jenifer
Daniel Carroll

Virginia

John Blair
James Madison Jr.

North Carolina

William Blount
Richard Dobbs Spaight
Hugh Williamson

South Carolina

John Rutledge
Charles Cotesworth Pinckney
Charles Pinckney
Pierce Butler

Georgia

William Few
Abraham Baldwin

New Hampshire

John Langdon
Nicholas Gilman

Massachusetts

Nathaniel Gorham
Rufus King

Connecticut

William Samuel Johnson
Roger Sherman

New York

Alexander Hamilton

New Jersey

William Livingston
David Brearley
William Paterson
Jonathan Dayton

Pennsylvania

Benjamin Franklin
Thomas Mifflin
Robert Morris
George Clymer
Thomas FitzSimons
Jared Ingersoll
James Wilson
Gouverneur Morris

Attest:
William Jackson, Secretary

Ratification

The Articles of Confederation called for all 13 states to approve any revision to the Articles. The Constitution required that 9 out of the 13 states would be needed to ratify the Constitution. The first state to ratify was Delaware, on December 7, 1787. Almost two-and-a-half years later, on May 29, 1790, Rhode Island became the last state to ratify the Constitution.

Constitutional Amendments

Note: The first 10 amendments to the Constitution were ratified on December 15, 1791, and form what is known as the Bill of Rights.

Amendments 1–10. The Bill of Rights

Amendment I

Congress shall make no law respecting an establishment of religion, or prohibiting the free exercise thereof; or abridging the freedom of speech, or of the press; or the right of the people peaceably to assemble, and to petition the Government for a redress of grievances.

Amendment II

A well regulated Militia, being necessary to the security of a free State, the right of the people to keep and bear Arms, shall not be infringed.

Amendment III

No Soldier shall, in time of peace be **quartered**[24] in any house, without the consent of the Owner, nor in time of war, but in a manner to be prescribed by law.

Amendment IV

The right of the people to be secure in their persons, houses, papers, and effects, against unreasonable searches and seizures, shall not be violated, and no **Warrants**[25] shall issue, but upon probable cause, supported by Oath or affirmation, and particularly describing the place to be searched, and the persons or things to be seized.

Amendment V

No person shall be held to answer for a capital, or otherwise **infamous**[26] crime, unless on a presentment or **indictment**[27] of a Grand Jury, except in cases arising in the land or naval forces, or in the Militia, when in actual service in time of War or public danger; nor shall any person be subject for the same offence to be twice put in jeopardy of life or limb; nor shall be compelled in any criminal case to be a witness against himself, nor be deprived of life, liberty, or property, without due process of law; nor shall private property be taken for public use, without just compensation.

Amendment VI

In all criminal prosecutions, the accused shall enjoy the right to a speedy and public trial, by an impartial jury of the State and district wherein the crime shall have been committed, which district shall have been previously **ascertained**[28] by law, and to be informed of the nature and cause of the accusation; to be confronted with the witnesses against him; to have compulsory process for obtaining witnesses in his favor, and to have the Assistance of Counsel for his defence.

Bill of Rights

One of the conditions set by several states for ratifying the Constitution was the inclusion of a bill of rights. Many people feared that a stronger central government might take away basic rights of the people that had been guaranteed in state constitutions.

Vocabulary

[24] **quartered** housed

[25] **Warrants** written orders authorizing a person to make an arrest, a seizure, or a search

[26] **infamous** disgraceful

[27] **indictment** the act of charging with a crime

[28] **ascertained** found out

Rights of the Accused

The Fifth, Sixth, and Seventh Amendments describe the procedures that courts must follow when trying people accused of crimes.

Trials

The Sixth Amendment makes several guarantees, including a prompt trial and a trial by a jury chosen from the state and district in which the crime was committed.

Amendment VII

In suits at common law, where the value in controversy shall exceed twenty dollars, the right of trial by jury shall be preserved, and no fact tried by a jury, shall be otherwise reexamined in any Court of the United States, than according to the rules of the common law.

Amendment VIII

Excessive bail shall not be required, nor excessive fines imposed, nor cruel and unusual punishments inflicted.

Amendment IX

The enumeration in the Constitution, of certain rights, shall not be construed to deny or disparage others retained by the people.

Amendment X

The powers not delegated to the United States by the Constitution, nor prohibited by it to the States, are reserved to the States respectively, or to the people.

Amendments 11–27

Amendment XI

Passed by Congress March 4, 1794. Ratified February 7, 1795.

The Judicial power of the United States shall not be **construed**[29] to extend to any suit in law or equity, commenced or prosecuted against one of the United States by Citizens of another State, or by Citizens or Subjects of any Foreign State.

Amendment XII

Passed by Congress December 9, 1803. Ratified June 15, 1804.

The Electors shall meet in their respective states and vote by ballot for President and Vice-President, one of whom, at least, shall not be an inhabitant of the same state with themselves; they shall name in their ballots the person voted for as President, and in distinct ballots the person voted for as Vice-President, and they shall make distinct lists of all persons voted for as President, and of all persons voted for as Vice-President, and of the number of votes for each, which lists they shall sign and certify, and transmit sealed to the seat of the government of the United States, directed to the President of the Senate;—the President of the Senate shall, in the presence of the Senate and House of Representatives, open all the certificates and the votes shall then be counted;—The person having the greatest number of votes for President, shall be the President, if such number be a majority of the whole number of Electors appointed; and if no person have such majority, then from the persons having the highest numbers not exceeding three on the list of those voted for as President, the House of Representatives shall choose immediately, by ballot, the President. But in choosing the

Vocabulary

[29] **construed** explained or interpreted

President and Vice President

The Twelfth Amendment changed the election procedure for president and vice president.

President, the votes shall be taken by states, the representation from each state having one vote; a quorum for this purpose shall consist of a member or members from two-thirds of the states, and a majority of all the states shall be necessary to a choice. ~~And if the House of Representatives shall not choose a President whenever the right of choice shall devolve upon them, before the fourth day of March next following, then the Vice-President shall act as President, as in case of the death or other constitutional disability of the President.~~—The person having the greatest number of votes as Vice-President, shall be the Vice-President, if such number be a majority of the whole number of Electors appointed, and if no person have a majority, then from the two highest numbers on the list, the Senate shall choose the Vice-President; a quorum for the purpose shall consist of two-thirds of the whole number of Senators, and a majority of the whole number shall be necessary to a choice. But no person constitutionally ineligible to the office of President shall be eligible to that of Vice-President of the United States.

THE CONSTITUTION

Vocabulary

[30] **involuntary servitude** being forced to work against one's will

Abolishing Slavery

Although some slaves had been freed during the Civil War, slavery was not abolished until the Thirteenth Amendment took effect.

Amendment XIII

Passed by Congress January 31, 1865. Ratified December 6, 1865.

1. Slavery Banned Neither slavery nor **involuntary servitude,**[30] except as a punishment for crime whereof the party shall have been duly convicted, shall exist within the United States, or any place subject to their jurisdiction.

2. Enforcement Congress shall have power to enforce this article by appropriate legislation.

Protecting the Rights of Citizens

In 1833 the Supreme Court ruled that the Bill of Rights limited the federal government but not the state governments. This ruling was interpreted to mean that states were able to keep African Americans from becoming state citizens and keep the Bill of Rights from protecting them. The Fourteenth Amendment defines citizenship and prevents states from interfering in the rights of citizens of the United States.

Amendment XIV

Passed by Congress June 13, 1866. Ratified July 9, 1868.

1. Citizenship Defined All persons born or naturalized in the United States, and subject to the jurisdiction thereof, are citizens of the United States and of the State wherein they reside. No State shall make or enforce any law which shall abridge the privileges or immunities of citizens of the United States; nor shall any State deprive any person of life, liberty, or property, without due process of law; nor deny to any person within its jurisdiction the equal protection of the laws.

2. Voting Rights Representatives shall be apportioned among the several States according to their respective numbers, counting the whole number of persons in each State, ~~excluding Indians not taxed~~. But when the right to vote at any election for the choice of electors for President and Vice-President of the United States, Representatives in Congress, the Executive and Judicial officers of a State, or the members of the Legislature thereof, is denied to any of the ~~male~~ inhabitants of such State, ~~being twenty-one years of age~~, and citizens of the United States, or in any way abridged, except for participation in rebellion, or other crime, the basis of representation therein shall be reduced in the proportion which the number of such ~~male~~ citizens shall bear to the whole number of ~~male~~ citizens ~~twenty-one years of age~~ in such State.

3. Rebels Banned from Government No person shall be a Senator or Representative in Congress, or elector of President and Vice-President, or hold any office, civil or military, under the United States, or under any State, who, having previously taken an oath, as a member of Congress, or as an officer of the United States, or as a member of any State legislature, or as an executive or judicial officer of any State, to support the Constitution of the United States, shall have engaged in insurrection or rebellion against the same, or given aid or comfort to the enemies thereof. But Congress may by a vote of two-thirds of each House, remove such disability.

4. Payment of Debts The validity of the public debt of the United States, authorized by law, including debts incurred for payment of pensions and bounties for services in suppressing insurrection or rebellion, shall not be questioned. But neither the United States nor any State shall assume or pay any debt or obligation incurred in aid of insurrection or rebellion against the United States, ~~or any claim for the loss or emancipation of any slave~~; but all such debts, obligations and claims shall be held illegal and void.

5. Enforcement The Congress shall have the power to enforce, by appropriate legislation, the provisions of this article.

Amendment XV

Passed by Congress February 26, 1869. Ratified February 3, 1870.

1. Voting Rights The right of citizens of the United States to vote shall not be denied or abridged by the United States or by any State on account of race, color, or previous condition of servitude.

2. Enforcement The Congress shall have the power to enforce this article by appropriate legislation.

Amendment XVI

Passed by Congress July 2, 1909. Ratified February 3, 1913.

The Congress shall have power to lay and collect taxes on incomes, from whatever source derived, without apportionment among the several States, and without regard to any census or enumeration.

Amendment XVII

Passed by Congress May 13, 1912. Ratified April 8, 1913.

1. Senators Elected by Citizens The Senate of the United States shall be composed of two Senators from each State, elected by the people thereof, for six years; and each Senator shall have one vote. The electors in each State shall have the qualifications requisite for electors of the most numerous branch of the State legislatures.

2. Vacancies When vacancies happen in the representation of any State in the Senate, the executive authority of such State shall issue writs of election to fill such vacancies: *Provided*, That the legislature of any State may empower the executive thereof to make temporary appointments until the people fill the vacancies by election as the legislature may direct.

3. Future Elections This amendment shall not be so construed as to affect the election or term of any Senator chosen before it becomes valid as part of the Constitution.

Prohibition

Although many people believed that the Eighteenth Amendment was good for the health and welfare of the American people, it was repealed 14 years later.

Amendment XVIII

Passed by Congress December 18, 1917. Ratified January 16, 1919. Repealed by Amendment XXI.

1. Liquor Banned After one year from the ratification of this article the manufacture, sale, or transportation of intoxicating liquors within, the importation thereof into, or the exportation thereof from the United States and all territory subject to the jurisdiction thereof for beverage purposes is hereby prohibited.

2. Enforcement The Congress and the several States shall have concurrent power to enforce this article by appropriate legislation.

3. Ratification This article shall be inoperative unless it shall have been ratified as an amendment to the Constitution by the legislatures of the several States, as provided in the Constitution, within seven years from the date of the submission hereof to the States by the Congress.

Women's Suffrage

Abigail Adams and others were disappointed that the Declaration of Independence and the Constitution did not specifically include women. It took many years and much campaigning before suffrage for women was finally achieved.

Amendment XIX

Passed by Congress June 4, 1919. Ratified August 18, 1920.

1. Voting Rights The right of citizens of the United States to vote shall not be denied or abridged by the United States or by any State on account of sex.

2. Enforcement Congress shall have power to enforce this article by appropriate legislation.

Taking Office

In the original Constitution, a newly elected president and Congress did not take office until March 4, which was four months after the November election. The officials who were leaving office were called lame ducks because they had little influence during those four months. The Twentieth Amendment changed the date that the new president and Congress take office. Members of Congress now take office during the first week of January, and the president takes office on January 20.

Amendment XX

Passed by Congress March 2, 1932. Ratified January 23, 1933.

1. Presidential Terms The terms of the President and the Vice President shall end at noon on the 20th day of January, and the terms of Senators and Representatives at noon on the 3d day of January, of the years in which such terms would have ended if this article had not been ratified; and the terms of their successors shall then begin.

2. Meeting of Congress The Congress shall assemble at least once in every year, and such meeting shall begin at noon on the 3d day of January, unless they shall by law appoint a different day.

3. Succession of Vice President If, at the time fixed for the beginning of the term of the President, the President elect shall have died, the Vice President elect shall become President. If a President shall not have been chosen before the time fixed for the beginning of his term, or if the President elect shall have failed to qualify, then the Vice President elect shall act as President until a President shall have qualified; and the Congress may by law provide for the case wherein neither a President elect nor a Vice President shall have qualified, declaring who shall then act as President, or the manner in which one who is to act shall be selected, and such person shall act accordingly until a President or Vice President shall have qualified.

4. Succession by Vote of Congress The Congress may by law provide for the case of the death of any of the persons from whom the House of Representatives may choose a President whenever the right of choice shall have devolved upon them, and for the case of the death of any of the persons from whom the Senate may choose a Vice President whenever the right of choice shall have devolved upon them.

5. Ratification ~~Sections 1 and 2 shall take effect on the 15th day of October following the ratification of this article.~~

6. Ratification ~~This article shall be inoperative unless it shall have been ratified as an amendment to the Constitution by the legislatures of three-fourths of the several States within seven years from the date of its submission.~~

Amendment XXI

Passed by Congress February 20, 1933. Ratified December 5, 1933.

1. 18th Amendment Repealed The eighteenth article of amendment to the Constitution of the United States is hereby repealed.

2. Liquor Allowed by Law The transportation or importation into any State, Territory, or Possession of the United States for delivery or use therein of intoxicating liquors, in violation of the laws thereof, is hereby prohibited.

3. Ratification ~~This article shall be inoperative unless it shall have been ratified as an amendment to the Constitution by conventions in the several States, as provided in the Constitution, within seven years from the date of the submission hereof to the States by the Congress.~~

Amendment XXII

Passed by Congress March 21, 1947. Ratified February 27, 1951.

1. Term Limits No person shall be elected to the office of the President more than twice, and no person who has held the office of President, or acted as President, for more than two years of a term to which some other person was elected President shall be elected to the office of President more than once. ~~But this Article shall not apply to any person holding the office of President when this Article was proposed by Congress, and shall not prevent any person who may be holding the office of President, or acting as President, during the term within which this Article becomes operative from holding the office of President or acting as President during the remainder of such term.~~

2. Ratification ~~This article shall be inoperative unless it shall have been ratified as an amendment to the Constitution by the legislatures of three-fourths of the several States within seven years from the date of its submission to the States by the Congress.~~

Voting Rights

Until the ratification of the Twenty-third Amendment, the people of Washington, D.C., could not vote in presidential elections.

Amendment XXIII

Passed by Congress June 16, 1960. Ratified March 29, 1961.

1. District of Columbia Represented The District constituting the seat of Government of the United States shall appoint in such manner as Congress may direct:

A number of electors of President and Vice President equal to the whole number of Senators and Representatives in Congress to which the District would be entitled if it were a State, but in no event more than the least populous State; they shall be in addition to those appointed by the States, but they shall be considered, for the purposes of the election of President and Vice President, to be electors appointed by a State; and they shall meet in the District and perform such duties as provided by the twelfth article of amendment.

2. Enforcement The Congress shall have power to enforce this article by appropriate legislation.

Amendment XXIV

Passed by Congress August 27, 1962. Ratified January 23, 1964.

1. Voting Rights The right of citizens of the United States to vote in any primary or other election for President or Vice President, for electors for President or Vice President, or for Senator or Representative in Congress, shall not be denied or abridged by the United States or any State by reason of failure to pay poll tax or other tax.

2. Enforcement The Congress shall have power to enforce this article by appropriate legislation.

Presidential Disability

The illness of President Eisenhower in the 1950s and the assassination of President Kennedy in 1963 were the events behind the Twenty-fifth Amendment. The Constitution did not provide a clear-cut method for a vice president to take over for a disabled president or upon the death of a president. This amendment provides for filling the office of the vice president if a vacancy occurs, and it provides a way for the vice president—or someone else in the line of succession—to take over if the president is unable to perform the duties of that office.

Amendment XXV

Passed by Congress July 6, 1965. Ratified February 10, 1967.

1. Sucession of Vice President In case of the removal of the President from office or of his death or resignation, the Vice President shall become President.

2. Vacancy of Vice President Whenever there is a vacancy in the office of the Vice President, the President shall nominate a Vice President who shall take office upon confirmation by a majority vote of both Houses of Congress.

3. Written Declaration Whenever the President transmits to the President pro tempore of the Senate and the Speaker of the House of Representatives his written declaration that he is unable to discharge the powers and duties of his office, and until he transmits to them a written declaration to the contrary, such powers and duties shall be discharged by the Vice President as Acting President.

4. Removing the President Whenever the Vice President and a majority of either the principal officers of the executive departments or of such other body as Congress may by law provide, transmit to the President pro tempore of the Senate and the Speaker of the House of Representatives their written declaration that the President is unable to discharge the powers and duties of his office, the Vice President shall immediately assume the powers and duties of the office as Acting President.

Thereafter, when the President transmits to the President pro tempore of the Senate and the Speaker of the House of Representatives his written declaration that no inability exists, he shall resume the powers and duties of his office unless the Vice President and a majority of either the principal officers of the executive department or of such other body as Congress may by law provide, transmit within four days to the President pro tempore of the Senate and the Speaker of the House of Representatives their written declaration that the President is unable to discharge the powers and duties of his office. Thereupon Congress shall decide the issue, assembling within forty-eight hours for that purpose if not in session. If the Congress, within twenty-one days after receipt of the latter written declaration, or, if Congress is not in session, within twenty-one days after Congress is required to assemble, determines by two-thirds vote of both Houses that the President is unable to discharge the powers and duties of his office, the Vice President shall continue to discharge the same as Acting President; otherwise, the President shall resume the powers and duties of his office.

Amendment XXVI

Passed by Congress March 23, 1971. Ratified July 1, 1971.

1. Voting Rights The right of citizens of the United States, who are eighteen years of age or older, to vote shall not be denied or abridged by the United States or by any State on account of age.

2. Enforcement The Congress shall have power to enforce this article by appropriate legislation.

Expanded Suffrage

The Voting Rights Act of 1970 tried to set the voting age at 18. However, the Supreme Court ruled that the act set the voting age for national elections only, not for state or local elections. The Twenty-sixth Amendment gave 18-year-old citizens the right to vote in all elections.

Amendment XXVII

Originally proposed September 25, 1789. Ratified May 7, 1992.

No law, varying the compensation for the services of the Senators and Representatives, shall take effect, until an election of representatives shall have intervened.

English and Spanish Glossary

MARK	AS IN	RESPELLING	EXAMPLE
a	alphabet	a	*AL-fuh-bet
ā	Asia	ay	AY-zhuh
ä	cart, top	ah	KAHRT, TAHP
e	let, ten	e	LET, TEN
ē	even, leaf	ee	EE-vuhn, LEEF
i	it, tip, British	i	IT, TIP, BRIT-ish
ī	site, buy, Ohio	y	SYT, BY, oh-HY-oh
	iris	eye	EYE-ris
k	card	k	KAHRD
ō	over, rainbow	oh	OH-vuhr, RAYN-boh
u̇	book, wood	ooh	BOOHK, WOOHD
ȯ	all, orchid	aw	AWL, AWR-kid
ȯi	foil, coin	oy	FOYL, KOYN
au̇	out	ow	OWT
ə	cup, butter	uh	KUHP, BUHT-uhr
ü	rule, food	oo	ROOL, FOOD
yü	few	yoo	FYOO
zh	vision	zh	VIZH-uhn

*A syllable printed in small capital letters receives heavier emphasis than the other syllable(s) in a word.

Phonetic Respelling and Pronunciation Guide

Many of the key terms in this textbook have been respelled to help you pronounce them. The letter combinations used in the respelling throughout the narrative are explained in this phonetic respelling and pronunciation guide. The guide is adapted from *Merriam-Webster's Collegiate Dictionary, 11th Edition; Merriam-Webster's Geographical Dictionary;* and *Merriam-Webster's Biographical Dictionary.*

A

abolition an end to slavery
abolición fin de la esclavitud

affirmative action an active effort to improve the employment or educational opportunities of members of minority groups and women
acción afirmativa iniciativas para mejorar las oportunidades laborales o educativas de las minorías y de las mujeres

AIDS acquired immune deficiency syndrome, a disease that affects the immune system, making patients vulnerable to infections
SIDA síndrome de inmunodeficiencia adquirida; enfermedad que afecta al sistema inmunológico y hace que los pacientes sean vulnerables a infecciones

Allied Powers a group of nations that allied to fight the Central Powers in World War I, and those countries in opposition to the Axis Powers in World War II
potencias aliadas grupo de naciones que se aliaron para luchar contra las potencias centrales en la Primera Guerra Mundial, y los países que se oponían a las potencias del Eje en la Segunda Guerra Mundial

al Qaeda the name of the terrorist organization headed by Osama bin Laden and responsible for the September 11, 2001, attacks
al-Qaeda nombre de la organización terrorista encabezada por Osama bin Laden, responsable de los ataques del 11 de septiembre de 2001

American Expeditionary Force the U.S. military forces sent to Europe during World War I and led by General John J. Pershing
Fuerza Expedicionaria Estadounidense fuerzas armadas de Estados Unidos bajo el mando del general John J. Pershing que fueron enviadas a Europa en la Primera Guerra Mundial

American Federation of Labor (AFL) an organization that united skilled workers into national unions for specific industries
Federación Americana del Trabajo (AFL, por sus siglas en inglés) organización que unió a obreros especializados en sindicatos nacionales para industrias específicas

American Indian Movement (AIM) a civil rights group organized to promote the interests of Native Americans
Movimiento de los Indígenas Americanos (AIM, por sus siglas en inglés) agrupación a favor de los derechos civiles que promueve los intereses de los indígenas norteamericanos

© Houghton Mifflin Harcourt Publishing Company

Anti-Imperialist League a group of citizens opposed to imperialism, and, specifically, to the peace treaty that gave the United States control of Cuba, Guam, Puerto Rico, and the Philippines
Liga Antiimperialista grupo de ciudadanos que se oponían al imperialismo y, más específicamente, al tratado de paz que daba a Estados Unidos el control de Cuba, Guam, Puerto Rico y Filipinas

apartheid a system of segregation practiced in South Africa
apartheid sistema de segregación practicado en Sudáfrica

appeasement the policy of giving into the demands of a nation in order to avoid war
apacigua miento contemporizacióno política de ceder ante las exigencias de una nación para evitar la guerra

Appomattox Courthouse the location where General Robert E. Lee was forced to surrender, thus ending the Civil War
Appomattox Courthouse poblado de Virginia donde el general Robert E. Lee fue obligado a rendirse, dando fin a la Guerra Civil

armistice a truce or cease-fire agreement between warring nations
armisticio tregua o acuerdo de cese del fuego entre dos naciones en guerra

arms race a growth in weapons based on the number of weapons an enemy country has
carrera armamentística aumento de armamentos según la cantidad de armas que tiene un país enemigo

atomic bomb a weapon that receives its explosive power from the splitting of atoms
bomba atómica arma cuyo poder explosivo es generado por la división de átomos

Axis Powers the coalition of nations in World War II that included Germany, Italy, and Japan
potencias del Eje coalición de naciones de la Segunda Guerra Mundial formada por Alemania, Italia y Japón

B

baby boom a sharp increase in the number of American births during the 1950s and 1960s
boom de la natalidad gran aumento en la cantidad de nacimientos en Estados Unidos durante las décadas de 1950 y 1960

Bataan Death March a forced march of American and Filipino soldiers captured by the Japanese along the Bataan Penninsula
marcha de la muerte de Bataán marcha forzada en la península de Bataán de soldados estadounidenses y filipinos capturados por los japoneses

Battle of Antietam (1862) a Union victory in the Civil War that marked the bloodiest single-day battle in U.S. military history
batalla de Antietam (1862) victoria del ejército de la Unión durante la Guerra Civil en la batalla de un solo día más sangrienta de la historia militar de Estados Unidos

Battle of El Alamein (1942) a turning point in World War II, in which Allied forces defeated the Afrika Korps of Germany
batalla del El Alamein (1942) momento decisivo en la Segunda Guerra Mundial, en el que las fuerzas aliadas derrotaron al *Afrika Korps* de Alemania

Battle of Gettysburg (1863) a Union Civil War victory that turned the tide against the Confederates at Gettysburg, Pennsylvania
batalla de Gettysburg (1863) victoria del ejército de la Unión durante la Guerra Civil que cambió el curso de la guerra en contra de los confederados en Gettysburg, Pensilvania

Battle of Leyte Gulf (1944) the largest naval battle in history, during which the American fleet destroyed most of the Japanese fleet
batalla del golfo de Leyte (1944) la mayor batalla naval de la historia, durante la cual la flota estadounidense destruyó la mayor parte de la flota japonesa

Battle of Midway (1942) battle of World War II that ended the Japanese advance in the Pacific
batalla de Midway (1942) batalla de la Segunda Guerra Mundial que puso fin al avance de los japoneses en el Pacífico

Battle of Shiloh (1862) a Civil War battle in Tennessee in which the Union army gained greater control over the Mississippi River valley
batalla de Shiloh (1862) batalla de la Guerra Civil en Tennessee en la que el ejército de la Unión adquirió mayor control sobre el valle del río Mississippi

Battle of Stalingrad (1942–1943) a major turning point in World War II; Soviet forces defeated Nazi forces after which the Nazis never recovered
batalla de Stalingrado (1942–1943) momento decisivo de la Segunda Guerra Mundial; las fuerzas soviéticas vencieron a las fuerzas nazis, que nunca más se recuperaron

© Houghton Mifflin Harcourt Publishing Company

Battle of the Bulge (1944–1945) the last German advance of World War II, which was stopped by Allied forces
batalla del Bulge (1944–1945) último avance alemán de la Segunda Guerra Mundial, que fue detenido por las fuerzas aliadas

Battle of the Coral Sea (1942) the first strategic defeat of the Japanese Imperial Navy by American forces during World War II
batalla del mar del Coral (1942) primera derrota estratégica de la armada imperial japonesa ante las fuerzas estadounidenses en la Segunda Guerra Mundial

Battle of the Little Big Horn (1876) "Custer's Last Stand"; battle between U.S. soldiers, led by George Armstrong Custer, and Sioux warriors, led by Crazy Horse and Sitting Bull, that resulted in the worst defeat for the U.S. Army in the West
batalla de Little Big Horn (1876) última batalla del general Custer; esta batalla entre las tropas de George Armstrong Custer y los guerreros siux al mando de Caballo Loco y Toro Sentado produjo la mayor derrota del ejército estadounidense en el Oeste

beats young people, many of whom were writers and artists, who discussed their dissatisfaction with the American society of the 1950s
beatniks jóvenes, en su mayoría escritores y artistas, que debatían acerca de su descontento con la sociedad estadounidense de la década de 1950

benevolent society an aid organization formed by immigrant communities
sociedad de beneficencia organización de ayuda formada por comunidades de inmigrantes

Berlin Wall a barrier of concrete and barbed wire between Communist East Berlin and West Berlin
Muro de Berlín barrera de concreto y alambre de púas que separaba la Berlín oriental comunista de la Berlín occidental

Bessemer process a process developed in the 1850s that led to faster, cheaper steel production
proceso de Bessemer proceso de producción de acero más económico y rápido, desarrollado en la década de 1850

Black Codes laws passed in the southern states during Reconstruction that greatly limited the freedom and rights of African Americans
Códigos Negros decretos aprobados en los estados sureños en la época de la Reconstrucción que limitaron en gran medida la libertad y los derechos de los afroamericanos

Black Power a social movement that called for African American power and independence
Black Power (Poder Negro) movimiento social que exigía el poder y la independencia de los afroamericanos

Black Tuesday October 29, 1929, one of the largest U.S. stock market drops
martes negro 29 de octubre de 1929, una de las mayores caídas de la bolsa de valores de Estados Unidos

Bonus Army a group of World War I veterans that demanded their bonus payments early
Bonus Army grupo de veteranos de la Primera Guerra Mundial que exigía el pago de sus bonos por adelantado

boomtown a Western community that grew quickly because of the mining boom and often disappeared when the boom ended
pueblo de rápido crecimiento comunidad del Oeste que se desarrolló con gran rapidez debido a la fiebre del oro, pero que desapareció cuando la fiebre terminó

border states Delaware, Kentucky, Maryland, and Missouri; slave states that lay between the North and the South and did not join the Confederacy during the Civil War
estados fronterizos Delaware, Kentucky, Maryland y Missouri; estados esclavistas ubicados entre el Norte y el Sur y que no se unieron a la Confederación durante la Guerra Civil

Boxer Rebellion (1900) a siege of a foreign settlement in Beijing by Chinese nationalists who were angry at foreign involvement in China
rebelión de los boxers (1900) asedio a un asentamiento extranjero en Beijing por parte de un grupo de nacionalistas chinos que estaban enojados por la participación extranjera en China

brinkmanship the Cold War foreign policy designed to "get to the verge without getting into the war"
política arriesgada política exterior durante la Guerra Fría diseñada para "llegar al borde de la guerra sin llegar a la guerra"

Brown v. Board of Education (1954) Supreme Court decision that ended segregation in public schools
Brown* contra la *Junta Educativa (1954) decisión de la Corte Suprema que puso fin a la segregación en las escuelas públicas

buffalo soldiers African American soldiers who served in the cavalry during the wars for the west
soldados búfalo soldados afroamericanos que sirvieron en la caballería durante las guerras del oeste

© Houghton Mifflin Harcourt Publishing Company

business cycle the rhythym in which an economy expands and contracts its production
ciclo económico ritmo al que la producción de una economía se expande y se contrae

buying on margin the process of purchasing stock with credit, hoping to sell at a high enough price to pay the loan and make a profit
compra a crédito proceso de comprar acciones con préstamos, con la esperanza de venderlas a un precio suficientemente alto para pagar el préstamo y obtener una ganancia

C

Camp David Accords (1978) an agreement between the heads of Israel and Egypt that began a process for peace in the Middle East
Acuerdos de Camp David (1978) acuerdo entre los líderes de Israel y Egipto que dio inicio a un proceso de paz en el Medio Oriente

capitalism an economic system in which private businesses run most industries
capitalismo sistema económico en el que las empresas privadas controlan la mayoría de las industrias

cattle drive a long journey on which cowboys herded cattle to northern markets or better grazing lands
arreo de ganado viaje largo en el que los vaqueros arreaban ganado para llevarlo a los mercados del Norte o a mejores pastos

Cattle Kingdom an area of the Great Plains on which many ranchers raised cattle in the late 1800s
Reino del Ganado área de las Grandes Planicies en la que muchos rancheros criaban ganado a finales de siglo XIX

Central Powers the coalition of nations in World War I that included the German, Austria-Hungary, and Ottoman empires
Potencias Centrales coalición de naciones de la Primera Guerra Mundial formada por los imperios alemán, austrohúngaro y otomano

Chinese Exclusion Act (1882) a law passed by Congress that banned Chinese from immigrating to the United States for 10 years
Ley de Exclusión de Chinos (1882) ley aprobada por el Congreso que prohibió la inmigración de chinos a Estados Unidos por 10 años

Chisholm Trail a trail that ran from San Antonio, Texas, to Abilene, Kansas, established by Jesse Chisholm in the late 1860s for cattle drives
Camino de Chisholm camino creado por Jesse Chisholm a finales de la década de 1860 que iba desde San Antonio, Texas hasta Abilene, Kansas, para arreos de ganado

Civil Rights Act of 1866 a law that gave African Americans legal rights equal to those of white Americans
Ley de Derechos Civiles de 1866 ley que dio a los afroamericanos los mismos derechos legales que tenían los estadounidenses blancos

Civil Rights Act of 1964 a law that ended discrimination based on race or gender
Ley de Derechos Civiles de 1964 ley que puso fin a la discriminación en base a la raza o al sexo

Cold War a period of hostility between Western powers and Communist powers
Guerra Fría período de hostilidades entre las potencias de Occidente y las potencias comunistas

collective bargaining a technique used by labor unions in which workers act collectively to change working conditions or wages
negociación colectiva método empleado por los sindicatos en el que los trabajadores actúan colectivamente para cambiar las condiciones laborales o los salarios

Communists people who believe in communism, or the political system in which all resources are shared equally
comunistas personas que creen en el comunismo, es decir, el sistema político en el que los recursos se distribuyen a todos por igual

Compromise of 1877 an agreement to settle the disputed presidential election of 1876; Democrats agreed to accept Republican Rutherford B. Hayes as president in return for the removal of federal troops from the South
Compromiso de 1877 acuerdo en el que se resolvieron las disputadas elecciones presidenciales de 1876; los demócratas aceptaron al republicano Rutherford B. Hayes como presidente a cambio del retiro de las tropas federales del Sur

Comstock Lode Nevada gold and silver mine discovered by Henry Comstock in 1859
veta de Comstock mina de oro y plata descubierta en Nevada por Henry Comstock en 1859

Congress of Industrial Organizations (CIO) a union that organized workers according to industry, not by skill
Congreso de Organizaciones Industriales (CIO, por sus siglas en inglés) sindicato que organizó a los trabajadores según la industria y no el nivel de especialización

© Houghton Mifflin Harcourt Publishing Company

conservation the planned management of natural resources to prevent their destruction
conservación administración planificada de los recursos naturales para evitar su destrucción

containment a foreign policy that attempts to stop the spread of communism without ending it in the countries in which it already exists
contención política exterior que intenta detener el avance del comunismo sin eliminarlo en los países en los que ya existe

contraband an escaped slave who joined the Union army during the Civil War
contrabando esclavo que escapó y se unió al ejército de la Unión durante la Guerra Civil

Copperheads a group of northern Democrats who opposed abolition and sympathized with the South during the Civil War
copperheads grupo de demócratas del Norte que se oponían a la abolición de la esclavitud y simpatizaban con las creencias sureñas durante la Guerra Civil

corporation a business that sells portions of ownership called stock shares
corporación compañía que vende algunas partes en forma de acciones

cotton diplomacy Confederate efforts to use the importance of southern cotton to Britain's textile industry to persuade the British to support the Confederacy in the Civil War
diplomacia del algodón esfuerzos de la Confederación por aprovechar la importancia del algodón del Sur en la industria textil británica para convencer a Gran Bretaña de apoyar a la Confederación en la Guerra Civil

Cuban missile crisis a threat to national security that occurred when the Soviet Union placed nuclear missiles in Cuba
crisis de los misiles de Cuba amenaza a la seguridad nacional que ocurrió cuando la Unión Soviética colocó misiles nucleares en Cuba

D

Dawes General Allotment Act (1887) legislation passed by Congress that split up Indian reservation lands among individual Indians and promised them citizenship
Ley de Adjudicación General de Dawes (1887) ley aprobada por el Congreso que dividía el terreno de las reservas indígenas entre sus habitantes y les prometía la ciudadanía

D-Day (1944) an invasion of Nazi-occupied France by Allied forces
día D (1944) invasión de las fuerzas aliadas en Francia, ocupada por los nazis

deficit the amount by which a government's spending exceeds its revenue
déficit cantidad en la que los gastos del gobierno superan sus ingresos

deflation a decrease in money supply and overall lower prices
deflación reducción de la disponibilidad del dinero y baja general en los precios

department store giant retail shop
tiendas por departamentos grandes comercios de venta al público

détente a period of closer diplomatic relations between the United States and the Communist powers of China and the Soviet Union
distensión período de relaciones diplomáticas más estrechas entre Estados Unidos y las potencias comunistas de China y la Unión Soviética

Disabled in Action (DIA) a group organized to promote the interests of people with disabilities
Discapacitados en Acción (DIA, por sus siglas en inglés) grupo organizado para promover los intereses de personas con discapacidades

dollar diplomacy influencing governments through economic, not military, intervention
diplomacia del dólar una manera de influir en otros gobiernos por medio del poder financiero mas no del poder militar

domino theory the idea that Communism would spread rapidly throughout Southeast Asia
teoría del efecto dominó idea de que el comunismo se extendería rápidamente por el sureste de Asia

doves opponents of the Vietnam War
palomas opositores a la guerra de Vietnam

dry farming a method of farming used by Plains farmers in the 1890s that shifted focus from water-dependent crops to more hardy crops
agricultura de secano método de cultivo que usaban los agricultores de las Planicies en la década de 1890 que provocó un cambio de los cultivos que dependían del agua a otros más resistentes

Dust Bowl an area of the United States that suffered a severe drought during the 1930s
Dust Bowl área de Estados Unidos que sufrió una grave sequía en la década de 1930

© Houghton Mifflin Harcourt Publishing Company

E

Eighteenth Amendment (1919) a constitutional amendment that outlawed the production and sale of alcoholic beverages in the United States; repealed in 1933
Decimoctava Enmienda (1919) enmienda constitucional que prohibió la producción y venta de bebidas alcohólicas en Estados Unidos; revocada en 1933

emancipation freeing of the slaves
emancipación liberación de los esclavos

Emancipation Proclamation (1862) an order issued by President Abraham Lincoln freeing the slaves in areas rebelling against the Union; took effect January 1, 1863
Proclamación de Emancipación (1862) orden emitida por el presidente Abraham Lincoln para liberar a los esclavos en las áreas que se rebelaban contra la Unión; entró en vigor el primero de enero de 1863

Equal Rights Amendment (ERA) a proposed amendment to the Constitution that would provide equal rights to women
Enmienda por la Igualdad de Derechos (ERA, por sus siglas en inglés) enmienda constitucional propuesta que otorgaría la igualdad de derechos a la mujer

escalation increased involvement in the Vietnam War
escalada mayor participación en la guerra de Vietnam

Exodusters African Americans who settled western lands in the late 1800s
Exodusters afroamericanos que se establecieron en el Oeste a finales del siglo XIX

expatriates citizens who leave their country to live elsewhere
expatriados ciudadanos que abandonan su país para vivir en otro lugar

F

Fair Deal President Truman's legislative plan for the nation that included antilynching laws
Fair Deal plan legislativo para la nación propuesto por el presidente Truman que incluía leyes en contra de los linchamientos

fascism a political system in which the state or government is seen as more important than the individual
fascismo sistema político en el que se considera que el estado o gobierno es más importante que las personas

Fifteenth Amendment (1870) a constitutional amendment that gave African American men the right to vote
Decimoquinta Enmienda (1870) enmienda constitucional que daba a los hombres afroamericanos el derecho al voto

54th Massachusetts Infantry African American Civil War regiment that attacked Fort Wagner in South Carolina
54to Batallón de Infantería de Massachusetts regimiento afroamericano de la Guerra Civil que atacó el fuerte Wagner en Carolina del Sur

fireside chats radio programs in which Franklin Roosevelt explained his plan for recovery from the Great Depression
charlas junto a la chimenea programas de radio en los cuales Franklin Roosevelt explicaba su plan para que el país se recuperara de la Gran Depresión

First Battle of Bull Run (1861) the first major battle of the Civil War, resulting in a Confederate victory; showed that the Civil War would not be won easily
primera batalla de Bull Run (1861) primera batalla importante de la Guerra Civil, en la cual ganó el ejército confederado; demostró que la guerra no se ganaría fácilmente

flappers young women who challenged traditional ideas of womanhood in the 1920s
flappers mujeres jóvenes que desafiaron las ideas tradicionales sobre la condición de la mujer en la década de 1920

Fort Sumter a federal outpost in Charleston, South Carolina, that was attacked by the Confederates in April 1861, sparking the Civil War
fuerte Sumter puesto de avanzada federal en Charleston, Carolina del Sur, cuyo ataque por parte de los confederados en abril de 1861 dio origen a la Guerra Civil

Fourteenth Amendment (1866) a constitutional amendment giving full rights of citizenship to all people born or naturalized in the United States, except for American Indians
Decimocuarta Enmienda (1866) enmienda constitucional que otorgaba derechos totales de ciudadanía a todas las personas nacidas en Estados Unidos o naturalizadas estadounidenses, con excepción de los indígenas americanos

Freedmen's Bureau an agency established by Congress in 1865 to help poor people throughout the South
Oficina de los Libertos oficina creada por el Congreso en 1865 para ayudar a los pobres del Sur del país

Freedom Rides a series of integrated bus rides through the South
Viajes de la Libertad serie de viajes en autobús por el Sur en los que se integraban las razas

© Houghton Mifflin Harcourt Publishing Company

frontier an undeveloped area
frontera área que no está siendo utilizada por el ser humano

fundamentalism a religious belief characterized by a literal interpretation of the Bible
fundamentalismo creencia religiosa caracterizada por una interpretación literal de la Biblia

G

genocide the complete destruction of a racial or ethnic minority
genocidio destrucción total de una minoría racial o étnica

Gettysburg Address (1863) a speech given by Abraham Lincoln in which he praised the bravery of Union soldiers and renewed his commitment to winning the Civil War
Discurso de Gettysburg (1863) discurso de Abraham Lincoln en el que alababa la valentía de las tropas de la Unión y renovaba su compromiso de triunfar en la Guerra Civil

Ghost Dance a religious movement among Native Americans that spread across the Plains in the 1880s
Danza de los Espíritus movimiento religioso de los indígenas norteamericanos que se extendió por la región de las Planicies en la década de 1880

GI Bill of Rights (1944) a law that offered veterans money for school, houses, farms, and businesses
Declaración de Derechos de los Soldados (1944) ley que ofrecía a los veteranos de guerra dinero para su educación, vivienda, granjas y negocios

globalization the process in which the United States is becoming more interdependent with other nations
globalización proceso por el cual Estados Unidos empieza a tener más interdependencia con otras naciones

global warming an environmental crisis in which the average temperature of the Earth is rising due to pollution
calentamiento global crisis del medio ambiente por la cual está aumentando la temperatura promedio de la Tierra debido a la contaminación

Great Depression a severe economic crisis that lasted for the entire decade of the 1930s
Gran Depresión grave crisis económica que duró toda la década de 1930

Great Migration a period of African American movement from the South to cities in the North
Gran Migración período en que los afroamericanos del Sur se fueron a ciudades del Norte

Great Society President Lyndon Johnson's legislative plan that included civil rights laws
Gran Sociedad plan legislativo del presidente Lyndon Johnson que incluía leyes a favor de los derechos civiles

H

habeas corpus the constitutional protection against unlawful imprisonment
hábeas corpus protección constitucional contra el encarcelamiento ilegal

Harlem Renaissance a period of artistic achievement during the 1920s
Renacimiento de Harlem período de logros artísticos durante la década de 1920

hawks supporters of the Vietnam War
halcones partidarios de la guerra de Vietnam

Haymarket Riot a riot that broke out at Haymarket Square in Chicago over the deaths of two strikers
Revuelta de Haymarket revuelta que se originó en la Plaza Haymarket de Chicago por la muerte de dos huelguistas

hippies young people who rebelled against the mainstream culture of the 1960s
hippies jóvenes que se rebelaron contra la cultura convencional en la década de 1960

Ho Chi Minh Trail a series of jungle paths that allowed Communist forces to travel from North Vietnam to South Vietnam
Camino de Ho Chi Minh serie de caminos por la selva que permitía a las fuerzas comunistas ir desde Vietnam del Norte hacia Vietnam del Sur

Holocaust a program of mass murder in which the Nazis tried to kill all Jews
Holocausto programa de asesinato en masa ideado por los nazis para exterminar a todos los judíos

Homestead Act (1862) a law passed by Congress to encourage settlement in the West by giving government-owned land to small farmers
Ley de Heredad (1862) ley aprobada por el Congreso para fomentar la colonización del Oeste mediante la cesión de tierras del gobierno a pequeños agricultores

© Houghton Mifflin Harcourt Publishing Company

Homestead strike (1892) a labor-union strike at Andrew Carnegie's Homestead Steel factory in Pennsylvania that erupted in violence between strikers and private detectives
huelga de Homestead (1892) huelga sindical en la fábrica de acero Homestead de Andrew Carnegie en Pensilvania, que produjo violencia entre huelguistas y detectives privados

horizontal integration owning all the businesses in a certain field
integración horizontal posesión de todas las empresas en un campo específico

Hull House a settlement house founded by Jane Addams and Ellen Gates Starr in 1889
Casa Hull casa de asistencia a la comunidad fundada por Jane Addams y Ellen Gates Starr en 1889

human rights the basic rights of all people
derechos humanos derechos fundamentales de todas las personas

hydrogen bomb a thermonuclear weapon that gets its power from splitting a hydrogen atom
bomba de hidrógeno arma termonuclear cuya potencia es generada por la división de un átomo de hidrógeno

I

impeachment the process used by a legislative body to bring charges of wrongdoing against a public official
juicio político proceso por el cual un cuerpo legislativo presenta cargos en contra de un funcionario público

imperialism the practice of extending a nation's power by gaining territories for a colonial empire
imperialismo práctica en la que una nación amplía su poder adquiriendo territorios para un imperio colonial

Industrial Workers of the World (IWW) a union founded in 1905 by socialists and union leaders that included workers not welcomed in the AFL
Trabajadores Industriales del Mundo (IWW, por sus siglas en inglés) sindicato fundado en 1905 por socialistas y líderes sindicales que incluía a los trabajadores que no admitía la Federación Americana del Trabajo

Information Revolution an increase in the ability to share information between people and locations brought about by the Internet
Revolución de la Información aumento de la capacidad de compartir información entre personas y lugares producido por Internet

initiative a method of allowing voters to propose a new law if enough signatures are collected on a petition
iniciativa método que permite a los votantes proponer una nueva ley si consiguen suficientes firmas para una petición

Internet a global system of computers that allows people across the world to communicate
Internet sistema global de computadoras que permite la comunicación entre personas de todo el mundo

internment the imprisonment of Japanese Americans in special camps during World War II
internamiento encarcelamiento de japoneses-americanos en campos especiales durante la Segunda Guerra Mundial

Iran-Contra affair a scandal during the Reagan administration in which government officials were accused of selling weapons to Iran and passing the profits to a revolutionary group known as the Contras
asunto Irán-Contras escándalo durante el gobierno de Reagan en el cual funcionarios del gobierno fueron acusados de vender armas a Irán y de entregar las ganancias a un grupo revolucionario conocido como los contras

Iran hostage crisis a crisis in which Americans were taken hostage by militants in Iran and held for over a year
crisis de los rehenes de Irán crisis en la cual varios estadounidenses fueron tomados como rehenes por militantes iraníes durante más de un año

ironclad a warship that is heavily armored with iron
acorazado buque de guerra fuertemente protegido con hierro

island-hopping the strategy used by U.S. forces in the Pacific during World War II that involved taking only strategically important islands
saltar de isla en isla estrategia de las fuerzas de Estados Unidos en el Pacífico durante la Segunda Guerra Mundial que consistía en tomar sólo las islas importantes desde el punto de vista estratégico

isolationism a national policy of avoiding involvement in other countries' affairs
aislacionismo política nacional de evitar involucrarse en los asuntos de otras naciones

© Houghton Mifflin Harcourt Publishing Company

J

Jazz Age a name for the decade of the 1920s based on the popularity of jazz music
Era del Jazz nombre que se le dio a la década de 1920 por la popularidad de la música de jazz

Jim Crow law a law that enforced segregation in the southern states
ley de Jim Crow ley que imponía la segregación en los estados del Sur

K

kamikaze Japanese pilots who flew suicide missions during World War II
kamikaze piloto japonés que volaba en misiones suicidas durante la Segunda Guerra Mundial

Kellogg-Briand Pact an agreement between nations proposing peaceful solutions to conflicts, signed after World War I
Pacto Kellogg-Briand acuerdo firmado entre naciones luego de la Primera Guerra Mundial que proponía soluciones pacíficas a los conflictos

Knights of Labor secret society that became the first truly national labor union in the United States
Caballeros del Trabajo sociedad secreta que se convirtió en el primer sindicato verdaderamente nacional en Estados Unidos

Ku Klux Klan a secret society created by white southerners in 1866 that used terror and violence to keep African Americans from obtaining their civil rights
Ku Klux Klan sociedad secreta creada en 1866 por blancos del Sur que usaba el terror y la violencia para impedir que los afroamericanos obtuvieran derechos civiles

L

League of Nations a coalition of governments designed to find peaceful solutions to disagreements, proposed by Woodrow Wilson
Liga de las Naciones coalición de gobiernos propuesta por Woodrow Wilson y diseñada para buscar soluciones pacíficas a los desacuerdos

Lend-Lease Act (1941) a law giving Franklin Roosevelt the power to sell, transfer, exchange, or lease military equipment to any country to help it defend itself against the Axis powers
Ley de Préstamo y Arriendo (1941) ley que dio a Franklin Roosevelt el poder de vender, transferir, intercambiar o arrendar equipo militar a cualquier país para la defensa contra las potencias del Eje

Liberty bonds loans to the government that aided its ability to prepare for World War I
bonos de la Libertad préstamos hechos al gobierno que le permitieron prepararse para la Primera Guerra Mundial

Lincoln-Douglas debates a series of debates between Republican Abraham Lincoln and Democrat Stephen Douglas during the 1858 U.S. Senate campaign in Illinois
debates Lincoln-Douglas serie de debates entre el republicano Abraham Lincoln y el demócrata Stephen Douglas durante la campaña de 1858 para el Senado estadounidense en Illinois

Little Rock Nine a group of nine African American students who began the integration of the Little Rock, Arkansas, public school system
los nueve de Little Rock grupo de nueve estudiantes afroamericanos que empezaron la integración del sistema de escuelas públicas de Little Rock, Arkansas

Long Walk (1864) a 300-mile march made by Navajo captives to a reservation in Bosque Redondo, New Mexico, that led to the deaths of hundreds of Navajo
Larga Marcha (1864) caminata de 300 millas que hizo un grupo de prisioneros navajos hasta una reserva indígena en Bosque Redondo, Nuevo México, en la que murieron cientos de ellos

Lost Generation the generation of young people who fought in World War I and eventually became disillusioned with the promise of American society
generación perdida generación de jóvenes que lucharon en la Primera Guerra Mundial y terminaron desilusionados con las promesas de la sociedad estadounidense

Lusitania a passenger ship bombed by Germany
Lusitania barco de pasajeros bombardeado por Alemania

M

Manhattan Project the U.S. effort to build an atomic bomb
Proyecto Manhattan plan de Estados Unidos de fabricar una bomba atómica

© Houghton Mifflin Harcourt Publishing Company

March on Washington a huge demonstration organized by Martin Luther King Jr. to protest racial discrimination
Marcha en Washington manifestación enorme organizada por Martin Luther King, Jr. en protesta por la discriminación racial

Marshall Plan the idea that the U.S. could help rebuild wartorn Europe with loans and other economic aid
Plan Marshall idea de que Estados Unidos podía contribuir con préstamos y otros tipos de ayuda económica a la reconstrucción de la Europa devastada por la guerra

Massacre at Wounded Knee (1890) the U.S. Army's killing of approximately 150 Sioux at Wounded Knee Creek in South Dakota; ended U.S-Indian wars on the Plains
masacre de Wounded Knee (1890) matanza de aproximadamente 150 indios siux en Wounded Knee Creek, Dakota del Sur; dio por terminadas las guerras entre estadounidenses e indígenas en las Planicies

mass culture leisure and cultural activities shared by many people
cultura de masas actividades culturales y del tiempo libre que les gustan a muchas personas

mass transit public transportation
transporte colectivo transporte público

Mexican Revolution a revolution led by Francisco Madero in 1910 that eventually forced the Mexican dictator Díaz to resign
Revolución Mexicana revolución iniciada en 1910 por Francisco Madero, que finalmente obligó al dictador mexicano Díaz a renunciar

militarism an increase in the importance of the military of a country
militarismo aumento de la importancia del ejército de un país

mobilize to prepare for war
mobilizarse prepararse para la guerra

Model T Henry Ford's automobile designed with the average American in mind
modelo T automóvil de Henry Ford diseñado para el estadounidense promedio

monopoly a complete control over the entire supply of goods or a service in a particular market
monopolio control absoluto de toda la oferta de bienes o de un servicio en un mercado en particular

Montgomery bus boycott a boycott of the Montgomery, Alabama, public bus system to protest its policy of segregation
boicot a los autobuses de Montgomery boicot al sistema público de autobuses de Montgomery, Alabama, en protesta por su política de segregación

Morrill Act (1862) a federal law passed by Congress that gave land to western states to encourage them to build colleges
Ley de Morrill (1862) ley federal aprobada por el Congreso que otorgaba tierras a los estados del Oeste para fomentar la construcción de universidades

moving assembly line an innovation of Henry Ford's that dramatically reduced the cost of production
cadena de montaje móvil innovación de Henry Ford que redujo significativamente el costo de producción

muckrakers a term coined for journalists who "raked up" and exposed corruption and problems of society
muckrakers término acuñado para nombrar a los periodistas que se dedicaban a investigar y exponer la corrupción y los problemas de la sociedad

N

National American Woman Suffrage Association (NAWSA) an organization founded by Elizabeth Cady Stanton and Susan B. Anthony in 1890 to obtain women's right to vote
Asociación Nacional Americana para el Sufragio Femenino (NAWSA, por sus siglas en inglés) organización fundada en 1890 por Elizabeth Cady Stanton y Susan B. Anthony para obtener el derecho al voto de las mujeres

National Association for the Advancement of Colored People (NAACP) an organization founded in 1909 by W. E. B. Du Bois and other reformers to bring attention to racial inequality
Asociación Nacional para el Progreso de la Gente de Color (NAACP, por sus siglas en inglés) organización fundada en 1909 por W. E. B. Du Bois y otros reformadores para llamar la atención sobre la desigualdad racial

National Grange a social and educational organization for farmers
National Grange organización social y educativa para los agricultores

National Organization for Women (NOW) a group that organized to promote the interests of women
Organización Nacional de la Mujer (NOW, por sus siglas en inglés) grupo organizado para promover los intereses de la mujer

© Houghton Mifflin Harcourt Publishing Company

National War Labor Board a government agency organized to help settle disputes between workers and employers in war industries
Junta Nacional del Trabajo en Tiempos de Guerra agencia del gobierno destinada a resolver disputas entre trabajadores y empleadores en las industrias relacionadas con la guerra

Nazis the National Socialist Party of Germany, headed by Adolf Hitler
nazis Partido Nacional Socialista de Alemania, liderado por Adolf Hitler

New Deal Franklin Roosevelt's legislative plan to end the Great Depression that included dramatic reforms of government agencies and powers
***New Deal* (Nuveo Trato)** plan legislativo de Franklin Roosevelt para poner fin a la Gran Depresión; incluía profundas reformas en las agencias y poderes del gobierno

new immigrant a term often used for an immigrant who arrived in the United States beginning in the 1880s
nuevo inmigrante término empleado a menudo para referirse a los inmigrantes que llegaron a Estados Unidos a partir de la década de 1880

Nineteenth Amendment (1920) a constitutional amendment that gave women the vote
Decimonovena Enmienda (1920) enmienda constitucional que dio a la mujer el derecho al voto

North American Free Trade Agreement (NAFTA) a treaty that eliminated trade barriers between Canada, the United States, and Mexico
Tratado de Libre Comercio de América del Norte (TLCAN o NAFTA) tratado que eliminó las barreras comerciales entre Canadá, Estados Unidos y México

North Atlantic Treaty Organization (NATO) an alliance of Western powers
Organización del Tratado del Atlántico Norte (OTAN) alianza de potencias occidentales

Nuremberg trials the war crimes trials of Nazi leaders
juicios de Nuremberg juicios de los crímenes de guerra de los líderes Nazis

O

old immigrant a term often used for an immigrant who arrived in the United States before the 1880s
antiguo inmigrante término empleado con frecuencia para referirse a los inmigrantes que llegaron a Estados Unidos antes de la década de 1880

Open Door Policy a policy established by the United States in 1899 to promote equal access for all nations to trade in China
política de puertas abiertas política establecida por Estados Unidos en 1899 para promover el acceso igualitario de todas las naciones al comercio con China

Operation Desert Storm the military effort to free Kuwait from Saddam Hussein's invasion
Operación Tormenta del Desierto acción militar para liberar a Kuwait de la invasión de Saddam Hussein

Organization of Petroleum Exporting Countries (OPEC) an alliance of oil rich countries that coordinates oil policies
Organización de Países Exportadores de Petróleo (OPEP) alianza de países ricos en petróleo que coordina las políticas petroleras

ozone layer a level of the Earth's atmosphere that is being depleted by pollution
capa de ozono nivel de la atmósfera de la Tierra que se está desgastando debido a la contaminación

P

Panama Canal an artificial waterway across the Isthmus of Panama; completed by the United States in 1914
canal de Panamá canal artificial que atraviesa el istmo de Panamá; Estados Unidos completó su construcción en 1914

pardon freedom from punishment
indulto liberación de un castigo

patent an exclusive right to make or sell an invention
patente derecho exclusivo para fabricar o vender un invento

Peace Corps a nonmilitary aid program introduced by John Kennedy
Cuerpos de Paz programa de ayuda no militar introducido por John Kennedy

Pearl Harbor a harbor in Hawaii that serves as the base of the U.S. Pacific fleet and was bombed in 1941 by Japan
Pearl Harbor puerto de Hawai que es la base de la flota del Pacífico de Estados Unidos; fue bombardeado por Japón en 1941

Pentagon the headquarters of the U.S. military, located outside of Washington, D.C.
Pentágono sede central del ejército de Estados Unidos, ubicado en las afueras de Washington, D.C.

© Houghton Mifflin Harcourt Publishing Company

Pickett's Charge (1863) a failed Confederate attack during the Civil War led by General George Pickett at the Battle of Gettysburg
ataque de Pickett (1863) ataque fallido del ejército confederado, al mando del general George Pickett, en la batalla de Gettysburg durante la Guerra Civil

Platt Amendment a part of the Cuban constitution drafted under the supervision of the United States that limited Cuba's right to make treaties, gave the U.S. the right to intervene in Cuban affairs, and required Cuba to sell or lease land to the U.S
Enmienda Platt parte de la constitución cubana redactada bajo la supervisión de Estados Unidos que limitaba el derecho de Cuba a firmar tratados, le daba a Estados Unidos el derecho de intervenir en los asuntos cubanos y le exigía a Cuba vender o arrendar tierras a Estados Unidos

Plessy* v. *Ferguson (1896) U.S. Supreme Court case that established the "separate-but-equal" doctrine for public facilities
Plessy* contra *Ferguson (1896) caso en el que la Corte Suprema de Estados Unidos estableció la doctrina de "separados pero iguales" en los lugares públicos

political machine a powerful organization that influenced city and county politics in the late 1800s
maquinaria política organización poderosa que influía en la política municipal y del condado a finales del siglo XIX

poll tax a special tax that a person had to pay in order to vote
impuesto electoral impuesto especial que tenía que pagar una persona para poder votar

Pony Express a system of messengers that carried mail between relay stations on a route 2,000-miles long in 1860 and 1861
Pony Express sistema de mensajeros que llevaban el correo entre estaciones de relevo a lo largo de una ruta de 2,000 millas en 1860 y 1861

popular sovereignty the idea that political authority belongs to the people
soberanía popular idea de que la autoridad política pertenece al pueblo

Populist Party a political party formed in 1892 that supported free coinage of silver, work reforms, immigration restrictions, and government ownership of railroads and telegraph and telephone systems
Partido Populista partido político formado en 1892 que apoyaba la libre producción de monedas de plata, reformas laborales y restricciones de la inmigración, además de asignar al gobierno la propiedad de los sistemas ferroviario, telegráfico y telefónico

Progressives a group of reformers who worked to improve social and political problems in the late 1800s
progresistas grupo de reformistas que trabajaron para resolver problemas sociales y políticos a finales del siglo XIX

Progressive Party a short-lived political party that attempted to institute social reforms
Partido Progresista partido político de poca duración que intentó establecer reformas sociales

Pullman strike (1894) a railroad strike that ended when President Grover Cleveland sent in federal troops
huelga de Pullman (1894) huelga del ferrocarril que terminó cuando el presidente Grover Cleveland envió a tropas federales

Pure Food and Drug Act (1906) a law that set regulatory standards for industries involved in preparing food
Ley de Alimentos y Medicamentos Puros (1906) ley que estableció normas regulatorias para las industrias de preparación de productos alimenticios

R

Radical Republicans members of Congress who felt that southern states needed to make great social changes before they could be readmitted to the Union
republicanos radicales miembros del Congreso convencidos de que los estados del Sur necesitaban hacer grandes cambios sociales antes de volver a ser admitidos en la Unión

realpolitik a foreign policy in which U.S. interests are put over ethical or principled concerns
realpolitik política exterior según la cual los intereses de Estados Unidos están por encima de los asuntos éticos o de principios

recall a vote to remove an official from office
destitución votación para sacar a un funcionario de su cargo

Reconstruction (1865–1877) the period following the Civil War during which the U.S. government worked to reunite the nation and to rebuild the southern states
Reconstrucción (1865–1877) período posterior a la Guerra Civil en el que el gobierno de Estados Unidos trabajó por reunificar de la nación y reconstruir los estados del Sur

© Houghton Mifflin Harcourt Publishing Company

Reconstruction Acts (1867–1868) the laws that put the southern states under U.S. military control and required them to draft new constitutions upholding the Fourteenth Amendment
Leyes de Reconstrucción (1867–1868) leyes que declaraban a los estados del Sur territorio sujeto al control militar estadounidense y los obligaban a reformar sus constituciones de manera que defendieran la Decimocuarta Enmienda

Red Scare a widespread fear of communism and Communists
Terror Rojo miedo ampliamente difundido al comunismo y los comunistas

referendum a procedure that allows voters to approve or reject a law already proposed or passed by government
referéndum proceso que permite a los votantes aprobar o rechazar una ley previamente propuesta o aprobada por el gobierno

reparations financial payments by the loser of a war
indemnizaciones compensación económica pagada por el bando que es vencido en la guerra

reservations federal lands set aside for American Indians
reservas territorios federales reservados para los indígenas norteamericanos

Roosevelt Corollary (1904) Theodore Roosevelt's addition to the Monroe Doctrine warning nations in the Americas that if they didn't pay their debts, the United States would get involved
Corolario de Roosevelt (1904) agregado del presidente Theodore Roosevelt a la Doctrina Monroe advirtiendo a las naciones de América que si no pagaban sus deudas, el gobierno de Estados Unidos intervendría

S

sanctions economic restrictions placed on a country in an attempt to change its policy decisions
sanciones restricciones económicas aplicadas a un país en un intento de cambiar sus políticas

Scopes trial a trial in which John Scopes was accused of teaching evolution illegally
juicio de Scopes juicio en el cual John Scopes fue acusado de enseñar ilegalmente la teoría de la evolución

search-and-destroy missions the strategy used in the Vietnam War in which enemy targets were located and attacked
misiones de búsqueda y destrucción estrategia de localización y ataque de objetivos enemigos usada en la guerra de Vietnam

Second Battle of Bull Run (1862) a Civil War battle in which the Confederate army forced most of the Union army out of Virginia
segunda batalla de Bull Run (1862) batalla de la Guerra Civil en la que el ejército confederado obligó a gran parte del ejército de la Unión a abandonar Virginia

Second Industrial Revolution a period of rapid growth in manufacturing and industry in the late 1800s
Segunda Revolución Industrial período de gran crecimiento en la manufactura y en la industria a finales del siglo XIX

segregation the forced separation of people of different races in public places
segregación separación obligada de personas de diferentes razas en lugares públicos

Selective Service Act (1917) a law that allowed the president to draft soldiers in times of war
Ley de Servicio Selectivo (1917) ley que permitía al presidente reclutar soldados en épocas de guerra

service economy an economy in which most jobs involve providing services instead of producing goods
economía de servicios economía en la cual la mayoría de los trabajos consisten en ofrecer un servicio en lugar de producir bienes

settlement houses neighborhood centers staffed by professionals and volunteers for education, recreation, and social activities in poor areas
organizaciones de servicio a la comunidad centros comunitarios atendidos por profesionales y voluntarios para ofrecer educación, recreación y actividades sociales en zonas pobres

Seven Days' Battles (1862) a series of Civil War battles in which Confederate army successes forced the Union army to retreat from Richmond, Virginia, the Confederate capital
batallas de los Siete Días (1862) serie de batallas de la Guerra Civil en las que las victorias del ejército confederado obligaron a las tropas de la Unión a retirarse de Richmond, Virginia, la capital confederada

Seventeenth Amendment (1913) a constitutional amendment allowing American voters to directly elect U.S. senators
Decimoséptima Enmienda (1913) enmienda constitucional que permite a los votantes estadounidenses elegir directamente a los senadores de Estados Unidos

© Houghton Mifflin Harcourt Publishing Company

sharecropping a system used on southern farms after the Civil War in which farmers worked land owned by someone else in return for a small portion of the crops
cultivo de aparceros sistema usado en las granjas sureñas después de la Guerra Civil en el que los agricultores trabajaban las tierras de otra persona a cambio de una pequeña porción de la cosecha

Sherman Antitrust Act (1890) a law that made it illegal to create monopolies or trusts that restrained free trade
Ley Antimonopolio de Sherman (1890) ley que prohibía la creación de monopolios o consorcios que restringieran el libre comercio

Siege of Vicksburg (1863) the Union army's six-week blockade of Vicksburg that led the city to surrender during the Civil War
Sitio de Vicksburg (1863) bloqueo de seis semanas realizado por el ejército de la Unión en Vicksburg para forzar la rendición de esa ciudad durante la Guerra Civil

sit-down strike a strike in which workers stay at their work stations so that strikebreakers cannot replace them
huelga de brazos caídos huelga en la cual los trabajadores permanecen en el lugar de trabajo para que los rompehuelgas no los puedan reemplazar

sit-in a form of protest in which African Americans sat at segregated lunch counters and requested service
sentada forma de protesta de los afroamericanos; se sentaban en los comedores que practicaban la segregación racial y pedían que les sirvieran

Sixteenth Amendment (1913) an amendment to the Constitution that allows personal income to be taxed
Decimosexta Enmienda (1913) enmienda constitucional que permite los impuestos sobre los ingresos personales

social Darwinism a view of society based on Charles Darwin's scientific theory of natural selection
darwinismo social visión de la sociedad basada en la teoría científica de la selección natural de Charles Darwin

socialism economic system in which the government owns and operates a country's means of production
socialismo sistema económico en el que el gobierno controla y maneja los medios de producción de un país

Social Security Act (1935) a law that instituted the pension plan Social Security
Ley del Seguro Social (1935) ley que estableció el plan de pensiones del Seguro Social

sodbusters the name given to Plains farmers who worked hard to break up the region's tough sod
sodbusters nombre dado a los agricultores de las Planicies que se esforzaron mucho para trabajar el duro terreno de la región

sphere of influence an area where foreign countries control trade or natural resources of another nation or area
esfera de influencia nación o lugar cuyos recursos naturales y comercio son controlados por otro país

Sputnik the first artificial satellite, launched by the Soviet Union in 1957
Sputnik primer satélite artificial, lanzado por la Unión Soviética en 1957

stagflation a term describing a slowing economy mixed with high unemployment
estagflación término que describe una economía que disminuye su ritmo, acompañado de un desempleo alto

stalemate a situation in which neither side can win a victory
punto muerto situación en la cual ninguna de las partes puede alcanzar la victoria

steerage the area on a ship in the lower levels where the steering mechanisms were located and where cramped quarters were provided for people who could only afford cheap passage
tercera clase nivel inferior un barco en el que se encontraban los mecanismos del timón y se ofrecían habitaciones reducidas para las personas que sólo podían comprar un pasaje barato

Strategic Arms Limitation Talks (SALT) negotiations between the United States and the Soviet Union designed to limit nuclear weapons
Tratados de Limitación de Armas Estratégicas (SALT, por sus siglas en inglés) negociaciones entre Estados Unidos y la Unión Soviética diseñadas para limitar el número de armas nucleares

Student Nonviolent Coordinating Committee (SNCC) a group organized to promote civil rights for African Americans through nonviolent protests
Comité Coordinador Estudiantil No Violento (SNCC, por sus siglas en inglés) grupo organizado para promover los derechos civiles de los afroamericanos con protestas no violentas

Students for a Democratic Society (SDS) a group organized to protest U.S. involvement in the Vietnam War
Estudiantes por una Sociedad Democrática (SDS, por sus siglas en inglés) grupo organizado para protestar por la participación de Estados Unidos en la guerra de Vietnam

© Houghton Mifflin Harcourt Publishing Company

suburb a neighborhood outside of a downtown area
suburbio vecindario en las afueras de una ciudad

Sun Belt the southern area of the United States from Florida to California that experienced an increase in population during the 1970s
Sun Belt área del sur de Estados Unidos, desde Florida hasta California, en la que hubo un aumento de la población durante la década de 1970

supply-side economics economic theory that focuses on influencing the supply of labor and goods; it usually involves sharp tax cuts
economía de la oferta teoría económica que pretende influenciar la oferta de mano de obra y de bienes; por lo general, implica grandes reducciones de impuestos

sweatshops hot, stuffy workshops in which workers prepare materials for low wages
fábricas explotadoras talleres calurosos y con el aire cargado en los cuales los trabajadores preparan materiales por salarios reducidos

T

talkie a film that includes sound
película sonora película que incluye sonido

Teapot Dome scandal a scandal under the Harding administration in which government officials were accused of taking bribes to allow oil to be mined from federal lands
escándalo de Teapot Dome escándalo durante el gobierno de Harding en el que se acusó a funcionarios del gobierno de aceptar sobornos para permitir que se usaran tierras federales para extraer petróleo

Teller Amendment (1898) a congressional resolution stating that the U.S. had no interest in taking control of Cuba
Enmienda Teller (1898) resolución del Congreso en la que Estados Unidos declaró que no tenía intención de tomar el control de Cuba

tenements poorly built, overcrowded housing
casas de vecindad viviendas mal constuidas y llenas de gente

Tennessee Valley Authority (TVA) a governmental agency designed to bring jobs and electricity to rural areas of the Tennessee River valley
Autoridad del Valle del Tennessee (TVA, por sus siglas en inglés) agencia del gobierno destinada a proveer empleos y energía eléctrica a las áreas rurales del valle del río Tennessee

Ten Percent Plan President Abraham Lincoln's plan for Reconstruction; once 10 percent of voters in a former Confederate state took a U.S. loyalty oath, they could form a new state government and be readmitted to the Union
Plan del Diez por Ciento plan de Reconstrucción del presidente Abraham Lincoln; si el 10 por ciento de los votantes de un estado que había sido confederado juraba lealtad a la nación, podían formar un nuevo gobierno y ser readmitidos en la Unión

terrorism the systematic use of fear or terror to gain goals
terrorismo uso sistemático del miedo o el terror para alcanzar objetivos

Tet Offensive (1968) a series of attacks by Vietcong forces that proved to many Americans the Vietnam War was not being won
ofensiva del Tet (1968) serie de ataques de las fuerzas del Vietcong que demostró a muchos estadounidenses que no estaban ganando la guerra de Vietnam

Thirteenth Amendment (1865) a constitutional amendment that outlawed slavery
Decimotercera Enmienda (1865) enmienda constitucional que prohibió la esclavitud

38th Parallel the boundary between North and South Korea before the Korean War
paralelo 38 límite entre Corea del Sur y Corea del Norte antes de la Guerra de Corea

Tonkin Gulf Resolution (1964) gave President Johnson the power to send combat troops to Vietnam
Resolución del Golfo de Tonkin (1964) otorgó al presidente Johnson la autoridad de enviar tropas de combate a Vietnam

totalitarianism a form of government in which every aspect of citizens' lives is controlled by the government
totalitarismo forma de gobierno en la cual todos los aspectos de la vida de los ciudadanos están bajo el control del gobierno

total war a type of war in which an army destroys its opponent's ability to fight by targeting civilian and economic as well as military resources
guerra total tipo de guerra en la que un ejército destruye la capacidad de lucha de su oponente mediante ataques a la población civil y a la economía así como a los recursos militares

transcontinental railroad a railroad system that crossed the continental United States; construction began in 1863
tren transcontinental línea ferroviaria que cruzaba Estados Unidos de un extremo a otro; su construcción se inició en 1863

© Houghton Mifflin Harcourt Publishing Company

Treaty of Fort Laramie (1851) a treaty signed in Wyoming by the United States and northern Plains nations
Tratado del Fuerte Laramie (1851) tratado firmado en Wyoming por Estados Unidos y las naciones indígenas de las Planicies del norte

Treaty of Medicine Lodge (1867) an agreement between the U.S. government and southern Plains Indians in which the Indians agreed to move onto reservations
Tratado de Medicine Lodge (1867) acuerdo entre el gobierno de Estados Unidos y los indígenas de las Planicies del sur en el que los indígenas aceptaron irse a las reservas

Treaty of Versailles (1919) brought an end to World War I, but was never ratified by the United States
Tratado de Versalles (1919) puso fin a la Primera Guerra Mundial, pero Estados Unidos nunca lo ratificó

Tredegar Iron Works a large iron factory that operated in Richmond, Virginia, in the early to mid-1800s
Tredegar Iron Works gran fábrica de acero que operaba a mediados del siglo XIX en Richmond, Virginia

trench warfare a new kind of warfare in World War I that involved troops digging and fighting from deep trenches
guerra de trincheras nuevo tipo de guerra utilizado en la Primera Guerra Mundial en el cual las tropas cavaban trincheras profundas y luchaban desde ellas

Triangle Shirtwaist Fire a factory fire that killed 146 workers trapped in the building; led to new safety standard laws
incendio de Triangle Shirtwaist incendio de una fábrica en el que murieron 146 trabajadores atrapados en el edificio; este suceso obligó a crear nuevas leyes de seguridad

Truman Doctrine a policy attempting to contain the spread of communism, beginning with military aid to the monarchies of Turkey and Greece
Doctrina Truman política que intentaba contener el avance del comunismo, ofreciendo inicialmente ayuda militar a las monarquías de Turquía y Grecia

trust a number of companies legally grouped under a single board of directors
consorcio varias compañías agrupadas legalmente bajo el mando de una sola junta directiva

Tuskegee Airmen a group of African American pilots who flew missions in World War I; they were the first African American military pilots
Aviadores de Tuskegee grupo de pilotos afroamericanos que volaron en misiones de la Primera Guerra Mundial; fueron los primeros pilotos afroamericanos del ejército

Twenty-first Amendment (1933) an amendment to the Constitution that ended Prohibition
Vigésimoprimera Enmienda (1933) enmienda constitucional que puso fin a la Ley Seca

Twenty-sixth Amendment (1971) an amendment to the Constitution that lowered the voting age to 18
Vigésimosexta Enmienda (1971) enmienda constitucional que redujo la edad mínima para votar a 18 años

U

U-boats German submarines or "untersee boats"
U-boats submarinos alemanes o "barcos untersee"

United Farm Workers a group organized to promote the interests of migrant farm workers, it eventually led to the Chicano movement
Trabajadores Agrícolas Unidos grupo organizado para promover los intereses de los trabajadores agrícolas migratorios; con el tiempo, dio origen al movimiento chicano

United Nations an alliance of nations that attempts to end disputes between countries peacefully
Naciones Unidas alianza de naciones que intenta resolver de manera pacífica las disputas entre los países

urban renewal a governmental program that attempted to rid cities of slums and replace them with low- and middle-income housing
renovación urbana programa gubernamental que intentó eliminar las barriadas de los centros urbanos y reemplazarlos con viviendas para personas de recursos bajos y medios

V

vertical integration the business practice of owning all of the businesses involved in each step of a manufacturing process
integración vertical práctica empresarial de poseer todas las empresas que participan en cada paso de un proceso de manufactura

ENGLISH AND SPANISH GLOSSARY

© Houghton Mifflin Harcourt Publishing Company

Vietcong the South Vietnam forces that were supported by North Vietnamese Communists
Vietcong fuerzas de Vietnam del Sur apoyadas por los comunistas de Vietnam del Norte

Vietnamization a policy introduced in an attempt to leave the Vietnam War, in which Vietnamese forces would take over the fighting
vietnamización política introducida en un intento de salir de la guerra de Vietnam, según la cual las fuerzas vietnamitas se harían cargo de la lucha

Vietnam Veterans Memorial a war memorial in Washington, D.C., dedicated to the veterans of Vietnam
Monumento a los Veteranos de Vietnam monumento conmemorativo de la guerra en Washington, D.C. dedicado a los veteranos de Vietnam

Voting Rights Act of 1965 provided new powers to the federal government to protect African Americans' voting rights
Ley de Derecho al Voto de 1965 dio nueva autoridad al gobierno federal para proteger el derecho al voto de los afroamericanos

W

War Powers Act (1973) a law that requires a president to get congressional approval before sending troops into combat
Ley de Poderes de Guerra (1973) ley que requiere la aprobación del Congreso para que el presidente pueda enviar tropas a la guerra

War Production Board a government agency set up to oversee production of war materials during World War II
Junta de Producción de Guerra agencia creada por el gobierno para supervisar la producción de materiales de guerra durante la Segunda Guerra Mundial

Watergate a scandal in which President Nixon resigned over accusations of illegal activity
Watergate escándalo que provocó la renuncia del presidente Nixon por acusaciones de actividades ilegales

weapons of mass destruction chemical, biological, or nuclear weapons that can kill thousands
armas de destrucción masiva armas químicas, biológicas o nucleares que pueden matar a miles de personas

Wilderness Campaign (1864) a series of battles between Union and Confederate forces in northern and central Virginia that delayed the Union capture of Richmond
Campaña de Wilderness (1864) serie de batallas entre la Unión y los confederados en el norte y el centro de Virginia que retrasaron la captura de Richmond por parte de la Unión

workers' compensation laws regulations guaranteeing a portion of lost wages to workers injured on the job
leyes de compensación laboral legislación que garantiza el pago de parte del salario a un trabajador lesionado en el ejercicio de su labor

World Trade Center a complex of several office buildings that were attacked by terrorists
World Trade Center complejo de varios edificios de oficinas que fue atacado por terroristas

Y

Yalta Conference a meeting between the leaders of the Allied powers that resulted in a plan for peace after World War II
Conferencia de Yalta reunión de los líderes de las fuerzas aliadas que produjo un plan de paz después de la Segunda Guerra Mundial

yellow journalism the reporting of exaggerated stories in newspapers to increase sales
prensa amarillista publicación de noticias exageradas en los periódicos para aumentar las ventas

Z

Zimmermann note a telegram from Germany to Mexico offering Mexico a return of territory in exchange for declaring war on the United States
telegrama Zimmermann telegrama de Alemania a México en el cual se ofrecía a México una devolución de territorios si le declaraba la guerra a Estados Unidos

zoot-suit riots a series of riots during which Mexican Americans were attacked by whites
disturbios *zoot-suit* serie de disturbios durante los cuales personas de raza blanca atacaron a mexicano-americanos

© Houghton Mifflin Harcourt Publishing Company

Houghton Mifflin Harcourt

Index

KEY TO INDEX

c = chart	*p* = photo
f = feature	*R* = Reference
m = map	

A

B

INDEX

C

D

E

F

G

H

I

J

K

L

INDEX

M

N

INDEX

O

P

Q

R

S

INDEX

U

V

W

Credits and Acknowledgments

HISTORY Unless otherwise indicated, all video reference screens are © 2010 A&E Television Networks, LLC. All rights reserved.

For permission to reproduce copyrighted material, grateful acknowledgment is made to the following sources:

Excerpt from *Bread Givers* by Anzia Yezierska. Text copyright © 1925 by Doubleday & Co., Inc.; copyright renewed 1952 by Anzia Yezierska, transferred to Louise Levitas Henriksen in 1970. Revised edition copyright © 1999 by Persea Books, Inc. Forward and Introduction copyright © 1999 by Alice Kessler-Harris. Reprinted by permission of Persea Books, Inc.

Excerpt from *The Diary of a Young Girl: The Definitive Edition* by Anne Frank, edited by Otto H. Frank and Mirjam Pressler, translated by Susan Massotty. Text copyright © 1995 by Doubleday, a division of Random House, Inc. Reprinted by permission of Doubleday, a division of Random House, Inc.

Excerpt from *The Grapes of Wrath* by John Steinbeck. Text copyright 1939 and renewed © 1967 by John Steinbeck. Reprinted by permission of Viking Penguin, a division of Penguin Group (USA) Inc.

Excerpt from *The Great Gatsby* by F. Scott Fitzgerald. Text copyright 1925 by Charles Scribner's Sons; renewed text copyright 1953 by Frances Scott Fitzgerald Lanahan. Reprinted by permission of Scribner, an imprint of Simon & Schuster Adult Publishing Group.

"I, Too" from *The Collected Poems of Langston Hughes* by Langston Hughes, edited by Arnold Rampersad with David Roessel, Associate Editor. Text copyright © 1994 by the Estate of Langston Hughes. Reprinted by permission of Alfred A. Knopf, a division of Random House, Inc. and Harold Ober Associates Incorporated.

Excerpt from letter of Gro Svendsen from *Frontier Mother: The Letters of Gro Svendsen*, translated and edited by Pauline Farseth and Theodore C. Blegen. Text copyright ©1950 by Norwegian-American Historical Association. Reprinted by permission of Norwegian-American Historical Association.

Excerpt from *Night* by Elie Wiesel, translated by Marion Wiesel. Text copyright © 1958 by Les Editions de Minuit; English translation ...t copyright © 2006 by Marion Wiesel. ...ed by permission of Hill and Wang, a ...Farrar, Straus & Giroux, LLC and W.W. Nor...t, Inc.

...*Days: A Memoir* ... Robert F. ... by McCall ... of

CREDITS AND ACKNOWLEDGMENTS

© Houghton Mifflin Harcourt Publishing Company